THE IRWIN SERIES IN ECONOMICS

CONSULTING EDITOR

LLOYD G. REYNOLDS
YALE UNIVERSITY

BOOKS IN THE IRWIN SERIES IN ECONOMICS

Economics

A GENERAL INTRODUCTION

Econo

1963

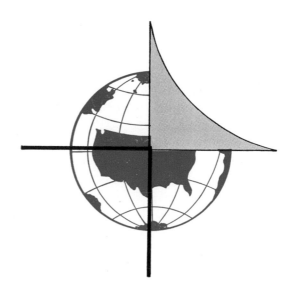

mics

A GENERAL INTRODUCTION

By Lloyd G. Reynolds

Sterling Professor of Economics and
Director, Economic Growth Center
Yale University

RICHARD D. IRWIN, INC., Homewood, Illinois

First printing, March, 1963
Second printing, August, 1963

Library of Congress Catalogue Card No. 63–14220

PRINTED IN THE UNITED STATES OF AMERICA

FOR MARY

To Teachers of Economics

WHAT ARE we trying to do in the elementary course? Surely not what we would have done ten or twenty years ago. The content of the subject and the preparation of our students are changing rapidly, and our teaching must keep abreast of change.

Students now enter college with considerable economic information from their high school courses in social studies and American history. They have learned something about business organization, the growth of the American economy, and the changing economic functions of government. They may even feel that they are already familiar with economics. But in this they are wrong, for they have not been exposed to the methods of thought which make economics a systematic study. This is essentially what the elementary course must do for them.

This is accordingly a book of ideas, with a minimum of descriptive material. A book of reasonable size cannot hope to be encyclopedic, and it is clear where the priority must lie. One must develop and apply the central tools of economic analysis. Factual information can be supplied readily enough through lectures and supplementary readings.

Most students who take the elementary course will never study economics again. (Sometimes this is *because* they took the elementary course!) Thus the course should be regarded as economics for the general reader. The problem is to give a student in one or two semesters something that he will remember and use later on for analysis of public issues and for effective performance as a citizen.

The objective is to train students to approach policy issues in the frame of mind with which economists approach these issues, to think like economists. The ideas needed for this are few and not very difficult. Keynes once remarked that "economics is an easy subject in which few excel." But because economic analysis so often runs counter to common-sense thinking, the main principles require illustration and application until they settle into a habitual method of thought.

Teachers of economics sometimes profess to want "a less theoretical book." Anyone who really means this is on the wrong track. There is no avoiding the necessity of theorizing. Schumpeter used to tell his classes that "theory is the systematic art of addressing questions to the facts." It is our searchlight in an uncharted sea of data that would otherwise surround and overwhelm us.

Surely what most teachers want is a smaller amount of *irrelevant* theory, less teaching of concepts that are not going to be used in the subsequent analysis. In this I am wholeheartedly on their side. At each stage I have tried to apply the following test: Is this concept essential, and will it actually be used, in analyzing economic activity and exploring policy issues? Concepts that do not clearly pass this test have been omitted or placed in appendixes, where they can be assigned by teachers who do consider them essential.

I have tried to present the central ideas in plain English, supplemented by simple geometry. The same ideas can be presented also in algebraic form. But symbols still frighten many students, and fear is not a good prelude to learning.

Several other judgments have guided the organization of the book:

1. The debate over whether macro- or microeconomics should be taught first will doubtless never be resolved. I have tried to organize the two halves of the book so that each stands on its own feet, and teachers can begin with Part One or Part Three as they prefer. My own preference is to begin with the micro material, because it seems odd to examine aggregates without first having looked at their components. This is particularly true in discussing economic growth, where a simplified aggregative presentation can lead to serious error.

2. In microeconomics, the whole is more than the sum of its parts. Micro theory often seems unappetizing to students because it is so *very* micro. The spotlight is held too long on the supposed operations of hypothetical business firms. The concept of a national economic mechanism, which transmits and absorbs changes occurring anywhere in the system, becomes lost in the shuffle.

I have tried to emphasize the interrelatedness of the market network, the results that a competitive economy is supposed to produce, and the extent to which the American economy meets these tests of efficient performance. As a minor theme throughout Part One, I examine the way in which the same problems of production and distribution are handled in Soviet-type economies, and the problem of appraising the efficiency of these economies.

3. In macroeconomics, long-run economic growth is emerging as the central problem of our time. The rapid growth of output in Soviet-type economies is asserted as proof of their superiority. The fact that U.S. economic growth has since 1950 lagged behind that of Western Europe and Japan gives cause for concern. The determination of the poorer countries of Asia, Africa, and Latin America to accelerate their economic development is a central fact of international relations. Thus the issues examined in Part Four now impress students as especially significant, and this may become increasingly true over the years ahead. In this respect the book can perhaps claim to be forward looking.

4. This claim can be made in another respect as well. In an age when the United States has willy-nilly assumed a position of world leadership, it seems odd that most elementary economics texts focus so heavily on the American economy. The standard allotment of space to the

Soviet-bloc countries and the underdeveloped countries combined is about 5 percent. This leaves the student ignorant of many matters on which he should be informed. It also breeds an ethnocentrism which regards our own economic institutions as right and proper, while all other nations are wrong-headed. The 20 percent of space that I have allotted to foreign economies is still not enough, but it is a step in the right direction.

I have worked hard to write a lean book rather than an overstuffed one, believing that most students will consider this an act of mercy. I believe there is very little in this edition which doesn't belong and cannot be used. A few things of consequence may have been omitted. But it is much easier to add than to cut, and additions which do turn out to be desirable will be made in later editions.

L. G. R.

New Haven
January, 1963

Acknowledgments

I AM GRATEFUL for several kinds of aid, without which this book could not have been completed. Ann Alker, William Albrecht, and Frederick Deming helped with data and bibliography. Daniel Waugh made preliminary drawings of the diagrams. Jean Banta, Olive Higgins, Rosemary Ingham, Peggy Johnstone, and Anne Phillips had a hand in the various stages of typing and mimeographing. Mary Reynolds prepared the index.

Most especially am I grateful to a number of colleagues who read part or all of the manuscript: James Blackman, University of North Carolina; Lang Cantrell, Los Angeles City College; Daniel Fusfeld, University of Michigan; William Greenwald, The City College, New York; Eric Gustafson, Harvard University; James Howell, Stanford University; the late Ward Macy, University of Oregon; Taulman Miller, Indiana University; Paul Montavon, University of Notre Dame; Kenneth Strand, Oberlin College; Leonard Weiss, University of Wisconsin; and John Arena, William Fellner, Edmund Phelps, Richard Porter, and Gustav Ranis, Yale University. Their comments were invaluable; but they should not, of course, be implicated in the outcome.

I should not fail to express appreciation to my students in elementary economics at Yale, whose skepticism and zeal for controversy has taught me more than they realized.

L. G. R.

Table of Contents

PART ONE

The Economics of Prices and Markets

PART TWO

Government and the Market Economy

PART THREE

The Economics of Income and Employment

PART FOUR

The Economics of Growth

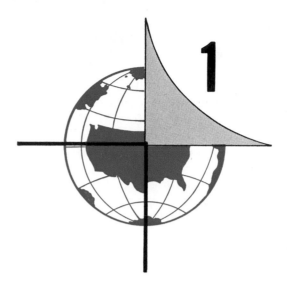

What Economics Is About

Political economy or economics is a study of mankind in the ordinary business of life; it examines that part of individual and social action which is most closely connected with the attainment and with the use of the material requisites of well-being. Thus it is on the one side a study of wealth; and on the other, and more important side, a part of the study of man.

ALFRED MARSHALL

The theory of economics does not furnish a body of settled conclusions immediately applicable to policy. It is a method rather than a doctrine, an apparatus of the mind, a technique of thinking, which helps its possessor to draw correct conclusions.

JOHN MAYNARD KEYNES

IN A GENERAL WAY, we all know what economics is about. It is concerned with the production, distribution, and use of material goods and services. It deals with the activities of the 4 million business concerns, 4 million farms, 70 million workers, and 50 million households that produced and consumed about $550 billion worth of output in the United States in 1962. As Adam Smith said, economics is "an inquiry into the nature and causes of the wealth of nations."

But just how is economics concerned with these things? What is its approach and method of analysis? What is the "apparatus of the mind" to which Keynes referred? This chapter is an informal chat about these things before we plunge into the subject in Chapter 2.

1

ECONOMICS AND BUSINESS

Students enroll in economics courses for many reasons—an interest in political issues, a desire to get ahead in business, a curriculum requirement that they would gladly escape. Someone may have told them that economics is practical, that it has something to do with business, that it might lead to success and fortune in the stock market. It is only fair to set this straight at the beginning. The study of economics is not a direct path to riches. The gibe often leveled at economists, "If you're so smart, why aren't you rich?" rests on a misunderstanding. Economists are not especially qualified for stock speculation, and several famous scholars have lost their shirts by ignoring this truth. Still less are they necessarily qualified to manage a business or teach anyone else how to do so.

Economics and business are related but distinct studies. Business administration looks at a business concern from the inside, as it were, while economics views it mainly from the outside. The student of business administration sets himself the problems faced by the business manager: How can this company be organized to perform most efficiently and profitably? What personnel, production, marketing, and financial policies will enable the company to survive, grow, and yield an adequate return on the stockholders' investment? The modern manager also wants his company to be considered a good citizen and to take its share of community responsibility. But efficiency and profitability lie at the heart of business management.

It is important that business units should be managed efficiently and that enterprisers should be enterprising. The national economy cannot operate efficiently unless this basic job is being done well. Even Russia has business schools, which have five-year programs of study, and which each year turn out thousands of accountants, bank personnel, statisticians, pricing and production experts, personnel managers, and economic planners. In addition, a high proportion of the top management of Russian industry is drawn from schools of engineering, as is true to a lesser extent in the United States.

The economist is concerned with the behavior of business units somewhat as a physicist looks at his neutrons and protons. Business concerns are the basic particles of the economic world. The economist views them from the outside, tries to understand their reactions, but does not try to change or improve them. He generally takes it for granted that business managers know their job and are doing it well. His interest is not in what goes on inside a particular company, but in its interaction with other companies in the larger economy. The economist does not try to find out how a particular textile mill can be managed most profitably. He does try to analyze what will happen to prices and production in the textile industry if the national demand for cotton cloth falls off.

This is not to say that economics is entirely impractical from a business standpoint. Many ideas first developed by economists have been applied in business management. Analysis of consumer demand, for example, has long been a standard subject in economics. Work in this area has obvious practical applications. If one can predict that a 3 percent increase in consumers' incomes will mean a 5 percent increase in sales of new automobiles, this is an important thing for automobile companies to know. It would also be important to know that a 5 percent rise in new-car prices will produce a 2 percent drop in the number of cars sold. Economists and statisticians have developed ways of making such predictions.

Management people also try to outguess the swings of the business cycle. Will national production and employment continue to rise during the next twelve or eighteen months? At what rate? Is there a danger that the economy may instead turn downward into a recession? Correct estimates can make the difference between large profits and serious losses. Economists have developed ways of analyzing fluctuations in national economic activity, and have even had some success in prediction. Most large companies now find it profitable to hire a few economists for this sort of weathervane work.

Basic training in economics is normally a required part of a business curriculum. Economists do not object to this—we need the customers. But it is wrong to regard business education simply as applied economics. Business administration is a multidisciplinary study, resting on economics as one pillar, but resting also on psychology, engineering, statistics, and a variety of other disciplines. Above all, it involves the adaptation and fusion of these tools in the solution of management problems.

Perhaps the best way to put the matter is to regard economics and business administration as intersecting circles with a small area of overlap. Business education is partly applied economics, but it is not *mainly* that. Economics has certain applications to management, but its *main* applications lie in another direction.

ECONOMICS AND GOVERNMENT

Economics is political economy. Its main applications are to the great issues of economic policy that have been debated for generations.

Who should pay the taxes? Should the rich have to pay a larger percentage of their incomes than the poor?

Should the government aim always to take in exactly as much as it spends? Is there sometimes a case for a budget surplus or deficit? If a country runs a deficit and increases its national debt, will it eventually become bankrupt?

Should manufacturers in the United States be protected against foreign competition by tariffs on imported products? Will goods produced by cheap foreign labor flood the country and cause widespread unemployment if this is not done?

Should the growth of giant corporations be viewed with approval as a step toward greater efficiency, or with alarm as leading to monopoly control of industry? If monopoly is a danger, what can be done about it?

Are farmers right in arguing that they have special problems calling for government aid? Is it sensible to guarantee farmers a certain price for corn, wheat, cotton, and other basic products?

What can government do to reduce the likelihood of business depressions? If a depression somehow gets started, what can be done to get out of it?

Why has the national output of the U.S.A. been rising more slowly since 1950 than the national output of the U.S.S.R.? What might be done to increase the growth rate of our economy?

Note that these issues have one thing in common. They all involve *action by government to influence the economy*. The key question in each case is what kind of government action is feasible and wise.

The main purpose of a course in economics is to train you to think systematically about economic issues, correct solution of which may determine the prosperity and even the survival of the nation in the decades ahead. The object is to produce citizens able to pull their weight in a democratic society. Reasonable literacy in economic affairs is also a hallmark of the educated modern man. A prominent economist was once asked by an alumnus why anybody should bother to study economics. He replied, "So as not to be embarrassed in conversation in your club!"

Economics is part of liberal education, of education for citizenship. "Ah," you say, "then economics is really the same thing as politics. The test of a good economist is whether he has correct opinions on political questions." Heavens no! Nothing could be farther from the truth. A left-wing Democrat may be a very good economist or a very poor one. So may a right-wing Republican. There are good and bad economists in every political camp.

The relation of economics to politics can be explained by a simple example. What should the federal budget look like for the fiscal year 1963–64? Should there be a surplus, a deficit, or an even balance? How can the economist contribute to a decision on this issue? Primarily, by raising three kinds of factual question:

a. *What is the present situation?* If present tax rates and expenditure levels were continued without change, what would the budget picture look like? What would be the size of the deficit or surplus at the end of the fiscal year? The answer depends on estimates of the level of business activity in the year ahead, since this has a large influence on tax receipts and some influence on government expenditures. Estimates of business conditions can never be completely accurate, and so economists can give only rough answers to the above questions. Many economists, however, are engaged in exactly this kind of calculation in the U.S. Treasury Department, the U.S. Bureau of the Budget, and private organizations.

b. *What are the policy alternatives?* Suppose a large budget surplus is in prospect, and the administration of the day decides it would be better to have a small surplus or an even balance. There are many different ways by which this might be accomplished. Tax collections may be reduced, or expenditures may be increased, or both. If it is decided to reduce tax collections, this can be done by raising personal income tax exemptions, reducing the basic tax rate, lowering the rates on higher bracket incomes, reducing the corporation income tax, cutting federal excise taxes, or doing several of these things together. Economists can estimate how much each of these steps would reduce tax collections and can make up various "package" proposals, each of which would have the same result of reducing the budget surplus by $3 billion or whatever the desired amount may be.

c. *What are the consequences of choosing a particular alternative?* The economist tries to determine, not merely what courses of action are open, but how the choice of a particular course will affect the operation of the economy. How would various ways of changing the personal income tax structure affect the equality of incomes in the country? What repercussions might be expected on spending, saving, effort, and initiative? How would a change in the corporate income tax affect corporate saving and investment? How would lowering the excise tax on particular products—tires, automobiles, cigarettes, transportation—affect the price and sales of these products? One mark of a professional economist is that he knows how to take hold of such questions.

On questions of fact, well-trained economists of any political shade should be in general agreement. Where they disagree, the differences can be pinpointed, spelled out in statistical terms, and perhaps reconciled.

Basic disagreement begins when one faces the question: *What should the government do?* Having looked at all the figures and all the alternatives, what is the wise course of action? Any answer to this question goes beyond economics in two directions. First, it involves value judgments. What is a just distribution of personal income? How active a part should government take in economic affairs? What kind of economic and political system do we want over the long run? The economist has no special competence to lay down the law on such matters.

Second, a statement that government *should* do a certain thing involves a judgment of what is feasible from a political and administrative standpoint. There is no point in drawing up a beautiful piece of legislation that is certain to be voted down by Congress; nor is there much point in passing a law that cannot be administered effectively. Judgments about what can and cannot be done politically are not within the province of the economist.

To reach decisions on economic policy, then, one needs:

1. A knowledge of economic facts, alternatives, and consequences—for this, see your nearest economist.
2. Judgments of value—for this, see the departments of philosophy and religion.
3. A knowledge of how to get things done through government—for this, visit lawyers and practicing politicians.

Steps 2 and 3 are *not* economics, and an economist has no special qualifications in these areas. But economists are also people, and have the same right as other citizens to hold personal values and make political judgments. Equally good economists may thus come out with different practical conclusions. There is nothing odd about this. When economists differ on what should be done, they are differing in their human capacity as citizens.

THE METHODS OF ECONOMICS

So much for what economists claim to do. How do they do it? What are the basic methods and techniques? What constitutes proof in economics?

The Necessity of Measurement

Economics has an advantage in dealing mainly with *quantities*. It is concerned with prices, hourly wage rates, numbers of people employed, amounts of goods produced and exchanged, quantity of money and credit in existence, government receipts and expenditures. These things are measurable in principle, though actual measurements fall short of perfection.

Precise measurement, then, is the basis for serious study of economics. Before trying to explain what goes on in the economy, we try to discover what actually *is* going on. If one man maintains that national output is higher this year than last, while another maintains firmly that it is lower, they cannot get any farther. Agreement on facts is an essential starting point. So we set out to measure total national output, production of specific goods and services, exports and imports, the money incomes of households, price levels and wage levels, and dozens of other things. One cannot approach economics without such measurements any more than natural scientists can operate without measures of mass or temperature.

Preparation and criticism of these measures is the task of *economic statistics*. There has been enormous progress on this front over the past two or three generations. In 1900 we had little more than the decennial

Census data plus a few skimpy price statistics. Today we have a great volume of measurements for almost every conceivable economic quantity, a volume that threatens at times to become overwhelming.

Explanation and Prediction

Measurement of what is happening is only the beginning. Our ultimate hope is to *explain* why things happen as they do. If we can explain past events, we have some chance of being able to *predict* future events. Science always aims at prediction; and practical men are especially intrigued by the possibilities of prediction in economics, since profits and votes may hang on the outcome.

Horseback predictions can sometimes be obtained directly from economic statistics. For example, if you look at statistics of personal income in the United States over the last 30 years, you will find that on the average about 92 percent of personal income after taxes has been spent on consumption while 8 percent has been saved. Except for the war years 1942–45, when goods were hard to get and savings were abnormally large, the savings ratio has not varied far from the 8 percent average. Thus if you have to make a quick estimate of what personal savings will be next year, your safest course will be to take 8 percent of expected personal income.

Such rules of thumb are all right as far as they go. Their limitation is that they give no explanation of *why* the figures behave as they do. It is as though an engineer looked at a machine and observed that a particular wheel always went around so many times a minute, but knew nothing about the principles governing the machine's operation. No engineer or physicist would be content to stop at this point. He wants to know *why* the machine behaves as it does. Until he knows this, he cannot be sure that another machine will behave in the same way, nor can he design a machine that would behave differently. Similarly, the economist wants to understand why the American people behave as they do about saving, food buying, working, and other things. He wants to discover the principles behind the statistics.

How can he go about getting this understanding? First, he can ask people why they made certain decisions. There are obvious drawbacks to this method. You can quiz only a small percentage of the population, and you can never be completely sure that you have a representative group. People do not always know why they did what they did, and if they do they may not be willing to tell. Interview questions have to be direct and simple, but the circumstances surrounding a decision are often complex. People can give more reliable answers about recent events than about events in the more distant past. Despite these difficulties, "survey research" has increased greatly in recent years and has added much to our economic understanding.

The standard method of physical science is the controlled experiment, but economists cannot use this method. We cannot shut people up in an isolated camp to observe their reactions. In any case people's reactions under such artificial conditions would be different from their reactions in everyday life.

So what are we to do? Deprived of the possibility of actual experiments, the economist resorts to *intellectual experiments*. The process of intellectual experiment begins with *observations of behavior*. The important thing is observation of large numbers of families, or business concerns, or what not, rather than of isolated individuals. It isn't very interesting to know that, when Mr. Jones got a $1,000 raise last year, he put $200 of this into extra saving. Mr. Jones may turn out to be an unusual specimen. But if we find out that all families in the United States received $20 billion more income last year and that $3 billion of this went into savings, this is significant. If we can break the total population down into groups, say by income level, and observe the different behavior in these groups, this is even more interesting.

The next stage is to sit down quietly in an armchair and try to reason out why people might have behaved as they did. One can think of many things that might influence family decisions about saving, including the family's present income, its expected future income, its accumulated wealth, fixed commitments for mortgages and time payments, and plans for children's education or other large future expenditures. From what we know of our own reactions, and from what we observe in statistical measurements, we try to estimate the probable strength of these various influences. This is the stage of *hypothesis building* or *theorizing*. At the end, we come out with a set of propositions that may be capable of explaining the facts. We can call this a *theory of household savings*.

Finally, we must go back to the facts and test our hypotheses against observed behavior. Our theory says, for example, that people will react in a specified way to a certain increase in their current income. Well, do they or don't they? The measures of what actually happens are the payoff. If they agree closely with our hypothesis, we can have some confidence that we are on the right track. If not, we must ask what went wrong and start over again. This step is termed *verification, hypothesis testing*, or *statistical inference*. Statistical inference is the economist's substitute for the laboratory he can never have.

It may be necessary to work back and forth several times between hypotheses and verification. We develop certain hypotheses in the first instance. We look at the facts. The facts don't quite fit. So we go back and change our hypotheses, perhaps making them more complicated to take account of things we had overlooked at first. Then we apply another test of statistics against our hypotheses. If we are lucky, the fit will be better, but the hypotheses may need still further revision; and so on and on. In the end, if we are clever as well as lucky, we may come out with a set of hypotheses that agree closely with observed behavior.

Building Hypotheses (Theorizing)

This may seem a bit abstract and difficult. So let's look at another illustration from one of the oldest branches of economics, the theory of consumer demand.

Our problem is to explain what determines the amount of butter bought by the U.S. population in a particular year. Since population is growing all the time, we had better correct this at once by changing the question to read: What determines the amount of butter bought per head of population? One's first thought is that purchases have something to do with price. It seems reasonable that people will buy more of an article when its price is lower than when it is higher. So our first hypothesis is: Purchases of butter vary inversely with the price of butter.

We now look at the statistics and find that the price of butter in 1962 was higher than in 1961; but purchases of butter were *also higher* in 1962, instead of lower as they should have been according to our hypothesis. Something obviously has been left out. A little more thought suggests that how much butter people buy depends partly on their income. If consumer incomes go up, they may buy more butter even though its price has risen.

Another look at the facts (and we should of course look at 20 or 30 years rather than just two or three) shows us that we still don't know everything about butter purchases. The figures jump about in a way which we can't explain satisfactorily by looking only at the price of butter and at consumer incomes. So we scratch our heads again and add hypotheses to take account of such things as:

1. People like butter but they can eat margarine. The lower the price of margarine compared with that of butter, the more people will shift to it to save money. So the price of margarine becomes another factor in our calculations.

2. Butter goes with bread. People usually don't eat spoonfuls of pure butter. So the amount of bread sold per year will affect the use of butter, and this must also go into our equation.

3. You can spread the butter thicker or thinner. As the slim figure and the calorie cookbook have become fashionable, most people spread it thinner. Some actresses even eat dry toast. So we add to our equation another item which the statisticans call a time trend. This shows that, apart from all other factors, butter purchases go down a certain amount each year for reasons which we don't entirely understand, but which we lump together as "changes in public taste."

We come out, then, with a more complicated theory including five factors influencing butter purchases instead of only one. If we have good measures of these five factors and of butter sales over a long period of time, we can get some idea of *how much* influence each factor has on the result. This is no place to explain the mysteries of statistical inference, but you can take them on faith. The job can be done. The end result is a formula which might look something like this:

$$\text{Butter purchases per capita} = 0.004 \text{ (consumer income per capita)}$$
$$-0.327 \text{ (price of butter)}$$
$$+0.673 \text{ (price of margarine)}$$
$$+0.018 \text{ (sales of bread)}$$
$$-0.007$$

Prediction and Proof in Economics

How do we test this complicated hypothesis about butter sales? By seeing how close it comes to explaining actual butter sales year by year. Suppose we take the year 1962. We fill in all the figures for 1962 on the right hand side of the equation—consumer income per capita in that year, butter prices, and so on—and carry out the calculations. The result tells us what butter sales per capita would have been in 1962 if the hypothesis were completely correct. We then look at actual butter sales in 1962 and see how far off we were.

The same process can be carried out for any year in the past. If the hypothesis predicts actual butter sales in most years within 1 or 2 percent, we can regard it as satisfactory. But if it is off by 10 percent on the average, it must be discarded and a new attempt made. Economists have developed demand equations of this type for wheat, sugar, meat, butter, milk, and other staple products; and these typically agree quite closely with actual sales.

Before concluding that economics is an exact science, let's look a little farther. Economic hypotheses are always tested by reference to the past. They have to be, since we have no figures for the future. Yet it is the future in which we are really interested. Are we safe in saying that a formula which fits the facts pretty well for the years 1940–60 will work just as well in 1965 or 1970? It will *if people continue to behave in the future as they have in the past.* This is an important qualification. Hypotheses about consumer purchases and savings are reasonably reliable because consumers' tastes and habits seem to change rather slowly. But suppose instead we were trying to predict how much companies will spend in 1965 on new plants and machinery. This is a quite variable and unstable figure. Our hypotheses about it are less complete than for consumer behavior, and predictions are likely to be farther from the mark.

Even at best, economic predictions have an "iffy" character. No economist in his right mind would say flatly "Butter sales next year *will* be 1,700 million pounds." Rather, he will say "*If* the price of butter is 63 cents, *if* consumer income is 380 billion dollars (and so on through several other ifs), *then* butter sales will be 1,700 million pounds." Even this statement is not sufficiently cautious. Statistical inference yields probabilities rather than certainties. So we must say something like "If butter prices, consumer incomes, and other relevant factors are as stated, then the chances are 95 out of 100 that butter sales will be between 1,675 and 1,725 million pounds."

Note also that economic predictions relate to a *group* of consumers, companies, workers, or what not; and the larger the group, the more reliable the prediction. It is sometimes argued that economics can't possibly be a precise subject, because it deals with human beings and human beings are unpredictable. If this means that we cannot predict the economic behavior of the Brown family very reliably, the argument is correct. But the economist is not interested in the Brown family. He tries rather to say what 5 million or 50 million families will do under specified conditions, which is a much more feasible undertaking.

MYTHS AND MISUNDERSTANDINGS

The Bogey of "Economic Man"

Economists are sometimes accused of supposing that man is perfectly rational and self-interested, that he responds only to money and is impervious to other motives. A best-seller entitled *The End of Economic Man* was devoted to destroying this economic bogey. The labor was fruitless, because the target was mythical. Economists are not congenitally stupid. They realize that human actions may be motivated by altruism, desire for power or prestige, the urgings of the subconscious, and many other things. It is obvious also that people don't always know what they are doing. Information may be incomplete and inaccurate, actions may be impulsive and mistaken.

But to develop economic hypotheses one need not suppose that people are *perfectly* informed and rational, or that they respond *only* to material advantage. We need suppose only that material advantage is an *important* motive, which operates along with others to shape personal behavior; and that there is *some* rationality and consistency in people's behavior patterns. If this is true, we can predict that most people will respond in a certain direction to certain stimuli.

In a community made up completely of ascetics or psychotics, economic reasoning would break down. But this is not the kind of world in which we live. Most workers prefer to get more pay rather than less, most consumers prefer to pay a lower rather than a higher price for the same product, most corporation officials prefer larger profits to smaller ones. To the extent that people are motivated in this way—whether this constitutes 25 percent, 50 percent, or 90 percent of their total motivation— economic reasoning can predict the general direction of their action. Remember that economists are interested in reactions of people in the mass rather than in predicting the behavior of individuals. If the Widget Company raises wages from $1.75 an hour to $2.00 an hour, I can't predict that Joe Doakes will quit his $1.50 job at the Ajax Company and rush over to

Widget. But I am safe in predicting that more workers will apply to the Widget Company for work at the new wage than were applying before. This is all that matters to the Widget Company and to the economist.

Why Bother with Theory?

Another common complaint is that economists spend their time making simple things difficult. Why bother with this difficult work of logical deduction, building up hypotheses, revising and testing them, and developing an elaborate body of theory? Why not simply go out and "look at the facts"? Surely the main currents in economic life are so obvious that one can draw conclusions from simple observation.

The difficulty with this approach is that the facts don't speak for themselves. And there are too many of them. How can one tell which facts are relevant to a particular problem? The facts need to be sorted out, arranged, focused. As soon as you begin to do this you are engaged willy-nilly in selecting hypotheses. You do not avoid theorizing but, since your theorizing is unconscious, it is likely to be bad.

A man who maintains that he is simply looking at the facts means really that he hasn't bothered to make his theory clear to his audience or to himself. He sees, for example, that prices have doubled over the past 20 years. Wages have gone up even more; and unions have been quite active, frequently going on strike for wage increases. From this he concludes, "It is obvious that unions are responsible for inflation." This is not a factual conclusion. It rests on a hidden structure of theory. What set of hypotheses does this man have in the back of his mind? The main hypotheses are:

1. Unions have the power to make wages go up faster than they would go up otherwise.
2. Unions exercise this power.
3. An increase in wages means an increase in production costs.
4. When the cost of producing an article is increased, its price must go up more or less proportionately.
5. Cost increases are the *main* reason why prices rise. Other reasons do not exist, or are of minor importance compared with this one.

These hypotheses may or may not be correct. That is not the point at issue. The point is that our observer has leaped to his conclusion without testing his hypotheses or even listing them clearly in his mind. If he had done so, he would have been forced to go through the careful procedure described in the last section. His "obvious" conclusion thus turns out not to be obvious at all. The assertion that a proposition is obvious usually means that the speaker is unwilling to undertake the hard work of finding out whether it is true.

Explanation requires theorizing. There is no escape from this. The only difference is between sloppy, naïve, unconscious theorizing and theorizing in which hypotheses are spelled out thoroughly and subjected to quantitative tests.

Never, never say to your economics instructor, "That may be all right in theory but it doesn't work in practice." His blood pressure will rise sharply, and the reason should be clear to you by now. The purpose of a theory is to describe and explain a certain body of facts. A theory which "doesn't work in practice" in the sense of not corresponding to the facts is simply a bad theory and should be rejected. A carefully constructed and tested theory *will* work, and one must keep improving it until it does.

A WORD ABOUT STUDYING ECONOMICS

Economics is different from any subject you have studied before. It is not like history, or literature, or physics. A few hints on how to approach the subject may save you time and worry.

1. Economics is not memory work. You will not become even an amateur economist by memorizing facts and figures. Economics is a method of thought, a way of taking hold of a problem, breaking it down for analysis, and working systematically toward a solution. It is also a special language, which uses words rather differently from ordinary usage. You become an economist by learning to use this language habitually and correctly, by learning where to find economic statistics and how to interpret them, and by practice in careful reasoning.

2. Economics is an additive subject. It unfolds in a systematic way, what comes later resting on an understanding of what went before. It may be possible in a history text to make sense out of the period 1850–75 even though you missed the chapter on 1780–1800. In economics you cannot skip steps in this way. So do not rush ahead without getting a firm grasp on what you have already read. If you stumble over a sentence or a paragraph, stop and clear it up then and there. If you do this, things will grow clearer as you proceed; otherwise, they are likely to grow foggier.

3. Forget what you think you know about economic issues, because much of what you "know" is wrong. The greatest difficulty in discussing economics is that people already know the answers. They see no need for examining evidence or for careful reasoning, and commit the simplest logical errors with unashamed cheerfulness. The purpose of this course is mainly to unteach you what passes for "commonsense economics" among the general public. Any positive knowledge you may acquire beyond this is a sheer bonus.

4. Care in reasoning, and a skepticism of facile arguments, goes without saying. You will learn as you go along that the commonest errors in economics stem from two sources. The first, known as the *fallacy of composition*, lies in supposing that what is true of the parts is necessarily true of the whole. A man who saves 90 percent of his income will grow rich. It does not follow that, if all families in a country save 90 percent of their incomes, the country will grow rich. This would, in fact, be an impossible situation. A company which cuts wages may raise its profits by so

doing. But if all companies try to cut wages at once, it is not at all clear that they will raise their profits.

> The other common fallacy consists in ignoring the *two-sidedness of economic events*. Consider the argument that a drop in farm prices will "reduce national purchasing power." The farmers who get the lower prices have certainly lost purchasing power. The city housewife, however, will find her food budget lower than before and will have more left over to spend on other things. Her purchasing power has been increased. So it is not at all clear that there has been a drop in national purchasing power. If by the end of the course you have developed the habit of looking automatically at both sides of any economic event, you will have made real progress.

APPENDIX: SOME QUESTIONS OF LANGUAGE

One difficulty with using plain English is that the words we use have an everyday meaning. The economist needs to use words precisely and often in a way which differs from ordinary usage. It will be well at this stage to define some of the key words which will be used in later chapters.

We have already spoken of goods and services. An *economic good* is any article which yields satisfaction to someone and which is scarce. It is *scarce* if there is less available than people would like to consume if they could have it free. In this case one will have to pay a *price* for the good. If there is enough to satisfy everyone's wants at a zero price, the article is a *free good*. The same article may be a free good in some circumstances but not in others. Drinking water from a mountain stream is a free good. But water flowing from a city tap is an economic good, since it costs something and users are charged for it in one way or another. Air is normally a free good, but cold air from an air-conditioner in summer is an economic good.

A *service* is an immaterial or intangible good. We speak of the services of the doctor, the entertainer, the teacher. These people do something which we want and for which we are willing to pay, though their product usually does not have a material form. The store clerk and the filling station attendant do not *make* anything, as a factory worker or a carpenter does. But they help us get something we want at the place where we want it, and for this service we are willing to pay.

Production is the making of an economic good or the performance of an economic service. Some early economists, including Adam Smith and Karl Marx, defined the term more narrowly to include only material production. The work of a farmer or shoemaker was considered productive, but the activities of a teacher or musician were labeled "unproductive labor." Modern economics draws no such distinction. Service production stands on the same footing as goods production.

The things which are necessary for production to be carried on are termed *factors of production* or *productive resources*. The most important of these is labor. In everyday usage, this term connotes factory work or some other manual activity. But in economics labor means any form of human effort exerted in production. The bricklayer, the accountant, the doctor, the business executive are all engaged in labor.

A second requisite for production is *capital*. This is a particularly tricky term in economics, because there is a major difference from everyday usage. When an individual speaks of his "capital" he usually means money or securities.

Thus it is essential to remember that in economics *capital is not money*. It is machinery, buildings, railroad track and rolling stock, inventories of raw materials, and other *physical* necessities for production. One classic definition runs, "Capital is produced means of production." *Capital goods* are goods which are produced, not for direct use by consumers, but as aids in the production of things which eventually will be used by consumers. Consumer goods are finished products for direct sale to consumers. All physical production can thus be divided into output of capital goods and output of consumer goods.

There is also a major difference from popular usage as regards *investment*. I think of buying a stock or bond as an "investment." A bank which makes a loan and receives a promissory note in return considers this an "investment." Here we are involved with money once more. In economics, however, *investment is the construction of a capital good*. Economics is concerned basically with physical processes rather than with the money which lubricates the wheels of industry. The amount of investment in the American economy in 1960 was *the quantity of capital goods produced during the year*, which had a money value of about $117.6 billion.

A third important element in production is *natural resources*. Strictly speaking, a natural resource is something given by nature and untouched by human hands, such as rivers, mineral deposits, virgin farm land, or virgin timber stands. As soon as human effort is applied, the resource becomes partly a capital good, a *produced* means of production. An Iowa farm today is partly a natural resource, because certain qualities of levelness, soil texture and composition, natural rainfall, and climate have been there for all time. But it is also partly a capital good, because generations of farmers have added fencing, drainage, tree and stone removal, artificial fertilizers, and other aids to production.

Labor, capital, and natural resources are coordinated in *production units*, such as farms, factories, stores, and transport networks. The work of coordination is done by *management*. Economists sometimes treat management as a separate factor of production, making four factors in all. But it may also be regarded as a specialized high-level kind of labor.

The total output of all production units in the economy, usually calculated on a yearly basis, bears the impressive title *Gross National Product*, usually shortened to GNP. The meaning of this total and the way in which it is calculated will be fully explained in Chapter 17.

For every dollar's worth of *output* produced there must be a dollar's worth of *income* created. Mysterious? Not at all. If a factory produces and sells $100,000 worth of output during a year, it receives $100,000 in return. All of this has to go somewhere. Any of it which is not paid out as wages and salaries, cost of materials purchased, taxes, or dividends must remain in the business at the end of the year (in which case it is still income belonging to the common stockholders who own the business). Thus income created must equal output produced; and instead of speaking of national product we can speak of *national income*, a term which will occur frequently in the chapters ahead.

A final matter of terminology: the difference between *money* quantities and *real* or *physical* quantities. National income and product are measured in dollars. They have to be, since this is the only way we can add up production of pig iron, soy beans, orchestra performances, and shoe shines. But is a dollar this year the same as a dollar last year? As a matter of fact, we know very well that how much a dollar will buy changes considerably over the course of time. Are we not, then, measuring with a rubber yardstick?

Suppose we observe that GNP in 1940 is $100 billion, and that GNP in 1950 is $200 billion. It looks as though production has doubled. But this would be a safe conclusion only if we knew that prices had remained unchanged. What may have happened instead is that the price of every article is double what it used to be, while production has remained unchanged. Thus we cannot draw any conclusion about physical production without making a correction for price changes.

The first step is to construct a *price index* showing what has happened to prices, on the average, year by year. Governmental statistical agencies prepare several such indexes, the most important being the Wholesale Price Index for goods at the manufacturing level, and the Consumer Price Index based on retail prices of goods and services bought by consumers. Armed with such figures, one can proceed to adjust or deflate the money totals.

For example, the money value of GNP rose from $100.6 billion in 1940 to $503.2 billion in 1960, or 500 percent. But over these years the level of prices rose by 235 percent. Dividing the percentage increase in GNP by the percentage increase in prices (500/235), we find that physical output rose by 213 percent. The result is termed *real GNP*, or *GNP in constant dollars*.

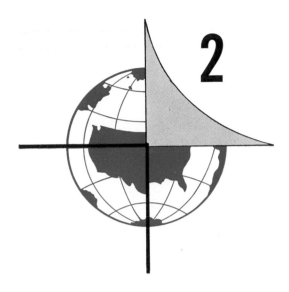

Some Dimensions of the American Economy

Young man, there is America—which at this day serves for little more than to amuse you with stories of savage men and uncouth manners; yet shall, before you taste of death, show itself equal to the whole of that commerce which now attracts the envy of the world.

EDMUND BURKE (1775)

THROUGHOUT PART ONE we shall be dealing with the idea of an economic system, the way in which different parts of the system interlock, and the problem of how one can judge whether the system is operating efficiently. Before discussing these things in general, it will help to have a description of an actual economic system. This could be the economy of Egypt, Australia, or Japan. But why not begin with things closest to home, with the economy of the United States?

An economy is marked off by the political boundaries of a national state. The physical area included may be a whole continent, as in the case of Australia, or the tiny territory of Belgium or Austria. National boundaries matter because the thing which knits an economic system together is free movement of labor, money, and commodities. These movements are typically easy *within* a country, but are subject to check at the national border. One cannot walk into an American grocery store and buy food with Austrian schillings. Movements of people from one country to another for permanent settlement are restricted by immigration laws. Movements of goods among countries are hampered by unfamiliarity of the products, transportation costs, tariff duties, and other restrictions.

In spite of these barriers there is a large international movement of goods and some international movement of people. There are also ways of converting the money of one country into that of another. Thus in a loose and figurative way one can speak of "the world economy." But the great bulk of economic transactions occur within particular countries, and this is why we use the term economic system to mean a *national* economic unit.

A second reason for emphasizing the national state is its importance in economic policy making. International organizations have little control over American economic activity. Our state and municipal governments exercise certain types of control, but the influence of the federal government is predominant. Washington is the focus for decisions on monetary policy, international economic relations, national defense, government spending, agricultural policy, and a host of other matters. Since economics aims to provide a better basis for decisions on these matters, the nation naturally bulks large in economic discussion.

The most striking characteristic of the American economy is its great size. This is not just a matter of geography. There are countries larger than the United States which have only a fraction of its productive capacity. Size for present purposes means *economic* size, as measured by total value of production. U.S. national output is now approaching the phenomenal level of $600 billion a year.

The great size of the American market permits us to use mass production methods. The enormous auto plants in Detroit make sense only in a country which buys six or seven million cars a year. They would not make sense in Chile or Ceylon. The size of our market also permits an unusually diversified pattern of production. In addition to the finished cars, we produce almost all the machine tools, aluminum, electrical apparatus, and other things necessary for automobile production. Almost every conceivable type of capital good and consumer good is produced somewhere in the United States.

The position of a small country is obviously different. It would not be feasible for Jamaica to produce a full range of industrial and agricultural products. It is more efficient to concentrate on items for which Jamaica's resources are particularly well fitted, to export a large part of this production, and to import much of what is needed for domestic consumption.

ACTORS ON THE ECONOMIC STAGE

A national economy includes *consumers* and *producers* of the national product. The basic unit on the consuming side is the family or *household.* There are about 45 million household units in the United States, plus some 10 million individuals living by themselves.

Households play a dual role in the economy. On one hand they buy the goods and services turned out by producing units. They provide the market toward which productive activity is oriented. On the other hand, households are the ultimate owners of productive assets. These assets are of several sorts. The most important is the labor of the family members. In most households this is the major source of family income. Households also own the capital assets used in business, either directly as in the case of small family businesses, or indirectly through ownership of stocks or bonds in a corporation. Finally, households own the bulk of the nation's agricultural land in the form of family farms.

The basic producing unit in the American economy is the *business concern.* The great majority of these are small family businesses conforming to the traditional picture of private enterprise. The same person owns and manages the business, takes all the risks, gets all the profit (if any), and can take cash from the till as he needs it. A large proportion of retailing, service activity, and building construction, and a good deal of light manufacturing is organized in this way. There are upwards of three million individual businesses in the United States, to which one might reasonably add some four million farms which are also managed on a family basis. "Little business" is obviously far from dead.

These millions of small businesses, however, produce only about one third of total private output. The remainder is produced by business *corporations.* The corporation is a very interesting institution which began to be important about a century ago and which has now assumed predominant importance in the economy. Its main features will be described in a moment.

It is not always recognized that *government agencies* are important producers, primarily of services rather than material products. Local governments produce police protection, fire protection, and educational services as well as streets and sewers. The state and federal governments produce highways, educational and research services, national defense, and the administration of justice. These services are important to the citizen, as would be apparent if they were suddenly eliminated. Unlike the product of business concerns, however, government services are usually not sold to individuals for a price. Their cost is assessed against the whole community through taxation. Decisions about how much of a particular service it is worthwhile to provide are made through the process of voting and political representation. How many television sets shall be produced on the other hand, is decided by individuals going to the store and "voting with their dollars" for this particular product. The former process is usually called *political or collective choice,* while the latter is termed *market choice.*

Households and producing units are linked in a dual fashion: (1) Households furnish resources for use in production. In return they receive wages, salaries, dividends, and other types of money income. This linkage is shown in the upper half of the diagram below. (2) The producing units take land, labor, and capital and combine them to turn out goods and services. These are then sold back to households, which pay for them with the money received in wages, salaries, and so on. This exchange is shown in the lower half of the diagram.

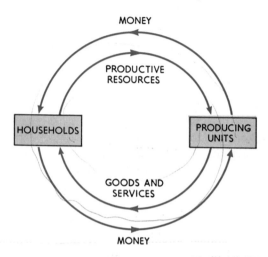

This is often termed *the wheel of wealth*, or *the circular flow of economic activity*. Money moves around the circuit in a counterclockwise direction. Physical quantities—factors of production and finished products—move in a clockwise direction. If we do our arithmetic correctly, the two flows must exactly balance each other. This sketch is highly simplified and ignores many real life complications, but it is a useful starting point in considering what one means by an economic system.

Concerning the Corporation

Most private production in the United States is carried on by business corporations. What is a corporation? How do you start one, and how does it operate?

To start a corporation you must apply to the government of one of the states, giving details of the proposed organization. If the application is approved, the state will issue a *charter* for the corporation. The corporation then becomes a legal individual, separate and distinct from any of the people who started it. It can sue and be sued, sign contracts in its own name, and so on. It has a further advantage over individuals in that it need not die with advancing age.

A corporation has the right to issue certificates of ownership, known as common stock. When the corporation is first formed, individuals acquire stock by subscribing a certain amount of money, say $100 per share, to get the company started. After that, the shares are transferable on the open market, and anyone can become part owner of a company by placing a buying order with his broker.

The common stock device enables many people to share in the ownership of the business, and this makes it possible to raise much more money than any individual could provide. A further advantage is that the stockholders of a company have *limited liability*. If I own a grocery store as an individual, and because of poor management the store runs heavily into debt, I am liable for every cent of the debt and can be put through bankruptcy proceedings if unable to pay. If I own common stock in a corporation, however, the worst that can happen is that the value of my stock may fall to zero. Beyond that, nothing can be done to me. My risk is limited to the amount I paid for the stock.

Each common stockholder owns a proportionate share of the buildings, machinery, and other property of the corporation. If there are 100,000 shares outstanding, of which I own 1,000, then I own one-hundredth of everything the company owns. If there are profits available to be passed out as dividends, one-hundredth of the total must come to me. Ownership of common stock also entitles me to a voice in electing the company's board of directors and making major policy decisions, such as to merge with another company or to issue additional stock. These decisions are normally made at an annual stockholders' meeting, at which each person has as many votes as he has shares of stock.

A corporation can also issue other types of security. The most important are *bonds* and *preferred stock*. A *bond* is a certificate of indebtedness. The buyer of the bond lends the corporation a certain amount of money. The corporation promises to pay a certain amount of interest each year, and to pay off the face value of the bond at the end of a set period. So long as these commitments are met, the bondholders have no voice in the management of the company. But if the company fails to pay the interest or principal they may take over the company's property and install a new management.

Preferred stock carries a promise to pay a fixed dividend each year, and these payments must be met before any dividends are paid to the common stockholders. It carries no right to participate in management so long as the promised payments are made.

While all corporations are similar in legal structure, they are by no means similar in size. Most of the half million business corporations in the United States are quite small. In 1952, about 60 percent of the corporations had assets of less than $100,000. They were no larger than a good-sized family business, and had adopted the corporate form mainly to achieve limited liability and other legal advantages.

At the other extreme are such corporate giants as American Telephone and Telegraph, DuPont, General Motors, and Standard Oil of New

Jersey, each with assets running into the billions. In 1952 the 250 largest corporations (excluding banks and other financial institutions), controlled about half of all nonfinancial corporate assets. These giants are found predominantly in transportation, in public utilities, and in certain branches of mining and manufacturing, which lend themselves to large-scale production. There are few large corporations in wholesale and retail trade, building construction, service industries, and other branches of the economy.

Who controls the large corporation? There are usually many thousands or even hundreds of thousands of stockholders. A.T.&T., the world's largest corporation, in 1962 had 1,700,000 stockholders and more than 200,-000,000 shares of common stock. The largest ball park would not begin to hold these people for an annual stockholders' meeting. In any event most of them take only a passive interest in the company. They may glance idly through the handsomely printed annual report. If they don't like the way things are going in the company, they sell their stock and that is that.

So who controls the annual meeting and elects the directors of the company? Sometimes one family or group owns a substantial block of stock. If the smaller stockholders are passive and unorganized, the large owners may achieve a dominant position. They may take an active hand in management, or they may leave this to salaried professional managers. In the latter case, the managers have wide discretion in managing the company's affairs, so long as they do not displease the dominant stockholding group.

In other cases no individual or group owns enough of the common stock to have any appreciable influence on the corporation. Here the management in charge, however it got there in the first place, is the dominant group and no one can effectively challenge its control. Each year management collects proxies from the scattered and powerless stockholders, and re-elects itself to office. As the top officers of the company near retirement age, they select their successors. Management becomes a self-perpetuating body, rather like a university faculty or the leadership of a political party.

The Organization Man and New-Style Capitalism

It is worth pausing to emphasize the gap between small individual business and large corporate business. In the large corporation, the property ownership of the common stockholders is largely divorced from control of the business, which is held by management. The top managers of American business are a new type of social group, controlling many billions of property which they do not own, setting their own salaries and other perquisites, obviously not subject to "the profit motive" in the same sense as a grocery store owner. What does motivate them? Why do they do what they do? The answers are important for the operation of the economy.

One must first distinguish personal motives from institutional drives. In personal terms, a top business executive is not very different from a politician, a general, or a college president. He is interested in income, but also in influence, public reputation, and professional excellence. Being president of A.T.&T. yields craftsmanlike satisfaction as well as a large salary.

If one looks beyond the individual and asks what motivates the management group as a whole, profit is clearly important. There are several reasons for this: (1) The company's profit rate is an indicator of professional success. A management which regularly turns in satisfactory profits, which does better this year than last year, or which does better than competitors in the same industry, is acclaimed in business circles. (2) Profits are necessary if the business is to grow and expand. Management generally regards expansion as normal and desirable. (3) Management often shares in the profits through bonus arrangements. (4) Consistent failure to make money can land a management in serious trouble. It may mean a cold shoulder from the bankers, loss of competitive position in the industry, possibly even the horrid specter of a stockholders' revolt.

Management thus seeks profit; but this is different from saying that it seeks only profit, or always seeks the last dollar of profit. There is a good deal to the conception of corporate management as sitting at the center of the enterprise, ringed in by pressures impinging from various directions. Customers are eager for better products at lower prices. The union wants its annual increase in wage rates and other benefits. The banker hopes that the company will remain solvent and repay its loans. The stockholders hope that the current rate of dividends will be maintained and preferably increased.

These pressures conflict at many points, and one cannot be sure that the stockholders' interests will always come out on top. There is evidence, for example, that prosperous companies often buy worker good will by paying more than prevailing wage rates in their areas. This may conflict with management's obligation to make the most money for stockholders, but the workers are nearby and can make more trouble for management than the stockholders can. Management's job is to live with these contending pressures, balance its books, and survive.

THE ORGANIZATION OF PRODUCTION

What is the relative importance of big business and little business in different sectors of the economy? It is easiest to get information on the size of *producing establishments*—farms, retail stores, manufacturing plants, and so on. This is obviously not the same thing as size of *companies*. One manufacturing company, such as U.S. Steel, may own many plants in different locations. Sears Roebuck or A&P own hundreds of retail outlets. But the individual store or plant remains the basic unit of production, and the size of these units is of considerable interest.

When one looks at the statistics, a striking conclusion emerges. The great majority of producing units are quite small. They seem barely large enough to yield a precarious living to their owner. This is true whether one looks at manufacturing, farming, retailing, or the service industries. The only type of industry in which large units are consistently the rule is public utilities, including railroads.

But while the small establishments predominate in numbers, they are much less important in production. The minority of large establishments in each industry typically produce the bulk of the industry's output.

Look first at the situation in manufacturing (Table 2–1). There are

TABLE 2–1

Size of Manufacturing Establishments, 1958*

SIZE CLASS (Number of Employees)	ESTABLISHMENTS		EMPLOYEES		PAYROLLS	
	NUMBER	PERCENT	NUMBER (000)	PERCENT	MILLIONS OF DOLLARS	PERCENT
1–4	105,641	35.4	218	1.4	738	1.0
5–9	50,660	17.0	340	2.2	1,297	1.8
10–19	46,820	15.7	644	4.2	2,615	3.5
20–49	46,307	15.5	1,443	9.4	6,058	8.2
50–99	21,764	7.3	1,513	9.8	6,416	8.7
100–249	16,132	5.4	2,497	16.2	10,939	14.8
250–499	6,240	2.1	2,150	14.0	9,709	13.2
500–999	2,757	0.9	1,893	12.3	9,176	12.4
1,000–2,499	1,363	0.5	2,047	13.3	10,852	14.7
2,500 and over	498	0.2	2,649	17.2	15,950	21.6
Total	298,182	100.0	15,394	100.0	73,750	100.0

* U.S. Department of Commerce, Bureau of the Census, *Census of Manufactures*, 1958, pp. 2–2, 2–3. In this and subsequent tables columns might not total precisely because of rounding.

almost 300,000 manufacturing establishments. But half of these are "holes-in-the-wall" with less than 10 employees. There are only about 27,000 plants in the country with 100 or more workers, or less than 10 percent of the total. Yet this small minority of plants employs about 75 percent of manufacturing workers in the country and accounts for 77 percent of factory payrolls.

In the case of retail stores (Table 2–2), the best measure of size is not number of employees but amount of business done per year. A highly automated supermarket may employ few workers but have a large sales volume. There are about 1 ¾ million stores in the United States. The dividing line between "small stores" and others may reasonably be set at sales of $100,000 per year, which would amount to about $300 per business day. On this basis almost three quarters of the stores operating in 1958 were small. Another 20 percent were medium-sized stores with annual sales volume between $100,000 and $1,000,000. Only 1.5 percent of the stores had a sales volume in excess of a million a year.

If one looks at business done, however, the picture is very different. The 1.5 percent of big stores did 31 percent of the retail business of the country, while the 20 percent of medium-sized stores did another 46 percent. This left less than one quarter of the business for the multitude of small retail outlets.

TABLE 2–2

Size of Retail Establishments, 1958*

Annual Sales (Thousands of Dollars)	Establishments		Sales	
	Number	Percent	Millions of Dollars	Percent
Less than 5	75,064	4.6	254	0.1
5– 9	146,805	8.9	1,014	0.5
10– 19	242,589	14.7	3,468	1.8
20– 29	201,886	12.3	4,884	2.6
30– 49	288,178	17.5	11,131	5.9
50– 99	316,998	19.2	22,288	11.8
100– 299	265,346	16.1	43,482	23.1
300– 499	49,125	3.0	18,766	10.1
500– 999	35,740	2.2	24,602	13.1
1,000–1,999	16,929	1.0	23,357	12.4
2,000–4,999	6,954	0.4	19,714	10.5
5,000 and over	1,295	0.1	15,520	8.2
Total	1,646,909	100.0	188,480	100.0

* U.S. Department of Commerce, *Statistical Abstract of the United States*, 1961, p. 836. Includes only stores which operated throughout the year.

The importance of large-scale retailing is even greater than these figures suggest. Many of the units which appear as small or medium-sized in Table 2–2 belong to large companies operating chains of retail outlets. Thus the true "independent retailer" is now confined to a small percentage of the market.

The situation in farming is shown in Table 2–3. The number of farms

TABLE 2–3

Size of Farm Units, 1959*

Size of Farm (Acres)	Farms		Acreage	
	Number	Percent	Acres (000)	Percent
Under 10	240,699	6.5	1,041	0.1
10– 49	811,118	21.9	21,807	1.9
50– 99	657,656	17.8	47,932	4.3
100–179	772,220	20.9	105,691	9.4
180–259	414,365	11.1	89,477	8.0
260–499	471,385	12.7	165,383	14.8
500–999	199,962	5.4	137,319	12.3
1,000 and over	136,278	3.7	551,713	49.2
Total	3,703,683	100.0	1,120,363	100.0

* Preliminary. U.S. Department of Commerce, *Statistical Abstract of the United States*, 1961, p. 619.

in the United States has been falling for a long time. From six and a quarter million in 1930, it has now fallen to less than four million. It is striking that almost half of these units contain less than 100 acres. This is scarcely a farm at all for grain growing or livestock production; but for poultry, fruits and vegetables, and certain specialty crops 100 acres may be quite adequate.

There are about two million farms of more than 100 acres. Only 136,000 farms, or about 4 percent of the total, contain a thousand acres or more. But note that these large units include almost half of total farm acreage. Once more a small minority of producing units is responsible for the bulk of economic activity in the industry.

One other feature of American farming may be noted in passing. About 80 percent of all farms are owned by the people who operate them. Only 20 percent of farm operators are tenants. This is a striking change from 1930 when 58 percent of farm operators were tenants and only 42 percent were owners. The change reflects the decline of cotton farming in the "old South," which was mainly on a tenancy basis. It also reflects the high prosperity during and after World War II, which enabled many tenants to leave the land for city jobs and many others to buy the land they occupy. Farm ownership, of course, is not always complete. About one third of the farm owners have mortgages, averaging more than $5,000 per farm, so that the local banker is often a silent partner in the enterprise.

The coexistence of large and small units in most American industries presents an interesting puzzle. It is not a new phenomenon. The picture shown here for recent years would not be basically different if one looked at 1930 or 1900. One would still find a minority of large units producing the bulk of the output in each industry, and a multitude of smaller units dividing the remainder.

How can "big fellows" and "little fellows" continue to exist side by side in a competitive economy? If large-scale operation is as efficient as we are brought up to believe, why don't the bigger concerns outproduce and undersell the small ones, and eventually force them out of existence?

The answer consists of several parts.

First, the industry classification used in Tables 2–1 to 2–3 is very broad. Manufacturing is not a single industry but a bundle of industries, which differ greatly as regards the most efficient size of plant. A steel mill or an auto assembly plant must be large to be efficient; but an efficient-sized cotton mill is considerably smaller, and a garment shop can be smaller still. The same is true in agriculture. Cattle ranching takes many acres, but thousands of chickens can be raised on a few acres. Thus if we made up tables for specific types of farming, or manufacturing, or retailing, the variation in size of units would be considerably reduced.

Second, even though a particular size of cotton mill may be most efficient, it may not make a great deal of difference whether the plant is somewhat larger or smaller. A plant half as large as the "right sized" one may be able to produce a yard of cloth at only 5 percent greater cost. Thus small plants can survive, though they will have lower profits than their more efficient rivals.

Third, the small operator may be able to offset his relative inefficiency in various ways. He can sometimes get a higher price for his product. Studies of retailing usually show that the small independent grocer or druggist charges more than the large chain stores. Yet many people continue to patronize the independent.

The small producer may get by partly by paying lower wages. Wage surveys typically show a direct relation between wage level and size of establishment in an industry. The bigger units pay out part of the gain from their higher productivity in the form of larger paychecks and fringe benefits to employees. This is good public relations and also good union relations.

Finally, the small businessman may survive by accepting a lower income for his effort. In farming, storekeeping, service and repair industries, and other one-man operations, the main cost is the owner's time; and he is free to value this at whatever he pleases. The less efficient he is in comparison with larger units, the less he will earn. Many thousands of small businessmen doubtless end up with less per year than they could earn by taking a salaried job. One can interpret this in various ways: as sheer ignorance and lack of foresight; as chronic overoptimism, an unwarranted expectation that "next year will be better"; or as a deliberate choice of independence even at a lower income.

Whatever the interpretation, the facts are clear. The small businessman survives partly by accepting a low income. Every year many thousands go bankrupt and pass from the scene, but there seems always to be an equal number of new recruits eager to step into their shoes.

FACTORS OF PRODUCTION: LABOR

Before examining what comes out of the production process, let us look at what goes in. The basic *inputs* or *factors of production* are labor, capital, and natural resources; and a few words on each of these is in order.

In the main lobby of the U.S. Department of Commerce building there is a "population clock," whose revolving hands show the population of the United States as of any hour and minute. The hands whiz around quite rapidly. Every 7 seconds a new arrival is registered on the clock, while every 19 seconds there is a subtraction through death. At 3:01 P.M. on November 30, 1961, the clock reached 185,000,000 people. By the time you read this, it will have passed the 190 million mark.

But this alone does not tell us how much labor the country can count on for production. Very young people, very old people, and a good many in between do not work for pay. Whether to work or not is partly a matter of preference and custom, and the percentage of the population which is at work varies considerably from country to country.

The situation in the United States in 1962 is shown in Figure 2–1.[1]

FIGURE 2–1

Percentage of Population in the Labor Force, United States, 1962

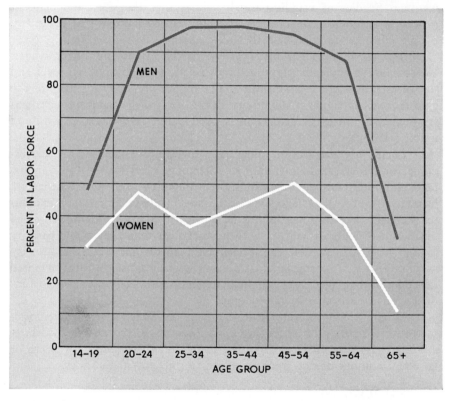

About 74 million people, or 58 percent of the population aged 14 and over were counted as members of the labor force at that time. More interesting than the total, however, is the distribution of the labor force. Note that more than 90 percent of men in the age range 20–65, and almost 40 percent of all women in this range, were available for work. There is a marked tapering off, however, under the age of 20 and above the age of 65.

This already tells us several things about the American economy and society:

1. For the able-bodied male in the prime of life, work is virtually obligatory.

2. The percentage of women at work, which has risen rapidly since

---

[1] Data from U.S. Department of Labor, *Monthly Labor Review*, April, 1962, p. 632.

1900 and is still rising, indicates a society in which women have high independence and status. There are many countries in which this would not be true. In Moslem countries, the percentage of women employed outside the home would be close to zero.

3. The low percentage of young people in the labor force indicates the high value placed on education in the United States. The proportion of those aged 16–25 who are enrolled in educational institutions has risen greatly since 1900 and is still rising. It must be a wealthy economy which can afford to keep young people out of the labor force for so long.

4. The American economy is also prosperous enough so that most people over 65 can and do choose to retire from work. Indeed, the retirement age has been creeping down and affects a good many people from 60 onwards.

A nation's labor supply is not just a matter of numbers. *Quality* is also important. Labor quality includes physical strength, health, trade skills, regularity of work performance, and responsiveness to material incentives. Some of these things are not susceptible to measurement. One tangible indicator of quality, however, is the *educational level* of the labor force. Education is partly a consumer good, which contributes to a fuller and more satisfying life whatever one's occupation. But it is also a capital good in the sense of inculcating attitudes favorable to high productivity and developing specific vocational skills. A more highly educated labor force can be presumed to be more skilled, more mobile, more aware of occupational possibilities and rewards.

Judged by this yardstick, the quality of the American labor force has risen sharply over the past century. Young people now complete, on the average, many more years of schooling than their fathers and grandfathers. Present-day workers in the prime ages 20–45 have had about three times as much education as people in the same age groups in 1900.

Some might still argue that this has no direct connection with productive efficiency, but they would be wrong. There is plenty of evidence that how much people earn is correlated with the length of their education. Thus if people get paid roughly what they are worth, their productive capacity must rise as their education rises.

Schultz's calculations on this are shown in Table 2–4 (page 30). By looking at the top right-hand corner of the table you can see that graduation from college will be worth about $150,000 to you over your lifetime. You will get back the cost of your college education 10 times over. Note also that the financial return on a college education has not decreased over the past generation, but on the contrary has increased considerably. The increased earnings resulting from a high-school diploma, however, have fallen (relatively) since 1939. Now that almost everyone goes through high school, the added value of a diploma is no longer what it used to be.

What do the people in the labor force do for a living? The kinds of job at which people were working in 1961 are shown in Table 2–5. In

TABLE 2–4

Additional Lifetime Income of U.S. Males, Ages 18 to 64, by Years of School Completed and Costs of Education, 1939 and 1958.

YEARS OF SCHOOL COMPLETED	1939	1958
College		
A. Added earnings (Dollars)	39,000	151,000
B. Added costs of education (Dollars)	4,348	13,780
C. Ratio A/B	8.97	10.96
High school		
A. Added earnings (Dollars)	25,000	70,000
B. Added costs of education (Dollars)	1,636	5,930
C. Ratio A/B	15.3	11.80
Elementary		
A. Added earnings (Dollars)	12,000	47,000
B. Added costs of education (Dollars)	344	1,169
C. Ratio A/B	34.9	40.2

Source: Theodore W. Schultz, "Education and Economic Growth," in *Social Forces Influencing American Education*, Sixtieth Yearbook of the National Society for the Study of Education, Part II (Chicago: University of Chicago Press, 1961), p. 79.

TABLE 2–5

Occupational Composition of the Employed Force, United States, 1962

OCCUPATIONAL GROUP	PERCENTAGE OF LABOR FORCE	
Professional, technical and kindred workers	11.7	
Managers, proprietors, and officials (except farm)	11.0	
Total		22.7
Clerical and kindred workers	14.9	
Sales workers	6.3	
Total		21.2
Service workers		12.9
Craftsmen, foremen, and kindred workers	12.9	
Operatives and kindred workers	17.5	
Laborers, except farm and mine	5.4	
Total		35.8
Farmers and farm managers	4.1	
Farm laborers	3.4	
Total		7.5
Total employed		100.0

Source: U.S. Department of Labor, *Employment and Earnings*, June, 1962.

broad terms, about one fifth are professional people, technical workers, executives, and business proprietors. Another fifth work in sales, clerical, and other white-collar jobs. About two fifths are manual workers at every level from laborers to highly skilled craftsmen. More than one tenth are in service occupations, and less than one tenth are in agriculture.

As industries rise and fall in relative importance, and as production techniques and organization change, the pattern of employment also changes. The occupational distribution of the labor force in 1900 looked quite different from the 1961 distribution. One striking tendency over the long run has been the rapid increase of professional, clerical, and other white-collar jobs. White-collar workers now form a majority of the urban labor force, and their preponderance is increasing. Another striking trend has been the relative decline of agriculture from more than half of the labor force in 1870 to less than 8 percent today.

FACTORS OF PRODUCTION: NATURAL RESOURCES

Most countries are not in the comfortable position of the United States. They have difficulty raising enough food to support their populations, even at a low level of living. Agriculture is their basic industry, and land their basic resource. It is an important resource in any country, at any stage of development.

The land *area* of a country does not reveal the amount of economically usable land. Most of the country may be desert or frozen tundra. Even in the United States, with its temperate climate, cropland is a minor part of the total area. The land area of the continental United States is 1,902 million acres. More than 40 percent of this is desert, mountains, forests, public grazing land, and other land not in farms. Almost another 40 percent is pasture and woodland. Cropland normally used for crops is only about 400 million acres, or 20 percent of the total.[2] In some countries (Belgium, Holland), the percentage of cultivated land would be much higher than this, but in others (Egypt, Saudi Arabia) it would be much lower.

We ordinarily think of the supply of usable land as fixed by climate and geography. It is something which is "just there." But this is not entirely true. The supply of land can often be increased by human effort. The most dramatic examples are large irrigation projects, which may reclaim millions of acres previously idle because of insufficient rainfall. Much can be done also through agricultural research. Development of dry farming methods, and of drought-resistant crops such as sorghum, enables cultivation to be pushed out into areas of scanty rainfall. Development of strains of wheat with a short growing season has enabled wheat growing to be pushed quite far north in Canada and the U.S.S.R.

---

[2] U.S. Department of Commerce, *Statistical Abstract of the United States*, Washington, 1961, p. 614. Data for earlier years may be found in U.S. Department of Agriculture, *Agricultural Statistics 1960*, Washington, 1961.

The fact that a certain amount of land is available for agriculture does not mean that all this land will be used. The amount of land actually used, and the intensity with which it is used, depends on population pressure in relation to the level of agricultural technology. If population pressure is severe and agricultural methods primitive, as in India, every possible acre will be pressed into service and a great deal of labor will be devoted to each one. But if population is sparser or agriculture more productive, it may not be necessary to put all of the usable land under cultivation. The United States is presently in a position to concentrate its agriculture on a limited acreage of the best land, while retiring less desirable land from active use.

When one turns to natural resources other than land, it is difficult to say much in general terms. The United States obviously has great supplies of water power, timber, coal, oil, minerals, and other products of nature. A listing of quantities of each of these things would be tedious and not very instructive. But it may be useful to comment on two aspects of resources which are often misunderstood in popular discussion.

First, when is a resource really a resource? This may seem like a silly question. Surely a resource is a physical quantity of something provided by nature. It is just there, for all time, unless or until it is used up in production. But this commonsense view turns out to be wrong. Resources are relative. Whether a physical object is or is not a resource to the economy depends on *discovery*, *demand* and *technology*.

The importance of discovery is obvious. A pool of oil has no economic significance until someone knows it is there. In most countries of the world geological exploration has been so scanty that no one knows what lies under the ground. Even in the better-mapped United States, there are undoubtedly many "strikes" still to be made.

Demand is also necessary. Someone must want the item in question, or want something which can be made from it. The Africans of Kenya and Uganda do not like rhinoceros meat, and so the rhinoceros is a nuisance rather than a resource.

Technical knowledge is a further ingredient. Crude oil was not a resource to the American Indian, but today we know how to extract from it a wide variety of useful products. Technical change can destroy resources as well as create them. Today we count our reserves of anthracite and bituminous coal as a basic resource. But suppose that a century from now developments in solar and atomic energy have provided cheaper sources of heat and power. Then coal may be just a strange black substance in the ground, with no economic value.

Thus natural resources turn out not to be so natural after all. To a significant extent, they are man-made.

Second, what about the scarcity and exhaustibility of natural resources? There is a popular impression that, since these resources are provided in fixed amounts by nature, and since we use up large quantities of them every year, we are bound in time to run out of many types of resources. What then? Will a shortage of basic resources eventually reduce our economic productivity, our military capacity, and our standard of living? Many conferences have been organized, many books written, many millions of dollars spent on research into this problem.

But is it really much of a problem? What happens as one continues year after year to use up the supply of a fixed resource? First, technical change may shift demand away from the item long before the supply has been exhausted. This seems likely to be the case with coal. With the present rapid pace of technical change, it is not much use to predict resource shortages 30 or 40 years ahead, since no one can really say what will be a resource at that time.

Second, as visible supplies of a resource dwindle, exploration for new supplies is intensified. In the case of oil this search has been spectacularly seccessful, to the point where many known fields are being held out of production to avoid flooding the market and breaking the world price.

Third, there are few natural products for which there are no substitutes. If the supply of a particular resource decreases, and if exploration does not provide a satisfactory offset, its price will rise. This will stimulate research to discover ways of doing without it and substituting other materials. Aluminum may be used in place of copper, stainless steel in place of aluminum, plastics in place of rubber.

The resource problem is eased also by the availability of international trade. Countries which are rich in resources are usually eager to sell them, and the United States has been drawing more and more raw materials from foreign sources. This involves the risk of wartime shipping dislocations and the consequent need for strategic reserves. But this is not a problem of resource scarcity.

FACTORS OF PRODUCTION: CAPITAL

Capital consists of *physical goods* used in the production of other goods and services. Capital goods are not directly consumed but they help to produce things which are desired and consumed by the public. A shoe factory constitutes capital because it turns out shoes for which consumers are willing to pay a price. A railroad's track and rolling stock are capital because they produce transportation services for which people are willing to pay. Fences, barns, and farm machinery are part of the capital used in agricultural production.

Most capital in the United States is privately owned, but ownership is not the essence of the matter. Publicly owned assets also yield services and may properly be considered part of the nation's capital. School and college buildings contribute to the production of educational services. Streets and highways provide transportation service. When the British railroads were bought out by the government in 1947 (partly because they were going slowly bankrupt!), they did not cease to be capital because of the transfer of ownership.

We sometimes say that capital goods are *durable*, while consumer goods are used up quickly. But this distinction is also slippery. What about an automobile, which may have a useful life of 15 or 20 years, longer than the life of most factory machinery? Should we not regard the automobile as a capital good, which "produces" the consumer good of transportation service year after year until it is worn out? And what about a home or an apartment house? Is this not a capital good, since it will yield housing service over a long period of time?

Government statisticians count all residential buildings as capital, on the ground that they resemble factories and commercial buildings in being very long-lived. Automobiles, stoves, refrigerators, and other household items are termed "durable consumer goods" and are not counted as capital. But this is a matter of definition, with no firm logical foundation.

Capital goods wear out over the course of time. This is termed *depreciation*, and is usually regarded as happening gradually and continuously. The fact of depreciation has important consequences. Suppose there are $1,000 billion worth of capital goods in existence in the United States at the beginning of 1963. If no new capital goods were produced during the year, the capital in existence at the end of the year would be less than at the beginning. The same buildings and machines might be standing around, but they would be more nearly worn out. The amount of service left in them would be less by the amount of the depreciation which had occurred during the year.

Production of new capital goods is termed *gross capital formation*. To see how much has actually been added to the capital stock over a certain period, however, we must deduct depreciation on the pre-existing capital goods. The result, gross capital formation minus depreciation, is termed *net capital formation*. This is the real addition to capital supply.

The United States has been adding to its capital stock for many years, and this stock has now reached a fantastic total. Goldsmith estimates that the net value of capital goods in the United States in 1958 was $1,367 billion.[3] Our national wealth at this time was thus almost three times the value of our annual output. We had about three years' production "stored up" in the form of capital assets. From another standpoint, our capital stock amounted to about $7,500 per head of population, or $20,000 for each member of the labor force.

Who owns all this wealth? About 40 percent of it belongs to business concerns (Figure 2–2). About the same amount consists of housing

---

[3] Raymond T. Goldsmith, *The National Wealth of the United States in the Postwar Period* (Princeton, N.J.: Princeton University Press, 1962). This total includes only *reproducible* tangible wealth. Land and other natural resources are excluded. Military installations are also excluded.

owned by families. The decision to count residences as capital is thus a major decision. Without this, national capital would be much smaller, and the ownership proportions would be quite different. Of the publicly owned capital, more than two thirds belongs to state and local governments. But remember that military facilities are excluded, which would have added almost a hundred billion to the total.

The United States is clearly a capital-rich country. We may note also that the supply of capital in the American economy has been rising a good deal faster than the supply of labor. The number of man-hours of

FIGURE 2–2

Net Reproducible Tangible Wealth by Sector, United States, 1958

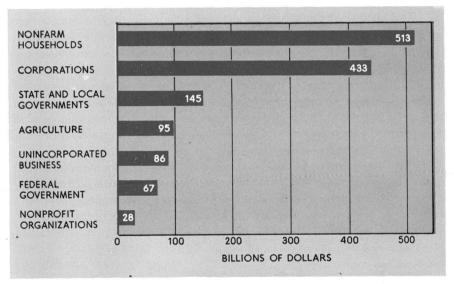

labor employed in private production in the United States doubled between 1890 and 1960; but the amount of capital in use increased more than five times.[4] *Thus capital per man-hour of labor* increased more than 2½ times over this period. This is a major reason why labor has become more productive over the years. Each man now works with much more machinery, power, and other physical aids to production. "Automation" is simply the latest expression of a trend which can be traced far back in our economic history.

Capital is not spread evenly over all industries in the economy. Some industries (oil refining, chemicals, air transportation) use a large amount of capital per worker employed. Other industries (clothing manufacture, retailing, cleaning and dyeing) use less equipment per man. The result is

---

[4] John W. Kendrick, *Productivity Trends in the United States* (Princeton, N.J.: Princeton University Press, 1961).

wide differences in output per worker. High-capital industries typically turn out more per man than low-capital industries, and they also pay higher wages to their employees. The benefits of *capitalism* to the worker have often been disputed. The benefits of *capital* appear to be beyond dispute.

THE PATTERN OF OUTPUT

What does all this labor and capital produce? How large is the national output? What does it look like, in concrete terms?

United States output, measured either as total or per capita output, is the highest in the world by a wide margin. National output per head of population in 1961 was $2,824. This does *not* mean that any family with three children could descend on local groceries and department stores and lay in 5 × $2,824 or $14,120 of goods during the year. A considerable part of national output—plant and equipment produced for sale to business concerns, military items and other products purchased by government—never shows up in the stores. The output of consumer goods and services in 1961 came to the smaller figure of $1,930 per capita. Remember also that income is unequally distributed within the population. If our five-person family were toward the upper end of the income scale, it would be able to command much more than the average quantity of goods, and conversely for low-income families.

The total output of the American economy, worth more than $550 billion in 1962, staggers the imagination. The number of separate products runs to hundreds of thousands. A list of even the major items would take many pages. Thus one cannot give any detailed description of the outflow of products. But by grouping products into certain broad "families," we can say something about the relative importance of these groups.

The importance of an industry may be gauged either by the number of people it employs or by how much it produces. Both measures are shown in Table 2–6. Value of output is perhaps the more significant measure, and we shall rely mainly on it.

Manufacturing is the most important branch of economic activity, a position which it attained about 1890 and has retained ever since. The proportion of national output coming from manufacturing plants has continued to creep up decade by decade, and now stands at about 30 percent of total production. Within this total are hundreds of different lines of manufacturing. These are usually grouped into two broad categories: "hard goods" or durable goods, which includes steel and other metal products, machinery, automobiles and transportation equipment, household appliances, and the like; and "soft goods" or nondurables, which includes food products, textiles, clothing, and so on. The durable goods group is now the larger of the two, and its preponderance is increasing.

Second most important is the trade sector, which makes up about one sixth of national output. The wholesalers and retailers in this category produce the service of getting goods from the producer to the ultimate user, of providing convenient locations in which families can have access to goods produced all over the world. With the growing size and complexity of the American economy, the task of distributing goods has become steadily larger relative to the task of physical production.

Third in order come the services produced by government. They now constitute one eighth of national output, a considerably larger percentage than a generation ago, due mainly to heavier military expenditures. Private service industries produce a bit more than 12 percent of national output. This group includes medical, legal, and other professional services; the entertainment industries; personal services such as barbering and beauty care; laundering and dry cleaning; and the work of servants in private households.

TABLE 2–6

Industrial Distribution of National Output and Employed Labor Force, United States, 1961*

Type of Industry	National Output (Percent)	Employed Labor Force (Percent)
Agriculture	4.3	7.6
Manufacturing and mining	29.6	25.0
Construction	5.2	6.2
Trade	16.3	20.2
Finance, insurance, real estate	10.4	4.6
Transportation, communication, and public utilities	8.3	6.0
Services	12.1	14.8
Government	13.8	15.9
Total	100.0	100.0

* U.S. Department of Commerce, *Survey of Current Business*, July, 1962.

Two impressions stand out from Table 2–6. One is the small size of the historic agricultural sector. Agriculture, forestry, and fisheries together now turn out less than 5 percent of national output. The political turmoil over agricultural policy relates to a shrinking part of the economy. A second striking fact is that industries concerned with physical production now constitute only half of national output. This is true even if we stretch a point and count transportation and utilities as part of the "goods" group along with manufacturing, mining, construction, and agriculture. The remaining "service" sectors—trade, finance, services, and government—make up half of national output, and their share is growing year by year. When we speak of the output of goods *and services*, therefore, the second term is not an afterthought. More and more of our productive activity takes an intangible rather than a physical form.

A different basis for classifying productive activity is according to the purchaser of the product, the ultimate customer. The customer may be a private household, a business concern, a government agency, or a foreign buyer. The relative importance of these groups in 1961 is shown in Table 2–7. This table is based on principles of national income accounting

TABLE 2–7

Gross National Product in 1961 by Type of Purchaser

	BILLIONS OF DOLLARS	PERCENT OF TOTAL
Consumer purchases	359.10	69.2
Durable goods	43.74	8.4
Nondurable goods	155.21	29.9
Services	139.10	26.8
Residential construction	21.04	4.1
Business purchases	48.22	9.3
Buildings	20.55	4.0
Machinery and equipment	25.54	4.9
Change in inventories	2.13	0.4
Government purchases of goods and services	107.43	20.7
Federal	57.00	11.0
State and local	50.43	9.7
Net exports of goods and services	3.98	0.8
Exports	27.27	5.3
Imports	23.29	4.5
Total	518.73	100.0

Source: *Survey of Current Business*, July, 1962, p. 6.

which we shall not examine in detail until Chapter 17. All that need be said here is that the table includes only *finished products*, at the stage of passing into use by an ultimate purchaser.

Consumers, as one might expect, are much the largest customers for the national output. They regularly buy around 70 percent of each year's production. Note the large proportion of this which consists of expenditure on services rather than on physical products. Purchases of services run well over $100 billion per year and make up about 40 percent of all household expenditure.

Government agencies are the second largest group of customers, taking about one fifth of all goods and services produced. State and local governments are the main buyers of ordinary or nonmilitary products, but heavy purchases of military items by the federal government make its total somewhat larger. This reverses the historic relationship which prevailed before 1940, when federal purchases were considerably smaller than state and local purchases.

Third in line come business organizations. Remember that the total here does not include purchases of materials which are to be worked over some more and then re-sold to someone else, such as purchases of leather by a shoe factory or cotton yarn by a weaving mill. Table 2–7 includes only business purchases *for final use.* This means basically purchases of buildings and machinery—in short, *capital formation.* This is not a big item, forming only about 10 percent of GNP. But it is a strategic item in the economy for two reasons. First, it is the source of new productive capacity and thus a major source of economic growth. National production is higher this year than last mainly because part of last year's output went into office buildings, factories, machine tools, commercial aircraft, and other things that will contribute to greater production over the years ahead.

Second, business purchases of plant and equipment are irregular from year to year, depending on sales and profits in the immediate past and businessmen's guesses about the future. Business purchases fluctuate considerably more than consumer purchases. These fluctuations are a major element in the "business cycle."

WHO GETS THE PRODUCT?

The Gross National Product of the United States in 1962 was about $550 billion. Now for every dollar of goods produced and sold there must be a dollar of income created. We can speak interchangeably of national *product* or national *income.* They come to the same thing.

Who gets all this money? And why do they get it? People receive income mainly because of their command over factors of production. They supply the services of these factors to producing units, and receive a cash payment in return. Factors of production can be divided broadly into animate (labor power) and inanimate (capital and natural resources). The return to the former is usually termed *labor income,* and that to the latter, *property income.*

Property income goes by various names—interest, dividends, profits, rents. These are all returns to ownership. Farmers, storekeepers, and other independent proprietors also receive income partly as a return on the land and capital which they own. Labor income appears mainly in the form of wage and salary payments, which alone make up about *two thirds* of national income in the United States. Farmers, small businessmen, and independent professional men do not pay themselves a salary; but most of what they receive is also a payment for personal effort.

Labor income and property income are hard to untangle statistically, mainly because it is hard to split the incomes of farmers and independent business and professional men into a "labor share" and a "property share." Making the best guess one can about this, however, it appears that more than three quarters of all income in the United States today is labor income, and less than one quarter is property income.[5]

Property owners do less well than these figures suggest, because they get considerably less than the income which theoretically "belongs" to them. About half of corporation profits are taken by the federal government in income taxes. Of the remainder, companies usually put about half back into the business and pay out the other half in dividends. Thus dividend payments come down to roughly a quarter of the original profit total. If one looks at income *actually received*, then, property income amounts to only about 15 percent of all personal income.

A different kind of question is how much income is received by each household in the economy, regardless of the source from which it comes. How many households fall in each "income bracket"? This bears directly on the degree of income equality or inequality in the country. The situation in 1960 is shown in Table 2–8, which covers all families of two or

TABLE 2–8

Distribution of Families by Annual Income, 1960

Annual Income (Before Income Taxes)	Number of Families (000)	Percent of Families	Aggregate Income Received (Millions)	(Percent)
Under $2,000	3,287	7.2	3,987	1.1
2,000–2,999	3,006	6.6	7,583	2.2
3,000–3,999	4,155	9.2	14,645	4.2
4,000–4,999	5,095	11.2	22,973	6.6
5,000–5,999	5,320	11.7	29,253	8.4
6,000–7,499	7,499	16.5	50,448	14.4
7,500–9,999	7,973	17.6	68,522	19.6
10,000–14,999	5,690	12.5	67,931	19.5
15,000 and over	3,345	7.4	83,824	24.0
Total	45,370	100.0	349,166	100.0

Source: U.S. Department of Commerce, *Survey of Current Business*, April, 1962.

more people living together, but does not include individuals living alone.[6]

Despite the growth of equalitarian beliefs and policies in recent decades, income distribution is still quite unequal. At the bottom, many households still have incomes at the incredibly low level of $2,000 or less. At

---

[5] The basis for this estimate, and the way in which labor and capital shares have changed since 1900, is explained in detail in Chapter 14.

[6] There were about 10 million individuals living by themselves in 1960. These were mostly young people just breaking into the labor market, or older retired people. On this account they fall heavily into the lower income brackets. To include them would give a biased view of "normal" family incomes.

the other extreme, the 7.4 percent of families with incomes above $15,000 receive about one quarter of all personal income. These high incomes come partly from concentration of property ownership in a minority of the population, but also from high business salaries and professional earnings. Most of the inequality of household incomes *must* be due to inequality of wages and salaries, since these provide the great bulk of all income received.

Remember, however, that the incomes in Table 2–8 are *before* payment of federal income taxes. The personal income tax rate rises steeply with rising income. People in the range of $20,000—50,000 a year pay about a quarter of their incomes in income tax, and people above $100,000 pay about half.[7] Thus the distribution of income after taxes is somewhat more equal than the distribution of pretax incomes. Whether we have gone too far, or not far enough, in leveling incomes through taxation is a hotly disputed political issue which will be discussed in Chapter 14.

SUMMARY

1. An economic system consists of *households* and *producing units*—mainly private business concerns in the United States, though government agencies are also important producers.

2. There is a circular flow of money and services between the two groups. Households sell services to producing units for money and spend this money on the output of the producing units.

3. Most producing units in the American economy are quite small. The minority of large units, however, produces the bulk of output in most fields.

4. The growth of the nation's labor supply depends on population growth, changes in the proportion choosing to work, changes in the working week, and improvements in the quality of labor through education and other means.

5. Natural resources are partly given by nature; but they depend also on discovery, demand, and technology.

6. Capital consists of buildings, machinery, and other durable goods used in the production of goods and services. Over the last century in the United States, the supply of capital has risen much faster than the supply of labor.

7. About 70 percent of our national output is bought by households for consumer use. About 20 percent is bought by government, and 10 percent consists of capital goods bought by business concerns.

8. More than three quarters of the income *earned* in the United States, and about 85 percent of the income actually *received*, is payment for work. The balance is income from property ownership.

9. Income distribution among households is still quite unequal. The top 15 percent of families receive almost 40 percent of all income (*before* payment of federal income taxes). The bottom 15 percent of families receive about 4 percent of total income.

---

[7] Tax rates are even higher than this. But because the rates are so high, tax lawyers and accountants have become very ingenious at discovering loopholes, deductions, and adjustments which bring down the tax actually paid.

PART | ONE

THE ECONOMICS
OF PRICES AND MARKETS

If you're going to write, don't pretend to write down. It's going to be the best you can do, and it's the fact that it's the best you can do that kills you.

DOROTHY PARKER

Not that the story need be long, but it will take a long time to make it short.

HENRY THOREAU

THE ECONOMIES of India, the U.S.A., and the U.S.S.R. seem on the surface to be very different from each other. Yet all economies perform the function of producing and distributing goods. To do this any economy must answer several questions:

1. Which members of the population shall engage in productive labor, how much work shall they do, and what shall they work at? This is the problem of *labor supply*.

2. How much effort shall be devoted to producing goods for immediate consumption, and how much to producing tools and equipment that will make possible greater production in the future? This is the problem of *capital supply*.

3. How much of each good and service shall be produced? What amount of resources shall be devoted to producing cotton cloth, television sets, super-

highways, and the thousands of other things included in national output? This is the problem of *resource allocation*.

4. What methods of production shall be used? Shall one grow corn with a great deal of hand labor and little machinery, or with much machinery and little labor? This is the problem of *production methods*.

5. How shall the national output be divided among the population? How much is each individual and household entitled to receive, and on what basis? This is the problem of *income distribution*.

The answers to these questions are interrelated. A man's income is related to how much work and what kind of work he does. Methods of production depend on available supplies of labor and capital. But the five questions are logically distinct, and each provides a vantage point for analyzing how an economy operates.

Every national economy answers these questions; but the institutional arrangements for reaching the answers differ considerably. Very broadly, one can distinguish *subsistence economies, planned economies*, and *market economies*. None of these ever exists in pure form. But it is helpful to think about them in pure form, just as it is useful to reason about pure chemical substances, frictionless space, and other things no one will ever see.

In a *subsistence economy* the basic unit is the family, clan, or tribe. Each unit produces all its requirements, and consumes everything it produces. The nation is simply a conglomeration of these self-sufficient units, each living in economic isolation. Economic decisions are made in patriarchal fashion by the family head or tribal chief, within the bounds of established tradition. Many rural areas of Africa, Asia, and Latin America come quite close to this pattern of subsistence organization.

In a *planned economy* the means of production and the authority to make economic decisions belong to the state. Control is concentrated in a central planning board, which decides what is to be done in every corner of the economy. The nation is organized, in effect, as a single giant corporation. In this pure form, a planned economy would be quite cumbersome and inefficient, and so complete central planning is never found in actuality. But the economies of the U.S.S.R. and other communist countries go a long way in this direction.

A *market economy* is the polar opposite of a planned economy in the sense that economic decisions are highly decentralized. Each member of the labor force chooses his job independently. Each household decides what to buy with its money income. Each business concern decides what to produce, what production methods to use, and where to sell the product. Anyone is free to go into any line of production, and to make or lose money by so doing.

The central mystery of a market economy is this: If economic decisions are made by millions of individuals, each doing precisely what he wants, what keeps the system from flying apart? May not the decisions of different people be so inconsistent that everything breaks down in confusion? How do conflicting interests and choices get reconciled with each other? This was long considered *the* central problem of economics, and it is still one of the most intriguing branches of economic study.

The market economy, like other pure types, is something no one will ever actually see. But the economies of the United States, Britain, the West European countries, and the British dominions come closer to this pattern than to any other.

Since each of these forms of organization is important in large areas of the world, each requires discussion in a general introduction to economics. There is no preordained sequence for this discussion. I choose to begin with subsistence economies and planned economies because they seem inherently simpler. The basic economic decisions are made by identifiable people, in one case a patriarch or tribal leader, in the other a central planning board. Thus the nature of the decisions stands out quite clearly. In a market economy, on the other hand, no one *makes* decisions for the economy as a whole. Overall decisions *get made* through an interlocking network of markets, in which the personal decisions of millions of individuals are registered and reconciled. To explain how this happens is a bit complicated, so it seems best to leave it until after the simpler cases have been considered.

An important issue running through Part One is: *What does it matter?* What does it matter whether an economy is organized on a market basis, a planned basis, or some mixture of the two? This raises the question of what we mean by efficient operation of an economic system. To judge whether one pattern of organization is likely to prove more efficient than another, we need some standard of efficiency to serve as yardstick.

Crudely, an economy is efficient if it produces a given volume of goods with minimum use of labor, capital, and other resources. Or, given the quantities of resources in use, an economy is efficient if it produces the maximum amount of goods and services. And the assortment of goods produced should correspond to the wishes of the population. This sort of statement is obviously fuzzy and incomplete, and we shall have to spell it out more fully and precisely. We shall then apply this yardstick to the American economy on one hand, and to the Soviet economy on the other.

The Subsistence Economy;
The Planned Economy

Q. What is the difference between capitalism and socialism?
A. Under capitalism, man exploits man. Under socialism, it's just the opposite.

OVERHEARD IN WARSAW

ANY NATION IS RIGHTLY concerned with total output and employment.
But this is not the whole of the economic problem. It is important, not
merely that people be employed, but they be employed efficiently. We
are interested in the pattern of output as well as its total amount. We
wouldn't want a GNP of $500 billion consisting entirely of ice cream
cones. People are also concerned with their shares of national output. Who
is to get how much? If the distribution is unequal, on what grounds does
one man receive a larger share than his neighbor?

This bundle of problems is usually called "the economics of production and distribution," "the problem of resource allocation," or simply "microeconomics." They will be our main concern throughout Part
One.

46

SCARCITY AND CHOICE

The Fact of Scarcity

Even with the great productive resources of the United States, we are not able to produce nearly as much as we should like to consume. The "economy of abundance" is not yet a fact. Perhaps we have as much as we *need* in the eyes of some austere outside observer, but we do not have as much as we *want*.

Any group which doubts this statement can convince itself by a simple experiment. Let each member of the group take a piece of paper. Write down the annual income which you would like to have when you are 35 years old, married, and have three children. Then average the figures for the group. It usually turns out that the group average is two or three times the *actual* average income of all families in the United States. It is not possible for everyone in the country to live at anything like the level which each of us considers desirable for himself.

The same result appears from household surveys in which families are asked how much additional income they need to live adequately and without worry. The figure mentioned is typically 10 to 20 percent higher than the family's current income, and this is as true of families with $10,000 a year as of families with $5,000 a year. Almost everyone wants just a little more. The doubling of real income per capita since 1935 has not made Americans noticeably more content with their lot. Appetite grows with eating, and the higher incomes in prospect for the year 2000 will still be inadequate to the needs which we shall feel *at that time.*

It may seem that this reduces economics to a dead end of complete futility. A Burmese student at Yale once wrote a doctoral thesis to prove that the main hope for the future lies in reducing man's wants instead of increasing his productive capacity. Leaving this issue to the philosopher, let us see how mankind adjusts to its urge toward consumption. Even in the wealthy United States there are still three million families with incomes below $2,000 a year. For these people scarcity of resources is no psychological fancy but a bitter fact of daily experience. In many other countries the average family reaches depths of poverty which have to be seen to be believed. In most countries the increase of economic resources, wise use of these resources in production, and careful distribution of the national output are matters of vital importance.

The Necessity of Choice

Scarcity lies at the root of economics. If all goods were free as air, there would be no need to economize resources and no economic problem. The central fact of scarcity forces hard choices. More of this means less of that. These choices somehow get made in every country and under every type of economic system. The main types of choice which must be made are:

1. *How much work shall people do?* If more people in the community engage in productive labor, or if everyone works more hours per week, total output will increase and everyone can consume more. This higher consumption, however, is purchased at the cost of less time for rest and recreation. There is a scarcity of *time* as well as of goods—indeed, this is the most basic and pervasive form of scarcity.

2. *How much effort shall be devoted to capital goods?* National output includes consumer goods destined for immediate use and capital goods which will make possible greater output in subsequent years. The proportion which capital goods form of total output varies widely from country to country. It is less than 10 percent in most of the underdeveloped countries, about 20 percent in the U.S., close to 30 percent in the U.S.S.R. A high proportion of effort devoted to capital goods reduces the current flow of consumer goods and holds living standards below what would be possible otherwise, but it lays the foundation for a larger flow of both consumer and capital goods in future years. This sort of choice, then, is often termed a "choice between present goods and future goods."

3. *What goods shall be produced, and in what quantities?* A glance through the U.S. Census of Manufactures reveals thousands of different products; and the number is further increased if we add agriculture, the service industries, and other sectors. Choices among these goods are of the "more or less" rather than the "all or nothing" variety. Shall we have more or less women's suits this year than last year? At a more detailed level, shall we have more or less of particular colors, sizes, patterns? In the field of capital goods, shall we have more or less road-building machinery, or oil-drilling equipment, or electronic computers? If the economy is running at full capacity, a decision to produce more of one item means producing less of something else. Someone must decide that the added production of A is worth more to the community than the sacrificed production of B. How do such decisions get made, and why does the list of quantities produced during the year look as it does?

4. *What production methods shall be used?* There are many ways to skin a cat or to produce a ton of steel. Specifically, there is often a choice between using elaborate machinery which needs only a few workers to operate, and using simpler machinery. This kind of choice may be termed "degree of mechanization," or "choice of labor and capital proportions." It is an important problem in the design and construction of new factories. It is important also in small-scale and flexible industries such as agriculture, where there are many feasible combinations of labor and capital. The ground may be turned over by hand with a spade, or by a

horse-drawn plow, or by a small tractor, or by a larger tractor capable of pulling several plows together.

This kind of choice may seem simple. Surely one should use the production technique which yields greatest output per dollar of cost or, what amounts to the same thing, yields lowest cost per unit of output. This is indeed a clue to the correct decision; but terms such as "more productive" or "least costly" are deceptively simple, and will have to be explored thoroughly in later chapters.

Choices in this area are obviously related to the supplies of labor and capital equipment available in the economy. Sweden, with a limited labor force but a large stock of capital goods, is well-advised to push mechanization. Countries with abundant labor but little capital, such as India or Indonesia, will have to use simpler production methods.

5. *Who shall get what is produced?* One might think of the national output of goods and services as heaped up at some central point, with each family being given "tickets" showing how much it is entitled to withdraw from the community stockpile. In a money economy these tickets take the form of dollars or whatever the national currency may be. How many dollars shall each family receive? Shall the distribution be equal or unequal, and on what grounds? This is naturally an important decision to the people involved, and is capable of generating intense controversy. It is only human to feel that one's own share is too small and that others are getting more than they deserve.

The basic economic choices, then, are work *versus* leisure, present goods *versus* future goods, more of one good *versus* more of another, more mechanized *versus* less mechanized methods of production, and more *versus* less equal distribution of money income.

A common thread runs through these choices. They are all of the "more or less" variety. Shall we have a little higher consumption standard at the cost of a little less leisure? Shall we have a little greater future productive capacity at the cost of a little less current consumption? Shall some families have a little more income at the cost of some others having less? And so on. In economic terminology, they are *marginal* choices, involving small plus and minus adjustments at the margin of decision.

If one were designing a new economy from the ground up, it would be necessary to consider an enormous variety of possible permutations and combinations. But no country is ever actually in this position. The economy is a going concern, adjusted to grinding out a certain bill of goods and distributing them in a certain way. The relevant and feasible decisions are to push out a bit in one direction and to cut back a bit in another. Over the course of decades, however, thousands of marginal adjustments can add up to major changes in the pattern of production and distribution.

Thus far we have spoken as though each type of decision could be made independently of the others. Each of the five types of decision *is* logically independent and can be singled out for separate analysis. But in practice all are interdependent, and a change in one area involves adjustment in the others as well. A change in the supply of labor in the economy, or in the supply of capital goods, or in the distribution of money income sets up repercussions which will spread to every part of the economy before the effects are exhausted.

Solution of the resource allocation problem thus involves simultaneous decision on a large number of questions, and decision on each point involves the decisions which are being made at the same time on all the others.

At this point the reader will surely throw up his hands and exclaim, "Why, that's impossible! Nobody in the United States supervises the economy in that fashion. And even if anyone wanted to, the human mind couldn't possibly cope with the problem." Yet all the decisions we have outlined do get made, in the United States and in every other country; and they were being made long before discovery of the electronic computer.

How can this be? The main task of Part One is to explore how the key economic decisions get made in a largely private economy such as that of the United States. Most decisions are left to the millions of workers, households, and business managers, and their choices feed back through markets in a way which regulates the course of economic activity. It will take many pages, however, to develop this cryptic statement.

Since analysis of a market economy is complicated, we shall approach it in easy stages by considering first two other kinds of economic organization: the subsistence economy, in which each family produces all its own needs; and the planned economy, using as an example the economy of the U.S.S.R. The reader will learn some basic economics from this exploration. He will also get a working familiarity with Soviet economic institutions, which are important in their own right.

THE SUBSISTENCE ECONOMY

A common gambit in elementary economics is to picture the economic problems and choices faced by Robinson Crusoe on his desert island. This is not as silly as it may seem. Crusoe is a shorthand symbol for any isolated household which meets its needs through its own efforts rather than through trade with other households. Crusoe, the hillbilly in the Appalachian Mountains, and the poor peasant of South India are brothers under the skin.

Consider a tribal village in western Uganda. There is one graveled road leading from the village to the capital city 250 miles away. Young men sometimes go to work in the city for a while, and bring back radios, bicycles, and other things which they have bought with their savings.

Apart from this, everything used in the village is produced and consumed on the spot.

The question of who shall work, and at what tasks, is settled by immemorial custom. Women till the fields and gather the crops. Children herd the cattle. Men do the heavier work of clearing new land, building irrigation ditches, house-building, and so on. They also hunt and fish and, in the happy days before the white man, used to engage in tribal warfare. In. the time left over, they sit under the banana trees and discuss village politics. The men show a strong preference for leisure as against productive effort, though they do not allow the same degree of choice to their women.

Even this small village with its simple agriculture produces a considerable range of products: grain, plantains, and bananas from the ground; milk and meat from the cattle; fish and wild game; alcoholic drinks brewed from the bananas; clothing woven and tailored by the women in the evenings; and simple articles of furniture fashioned from wood by the men. This raises a typical economic problem of distributing the available labor time among various lines of production in such a way as to achieve greatest satisfaction. Note that decisions will be based both on the villagers' liking for different articles of consumption and on the difficulty of producing them. The men may catch few wild antelope *either* because they do not find them very tasty or because the time required is much greater than for other foods.

There is also a problem of capital supply. The villagers might devote their full time to producing goods for immediate consumptions. Alternatively, they may spend some time fashioning crude fish nets, spears, bows and arrows, shovels, hoes, and the like. These things will increase the productivity of their work and enable them to live better in future. They may also spend time on land clearing, terracing, drainage and irrigation ditches, road building, and other agricultural improvements. They may build larger and more comfortable houses, perhaps substituting tin roofs for the traditional thatched roofs. And by eating less meat for the time being, they can gradually build up the size of their livestock herds, which are a major capital asset.

These are all primitive forms of saving and capital formation. By consuming less than they might during the current year, the villagers can enjoy a larger income in later years. The basic condition for capital formation is also apparent: natural resources and the people's productive capacity must be large enough so that it does not take their full time every day just to win a bare livelihood. If it did, they could never get ahead of the game, never set aside enough of their basic resource—labor time—to improve the tools of production.

The income distribution problem is simple. Each family consumes what it produces. The family, however, is an "extended family," a group of perhaps 30 or 40 people linked by blood and marriage, instead of the smaller individualistic family which is customary in the West. Each member is entitled to his share of the family food supplies. Thus how much a particular villager gets depends on the output of a large group rather than on his personal productive effort.

The Uganda village, in short, contains most elements of the economic problem. There are worker-consumers with certain attitudes toward work, leisure, savings, and consumption; with a stock of technical knowledge and personal skills; and with preferences among different consumption goods. There is a more or less plentiful supply of natural resources. There is a supply of capital goods which can be added to, simply maintained, or allowed to wear out without replacement. These are the same elements which underlie economic choice in complex economies. And whether in a complex economy or a self-sufficient village, economic decisions are shaped by *natural resources, technical possibilities,* and *personal preferences.*

THE PLANNED ECONOMY

There is no fully planned economy in the world, nor is there ever likely to be. Central planning implies that in the center of the economy sits a group of controllers who issue detailed orders on the quantity of each product to be produced in the coming year; how much labor and materials each factory shall have to produce its output quota; how many people in the country shall be employed, where they shall work, and what they shall be paid; and all other details of economic life.

Even with high-speed computers and a large statistical staff, it would be difficult to draft and enforce a consistent plan embracing all these matters. Nor is there any need for such comprehensive control. One can control the essentials without controlling everything; and there is an obvious advantage in allowing plant managers, workers, and consumers to exercise some initiative within the framework of the overall program.

The economies of the communist countries, then, are partially planned economies. One could also call them *priority* economies. Industries to which the government attaches high priority for military or development reasons are closely planned and supervised. Others are left to ride along with looser controls. Moreover, alongside the element of central direction, these countries provide opportunities for individual choice similar to that exercised in capitalist countries. The blending of direction and choice, and the way in which the blend has changed over the course of time, is in fact the most interesting feature of these economies.

The U.S.S.R., as the oldest and most productive of the communist countries, is the natural one to select for illustrative purposes. One should bear in mind that many things about the Soviet economy are still not known to Western scholars, and also that economic institutions are still evolving, so that what one says today may be outmoded tomorrow. What we have to say can be organized under four heads: (1) planning organizations; (2) decisions on what shall be produced; (3) decisions on production methods; and (4) income distribution, including the question of who works and at what jobs.

Planning Organization

Production targets for key raw materials and finished goods are set in Moscow. Planning is not all-inclusive, and targets are not always achieved, but the development of the economy in its broad outlines is guided from a central point.

Who does the planning? The main groups involved in economic planning at present are these:

1. *The Council of Ministers (Cabinet) of the U.S.S.R.*, headed by the Premier, which is the supreme policy-making body. It might be argued that the Presidium of the Communist Party, which dominates political life under the Soviet one-party system, is really the supreme governing authority. But the leadership of the Party and the government is so closely intertwined that one cannot draw any significant distinction between them. Major questions of economic policy are usually discussed first at Party Congresses, and decisions of the Council of Ministers are then made within the framework of Party directives.

The Council of Ministers makes strategic decisions on such matters as: the feasible growth rate of the economy over the next several years; the division of national output between consumer goods and capital goods; the allocation of capital goods among public utilities, manufacturing, agriculture, housing, and so on; the pace of development in different regions of the country; and the distribution of new plants among these regions.

2. *The State Planning Commission (Gosplan)* takes these general directives and turns them into a detailed draft economic plan, containing production targets for each controlled commodity and a division of the proposed output among the various republics. It discusses this draft plan with officials of the republics, and eventually brings back an agreed plan for final ratification by the Council of Ministers. It also collects a great deal of statistical information on the operation of the economy.

3. The U.S.S.R. is divided into 15 republics, which correspond somewhat to American states, except that two republics—the Russian Federated Republic and the Ukraine—contain two thirds of the country's population and more than two thirds of its economic activity. The *republic Council of Ministers* is responsible for production carried on within its borders. For products produced and consumed entirely within the republic, it is the sole authority. For "all union commodities," where production and allocation must be coordinated for the country as a whole, each republic negotiates with Moscow concerning its share in the total program. Once a final plan is agreed on, officials of the republic are responsible for meeting the specified targets.

4. The *republic Gosplan* carries on the detailed work of planning and supervising production within the republic, under general direction of the Council of Ministers. The relation is the same as that between the U.S.S.R. Council of Ministers and the U.S.S.R. Gosplan.

5. *The Regional Economic Council (Sovnarkhoz)*. The larger republics are divided into a number of regional economic units, though a small republic may have only one such unit. There are presently upwards of a hundred regional economic councils in the U.S.S.R. Each sovnarkhoz has planning and supervisory responsibility for plants in its region. The sovnarkhoz usually has a staff of several hundred people. It is divided into industry divisions covering the main types of production in the region, and also has functional or staff divisions concerned with manpower, finance, transportation, and the like.

6. The lowest operating unit is the plant or *enterprise*. The enterprise director is appointed by the sovnarkhoz of his region and is responsible to it. Management is based on "one-man responsibility." While lower officials of the enterprise may criticize and discuss matters of policy, decision rests with the director and he alone is responsible for success or failure. Most enterprise directors are engineers, and the Russians find it difficult to understand how we can allow men to rise to top management positions in the United States without engineering training.

This does not indicate the full complexity of Soviet economic organization. For example, certain products of major military importance are managed directly from Moscow, and regional officials have no authority over them. At the other extreme, industries of purely local importance operate under the city council and higher planning bodies take no account of them. This includes service and repair establishments, baking and other local food processing, and even plants below a certain size engaged in producing bricks and other building materials.

Planning procedures. Having brought the actors onto the stage, let us examine what they do. There are three types of plan: the long-range plan, the annual plan, and the quarterly plan. Long-range targets are necessary as a guide to current planning, and particularly as a guide to development projects which will take several years to complete. If steel production is to rise by 30 percent five years from now, development of new ore mines may be necessary at once. A major hydroelectric project may take five to ten years to complete. While five years is the commonest planning period, the current plan runs from 1959 through 1965.

The annual plan, however, is the yardstick for current industrial operations. Preparation of this plan begins about a year in advance of the period which it is to cover. Early in 1963, Gosplan U.S.S.R. began drafting the plan for production of all-union commodities during 1964. By April this may be far enough along to be broken down by republics and passed on to the republic governments. Each republic gosplan must then break down its quota of each product among the sovnarkhoz units.

It must also add plans for articles produced and controlled within the republic, for which Moscow prepares no figures. Republic gosplan then sends down to each sovnarkhoz tentative output quotas for each item to be produced in its region. The sovnarkhoz, finally, breaks these figures down into quotas for individual enterprises. As the plan moves downward, it takes on more and more bulk and detail, and more of a concrete operating character. As one official put it, "The plan rolls up like a snowball."

Even before this downward process is completed there has been set in motion a reverse current of plans and proposals, often termed "planning from below." This begins at the grass roots with the individual enterprise, which has the advantage of knowing better than anyone else what it is capable of producing. Each enterprise passes up to its sovnarkhoz its own proposed plan for 1964—how much it can produce, and how much labor, materials, and supplies it will need to produce this amount. There is a good deal of gamesmanship in drafting these enterprise plans. A Soviet manager is judged, promoted, and to some extent paid by his success in achieving the plant's output quota for the year. Failure is regarded at best as inefficiency, at worst as sabotage. It pays, therefore, to get as low a quota as possible by concealing the true productive capacity of the plant. If things go poorly during the year, there is a safety factor. If things go well, the manager may be able to exceed his plan targets and earn a good bonus.

Sovnarkhoz officials, of course, are supposed to discover any such minimizing of capacity. It is quite common for enterprise plans to be adjusted upward by 5 to 10 percent at the sovnarkhoz level. The sovnarkhoz then puts all its enterprise plans together and transmits them to the republic Gosplan, which after further scrutiny and adjustment passes them on to Moscow. Gosplan in Moscow thus finally gets in its hands a picture of what everyone at lower levels believes the economy is capable of producing.

These "feasible figures" often fall short of the "desirable figures" which were passed down originally from Moscow. Moreover, the discrepancies will vary from one product to another, so that the original program is thrown out of balance. This leads to much additional adjusting and reconciling of targets in Moscow, and to much bargaining between Moscow and the republics, the republics and the sovnarkhozy, and so on down. Finally the revised plan is brought back to a full-dress conclave in Moscow attended by the Council of Ministers, key Gosplan officials, and representatives of the republics. When approved by this meeting the figures are final and binding. If the process is completed by November of the year before which the plan is to take effect, everyone is well satisfied. It is not uncommon, however, for the new year to begin before final targets have been approved.

The final plan has three main components: (1) A list of the outputs expected from each industry of all-union importance. This means capital goods industries, industries of military importance, key foodstuffs, and a few other key consumer goods industries. (2) Balance sheets for the materials necessary to produce these outputs, showing how much of each material will be available during 1964 from current production, reserves, or imports, and where the available supply will go. Control sheets of this sort currently are prepared for upwards of a thousand materials. There is also prepared a balance sheet of available and required manpower, broken down by industries and regions. (3) A production and cost plan for each enterprise, showing the list of products which it is expected to produce, and the quantities of labor, fuel, materials, and other supplies which it is allowed to purchase during the year. These three elements of the plan are interrelated and should ideally be fully consistent.

Little need be said of the quarterly plans which are prepared for each enterprise. They make the production targets more concrete by reducing them to months and calendar quarters, provide a basis for reporting current operations, and introduce some flexibility into the annual plan. A plant which turns out to have unexpectedly great productive capacity may find its quota increased during the year, while a plant which runs into legitimate difficulties may argue for a reduction in its original schedule.

Enforcing the plan. The fact that production goals are announced with much fanfare does not mean that these goals will be met. What controls are available to ensure that production during the year will go roughly according to plan? Four main devices are used for this purpose:

1. *Control through the State Bank (Gosbank).* Each enterprise has an account at Gosbank, and all payments between enterprises are made by bookkeeping transfers. Cash is drawn out for the weekly payroll, and this also is charged against the enterprise's account. The manager of the Gosbank branch with which an enterprise deals thus has his finger on the pulse of the enterprise. The enterprise's output plan for the year is accompanied by a financial plan, showing how much it will receive from sale of its products, how much it is allowed to spend for labor and materials, and how much short-term credit it may have to cover inventories and goods in transit. The enterprise may overdraw its account for good cause, but this requires the consent of Gosbank. If the enterprise seems to be departing seriously from plan, this consent presumably will not be given.

2. *Supervision by the Sovnarkhoz.* Each industry division of the sovnarkhoz is expected to keep in close touch with plants in its industry, to obtain and analyze their operating reports, to help them out with production problems, and to call them to account for serious failures. As a last resort, the enterprise director may be removed and replaced. In American terms, the Soviet enterprise corresponds somewhat to a branch plant of a parent corporation (the sovnarkhoz), which has ultimate responsibility for its performance.

3. *Multiple Channels of Information.* In an effort to prevent enterprise directors from concealing a record of poor performance, the system provides numerous channels through which independent reports can be passed up to higher authorities. The chief accountant of the enterprise has a direct line to the accounting department of the sovnarkhoz, and has considerable independence in his dealings with the director. He is expected to act as the "financial conscience" of the enterprise and to report discrepancies between plan and performance. There is a Communist Party cell in every enterprise, and from this group reports can travel up to Moscow via party channels. Large enterprises and enterprises of military significance usually have members of the security police attached to them, who report directly to their superiors. The chairman of the trade union organization in the plant can make reports to higher union bodies.

All these precautions are not necessarily sufficient. Everyone connected with an enterprise has some interest in forming a common front against higher officialdom. It is not uncommon for the director, accountant, and other local officials to form a coalition to present misleading reports of performance or even falsify records and accounts. Having done this, they are all involved and must stick together to make their story hold up.

4. *Financial Incentives.* The system makes it worthwhile for management officials and workers to produce effectively. Most workers are paid on a piece-rate basis under which earnings rise proportionately, or even more than proportionately, with the quantity produced. Management officials, in addition to a basic salary, receive a bonus geared to fulfillment of the plant's output plan. The director of a successful enterprise draws a large part of his income from this source. Part of any profit earned by exceeding the output target also goes into an Enterprise Fund, which may be used in part for building worker apartments (still scarce and highly valued by Russian workers), for health and recreational facilities, and other employee benefits. To the extent that these direct incentives are effective, the need for outside supervision and control is reduced.

Decisions on What to Produce

No general rationale for planning decisions has ever been set forth in Soviet writings. One leading Western student of the Soviet system says simply: "They do it the way they do it." But one can say a little more than this. First, Soviet plans have always had a strong bias toward capital goods production. Resources have been poured unstintingly into steel, machinery, electrical equipment, power production, and other lines of heavy industry. Close to 30 percent of gross Soviet output each year goes into capital goods, compared with about 20 percent in the United States. This is a high rate of investment. It has meant holding back on production of consumer goods and keeping living standards below what would have been possible otherwise—certainly below what people would have chosen of their own accord.

If pressed for a justification of this austere policy, Soviet leaders would say that it was essential to build a powerful industrial base to protect the country against military attack. There is historical warrant for this view. Without the rapid industrialization of the country from 1928 to 1940, there is little doubt that it would have been conquered by Germany in 1942–43 and world history would have taken a decidedly different turn. Soviet leaders would also argue that higher saving today will mean greater consumption tomorrow. The rapid build-up of basic industrial capacity will eventually make possible a great outpouring of consumer goods, and a much higher standard of living. Soviet leaders surpass even Americans in their confident belief in material progress.

The basic planning decision, then, is what proportion of resources shall be devoted to capital goods. Next one faces the question: What types of capital goods? This is in effect a decision about which lines of industry are to be expanded most rapidly. A decision to build a major hydroelectric project on the Volga implies a need for certain quantities of earth-moving equipment, trucks, cranes, turbines, steel, cement, and labor. A staff of engineers can translate the finished project into the components necessary to produce it, and these can then be fitted into current production schedules. Since capital goods form such a large part of national output, much of the production plan follows automatically from decisions about industrial expansion.

But how is it decided which lines of production are to be expanded in the near future, and at what rate? This is a major policy decision, and is arbitrary in the sense that it rests on no single rule. During a particular five-year plan, two or three sectors of the economy are singled out as the main obstacles to further development and productive resources are channeled heavily into these sectors. After a time this means that these sectors become overdeveloped relative to other parts of the economy, and new bottlenecks emerge which are attacked in the next plan period. At various stages of Russian economic development the leading role has been played by steel and machinery, electric power, transportation, military equipment, light metals, and chemicals. At the present time chemicals, power, and machinery are receiving primary emphasis, but there is also considerable emphasis on housing and farm equipment.

It is difficult to find any guiding principle for the planning of consumer goods output. Certainly production is not guided, as it is in a capitalist system, by consumers' preferences expressed through purchases in the market. How, then, can the authorities discover "what people really want"?

This problem is not yet as serious in the Soviet Union as it would be in the United States. The reason is that most consumer goods production in the Soviet Union still consists of basic necessities. Luxury goods, where consumer fancy has widest sway, play a minor role in the economy. For basic items of food, clothing, and housing one can set up rough standards of physical need. Nutritionists can say how many calories per day, how much fat and protein, how much minerals and vitamins, are necessary to sustain health and working efficiency. These requirements can be converted into pounds of bread, potatoes, vegetables, meat, and other foods. Housing standards are more arbitrary; but once one decides on so many square feet of floor space per person, one can calculate how many new houses and apartment buildings will be necessary to attain this standard. The housing deficit in the Soviet Union is still so staggering that one cannot make any mistake in building as much as resources permit. Clothing requirements are also flexible, but one can set minimum targets for coats, suits, shirts, shoes, and other items; and these can be converted into yards of cloth, quantities of leather, and so on.

Minimum consumer requirements seem to be scheduled into the annual plan in the same way as capital goods. Consumer goods production above the minimum is largely an unplanned residual, both in the sense that output targets are not even set for many products, and in the sense that fulfillment of targets is not viewed with the same urgency as would be true of steel, power, or machine tools. If there is steel left over after priority needs have been met, some of this may go into passenger cars, refrigerators, and other consumer goods; but it is not considered urgent that any particular output of these items be attained in a particular year. There is a general intent to raise the output of most consumer goods year by year, and gradually to approach the consumption levels of Western Europe and the United States. But there is not the feeling of driving urgency about this that one encounters in the realm of investment goods.

Agricultural production is not as thoroughly planned as industrial production. The basic unit of Soviet agriculture is the collective farm. These farms are large by American standards—there are less than 100,000 of them, compared with our 4 million farms. Even a small collective has several thousand acres of land and several hundred people. The workers on the farm are divided into work teams, each under a foreman, somewhat in factory fashion. They are paid partly through an allowance of grain, potatoes, and other farm produce, and partly through a cash wage per hour. How much one gets depends on his work assignment and the skill involved in the work. A tractor driver gets more than a milkmaid. Families on the farm may also rent small plots of land, usually half an acre to two acres, for private cultivation. What a farmer raises on his private plot can be sold in the nearest town market and the money is his.

Total agricultural production really is not planned at all. What is planned is the amount of grain, potatoes, meat, and other staples which the government expects to buy from the farms and ship to the city to feed the urban population. State purchasing agencies contract with each farm to buy specified amounts of produce at specified prices, and the farm must treat these deliveries as a first obligation. What is left over is theirs. If they work hard and the weather is good, they will eat well. If not, they will eat poorly.

Production from the private plots is of course unplanned, and this is an important part of total farm output. The private plots produce almost all the poultry and eggs, and more than half the meat, milk, potatoes, fruits, and vegetables. Collective cultivation, on the other hand, accounts for the great bulk of the grain, feed and forage, cotton, sugar beets, and industrial raw materials. Soviet officials do not like the private plot system, which they regard as old-fashioned and capitalistic; but it is so productive that they have not yet been able to get rid of it.

Production Methods and Operating Efficiency

The problem of production methods divides into two subproblems: (*a*) the basic design of plant and equipment; (*b*) utilizing each plant so as to obtain greatest output from a certain amount of labor and materials.

Basic production design. The central fact here is the severe shortage of capital goods. Despite strenuous efforts to build up steel and machinery capacity, there has never been anything like enough capacity to meet all military and industrial needs. Labor is not abundant either, but it is relatively more plentiful than capital. Logically, this should lead to production methods which use a good deal of labor and which economize on capital—*labor-intensive methods*, in economic parlance.

The Soviet economy has in fact been bent in this direction, and in two main ways. First, whole sectors of the economy have been starved of capital and have had to make out with simple production methods. Agriculture is the outstanding example. The number of tractors, cultivators, combine harvesters, milking machines, and other machines on Soviet farms is tiny compared with the technical possibilities and with the amounts used in more advanced countries. Soviet agriculture depends mainly on human and animal power. In 1960 there were still more than 10 million horses on Russian farms. (How many would one see in a day's drive through Illinois or Iowa?) It takes 40 percent of the Soviet labor force to feed the Soviet population, while less than 10 percent of the labor lorce suffices for this purpose in the United States. This means that each Soviet farm worker is turning out much less output than the American farmer. This is due partly to difficulties of supervision and management, less use of fertilizers, poorer seed and livestock strains, and other factors. But it is due above all to the low level of farm mechanization.

The transportation system has also been kept on short rations. Road mileage and numbers of trucks and buses are low by American standards, so that the work of moving goods and people piles up on the railroads. In 1957 railroads still were carrying 90 percent of all freight traffic in the U.S.S.R., compared with 39 percent in the U.S.A. The Soviet rail system even carried three fourths of all passenger traffic, which has almost disappeared from American rail lines. An American railroad official would be happy if he could have the volume of business handled by his Soviet counterpart. But he would be unhappy with the equipment given him to do the job. The supply of freight cars, passenger cars, and locomotives is deficient in both quantity and quality. The steam locomotive is almost a museum piece in the United States. The U.S.S.R. in 1958, however, was still using 11,000 steam locomotives and only 2,000 electric and diesel-electric engines.

Second, even in the preferred industrial sector capital has been economized by using methods which are more labor-intensive than those used in the United States. The central production operations are quite well mechanized. The carding, spinning, and weaving departments of textile mills, the main assembly lines in auto and truck plants, look much like their counterparts in the United States. But supplementary operations—getting materials to the machines, finishing and packing, getting finished products to the shipping room, and so on—make more use of hand labor than is true here. One sees few automatic conveyor systems or mechanical lift trucks in Soviet factories.

Current operating efficiency. In addition to the grand strategy of plant design, there are a multitude of detailed, tactical problems of production method. Given the same machinery, materials, and labor, some managers will get more output than others. The job of the enterprise director is to produce the maximum from the supplies allotted him by higher authorities. How much output he gets will depend on his skill in arranging the plant layout, subdividing production processes, scheduling production, hiring the right quantity and quality of labor, and motivating workers and supervisors to a high rate of effort.

The Soviet manager is stimulated to efficiency by a carrot and stick technique. On the negative side, he must operate within the framework of the plan. He may spend only certain amounts on labor, materials, and other supplies, and he must produce a certain volume of output. His success is judged by conformity to the cost side of the plan as well as the output side. Moreover, he is expected to do better year by year. Rising productivity is built into the system in the sense that each year the planning authorities specify that the plant must increase output and reduce costs.

A manager who falls seriously short of the planned targets can expect demotion. In the Stalin era he would have been accused of "wrecking" or "sabotage," and might have been shot or sent to Siberia. In the more relaxed atmosphere of today, he will suffer only a loss of status and salary. The successful manager, on the other hand, can expect promotion to a larger enterprise or may become an official of the sovnarkhoz or the republic. Most Soviet managers seem to feel that directing a large enterprise is the best job available in the system. This is partly because the director of a successful enterprise earns substantial bonuses, while a salaried official of the republic or national government does not. (American businessmen resist taking jobs in Washington for the same reason!) If the enterprise succeeds in increasing output above or reducing costs below the planned level, part of the resulting profit comes back to management officials as bonus. This may run to 50 percent or more of the manager's basic salary.

The incentive system of Soviet managers, in short, bears considerable resemblance to that of American business executives. The intrinsic satisfaction of doing a good administrative job, desire for the esteem of one's superiors and inferiors, hope of promotion to larger responsibilities, and financial incentives combine to induce managers to put forth their best efforts.

Even with these incentives, the efficiency of Soviet industry leaves much to be desired. There are several reasons for this. First, the cost and output norms are matters of bargaining rather than scientific determination. The enterprise director may agree to ambitious targets, and then struggle to fulfill them. Or he may, by hard bargaining and concealing his true productive capacity, secure low targets which can be met with little effort. It is not surprising that managers prefer the second course, which gives them a safety margin in case of trouble and a chance of earning large bonuses by overfulfilling a plan which was too low in the first place.

Another difficulty is that the output norms are not entirely clear. Greatest importance usually is attached to total value of output in rubles. The plant also is given physical targets for its various products and is expected to produce the right assortment of products as well as the proper total value. But if some of the products are overpriced relative to the cost of producing them while others are underpriced, the enterprise has a strong incentive to fulfill its value plan by concentrating on production of the high-priced items. Enterprises often depart from their assortment for this reason, and these departures are not effectively policed.

Difficulties may arise even if the production targets are specified solely in physical terms. Textile plants have sometimes been given targets of so many million yards of cloth, without specifying how wide the cloth is to be. Since it is cheaper to produce a yard of 30-inch cloth than one of 50-inch, there is a tendency to concentrate heavily on the narrower widths even though this may not meet the preferences of buyers. Moreover, a plant may produce goods which are adequate in quantity but not in quality. In a sellers' market where goods of every sort are scarce, the customer has little alternative but to accept the faulty goods and make the best of it. Quality control has been a major problem in Soviet industry from the beginning.

Finally, greater importance is usually attached to the output plan than to the cost plan. Controls over expenditure on labor and materials are not very firm. If a director meets his output quota, there is a tendency

to wink at how he did it. Success thus may be achieved by using more inputs than were really necessary. The combined effect of these things is to
produce a lower level of operating performance than exists in comparable
plants in the United States.

The Distribution of Income

Farm incomes versus city incomes.   About 40 percent of the Soviet
labor force still works the land. How much they get for what they grow
thus has a great effect on the distribution of income. This is a major political issue in almost every country. In the Western countries, government
typically intervenes on the side of the farmer. By supporting prices above
the level which they would reach in a free market, government transfers
income from city consumers to farm producers.

In the Soviet Union, government policy for many years worked in
the opposite direction. The collective farms were obliged to deliver
specified quantities of farm produce to the government at artificially depressed prices, prices which yielded very low incomes and living standards. These foodstuffs were resold to the city population at much higher
prices, and the government pocketed the difference. This policy served a
dual purpose. The fact that farm incomes were held much below city incomes provided a strong incentive for people to move to the city, and
this was necessary to provide labor power for the rapid expansion of
urban industry. The food extracted from the remaining farm population
served to feed the urban labor force as it worked on the enormous program of construction and heavy industrial development.

There is no doubt, however, that this policy was pushed too far and
that farmers were squeezed too hard during the Stalin era. The prices
which the government paid for food hardly rose at all between 1937 and
1950. Meanwhile, the prices which farmers had to pay for manufactured goods doubled and redoubled. Even considering the fact that
farmers were able to sell part of their production outside government
channels at higher prices, they suffered severely during these years. One
expert has estimated that the real income of the farm population was cut
in two.

Small wonder that the farmers did not produce enthusiastically. The
peasant has an infinite capacity for quiet sabotage, and the government
paid dearly for its niggardliness. Farm workers spent as much time as
possible on their private garden plots and as little as possible on the main
farm operations. Farm production consistently fell short of the planned
targets, and in many lines was not much higher in 1950 than in 1910.

After the death of Stalin there was a drastic shift to a pro-farmer
policy. There was a thorough reorganization of controls over agriculture
and a substantial increase in farm prices. Government prices for food purchased from collective farms were about seven times as high in 1958 as
in 1950. Farm income from all sources is estimated to have tripled during

this period. Incomes on the more efficient farms seem now to have risen close to parity with the incomes of factory workers.

Wage and salary incomes. Urban wages and salaries are set in a labor market which does not differ strikingly from our own. Workers in practice have the right to move freely from one job to another. Labor is so scarce that a good worker knows he can find a job wherever he goes.

This means that each enterprise has to work out a "package" of wages and other conditions which is attractive enough to recruit and hold the labor it needs. Wage schedules have to be tailored to hiring requirements. Steel, machinery, and other heavy industries offer considerably higher wages than light manufacturing, partly because of the nature of the work, but also to make sure that these high-priority industries can get all the labor they need. Wages are also considerably higher in the colder eastern regions of the Soviet Union. The government can appeal to people's Soviet patriotism to go out and colonize these unattractive areas, but a good lacing of money is a wonderful help to patriotic spirit.

Other important characteristics of the wage-salary structure are:

1. A substantial spread between rates for skilled and unskilled labor. It is common in manufacturing plants to find skilled mechanics earning two to three times as much as common laborers—a wider spread than one would find in most industries in the United States. This is meant to induce workers to better their skills, and thus meet the needs of an expanding industrial economy which has a chronic shortage of skilled labor.

2. Extensive use of piece-rate systems, under which a worker's earnings are based on how much he produces. Piece-rate payment is used even more widely in Russia than in the United States, and for the same reason —to stimulate each worker to produce up to the limit of his individual capacity. Under piece-rate payment, a worker's official wage rate may give little clue to his earnings. His job may call for a basic rate of 100 rubles a month; but if he is proficient and hard working, he may turn out enough product to earn 150 rubles or more.

3. High rates for manual work compared with those for white-collar jobs. It is startling at first glance to find that the girl on a spinning machine in a Tashkent cotton mill earns 100 rubles a month, while a typist in the office of the same plant earns 50 rubles. Plant officials explain, "We pay for what is important—for production." The decisive point, however, is that they can *get* enough typists at the 50-ruble wage.

4. Good salaries and perquisites for industrial managers. The Russians have from an early stage recognized the key importance of skilled management and have been willing to pay for it. The director of a medium-sized industrial plant earns, in salary and bonuses, five or six times the earnings of a common laborer in his plant. In addition, he usually is provided with a car, a house, vacation allowances, and other perquisites. When one considers that the top income tax rate in Russia is only 13

percent, the income difference after taxes between laborer and chief executive is probably about the same in Russian industry as in American industry.

Income distribution among households. Information on family incomes comparable to that given for the United States in Chapter 2, is not available for the U.S.S.R. But it seems likely that household income distribution is more equal there than here. Property income, which in the United States flows mainly to the upper income brackets, is almost absent in the U.S.S.R. Moreover, a number of services are provided free by government. All medical and hospital services are free. Not only is college education free, but students receive living allowances from the government. Housing is heavily subsidized and rents are low by Western standards. Since these free and subsidized services count as part of family income, and since they are open to all comers, the result is a considerable equalization of living standards.

The Soviet System: A Mixed Economy

This completes our tour of the Soviet economy. We have seen how the Soviet system works out, on a much larger scale, the same basic decisions which must be made in a subsistence economy. These decisions are made partly through administrative orders, but also partly through individual choice and initiative similar to that which operates in a market economy.

Administrative decisions determine (1) the broad division of national output between consumer goods and capital goods; (2) the distribution of capital goods among different lines of industry, which determines their relative rates of expansion; (3) specific production targets for a long list of industrial raw materials, metals, machinery, building materials, housing, foodstuffs, and other basic consumer products. This planned sector accounts for most of national output, and shapes the broad contours of economic development.

What does this leave for individual choice and initiative? Mainly the following:

1. Workers can choose where to work, what kind of work to do, and how hard to work. These choices are made in much the same way in the U.S.S.R. as in the U.S.A. and other industrial countries. The main inducement which steers workers in one direction or another is the money earnings and fringe benefits offered by various jobs.

2. Consumers can decide how to spend their money incomes. Until recently choice has been limited by the fact that incomes were too low to cover more than basic necessities. As income levels rise, however, and as the variety of consumer goods increases, consumer choice will take on greater meaning; and it seems likely that there will be pressure on government to give greater weight to consumer preferences in planning production.

3. A considerable part of production is subject to local decision rather than central control. This is notably true of farm output, and particularly of production on farmers' private plots. It is true also of local manufacture for local use, and of local service industries, which comprise a sizable percentage of Soviet output.

4. Even where output targets are centrally determined, how much is actually produced and how efficiently it is produced depends on the effort and initiative of management officials. These people are motivated by a mixture of prestige and power considerations, material rewards, promotion possibilities, and other incentives which does not seem to differ greatly from that of their counterparts in capitalist countries.

It has become fashionable to refer to the United States as a "mixed economy," meaning that government carries on a considerable part of national production and also intervenes in many ways in the private economy. What is not so widely recognized is that the U.S.S.R. is also a "mixed economy." The mixture is quite different from our own, but the difference is one of degree rather than of black-and-white contrast. Moreover, the Soviet mixture has been changing rapidly since the early fifties, and will undoubtedly continue to change in the future.

Western economists, to the extent that they have any missionary urge to save souls abroad, can hope that Soviet officials will gradually discover the advantages which (we believe) are inherent in individual initiative, price "cues" as against administrative orders, and wide use of market mechanisms. There is no doubt that some Soviet administrators do realize these things. The main obstacle to acting on this knowledge is doubtless the *political* centralism of the Soviet system, and the difficulty of reconciling free choice in economic matters with the tight discipline of a one-party state. There is also the ideological need to avoid any obvious imitation of capitalist methods and to sanctify any new departures by copious quotations from Marx. Fortunately Marx wrote several thousand pages, many of them reasonably obscure, and this simplifies the task.

SUMMARY

1. Our productive resources are not sufficient to turn out nearly as much as we would like to consume.

2. Scarcity of resources forces hard decisions concerning (1) how much work the population shall do; (2) how much effort shall be devoted to providing for the future through production of capital goods; (3) how much of each consumer good and service shall be produced; (4) what production methods shall be used; (5) how much of the national output each household shall receive.

3. In a subsistence economy these decisions are heavily influenced by custom, family structure, and the authority of family heads and village officials.

4. In the planned economy of the U.S.S.R., the division of national output between consumer goods and capital goods is a strategic decision made at the highest level of government.

5. Production of basic foodstuffs, standard clothing, and other key consumer goods is planned to meet minimum standards of physical need. Non-

essentials receive lower priority and output typically falls short of official targets. Agricultural production by its nature cannot be planned as tightly as industrial production.

6. Industrial managers are stimulated to operate their plants efficiently by a combination of plan controls, promotion and prestige rewards, and money incentives.

7. Decisions about how much to work and where to work are left largely to the individual worker. The system of wage rates is so constructed as to enable high-priority industries to recruit the labor they need.

8. Wage differences between laborers, skilled workers, managers, and professional people are probably about as wide in the U.S.S.R. as they are in the U.S.A. Differences in household income are smaller, however, because property income is absent and because many services are provided free by government.

9. The Soviet system is a mixed economy. Many things are planned, some more tightly and effectively than others. But a good many other things are left to individual choice and initiative.

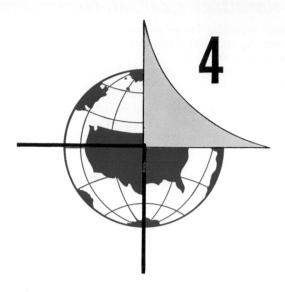

The Market Economy

"'Tis so," said the Duchess; "and the moral of it is 'Oh! 'tis love, 'tis love that makes the world go round!' "

"Somebody said," whispered Alice, "that it's done by everybody minding their own business!"

"Ah, well! It means much the same thing," said the Duchess.

Alice's Adventures in Wonderland

Once you have gone to market you have told the whole world.

RUSSIAN PROVERB

MARKETS AND PRICES

FEW PEOPLE in the United States live as isolated Crusoes. Nor does anyone sit in Washington deciding how much of each good shall be produced. How, then, are the key economic decisions made? Russian leaders refer to capitalist economies as "unplanned," "chaotic." Yet these economies actually show a great deal of order and stability. What is it that produces order rather than chaos?

I go down to the supermarket on Saturday afternoon and lay hands on a market basket. No one has any notice of my coming. Yet the goods I want are usually there, and at about the prices I had expected to pay. The people who produced the goods may be thousands of miles away.

They know nothing about me and care less. Yet their activities are somehow coordinated with my desires. Writers with a poetic bent have sometimes compared a market economy to an astronomical system, with self-interest playing the role of gravity, and millions of consumers and producers whizzing harmoniously about in their respective orbits.

What holds the economy together? A brief answer, which will take several chapters to develop, is that the system is coordinated through an interlocking network of *markets*. The key feature of each market is the *price* prevailing in the market. These two terms have a special meaning in economics and require a word of explanation.

Markets

The term "market" does not refer just to fishmarkets or fresh vegetable stalls, or even to retail trade in general. Every good and service is regarded as having a market, in which supplies of the good are bought and sold. There is a market for basic steel, electric power, textile machinery, cotton cloth, dry cleaning, barber services, and every other item produced in the economy. Moreover, a product may pass through a series of markets before reaching the ultimate user. A farmer sells wheat to a miller, who sells bran to a food manufacturer, who sells bran flakes to wholesale distributors, who resell to retail grocers, who supply consumers in the retail market.

There are also markets for the basic services used in production—for land, labor, and capital. Thus we speak of the "money market," in which lenders provide funds to borrowers at a specified rate of interest. In the "labor market" employees deal with employers, exchanging so many hours or weeks of labor for a certain wage.

A market is not necessarily, or even usually, a single place. The distinguished British economist, Alfred Marshall, stated that: "A market is an area within which buyers and sellers are in such close communication with each other that price tends to be the same throughout the area." Some markets are virtually worldwide. This is true of many basic raw materials, and also of securities of the U.S. government and of leading U.S. business concerns. The requirements for a wide market are that the product be sufficiently standardized that it can safely be bought and sold without being seen, and that its value be high relative to the cost of transporting it. Gold, precious stones, and gilt-edged securities, whose value is high and transport cost low, are the international commodities par excellence. But other staples such as copper, aluminum, rubber, coffee, cocoa, wool, and cotton also enjoy a world market.

Other markets are national in scope. Men's and women's clothing can be shipped anywhere in the United States at a cost which is small relative to the value of the merchandise. A clothing manufacturer in any part of the country, then, is in direct competition with makers of the same item in other regions and must watch their prices. This is true also of other light manufactured goods. As one gets into heavier products with a low value per pound, shipment to distant points becomes less feasible and the market shrinks to regional or local proportions. Each city has its own sand and gravel quarries, which do not compete with suppliers in other cities. Brick factories have a narrow market area because of the great weight and low value of their product.

Retail markets, particularly markets for groceries and other staple necessities, are centered in a single town or city. But the rise of the automobile has made retail markets larger than they used to be. An enterprising housewife will drive to a suburban market or even to the next town if she detects a substantial advantage in quality or price. The market area of each town thus interlocks with that of neighboring towns in an endless chain.

The size of the labor market depends on the level of labor in question. An outstanding business executive, scientist, actor, or surgeon enjoys a national market. He is known throughout the country, is well informed about opportunities in other areas, and will move to another location if it offers sufficient advantage. For most manual, clerical, and subprofessional jobs, however, one can take the locality as the relevant market area. A worker who is settled in a community and perhaps owns a home there is unlikely to know about or to be much interested in jobs in other cities. These local labor markets are linked, however, by the possibility that people *might* move if the wage level of City A rose much above that of City B. This possibility is sufficient to keep wage levels of nearby cities reasonably well in line with each other.

Prices

A "price" is the amount paid for a specified quantity and quality of any good or service, the amount for which it exchanges in the relevant market. Bricklayers are paid, say, $4.00 an hour in Minneapolis. This is the price at which this kind of labor is sold by workers in the Minneapolis labor market. Thus a wage rate is a price. An interest rate is also a price— the price paid for use of a certain quantity of money for a stated period of time. Most frequently price is used in its everyday meaning of the amount paid for a pair of shoes or a pound of butter. But when the term is used in a general way, when one speaks of "competitive pricing" or "the price mechanism," it should be taken to include wage rates, interest rates, rents, and other payments for productive services.

A SIMPLIFIED MARKET SYSTEM

We are now going to engage in a typical bit of economic abstraction. We shall set up a simple model of a market economy, designed to highlight certain key markets and prices and to show their interrelations. The excuse for doing so is that the real world bears some resemblance to this simple model. An understanding of this simplified system will help us in exploring the complexities of the actual American economy at a later stage.

Our model rests on several foundation stones, or *assumptions*, which should be kept clearly in mind for the rest of this chapter. These are suppositions about the setup of markets and the behavior of people in the system, without which we should be unable to reach definite conclusions. The main assumptions are:

1. Government is left on the sidelines for the time being in order to explore the operation of a *purely private economy*. All production in the system is carried on by private business units.

2. All markets in the system are characterized by *pure competition*. This implies that:

> *a*) Any person in the economy can enter any market if he sees a chance of gain by so doing, and can operate on either the buying or selling side. There are no legal or other barriers to entrance into any market.
> *b*) There must be large numbers of buyers and sellers so that the dealings of any individual are a small part of total transactions in the market, hence will have little influence on the prices established.
> *c*) Buyers may not get together to beat down the market price, nor may sellers conspire to raise it. "Rigging" of the market is forbidden.

Few actual markets meet these requirements. The New York Stock Exchange comes very close, however, and so do the commodity exchanges for wheat, corn, cotton, sugar, cocoa, and other staples. Most other markets fall short of these specifications to a greater or lesser degree.

3. Everyone willing to work at existing wage scales can find work. The model is one of a *full-employment economy*. This does not mean that we ignore the importance of depression and unemployment in actual economies, but this problem is reserved for later treatment in Part Three. Meanwhile, the full-employment assumption means that increased output of any product in the system must be accompanied by reduced output of one or more other products. Since everyone is at work, increased employment at one point in the system means reduced employment somewhere else.

4. The workers, housewives, business executives, farmers, and others in the system are reasonably well informed about prices in the markets in which they operate. But they do not need to be perfectly informed for the system to operate effectively.

5. People in the system are interested in material well-being, in monetary gain. We suppose that a worker will normally prefer a higher wage to a lower wage for the same kind of work, that a housewife will prefer a lower price to a higher price for the same article, and that a businessman will prefer larger profits to smaller ones.

So much for the underpinnings of the model. Now what does it look like? The system is sketched in Figure 4–1. It includes three types of organization: households, producers of goods and services, and retailers. These groups are linked by four types of market: labor markets, money markets, producers' markets, and retail markets. The curlicues in each market are steel springs, intended to suggest that tension is being exerted on the market from both sides—the buying or demand side, and the selling or supply side.

Goods move from left to right across the chart, while money flows in the opposite direction. Since the households at the extreme left are the same households which appear at the extreme right, the chart could be

FIGURE 4–1

The Market Mechanism

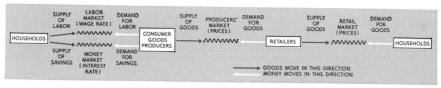

Each market in the system is linked to many other markets.

curled over to form a continuous circle, the "wheel of wealth" shown in Chapter 2.

The drastic simplification of reality involved in this diagram is apparent. The American economy includes millions of households, producing units, and retail outlets. Listing each of these separately would extend the chart downward for several miles. Moreover, rarely is all the work of producing a finished good done in a single enterprise, as suggested by our one box for producers. There are usually numerous stages of processing on the way from raw materials to final sale, and inserting these stages would stretch out the diagram in the horizontal direction. What we have done is to collapse or condense the "real world diagram," both horizontally and vertically, to make it printable and comprehensible.

SOME CHARACTERISTICS OF THE MARKET ECONOMY

Figure 4–1 was constructed to explain the key economic decisions made in a market economy. Before turning to that problem, however, let us look at some general characteristics of this kind of economy.

One Market, One Price

Under pure competition, there can be only one price for a specified product. If one seller tries to charge more than the prevailing price, buyers will abandon him and buy elsewhere. If he offers goods below the prevailing price, buyers will flock to him so fast that he will conclude that he can safely raise prices. The large number of buyers and sellers in the market, and the possibility of shifting from one to another, forces all dealings in the direction of a single price. This price gives a "thermometer reading" of the situation prevailing in the market in question. The economic mechanism may be thought of either as a network of interconnected *markets*, or as a network of interconnected *prices*, each indicating the situation in the market to which it relates.

Price Determined by Supply and Demand

A nineteenth-century wit remarked, "Teach a parrot to say 'supply and demand' and you have an economist." The fact that the term has become a cliché should not blind us to its remarkable usefulness. Price obviously *is* influenced by pressure from both sides of the market—from sellers supplying the good or service who will cease supplying it if the price falls too low, and from buyers who want the product but will feel obliged to stop buying it if prices rise too high. The markets in Figure 4–1 have been represented as steel springs to indicate that tension is exerted on the market from both the supply and demand sides. A tug on the spring from either side will be felt at the other side, and will lead to a different quantity of the product being exchanged in the market at a different price.

The Interrelation of Prices and Markets

Each market is related to every other market in the system. This means that the prices which measure the state of the market also are interrelated. What will happen if consumers decide to buy more television sets and fewer radios? Retailers of television sets will find merchandise moving off their shelves at a brisker pace (right-hand side of Figure 4–1). They no longer will feel obliged to offer special discounts and clearance sales, which amounts to an increase in their selling price. Next they will order more sets from the manufacturers. Faced with this rush of business, manufacturers may raise their prices. Certainly they will try to increase production, and the prosperity of the industry may cause new companies to set up in television production. This will increase the demand for metals, glass, and other materials going into the sets, for certain kinds of machinery, for bank loans, and for labor to produce the increased output. Thus the impact is felt finally in the markets for productive services (left-hand side of Figure 4–1). Higher wages may be offered voluntarily to attract the necessary number of workers, or if there is a union, it may take advantage of the situation to demand a wage increase.

Even this is not the end of the story. Increased demand for television parts will cause expansion of all the industries supplying those parts, and the impact will stretch back to iron and copper mines, lumber mills, and silica sand for glass production. Movement of labor to the expanding television industry will force other companies to recruit more actively and probably to raise their wages. The effects will be felt eventually in thousands of markets, many of them remote from the initial point of impact.

Meanwhile, the hapless radio producers will be faced with an opposite sequence of events. Some of them may manage to convert their plants and become television manufacturers. Unless they do this they will be faced with declining sales and profits, and their material suppliers and workers will suffer along with them. The reader can trace out for himself the sorry sequence of events resulting from a permanent *drop* in demand for a product.

It is now clearer why we are justified in speaking of an economic *system*. Using the dimensions of Figure 4–1, markets are linked in a horizontal direction by technological processes, by the flow of materials through successive stages of processing and distribution until the finished good reaches the ultimate user. They are cross-linked in a vertical direction by the existence of alternatives and the consequent possibility of choice. Consumers may decide to use more of commodity A and less of B. Producing units may decide that one sort of machine or material does the job better than another. Workers may decide that they prefer to work at Company X rather than Company Y.

A shift in one market is transmitted through these vertical and horizontal linkages into markets which on the surface seem quite remote from the first. A market economy may be visualized as a kind of giant computer, constantly receiving information from all parts of the system and working out correct adjustments. A shift in one market starts lights flashing all through the machine and many prices and outputs may have to change before the computer settles down once more with a sigh of contentment. A major function of economics is to analyze and predict these indirect effects, which the man on the street typically overlooks.

The Basic Data: Individual Preferences and Production Possibilities

A market economy is individualistic in the sense that its operation depends on the preferences and choices of the millions of individuals in the system. This obviously cannot mean that each person's preferences are independent of those of others. Any social psychologist could demonstrate that this is not so. But however preferences are determined, whether people are herd-minded or as independent as Crusoe, their choices are *registered* by individual acts of buying and selling in various markets. These are the ultimate pressures to which the market economy responds.

The term *preference* may suggest something whimsical or intangible, simply a vague attitude of mind. But economists use the term in a more precise sense. *Consumer preference* implies that a man knows how much a particular product is worth to him relative to each other product he buys. He knows how much of product A he would give up to get a certain amount of product B; and since he has only so much income, he has to make this kind of decision every day. Similarly one can speak of *worker preferences*. If a man can choose his working hours, as many people can to some extent, he must balance the attractiveness of extra income and extra leisure. In choosing among jobs, he may decide that a strenuous and uncomfortable job should pay him 50 cents an hour more than a light, pleasant job; and so on.

The other thing which we take as given in analyzing a market economy is *methods of production*. Even for a single product, we speak usually of *methods* rather than of a single method. There are many different ways of using land to grow wheat. The farmer may use a great deal of machinery and little labor, or simpler tools and more labor. He may spend more or less on drainage, fertilizers, improved seed, and other supplies. We assume that the producer knows all these alternative possibilities and makes an informed choice among them. But we do not at this stage ask where new production methods come from, any more than we ask where consumer and worker preferences come from.

Some of the tools which economists have developed for analyzing individual choice and production decisions are outlined in an Appendix to this chapter.

Equilibrium and Disturbances of Equilibrium

The term *equilibrium* will occur frequently in later chapters, so it is best to get the general sense of it at the outset. In economics as in mechanics, equilibrium is a state of balance, a condition which will continue unchanged until disturbed by some outside event. If the market price of a product is $3.00, and if at that price the quantity which suppliers wish to sell exactly equals the amount which users are willing to buy, the market is in equilibrium. The same quantity will continue to be exchanged at the same price, week after week and month after month, until there is some change in behavior on either the buying or selling side.

One can even imagine a situation in which all markets in the economy would be in equilibrium at the same time. Suppose each individual has preferences as regards working and consuming, and that these preferences continue unchanged over time. Suppose also that no one upsets the applecart by inventing new products or new production methods. We might then expect that the economy would settle down gradually into a stationary state—producing the same quantities of each good month after month, hiring the same amounts of labor for each job, and so on.

Now we know that no actual economy operates in this fashion. Why is this?

1. One important disturbing factor, general waves of prosperity and depression, has deliberately been left out of the picture and will continue to be ignored until Part Three.

2. A major source of disturbance is the invention of new products and new methods of production. When a major new product appears and

catches on, other products have to move over, as it were, to make room for it. Some existing products suffer a loss in sales and some disappear entirely.

3. There are spontaneous shifts in consumer preference. Even without the appearance of new products, taste and fashion may shift away from certain goods and toward others. As slimness becomes fashionable, people will eat less potatoes and more lettuce.

4. There are spontaneous shifts of preference at the other side of the diagram. An increased preference for leisure, or increased preference for white-collar jobs compared with blue-collar jobs, will clearly have important repercussions. So will a decision to save more and consume less, or vice versa.

5. War obviously produces severe dislocations in the economy. Less important short-term disturbances can result from unusually good or bad harvests, shifts in economic conditions in other countries, long strikes in key industries, and a variety of other factors.

A market economy can be regarded as a basically stable and self-adjusting mechanism which is constantly being jolted and modified by these various disturbances. The water level of the ocean is essentially stable; but on top of this one finds tidal movements, the long "rollers" of mid-ocean, smaller waves, and tiny ripples whipped up by surface winds. Any actual economy displays a similar "choppiness." Basic, slow-moving changes are in process, and on top of these are a multitude of transient disturbances. Economics helps one to sort out these various layers of disturbance and assess their relative importance.

ECONOMIC DECISIONS IN A MARKET ECONOMY

It may seem that we have made a long detour from the problem with which this chapter began: how the key economic decisions are made in a market economy. Having gone this long way round, however, we can now take a shorter route home.

Work and Leisure

Decisions in this area are made by many millions of workers and potential workers. They have to decide three things: whether to work at all, how much work to do, and what to work at.

1. The decision whether to work at all is heavily influenced by economic necessity and social pressure. Except for the wealthy, a decision not to work means a decision not to live very well; and in the United States it is unfashionable for an able-bodied male to remain idle even if he can afford to do so. Single women are also expected to work from school-leaving to marriage. Married women, on the other hand, usually have a real alternative between taking jobs and not taking them. This group shows a growing preference for work outside the home. The reasons include smaller families, mechanical aids to housekeeping, and a steady

widening of the range of occupations considered normal and proper for women. The percentage of women aged 25–44 who are in the labor force increased from 18 percent in 1890 to almost 40 percent at present.

2. Having decided to enter the labor force, one must next decide how much work to do. This depends on the shape of individual preference systems. A man who values income highly because he has a large family or expensive tastes may prefer to work long hours for a large paycheck. A man with fewer responsibilities or of a more idle temperament may prefer to work fewer hours.

This kind of decision is also influenced by social custom and industrial practice. In modern industry, it is not feasible for each worker in an enterprise to choose his own working hours. All must abide by a standard schedule. Throughout a large part of American industry, the standard is now eight hours a day, five days a week, with two to four weeks of vacation during the year. Standard hours have fallen greatly since 1900 and undoubtedly will continue to fall in the future.

The existence of a standard schedule in each establishment does not mean that the individual is entirely without choice. Different industries have different practices, ranging from 30 hours a week in some to 50 hours or more in others. A man can choose to enter a long-hour or a short-hour industry. Many plants also work overtime during busy periods, and workers have the option of putting in for overtime or avoiding it. A worker with a high preference for income may even hold two jobs at the same time. These people are often called "moonlighters," and there are now several million of them. On the other hand, people with a low income preference can often find part-time employment. Married women who need time for household duties often adjust in this way. Of the seven million part-time workers in the United States, more than four million are women.

3. Each person also must decide *where* to work—at what kind of job, for what company, and in what part of the country. True, the middle-aged machinist cannot suddenly decide to become a doctor. A long-time resident of Oakland isn't really concerned with jobs in Youngstown. In the formative high school and college years, however, the range of choice is potentially as wide as the economy itself. This means that, *given sufficient time*, the number of people choosing to work in certain occupations or areas may rise substantially while preference for other types of work may decline. Even the factory operative usually has a modest range of choice among specific jobs and employers.

Each worker presumably chooses the job which yields maximum advantage in view of his own preference system. This does not mean that he necessarily chooses the highest-paying job he can find. He may be influenced by whether the job is close to home, whether he has friends in the plant, whether the work is hard or easy, and any number of other things. Adding all these things together, he chooses the job which offers him the most attractive "package" of conditions. If it should happen that two jobs are alike in every respect except wages, most people will doubtless choose the higher wage.

Each employer competing in the labor market, then, must work out a package of conditions good enough to attract and hold the number of workers he needs. If he wants 750 employees, then there must be 750 people in the community who value his terms of employment more highly than the terms offered by rival employers. Some workers may be firmly wedded to the plant by long habit, or because they find the work inherently congenial and attractive. But there will be others who are closer to the margin of decision, who are wavering between a job in plant A and plant B. It is these "marginal" people who must be persuaded. Wages are typically a key device for persuading them, partly because money is after all important, and partly because wage levels can be adjusted more rapidly than most other conditions of employment.

Thus workers' preferences encounter the terms offered by employers in the labor market. Through the market there is worked out a pattern of wages and other terms of employment such that each worker is reasonably content with his job choice and each employer is able to hire the number of workers he needs.

Capital Goods and Consumer Goods

Business units need more than labor to set up in production. They need buildings and machinery, which may be elaborate and expensive. How can they get the money to buy these things? In our simplified economy, they would have to borrow from households. This would be done in the "money market." In this market the individual hands over a certain amount of money (say $100) and gets in return either a definite promise (in the case of a bond or preferred stock) or a reasonable expectation (in the case of a common stock) of receiving a certain money payment each year (say $5). In this case the rate of interest is $\frac{5}{100} = 5$ percent. The rate of interest is the "price" of money in the capital market, just as the rate of wages is the governing price in the labor market.

Where do households get the money which they hand over to business? Presumably from saving, i.e., from spending on current consumption something less than their current income. The inducement to save is that, by reducing current consumption, one can earn interest payments and thus enjoy higher consumption in future years. This kind of choice, indeed, is often termed a "choice between present goods and future goods."

Whether a person is more or less savings-minded will depend on such things as: whether his earnings may be expected to rise or decline in future years; whether family responsibilities are increasing or decreasing; whether savings are needed for some major expenditure such as a house or college education of children; plans for retirement; and whether the person is temperamentally farsighted or shortsighted, reckless or conservative. The amount saved will also be influenced strongly by the size of the family income. People with large incomes save on the average a much higher percentage of their incomes than people in the low-income brackets.

The supply of savings, shaped by these personal preferences, encounters the demand for savings by business units on the capital market. Through the working of the market a rate of interest is established and a certain volume of savings is exchanged. How does this affect the operation of the economy? Suppose that in a particular year the net output of our model economy is worth $500 billion. Under the simple conditions assumed here, all of this will be distributed to individuals in income payments. Personal income = net national product = $500 billion. Now suppose that 20 percent or $100 billion of this is put into savings while the remaining $400 billion is spent on current consumption. If the economy is to be in balance, the output of consumer goods cannot exceed $400 billion, since this is the amount that households have allocated to purchase of consumer goods. But we supposed originally that total output of the economy was $500 billion. What has become of the other $100 billion? This consists of capital goods production. The $100 billion which savers hand over to business concerns is used to buy this quantity of capital equipment.

The situation may be sketched as follows:

$$
\text{Total Income } 500 \left\{
\begin{array}{l}
\dfrac{\text{Spent}}{400} = \dfrac{\text{Consumer goods output}}{400} \\[2em]
\dfrac{\text{Saved}}{100} = \dfrac{\text{Capital goods output}}{100}
\end{array}
\right\} \text{Total Output } 500
$$

For our simple economy to be in balance, the distribution of national output between capital goods and consumer goods must precisely correspond with the distribution of personal income between savings and consumption. Money flows and goods flows must match. If people decide permanently to increase the proportion of income saved, the structure of production will gradually respond to this decision. The percentage of output going into capital goods will rise and the percentage going to consumer goods will fall.

Whether an economy is a low-savings economy or a high-savings economy is clearly very important. Where households are unwilling to postpone consumption and insist on spending almost all their incomes, the supply of loanable funds will be small and the rate of interest high. Only business ventures which promise high returns can be undertaken. Additions to the country's stock of plant and equipment will be slow. Production methods will be simple and labor-intensive, output per worker small, and living standards low. These conditions characterize many of the under-developed countries, where the level of savings is close to zero.

A high propensity to save, on the other hand, makes for moderate interest rates, a rapid build-up of the country's capital stock, use of increasingly elaborate techniques and equipment, and a steady rise of living standards. Rising incomes, of course, make it still easier to save in the future, and the build-up of capital goods becomes cumulative.

What Kinds of Consumer Goods?

The choices examined thus far determined the amount of labor available in the economy, which sets a ceiling on total output, and the broad division of output between consumer goods and capital goods. This leaves unsettled the question of what kinds of consumer good shall be produced, and in what quantities. Why do we turn out seven million cars this year rather than five million or nine million? Why six hundred million pairs of shoes rather than a larger or smaller quantity? We have already seen that this is a difficult problem under central planning and is not solved very satisfactorily. How is the same problem solved in a market economy?

A rough answer, which will be spelled out more fully in the next several chapters, is that the amount of each good produced is determined by weighing costs of production against the price which consumers are willing to pay. Under pure competition, business concerns will grind out more and more of a product as long as consumers will buy it at a price sufficient to cover the cost of making it. Production is thus guided by consumers' preference systems as expressed by their purchases in retail markets.

Suppose that at a particular time men's shoes could be produced and retailed at $15 per pair, including a reasonable profit to all concerned. Consumers are so avid for shoes, however, that they are willing to pay $25 and the market price settles for the time being at this level. This price obviously yields handsome returns to all the sellers in this particular chain of markets—retailers, wholesalers, shoe manufacturers, leather makers, and the rest. The result will be a strenuous effort to turn out more of this profitable item. Existing shoe companies will expand their production and new companies may be set up.

As the production of shoes rises, however, two things will happen. The price offered for shoes in the market will fall, following the general principle that increased quantities of any product can be sold only by lowering its price. The cost of producing additional shoes may also rise, but it may not. In any event, the fall in price will gradually reduce the gap between price and cost, and eventually a point will be reached at which there is no incentive to expand shoe production further.

Under pure competition, in short, a positive price-cost gap signals an expansion of production, while a negative gap (a loss) signals curtailment of production.

The concept of "cost" deserves additional comment. Cost of production is on the surface a certain quantity of money. The shoe producer must pay certain amounts for labor, for leather, for other supplies and materials, and for interest on the capital invested in the enterprise. But these money costs have a deeper economic significance. Consider labor, which is the most important cost item for the economy as a whole. Our shoe producer has to pay, say, $2.00 an hour to hire an additional worker. Why must he pay this? Because the worker is worth this much to some other employer—say, a furniture manufacturer. If the labor market is competitive, as we have supposed it to be, the shoe producer must pay at least as much as the man would be worth elsewhere in order to bid him away into shoe production. If the man goes to work on shoes, however, he cannot work on furniture, and the output he might have produced there is lost to the economy. The real cost of his shoe output is thus the value of the furniture output which he does not produce. Economists term this *opportunity cost*—the value of foregone opportunities.

The significance of equality between price and cost now becomes more apparent. Price measures the valuation which consumers place on an additional pair of shoes, the benefit which they expect to derive from this item. Cost, traced back to its root meaning of *opportunity* cost, measures the valuation placed on the articles which must be sacrificed to make possible production of the extra pair of shoes. When these two valuations are precisely equal, consumers cannot be benefited by any further shifting of resources into or out of shoe production. If all product markets are in this sort of equilibrium, one can argue that the economy is doing the best possible job of satisfying consumer preferences.

The Choice of Production Methods

When one speaks of "cost of production," one means cost of production *by a certain method*. Different methods will yield different levels of cost. How, then, does a business concern decide what method to use for a particular product? This is an especially important question in designing a completely new plant. Once the plant has been built, the range of choice is narrower; but one can still make modifications so as to save labor by using more machinery, or vice versa.

Decision on this point requires two kinds of information. First, one must know the production possibilities system (Appendix Figure 3). One must know what alternative combinations of labor, capital, and other factors are *technically possible* for the level of output desired. But this alone cannot determine which alternative is *economically preferable*. To determine this we must know the prices of the various factors. Then we can calculate production costs by each method, and choose the method which yields lowest cost.

The way in which this will work itself out is almost self-evident. In an economy where labor is scarce and expensive, as it is in the United States, the scales will be tilted in favor of mechanization and automation.

Countries with abundant labor and little capital, on the other hand, will lean toward simpler methods. The relative scarcity of labor and capital is reflected in their relative prices; and these prices lead producers to choose methods which economize on the scarcer factor and make more use of the abundant one. This is efficient from the standpoint of the individual producer and also makes best use of national resources.

But haven't we assumed too readily that businessmen are invariably well-informed and rational? How do we know that they will select and use the lowest-cost methods of production? The answer is that under pure competition efficiency is the price of survival. If some companies can produce shoes for $15.00 per pair, others must learn to do the same if they are to continue in the industry.

Competitive pressure forces each producer to make correct decisions about production methods and to run his plant efficiently. If anyone in an industry develops improved methods leading to lower costs, other producers must eventually fall in line. The penalty for being inefficient is elimination from the economy. This is a major argument for competition as a method of economic organization.

The Distribution of Income

The final question which our market economy must answer is what share each individual or family shall receive of the national output. Why do some people receive 10 or 20 times as much as others? To what extent are these differences inherent in a market economy, and to what extent can they be altered by community action?

In a market economy people receive income as *owners of labor and capital* which they contribute to the production process. Each person's income depends on the *quantity* of resources which he contributes multiplied by the *price* which these resources fetch on the market. The problem of resource prices has already been examined. The rate of interest is determined in the capital market, the wage rates for various types of labor in the labor market. But what determines the quantity of resources which each person owns?

How much capital a man owns depends on how much he has inherited and how much he has added to or subtracted from this amount. He can add to his inheritance by saving or subtract from it by spending beyond his current income. If it were not for the inheritance factor one could say simply, "How much you own depends on how much you save." Inheritance is quite important in practice, however, and this weakens the argument that property income is justified by personal merit or sacrifice. The feasibility of passing on property intact depends a good deal on the inheritance laws of the country, and on whether the government levies estate taxes at death.

Capacity for productive labor is partly inborn. Some occupations require natural talents which occur only rarely in the population. One cannot mass produce concert violinists, ballerinas, or big-league pitchers capable of winning 20 games a year. People with these talents are bound to command a premium price. Capacity to perform most jobs, however, is largely a matter of training. There are many young people in the country who are capable of being average machinists, accountants, professors, sales clerks, or lawyers. But how many people, and *which* people, actually get into these occupations depends on opportunity to acquire the necessary education and experience. This is particularly important for law, medicine, science, and other professional occupations. Even in the United States, and to a greater extent in most other countries, cost of education and limitations of university capacity restrict the number of people who can get into the higher occupations. Thus these occupations, in addition to the earnings which they could command in a free market, receive an additional premium resulting from artificial restriction of supply.

It follows that the distribution of income in a country depends partly on its institutional structure and is in no sense immutable. One can always alter income distribution by changing the pattern of resource ownership. If one would like to see a more equal distribution, one can try to enlarge the educational bottlenecks which restrict access to the higher occupations; and one can try to bring about a more equal distribution of property ownership. Such measures tackle the income distribution problem in a fundamental way, and in a way which does not interfere with the operation of the market mechanism.

In addition, of course, government can alter income distribution through taxation, and most governments do a good deal of this. How far this tendency should be carried is a subject of intense political controversy, to which we shall return in Chapter 14.

CONCLUDING COMMENTS

The Market Provides Answers

We have tried to demonstrate that a market economy is capable of answering the key economic questions posed at the outset. Given the distribution of resource ownership, personal preference systems, and the production possibilities set by technology, one can deduce how much of each product will be produced and what it will sell for, where each person will work and how much he will be paid. One may think of the appropriate price-production pattern as being worked out in a flash by solving a large number of equations in a computer or, more realistically, as being approximated through the trial-and-error process which goes on in any actual economy.

An attractive feature of the market economy is that the answers are worked out on a *decentralized* basis, through millions of individuals making their own decisions in thousands of different markets. There is no need for a central planning board to supervise the process from on high.

The decentralized system has advantages in terms of flexibility, speed, and opportunity for personal initiative.

The Interdependence of Markets

This point has already been made but deserves to be emphasized. A shift in preferences or technology, while its initial impact may be mainly on one market, sets up repercussions which will be transmitted to many other markets before the system settles down into a new equilibrium. The self-adjusting character of the system depends on this linkage and interdependence of markets.

Space does not permit detailed illustration of this point; but the reader will find it instructive to do a few "finger exercises" on his own account, starting with a change somewhere in the system and trying to trace out the repercussions of the change. Consider, for example, the following:

1. A shift of workers' preferences *away* from bituminous coal mining.
2. A shift of consumers' preferences *away* from potatoes and *toward* lettuce.
3. Introduction of a completely new product—choose your own—into the economy.
4. A shift of workers' preferences toward leisure, leading to a general shortening of the work week.

If you can work out cases of this sort successfully, you will have absorbed the essence of this chapter.

A Guiding Thread: The Marginal Principle

This chapter has tried to explore the full range of decisions which have to be made in any economy. These may seem on the surface to be quite different from each other, yet there is a unifying principle which runs through them all. This is commonly termed the *marginal principle*. It means that economic choices are typically between small or *marginal* quantities. The consumer does not choose between buying a great quantity of beef and giving up beef altogether. He asks rather: "Seeing how prices are this week, will it be worthwhile for me to buy *a little more* beef and perhaps *a little less* pork?" He is comparing, not *total* quantities, but *marginal* quantities. He is weighing the possible advantage of making small adjustments at the boundaries of his present consumption pattern.

Similarly, our shoe manufacturer is not in the position of deciding between building six new shoe factories and going out of business completely. His typical problem is this: "I'm turning out 500 pairs a day. If I went up to 550 pairs a day, could I sell the extra 50 pairs for enough to cover the cost of making them"? Would the extra income or revenue cover the extra costs? The manufacturer is not reasoning about his total output, but about a small or marginal change in his rate of output.

The worker considering whether the money he would get for working overtime on Saturday morning is attractive enough to outweigh not being able to take his son fishing is engaged in a marginal calculation. So is the householder wondering whether the interest he will get on a $100 U.S. saving bond outweighs the pleasure of spending the money right away. So is the plant manager trying to calculate whether the savings from an improved machine will repay the cost of the machine.

Individuals throughout the economy are constantly engaged in millions of calculations of this sort. Each tries to work out a pattern of behavior which will yield greatest satisfaction in terms of his preference system. If these calculations are being made correctly, then the system is performing as efficiently as it can within the limits of people's preferences and the basic resources available.

The Market as Reconciler of Conflicting Interests

A competitive economy performs another important function, so obvious that it is in danger of being overlooked. It produces a working compromise among the conflicting interests of individuals and groups in the economy. Indeed, it is the only way of achieving such a compromise without central economic control.

Consider the inevitable difference of interest over income distribution. Everyone wants more, and there just isn't enough to go round. This could lead, and in some societies has led, to armed conflict. Competitive pricing of labor and capital on free markets at least provides a clear principle for income distribution, a principle which can readily be explained and which has managed to win a considerable measure of public agreement.

Consider also the fact that the things consumers want to have produced may not correspond at all closely to the kinds of work people would like to do. Some of the products in greatest demand may require work which is heavy, hot, and generally uncongenial. Men might prefer to spend their days in work which is light, leisurely, and creative, but which yields products of little market value. This conflict is resolved by pressures from the two sides meeting in the market and reaching a working adjustment. The product in great demand commands a relatively high price. This means that the industry can afford a relatively high wage rate. High wages are sufficient, at least for some workers, to offset the natural unpleasantness of the work and the industry is able to recruit a labor force. Coal mining is a good example.

In the opposite case of work which is naturally congenial, one can hire people at low wage rates, the low wages being offset by the pleasantness of life on the job. These wages permit the product to be offered at low prices; and low prices induce the public to take more of the product, even though their preference for it is not high. Thus some people are able to work in these pleasant occupations. There are people who say they would paint, act, or play the violin "for nothing"—and they must mean it, because most artists earn very little. By performing for next to nothing they create a market for their services and are able to follow their career preference.

Consider finally the conflict of interest between each group of producers in the economy and the consuming public. Each producer group—the farmers, the steel producers, the retail druggists, and the rest—would really like to mulct consumers by charging a high price for their wares. Talk about "public service" is a thin veil for mercenary motives.

Where pure competition prevails, however, producers are obliged to work for minimum returns. Each producer is compelled to work at full efficiency and to provide the community with goods at minimum cost. This is not done out of altruism. Producers continue to be as selfish as ever, but competition channels their selfishness in a direction useful to the community. As Adam Smith concluded, ". . . thus each is led, as though by an invisible hand, to promote a good which was no part of his intention."

The Best of All Possible Worlds?

Is the competitive market economy, then, a kind of economic Utopia? Many economists have argued persuasively that a purely competitive system does (or more correctly *would*, if it could be brought into existence) produce better results than any other kind of economic organization. The argument is that such a system gives greatest possible weight to the preferences of people in the economy. Guided by these preferences, the system works out a pattern of production which is as good as one can do with the resources available. If all individuals have made their marginal calculations as best they can, then any change which might be made would leave people worse off than before. Broadly, the argument is that people can do better for themselves than anyone else can do for them.

It would be pleasant if this argument could be accepted and applied without question. The duty of government then would be to go out and promote competitive conditions in every realm of economic life; and if it succeeded in this, it need do little more. This outlook, associated historically with "Manchester liberalism," still commands considerable support in Western Europe, Britain, and the United States. But matters are not so simple. Several reservations must be entered even at this early stage:

1. Our model of a market economy is limited to production by private business units. It gives us no principles for deciding what services should be provided by government, and how much of these services should be provided. We still have the problem of drawing an appropriate boundary between private and public production.

2. The argument for competitive organization is not immune to criticism. The competitive model professes to produce maximum output at minimum cost in human effort. This is an important economic goal, but it is only one goal among others. A market economy contains little provision for personal security, and it is likely to produce a quite unequal dis-

tribution of income. It may or may not produce as high a rate of technological progress as an economy based on private monopolies or state enterprises. Nor does the market economy provide any guarantee against business depressions. There is an open-and-shut case for the market economy only if one attaches great weight to current operating efficiency compared with stability, growth, equality, and other possible objectives.

3. It can be argued that the American economy has already departed so far from the competitive pattern that this pattern is no longer a useful guide to public policy. We have with us the railroads, electric power companies, and other "natural monopolies"; the many lines of industry dominated by a few giant firms—steel, petroleum, automobiles, and the rest; the farm organizations insisting on government price fixing and subsidies; the unions doing their best to abolish competition in labor markets. Any model of the economy which assumes the general prevalence of competition may thus be attacked as irrelevant to practical affairs.

The advocates of competitive markets, however, have a rebuttal to this line of argument. They say, in effect, "The fact that crime has flourished in the past doesn't mean that it need flourish in the future. Certainly there is much suppression of competition in the American economy. But the answer is not to throw up our hands and accept this. We should go out and try to stop it." Economists of differing mind are apt to reply: "That is easier said than done. In many parts of the economy it would be entirely impossible to establish competitive markets. Even where competition could be established, this would often do more harm than good."

This kind of dialogue, with excellent economists on both sides, runs like a fugue through contemporary economic writings. We shall encounter it frequently throughout Parts One and Two.

The Strategy of Part One

This chapter is a preview of Part One. It contains the essentials of microeconomics, but in barest outline and at a quite superficial level. The task now is to put flesh on the bones by probing more deeply into the operation of specific types of market—markets for goods and services (Chapters 5–7), and markets for labor and capital (Chapters 8–9).

In Chapter 10 we shall summarize and review the market system at a more advanced level, and wrestle with such issues as: To what extent, if at all, can the competitive market economy be considered an economic ideal? How is the performance of such an economy likely to compare with that of Soviet-type economies? Could performance of the Soviet economy be improved by building more market devices into the system?

SUMMARY

1. This chapter analyzes the operation of a private economy in which all markets are characterized by pure competition. (Review the definitions of *market, price,* and *pure competition* given at the beginning of the chapter.)

2. Important characteristics of this economy are: there can be only one price in a particular market; each price is influenced by supply and demand; all prices and markets in the system form an interlocking network.

3. The results which the economy produces depend on individual preferences and production possibilities. Specifically, there are (*a*) *consumer preferences among products*; (*b*) *worker preferences between income and leisure*; (*c*) *preferences between present consumption and future consumption*, which determine the amount of saving; (*d*) known alternative methods of producing a particular good, described by its *production function.*

4. Decisions about working are made by individual workers in response to the terms offered in the labor market.

5. The division of national output between consumer goods and capital goods depends on decisions about saving.

6. The amount of each consumer good which will be produced depends on a balancing of its cost of production against the price which consumers are willing to pay. Price is significant because it measures benefit to consumers. Money cost is significant because it measures real or opportunity cost. (Review the definition of this term.)

7. Each product will be produced by the method which, given the price of labor and capital, yields lowest total cost per unit of output.

8. Each person's income depends on the quantity of resources which he contributes to production and on the price which these resources command in the market.

9. Through all these decisions runs the guiding thread of the *marginal principle*. Economic choice typically involves small adjustments at the margin of decision.

10. One can make a strong argument that a purely competitive economy leads to a pattern of production which is the best one can do with the resources available. But this argument is subject to important qualifications, which will be spelled out more fully in later chapters.

APPENDIX: THE FOUNDATIONS OF THE MARKET ECONOMY —INDIVIDUAL PREFERENCES AND PRODUCTION POSSIBILITIES

We mentioned early in Chapter 4 that individual preferences and production methods are taken as given in analyzing a market economy, and that economists try to use these terms in a precise way. A brief elaboration of this point may be helpful.

Consumer Preference

Consider the case of Mr. Bibber. He has a fixed amount of money per month to spend on food and he eats only two foods, meat and potatoes. He is entitled to choose various combinations of these; but since his income is limited, he can get more of one item only by giving up some of the other. His food preference system may be shown as a curve, *I*, indicating different combinations of the two articles which would be equally acceptable to him. He would be equally content with much meat and very little potatoes (Point *A*), or far more potatoes and a small meat allowance (Point *B*). As we move down the curve from *A*, its shape tells us how much additional potatoes it would take to get Mr. Bibber to sacrifice a certain amount of meat. It shows the terms on which he is willing to substitute one product for the other. As we move closer to *B* and the amount of meat diminishes, it will take more and more potatoes to get Mr. Bibber to give up a pound of meat. This seems like a reasonable supposition. Finally we may reach a rock-bottom level at which Mr. Bibber is unwilling to give up any more meat no matter how much potatoes he is offered. At this point I becomes a horizontal line.

This type of diagram, known in economics as an "indifference curve," is a very flexible and useful device. Different attitudes toward the two commodities can be shown simply by differences in the shape of the curve. If the consumer regards the two products as close substitutes, almost interchangeable with each other, I will be a shallow curve, close to a straight line. If he does not regard them as very good substitutes for each other, the curve will bend down more toward the origin. In the extreme case, where Mr. Bibber insists on a specific "package" of so many pounds of meat and so many pounds of potatoes

FIGURE 1

Mr. Bibber's Food Preference System

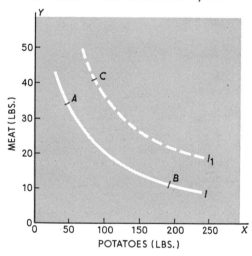

I shows combinations of meat and potatoes which would be equally acceptable to Mr. Bibber. So does I_1. The higher curve shows a higher level of satisfaction, since on it he can have more of both items.

and is unwilling to substitute at all, the indifference curve would become a right angle with the point of the angle showing the one preferred combination.

"But," you may ask, "what about a point like C? Here he has *both* more meat and more potatoes than at A. So why won't he simply move up to C and stay there?" The reason is that we limited his income at the outset. Of course Mr. Bibber would prefer C to A if he had enough money to buy greater quantities of both products. C lies on a higher indifference curve representing a higher level of living. This second curve is shown by I_1. There are in fact a large number of indifference curves from Mr. Bibber, lying one above the other, and filling the whole space in the diagram. Each corresponds to a different consumption level, and Mr. Bibber naturally will climb to the highest one that his actual income level permits. The totality of his indifference curves for all levels of consumption is termed his *preference system*.

The notion of a preference system seems quite abstract and unreal on first acquaintance. One reason is that the usual illustrations consider choice between two commodities only, whereas real-world choices are obviously more complex. But there is no logical difficulty in extending the idea of a preference system to embrace 10, 50, or any number of commodities which may be available for consumer choice.

At the right-hand side of our market diagram, then, stand individuals as consumers, expressing their preferences among the multitude of products on the market—"voting with their dollars." This provides a general guide to production targets for the economy. At the opposite side of the diagram are these same people deciding how much work to do, what jobs to work at, how much to save, and how to dispose of these savings. The feasibility of production, which is shaped by the available supplies of labor and capital, rests on these decisions.

Worker Preference

The preferences which operate at the left-hand side of the diagram may also be analyzed by the indifference curve technique. Consider, for example, Mr. Restwell's preference between income and leisure as shown by Figure 2.

FIGURE 2

Mr. Restwell's Work Preference System

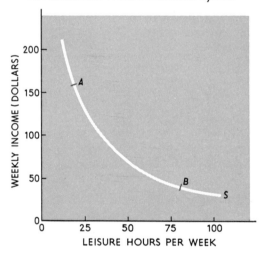

S shows combinations of income and leisure which would be equally acceptable to Mr. Restwell. Note that as his work week becomes longer, it takes more and more money to persuade him to work an extra hour.

We suppose that Mr. Restwell is a commission salesman, who can work as few or as many hours per week as he wishes. He can get more income by working longer hours, but this means a sacrifice of leisure. On the vertical axis of Figure 2 we show weekly income, while the horizontal axis shows leisure, i.e., hours *not* worked. This is a bit tricky and requires a little thought. As we move to the right along *OX* leisure is increasing, which means that hours work per week are *decreasing*. Conversely, as we move leftward toward the origin the work week is *increasing*.

The curve *S* shows different combinations of income and leisure which Mr. Restwell would consider equally attractive. At a very low income level, such as point *B*, he will be willing to sacrifice a good deal of leisure for an extra dollar of income. As we move up toward *A*, however, and his income becomes increasingly adequate, he will sacrifice less and less leisure for an extra dollar. This seems plausible on a common-sense basis. As in the previous case, we can show different outlooks for Mr. Restwell by the way we draw the curve. With a stroke of the pencil we can make him greedy or abstemious, idle or diligent. It is also true, as before, that Mr. Restwell would be still happier were he on a higher indifference curve where he can have *both* more income and more leisure. To do this, however, he would have to be in an occupation paying more per hour. He will climb to the highest indifference curve which his capacities and job classification permit.

Looking back to Figure 4–1 in Chapter 4, we can say that the left-hand side of the market diagram represents the ultimate *cost* of production in terms of human effort, while the right-hand side represents the ultimate *benefit* of production in terms of consumer satisfaction. The economic problem is to adjust the tension between these two forces in a way which attains greatest net benefit for the population involved. In a private market economy, business units are the middlemen through which the necessary adjustments are made.

What about these businessmen who stand in the middle of the market diagram? Do they also have preference systems? Not in the same sense as consumers or workers. A businessman does not decide to produce fried shrimp because he likes to eat fried shrimp, nor will he refrain from producing canned spinach because he hates the stuff. His task is threefold: (1) to discover some good or service which can be marketed at a price which will cover production costs; (2) to decide how much of this product it pays to produce, i.e., how much he can sell at an acceptable price; (3) to choose a method of production which will yield lowest costs per unit of output. These are technical problems, not personal problems. We do not assume any personal preferences in his business role, except a preference for larger profits over smaller ones.

Production Methods

The choice of production methods can be analyzed in a way similar to the problems of personal choice already explored. Mr. Grosslander has just bought a 500-acre wheat farm in Kansas. There is no equipment on the farm as yet, and no labor except his own. With proper management and favorable weather, he should be able to produce 12,000 bushels of wheat per year. But there are many possible ways of doing this. He may do all the work himself with a lot of mechanical equipment. Or he may use smaller quantities of machinery and more hired labor. He *could* conceivably cultivate the farm coolie-fashion, with a large number of hand workers and hardly any equipment.

The curve P in Figure 3 shows different combinations of labor and

FIGURE 3

Mr. Grosslander's Production Function

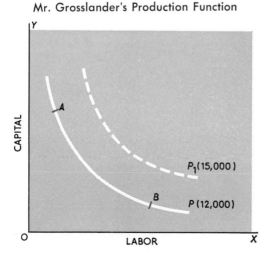

P shows combinations of labor and capital capable of producing the same output, 12,000 bushels of wheat. The (larger) combinations shown on P_1 would produce 15,000 bushels from the same land.

capital which might be used to produce the same product, 12,000 bushels of wheat. Point *A*, for example, represents a production method using little labor, while *B* represents a much more labor-intensive method. Different points on *P* are *indifferent* from a production standpoint—they all yield the same output. This type of curve is usually termed an *isoquant* (for *equal quantities* of output). The underlying basis for this curve is *technological*, and it will change its shape as invention reveals new possible labor-capital combinations. The underlying basis for the indifference curves in Figures 1 and 2, on the other hand, is *psychological*.

Suppose that Mr. Grosslander wants to work his land harder and turn out 15,000 bushels of wheat instead of 12,000. Then he will have to use *both* more capital and more labor than would be needed for a smaller volume of output. P_1 shows different labor-capital combinations which would produce 15,000 bushels. By drawing more and more such lines one can fill the entire diagram, each referring to a different level of production. The totality of these lines is usually called a production function.[1]

To sum up: the results which the market mechanism produces depend on basic psychological preferences and technological possibilities. These are the fuel for the motor, and give a particular economy its distinctive pattern of output and resource use.

------

[1] Also often termed a *production surface*. Quantity of output may be represented in the third dimension, by vertical distances above the surface of the diagram. Then as we move outward from the origin we are moving up a mountain slope toward higher and higher output levels. Each isoquant represents a contour line circling the mountain at a constant height, similar to the contour lines on topographical maps.

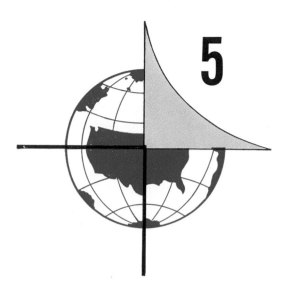

Pricing in Product Markets:
Demand-Supply Analysis

John Stuart Mill
By a mighty effort of will
Overcame his natural bonhomie
And wrote "Principles of Political Economy."
EDMUND CLERIHEW BENTLEY

IN CHAPTER 4 we presented a general view of the market mechanism. In Chapters 5 through 9 we focus our microscope on different parts of the system. We begin in this chapter with product markets, and ask what determines how much of a particular good will be produced and how much it will cost. We continue to assume the existence of pure competition with free entry, many buyers and sellers, no collusion or price fixing, and adequate information.

Consider a manufactured product sold to consumers. This good is produced by many manufacturers and is bought by consumers throughout the country. We ignore the existence of middlemen, which does not change the essentials of the picture, and speak as though the product were priced and distributed directly by the manufacturer. What will go on in this manufacturer-consumer market? How much of the product will be exchanged, and at what price?

There are obviously two kinds of pressure at work in the market. On one side is the willingness of consumers to buy larger or smaller quantities of the product, depending on its price. On the other side is the willingness of manufacturers to produce and bring to market various amounts of the product, depending on the price which they expect to receive. Demand-supply analysis is a way of separating these forces, analyzing each in turn, and then bringing them together to explain price and output.

Beginning with the consumer side of the market, the central principle is simple. If the price of a good is reduced, everything else remaining unchanged, more of it can be sold than before. Each individual purchaser will normally take more at a lower price. Thus when these purchases are added together, the total amount sold increases.

THE INDIVIDUAL BUYER

The notion that people will buy more of a product at a lower price may seem so commonsensical that no explanation is needed. It will nevertheless be worthwhile to explore this behavior further. There are two alternative approaches to the subject. The first involves the concept of *utility*, the satisfaction derived from consumption. The second, which involves use of indifference curves, is more precise but also more advanced, and has consequently been placed in an Appendix to this chapter.

The Individual Demand Schedule

Suppose that Mr. A, a confirmed coffee drinker, could have only one pound of coffee a month. This would yield a large amount of satisfaction or *utility*. It would give him that first morning cup of coffee which makes it possible to face the day's work.

But perhaps instead of one pound a month he can have two. Now he can have a second cup of coffee at breakfast, or perhaps a cup in mid-morning. This will yield additional utility, though not as much as that yielded by the first pound. A third pound per month will mean that he can drink coffee at lunch or in the evening. This will add to his satisfaction, but probably by less than the second pound. And so on. Eventually, when he has enough coffee to drink all that he can hold, an additional pound will yield no utility at all.

We define *marginal utility* as *the utility of the last pound of coffee which Mr. A consumes.* What we have been saying, then, is that as Mr. A's coffee consumption rises, the marginal utility of coffee to him will decline. This is called the *principle of diminishing marginal utility.* If Mr. A had time and inclination, he could work out on paper a *utility schedule*, showing the satisfaction yielded by each additional unit of coffee purchased.

He will actually not do this; but he or his wife will carry a rough impression in their minds as they go about their weekly shopping. Even if the price of coffee is very high, he will still buy that first pound, because the utility which it yields is also very high. If the price is lower, so that he does not have to give up so much of other things for a pound of coffee, he may buy a second or a third pound. Their utility is lower, but still sufficient to make the purchase seem worthwhile. If the price is still lower, he will go on to buy additional pounds with lower marginal utility.

On this basis we can construct Mr. A's *demand schedule* for coffee, which might look like this:

PRICE PER POUND (Dollars)	POUNDS BOUGHT PER MONTH
2.50	1
2.25	2
2.00	3
1.75	4
1.50	5
1.25	6
1.00	7
0.75	8
0.50	9
0.25	10

If the price is $2.50, he will get along with that first pound. At lower prices he will buy more until, if the price fell to 25 cents, he would buy 10 pounds a month.

The same information is shown graphically in Figure 5–1. Since coffee is usually bought in pound packages, the graph consists of a series of disconnected points. For products where the quantity purchased can be

FIGURE 5–1

Mr. A's Demand Schedule for Coffee

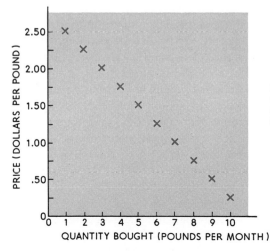

Each point means that, if the price were as shown on the vertical axis, Mr. A would buy the number of pounds shown on the horizontal axis.

varied by very small amounts, the demand schedule would appear as a continuous line or *demand curve*.

The concept of diminishing marginal utility has another important application. Mr. A consumes not only coffee but beefsteak, potatoes, shoes, movie theatre tickets, and hundreds of other things. Each of these products obeys the principle of diminishing marginal utility—the more units he is already consuming, the less satisfaction will he derive from an additional unit.

This presents a problem of how he should distribute his income over the many products competing for his dollar. It will not pay him to buy so much of one product that its marginal utility becomes very low, while skimping on another to the point where its marginal utility is very high. He should distribute his income so that the utility yielded by the last dollar spent on coffee just equals the utility from the last dollar spent on every other product he buys. This is what people have vaguely in mind when they talk about "getting their money's worth" from each expenditure. If a consumer is not doing this, if the satisfaction derived from the last dollar spent on product A is *higher* than that of the last dollar spent on product B, he can increase his satisfaction by shifting income from B to A until equality is reached.

This line of reasoning provides a definition of *rational consumer behavior*. In actuality, most consumers do not calculate this precisely, and it may not be worth their while to do so. Beyond a certain point the gain in satisfaction would be outweighed by the mental effort required. It is irrational to strive too hard for perfect rationality.

Some Qualifications to the Demand Schedule

We seem to be on safe ground in concluding that consumers will buy less of a product if its price rises, and more if its price falls. But the ground is more treacherous than it appears. We can be sure of this result only if we specify a number of conditions. The most important are:

1. Buyers' preferences must remain unchanged. If we allow Mr. A's preference system to jump about at the same time that the price of coffee is shifting, we can no longer be sure of the outcome.

2. Buyers' preferences must be *independent* of the market price itself. Without this stipulation, a price cut might sometimes *reduce* the quantity sold. If the price of diamonds fell drastically, they might cease to be prestige symbols and engagement rings might contain emeralds instead.

3. Buyers' incomes must remain unchanged. If Mr. A's income rises at the same time that coffee prices rise, he may end up buying more coffee rather than less.

4. Prices of other products must remain unchanged. This is especially important for closely related products, such as, in the present case, tea, cocoa, soft drinks, sugar, and cream. We must hold these prices con-

stant if we wish to observe the pure effect of a change in coffee prices on coffee sales.

5. Prices must be expected to continue at about their present level. If coffee rises 10 cents a pound and consumers fear it will rise another 10 cents next month, they may rush out and buy heavily to beat the price rise. *Speculation on price changes* may mean that a price increase, at least for a while, will *raise* sales of the product instead of reducing them.

The principle of demand may now be restated in stricter form: A consumer will purchase less of a product whose price has risen, and more of a product whose price has fallen, *provided* that his income and his preference system remain unchanged, that the prices of all other products remain unchanged, and that present prices are expected to continue indefinitely in the future.

THE MARKET DEMAND SCHEDULE

Will *total* purchases of a product obey the same principle as purchases by an individual consumer? Will a decline in shoe prices, everything else in the economy remaining unchanged, lead to an increase in shoe purchases? Yes, it will. The reason is that total national demand is sim-

TABLE 5–1

Market Demand Schedule for Men's Shoes,
United States, January 30, 1963

PRICE PER PAIR (Dollars)	QUANTITY SOLD (Millions of Pairs per Year)
30	85
27	110
24	130
21	160
18	190
15	240
12	300
9	375
6	500

ply the sum of the demands of individual households. A drop in shoe prices will cause at least some families to buy more shoes, and thus there will be more shoes bought in the country as a whole.

A hypothetical list of how many pairs of shoes might be bought at various price levels is shown in Table 5–1. This is termed a *market demand schedule*. As we go down the price column to lower and lower prices, we find larger and larger quantities appearing in the purchases column. The same information is shown graphically in Figure 5–2. *DD* shows the amount which purchasers would be willing to buy at various alternative prices. This is known as a *demand curve*, and is a central tool of economic analysis. It is drawn as a continuous line, indicating that price can be varied by very small amounts and that sales will always respond.

Figure 5–2 looks deceptively simple. Since we shall be using demand curves frequently in later chapters, we had better pause to consider

FIGURE 5–2

Market Demand Schedule for Men's Shoes

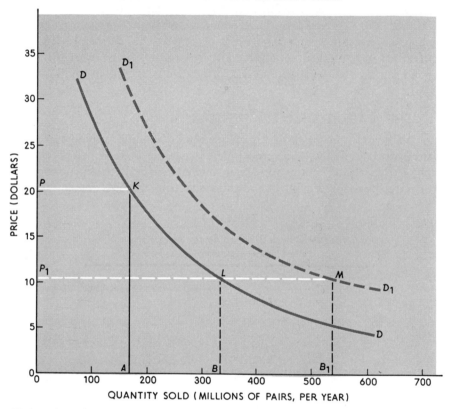

DD is a demand curve. Each point on the curve shows how many pairs of shoes consumers would be prepared to buy at a specified price. D_1D_1 indicates a change in demand to a higher level.

exactly what they do and do not mean. Three main points should be kept in mind:

1. A demand curve is *not* a historical chart showing the course of events over a period of time. The demand curve does *not* say that if price falls from OP in 1963 to OP_1 in 1970, then the quantity sold will increase from OA to OB. Over this period preferences, incomes, and other prices will certainly have changed, and thus the basis we laid down for constructing a demand schedule has been swept away.

The demand curve is an analytical concept, not a historical concept. All the points on the curve hold true *simultaneously* and at the same moment of time. They represent alternative possibilities, only one of which can actually be realized. *If* price were to be *OP*, then quantity sold would be *OA*. If instead the price were to be OP_1, then quantity sold would be *OB*. But only one of these possibilities can be realized in a particular market at a particular time.

2. The term *change in demand* is often used incorrectly. If price in Figure 5–2 rises from OP_1 to *OP*, and sales consequently fall from *OB* to *OA*, many people would say that "demand has fallen." This is wrong. Consumer preferences have not changed, and the demand curve is exactly where it was. There has simply been a *change in the quantity sold* in response to a change in price.

Movement from one point to another *on the same demand curve*—in this case, from *L* to *K*—is *not* a change in demand. A change in demand occurs only when *the whole demand curve shifts to a new position.* Suppose *DD* moves upward to the position D_1D_1. This is truly an increase in demand, because whatever the price it will now be possible to sell more than with the previous demand curve. At price OP_1, for example, one can now sell OB_1 units of product instead of *OB*. The movement from *L* to *M* does represent a change in demand, while that from *L* to *K* does not.

Why might demand rise from *DD* to D_1D_1? Basically, because of a change in one or more of the things which we specified earlier as constant: people's preferences, their incomes, and the prices of other goods.

3. The figures for Table 5–1 and Figure 5–2 were pulled out of the air to illustrate the principle that demand curves slope downward to the right. But if we were dealing with a real product in the real world, we could not make up figures in this way. Any actual demand curve has a specific shape, which depends on the role of the product in consumers' preference systems. Some products have a very steep demand curve, indicating that consumers will buy almost as much at a high price as a low price. In other cases, purchases may fall off sharply as the price rises, which would mean a flat demand curve. The shape of a particular demand curve depends on such things as:

a) Whether the product is basic to the consumption pattern of most households, or an optional item which can readily be sacrificed. The demand curve for bread obviously is less elastic than that for silk scarves.

b) Whether there are close substitutes for the product. If close substitutes are available, people will shift to these as the price rises and sales will fall off rapidly. Salt, on the other hand, has a steep demand curve precisely because there is no good substitute for it.

c) Whether the product is consumed mainly by higher income groups, or mainly by lower income groups, or by both. A demand curve may change its shape one or more times as price declines to a level which taps poorer and poorer groups of customers.

d) Whether the product is a large or a small item in consumers' budgets. Minor items of expenditure are apt to have steeper demand curves than major items. A rise in the price of toothpaste does not reduce my real income appreciably.

Elasticity of Demand

The shape of demand curves may strike the reader as a highly abstract and unreal subject. To businessmen, however, it is a matter of intense practical concern. If a company cuts its price by 10 percent, will sales increase by 5 percent, or 15 percent, or 25 percent? If costs are rising and the company is considering a price increase, will sales fall off only slightly or a good deal? The answer can make the difference between good profits and large losses. Companies and management consulting firms spend large amounts of money trying to find out what the demand curves for various products look like.

In a matter of such importance it is not very satisfactory to refer to demand curves simply as "steep" or "flat"—especially since this depends on the scales used on the axes of our supply-demand diagram. We need a more precise measure of just how quantity sold responds to a change in price. The measure which economists use for this purpose is termed *elasticity of demand*. This measures the relative effect on quantity sold of a (small) change in price. More precisely, elasticity $e = -\dfrac{\% \text{ change in } Q.}{\% \text{ change in } P.}$ If elasticity is greater than one, so that a 1 percent change in price produces more than a 1 percent change in quantity sold, we say that demand is *elastic*. If elasticity is less than one, so that a 1 percent change in price produces a less than 1 percent change in quantity sold, demand is said to be *inelastic*. The borderline case, where elasticity is equal to one, is referred to as one of *unit elasticity*. Since we are dividing a positive Q change by a negative P change, or vice versa, the result would be negative. Hence we add a negative sign to the elasticity formula to convert this back to a positive number.

The practical importance of this is that it tells sellers of a product whether a price change will increase or decrease their total receipts from sales. How does this work? If demand is elastic, i.e., a 1 percent drop in price produces a more than 1 percent increase in sales, then sales revenue must be larger after the change than before. Conversely, a 1 percent rise in price, by causing a more than 1 percent drop in sales, will reduce sales revenue. Where demand is elastic, *sales revenue moves in the opposite direction to price* in the event of a price change.

But suppose that demand is inelastic. A 1 per cent cut in price increases sales less than 1 percent, so sales revenue must fall. Conversely, a rise in price will raise sales revenue. Where demand is inelastic, then *sales revenue moves in the same direction as price*. In the borderline case of unit elasticity, finally, *a price change leaves sales revenue unchanged*.

These concepts may be illustrated by Table 5–2 and Figure 5–3, which show a hypothetical demand schedule for men's shirts. In addition to showing the quantity sold at each price, we show total sales revenue and the elasticity of demand. Demand is elastic down to a price of $5.00 per

TABLE 5–2

Market Demand Schedule for Men's Shirts, United States, January 30, 1963

Price (Dollars)	Quantity Sold (Millions per Year)	Sales Revenue (Millions of Dollars per Year)	Additional Revenue (Millions of Dollars)	Additional or Marginal Revenue per Unit Sold (Dollars)	Elasticity of Demand*
12	25	300			
				8.50	3.83
11	35	385	85		
				7.70	3.71
10	50	500	115		
				5.70	2.48
9	65	585	85		
				4.75	2.27
8	85	680	95		
				3.60	1.92
7	110	770	90		
				2.30	1.56
6	140	840	70		
				0.60	1.13
5	172	860	20		
				0.00	1.00
4	215	860	0		
				−0.60	0.86
3	275	825	−35		
				−0.75	0.77
2	375	750	−75		
				−1.10	0.57
1	550	550	−200		

* Strictly, each figure is the average elasticity over the one-dollar interval involved. Thus the first figure is $-\dfrac{10/30}{-1/11.5} = 3.83$.

shirt. Sales revenues rise as the price is reduced. The drop from $5.00 to $4.00 leaves revenue unchanged, so that we have unit elasticity over this range. Below $4.00 demand becomes inelastic and sales revenue declines with each drop in price.

This illustrates an important point. The same demand curve may have $e < 1$, $e = 1$, and $e > 1$ over different ranges of price. It is dangerous, therefore, to refer to an entire demand curve as "elastic" or "inelastic." One should speak only of elasticity at a particular price, or over a small range of prices.

It is clear also from Figure 5–3 that one's visual impression of the shape of a demand curve can be quite misleading. The upper part of the curve appears quite steep, yet it turns out to be elastic. The lower portion looks flatter, yet it is inelastic. How can this be? The explanation is that

FIGURE 5–3

Demand and Revenue Curves for Men's Shirts

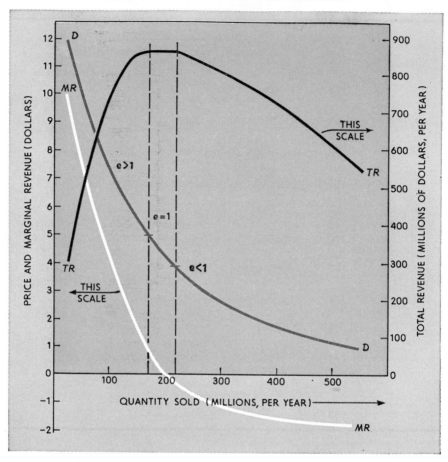

The demand curve *DD* and the marginal revenue curve *MR* are drawn with reference to the left-hand vertical axis. The total revenue curve *TR* refers to the right-hand axis. Note that when **e > 1,** TR is rising and MR is positive. When e = 1, TR is constant and MR is zero. When **e < 1,** TR is falling and MR is negative.

elasticity is based, not on *absolute* changes in prices and quantities, but on *percentage* changes. In the upper range of Figure 5–3, a dollar cut in price is only a small percentage change, because we are starting from a high base. A sales increase of 1,000 shirts, however, is a *big* percentage increase because we are starting from a low sales volume. Hence our elasticity measure, $\dfrac{\%\ \text{change in } Q}{\%\ \text{change in } P}$, turns out to be large and demand is elastic. In the lower range of the curve, the percentage price changes are getting steadily larger and the percentage quantity changes steadily smaller. Thus elasticity falls farther and farther below 1.

Marginal Revenue

Marginal revenue is the change in total revenue which results from selling an additional unit of output. Look again at Table 5–2 and see what happens if the price of shirts is reduced from $12 to $11. It is now possible to sell 10 million more shirts per year. One might think that sales revenue is increased by $11 × 10 million or $110 million. But this is incorrect. For in order to sell this amount, one has to cut the price on *all* shirts sold during the year. The 25 million shirts which one could sell anyway at $12 are now being sold at $11, which *reduces* sales revenue by $25 million. So the addition to total revenue is only $100 million—$25 million = $85 million, as one sees from column 4. *Marginal revenue* per additional shirt sold, shown in column 5, is $85 million/10 million = $8.50.

The key point is that *marginal revenue is always lower than price.* The reason is the price cut on earlier units which is necessary to sell the additional units. Go down the table and note that as price falls, marginal revenue also falls, but at each level *MR* is lower than price. When one reaches the point of unit elasticity, where additional sales add nothing to total revenue, *MR* becomes zero. And when we pass into the zone of inelastic demand, where further sales reduce total revenue, *MR* is negative.

This is shown graphically by the *MR* line in Figure 5–3. Note that *MR* lies consistently below *DD*, intersects the *x*-axis in the zone of unit elasticity, and is negative from then on.

The marginal revenue concept is useful in calculating how a producer can make most money. Suppose you own a spring of mineral water, from which you can draw off as much or as little as you like each day. The water costs nothing to produce. You have a demand curve which looks like *DD* in Figure 5–3. Your problem is to set a price and rate of output which will yield greatest revenue. Total revenue will be largest where marginal revenue is zero, that is, where the *MR* curve intersects the *x*-axis. So this is the rate of output you should choose. For goods which cost something to produce, the problem becomes more complicated, but the central principle remains the same: it will pay to expand output so long as the marginal revenue yielded by an additional unit exceeds the cost of producing it.

Special Cases of Demand

A few special demand situations are shown in Figure 5–4. D_1D_1 shows completely inelastic demand, with the same quantity being sold regardless of price. This obviously couldn't go on forever—price couldn't climb up into the sky without having some effect on sales. But one might find something close to zero elasticity over a certain range. Whether a small part for a Chevrolet costs $1.00, $1.50, or $2.00 is not going to have much effect on the number of parts sold.

D_2D_2 shows the opposite case of a demand curve which is infinitely elastic. The amount sold has no effect on price. The classic illustration is the demand for wheat from a particular farm. The farmer can sell 1,000 bushels, 5,000 bushels, or 10,000 bushels. The market price will be the same. But if this farmer expanded to the point of owning half the wheat land in Montana, he could no longer sell as much as he chose without af-

FIGURE 5–4

Special Cases of Demand

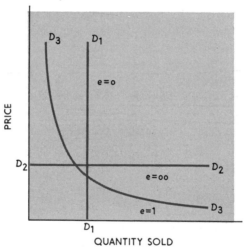

fecting the market price. Only a small seller in a large industry can safely assume that his demand curve is horizontal.

D_3D_3 shows a demand curve which has unit elasticity throughout. Whether the price is high or low, sales revenue will be the same, a change in price being just offset by an opposite change in quantity.

Derived Demand

Our illustrations to this point have involved articles bought by consumers. What about the multitude of products—raw materials, semifinished goods, machinery, building materials—which are bought by one business concern from another and never enter the retail market? Do such goods have demand curves? Of course they do. Since the demand for these things rests on, or is derived from, the demand for some final product to which they contribute, it is termed a *derived demand*. The demand for bricks is derived from the demand for buildings. The demand for steel is derived from the demand for finished goods using steel. The demand for a particular kind of labor is derived from the demand for the finished product of that labor.

The shape of a derived demand curve has the usual meaning. It's elasticity shows whether sales are very responsive to price changes or only slightly responsive. This depends mainly on three things:

1. *Elasticity of demand for the final product.* An increase in the price of materials or labor going into a finished good will raise its cost of production and this will normally raise its price. If, as the price of the final product is raised its sales fall off rapidly, then sales of the materials used in making it will also fall off rapidly. Thus the more elastic the demand for the product, the more elastic will be the demands derived from it.

2. *The importance of the item in total cost.* Suppose a certain item constitutes $10 of the cost of a $100 product. The price of the material now rises 10 percent, so that the same quantity costs $11 instead of $10. To "cover" this cost increase, the price of the final product would have to be raised from $100 to $101, or by 1 percent. Suppose elasticity of demand for the final product is unity. Then its sales will fall 1 percent, and sales of the material will also fall 1 percent. Note that, although demand for the final product has unit elasticity, demand for the material in question is very inelastic—a 10 percent price increase causes a drop of only 1 percent in sales. The reason is that the material is such a small part of total cost that an increase in its price has only a small impact on price and output of the final product. This is sometimes termed "the importance of being unimportant."

Suppose the material had cost $60 out of the $100 price of the product. Then, if we suppose the product demand curve has unit elasticity as before, a 10 percent increase in the price of the material may produce a 6 percent increase in the price of the product, and sales of both product and material will fall 6 percent. Demand for the material is considerably more elastic than before. This leads to a second principle of derived demand: demand for an intermediate good or a factor of production will be more elastic the larger its share in the cost of the final product.

3. *The availability of substitutes.* We have been supposing that, when the price of a material or component is increased, producers of the final product will have to go on using it anyway. This may or may not be true. There will often be some possibility of substitution. As cotton becomes more expensive, rayon and other synthetics will be used instead. As the price of steel rises, it may be feasible for some purposes to substitute aluminum, copper, or other metals. As wage rates rise, employers will make greater use of automatic processes which use less labor. The greater the possibilities of substitution, the more elastic will be the demand for the intermediate good in question.

Elasticity of a derived demand curve, in short, varies directly with elasticity of demand for the final product, with the percentage which the item forms of total production costs, and with the availability of substitutes in the production process.

SUPPLY AND EQUILIBRIUM PRICE

Demand is only one of two sets of forces influencing price. Buyers are only one side of the market. What about the manufacturers or the other side of the market? How is the price which exists in the market going to affect the amount they will be willing to produce and sell?

The Supply Schedule

This is a complicated question. The answer depends on the nature of the industry. It depends also on the period of time which we take into account. The amount which will be supplied at a particular price next

FIGURE 5–5

The Market Supply Schedule

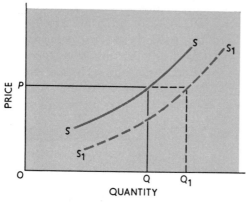

SS is a supply curve. Each point on the curve shows how much of the product sellers will offer at a specified price. S_1S_1 shows an increase in supply —more offered at each price than was true previously.

year may be larger or smaller than the amount which will be supplied today. These and other factors influencing the shape of the *supply schedule* will be examined in the next chapter.

The purpose here is simply to show how supply conditions interact with demand conditions to determine the market price and quantity sold. So for illustration let us select a situation, quite common in practice, in which larger quantities are offered on the market as the price rises. This possibility is shown pictorially in Figure 5–5. SS is a *supply schedule* or *supply curve*. Each point on it shows the amount which sellers of the product will be willing to bring to market at the price in question. The fact that the curve slopes upward to the right says that producers will offer more goods at higher prices.

We must observe the same cautions about the supply curve which we noted earlier in the case of demand. Specifically:

1. The supply curve is *not* a historical curve linking prices and quantities sold in different time periods. It shows alternative possibilities

available *at a moment of time*. If price *were* at a certain level, *then* a certain quantity would be offered on the market. But only one of these possibilities will actually be realized at a particular time.

2. The supply curve for each good has a specific shape, depending on how easy or hard it is to expand production. The shape of the supply curve is of great importance to buyers. If the supply curve slopes up steeply, this means that an increased demand can be gratified only at substantially higher prices. Conversely, a gently sloped supply curve indicates that production can be expanded readily and that higher demand will not cause much increase in price. *Elasticity of supply* is defined and measured in exactly the same way as for demand.

3. The supply curve, like the demand curve, can be given a definite shape only if we suppose that certain other things remain constant. In the case of demand, we assumed that buyers' preferences, their incomes, and the prices of substitute products were known and constant. In the case of supply, the most important things which we hold constant are the methods of production and the supply conditions of the materials, labor, and other things needed for production. If any of these things should change, the old supply curve vanishes and a new one appears.

4. A movement from one point to another on *SS* is *not* a change in supply. It is simply a change in the quantity offered in response to a change in price. A change in supply means *a shift of the entire curve to a new position*, such as S_1S_1 in Figure 5–5. Note that at any price sellers will now offer more goods than before. At the price *OP* they will now supply OQ_1 units instead of *OQ*. Thus a rightward shift of the supply curve indicates an *increase in supply*. This might happen because improved production methods have been developed, which make it possible to turn out the product at a lower cost and offer it at a lower price. In the converse case of a decrease in supply, *SS* would move upward to the left.

Market Equilibrium

We are now in a position to bring the demand and supply curves together on the same diagram, as is done in Figure 5–6. What is the point of this diagram and what does it tell us? The intersection of *DD* and *SS* defines a price (*OP*) and a quantity sold (*OQ*) which have a special significance. We call these the *equilibrium price and quantity* in the market. This means two things:

1. If the price *OP* somehow gets established, it will persist. It is in fact the only price which precisely "clears the market," the only price at which the amount consumers are willing to buy exactly equals the amount producers want to sell. This being so, there is no reason for the price to change until there is a shift in *DD* or *SS*.

2. If the market price starts out either above or below *OP*, forces will operate to move it toward *OP*. Suppose, for example, the market

"opens" on a particular morning at price OP_1. What will happen? At this price the amount sellers stand ready to offer (P_1K) is much larger than the amount buyers are willing to take (P_1L). As soon as this becomes apparent, some sellers will begin to offer the product at lower prices. Thus the market will begin to slide down the demand curve, with no logical stopping point until it reaches point A.

FIGURE 5–6

Demand, Supply and Equilibrium Price

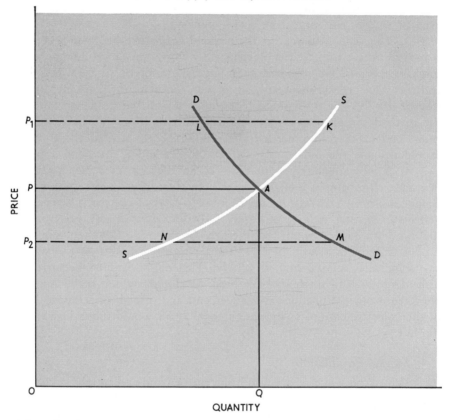

If demand and supply are in this position, the market price will be OP and the quantity exchanged will be OQ. Other prices, such as OP_1 and OP_2, will not be feasible. Explain why.

Suppose, on the other hand, that the market starts off at OP_2. At this low price, the amount buyers want (P_2M) is much larger than the amount producers are willing to supply (P_2N). Some of the eager buyers will now begin to bid up the price, preferring to pay a bit more rather than go unsatisfied. As this process goes on, the market travels up the demand curve and there is no reason for it to stop short of *A*.

OP, in short, is the only price which is stable and will maintain itself so long as the underlying demand and supply conditions continue unchanged.

Does the supply-demand diagram *explain* price and output? Not in any ultimate sense. A full explanation requires that one know everything which lies behind the *SS* and *DD* curves. Behind the demand curve lies the whole array of consumer preferences. Behind the supply curve lie many things which we still have to examine—notably, costs of production. But these things affect price *through* their effect on the position of the demand and supply curves. Anything which affects the price of a product must do so either by altering the willingness of consumers to buy (*DD*) or the willingness of producers to bring various quantities to market (*SS*). The demand-supply apparatus thus gives us a basis for *classifying* the ultimate determinants of price and for reasoning about them in an orderly manner.

The supply-demand diagram is often called the "Marshallian cross" after one of its early exponents, the great Cambridge economist Alfred Marshall. The reader will encounter it repeatedly in later chapters, in a wide variety of practical applications. It is important at this stage, therefore, to master the logic of the diagram so thoroughly that it becomes a habitual method of thought.

APPLICATIONS OF DEMAND AND SUPPLY: THE ECONOMICS OF PRICE FIXING

The reader may already have asked himself: Suppose the government just steps in and *fixes* a price? "The price of bananas will be so-and-so, on penalty of fine or imprisonment." What happens then to all our reasoning about supply and demand?

It is certainly possible for government to pull a price out of the air and enforce it by legal decree. This is the general rule in planned economies and happens quite often in other countries. This does not mean, however, that demand-supply analysis becomes irrelevant. On the contrary it is essential to an understanding of *what will happen as a result of the fixed price.*

Price Supports and Farm Surpluses

Suppose the government guarantees farmers a minimum price for wheat, and that this is above the equilibrium price which would exist in a free market. This situation is illustrated by Figure 5–7. The equilibrium price with this supply-demand situation would be $1.50 per bushel. At this price *OC* bushels of wheat would be produced and sold, and the market would be cleared. Farmers maintain, however, that $1.50 per bushel is not a fair return for their efforts and persuade Congress to intervene. Congress decrees that the price shall be $2.00 per bushel, and enforces this by binding the government to buy wheat at this price.

What will happen? Farmers respond to the higher price by increasing wheat plantings and now turn out *OB* bushels per year. Consumer purchases, however, are reduced by the higher price and fall to *OA*. The difference between production and sales is *AB*. This "surplus wheat" piles

FIGURE 5–7

A Price Support System for Wheat

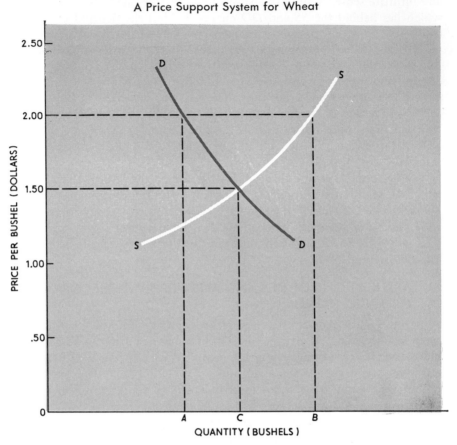

At a guaranteed price of $2.00 per bushel, the supply of wheat exceeds the quantity demanded. What might be done to equalize supply and demand?

up in the hands of government which, unless it can ship the excess abroad at bargain prices, must simply hold and store it. But this is only a short-range solution. Next year's crop will bring in more surplus wheat, and the government's stockpiles will eventually become unmanageable.

One possible avenue of escape is to take away from farmers the right to grow and sell as much wheat as they choose. Each wheat farmer might be required, for example, to reduce the number of acres sown to wheat by one third. But reduction of acreage may not be very effective. Farmers take their poorest land out of cultivation, and then pile as much fertilizer, labor, and equipment as possible onto the remaining acres. Thus they may end up growing about as much as before on the reduced acreage.

A more drastic approach is to set a marketing quota for each farmer, which permits him to sell only so many bushels per year at the controlled price. By careful calculation, it might be possible to make these quotas add up to just the amount OA. There would then be a *managed equilibrium* in the sense that consumers would be willing to buy at $2.00 all the wheat that farmers were legally permitted to sell. But the price to the consumer is still an inflated price.

The complexities of actual farm price support legislation are examined in Chapter 12. The point here is simply to demonstrate that one cannot decree a price and leave it at that. Certain consequences follow, which necessitate further controls. *Price* regulation usually leads quite quickly to *quantity* regulation as well.

Price Ceilings and Black Markets

The same conclusion is reached by examining a situation in which government sets a *price ceiling*, a maximum price which is *below* the market equilibrium. This was done on a large scale during World War II. The resulting situation is shown in Figure 5–8. The market equilibrium is OP, the legal ceiling OP_1. Instead of a "surplus" as in the wheat case, we now have a "shortage." At the ceiling price consumers would like to buy OB units of the product, but only OA units are available. The difference, AB, represents unsatisfied demand for the product.

Which lucky customers will get the limited quantity available? Unless some control system is installed, people may simply line up in front of the store. The early-comers at the head of the line will be served while those at the end get nothing. Favoritism and bribery spring up. The storekeeper keeps a stock of the product "under the counter" for favored customers, or he insists on "tie-in sales." This means forcing the customer to take some slow-moving item which he doesn't want in order to get the scarce item he does want.

If the good is a necessity, and if one wants to achieve a fair distribution of the available supply, this can be done through *rationing*. Ration coupons can be issued to each family, entitling it to buy a specified quantity of the product. Storekeepers are forbidden to sell the product except to people holding ration coupons. If the system is well managed, the number of coupons issued should just add up to the supplies available (OA). Once more we have a managed equilibrium, in which price control is supported by quantity control.

Rationing was used on a large scale during World War II for gasoline, tires, fuel oil, meat, canned goods, dairy products, coffee, sugar, and other foods. Supplies of these things were well below what people would have liked to buy with their high wartime incomes. Rationing helped to distribute the scarce supplies in an equitable way. The system led, however, to difficult problems of evasion and enforcement. A buyer whose ration coupons had run out could often get supplies by offering more than the official ceiling price. This was illegal, but some sellers were willing to break the law for enough money. A new class of middlemen grew up who specialized in getting scarce goods from producer to consumer

FIGURE 5–8

Price Ceilings and Black Markets

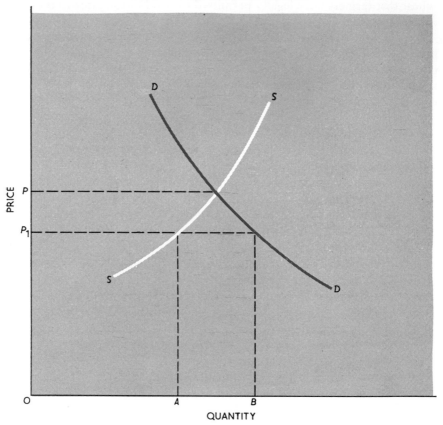

At a ceiling price of OP₁ the quantity demanded exceeds the available supply. What is likely to happen next?

outside the rationing system and at premium prices. These deals were called *black market* transactions.

Pricing Consumer Goods in the U.S.S.R.

We saw in Chapter 3 that production of consumer goods in the U.S.S.R. is not geared very closely to consumer preferences. Yet consumer goods are distributed through retail outlets at a market price, and consumers have free choice of goods within the limits of their incomes. This seems contradictory. What is the explanation?

The matter may be cleared up by a diagram. Figure 5–9 shows the demand and supply curves for washing machines in the U.S.S.R. If this were a market economy, production would be carried to the intersection point of *DD* and *SS*. Output of washing machines would be *OG* and price would be *OF*.

But the Soviet authorities do not use this type of reasoning. Washing machines use metal and other scarce resources which might better, they conclude, be going into tractors and machine tools. So Gosplan decides to limit washing machine production for 1963 to OA. The authorities want to distribute this output through stores in the usual way and without the necessity of rationing. How to do it? Simple enough. Just

FIGURE 5–9

The Washing Machine Industry in the U.S.S.R.

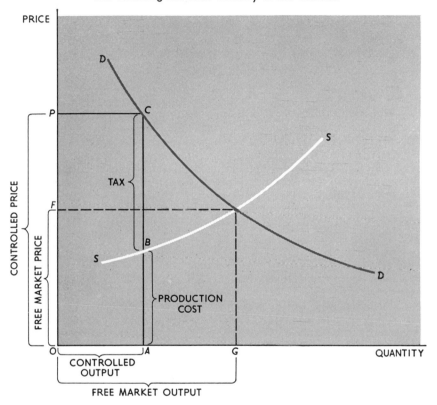

In a market economy, output would be OG and price OF. But central planners may decide to produce a smaller quantity, such as OA, and sell it at OP. The price includes a tax of BC in addition to production cost AB.

add on to the production cost AB an excise tax (called in Russia a turnover tax) of BC and set the retail price at $AC = OP$. At this high price consumers are willing to buy just the number of washing machines (OA) which the planners have decided to produce. A managed equilibrium once more!

But Soviet planners have to guess where DD is, just as capitalist producers do, and they don't always succeed in setting prices which will exactly "clear the market." One hears of shortages of certain items, and of people bribing storekeepers to let them know when a consignment of some scarce article is due to arrive. This means that the articles in question have been underpriced. Note that any price below *OP* in Figure 5–9 would create a "shortage" of washing machines.

Other articles, however, are sometimes overpriced. Around 1960 the authorities found that some expensive items—cameras, wristwatches, radio and television sets—were not moving off retail shelves as rapidly as they were being produced. One could conclude that the turnover tax on these articles was too high, leading to a price above the level corresponding to *OP* in Figure 5–9. A simple remedy would have been to cut the turnover tax and the retail price. The government did not want to do this, however, and gave as a reason that it would reduce the Treasury's tax collections. Instead, an effort was made to raise demand curves by introducing the capitalist device of installment credit.

SUMMARY

1. As one consumes additional units of any product (per period of time), the satisfaction yielded by the last unit decreases. This is known as the *principle of diminishing marginal utility*. It explains why a consumer will normally buy more of any product at a lower price.

2. Since total demand is the sum of individual demands, it behaves in the same way. A reduction in price leads to an increase in quantity sold. The *demand curve* slopes downward to the right.

3. Movement from one point to another on the same demand curve is *not* a change in demand. A change in demand means that the whole curve has shifted to a new position.

4. Elasticity of demand is $-\dfrac{\%\ \text{change in } Q}{\%\ \text{change in } P}$. It is measured at a point or over a small distance on the demand curve. The same demand curve will have different elasticities at different points.

5. Where $e > 1$, demand is elastic; where $e = 1$, demand has *unit elasticity;* where $e < 1$, demand is *inelastic*. This is of practical importance in determining whether a price change will increase the sales receipts of the sellers, lower them, or leave them unchanged.

6. Demand for raw materials, semifinished products, and factors of production is *derived* from the demand for the finished product. The elasticity of a derived demand curve increases with the elasticity of demand for the final product, with the percentage which the item forms of production costs, and with the availability of substitutes in the production process.

7. The *supply curve* shows the quantities which sellers of a product will offer at various market prices. It is taken here as sloping upward to the right; but the factors determining its shape will be examined in the next chapter.

8. The intersection of the supply and demand curves defines an *equilibrium price and quantity exchanged*. Equilibrium means that the price is stable and will continue so long as the underlying demand and supply conditions continue unchanged.

9. It is possible to fix prices by law above or below the market equilibrium. But awkward consequences may follow. If farmers are guaranteed a support price *above the equilibrium level*, there will be excess supply and government will have to buy the surplus output. If it does not want to accumulate these surpluses, it must regulate farm production. If government sets a price

ceiling *below the equilibrium level*, the result will be excess demand leading to rationing of the product.

10. Soviet planners try to price each consumer good at a level such that consumers will buy just the quantity which the planners have decided to produce. They try to hit the demand curve; but they do not take the demand curve as a guide in deciding how much to produce.

APPENDIX: THE INDIFFERENCE CURVE APPROACH TO DEMAND

The marginal utility approach is open to logical objection because it implies that we can measure consumer satisfaction as a thermometer measures temperature. Economic theorists today generally reject this assumption. They prefer to approach demand analysis via indifference curves, which do not imply measurability of utility.

Let's go back to Mr. Bibber of Chapter 4, and his preference system for meat and potatoes. Figure 1 here is the same as the previous diagram. We did not try in Chapter 4 to explain how much meat and potatoes Mr. Bibber will actually buy. This turns out to depend, not just on Mr. Bibber's preferences, but also on the prices of the two commodities. Suppose the price of meat is 50 cents a pound and the price of potatoes is 10 cents a pound; and suppose Mr. Bibber has $20 a month to divide between the two articles. Then he could buy 40 pounds of meat and no potatoes, or 200 pounds of potatoes and no meat, or various intermediate combinations.

By joining these points we get the line *MP*. This may be called Mr. Bibber's consumption possibilities line, since any combination of meat and potatoes which he can afford to buy will be represented by a point on *MP*. It is also sometimes called the price line, since its slope depends on the relative prices of the two products. If the price of meat were $1.00 a pound, *M* would be at 20 rather than 40 on the vertical axis, and *MP* would be much flatter than it is. Conversely, a higher price for meat would mean a steeper price line.

The area of Figure 1 is filled, as we saw in Chapter 4, by a large number of indifference curves lying one above the other. As one moves upward ("northeast") on the diagram, one reaches higher indifference curves representing higher levels of satisfaction. A particular indifference curve is drawn to show that Mr. Bibber derives *the same level of satisfaction* from various combinations of meat and potatoes. They are substitutable for each other in his consumption budget. The whole set of curves shows that he can get *greater satisfaction* if his income allows him to move to a higher indifference curve.

How much meat and potatoes will Mr. Bibber actually buy? He must settle for some point on *MP*, since this line contains all the combinations he can afford with his income. Given this limitation, he will naturally try to reach the highest possible indifference curve. The highest indifference curve which is touched by *MP*, therefore, will be the best he can do. This is *II* in Figure 1, and his preferred consumption pattern is shown by *A*, the point at which *MP* is tangent to *II*. By running lines from *A* to the two axes, we discover that he will buy 22 pounds of meat and 90 pounds of potatoes per month.

A little thought reveals why Mr. Bibber cannot profitably move in any direction from *A*. If he tries to move to right or left along *II*, he will not be able to do so because all points except *A* lie *above MP*, i.e., they represent combinations which cost more than his income. If he tries to move up or down along *MP*, he can do so but will find himself on a lower indifference curve representing a lower level of satisfaction.

Suppose now that the price of meat rises from 50 cents to 65 cents a pound, while the price of potatoes remains the same. M moves down to M_1, because even if Mr. Bibber spends all his income on meat he can buy only about 31 pounds instead of the previous 40. The price line thus becomes M_1P. The best position which Mr. Bibber can reach now is A_1, the point at which M_1P just touches the lower indifference curve I_1I_1.

FIGURE 1

Mr. Bibber's Food Preference System

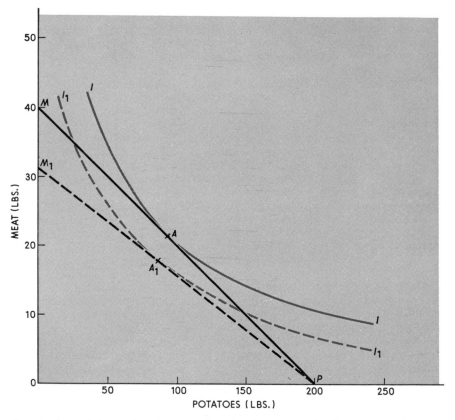

The price line MP shows all combinations of meat and potatoes which Mr. Bibber can buy with his income. He will select the combination shown by A, where MP touches the highest indifference curve (= satisfaction level) he can attain. M_1P shows what happens if the price of meat rises.

At the higher price, Mr. Bibber buys only about 18 pounds of meat instead of the previous 22. His meat purchases have fallen for two reasons: (1) The fact that meat prices have risen while his money income remains unchanged means that his purchasing power is reduced. He is less "well off" than before. Note that he even buys less potatoes than before, even though potato prices are unchanged. This is usually termed the *income effect*. (2) Since potatoes are now *relatively* cheaper, he buys *relatively* more potatoes and less meat than he did before. He substitutes potatoes for meat in his consumption pattern. This is termed the *substitution* effect.

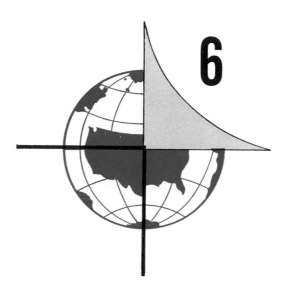

Cost and Price
under Pure Competition

"The cause of lightning," Alice said very decidedly, for she felt quite sure about this, "is the thunder—no, no!" she hastily corrected herself, "I meant it the other way."

"It's too late to correct it," said the Red Queen: "When you've once said a thing, that fixes it, and you must take the consequences."

Through the Looking-glass.

IN CHAPTER 5 we were deliberately vague about the forces behind the supply curve. We said that producers will typically turn out more at a higher price than at a lower one. But how do we know this is true, and why should business concerns behave in this way?

How much business concerns are willing to produce, and the price which they will expect to get for their product, is related to their costs of production. The task of this chapter is to examine the behavior of costs and their effect on production decisions. The central question to be answered is this: What difference does the level of production make to cost per unit of output? If the shoe industry expands and turns out 20 percent more shoes than before, will the cost of making a pair of shoes rise, or fall, or remain about the same?

To get a definite answer to this question we must set up strict ground rules. We must suppose that, as the level of shoe production changes, everything else in the economy remains unchanged. Only in this way can we isolate and examine the effect of an output change.

Three kinds of ground rule are necessary:

1. The cost of producing a pair of shoes will be affected by the *method of production*. There may be several methods available at a particular time, some requiring only simple equipment, others using more equipment and less labor. These known alternatives are usually summed up as *technology* or *the state of the industrial arts*. We suppose that producers in the industry are familiar with existing technology and that they select the method which, given the prevailing prices for labor and capital, will yield lowest production cost. If someone should discover a much more efficient method of shoe production, production cost would drop. So we must rule out this possibility if we want to examine the effect of an output change pure and simple.

2. Even with the same method of production, cost may be higher or lower depending on the *efficiency of management*. Lazy and backward management will mean a higher cost than hard-working and progressive management. To control this factor we assume that management is always perfectly efficient in organizing and supervising production, that it gets the best results which are technically possible. Thus the costs discussed below are *minimum feasible costs* of production by a given method. Everyone knows that this assumption is not fully justified in practice, but it can serve as a first approximation. In a competitive industry with many producers, there is strong pressure on each company to keep its cost near the minimum level.

3. Finally, the cost of producing a pair of shoes depends on the *prices of the materials and services used in production*—the wage rates of shoe workers, the cost of machinery and equipment, the price of leather, and so on. A change in any of these prices will change production cost. If shoe workers' wages rise, everything else remaining unchanged, there will be an immediate increase in cost. Producers will also have an incentive to adopt methods using more machinery and less labor, which will have further effects on cost.

What we are after is a *cost schedule*, showing how cost varies with changes in the level of output. In order to isolate the effect of output changes, we must freeze everything else which affects cost: the state of technology, the efficiency of management, and the prices of the factors of production. This means that the cost schedule is valid only at a moment of time. If any of the underlying conditions changes, the cost schedule will also change. One additional point of method. In economics, *the cost of a product means all the expenses necessary to induce producers to bring it to market*. Over the long run, this must include a *normal rate of profit* to the owners of the enterprise. What is a normal profit? Operationally, it is a profit rate which provides no inducement for more producers to enter the industry or for existing producers to leave it. It is an equilibrium rate, which holds plant capacity in the industry at a constant level.

Normal profit is in fact not profit at all. It is a necessary interest return on the owners' investment, required to induce them to devote their funds to this line of production instead of something else. This level of return *is always included in the cost schedule*. When price equals cost, then, the industry is earning a normal rate of return. If price is above cost, this means that the rate of return is abnormally high.

If this is the meaning of cost, what do we mean by profit? In economics, *profit is the difference between the actual rate of return and the normal rate*. For this reason it can be either positive or negative. If price is above cost, there is positive profit in the economic sense, and of course in the business sense as well. If price is below cost, economic profit is negative, though business profit may still be positive. *Example:* a company is earning 3 percent on the owners' investment. The normal rate of return in the industry is 6 percent. Business profit is +3 percent, but economic profit is −3 percent.

In the following chapters we shall try to use profit consistently in its economic meaning. This meaning should be mastered at the present stage to avoid later confusion.

SUPPLY AND PRICE: THE MARKET PERIOD

In analyzing the demand schedule we saw that its shape depends on *how much time* is allowed for adjustment to a change in price. So too in the case of supply. The shape of the supply curve, and the reasons for this shape, differ depending on the length of time which we take into account. We can usefully distinguish three periods:

1. The *market period* is defined as one which is too short to permit any change in supply.
2. The *short period* or *short run* is long enough to allow changes in the rate of production from existing plants, but not long enough to allow construction of new plants.
3. The *long period* or *long run* is long enough for new plants to be built and new producers to enter the industry.

Note that these are *functional* definitions rather than clock-time definitions. They run in terms of *what happens* over the course of time, rather than in terms of so many weeks or months. Thus the market period, during which available supplies remain fixed, may be one day for fresh fish, a month for cotton textiles, 12 months for corn production or labor supply.

Price determination in the market period is illustrated by Figure 6–1. The supply curve is a vertical line, indicating that supply is fixed for the time being. This being so, price is determined solely by the level of demand. The higher the demand, the higher the price, and vice versa.

This diagram is useful in explaining the gyrations of prices for perishable products. Fresh fish is the classic example. The catch on a particular day determines market supply, and this supply has to be sold for whatever it will bring. (This illustration, however, dates from before the invention of the deep-freeze. What effect would you expect the possibility of freezing fish to have on the shape of the supply curve?)

FIGURE 6–1

Supply and Price in the Market Period

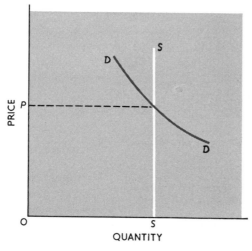

With supply fixed at OS, price depends solely on the level of demand. If demand is DD, price will be OP.

SUPPLY AND PRICE: THE SHORT PERIOD

During the short period, the number of plants in the industry is fixed and cannot be increased. Supply can be altered, however, by varying the rate of production from existing plants. They can be operated at full capacity, or at 80 percent of capacity, or at still lower rates.

Let us look for a moment at the short-period behavior of the widget manufacturing industry. This is a purely competitive industry, in which many companies are engaged in turning out an identical product. Each is so small a part of the industry that he can sell more or less without affecting the market price. He has no price-setting problem, price being determined for him in the market. His problem is simply how much to produce at the going price.

How much a company will produce for a certain price must have something to do with its costs of production. So we must look further into production costs, and particularly into how they change at different levels of plant operation. Remember throughout this section that the *plant and equipment does not change.* We simply produce more or less from it by using more or less labor and materials.

Costs and Rate of Plant Operation

We must first distinguish two kinds of cost:

1. *Fixed (or Overhead) Costs.* These are costs whose amount is not influenced by the plant's production level. They would continue even if the plant were to stand idle, and they do not increase when it is run at full capacity. Property taxes, fire insurance, interest on borrowed money, and salaries of top management officials are examples of overhead costs. Machinery will deteriorate and become obsolete whether or not it is used in production, and so part of the depreciation cost of equipment is overhead.

The important thing for present purposes is that *overhead costs have no bearing on production decisions.* The producer is stuck with his overheads, which for this reason are sometimes called "sunk costs." He cannot reduce them by producing less or even by shutting down. The only costs pertinent to his problem of how much to produce are:

2. *Variable (or Direct) Costs.* As the name implies, these are costs which do vary with the rate of production. As more is produced, more materials must be used, more labor hired, more electric power consumed, and so on. Thus direct costs rise and fall with output.

But *how rapidly* will direct costs increase as output increases? Will costs go up less than proportionately, or precisely in proportion with output, or more than proportionately? This is important from a profit standpoint. If direct costs increase proportionately with output, then cost *per unit produced* remains constant. But if costs rise faster than output, cost per unit will be rising.

What will actually happen depends on the type of production in question. In most cases, it seems reasonable to expect that direct costs will for a time increase about in proportion to output. Each additional unit of production will require about the same amount of material, the same number of man-hours of labor, the same amount of machine time for processing, and so on. Thus over a considerable range output can be stepped up without producing any increase in direct cost per unit.

But this cannot go on forever. The very notion of plant capacity implies that there are limits beyond which it will be difficult or impossible to increase production. As a company tries to squeeze more and more production out of the same plant, the cost of additional output will eventually begin to rise. Why is this? The normal plant work force will have to be increased, and the new workers may be less efficient than the old. Overtime work becomes necessary, and this has to be paid for at premium rates. If second or third shifts are used, efficiency will be lower on these than on the day shift. When equipment is in constant use, it cannot be maintained so effectively and machine breakdowns will increase. The plant may become so crowded that men and materials get in each others' way, with a loss of time and output.

One might expect, therefore, that the costs of a typical widget company would behave as shown in Table 6–1 and Figure 6–2. The basic information is contained in Table 6–1, which should be studied first. Figure 6–2 presents some of the same information in graphic form.

TABLE 6–1

Costs and Rate of Operation, The ABC Manufacturing Company

Output (Units)	Fixed Cost (Dollars)		Variable Cost (Dollars)			Total Cost (Dollars)	
(1)	Total (2)	Average (3) = (2)/(1)	Marginal (4)	Total (5)	Average (6) = (5)/(1)	Total (7)=(2)+(5)	Average (8)=(3)+(6)
1	100	100	12	12	12	112	112
2	100	50	12	24	12	124	62
3	100	33.3	12	36	12	136	45.3
4	100	25	12	48	12	148	37
5	100	20	12	60	12	160	32
6	100	16.7	12	72	12	172	28.7
7	100	14.3	12	84	12	184	26.3
8	100	12.5	12	96	12	196	24.5
9	100	11.1	13	109	12.1	209	23.2
10	100	10	14	123	12.3	223	22.3
11	100	9.1	15	138	12.5	238	21.6
12	100	8.3	17	115	12.9	255	21.3
13	100	7.7	19	174	13.4	274	21.1
14	100	7.1	21	195	13.9	295	21.0
15	100	6.7	23	218	14.5	318	21.2
16	100	6.3	26	244	15.2	344	21.5
17	100	5.9	29	273	16	373	21.9
18	100	5.6	32	305	16.9	405	22.5
19	100	5.3	36	341	17.9	441	23.2
20	100	5	40	381	19.1	481	24.0

Since we want to examine the effect of changes in output, column 1 shows different possible production rates, ranging from 1 widget per hour to a maximum of 20 per hour. Fixed costs, by definition, remain the same regardless of output; and so column 2 always shows the same fixed cost of $100. When we divide output into this, to get average fixed cost per unit (column 3), we notice an interesting thing. The higher the rate of production, the lower is average fixed cost. The popular term for this is *spreading the overhead*. As output rises, overhead costs are spread over more and more units, so that the cost chargeable to each unit falls steadily. In Figure 6–2 average fixed cost is shown by *AFC*.

Now let us look at the behavior of direct or variable costs. Column 4 shows the direct cost of producing each additional unit as output is increased. This is termed *marginal cost*, and is a basic concept. We have supposed that marginal cost remains unchanged up to a production rate of 8 units.[1] Beyond this, as output continues to rise, marginal cost turns upward for the reasons suggested above. This behavior is shown by *MC* in Figure 6–2, which is simply a charting of column 4.[2]

The remaining columns require little explanation. Column 5 is a summing up of the items in column 4, which shows us the *total* variable cost for each level of production. Dividing the number of units produced into this we get average variable cost, shown in column 6 and *AVC* in Figure 6–2.

FIGURE 6–2

Costs and Rate of Operation

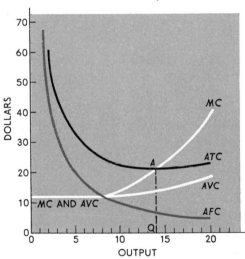

ATC is the sum of AFC and AVC at any given point. It falls for a time because AFC is falling faster than AVC is rising, but eventually the opposite becomes true and ATC turns upward. Production OQ, for which ATC is a minimum, is defined as the *capacity* of the plant.

The company manager, of course, is interested in how he comes out overall when fixed and variable costs have been added together. This addition is performed in column 7. We can then calculate average total cost per unit of output in either of two ways: by dividing output into total cost, or by adding average fixed and average variable cost. The result will be the same and is shown in column 8. In Figure 6–2, average total cost is shown by *ATC*.

---

[1] In actuality, low production rates are likely to be quite inefficient; and so marginal cost will often fall for a while as production is increased, before leveling off and eventually turning upward. This makes little difference to the outcome of our argument, and it seems best to ignore it in a simplified illustration.

[2] The fact that *MC* turns up just after crossing *AFC* has no significance. The illustrative figures chosen for Table 6–1 just happen to work out this way.

Note that average total cost falls for a long time, because average fixed cost is falling fast enough to more than offset the rise in direct costs. Eventually, however, the rise in direct costs begins to predominate and *ATC* turns upward. Lowest cost per unit is achieved at point *A*, with an output of 14 units. This is the most efficient rate of operation, and is usually defined as the *capacity* of the plant. The plant can produce more or less than this, but at any other rate of production unit cost will be higher.

The fact that *MC* intersects *ATC* at *A* is not an accident, and we can show that this must always be true. Take a group of boys averaging 6 feet in height and add another boy 5 feet 8 inches tall. The average of the group will now be lower than before. But if we added a boy taller than the previous average, say 6 feet 2 inches, the average height of the group would rise. The same principle holds here. So long as the cost of an additional unit of output is *below* the average cost of previous units, i.e., so long as *MC* is below *ATC*, then *ATC* must decline. But when we begin adding units whose cost is *above* the previous average, i.e., when *MC* rises above *ATC*, then *ATC* must begin to rise. Hence *MC* must intersect *ATC* at its minimum point.

It should be emphasized that *ATC* includes *all* necessary costs of production, including a normal rate of return on invested capital. Thus any time the producer is getting a price above *ATC*, he is making a positive profit and has an incentive to expand. If he is getting less than *ATC*, his profit is negative, and if the situation continues he will probably consider dropping out of the industry.

Supply and Price in the Short Run

We can now return to our original question: How many units will it pay the ABC Manufacturing Company to produce? What will be the actual operating rate of the plant? This question cannot be answered without knowing the price of the product. So in Figure 6–3 we show several possible prices, in order to see what will happen in each case.

Suppose first that the market price of widgets were $10. At this price, and in fact at any price below *OM*, the plant cannot afford to operate. The direct cost of producing each widget would be higher than its price, and the company would be out of pocket on every unit sold. So it is best to shut down the plant completely. The company will be losing money to the extent of its overhead costs, but it will lose less by shutting down than by operating.

What if the market price rises to $15, indicated by P_1P_1? Now the plant can afford to operate, since the price of a widget is sufficient to cover the direct cost of producing it. How much will it pay to produce? The answer is OQ_1, or 11 units per day. Why is this? Because up to this point the price is more than sufficient to cover the marginal cost of producing additional units. The marginal cost of the eleventh unit, however, is just equal to its price, since P_1P_1 intersects MC at this point. And if production were pushed beyond OQ_1, marginal cost would rise above the price line. Units to the right of Q_1 would cost more to produce than could be gotten for them on the market, and so their production is unprofitable.

FIGURE 6–3

Determining the Rate of Output

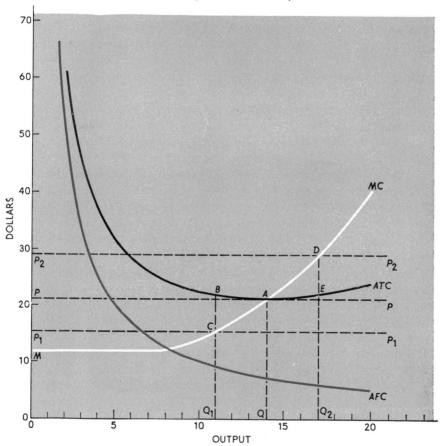

To determine the proper rate of output, look at the price line and the MC curve. The firm will make most profit (or least loss) by producing the output for which price = MC. To determine the profit level, look at the price line and the ATC curve. If price is above ATC, there is positive profit; if it is below, there is negative profit.

Note that at output OQ_1 profits are negative, since price is below average total cost by the amount BC. This is too bad, but the company can't do anything about the market price, and it will lose less by producing at OQ_1 than at any other rate.

A happier situation is shown by the price OP. It will now pay to increase production to the intersection of PP and MC, which occurs at

$OQ = 14$ units. At this point price just equals average total cost. If price should rise to OP_2, it will pay to increase production further to $OQ_2 = 17$ units. And now the company will be making positive profits, since the price of each unit exceeds average total cost by the amount DE.

This leads to a rule for production decisions under pure competition: *A producer will make maximum profit (or minimum loss) by producing that output at which marginal cost is equal to price*. The principle can be interpreted in either of two ways. First, it can be taken as a statement about how business concerns behave in the real world. As such, it is open to numerous objections and qualifications. It assumes that executives have full knowledge of present and prospective costs and prices, so that they know exactly what they are doing. It assumes that their sole objective is maximum profit. It assumes competitive conditions under which no producer has any influence over price. But in most industries producers do have some degree of control over prices; and since they have to decide about price as well as output, their calculations are more complicated than in this simple example. Thus it is easy enough to show that Figure 6–3 gives an oversimplified picture of actual business behavior.

Why, then, have we bothered to develop the $P = MC$ principle at all? Partly because it serves a second purpose as a *criterion of economic efficiency*. Consider the question which has come up several times in earlier chapters: how much of each good and service should an economy produce? Here we are thinking, not of the profits or losses of particular companies, but of using the nation's productive resources most effectively to satisfy the wants of the consuming public. It is obviously possible to produce either too little or too much of a particular product, so little that consumers are starved for the product, or so much that they are completely satiated. Somewhere in between there must be a rate of production which is just right. How can we tell when we have reached the margin beyond which production should not be carried?

It seems reasonable that production of a good should be expanded so long as the importance which consumers attach to it, as measured by the price they are willing to pay, exceeds the necessary cost of producing it. As production is increased, however, price will fall and costs are likely to rise. Eventually we shall reach a situation in which the price that can be secured for an additional unit of output just equals the cost of producing it. This is a signal that production should not be expanded further. But this is just the $P = MC$ principle. This principle thus provides a guide to the proper allocation of resources among different lines of production, and this is true regardless of whether the economy actually achieves such an allocation in practice.

For the individual producer under pure competition, then, *the marginal cost curve is the supply curve*. We can read off the company's response to a price change simply by noting where the price line intersects the marginal cost curve. The supply curve rises because marginal cost eventually rises as production is increased.

What about the widget industry as a whole? The industry consists of a large number of companies, each with cost curves similar to those shown in Figure 6–3. For simplicity, let us assume that *the cost curves of all companies in the industry are identical.* A higher price, then, will lead each company to increase its output in conformity with the $P = MC$ principle. But the total output of widgets is the sum of the outputs of individual companies. Hence total output will rise with an increase in price. The industry's short-run supply curve slopes upward. Behind this rising supply curve lies the difficulty of forcing more and more product out of a fixed number of plants.

Price and output determination in the short run is illustrated by Figure 6–4, which is a replica of the demand-supply diagram in Chapter 5. The supply curve slopes upward to the right for the reason just given. The demand curve slopes downward to the right in the usual way. The intersection of the two curves defines an equilibrium price and output.

Transition to the Long Period

Is the short-run equilibrium price shown in Figure 6–4 the final word? Will this price continue indefinitely into the future? Not necessarily.

FIGURE 6–4

Price and Output in the Short Run

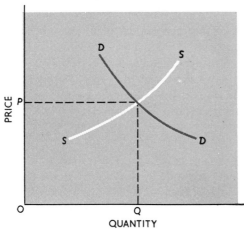

The short-run supply curve for an industry slopes upward to the right. This is because each producer has rising marginal costs, and so will produce more only at a higher price.

Suppose the short-run equilibrium price is at the level shown by OP_2 in Figure 6–3. All companies in the industry are making positive profit. Then there will be an incentive for new producers to enter the industry. Given sufficient time, new plant capacity will be built and put into operation. The supply curve SS in Figure 6–4 shifts outward to the right, intersects DD at a lower point, and the price falls.

Suppose on the other hand that in the short run price settles at the level of OP_1 in Figure 6–3, so that all companies are making negative profit. Then producers will have an incentive to get out of this industry and into something else—indeed, if the price is low enough, they will have cash losses and be forced into bankruptcy. As companies are squeezed out of the industry, SS in Figure 6–4 shifts to the left, intersects DD at a higher point, and the price rises.

Over the long run, then, the industry can be in equilibrium only at the price OP in Figure 6–3. Why is this? Because this price just equals average total cost. Thus by definition it provides a normal rate of return, and there is no incentive for producers to enter or leave the industry. Any short-period price higher or lower than OP will cause the industry supply curve to shift in such a way that price moves back toward OP.

When the industry is in long-run equilibrium at OP, price equals average total cost as well as marginal cost. Moreover, each plant is operating at the most efficient rate, i.e., at the minimum of its ATC curve. This situation, in addition to being acceptable to the private producers, is one of maximum efficiency from an overall economic standpoint. If each industry in the economy has reached this sort of adjustment, the economy is doing as well as it can with the resources available. On this ground one can argue that a purely competitive organization of the economy leads to an optimum allocation and use of resources.

SUPPLY AND PRICE: THE LONG PERIOD

In speaking of the addition or subtraction of plant capacity we have already moved from short-period to long-period problems. In a growing economy most industries are experiencing increases in demand and are increasing their productive capacity over the years. What does this do to cost and price? Will addition of more plants raise the level of costs in the industry, or lower it, or leave it unchanged?

Cost and the Scale of Production

Before tackling this question we must clear up a related question which so far has been left in the background. In showing the cost situation of a typical widget company in Figure 6–3, we simply *assumed* that the company was of a certain size. We did not ask how it got to be this size, or whether this is the best size for it to be. So we must pause to ask what determines the size of companies in a competitive industry, and how size affects the level of costs.

It is usually taken for granted that there are *economies of large-scale production* which mean that a large plant can produce more cheaply than a smaller one. Up to a point this is certainly true, and it is not hard to see why. First, a larger plant can achieve greater subdivision and specialization of production processes. In a small custom workshop, a shoemaker may perform all the operations needed to turn out a shoe. In a large factory these operations are finely subdivided. It may be boring for the worker to make the same few motions all day long, but he learns to do them faster, he wastes no time in changing from one task to another, and he can use tools which are specialized to a particular job. Subdivision of production operations is an essential basis for mechanization.

In some industries the basic production equipment is very large. The huge machines which stamp out auto bodies, the automatic equipment which drills all the holes in the cylinder block in one operation, the miles of assembly line, and the large ovens which spray and bake paint on the car would be quite beyond the means of a small producer. But when thousands of cars a day are fed through the plant, the cost per car can be cut to a low level. Large plants can also afford to mechanize many supplementary operations, such as bringing materials to the production floor, and packaging and shipping the finished produce.

Eventually one reaches a point at which the plant is large enough to take full advantage of existing technology, and a still larger plant would not have lower unit costs. But we are interested here mainly in *size of company* rather than size of plant; and there may still be cost savings in having several plants operated by the same company. Certain general expenses must be borne regardless of output. Every company must have a president, treasurer, personnel director, sales manager, and so on. If these overhead costs can be spread over a million units of output per year instead of a hundred thousand, unit cost will be lower. A large company can afford expert staffs for research and development, production engineering, and other activities. And a company which buys materials and supplies on a very large scale may be able to get them at lower cost. It is also conceivable that a company may become too large, and that its costs may be higher than those of smaller concerns. The wastes of bureaucracy are not confined to government. A very large corporation may have so many layers of executives, so much delay and error in transmission of instructions and information, so wide a gap between top executives and factory personnel, that it becomes muscle-bound. Actual evidence on this point is difficult to secure. Large companies are often in a semimonopolistic position in their respective industries. And so if one sees indications of inefficiency, it is hard to tell whether this is due to size *per se* or to the fact that the company is not subject to effective competition.

Suppose, then, that I am planning to start a new company for widget production. I hire a firm of management consultants and put the following question to them: If I set up an organization to produce 50,000 widgets a year, what is the lowest cost I can obtain per widget? What will the cost be if I plan for a capacity of 100,000, or 150,000?

The consultants' report might look somewhat as shown in Figure 6–5. A very small company would have high unit costs, and for a while larger size would reduce costs rapidly. After a while, however, the economies of scale begin to taper off and *CC* falls more gradually. Research studies indicate that in many manufacturing industries there is a cost difference of only a few percent between a medium-sized company and one several times as large. Eventually, as the company becomes larger and larger, unit costs may turn up again because of administrative difficulties.

FIGURE 6–5

The Effect of Size on Cost

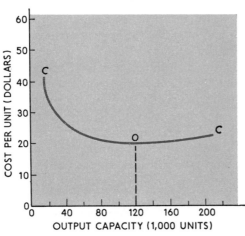

CC is a *planning curve or long-run average total cost curve*. It shows the lowest unit cost which could be attained by companies of various sizes. Its shape shows that up to a point large-scale production reduces unit cost, but eventually cost turns upward again. The size OQ, corresponding to the minimum point on CC, is called the *optimum size* or optimum *scale* of company.

The curve *CC* is often termed a *planning curve*, since it is used in reaching long-run decisions about expansion. It is also called a *long-run average total cost curve*. The minimum point of the curve, *O* in Figure 6–5, is called the *optimum size* of company. A company of this size, with annual production capacity of 120,000 units, could attain lower unit cost than either a smaller or larger company.

The concept of optimum size is important. For an economy to operate most efficiently, all companies should be of optimum size for their respective industries. This size will of course vary widely from one industry to another because of differences in production methods. It will be smaller for a shoe repair shop than for a grocery, smaller for a cotton mill than for a steel plant. Efficiency does not require that *all* producers be large. Largeness is entirely relative, and the requirement is merely that each enterprise be of optimum size for its type of production.

Optimum size also changes over the course of time as a result of technical developments. Invention of ever-larger and more specialized machinery tends to increase the most efficient size of *plant*. And as business school researchers develop better methods of coordinating large enterprises, this will increase the optimum size of *companies*. It is probably a safe guess that optimum size in most industries is rising over the course of time.

What is the likelihood that companies in each industry will actually achieve optimum size? This depends partly on the level of demand for the product. It is not uncommon to encounter the situation shown in Figure 6–6. *DD* for the product intersects *CC* to the left of *O*. Then there will be room in the industry for only one producer, and this producer

FIGURE 6–6

The Feasibility of Competition

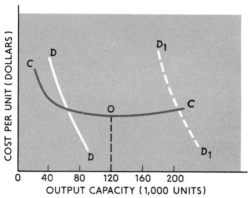

With demand at DD, there could be only one producer in this industry. With D₁D₁ there could be only two efficient-sized companies. Pure competition is feasible only if DD lies so far to the right that there is room for many producers, each of the optimum scale OQ.

will be unable to attain optimum size. If demand should increase to D_1D_1, however, and if *CC* has not been altered by technical changes, there will be room for two companies of about optimum scale.

This illustration helps also to explain why pure competition is a rare situation. Under pure competition there is no market barrier to expansion. Each producer is a small part of the industry, and can sell as much as he chooses at the market price. If a company is operating to the left of *O*, therefore, it has an incentive to expand and reduce its unit cost of production. But suppose all companies in the industry do this, and all arrive eventually at *O*. Will we still have pure competition? *Only if the market is large enough to absorb the output of many producers, each one of optimum size.* Or, to put the point in reverse, *only if optimum scale is small relative to the size of the market.* This is the typical situation in agriculture; and it is approximated in some manufacturing industries, such as cotton textiles and garment production. In many industries, however, optimum scale is large enough so that only a few efficient-sized producers can survive.

The Long-Run Supply Curve

The key question about long-run supply can now be stated more precisely. Consider a purely competitive industry in full equilibrium. Each company is operating at capacity, and *each is of optimum size*. Price just equals average total cost and all is well. Now demand increases, so price rises and positive profits appear. This causes new companies, presumably also of optimum size, to enter the industry. What will this do to the cost level of existing producers? Will costs be increased, or decreased, or remain unchanged? Where will cost and price settle down after the industry has adjusted fully to the new level of demand?

There are three possibilities, usually termed *constant costs, increasing costs,* and *decreasing costs*. Let us look at these in turn.

Constant costs. One possibility is that new companies entering the industry will have the same cost level as the old ones, and that the cost level of existing producers will remain unchanged. This requires that this industry's demand for labor, materials, and other factors of production form a small part of total demand for these factors, so that expansion of the industry will not affect factor prices. If it is true that expansion of capacity leaves everyone's costs unchanged, then the industry's long-run supply curve will be horizontal. Production can be expanded to any desired extent without any increase in cost and thus without any need for a permanently higher level of prices.

Increasing costs. There are industries in which productive capacity can be added only at higher cost, and where the long-run supply curve consequently slopes upward. A classic illustration is wine growing. Good wine land requires an unusual combination of soil composition, rainfall, slope, exposure to sun, and shelter from storms. The amount of first-class land available is limited. If wine growers know their business, as they should after several hundred years, the best land will be put into cultivation first. As demand continues to increase, land will have to be used which is less and less well adapted to vineyards. This land will produce smaller yields for the labor and materials used, which means higher marginal costs for added units of output. The more demand increases, the more marginal costs will rise. The top-quality land will also be worked more intensively by using more labor, fertilizers, and equipment per acre. But this also lends to rising marginal costs as extra gallons of wine are won with greater and greater effort.

This is a common situation in the extractive industries. It is easy to take out the largest and most accessible trees from a stand of virgin timber. As one goes farther away from transportation and into smaller trees, marginal costs will rise. Copper mines differ greatly in depth of the ore body below the surface, thickness of the veins, and copper content of the ore. The cheapest known sources of ore will be exploited first. As demand increases, it becomes necessary to use thinner veins and lower-grade ores at higher cost per pound of copper produced.

Decreasing costs. Are there cases of the opposite sort, cases in which adding more plants to an industry will lower everyone's production costs? One can think of some reasons why this might happen. Where an industry has become localized in certain areas, it gradually creates a pool of skilled and experienced labor which did not exist in the first instance and which raises labor efficiency throughout the industry. Larger output for the industry may make possible a finer subdivision and specialization of work in individual plants. One set of plants may do nothing but spin cotton yarn, another group nothing but weaving, and another group may dye and finish the cloth, and so on. In this way each plant may get larger production volume and lower unit costs *on a specific operation* than could be had if each plant performed the full range of operations from raw material to final product. Similarly, production of key materials and supplies can be delegated to supplementary producers, who can achieve large output volume and lower costs as the industry expands. The Akron tire plants can get vulcanizing chemicals more cheaply by buying them from a nearby chemical plant than by producing them themselves, but this chemical plant could not be built until the tire industry became large enough to make the venture profitable. Such savings are usually termed *external economies*, since they are external to any single company.

A Summary Word on Supply

To sum up the discussion to this point: the shape of a supply curve depends on the period of time taken into account. If one takes a very short period, supply is completely inelastic. Over a period long enough for existing producers to alter their rate of production, one faces an upward-sloping supply curve. The upward slope is due to the rising marginal cost of squeezing more production out of a fixed number of plants. Finally, if one allows enough time for additional producers to enter the industry, the supply curve may still slope upward in the case of extractive industries exploiting a scarce natural resource. But in many cases the long-run supply curve will be horizontal, and in some cases it may slope downward because of external economies.

The general principle is that the longer the period of time considered, the more elastic will be the supply curve. This makes good common sense. The shape of the supply curve indicates basically the strength of resistances to an increased supply of the product, the costs which must be overcome to get increased production. The more readily and cheaply supply can be expanded, the more elastic the supply curve will be. Since expansion takes time, it seems clear that supply should be more expansible over long periods than short ones; and this is precisely the conclusion which we have reached.

THE WORKING OF THE MARKET MECHANISM: SHIFTS IN DEMAND AND SUPPLY

Having explained the forces behind the demand and supply schedules, we are in a position to put the apparatus to work in analyzing economic events. We live in a dynamic, ever-changing economy. Few markets are ever in equilibrium, and if so they would not stay there long. Demand and supply curves for various products are constantly changing their shape and position. The practical purpose of demand-supply analysis, then, is mainly to explain *change* rather than stability. We use it to explore the train of events which will be set off by a shift in demand or supply conditions.

Shifts in Demand

Consider first the repercussions set off by a rise in demand for a product. Why may demand increase? Presumably because one or more of the things which we held constant in constructing the demand curve have changed. People's incomes may have risen. There may have been a shift in preferences. Or the price of some other product may have changed. There are two possibilities here. If products A and B are *substitutes*, a reduction in the price of A will *lower* the demand curve for B. A cut in butter prices reduces the demand for margarine. But if A and B are *complementary* products which are normally used together, a reduction in the price of A will *raise* the demand curve for B. A lower price for cars raises the demand for gasoline.

So, for whatever reason, DD in Figure 6–7 shifts upward to position D_1D_1. What will happen? Immediate consequences are one thing, eventual consequences another. To trace out the chain of events, we show in Figure 6–7 three supply curves, corresponding to our three time-periods. S_m is the market supply curve, its vertical shape indicating that supply cannot be increased immediately. S_s is the short-run supply curve, indicating the possibility of increasing production from existing plants. S_l, the long-run supply curve, reflects the costs involved in adding fresh plant capacity. S_l has been drawn horizontal on the assumption that we are dealing with a constant-cost industry, but it could also be drawn to show increasing or decreasing long-run costs.

The first effect of the demand increase will be a rise in price. Price will rise from the old equilibrium P toward P_1, corresponding to the intersection of S_m with the new demand curve D_1D_1. At this attractive price, the industry will rush to get out more product. Additional labor will be hired, more materials bought, and plants worked longer hours.

The industry will expand along S_s, which rises because of the rising marginal cost of working plants closer to capacity. Output will move from Q toward Q_1, and as this happens price will decline from P_1 toward P_2. At B, where S_s intersects D_1D_1, the industry will be in short-run equilibrium.

FIGURE 6–7

Increase in Demand with Constant Costs

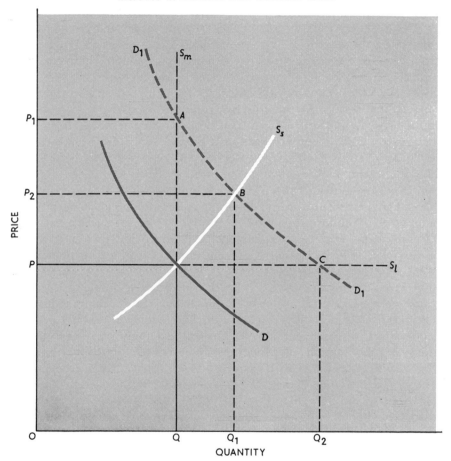

S_m, S_s, and S_l are the market, short-run, and long-run supply curves for this industry. If demand rises from DD to D_1D_1, the industry will move immediately to the market equilibrium at point A, then to the short-run equilibrium at B and finally back to long-run equilibrium at C. The permanent effect is a rise in productive capacity from OQ to OQ_2.

But price P_2 still yields positive profits. So if the higher demand is expected to be permanent, companies will begin planning to expand, and new producers will move into the industry. As new plants come into production, the industry's output expands beyond Q_1 toward Q_2. The industry travels down the demand curve toward C, price declines from P_2 toward the old level P, and returns in the industry recede toward a normal level.

The end result, then, is as follows: the industry's productive capacity has been enlarged; output has expanded from Q to Q_2; profit is zero, as it was at the beginning; and the price is also just what it was originally. (This last conclusion, of course, depends on the assumption of constant costs. If S_l sloped upward, the new permanent price would be higher than before.)

The consequences of a permanent decline in demand can be traced out in the same way. The short-run effect is a drop in price, output, and rate of return. Negative profits, if continued long enough, will force some companies to liquidate or shift to other products. New producers will be discouraged from entering the industry. Thus the industry's productive capacity will shrink. As this happens, price and rate of return gradually rise toward the original level. When earnings have returned to normal, the thermostat clicks and contraction of the industry ceases. The long-run results are: smaller capacity; smaller output; zero profit, as before; and (under constant cost) no change in price.

Note the nicety of this mechanism. Upward or downward shifts of demand trigger off upward or downward price-profit movements. These induce an appropriate expansion or contraction of productive capacity. As adjustments in capacity are completed, prices and profits return to normal levels. The end-result is a reallocation of resources corresponding to the new pattern of demand.

True, the market is more effective in directing resources into expanding industries than in squeezing them out of declining industries. The latter process is slow and painful. But fortunately it is not often necessary. The reason is that in a growing economy total demand for goods and total supply of productive resources are normally rising. So what mainly happens is that *some industries expand faster than others*. The market operates to channel new resources into industries whose demand curves are rising most rapidly. And other industries can shrink relatively without suffering an absolute decline which would force them to release labor and capital.[3]

Shifts in Supply

The supply curve may shift as well as the demand curve. An *upward* shift of SS would mean that it is more difficult than before to produce

---

[3] A forthcoming study by Professor George Stigler for the National Bureau of Economic Research finds that, out of 98 manufacturing industries examined over the years 1947–56, only a half dozen actually lost capital. At the other extreme, the seven most rapidly growing industries increased their capital at more than 11 percent per year. The average rate of increase for all industries was about 6 percent a year.

any given amount of the product. Such a shift is unusual in practice. Much more typical are *downward* shifts of SS. These result mainly from a factor which has been ruled out of consideration up to this point, progress in science and technology. Technical progress can take the form of turning out a better product at the same cost, or the same product at lower cost, or most commonly both together. In the early years of a new industry costs often fall dramatically, though progress may slow down as the industry matures.

FIGURE 6–8

A Shift in Supply over Time

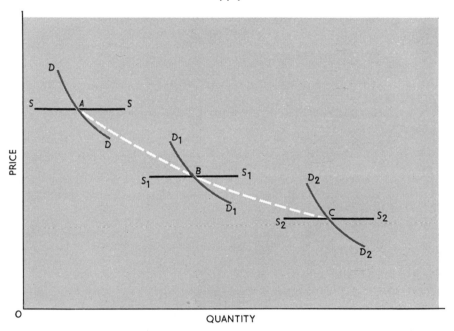

DD and SS refer to 1960. D_1D_1 and S_1S_1 show the same industry in 1970, and D_2D_2 and S_2S_2 in 1980. Demand is rising, while at the same time the long-run supply curve is being lowered by technical progress. The industry expands along the dotted line ABC, usually termed a *historical cost curve*.

The effect of downward supply shifts is shown in Figure 6–8. Each of the small supply-demand sketches relates to a different period of time— say 1960, 1970, and 1980. We assume that demand for the product is growing over time, and that at any given time the industry is subject to constant costs. In the absence of technical progress, the growth of demand would lead simply to greater production at the same cost and price level. The industry would travel to the right along SS. But instead technical progress drops the level of costs, first to S_1S_1, then to S_2S_2. So the industry travels along the path shown by the dotted line linking the equilibrium points *A*, *B*, and *C*. This line is sometimes called a *historical cost curve*.

The rate of technical progress differs widely from one industry to another, and this has important consequences for the production pattern of the economy. All industries are in competition with each other for the consumer's dollar. Those which are most successful in reducing costs and prices will be able to travel out fastest along their demand curves. If one takes two cross-sections of the economy 10 or 20 years apart and observes which products have shown greatest increase in output, one finds a strong association between increases in output and *relative* decreases in price.

SUMMARY

1. In analyzing costs and supply we take *technology, management, efficiency*, and the *prices of factors of production* as known and constant.

2. Cost is defined to include a *normal rate of return* to the owners of capital, that is, a rate of return which provides no inducement for expansion or contraction of productive capacity in the industry.

3. *Profit* is the difference between the actual rate of return and the normal rate. It can be either positive or negative.

4. In the *market period*, supply is fixed. Price depends solely on the level of demand.

5. In the *short period* or short run, plant capacity is fixed. Production costs can be divided into *fixed or overhead costs*, and *variable or direct costs*. *Marginal cost* is the direct cost of producing an additional unit of output, and it always rises beyond a certain point. When it becomes equal to *average total costs*, *ATC* also begins to rise. The output for which *ATC* is a minimum is defined as *plant capacity*.

6. Each plant will produce the output for which *price equals marginal cost*. The supply curve of each producer is identical with its marginal cost curve, hence slopes upward to the right. And since total output is the sum of the outputs of individual companies, the supply curve of the industry also slopes upward to the right.

7. While a company is in short-period equilibrium where price equals marginal cost, it will be in long-run equilibrium only if price also equals average total cost, that is, if the price line touches the *ATC* curve at its minimum point. If price is above *ATC*, there is positive profit and the company has an incentive to expand capacity; and conversely if the price is below *ATC*.

8. In the *long period* or long run, new plant capacity can be constructed and companies can become larger or smaller. Up to a point, increasing size will mean lower unit cost; but eventually unit cost will begin to rise. The size of company which yields lowest unit cost is termed the *optimum size*.

9. Under pure competition there is no barrier to a company's expanding until it reaches optimum size. But this means that pure competition can continue only if the market is large enough to absorb the output of many optimum-sized producers.

10. The long-run supply curve depends on what happens to an industry's cost level as production capacity is increased. Extractive industries may be subject to *increasing costs* due to their use of a scarce natural resource. In most other industries it seems reasonable to expect *constant costs*. But in some cases one may find *decreasing costs* arising from *external economies*.

11. Demand-supply analysis is useful mainly in tracing the results of a

shift in demand or supply conditions. The *immediate effect* of a permanent increase in demand is a higher price and positive profits. The *short-run effect* is an increase in the rate of operation of existing plants. The *long-run effect* is construction of new productive capacity. In a constant-cost industry, after all adjustments have been completed, unit cost, price, and earnings will have returned to their original level.

12. If we admit technical change to the picture, an industry's supply curve may shift downward over time as a result of technical progress. The industries which are most successful in reducing unit cost and price tend to show largest increases in output over the years.

Monopoly Power in Product Markets

Here's the rule for bargains: "Do other men, for they would do you."
That's the true business precept.

CHARLES DICKENS

Business is really more agreeable than pleasure; it interests the whole
mind, the aggregate nature of man more continuously and more deeply. But
it does not look as if it did.

WALTER BAGEHOT

IT IS USEFUL to examine the logic of a purely competitive economy. Since
our own economy is partially competitive, a clear picture of how competitive markets operate helps to explain what goes on around us. Competitive theory is useful also for yardstick purposes, for analyzing the
meaning of economic efficiency.

But we should not confuse this theoretical model with the actual
economy of the United States or any other country. There never has been
and never will be a fully competitive economy. We must now examine
some of the ways in which the American economy departs from the competitive model and the consequences of these departures.

THE MEANING OF MONOPOLY POWER

Pure competition is a situation in which no buyer or seller is able to
influence the market price. The large number of buyers and sellers, and
the complete independence of their actions, prevents any of them from

having significant influence on the market. Such competition is often termed *atomistic*.

Monopoly power exists in a market when a single seller or buyer, or a group of sellers or buyers, *is* able to influence the market price. This is a mirror image of the definition of pure competition. Either no one can influence the price, in which case the market is purely competitive; or someone is able to influence price, in which case monopoly power is present.

Monopoly power may exist on one side of the market and not on the other. A large mail-order house dealing with many small shoe manufacturers illustrates monopoly power on the buying side. A large automobile manufacturer selling to thousands of small car dealers illustrates monopoly power on the selling side. In some cases monopoly power exists on both sides of the market—for example, when the United Mine Workers negotiates over wages with an association of all the anthracite coal companies.

In discussing monopoly power in product markets it is usual to focus on the selling side. We shall follow this approach here, bringing in large buyers only where they help to explain sellers' behavior. Viewed from the selling side, one finds three main types of market situation:

1. *A single seller provides the whole supply of a good or service.* This is *monopoly* in its everyday meaning. It is the standard situation in railroad transportation, power production, telephone and telegraph communication, and other public utilities. It is also found occasionally in manufacturing and in local trade and service industries.

2. *There are a few sellers of a product.* What do we mean by "a few"? This is not a matter of numbers, but a matter of behavior. We say that there are "few" sellers if a price change by one seller will be noticed and reacted to by other sellers. Few means few enough so that they can keep track of each other. By the same token, there are "many sellers" when no one is important enough for others to pay attention to his actions. The market with many sellers is an anonymous market, in which each company is free to make its own decisions without worrying about the reactions of its rivals.

Since "monopoly" comes from Greek roots, the situation of few sellers has been labeled *oligopoly*. It is a common situation in manufacturing, construction, wholesale and retail trade, and the service industries.

3. *There are many sellers, but the product of one seller is not a perfect substitute for that of another.* This may be because the products are actually different, or because buyers have become convinced through advertising that they are different, or because they are available at different locations, or because the seller provides a variety of personal services along with the product. The best illustrations are found in retailing and service. A box of Wheaties sold in two different groceries is not the same product to me as a buyer. One grocery may be nearer to my home than the other. One grocer may be more accommodating as regards credit, de-

livery, and other services. I may prefer the personality of the check-out girl in one store to that of her opposite number. For these or other reasons, I may prefer to buy at one store rather than the other. This preference, which ties me in some measure to one seller, means that the market is no longer purely competitive.

This situation has been termed *imperfect competition* or *monopolistic competition*. The latter term underlines the fact that each seller has a distinct product and a group of regular customers who prefer that product. As regards this group, he has a limited degree of monopoly power. He has his own demand curve, and is not tied to a uniform market price. If he raises his price above that of other sellers, he will lose some but not all of his customers. If he cuts his price below others he will gain some customers, but everybody will not rush to him. Some will remain loyal to their customary seller. The strength of dealer loyalties or brand loyalties can be judged from the elasticity of the demand curves of the various sellers.

Where many sellers compete in this way, the demand curve for each is likely to be elastic and the market power of each seller quite limited. People may pay a little more to buy at their favorite grocery or filling station, but they will not sacrifice very much for very long. The results of monopolistic competition with many sellers are thus not likely to differ strikingly from those of pure competition. Entrance to the market is easy, rivalry is anonymous, profits are moderate, and the market adjusts to supply and demand shifts in the way described in the last chapter.

We shall accordingly say little about monopolistic competition here, concentrating rather on the novel problems posed by monopoly and oligopoly.

THE SINGLE SELLER

A monopolist in ordinary parlance is someone who controls the entire output of a particular product. But what is "a product"? We think of it as being something distinctive, something for which there is no ready substitute. But there are few things for which there is no substitute. The producer of Dairy Maid butter has a monopoly of his own brand; but since other brands are close substitutes, his market power is small. Does butter as a whole, then, constitute a product? In various times and places oleomargarine, lard, peanut butter, and other things have been used on bread instead of butter. So perhaps it is bread spreads of every type which should be considered "a product." The contribution of these spreads to the diet is primarily fat. But fat may also be obtained from meat, vegetable oils, and other sources. So should not the whole category of fats and oils be treated as a product? The chain of substitutes goes on and on, in ever-widening circles. A monopolist in the strict sense would have to control everything produced in the economy.

We get around this difficulty by defining a product on the basis of *a major gap in the chain of substitutes.* Goodyear and Firestone tires are close substitutes for each other, and it would not make much sense to treat them as separate products. But there is no good substitute for automobile tires as a whole. When we come to such a gap, we consider everything inside it as a single product. A company which produces all of such a thing has a monopoly.

In this case the demand curve for the product belongs to one company. The company *is* the industry. The power of the monopoly is shown by the elasticity of demand. No monopoly is ever perfect. The Aluminum Company of America had a monopoly of aluminum production for 50 years; but there are considerable possibilities of substitution among aluminum, copper, steel, and other metals. The New Haven Railroad has a monopoly of rail transportation between Boston and New York, but people can and do make this trip by airplane, bus, and automobile. These things are all reflected in the demand curve.

Bases of Monopoly Power

There are several possible reasons for the appearance of monopoly. In some cases the *conditions of production* make it uneconomic to have more than one producer. Suppose the optimum scale of enterprise is very large relative to market demand, as in railroading, subway and interurban transportation, telephone communication, and electric power generation and distribution. While it might be possible to have several rival producers operating in the same area, each would have considerably higher unit costs than a single consolidated concern. So we accept monopoly. Industries of this sort are in fact commonly termed *natural monopolies.*

A second important reason for monopoly is *limited size of the market* for the product. Demand may be small enough so that one efficient-sized plant can provide all the necessary output. If one company gets an early start, and if it expands as rapidly as demand rises, there may never be room for anyone else to break into the industry. Most monopolies in manufacturing are monopolies of little things, not of big things. The complex and mechanized industry of the United States requires thousands of small parts and components, tools, gadgets, chemical materials, specialty products of every sort. These are sold usually to other companies rather than to the general public. A small gadget may be an essential component of some larger product, yet a single plant may be able to handle the national demand quite easily. In villages and small towns, monopoly in trade and service industries is quite common. Everyone has seen towns with one bank, one hotel, one movie theatre, one electric repair shop, one dry cleaner. Smallness of the local market is the main explanation of these cases.

In other cases there is enough demand to support two or more producers, but one company gets a head start and is able to keep out would-be competitors. One way of doing this is through *patent control.* If the product involves some new production process, the company can secure from the U.S. Patent Office an exclusive right to this process for a period of 17 years. Anyone who tries to duplicate it is liable to suit for infringement of patent. Threat of an expensive patent trial can be a powerful weapon in the hands of an established concern, even when its legal case is not strong. And if enough new features can be added to the process to warrant new patents, exclusive rights can be extended over a longer period.

Another possibility is *control of an essential material.* The Aluminum Company of America for many years bought up newly discovered deposits of bauxite ore, either using them itself or at least preventing any rival producer from using them. In this way it managed to keep control of the industry for a long time after its original patent protection had run out. *Control of labor supply* is another possible device, found mainly in local rather than national industries. Local associations of building contractors, trucking concerns, laundry and dry cleaning establishments, and the like have sometimes signed union agreements under which the union promises that its members will not work for anyone who is not in the association. This does not make it impossible for new companies to get established, since they can try to recruit nonunion labor; but it certainly makes it more difficult.

Still another possibility is *amalgamation.* Put all producers in the industry together into a single corporation. Corporation lawyers and investment bankers are expert in working out merger terms. Many of the famous early "trusts" in the United States were formed in this way, including American Tobacco, Standard Oil, and United States Steel. Today, however, a merger which controlled all or most of the output in a national industry would be subject to attack under the antitrust laws. Thus this approach to monopoly has been at least partially blocked.

Cost, Price, and Output under Monopoly

How will a monopolist set about doing the best for himself? And how does the result differ from that which would be reached under competitive conditions?

It is best to consider these questions in terms of the long run rather than the short run. The long-run problem, as we saw in the last chapter, is how much plant capacity will be constructed in a particular industry. Will the amount of capacity built be larger or smaller under monopoly than under atomistic competition? The answer will largely determine the level of current output and the price of the product.

We must also specify the characteristics of the industry. Consider an industry in which demand is very large relative to the optimum scale of plant. It is technically possible to have a large number of plants in the industry. Suppose also that new plants can be added at constant cost, so that the long-run supply curve is horizontal (*PS* in Figure 7–1). The cost *OP* includes a normal rate of profit on invested capital. *DD* is the demand curve for the product.

If each plant belonged to a separate company, and if these companies competed atomistically with each other, one would expect the industry to expand to the demand-supply intersection at *C*. Equilibrium price would be *OP*, which is just sufficient to cover cost, and output would be *OQ*. The reasoning behind this conclusion has been explained in previous chapters.

But suppose instead that there is only one company in the industry, with power to decide how much capacity shall be built. The monopolist could, of course, build enough plants to produce *OQ* and sell this output

FIGURE 7-1

Monopoly Price and Output in the Long Run

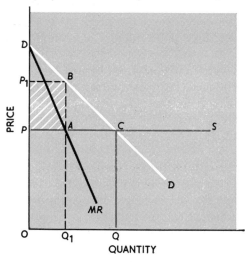

DD and PS are the demand and long-run supply curves for the product. Under pure competition the intersection of these curves would define a price OP and output OQ. A monopolist, however, would make greatest profit by restricting output to OQ_1, where marginal revenue equals marginal cost. His price is OP_1 and his profit is the shaded area $PABP_1$.

at price *OP*. But then there wouldn't be much point in his having a monopoly. He can profit from his monopoly position only by selling less at a higher price.

It is not correct to say that the monopolist will charge the *highest possible price*. If he charged *OD*, he would have no sales and would be out of business. What he will do, if he has all the necessary facts and thinks only of profit, is to choose the output which yields *maximum profit*. This output can be determined by using the concept of *marginal revenue* explained in Chapter 5. In Figure 7-1, *MR* shows the addition to sales revenue from each additional unit sold. It will always be less than the *price* of the additional unit, since to sell another unit one has to cut the price not only on that unit but also on all previous units produced. Thus *MR* always lies below *DD*.

The best level of output for the monopolist will be OQ_1, corresponding to point A at which MR intersects PS. Why is this? Because up to this point the revenue added by each unit exceeds the additional cost of producing it. Beyond A, however, marginal revenue falls below marginal cost, so that additional output would reduce profit. Profit is maximized at OQ_1, where marginal revenue and long-run marginal cost are equal.

Looking up to the demand curve, we see that an output of OQ_1 can be sold at a price of OP_1. The monopolist's total revenue from sales (price × quantity sold) is OQ_1BP_1. But his total production costs, including a normal return on capital, are only OQ_1AP. So he has left over the shaded area $PABP_1$. This profit area is larger than it would be at any other level of output.

What's Wrong with Monopoly?

One can't help feeling that there is something wrong with the price-output adjustment under monopoly. But what precisely is wrong with it? One can single out at least three disadvantages of monopolistic conditions.

1. The most striking thing which stands out from Figure 7–1 is that too little of the product is being produced. Why can we say this? Because at the monopoly output OQ_1, there is a large gap between the price (Q_1B), which indicates how badly buyers want the product, and the marginal cost of producing it (Q_1A). This gap is shown by the distance AB.

We emphasized earlier that in a competitive market economy the output of each product will be carried to the point where social cost and social benefit exactly balance, where the price people are willing to pay for the last unit produced is just sufficient to cover the cost of producing it. In the present case, the socially desirable output is OQ, and if the industry consisted of many competing firms this would be the actual output.

Under monopoly, however, output is restricted to OQ_1. This means that too small a quantity of economic resources is being used in the industry. Some labor, capital, and other resources which consumers would prefer to see devoted to this product are not being devoted to it. Instead, they are forced to seek employment elsewhere in the economy which means that one or more other products are being *over*produced. This misallocation of resources is the basic disadvantage of monopoly.

2. A second consequence is that the monopolistic company makes profits for which it performs no economic function. This is sheer tribute levied on the hapless buyer. Consumers are likely on the average to have smaller incomes than the owners of stock in the monopoly business, and the effect is thus a transfer of income from lower brackets to higher brackets. But this is not the essence of the matter. Even if the buyers were richer than the monopolistic seller, exaction of monopoly profits could not be justified on efficiency grounds.

3. Price isn't everything. Service, quality, and other aspects of the bargain are important. One disadvantage of dealing with a monopolist is that he can push you around on these things as well as on price. A competitive seller cannot do this. If he falls down on service or quality, the customer simply says good-bye and goes across the street. But when you can't go anywhere else, and the seller knows this, he may take advantage of it by being slow on deliveries or service calls and unreliable in performance.

There are few propositions on which one can get such widespread agreement among economists as that uncontrolled private monopoly is undesirable. What can be done about it is another matter, which must wait until Part Two.

A Qualification: Monopoly Cost and Competitive Cost

In drawing Figure 7–1 we supposed that the long-run supply curve of the industry would be the same whether the industry was operated by a single large company or by many small companies. Production cost was set at the same level, *OP*, in both cases. This is unlikely to be true in practice. It seems more likely that cost levels will differ under the two forms of organization. But in which direction? Few subjects are more warmly debated among economists, with eminent authorities on both sides. On one side it is argued that a very large company can achieve economies in selling, purchasing, financing, and other types of expense which will reduce costs per unit of output; that the giant company can hire top-quality professional management and thus achieve greater operating efficiency; and that part of monopoly profits can be plowed back into research activities which will make for a more rapid improvement of products and processes. Against this it is argued with equal vigor that a large company can easily become *too* large to manage efficiently; that absence of competition can lead to slack management and needlessly high costs; and that the small competitive producer will be more efficient and inventive than the monopolist because he *has* to be to survive in the competitive struggle.

There is as yet no conclusive evidence in either direction. One cannot rule out the possibility that cost per unit of output *might* be lower under monopoly than under competition. It is conceivable, though unlikely, that the monopolist's costs might be enough lower so that his price and output would work out at about the same levels as under pure competition.

A Qualification: Will Profits Be Maximized?

We also supposed in the earlier discussion that a rational monopolist, after reviewing his cost and demand position, would set price and output so as to make maximum profit. But will he always do this? May there not be reasons why price will sometimes be set either above or below the most profitable level?

The only reason for setting price above the most profitable level would be ignorance. Conservative and tradition-bound industries sometimes refuse to lower prices even though they could increase profits by doing so. This behavior may arise from a mistaken belief that demand is very inelastic and that lower prices will make little difference to sales. The railroads, for example, have typically resisted pressure for lower passenger fares. When forced to reduce fares, they have sometimes been surprised to find that demand was more elastic than they had supposed, and that profits were higher or losses smaller at the lower rates.

A stronger possibility, however, is that the monopolist may charge less than the price which would yield largest immediate profit. Unless the company's monopoly position is very secure, it may fear that large profits will tempt new producers to enter the industry. It will therefore try to make its profits *look* as small as possible, partly by bookkeeping devices, but partly by accepting genuinely lower profits than it could get. Another possible reason for not charging maximum prices is that large profits stimulate the union's appetite for wage increases. Thus large profits resulting from high prices may turn out to be purely temporary. It may be wiser strategy to set prices at a lower level, earn good but not exorbitant profits, and be in a position to take a firmer stand on wage rates. This may also be good public relations vis-à-vis government agencies.

To the extent that such motives are operative, our conclusions need to be qualified. Monopoly price still is likely to be higher than competitive price, and output correspondingly lower. But the difference is not as great as it would be if the urge toward profit maximization operated without restraint.

THE SMALL GROUP: OLIGOPOLY

Very often one finds a few sellers sharing a particular market. This is especially common in local markets—the small city with its half-dozen banks, three or four building contractors, a few movie theatre operators, and so on. But it occurs also in many industries producing for the national market. The list of industries in which a few companies provide most of the output reads like a *Who's Who* of American manufacturing. It includes aircraft, automobiles, basic steel, cigarettes, copper rolling, distilling, heavy electrical equipment, railroad cars and locomotives, soap, sugar refining, synthetic fibres, telephone equipment, and tires.

The seller in this sort of market is in a very different position from the seller under pure competition. An outstanding characteristic of pure competition is its anonymity. Each seller keeps his eye fixed on the market price, and decides how much to produce and sell independently of anyone else. He doesn't need to know who the other sellers in the market are or to take any account of their reactions.

Suppose, however, that you are the vice-president in charge of sales at Goodyear Tire. You are not selling at a fluctuating market price. You are selling at a list of quoted prices for different tire sizes and types, which you determine and which stays unchanged for weeks or months at a time. In setting these prices you are not a free agent. Your price list has to look much like those of Firestone, U.S. Rubber, and General Tire. Indeed, prices will normally be identical, because any company which was above the others would lose business. You can be certain that if you lower your prices, the other companies will follow, and if anyone else cuts prices, you will have to come into line. In short, you have to take account of rival sellers and to estimate their reactions to your decisions. This is the characteristic feature of oligopoly.

Setting the "Right" Price

There is no generally accepted theory of pricing under oligopoly, and probably cannot be because of the great variety of conditions in different industries. But we can indicate some of the things on which the outcome may depend.

As a beginning, look back at Figure 7–1. Suppose this industry, instead of being controlled by one company, is divided among several companies. For simplicity, suppose that all companies have the same level of production costs, OP. The industry demand curve is DD as before.

What will happen? If company executives are interested in maximum profit, one might expect them to do just what a monopolist would do in the same situation. They will put their heads together and agree on the maximum-profit price OP_1. Total output of the industry will then be OQ_1 as before. The main difference from the monopoly case is that the industry's sales are now divided among several companies, and this may lead to argument over what share of the total business each company should have.

Prices doubtless are fixed at or near the maximum-profit level in some cases. But this may not happen, and it is important to explore the various reasons why it may not happen.

One difficulty is that private price fixing is illegal in the United States. If rival producers get together and agree to observe a set price for a product sold in interstate commerce, they are violating the antitrust laws. This prevents open, formal arrangements to control prices and production. In some countries members of an industry can legally form a trade association or cartel which sets prices, allots production quotas to each company, and regulates admission of new companies to the industry. Such associations are illegal in the United States and have never gained a firm foothold.

So price fixing is illegal. But most businessmen do not feel that it is *wrong*. Indeed, when demand is falling and profits are low they are apt to argue that it is essential. When the law prohibits something which many people still want to do, the effect is to drive the prohibited practices underground. There is much informal evasion of the antitrust laws, which is hard to discover and eliminate. The telephone still works, and the quiet talk in a corner of the golf club can be quite effective.

A common control device is *price leadership*. Price changes are announced first by some bellwether company, perhaps U.S. Steel for steel prices, one of the Standard Oil companies for oil products, and so on. The "leader" in an industry need not always be the same company, but may change from time to time. Once the leader has spoken, everyone else in the industry announces an identical price change.

How does the leader decide where to set prices? In some cases, leadership is a cloak for a secret price agreement. The industry confers on a change, and one company is selected to announce it. But this is not necessarily the case. The leader may have some independence of judgment and action. Other members of the industry, in effect, delegate to one company the responsibility of working out price strategy for the group. This company may be selected because it is big, because it is the traditional pacesetter, or because of a strong figure in the company's management. But the leader is not free to do anything he may feel like. Unless he takes account of the interests and views of other companies, he will not remain leader indefinitely.

This is one way of getting controlled pricing without the necessity of a conference before every price move. Some court decisions have termed this method "conscious parallelism of action." The U.S. Department of Justice has attacked it under the antitrust laws, but its legal status is still unclear. It is difficult to see what could be done about it even if it were eventually held illegal. One can scarcely forbid rival companies to match each others' price changes, since an identical product must be sold at about the same price by all producers.

Some Obstacles to Price Agreement

The antitrust laws are not the only obstacle to price fixing. There are other reasons why "gentlemen's agreements" about prices may break down or may lead to prices below what a monopolist would charge:

1. It makes considerable difference whether there are three companies in an industry or 30 companies. If there are only two or three producers, prices can be controlled by telephone or mental telepathy. If there are several dozen companies, it takes a good deal of discussion and paperwork. This leaves a trail which antitrust investigators can pick up.

2. If there are enough producers, there are likely to be a few "uncooperative" ones. One reason may be the existence of substantial cost differences in the industry. The assumption that all producers have the same cost level is usually not justified in practice. Consider an industry in which production costs for most companies fall in the range $1.00 to $1.10 per unit. Several companies, however, are able to produce for $0.80 per unit. These low-cost producers have the whip hand. They may decide to follow a policy of "live and let live," and go along with the in-

dustry on a price of, say, $1.10. This will cover the costs of all companies and yield the low-cost concerns a handsome profit. On the other hand, they may prefer a strategy of "cut and expand." They may cut prices to, say, $0.90 per unit. This will gradually force higher-cost companies out of the industry and allow the low-cost companies to take over more of the market. To the extent that there are low-cost companies with expansionist aspirations, it will be hard for the industry to follow a high-price policy.

3. In some cases an industry is divided between producers of advertised national brands sold at a relatively high price, and producers of unbranded merchandise who must undersell the national brands in order to win a market. It is difficult to line this second group up behind a price agreement, since their very existence depends on lower and more flexible prices. Producers of unbranded nylon hosiery, for example, have never been willing to cooperate with the big-name manufacturers on price strategy.

4. There may be other differences of economic interest among members of an industry. There may be honest differences of opinion about the location of the industry demand curve. Or there may be old-fashioned individualists in the industry who object to price fixing as a matter of principle. Harvey Firestone, Sr., was such a person, and his insistence on independent action was one reason for severe price competition in the tire industry during his lifetime. Henry Ford played a similar role in the early days of automobile manufacturing.

5. The pressure of large buyers such as Sears Roebuck, Macy's, or A & P helps to break down price agreements among manufacturers. By dangling a large order under a manufacturer's nose, and by threatening to shift the order to another manufacturer, they can sometimes induce a company to cut prices. Some large retailers have also set up their own manufacturing units.

Where the mass distributor buys from a multitude of small pea canneries, shoe factories, or pants producers, it may exert pressure which is severe and even unfair. But the situation is different for the large manufacturers of electric appliances, tires, paint, or window glass in their dealings with Sears Roebuck or Montgomery Ward. These people are big enough to hold their own, and without some counterweight would probably take advantage of the consumer. The mass distributor, by exercising what Galbraith has termed "countervailing power," produces a more equal balance of forces in the market and a lower level of prices.

6. Even though a few companies produce 60 or 70 percent of an industry's output, there may be numerous small producers who share the remainder of the market. Their existence depends on being able to sell at lower prices than their larger rivals. If the big fellows raise prices too much, the advantage of the small companies increases, their sales expand and begin to cut seriously into the sales of the big companies, and the lat-

ter may be forced to beat a retreat. The existence of a fringe of small competitors thus exerts a restraining influence on the price policies of the industry leaders.

Where entrance to an industry is easy, *potential* competition also has a restraining influence. If prices are high and profits attractive, new companies will come in. Unless the leading companies are astute enough to follow a moderate price policy, they will gradually lose ground. There are numerous cases in which a "trust" once controlled 70 percent of an industry but now has only 20 or 30 percent.

For these reasons all one can really say about pricing under oligopoly is, "it depends." Price will usually settle at a level somewhere *between* that which would be charged by a single monopolist and that which would exist under pure competition. It is probable that the larger the number of companies in the industry, the more closely will price approach the competitive level. But this is simply a hypothesis, and it would be difficult to prove that it *must* be so.

Other Reasons Why Profit May Disappear

1. *New producers.* Take a case in which price does get set at a level which yields profit to companies in the industry. This is not necessarily the end of the matter. Forces may be set in motion which will erode the profits and bring producers out no better off than they would be under pure competition.

The solid lines in Figure 7–2 show the position of one company in our profitable oligopoly industry as the curtain rises. *ATC* is the average total cost curve of Chapter 6. Since it includes a normal return, any price above *ATC* yields profit.

DD is a new kind of demand curve—a demand curve, not for the industry as a whole, but for this particular company. It shows how much the company will be able to sell at various price levels, assuming that everyone in the industry charges the same price and that this company's share of the market does not change. *DD*, in short, is a small replica of the total demand curve for the product. If the company's market share should change for any reason, *DD* will shift correspondingly—upward for a larger share, downward for a smaller one.

The illustration works out best if we assume that the cost and demand curves of all companies in the industry are identical. When the company shown in Figure 7–2 is making money, everybody is making money. What happens to it happens to everybody.

Suppose members of the industry get together and agree on the price *OP*. Our company will then produce *OQ*, and will enjoy a substantial profit. Unless it is possible to bar people from the industry, however, this high profit level will attract a flow of new producers. The available business will be split up finer and finer and the market share of the old companies will decline, i.e., their demand curves will shift downward to the left. This can go on until each company is earning no more than a normal competitive return. This would happen if demand fell to the position D_1D_1 where it just touches the ATC curve. Each company still is getting the agreed price OP but is able to sell only OQ_1, about half as much as before.

Things cannot get worse than this—at least, they cannot *remain* worse. If still more newcomers enter the industry and demand falls completely below ATC, some companies will decide to go out of the business,

FIGURE 7–2

Possible Oligopoly Adjustments

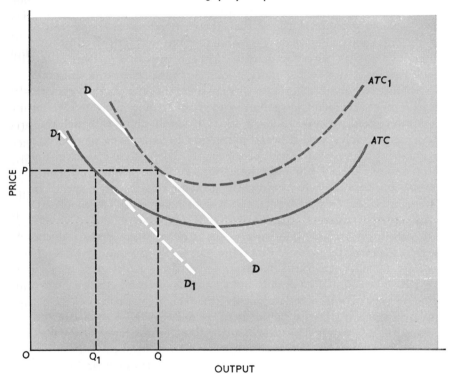

DD and ATC are the demand and cost curves for a typical company in an oligopoly industry. The company is able at the outset to earn profit by selling OQ units at price OP. But this surplus may be eliminated *either* because entrance of more companies forces this company's demand curve down to D_1D_1, or because competitive selling expenditures force its cost curve up to ATC_1.

and D_1D_1 will begin to rise again. The position in which D_1D_1 is just tangent to ATC is thus an equilibrium position for an oligopoly group with no limits on entrance. It corresponds to the equilibrium adjustment under pure competition, in which the horizontal price line just touches the minimum of the ATC curve.

What is wrong with this equilibrium from a public standpoint? Companies in the industry are making only normal returns. Each company, however, is operating much below capacity, i.e., below the minimum point on its *ATC* curve. Plants are partially idle because too many companies have come in to take advantage of the fixed price. The commitment of resources to the industry is greater than needed for the volume of output, and this constitutes economic waste. The monopoly gap between price and unit cost has been closed, not by price coming down, but by unit costs being forced up. Price remains too high and output too low compared with competitive standards.

2. *Selling expenses.* Suppose companies in the industry are able to maintain the fixed price *OP and* to bar new producers. Are their profits then completely secure? Not necessarily. Some companies in the industry may want to get more business than they are getting at the agreed price. If we look back at Figure 7–2, we note that output *OQ* is well below production capacity. Any company which can put some of this excess capacity to work by selling more goods can raise its profits substantially.

How to get more business? It may seem that the obvious answer is to put on more salesmen and spend more on advertising. This involves an assumption about the product itself. It must be something to which the producer can attach a special brand name, and he must have some chance of persuading buyers that it has special merits not possessed by rival brands. In economic parlance, it must be a *differentiated* product rather than a *standardized* product. It would make no sense to advertise a special brand of spring wheat or steel billets; but it does make sense for toothpaste, or soap, or cigarettes.

How does advertising operate? It is often asserted that advertising *creates* demand. But it would be more correct to say that advertising tries to *shift* demand. American Tobacco's advertising is designed to get people to smoke more of its brands and to raise its demand curve by lowering those of other companies. It is possible that the intense barrage of cigarette advertising to which the public is subjected may raise *total* demand for cigarettes. But where does this demand come from? Since consumers' incomes are the same as before, it must come from *reduced* consumption of some other product. Once more, the effect is a *shift* in demand rather than an addition to total consumer demand. Advertising could *create* demand only if, by making the public more eager for goods in general, it raised the percentage of total consumer income spent and reduced the proportion saved.

In the present case, each company tries through increased advertising to shift its demand curve to the right. How will this work out? If one company's advertising agency comes up this year with an especially ingenious slogan, it may win sales for the time being. Over the long run, however, these temporary victories tend to cancel out. If the agencies working for competing companies are equally expert, the result may be to leave everyone's demand curve in about the same position. The advertising race in fact bears some resemblance to an armaments race among nations. When country A raises its arms budget, country B must do likewise. So too with advertising. If Ford appropriates more money for advertising next year, Chrysler and General Motors must do the same.

But while advertising may not affect demand curves very much, it certainly affects cost curves. Substantial sales costs are now added on top of production costs, and ATC shifts upward to the right. There is no natural check on this process until costs reach the level shown by ATC_1 in Figure 7–2. Here the cost curve just touches the demand curve, which we suppose has not been changed by the advertising struggle, and each company is making only normal returns.

It may be regarded as irrational to carry selling expenses to this length. Companies could reduce costs and increase profits by holding a "disarmament conference" and agreeing to cut their advertising budgets. Why don't they do this? Well, why do international disarmament conferences seem always to end in failure? There may be some parallel between the rivalry of national states and the empire-building proclivities of big business executives. In addition, the advertising industry has worked long and successfully to create a certain mystique of advertising, a conviction in the business world that it *must* somehow pay off.

Oligopoly, Monopoly, and Competition

Oligopoly resembles monopoly in that sellers possess market power and may agree to hold prices above the competitive level. But under oligopoly this result is not so certain. The larger the number of producers, the less likely it is that they will be able to maintain a firm price agreement. Oligopoly control of a market is shakier than monopoly control, and this is an advantage to consumers. Moreover, the fact that oligopolists compete actively with each other in areas other than price may generate more rapid improvement of products and production methods than would occur under monopoly. If automobile production had been monopolized by a single company since 1900, it seems unlikely that we should have the variety and quality of automobiles available at present.

There are some costs to be weighed against these advantages. An oligopoly group may subject itself to heavy advertising and selling expenses which a single monopolist could avoid; and it may be plagued by idle plant capacity which raises unit costs and wastes economic resources. On the whole, however, oligopoly seems preferable to monopoly in most situations.

Oligopoly does not, however, attain the standard of economic efficiency which one would expect of a purely competitive industry: absence of surplus profit, full use of capacity, absence of competitive selling costs, flexible pricing, and quick responsiveness to demand or cost changes. But this conclusion is perhaps academic. The industries in which oligopoly now prevails cannot be converted into purely competitive industries. We must live with oligopoly, like it or not. What might be done to improve the economic performance of oligopolistic industries will be explored in Chapter 11.

MONOPOLISTIC COMPETITION

Even when there are many sellers in a market, their products may not be identical in the eyes of consumers. Hence the conditions of pure competition are not met. *Monopolistic competition* is a situation in which there are many sellers but buyers have preferences among them. Each seller has his own demand curve, its elasticity reflecting the strength of buyers' preferences for his particular shop, brand, or what not.

The most important actual cases of this sort are probably in the retailing and service industries. The most important basis for buyer preference in these cases is geography—the cost and inconvenience of going long distances to shop. If it were not for this factor, everyone in a city might buy groceries at a single enormous supermarket. But most people prefer to shop close to home, and this provides the basis for a network of small and medium-sized stores throughout the city.

Another important possibility is *brand preference* for the product of a particular manufacturer. Cases of brand preference, however, are usually also cases of oligopoly, in which case they are covered by the discussion of the previous section.

The main economic consequence of monopolistic competition is that there will be more sellers in the industry than there would be under pure competition, and that their average size will be smaller. The fact that stores or other producing units are smaller may mean higher costs per unit of goods sold, in which case consumers will have to pay higher prices than under pure competition. But this cannot be considered economically inefficient, since the smaller scale of operations is a *result* of consumer preferences. If we accept these preferences, we must accept the results which follow from them. Where the preference is based on *location*, consumers get an obvious *quid pro quo* through not having to travel so far to shop.

The demand curves of individual sellers are likely to be quite elastic, so that each seller has little market power and will not deviate much from the prices charged by other sellers. Where this is true, the consequences of monopolistic competition do not differ importantly from those of pure competition. People will move into and out of the industry in response to demand shifts, price will just cover average unit cost, and both cost and price will be near the competitive level.

THE USEFULNESS OF COMPETITIVE REASONING

In Chapters 5 and 6 we developed the central ideas of supply-demand analysis under conditions of pure competition. But it now turns out that some industries are monopolistic, others oligopolistic, still others characterized by monopolistic competition. Together such situations make up most of the economy, and pure competition is a rarity. What does this do to the practical usefulness of supply-demand analysis? Is there "life in the old dogmas yet"? Or must we discard the theory of competitive markets?

One can work up a heated argument on this subject in a group of economists. Certainly we cannot decide the issue here. But a few comments are in order:

1. The idea of an *economic system*, a mechanism of interrelated product and factor markets, is largely unaffected by the presence of monopoly power in the economy. It remains true that events in one market will have repercussions throughout the system, and that it is important to trace out these repercussions.

2. The direction of *adjustment to change* remains the same under different types of market structure. A rise in an industry's demand curve normally will produce an increase in output under monopoly as under competition, and conversely for a decrease in demand. A decrease in costs normally leads to lower prices and larger output in any market context.

3. A telling point on the other side is that if one takes a "slice" through the economy at any moment of time, a flashbulb picture rather than a time exposure, one will *not* find things working out as they would under atomistic competition. Some industries will have unduly high prices and unduly small outputs. Some companies will be making profits which they could not make under pure competition.

4. But the monopoly or oligopoly price may not be as different from the competitive price as one might think. If sellers were always perfectly organized, perfectly informed and self-interested, and confronted only by small unorganized buyers, one would expect to find excessive prices. But one or more of these conditions may fail. Monopolists will not always seek the largest immediate profit. Oligopolists may fall out. It may prove impossible to bar new competitors from the industry. The market power of large buyers may partially offset that of sellers.

5. Atomistic competition, interpreted broadly to include monopolistic competition, still covers a sizable segment of the economy. Agriculture remains atomistic on the production side, despite government price controls. Most retailing and service activity, much of building construction, and perhaps a third of manufacturing output approaches conditions of atomistic competition.

6. The *tools of analysis* developed for competitive markets may be useful in other situations even though the *results* of the analysis differ. Note that in reasoning about monopoly and oligopoly behavior we found ourselves using the demand and cost concepts developed in earlier chapters. Until someone comes along with a superior toolkit, it makes sense to keep on using what we have.

SUMMARY

1. Monopoly power exists in a market when a single seller or buyer is able to influence the market price. Viewed from the selling side, one can distinguish three situations: (*a*) *monopoly*, where one seller provides the entire supply of a good or service; (*b*) *oligopoly*, where there are few enough sellers so that each must take account of rival sellers and estimate their reactions to his own decisions; (*c*) *monopolistic competition*, where there are many sellers, but the product of one seller is not a perfect substitute for that of another.

2. Under monopoly, price will be higher and the quantity produced smaller than would be the case under pure competition. Monopoly distorts the allocation of resources by admitting too little labor and capital to the monopolized area, thereby forcing more resources to seek employment in other (competitive) sectors of the economy.

3. Under oligopoly, price may settle anywhere between the level which would be charged by a single monopolist and the level which would exist under pure competition; and quantity produced will vary correspondingly. While it might be logical for oligopolists to agree on the monopoly price, there are several reasons why this may not actually happen: price fixing is illegal; there may be differences of economic interest among the oligopolists; pressure by large buyers may break down the united front of sellers; and numerous small producers may exert a restraining influence on the large producers.

4. Even if oligopolists can agree on a profitable price, profits may be eroded by the entrance of new producers or by the growth of selling expenses. Below-capacity operation and excessive selling expenses are common sources of waste in oligopoly industries.

5. Monopolistic competition leads to sellers being smaller and more numerous than would be the case under pure competition; but this cannot be considered wasteful, since it occurs in response to consumers' preferences.

6. The theory of pure competition developed in Chapters 5 and 6 is useful even when monopoly power is present. The results of monopolistic competition do not differ basically from those of pure competition; and the two situations together cover perhaps two thirds of total production. Even a monopoly or oligopoly price may not be as different from the competitive price as one might expect. Moreover, competitive theory continues to be useful in predicting adjustments to change in demand or cost conditions.

Labor Markets and Wage Determination

A man's value is that which he sets upon himself.

RABELAIS

As in other things, so in men; not the seller but the buyer determines the price.
For let a man (as most men do) rate themselves at the highest value they can;
yet their true value is no more than it is esteemed by others."

THOMAS HOBBES, Leviathan

THE LAST THREE CHAPTERS were concerned with the product markets at
the right-hand side of our economic flow chart. We turn now to examine
the markets in which households supply labor and capital to business organizations.

The linkage between what we have been discussing and what we
are going to discuss comes through the concept of *cost*. We have said that
a business concern has production costs, and that the shape of supply
curves depends on how costs change as the quantity of production
changes. But the nature of costs has been left in the background. We must
now look more carefully at what these costs are and how they are determined.

Much the most important cost item in the economy is labor. Wages
and salaries form about 80 percent of the value of output originating in
manufacturing. In fields which use less labor and more capital, the labor
cost ratio is lower. In electric and gas utilities, for example, it is about 50
percent. For the economy as a whole, however, employee compensation

is better than 70 percent of national income produced. If we can explain how wages and salaries are determined, then, we shall have done most of the job of explaining production costs.

Remember that *labor* means every kind of human effort exerted in production. It does not mean manual labor only. One can speak of the labor of an executive vice-president and the price (salary) of that labor. The doctor and lawyer are selling labor, for which their fee is the price. Whenever anyone receives payment for personal effort, we treat the effort as labor and the payment as a wage.

Why was John Andrews, a Grade A machinist in the Kaiser Steel mill in Fontana, California, earning $3.75 an hour in June, 1963? Why not $2.00 or $5.00? Andrews' earnings are influenced by several things: (1) The *general level of wages* prevailing in the United States. If Andrews were a machinist in Italy, Japan, or India his earnings would be different. This is the most important single factor in the situation.

2. Andrews belongs to a particular *occupation*, which occupies a certain niche in the American wage structure. Machinists earn more than janitors but less than locomotive engineers or dentists.

3. Andrews is employed in a particular *company* and *industry*, in a certain *locality*, and in this case under the terms of a *union* contract. Each of these things will have some influence on his earnings.

In order to explain Andrews' earnings, then, we must explain the general wage level of the United States, the wage level for machinists relative to other occupational groups, and the variation of machinists' earnings depending on the locality, industry, and company in which they are employed. To do this is the task of the next three sections. The procedure is to work downward from the general to the specific, seeking by successive approximations to explain Andrews' $3.75 an hour as completely as possible.

THE GENERAL WAGE LEVEL: MARGINAL PRODUCTIVITY ANALYSIS

What determines the level of real wages in a country and the rate of increase in wages over the course of time? This is the most basic question one can ask about wage determination. The explanation offered here, usually termed the *marginal productivity theory* of wages, was worked out by Alfred Marshall of Cambridge and John Bates Clark of Columbia around 1890. While the theory has been refined since their day, it has not been changed basically by later economists.

It seems reasonable that what workers receive is related to what they produce. But what determines how much labor will produce at a particular time and place? Two things, say Marshall and Clark: the quantity of labor employed, and the quantities of land, capital, and other resources available to support labor's efforts.

Let us explore this idea through a simple illustration. Imagine a small agricultural country containing 10,000 square miles of arable land. The owners of the land do not work it themselves, but employ hired labor for this purpose. There are certain known methods of cultivation, which remain unchanged. The supply of tools and equipment also remains constant, but the *form* of this equipment can be varied so as to cooperate most effectively with whatever quantity of labor happens to be available. If there are only a few workers, they can ride combine harvesters; but if population is extremely dense, each man may have to get along with a spade. This may seem at first an odd and unrealistic assumption. Yet given enough time, there is no doubt that the form taken by capital in a country *is* adapted to the amount of labor available.

The supply of *all productive resources other than labor* is thus constant, and we ask what will happen to output as the quantity of labor is varied. If only 10,000 hired workers are available, each will have a square mile of land and a lot of equipment at his disposal, and output per man should be high. If another 10,000 are added, the new workers may still produce almost as much as the earlier ones. Each will have half a square mile, which is still a good deal of land, and each acre can be cultivated more thoroughly than before. As more and more workers are added, however, the amount which each adds to total output—the *marginal productivity of labor*—will decline steadily, since each man has less and less land and equipment at his disposal. At the extreme, one would reach the situation of some Asiatic countries, where each man digs with his simple tools on an acre of land and produces very little.

The classical economists called this *the law of diminishing returns*. If increasing quantities of one factor (in this case labor) are employed in production, the quantities of all other factors remaining unchanged, additional units of the variable factor will after a certain point add decreasing amounts to total output. While we have developed this principle for an agricultural economy, it applies to industrial operations as well. If the quantity of buildings, machinery, and other capital goods remains fixed, adding more and more labor will add less and less to total output.

The operation of our hypothetical economy is illustrated by Figure 8–1. *DE* shows the marginal product of labor, i.e., the amount added to national output by employment of additional workers. It slopes downward because of the law of variable proportions. Suppose the number of workers available for employment at a particular time is *OA;* and suppose also that these workers are identical in skill and efficiency, so that no one man is worth more to employers than any other. What will be the price of labor in this situation?

If all *OA* workers are employed, the last man added will have a marginal product of *AB*. This is what he adds to total output. His wage rate cannot be more than *AB*, for then it would not pay to employ him. If the labor market is competitive, his wage cannot be less than *AB;* for if it were, employers would see a chance to make a profit by hiring him for less than his marginal product and would bid for his services. Competition among employers for labor will insure that the worker receives his full marginal product, *AB*, but no more than this.

It follows that no worker in the system can receive a wage higher than *AB*. It may seem that the men above the margin—the men to the left of *A* on the *x*-axis—are being cheated by this arrangement. They seem to be producing more than they are getting. If all workers are of equal efficiency, however, they are interchangeable with each other. The "marginal man" is not marginal in the sense of being particularly stupid or incompetent. He is simply the last man on the scene. If a man doing a particularly vital job were to drop out, a man could be taken from the margin

FIGURE 8–1

Determination of the General Wage Level

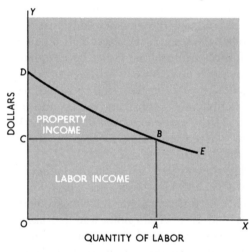

DE shows the marginal physical productivity of labor. It is also the demand schedule for labor. If the amount of labor available is OA, the rate of wages will be OC.

to replace him. Hence one man cannot earn more than another. This follows also from the definition of a competitive market. In such a market there can be only one price for the product—in this case only one wage for a specified quality of labor.

The total output of the economy in this situation is the area *OABD*. Of this amount labor receives *OABC*, the wage rate *AB* multiplied by the number of workers employed *OA*. The remaining area *BCD* goes to the owners of land and capital. The analysis thus yields a division of national output between labor income and property income.

SOME APPLICATIONS OF MARGINAL PRODUCTIVITY

This simplified reasoning may seem remote from the conditions of real life. Yet it leads to sensible conclusions, which could almost (but not quite!) have been reached by commonsense methods. The main conclusions are:

1. *The level of real wages varies inversely with the quantity of labor available in the economy.* Other things equal, the *larger* the supply of labor the *lower* will be the level of real wages. This helps to explain why densely populated countries such as India have lower wage levels than more sparsely populated countries such as Canada or the United States.

2. But this is clearly not the whole story. Britain is very densely populated, yet has one of the highest wage levels in the world. The wage level depends, not only on the quantity of labor OA, but on the height of the productivity curve DE. *Real wages vary directly with the productivity of labor.*

What determines the height of DE? The main factors are:

a) Availability of *natural resources*—soil fertility, climate, mineral and oil deposits, and so on.

b) The *quantity of capital goods* available. An economy which is rich in productive equipment will have greater output per man than one which is not.

c) The *state of technology.* A single invention, such as hybrid corn or synthetic fibers, may enable the same quantities of labor and capital to turn out several times as much product as before.

d) The *quality of the labor force.* The same number of people may turn out more or less product, depending on their health, education, technical training, and motivation.

e) The effectiveness of *economic organization.* This includes management efficiency in particular plants and industries. At a higher level, it means the effectiveness with which the whole production apparatus of a country is coordinated through the market mechanism or in other ways. Particularly important is the speed with which resources can be shifted from areas of the economy where their productivity is relatively low to other sectors where their output would be greater.

Labor productivity depends, in short, on the supplies of the other resources which cooperate with labor in production. Any increase in these supplies will raise the productivity curve and the level of real wages, while a reduction will have the opposite effect.

3. Marginal productivity analysis helps to explain *changes in the wage level* over the course of time. One basic consideration is the behavior of labor supply. Population is normally growing, which tends to increase the supply of labor. But this may be partially offset by a reduced propensity to work as income levels rise. Man does not live by consumption alone. Leisure is also one of the good things of life, and as incomes rise people may decide to enjoy greater leisure. Thus the number of man-hours of work forthcoming from a given population is likely to fall.

While labor supply tends to rise less rapidly than population, it is still likely to rise somewhat. Increased labor supply by itself would make for lower real wages. But here enters a second element in the situation: In a progressive economy the productivity curve DE will normally be shifting upward because of technical progress and increases in capital supply, and this tends to *raise* wages. The actual course of wages, then, depends on a race between population and productivity. If the labor force is growing rapidly while the rise of productivity is sluggish, real wages may stagnate or decline. Many of the less developed countries are in this situation. But if increases in productivity keep ahead of the growth of the labor force, real wages will rise. This has been the normal situation in the United States over the past century.

Our most reliable information on wage changes relates to manufacturing industry. The increase in real hourly earnings in manufacturing from 1889 to 1957 is shown in Figure 8–2. The size and steadiness of the increase is impressive. In 1957 an hour of work yielded almost five times as much real income as did an hour of work in 1889. Note also the close parallel between the rise of real wages and the increase in physical output per man-hour.[1] Rising productivity (which of course must itself be explained) is the proximate explanation of the rapid rise in wage levels.

4. This analysis throws light on the possible influence of unionism on wages. There is no question that unions can sometimes raise wages for a particular occupation, plant, or industry. But can they raise wages appreciably for the labor force as a whole? If so, they would have to do it in one of the following ways:

a) Reducing the supply of labor, or at least reducing the *rate of increase* in labor supply. Unions might press for legislation restricting work by young people, or encouraging earlier retirement of older workers, or reducing the flow of immigrants from other countries. Shorter hours of work and longer vacations also reduce labor supply by cutting the number of hours each person works in a year's time.

b) Unionism might shift the productivity curve upward or downward. Many management people argue that union restrictions on work speeds and production methods have reduced productive efficiency. Unionists, on the other hand, often argue that union pressure for higher wages stimulates efficiency by making management work harder to improve production methods and find ways of paying the higher wages. Both effects doubtless exist, but it is hard to judge their relative importance.

c) We have been supposing that labor markets are perfectly competitive. But, argues the unionist, this is often not true. Consider the one-company town, where the employer sets the wage and says, "Take it or leave it." Workers may take it because of the lack of nearby opportunities, even though the wage is below rates in other areas and the company is making surplus profits. If these workers organize a union and put pressure on the employer by threatening a strike, they may be able to raise

---

[1] The productivity index covers the entire private economy, while the wage index relates to manufacturing only. The two are thus not strictly comparable. If we had a wage index for the whole economy, however, it would probably not move very differently from the index for manufacturing.

FIGURE 8–2

Man-hour Output and Real Hourly Earnings in Manufacturing, United States, 1889–1957 (Indexes, 1929 = 100)

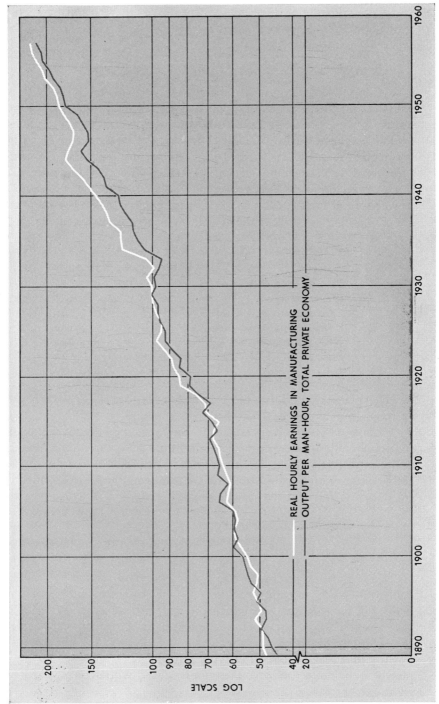

Source: Solomon Fabricant, *Basic Facts on Productivity Change*, National Bureau of Economic Research, 1958.

wages considerably at the expense of profits. If there are many such cases throughout the economy, unionism can produce some increase in the general wage level.

WAGES FOR A PARTICULAR OCCUPATION

George Jackson, a coal miner in Harlan County, Kentucky, is not interested in the average wage level of the country. He is interested in wages for coal mining. Every occupational group is interested in its specific wage, and there are wide differences in earnings above and below the general average. In April, 1962, manufacturing workers received an average of $2.39 an hour. At the bottom of the scale, however, limited price variety store employees averaged only $1.18, while at the top electrical contract construction workers were earning around $4.00. Average hourly earnings of production workers in various fields in April, 1962, were as follows:

Mining	$2.71
Contract construction	3.26
Manufacturing	2.39
Durable	2.56
Nondurable	2.16
Wholesale trade	2.35
Retail trade	1.74
Banks	1.92

What explains these differences? Why may one sort of work pay three or four times as much as another?

Look at a particular occupation, such as coal mining. It will be useful to begin by asking how the wage rate for coal miners would be determined under pure competition. Supply-demand analysis will carry us a considerable distance on this problem, and we can bring the United Mine Workers onto the stage at the proper point.

The Supply of Labor

It seems reasonable that the supply curve will slope upward in the usual way (Figure 8–3). More people will be willing to work as coal miners at a high wage level than at a lower one. Coal mining is difficult and dangerous work. If employers offer low wages, many men in the minefields will say, "It just isn't worth it," and drift away in search of other jobs. As the wage rate is raised, however, more and more people will stomach their dislike of the work and conclude, "Well, I still don't like it; but for that much money I'm willing to do it." Unless people are completely oblivious to money, the supply curve will slope upward to the right.

But it may slope upward more or less steeply. What determines the position of the labor supply curve? One can think of several influences:

1. Only a certain number of people have the native abilities required for such occupations as wine tasting, opera singing, or championship tennis. In this event the number of workers cannot be increased by offering more money, and supply is completely inelastic.

2. Some people may have such a strong preference for a particular career that money has little influence on them. The supply of would-be novelists or painters is probably quite inelastic on this account.

FIGURE 8–3

The Wage Rate for Coal Miners

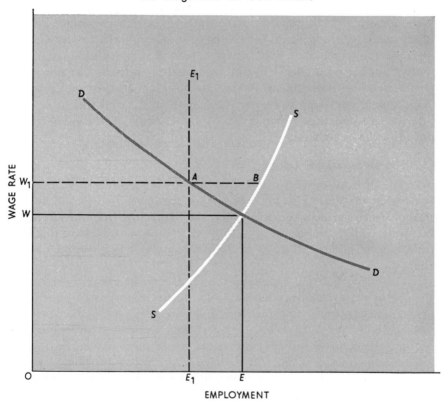

DD and SS are the demand and supply curves for coal miners. Under pure competition, OE workers would be employed at a wage of OW. A strong union might insist on the wage OW₁, but in this event only OE₁ workers would be hired.

3. Some occupations have a long training period. If more college freshmen decide in 1965 to become doctors, this will not increase the supply of doctors in practice until about 1975. This is almost as true of lawyers, scientists, and college teachers. In this situation the supply curve will be highly inelastic for short periods, but its elasticity will increase with the length of time considered. The "10-year elasticity" will be considerably higher than the "one-year elasticity."

4. Entrance to an occupation may be controlled by a licensing system, a trade association, or a union. In this case there is no necessary connection between the number who would like to work in the occupation and the number actually admitted to it. The potential supply may be quite large, but the number actually working may be fixed.

5. Geographical isolation is an important factor in some situations, including our coal mining case. Mining areas are usually one-industry areas, with few alternative opportunities available nearby. This ties workers more closely to their jobs than would be true in a diversified industrial area, and labor supply is quite inelastic.

What practical difference does the shape of the supply curve make? A completely inelastic supply curve would mean that the wage is determined *solely* by the demand for the labor in question. If the demand for opera stars is high, they will live well, and if it is low they will live poorly, but their number will not be affected. Shifts in demand affect only wages, not employment. In the case of an occupation with a highly elastic supply curve, on the other hand, shifts in demand will make little difference to the wage but will have a large effect on the number employed in the occupation.

The Demand for Labor

The demand curve for coal miners is shown by *DD* in Figure 8–3. The higher the wage rate for coal miners, the fewer miners will be employed. We learned in Chapter 5 that the higher the price of anything, the smaller will be the quantity purchased. It is easy to see why this is so in the case of goods and services. But why should it be so in the case of labor?

Consider what will happen as the wage rate for miners is increased. A wage increase raises production costs. Some of the more poorly endowed mines will now find that their costs are above the market price of coal, and will have to shut down. Others may find that it no longer pays to work the deepest and thinnest seams where costs are highest. They will continue operating but will produce less than before. The output of coal will fall off and its price will rise. In the case of an atomistic industry such as bituminous coal, the rise in price and fall in output will be gradual and unplanned. Where price is controlled under monopoly or oligopoly, the sequence of events is more rapid and direct. Producers, seeing that production costs have risen, will mark up prices to cover the increased cost.

The next step involves the effect of higher coal prices on sales of coal. Coal is in competition with oil and other fuels, and U.S. coal competes to some extent with coal from other countries. The demand curve for U.S. coal is thus rather elastic. Price increases will involve a considerable drop in sales, and therefore in coal production. This is the first reason why higher wages will mean reduced employment.

There is a second reason for the slope of the labor demand curve.

An increase in wage levels stimulates employers to look around for labor-saving machinery which will enable them to produce the same output with fewer workers. It will pay to install mechanical equipment whenever the saving in labor costs is more than sufficient to cover the cost of the machine. The higher that wage rates go, the greater the replacement of labor by machinery, and the lower the volume of employment.

Take a simple example. A company is considering buying a machine which can do the work of three men and will cost $10,000 a year for depreciation, interest, and other charges. If a man's yearly earnings are $3,000, say 2,000 hours at $1.50 an hour, the saving in labor costs is $3 \times \$3,000 = \$9,000$. Since the saving is less than the cost of the machine, it will not be purchased. But if wages rise to $1.75 an hour, the saving becomes $3 \times \$3,500 = \$10,500$. Now it will pay to buy the machine, and there will be three fewer workers hired.

This has been an important factor in coal mining. There has been a great increase in use of power coal-cutters, conveyor systems, open-strip mining, and other mechanical devices. The rapid rise of wage levels, by stimulating these developments, has made for a faster drop in employment.

Note that this argument is carried out under the strict rules of supply-demand analysis used in Chapter 5. The basic rule is that conditions outside the market we are studying are given and constant. Specifically, all other wage rates and prices in the economy remain unchanged, general business conditions remain unchanged, and methods of production are constant. To put the point differently: we are analyzing the consequences of a change in miners' wages *relative to other wage rates*. If miners' wages rise 5 percent, but at the same time all other wages rise 5 percent, this amounts to *no change* in miners' wages for present purposes. But if miners' wages rise 5 percent *more* than other wages, our supply-demand results become applicable. We can say that, if wage rates for coal miners rise *relative to* the general wage level, then one should expect a drop in the number of coal miners *relative to* employment in other occupations.

In the case of coal mining, this is precisely what happened in the United States between 1945 and 1960. Miners' wages rose by 264 percent, compared with an increase of 223 percent in average earnings in manufacturing. Meanwhile employment in bituminous coal mines *fell* by 55 percent, compared with an *increase* of 31 percent in general employment. A *relative* increase in miners' wages was accompanied by a sharp *relative* decline in employment. The reasons for the drop in coal employment were more complex than this, but students of the industry would agree that the rapid rise in wages was an important factor.

What determines the elasticity of demand for a particular kind of labor? Labor demand is derived from demand for the product, and follows the rules of derived demand explained in Chapter 5. The elasticity of demand for labor depends on: (1) the percentage which this type of labor forms of total production cost. If painters' wages are only 10 percent of the cost of building a house, then a 20 percent wage increase can be covered by a 2 percent increase in house prices, which will cause little reduction of sales and employment. Labor demand is inelastic. (2) The elasticity of demand for the product. The greater the elasticity of product demand, the larger the drop in output and employment which will be caused by a specified wage-price increase, and the greater is the elasticity of demand for labor. (3) The availability of mechanical substitutes. The greater the susceptibility of a production process to mechanization, the greater the elasticity of demand for the workers in question. (4) The supply conditions of other factors used in producing the product. If some other factor has a very inelastic supply curve, so that a small drop in output of the finished product means a sharp drop in the price of this factor and therefore in production costs, this will help to offset the effects of any wage increase, i.e., it will make the labor demand curve more inelastic.

The demand for a particular sort of labor is inelastic, then, to the extent that demand for the product is inelastic, that the labor in question forms a small part of total cost, that the workers cannot readily be replaced by machinery, and that there is inelastic supply of other factors of production. A union is in a strong position if the demand for the labor of its members is highly inelastic, because then the union can raise wages a good deal (always *relative* to the general wage level) with little reduction in the number of people employed. Where the labor demand curve is elastic, however, a union will have to pay for wage gains by a substantial reduction of employment opportunities.

Competitive and Regulated Wages

If coal miners are hired in a competitive market, and if we know the position of the supply and demand curves for miners' labor, we can say how many miners will be employed and how much they will be paid. The intersection of DD and SS in Figure 8–3 determines a *price*, the wage rate OW, and a *quantity exchanged*, the employment level OE. This is an equilibrium position in the sense that, if it were to be established, no one would have any reason to alter it. At the wage OW, employers want to hire OE workers, and just this number of workers will seek employment in the industry. The quantities offered and demanded balance, and the market is cleared. If demand or supply should shift, there will be a new equilibrium wage and employment. The mechanism works in the same way as for product markets.

The fact that OW would be the wage rate under competitive conditions does not mean that this wage will actually be established. It is perfectly possible to set a higher wage level through legislation or collective bargaining. There are at least three ways in which a union might seek to establish a wage higher than OW:

1. The union might try to raise the demand for its labor. One way of doing this would be to raise demand for the product. The Ladies' Garment Workers' Union has helped New York dress manufacturers to finance advertising campaigns designed to establish New York as a world fashion center and to raise the demand for clothes made there. A union will normally join employers in its industry in lobbying for tariff protection which, by reducing the flow of competing imports, raises the demand for domestically produced goods. If the labor demand curve can be raised, it may be possible to raise both wages *and* employment. (Trace how this would work out on Figure 8–3.)

2. The union might try to restrict the number of workers admitted to the occupation. Suppose the United Mine Workers could hold down the number of coal miners to OE_1 in Figure 8–3. This would amount to establishing a new vertical supply curve for labor, E_1E_1. No more workers than this can get into the industry, regardless of how many might like to. The wage will then be determined by the intersection of E_1E_1 and DD, yielding a wage OW_1 which is well above the competitive level.

A few unions have tried to restrict labor supply in this fashion; but these efforts are usually not successful. Moreover, they are not really necessary, for there is a more direct and effective route to the same end. This is:

3. The union may simply insist that employers pay the wage OW_1, under threat of a strike. This amounts, in a sense, to making the supply curve of labor horizontal along W_1AB. Below OW_1 employers will get no labor at all, since everyone will walk out. At this wage, they can get any number of workers they want up to W_1B. The end result is the same as in case (2). At the union wage OW_1, employers find that it pays them to hire only OE_1 workers, so only this number of workers can find a place in the industry.

All this sounds easier than it actually is. Employers do not simply lie down under union demands, and there are other reasons why a union may have difficulty in maintaining wages much above the competitive level. These practical difficulties will be explored further in Chapter 13.

WAGE DIFFERENCES AMONG OCCUPATIONS

The economy contains hundreds of different occupations, ranging from corporation presidents and surgeons down to domestic servants and farm laborers. How are the earnings of these groups related to each other? How are the markets for different types of labor linked in a general market system?

The linkage comes through the fact that people have a choice among alternative occupations. In a purely competitive economy, anybody could enter any occupation which seemed attractive to him. It is worth exploring this idea a bit to see what pattern of relative wages will result. Labor will flow into a particular occupation so long as people see a net advantage in choosing that occupation rather than something else. The higher the wage for occupation A, the more people will prefer it to other types of work. This upward-sloping supply curve, together with the demand curve for occupation A, will determine a market wage. The same is true for occupations B, C, D, and so on. If the whole system is to be in equilibrium, the last man engaged in occupation A, the *marginal* man,[2] must consider it just worth his while to remain there rather than shift to something else. So too for the marginal men in each of the other occupations. This has been termed *the principle of equal net advantage*—equal, that is, from the viewpoint of the people at the margin of decision. When the economy reaches a position in which no one feels that he can gain by switching occupations, then all labor markets are in balance and the relative wages for various occupations are in equilibrium.

Does this mean that wage rates for various occupations must be equal? Obviously not. *Equal advantage* does not mean *equal hourly wages.* Occupations differ in natural attractiveness, the ease or difficulty of learning them, and many other respects. If a particular occupation has poor working conditions, high training costs, or other disadvantages, a higher wage will be necessary to offset these things and tempt enough people into the occupation. Concretely, a higher wage might be necessary to compensate for:

1. Unpleasant or hazardous working conditions. One reason why coal mining carries a high wage rate is that the chances of accidental death are higher than in most other jobs.

2. A high degree of physical or mental effort. Heavy manual labor ordinarily pays more than light jobs such as floor sweeper, elevator operator, or night watchman.

3. Irregularity of employment. One reason for high hourly wage rates in the building trades is that construction drops off during the winter months and most workers get considerably less than a full year's work. High hourly earnings are necessary to yield reasonable annual earnings.

4. Risk of failure. A man can be less certain of succeeding as a lawyer, storekeeper, or corporation executive than he can as a bricklayer or gardener. If people are deterred by risk, a higher level of earnings in business and the professions will be necessary on this account. On the other hand, if you do succeed in these fields there is a chance of great success. Adam Smith argued that the existence of a few big prizes, plus the "over-weening confidence" which most men have in their own ability and good fortune, would lead *more* people to enter these risky fields than would be true if returns were perfectly certain. Many people participate

---

[2] Note that here we are using *marginal man* in a somewhat different sense from a few pages back, where we were considering the economy as a whole and assuming all labor to be homogeneous.

eagerly in lotteries, in which ticket holders as a group are sure to lose, but a few will win large amounts.

5. Time and expense of training. To set up in medical practice may take 10 years of higher education at a cost of $25,000 or more. There is a further cost in that during these years the student could have been earning a salary in some other occupation. The doctor's earnings over his working life must be enough to repay these initial costs with interest. The same is true of other occupations requiring higher education such as law, engineering, and teaching.

In a purely competitive economy, wage differences among occupations would be *equalizing* differences. They would equalize the net advantage of various occupations to people on the margin of decision. Most people would be within the margin and would regard their occupations as clearly preferable to anything else. Those least attached to their present occupation, the marginal men, would be indifferent as between their present job and the next best thing. No one could make a net gain by changing jobs. This would be a "correct" system of wage differences in the sense of corresponding to peoples' occupational preferences.

What would a system of purely competitive wage differences look like? Looking at actual wage relations does not give a reliable answer, because of the numerous restrictions on competition in actual labor markets. Competitive wage differences would probably be somewhat smaller than the differences presently existing in the United States. Business and professional earnings would be less far above manual workers' earning than they actually are, and the earnings of skilled labor would not be so far above those of common labor. But this is only a surmise, which would be hard to test statistically.

Labor markets in practice are far from fully competitive. Various restrictions impede the free flow of labor and affect relative wage rates. One such interference has already been described. A particular group may organize itself and insist on a rate of payment above the competitive level. Trade unions and professional associations have this as one of their major purposes. If they succeed, the result is that fewer people can be employed in the occupation than would be able to work there at the competitive wage.

Another restriction on free choice of occupation is the cost of higher education, which is essential for the professions and important for a business career. Millions of families in the United States cannot afford to finance a long period of college training, and some who could afford it do not encourage their children to go to college because of limited knowledge and foresight. Government and private scholarship systems help somewhat, but are far from adequate to the need. For some occupations there is a physical bottleneck in training capacity. There is considerable agreement, for example, that too few places are available in medical schools and that too few doctors are being graduated. It is expensive to build medical schools, however, and the federal government which could provide the necessary resources has not moved vigorously in this direction. These barriers reduce the flow of people into the higher occupations below what it would be if there were complete freedom of choice. The result is to raise earnings in these occupations above the competitive level.

OCCUPATIONAL WAGE DIFFERENCES IN THE UNITED STATES

We have approached the problem of wage differences by starting with the concept of purely competitive labor markets, and then bringing in restrictions which may cause actual wages to differ from the competi-

Table 8–1

Median Income of Male Full-time Workers, by
Occupation Group, United States, 1959*

Occupation Group	Median Annual Earnings, 1959
Professional, technical, and kindred workers	
Self-employed	$11,765
Salaried	7,052
Managers, proprietors, and officials (except farm)	
Self-employed	5,648
Salaried	7,268
Clerical and kindred workers	5,259
Sales workers	5,713
Craftsmen, foremen, and kindred workers	5,706
Operatives and kindred workers	4,744
Laborers, except farm and mine	4,041
Private household workers	. . .
Service workers, except private household	4,088
Farmers and farm managers	2,056
Farm laborers and foremen	1,750
All civilian workers	5,273

* *Statistical Abstract*, 1961, p. 322. "Full-time workers" are those who worked 35 hours or more for 50 weeks or more during the year.

tive pattern. Let us now look at actual wage differences in the United States and see whether they are understandable in these terms. We do not have wage rates for each type of work in the economy, but we do have information about yearly earnings, and this can serve as a rough substitute. Table 8–1 shows the median annual earnings of men employed full-time in various types of work in 1959.

Several things stand out from this table. Earnings of *self-employed business proprietors* are lower than one might have expected. Grocers, filling station operators, and other small independent businessmen earn less in a year than the skilled manual worker. Why is this? Some people may prize independence so highly that they deliberately choose self-employment knowing that it will mean lower earnings. But the more important reason is that small businessmen *expect* to make more than they do. The man who puts his life's savings into a corner grocery visualizes himself as the founder of a new A & P. Most of these people turn out not to have much business ability and end up in bankruptcy. But Adam Smith's principle of large prizes and overoptimism keeps a fresh supply of would-be businessmen springing up every year.

Salaried executives do considerably better than independent proprietors. Yet note that the average for this group is only $1,500 a year above that for skilled craftsmen. The president of a large corporation may receive several hundred thousand dollars a year in salary and fringe benefits. Looking at these peak salaries, one is apt to forget that for every president of General Motors there are hundreds of department heads within General Motors earning modest salaries. And for every General Motors there are hundreds of small corporations with lower salary levels. The chance of a large income induces many people to go into business careers in the hope of hitting one of the big prizes, but few actually do.

What about the small group of top management people who in effect set their own salaries? There is not a perfect market for corporation presidents, and their salaries are influenced more by personal leverage than by demand and supply. Research studies suggest that a major factor is the size of the organization: the larger the company, the higher the president's salary. This may be partly because increasing size of company means more layers of administrative organization. Companies often reason that salaries at each level should be a certain percentage above those at the next lower level. Thus if one goes up through six layers of superstructure instead of three, one comes out with higher salaries at the top.

The highest-paid group in the economy are the *independent professional practitioners,* such as doctors, lawyers, dentists, and engineers. Medicine yields highest average earnings of any occupation; and the independent professional group as a whole earns 60 percent more than the average salaried man in business. Part of these higher earnings can be traced to the cost of extra years of education, but only part can be explained in this way. The remainder is a monopoly gain arising from the fact that many people who would like to train for the professions cannot afford to do so. If scholarship or loan funds were adequate to support all qualified candidates through the training period, the increased supply of professional people would gradually lower the price of their services, and this monopoly gain would disappear.

The man with a *white collar* has traditionally enjoyed more prestige than his blue-collared neighbor, and for most of our history he has enjoyed higher earnings as well. As recently as 1940, the annual earnings of clerical workers were above those of manual workers. More recently, however, the manual workers have pulled ahead. The average skilled craftsman is now well ahead of the average clerical worker, and the semi-skilled factory operative is almost abreast of him. An important reason is the great increase in the percentage of young people finishing high school. High school graduates often regard manual labor as beneath them and white-collar jobs as their natural right. The rise in educational levels has thus increased the supply of white-collar workers, which tends to lower their price, and at the same time depleted the supply of manual workers, tending to raise their price.

The reversal of the traditional relation between white-collar and blue-collar earnings is thus explained partly by shifts of labor supply curves. But two other factors are probably important. The high level of business activity since 1940 has meant that most manual workers now get closer to a full year's work than they did during the thirties. This would raise annual earnings even without any change in relative wage rates. Moreover, the growing strength of unionism among manual workers, while white-collar workers remain largely unorganized, may have something to do with the shift in relative earnings.

Semiskilled workers earn about 20 percent more than *laborers*, and *skilled workers* about 40 percent more. The advantage of the upper manual groups has decreased considerably over the course of time. Fifty years ago, hourly wage rates for craftsmen were typically double those of laborers in the same industry. Today, they usually receive one third to one half more than laborers. This shrinkage of the gap between skilled and unskilled workers can be explained on a supply-demand basis. Fifty years ago, the supply of unskilled labor was inflated by mass immigration of un-trained workers from Europe, large-scale movement of American farm boys from country to city, and much dropping out of school at an early age. This ample supply depressed laborers' wages and gave the craftsman a large wage advantage. Today the supply of unskilled labor is much diminished. Mass immigration ended in 1923, the farm population is now too small to make its former contribution to the urban labor supply, and far fewer students drop out before the end of high school. So, it is not surprising that the price of unskilled labor has risen faster than the price of higher grades of labor, narrowing the gap between them.

At the bottom of the income pyramid stands the *farm population*. At no time during the past 50 years has the average farm laborer earned half as much as the unskilled factory worker, even including the value of board and room which the farm laborer often receives. Farm operators do better, but not a great deal better. How can this be? Why don't all the farm workers rush off immediately to the city?

There are probably several reasons for the depressed level of farm wages. The demand for farm labor has been falling off for a long time. Agricultural production has not been expanding as fast as other sectors of the economy. A country can eat only so much, no matter how rich it may become. In addition, the rapid mechanization of agriculture—tractors, combine harvesters, cotton pickers, milking machines, and the rest—has enabled more to be produced with less labor. On the supply side, rural birth rates are relatively high and this holds up the supply of farm labor. Growing supply combined with shrinking demand is the basic explanation of the low level of farm incomes.

This still does not explain why the farmers do not rush off to the city. If enough of them did this, the supply of farm labor would shrink, that of factory labor would rise, and the income gap would gradually close. But there are serious obstacles to this movement. Country people do not have a clear picture of job opportunities in the city, they are attached to their home areas, and they hesitate to face the costs and risks of movement. Many people do move from country to city despite these obstacles. But the *movement is not fast enough* to drain off the chronic excess of rural population and to close the income gap.

It does seem that supply-demand reasoning, modified by a recognition of imperfections in actual labor markets, is helpful in analyzing wage differences among major occupational groups. The finer details of the wage structure will always defy precise analysis. No demand-supply diagram will tell us why one job in a factory pays precisely four cents an hour more than another. But such questions, while they may be important to the personnel manager, are not of much interest to the student of the national economy. The economist is interested in explaining the broad contours of the national wage structure, and how these change over long periods of time. For this purpose, one can get a good deal further with supply-demand analysis than without it.

WAGE DIFFERENCES WITHIN AN OCCUPATION

We must now take a further step toward reality by exploring why workers earn different amounts even within the same occupation. Take any occupation you wish—machinists, carpenters, laborers, domestic servants—and go around the country inquiring how much people earn. You will usually find sizable differences even within the same city, and still larger differences among geographical regions.

Regional Wage Differences

The highest wages in the United States are found on the Pacific Coast, particularly in Seattle, Portland, and San Francisco. Another high-wage belt runs from New York through Pittsburgh to Detroit and Chicago. Wages then taper off as one goes west into the farm states, north into New England, or south toward the Gulf Coast. The lowest wages in the country are found in rural areas of the deep South.

These differences are partially offset by differences in living costs. It costs less to live in a small town in Minnesota than it does in Chicago or Detroit, and it costs still less in a small town in Mississippi. The difference in *real* wages is thus less than the difference in *money* wages. But the offset is not complete. There are still sizable differences in real wages, and these require explanation.

Broad regional differences can be explained largely on a supply-demand basis. The southeastern states have a relatively high rate of population increase. Until recently the main outlet for this labor was in agriculture, where labor productivity and wage rates are low. A factory could come into a southern town with a wage level high enough to recruit labor out of agriculture, yet considerably below the level of competing factories in other regions. Suppose farm workers in South Carolina are getting $0.50 an hour, while the wage level in northern textile mills is $1.50 an hour. A textile mill setting up in South Carolina with a wage level of $1.00 an hour will be able to draw as much labor as it needs out of agriculture and also to undersell its northern competitors. (There is no evidence, incidentally, that a worker in Birmingham or Atlanta produces less than a worker in Boston or Chicago, given identical equipment, training, and supervision.)

This situation should set off a chain reaction: many new plants should spring up in the South to take advantage of lower labor costs. Their lower costs will enable them to undersell and take business away from northern plants. Northern production will decline, or at least fail to expand as fast as southern production. The demand for labor in the South will rise rapidly, while labor demand in the North will stagnate. This means that wage rates in the South will rise relative to those in the North, and the gap between the two regions will gradually shrink. The original situation, in short, was not an equilibrium situation. Through the normal working of economic forces, through movement of industry from North to South and movement of labor from South to North in search of higher wages, the system should gradually approach an equilibrium. Wages would not necessarily become equal in the two regions, but they would come a good deal closer together.

Something like this has actually been going on over the past 50 years. The rate of industrial expansion in the South has been considerably faster than anywhere else except the West Coast, and a number of manufacturing industries are now largely southern industries. As this has happened, wage levels in the South have risen and there has been a gradual shrinkage of the North-South differential in many industries, though not in all.

Differences by Size of City

There is usually a considerable difference in wage levels between large cities and small towns in the same region—between Chicago and West Bend, Wisconsin, or between Atlanta and Newton, Georgia. Even after adjusting for the lower living costs in small towns, there remains a difference in real wage levels.

One reason for the lower wage level of small towns is that they can attract labor readily from the farm population. High rural birth rates produce a surplus of labor which has to seek urban employment. A small town personnel manager can usually pull in all the labor he needs by spreading the word through the surrounding countryside. The large city has to attract labor mainly from smaller towns and cities, and it must offer enough of a wage premium to induce people to move.

There is a natural corrective to unduly large city-town differences, just as there is to interregional wage differences. The lower wage level of the small town offers employers a standing inducement to move there from the city. This is particularly true of "footloose" types of manufacturing with little fixed equipment and a high labor cost ratio, such as garments, shoe manufacture, textiles, furniture, canning, and meat packing. There has been considerable movement of these industries into smaller communities in recent decades.

Wage Differences in the Same City

One of the most puzzling things about labor markets is the fact that companies in the same city often pay considerably different rates for what seems to be the same kind of labor. Studies of many occupations in many cities by the U.S. Bureau of Labor Statistics show that the highest plant in the city often pays 50 percent above the lowest plant for the same job. This conflicts sharply with the principle that there can be only one price in a competitive market. What is the answer?

The apparent differences may be partly spurious. The different wage rates may not apply to the same *quality of labor* applied to the same *job duties*. Even "common labor" is not identical from one plant to another. The work may be heavy and exhausting in one plant, lighter and easier in another. Working conditions, fringe benefits, and other job characteristics may differ. The workers involved may also differ in personal efficiency. A high-wage company may set strict hiring specifications designed to fill the plant with people of superior efficiency; and because its jobs are attractive and people want to hang on to them, it may be able to demand a better level of performance. The fact that the wage level of company A is 25 percent above that of company B does not mean that company A's *labor cost per unit produced*, which is what really matters to management, will be 25 percent higher. Labor cost may not be higher at all, if the high-wage policy is accompanied by careful hiring and effective supervision.

Suppose that after correcting for these things one still finds "genuine" differences in wages for precisely the same quality of labor and type of work. How are these differences to be explained? One possible explanation is union pressure. A union sometimes pushes a particular company out of line with the rates paid by other employers. There are other cases, however, in which a company apparently just chooses to pay wages above the general level in the area.

These cases are rather puzzling. Why should any company choose to pay more than the prevailing market rate for labor? Does this not run counter to the natural urge to maximize profits? The companies following a high-wage policy are usually large, well managed, and often sheltered from price competition by a monopoly or oligopoly position. They usually enjoy profits which are large and secure enough so that management can allow itself the luxury of paying superior wages. As executives walk through the plant, it is nicer to be greeted with genuine friendliness than veiled hostility, and paying "the best wages in town" certainly contributes to this. A high wage level makes it easier to recruit high-quality workers and to demand good job performance, and may help the company to stave off the union or live with the union. It is understandable, therefore, that some managements should choose a high-wage policy in preference to squeezing out the last drop of profit.

At the other end of the scale one finds plants which are paying below-average wages, and even so are making little or no profit. This may happen in an atomistic industry where demand is falling; or it may be because the plant has antiquated methods or machinery, poor location, or some other handicap; or it may be due to poor management. Low wages are more apt to reflect managerial incapacity than managerial greed.

Differences in Personal Efficiency

There are wide differences in personal capacity among people in professional, administrative, scientific, and artistic work, which go far toward explaining differences in earnings in these occupations. Even in the simplest manual operations, some people have greater physical stamina, faster reflexes, better concentration, and other advantages which enable them to turn out a good deal more in an hour's time.

This reflects itself partly in the job area to which people gain admission. Proficient and eager workers stand the best chance of getting into the high-wage plants which have first pick of the area labor force. They also have best chance of promotion to higher occupational levels. Both things mean higher earnings for able people.

Even within the same plant and work group, one may find substantial differences in personal capacity. This is sometimes recognized by establishing a "rate range" rather than a single rate for each job. Machinists may be placed in a rate range of $2.50 to $2.90 per hour, and may be given "merit increases" within this range based on the foreman's judgment of their work.

Differences in ability may also be recognized through *piece-rate* or *incentive* payment, under which how much the worker receives depends on how much he produces. This is widely used in manufacturing processes where each worker's output can be identified, and where quantity of output rather than quality is the main consideration. The hope is that payment by results will stimulate each worker to produce up to the limit of his ability. This objective is never entirely accomplished. There is typically pressure on the faster members of a work group to hold back so as not to show up their slower colleagues. Workers also have a well-grounded suspicion that, if they produce so much that their earnings become "unreasonably high" in the eyes of management, the piece-rate is likely to be cut. Incentive payment doubtless produces a higher level of effort than one would get under time payment. It also produces a quiet but determined battle of wits between workers on the one hand and foremen and time-study men on the other.

SUMMARY

1. The level of real wages in a country varies *directly* with the productivity of labor, and *inversely* with the quantity of labor.

2. Labor productivity depends on supplies of natural resources and capital equipment, the state of technology, the quality of the labor force, and the effectiveness of economic organization.

3. Unionism could raise the general level of real wages by raising labor productivity, by reducing the supply of labor, or by eliminating undue employer power in the labor market.

4. The equilibrium wage for any occupation is determined by the labor demand and supply curves for that occupation. The supply curve slopes upward to the right because of alternative job opportunities. The demand curve slopes upward to the left because machines can be substituted for men, and because other products can be substituted for the one in question.

5. Some variation of wages is necessary to equalize the net advantage of different occupations. These may be termed *natural, equalizing,* or *competitive* wage differences. But part of the variation which one observes in actuality arises from barriers to free movement of labor among occupations. This is particularly important for the professional and managerial occupations, where costs of higher education are a significant barrier.

6. Interesting characteristics of the earnings structure in the United States include: relatively high earnings of independent professional people; relatively low earnings of small independent businessmen; earnings for routine sales and clerical work which are little above the level of manual labor; and a depressed earnings level for both farm laborers and farm operators.

7. Wages for the same kind of labor vary considerably according to region of the country, size of city, size of company, type of industry, and efficiency of the individual worker. These differences are largely, though not completely, explainable in terms of supply-demand reasoning.

Money Markets, Interest, and Profit

Get money, by fair means if you can; if not, get money.

HORACE, *Epistles*

There are few ways in which a man can be more innocently employed than in getting money.

SAMUEL JOHNSON

IN THE LAST CHAPTER we examined incomes from personal effort. We turn now to examine incomes derived from property ownership.

In an industrialized capitalist country, property income takes mainly the form of *interest* or of returns which are closely akin to interest: Interest rates are determined in *money markets*, so we must begin by looking briefly at what goes on in these markets.

MONEY MARKETS

The typical money market transaction is simple. A man wants to build a house and needs $10,000 more than he has. He has a mortgage made out for this amount, signs it, hands it over to a savings bank or some other buyer, and gets the money he needs. A businessman needs a six-month loan to cover increased purchases of raw materials. If his credit rating is good, a bank will provide the money in return for a promissory note, which is a promise to repay the money with interest by a certain date. The federal government finds itself running a $5 billion deficit this year. It borrows the money from investors, giving in return a promise to repay the money after, say, five years, and to pay interest at a specified rate in the meantime.

Note that each of these transactions involves an *exchange of securities against money*. On one side of the market are people who want money and issue securities in order to get it. On the other side are people who have money and are willing to hand it over and take securities in return. We may regard this sort of market, then, either as a *market for securities* or a *market for money*. It is convenient to follow the latter course, and to describe such exchanges as taking place in *the money market*. Alternatively, we could speak of the *loan market* or the *market for loanable funds*.

From this standpoint, the borrowers in our illustration—the businessman, the government, the householder—stand on the *demand* side of the market. They are demanding money and offering securities in return. The people who provide the money, the lenders, are on the *supply* side of the market.

Interest Rates and Security Yields

A characteristic of any market is that something is being exchanged *at a price*. What is the price in this case? What does one mean by the *price of money?* A man with $1,000 always has the option of spending it immediately or holding it. He will presumably not give it up unless he expects to get back *something more* than his original $1,000. This something more, which we call *interest*, is the price for parting with money.

Some securities carry the rate of interest on their face. A house mortgage carries a promise to pay interest at, say, 5 percent over the life of the mortgage. Or suppose a business concern borrows $100,000 from its bank for a year, agreeing to pay back $106,000. Then the rate of interest is clearly 6 percent.

In the case of stocks and bonds, however, we usually speak of the *yield* of the security. A yield *is* a rate of interest. It is the return for the money advanced by the buyer of the security. But the yield is usually not stated on the surface and requires a little calculation.

Suppose I buy a hundred shares of A. T. & T. common stock at $120 a share. There is no promise to pay any set dividend on this stock. So where is my rate of interest? In this case, while there is no definite promise, the company has for years customarily paid a dividend of $3.60 per share. A. T. & T. is a well-managed concern with an expanding market, which seems well able to continue this dividend in future. I can expect, therefore, to receive a return on these securities of 3.60/120 = 3 percent per year. This is termed the *yield* of the security. It is a rate of interest just as truly as in the mortgage case, the only difference being that it is an expected return rather than a guaranteed return.

The concept of yield is applicable also to fixed-income securities. Consider a very long-term bond (ideally, the British consol, which has no repayment date). It may have been issued originally at a face value of $1,000, and carries guaranteed interest of $40 per year. Does this mean that it yields 4 percent? Not at all. After a bond is issued, its price will fluctuate with conditions in the money market. What matters to me as a buyer is how much interest I receive relative to the *current price* of the bond. If the price of this bond falls to $800, then it will yield me 40/800 = 5 percent. But if its market price rises to $1,333, it will yield only 40/1,333 = 3 percent.

This underlines an important principle: *the yield of a fixed-income security moves in the opposite direction from its price.* Rising bond prices mean falling bond yields, or a drop in interest rates. Falling bond prices mean rising interest rates. The same is generally true of stock prices. If stock prices are rising, then unless dividend payments are rising equally fast, the yield must be falling; and vice versa. Thus we can generally speak either of a *rise in the rate of interest* or a *fall in security prices* as meaning the same thing.

Instead of working forward from the price of a security to its yield, we can work back in the other direction from yield to price. Suppose we have a very high-grade bond, that is, one on which the payments of interest and principal are almost certain to be met. It carries a promise to pay $10 interest per year. How much is it worth in the market? This depends on the yields which can be obtained from other securities of the same quality. If other top-quality bonds are currently yielding 4 percent, then this one should yield about the same. Its price, P, should satisfy the condition $\frac{10}{P} = \frac{4}{100}$, or $P = \$250$. If its price were less than this, it would be yielding more than 4 percent, and people would sell other bonds to buy this one, causing a rise in its price. If its price were above this, the opposite sequence would follow and its price would fall to the equilibrium level of $250. Securities markets are full of experts at this sort of calculation, and this holds the yield of one security closely in line with those of other securities with the same characteristics. This process of working back from the income yielded by an asset to its price is termed *capitalization*.

One usually thinks of interest as a return to owners of securities, pieces of paper. But tangible assets can also be construed as securities of a sort; and the return on tangible assets can properly be regarded as interest. Suppose I buy an apartment building for $100,000 and after paying all operating expenses for the year have $6,000 left at the end. The tenants pay me "rent," and my income is classified statistically as "rental income." But surely my situation is no different than if I had bought $100,000 of bonds which pay me $6,000 interest. In either case I have exchanged cash for an asset, on which I am getting a 6 percent return. It is legitimate to call this interest in either case. The great bulk of property income, in short, can be treated as interest, and we can regard personal income as divided into wages and interest without being far off.

Money Market Operators

The groups operating in the money market can be classified as *borrowers, lenders,* and *intermediaries.* While a great deal could be said about each of these groups, a few words must suffice here.

The most important borrowers are *business concerns.* In good years, U.S. businesses put something like $75 billion into new office buildings, stores, factories, machinery, and equipment. Most of this is paid for from internal sources, from depreciation allowances plus retained profits which are put back into the business. But after mobilizing all the resources which can be obtained in this way, businesses have to raise many billions by selling securities in the outside market.

A second important group of chronic borrowers are the *state and local governments.* State and local borrowing through bond issues now runs around $10 billion per year. The *federal government* is a large but intermittent borrower. In years when the budget is in balance, it does no net borrowing; but in deficit years it may have to borrow $5 to $10 billion. Even when it is doing no net borrowing, it has to sell enough new securities each year to pay off the holders of old securities which are falling due. Through these *refunding operations,* the U.S. Treasury is active in the money market all the time, and has a strong practical stake in the movement of interest rates.

The main group on the lending side of the market is *households.* Families of course operate to some extent on both sides of the market. They borrow as well as save. But the borrowings of some households are much more than offset by the savings of others. On balance, the household sector is a net supplier of funds to the tune of about $25 billion a year.

Another important lending group, the *commercial banks,* are omitted here and left for discussion in Part Three. Their characteristic function is to make short-term loans to business concerns, usually repayable in six to twelve months. Unlike households, which must save money before lending it, the banking system can *create* money. It can do so only within limits, and operates under controls imposed by the Federal Reserve System. But there is a flexibility to bank lending operations which is not possessed by any other group.

Financial intermediaries are so called because they are middlemen standing between the ultimate lenders and borrowers of funds. They do not save or create the money in which they deal. Their function is to collect money from household savers and to put it into mortgages, government bonds, corporate bonds and stocks, and other types of security. The most important of these intermediaries are *life insurance companies, savings banks,* and governmental and private *pension funds.*

THE RATE OF INTEREST

What determines the rate of interest? An initial complication is that there are many different securities, yielding anything from 1 percent to upwards of 10 percent. This requires the same procedure which we used in analyzing wage determination. We shall first explore what determines the *general level* of yields, and then consider why yields vary so much from one security to another.

The rate of interest might be regarded as simply an average of the yields on all securities in existence at a particular time. It is more precise, however, to define it as the yield on an *ideal security*, a very long-term bond with no risk that interest and principal payments will not be met. The classic example is the British *consol*, a government bond with no expiration date, carrying a fixed interest amount backed by the full credit of the country. A 20-year bond of the United States government is a reasonably close approximation. The yield on such a bond happens to fall in the middle range of prevailing yields on other securities. The main reason for using this as a reference point, however, is that it has a clear meaning: the charge for the use of money where there is minimum risk that the money will not be repaid. It is in fact often termed *the pure rate of interest*.

The yield of long-term U.S. government bonds from 1919 to 1962 is shown in Figure 9–1.[1] Note that the figure reached about 5½ percent in 1920, at the peak of the boom following World War I. It then sagged to a low of little more than 2 percent at the end of the depressed thirties. During World War II, when the federal government was the major borrower, the interest rate was fixed by government policy along with most other prices and wages. About 1950 yields began to rise once more, and have been around 4 percent in recent years.

An index of yields on top-quality corporate bonds (Moody's Aaa rating) is included for comparison. Note that this fluctuates closely with government bond yields, but is normally ½ percent to 1 percent higher. The reason is that even the best corporate bonds are not quite as secure as a government bond. This illustrates a general principle: the riskier a security, the more it must yield to induce investors to buy and hold it. The difference between the government bond yield and the corporate Aaa bond yield is a *risk premium*.

A still longer perspective is provided by Figure 9–2, which runs back to the nineteenth century. The figures show ups and downs in interest rates, with a declining tendency over the long run.

Why do Figures 9–1 and 9–2 have the shape that they do? Why do bond yields in the United States show a sagging tendency over the past century? Why were yields particularly depressed during the thirties, and why did they revive markedly during the fifties?

---

[1] Data are from the *Federal Reserve Bulletin*, July, 1962, p. 864.

FIGURE 9–1

Yield on Long-Term U.S. Bonds and High-Quality
Corporate Bonds, 1919–62

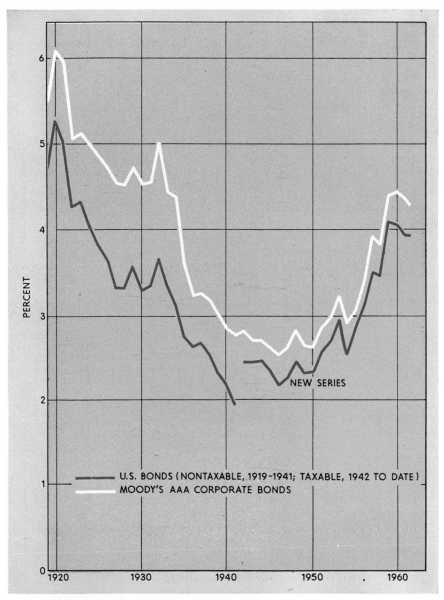

Looking at the matter on a world scale, why do interest rates differ substantially in different countries? In 1961, for example, the yield of long-term government bonds was as follows:[2]

_____

[2] U. N. *Statistical Yearbook*, 1961, pp. 529–30.

FIGURE 9–2

Yields on Selected Types of Security, United States, 1857–1960

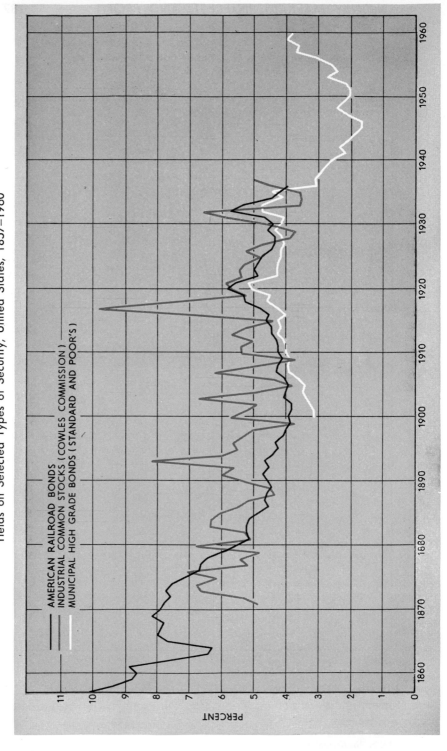

Switzerland	3 07%	Canada	4.96%
Egypt	3.42	France	5.04
Pakistan	3.70	Peru	5.18
Portugal	3.85	Italy	5.22
India	4.14	Australia	5.34
Belgium	4.35		

Private lending rates in these countries varied even more widely. What is the basis for these differences?

The main forces influencing long-term movements in the rate of interest may be analyzed by considering a simplified case in which the demand for funds comes entirely from business concerns and the supply of funds entirely from households. We assume that the economy is working at full capacity and ignore the short swings of the business cycle.

The Demand for Funds

Looking first at the demand side, why are business concerns willing to pay a price for the use of money? In the case of labor, we found an objective basis for wage determination in the value of the worker's produce. But how can money produce a product?

Borrowed money is valued, not for itself, but for the equipment which can be bought with it; and this equipment has a productivity which makes payment of interest feasible and worthwhile. Consider a wheat farmer who has been harvesting his 300 acres in the old-fashioned way, using a binder to tie the sheaves, hiring labor to set up the sheaves in the field, and then carrying them in hayracks to the threshing machine. This costs him 60 man days of labor at $10 per day, or $600, plus $300 for upkeep of the binder and other expenses, or a total of $900. He now has an opportunity to buy for $4,000 a combine harvester which does the whole operation at once and eliminates the need for the hired labor. It will last for 10 years, so he will have to set aside $400 each year for depreciation. Repairs, gasoline, and other operating expenses are estimated at $100. His total harvesting cost, then, is $500, and he can save $400 per year compared with the old method.

The combine harvester each year saves $400/4,000 = 10$ percent of its cost. It may thus be said to have a *productivity* of 10 percent. If the farmer can borrow money to buy the machine for anything less than 10 percent, he will profit by doing so. Suppose he can borrow $4,000 at 6 percent interest. His interest charges will then be $240 per year. But since he saves $400 a year in operating expenses, he is $160 better off than before. If the rate of interest were above 10 percent, however, it would no longer be worthwhile to borrow money to buy the machine.

Large corporations are constantly engaged in calculations which, while much more complicated than this, have the same general character. A. T. & T. has been gradually replacing long-distance telephone operators by automatic equipment for direct dialing. This involves estimating the cost of the new equipment, the consequent saving in operating expenses, and converting this to a yield on cost. If expenditure of a hundred million dollars on equipment will save eight million dollars annually in operating costs, the yield is 8 percent. These calculations are not revealed to the general public. We know, however, that A. T. & T. has been raising large amounts of money for new equipment by selling securities at interest rates running up to 5 percent. The prospective yield of the new equipment, therefore, must be above 5 percent.

These examples involve changes in production methods. But the same sort of calculation is required in starting a new company, increasing its production capacity, launching a new product line, or doing anything else which means spending money on plant and equipment. The basic question always is how the prospective return from the investment, after deducting all the attendant expenses, compares with the initial cost. If the yield of a project is above the market rate of interest, the company can make money by undertaking it. If the reverse is true, the project is not worthwhile and should be abandoned.

FIGURE 9–3

Determination of the Rate of Interest

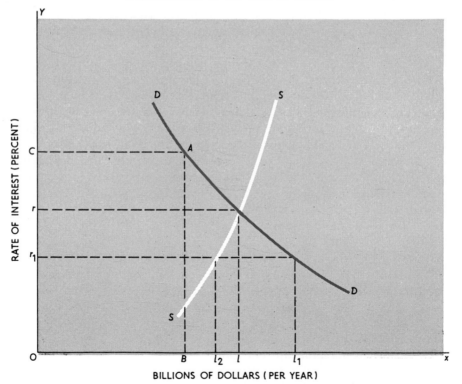

DD and SS show the total demand for and supply of funds in the money market. In this situation O*l* billion dollars will be borrowed and the interest rate will be O*r*.

We can now build up a demand curve for funds in the following way: Suppose the rate of interest were very high, say 20 percent. Even at this rate some investment projects would look as though they would "pay off," and some money would be borrowed to undertake them. If the rate were only 15 percent, a good many more projects would "pay off" and the demand for funds would be greater. At 10 percent, the demand would be still greater. Thus one can lay out a series of points defining a demand curve of the usual shape (Figure 9–3).

A particular point on the curve shows that, if a certain amount of new equipment were to be constructed in a particular year, the last or *marginal* item of equipment would have a yield on cost which can be read off from the *y*-axis. Point *A*, for example, means that if *OB* worth of new capital were brought into production this year, the least effective part of this would have a yield of *OC*. The downward slope of the curve means that construction of more and more capital, everything else being given, will bring declining yields.

The general shape of the demand curve would be the same if we included government borrowers as well as business borrowers. The demand of state and local governments for funds is probably more inelastic than that of business concerns, but it is not entirely inelastic. Government units will not borrow as readily at 8 percent as at 4 percent. A demand curve including government borrowing, then, would be farther to the right than *DD*; it would probably be less elastic; but it would slope downward to the right in the same way.

The Supply of Funds

What about the supply of funds from households? Specifically, how will household savings be influenced by changes in the rate of interest? It seems reasonable to expect that the supply curve will slope upward to the right, that more will be saved at higher rates of interest. Saving involves sacrifice. It means giving up money which might be used to gratify immediate wants. People should be more willing to make this sacrifice if they are offered a larger reward. It also seems likely that higher rates of interest will discourage consumer borrowing (negative saving), which amounts to an increase in the *net* savings of households.

Against this it may be argued that most saving is habitual and even automatic. I get accustomed to certain payroll deductions for old age pensions, to a monthly mortgage payment on my house, to putting so much in the savings bank or a stock-purchase fund every month; and I may continue to do this whether my savings earn 2 percent or 5 percent. It is also argued that many people are *target savers*, who are trying to build up a certain retirement income or reach some other limited goal. If I want a retirement income of $4,000 and the rate of interest is 4 percent, I will have to accumulate $100,000. But if the interest rate were 8 percent, I would have to save only $50,000. On this basis *less* would be saved at higher interest rates, and the supply curve would bend backward to the left.

Statistical studies have not yet presented clear evidence on these matters. We have compromised here by drawing SS as sloping upward in the conventional way, but making it quite inelastic to suggest that people's savings habits may be rather fixed at a particular time.

The Rate of Interest

The logic of the supply and demand curves in Figure 9–3 is the same as in our earlier supply-demand diagrams. They represent the situation at a moment of time. They rest on underlying factors which are taken as given and constant. Technology, and the array of investment opportunities resting on known techniques of production, is constant on the demand side. People's attitudes toward saving, and also their incomes, are constant on the supply side.

Intersection of SS and DD yields an equilibrium rate of interest, Or, and a quantity of funds which will be lent and borrowed, Ol. Or is the equilibrium rate because only at this rate does the amount of money which businesses are willing to borrow exactly equal the amount which households are willing to supply. This line of explanation, in short, makes the rate of interest depend on the thriftiness of the population (SS) and the productivity of capital (DD), which depends on the stock of known investment opportunities. In equilibrium the market rate of interest must just equal the marginal productivity of capital. The reasoning is the same as that used in determining the general level of wages.

Using the Supply-Demand Mechanism

This old-fashioned "neoclassical" theory of interest, properly qualified and applied, is a useful explanatory device. But the reader should be warned against relying on it for more than it is worth. It does *not* explain the gyrations of interest rates over short periods of time. One cannot safely conclude that, if the demand or supply curves shift, the system will adjust smoothly and quickly to a new equilibrium position. On the contrary, if people's urge to save increases or businessmen's willingness to borrow declines, the immediate effect will be a drop in spending and business activity; and instead of the system righting itself rapidly, things are likely to get worse before they get better. All this will be explained in Part Three. We insert a word here simply to warn the reader that he doesn't yet know all there is to know about interest.

What, then, *is* neoclassical interest theory good for? It is helpful mainly in reasoning about the movement of interest rates over long periods of time. This can be viewed as the outcome of a race between SS and DD, both shifting rightward over the course of time, but not necessarily at the same rate.

On the supply side, personal incomes in the United States have been rising with the growing productive power of the economy. This provides a possibility of larger savings, though it does not guarantee it. Actually, the percentage of personal income saved in the United States does not seem to have changed much over the past 75 years. Savings have risen more or less proportionately with income. But even this means that SS is shifting quite rapidly to the right.

On the demand side, conflicting tendencies are at work. The fact that a large amount of investment is undertaken each year means that some of the known investment opportunities are being used up. Once A. T. & T. has completely eliminated the long distance operator, they can't do it again. This particular opportunity is gone. If this were the only thing happening, it is clear what the outcome must be. All the projects yielding 6 percent or more would eventually be used up, then those yielding at least 5 percent would be exploited, and so on down the ladder of declining yields. The interest rate would have to fall steadily in order to keep investment going.

But while known investment opportunities are being used up, new ones are constantly being created by science and technology. Discovery of a major new product may suddenly open up the possibility of large yields on new types of investment. Witness the heavy expenditure in recent years on plants to produce space rockets and fuel for them, electronic calculating equipment, atomic power and other fission by-products, jet passenger planes, television receivers, fully automated machine tools, and many other things which did not exist in 1940. If technical progress is rapid enough, it can more than offset the using up of known opportunities, and keep DD shifting to the right over the course of time.

The long-term course of interest rates, then, depends on a race between thriftiness and technology, on whether the supply or demand for funds is rising more rapidly. In the United States over the past century, it seems technology has not quite kept up in the race. The demand curve for funds has risen greatly, but the supply curve has moved rightward so rapidly that it now intersects the demand curve at a lower rate of interest. This hypothesis is illustrated by Figure 9–4, where DD, SS and r indicate the situation as of 1860, and D_1D_1, S_1S_1, and r_1 the situation as of 1960. The long-term course of interest rates is shown by the dotted line connecting points A and B.

Money Flows and Goods Flow

We have analyzed the rate of interest in monetary terms, as though all that mattered was the meeting of the supply and demand for funds in the money market. But these money flows have their physical counterpart, and it is the physical processes which are important for the functioning of the economy. The fact that all income is not spent on consumer goods means that not all the resources of the economy need be devoted to producing consumer goods. Corresponding to the transfer of

FIGURE 9–4

A Possible Explanation of Interest Rates Changes

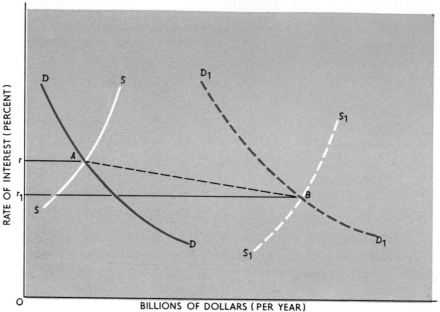

DD and SS show a possible money market situation as of 1860. D_1D_1 and S_1S_1 show the situation as of 1960. In this event the rate of interest would have fallen from Or to Or_1 over the intervening period.

purchasing power from lenders to borrowers is a transfer of resources to production of factories, machinery, and other capital goods; and the size of these two transfers is closely linked. If 10 percent of national income is saved, then this percentage of the country's annual output will take the form of capital goods.

Thinking in terms of physical processes helps to avoid certain confusions. For example: why should mere money ever be an obstacle to the creation of useful new facilities? If the interest rate is too high for a project to "pay off," why cannot government simply force down the interest rate? Why shouldn't government hold down the interest rate anyway to protect borrowers against the "monied class?" And if borrowers can't get enough funds, why not have the banking system create whatever new money is needed?

During war periods, when government is the chief borrower, government does fix the interest rate below the equilibrium level, and this has sometimes been done even in peacetime. But the consequence of doing this is an excess of demand over supply at the fixed price. Look back to Figure 9–3. Suppose government decides to fix the interest rate at Or_1. At this rate borrowers will want Ol_1 of funds, but only Ol_2 is available.

The demand for funds exceeds the available supply. This means basically that the demand for *physical* resources for investment projects is greater than the resources available. What to do? One solution would be for government to ration the available funds among would-be borrowers according to some scale of social priorities. "Capital rationing" was practiced by many European governments during the period of heavy reconstruction following World War II, mainly by requiring a license for any new construction. Licenses were issued more freely for machine tool plants than for race tracks, and the amount of investment activity was held within the resources available. This is a workable system, but it is a major modification of private enterprise. Which projects shall be undertaken depends on the judgment of a government board rather than on businessmen's calculations of prospective yield.

It may be thought that there is still another course. Why not close the gap between supply and demand for funds by creating additional bank credit? This can be done, but creating more money does not create more productive resources. Suppose the economy in Figure 9–3 is operating at full capacity. The interest rate is Or and the economy is in balance. Now government pegs the interest rate at Or_1 and an excess demand for funds appears. This excess demand, $Ol_1 - Ol_2$, might be met by creating additional money. But what can the borrowers do with their new dollars? All resources in the economy are fully employed. The new money can only go into hiring resources away from their present users, which will raise wage rates and other resource prices. The result will be a general rise in the price level. If one wants to avoid this result, one is forced back to the previous solution of capital rationing.

Interest thus serves a thermostatic function in the economy. The equilibrium rate of interest holds the demand for funds within the limits of available savings. More importantly, it holds the demand for physical resources for use in investment projects within the limit of available resource supplies, and enables investment to proceed without inflationary pressure on the price level.

Further, within the total volume of investment activity, the interest rate provides a simple way of determining *which* investment projects shall be undertaken. Projects which promise a yield higher than the rate of interest will be undertaken, and those which promise a lower yield will not be. Higher yields will always be preferred to lower ones. Since the yield of a new factory or any other project depends on product prices which reflect consumer preferences, an allocation of resources in this way will be economically correct. This is the argument for allowing allocation of funds to be determined through competition in the money market.

DIFFERENCES IN INTEREST RATES

We must now move a step toward reality by recognizing the wide variety of interest rates in the money market. The movement of some of the key rates since 1945 is shown in Figures 9–5, 9–6, and 9–7.[3] Note the substantial differences in yield at any time. In mid-1962, for example, the rate on three-month Treasury bills was 2.70 percent. Long-term U.S. government bonds were yielding 3.90 percent. Top quality (Moody's Aaa rating) corporate bonds yielded 4.28 percent. The average rate charged on business loans by New York City banks was 4.78 percent. Banks in Southern and Western cities were charging 5.33 percent on the average.

FIGURE 9–5

Yields on U.S. Securities of Differing Length, 1945–62

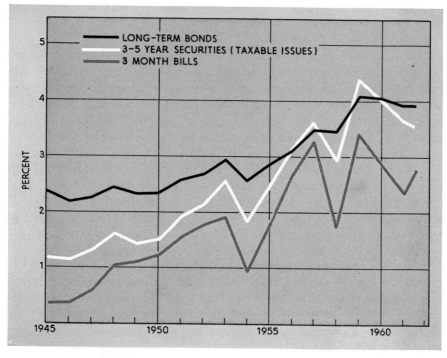

Nor does this reveal the full range of variation. Interest rates on home mortgages at this time averaged about 6 percent. Many small-town banks were charging rates in the range of 6 to 8 percent on business and agricultural loans. Consumer loans by banks and finance companies often carry rates of 10 percent or more.

The main reasons for this variation of interest rates are:

1. *Length of the loan.* Anyone who buys a three-month Treasury bill knows that he will have his money back in 90 days. Such a security has great *liquidity*, because the commitment is for a very short period. Liquidity is an advantage because after 90 days it may turn out that the money will bring a better yield somewhere else. Commercial banks typi-

---

[3] Data from the *Federal Reserve Bulletin*, July 1962, and earlier issues.

cally put funds which are not needed immediately for customer loans into short-term Treasury bills and certificates. If the demand for customer loans rises, they claim payment from the government as the issues mature and shift the funds over into business use. The convenience of Treasury bills means that the Treasury can sell them at a low interest

FIGURE 9–6

Yields on Corporate Bonds and Stocks, 1945–62

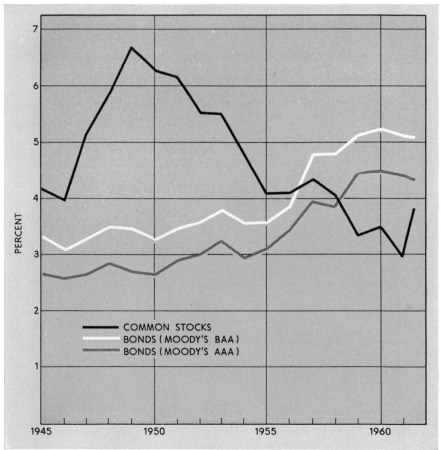

rate. But if the Treasury asks people to tie up money in a 5-year bond it will have to offer a higher rate, and a 20-year bond typically yields still more. This normal relationship of rates stands out in Figure 9–5.

2. *Riskiness of the security.* The riskier a security, the higher a yield it must offer to induce investors to buy it rather than something else. Even the best corporate bonds (Aaa) are a bit riskier than governments, and must therefore yield a little more; and corporate bonds at the next quality level (Baa) must yield still more. In mid-1959, 20-year gov-

ernment bonds yielded about 4 percent, corporate Aaa bonds about 4¼ percent, and corporate Baa bonds a bit over 5 percent. Bonds are classified by expert analysts in such organizations as Standard and Poor's or Moody's Investment Service, whose ratings have wide acceptance in the financial community. The basis of rating is the likelihood that interest and principal payments will be met, as indicated by past and prospective

FIGURE 9–7

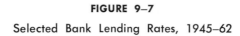

Selected Bank Lending Rates, 1945–62

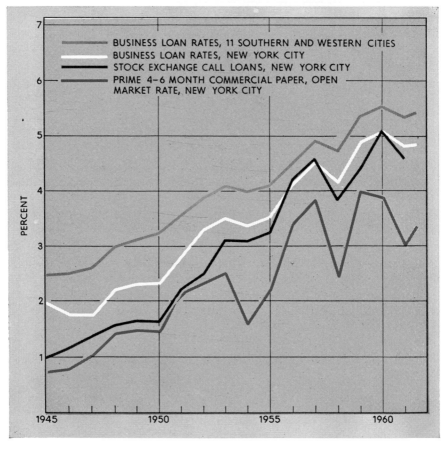

earnings of the company. One can always find bonds which *promise* yields of 8 or 10 percent—if the interest is actually paid! A yield of this size usually indicates a high risk that the company will not meet its commitments.

A common stock is riskier than a bond issued by the same company, since it carries no guarantee of dividend payments. One might expect, therefore, that the yield on stocks would have to be higher than that on bonds. This is usually, but not always, the case. In mid-1962, for example, the average yield on common stocks was 3¾ percent, compared with 4¼ percent on good quality bonds. This suggests that there are complicating factors at work. These factors include:

a) What is the yield on a common stock? The 3¾ percent figure includes only cash dividends paid to stockholders. But profits plowed back into expansion of the business also belong to the stockholders, and may be expected to raise earnings and dividend payments at some later date. On the basis of *total earnings*, corporate stocks were yielding more than 5 percent in mid-1962.

b) People do not buy a stock for dividends alone. They hope also that the price of the stock will rise over the years. In the case of so-called "growth stocks" this is the main consideration. These are companies which deliberately pay little or no dividends and put most of their profits back into the business. As the business grows and its profits increase, the value of its stock naturally rises. Stock in an expanding and profitable company can double or triple in value without the company having paid a cent of dividends. Thus the owner secures a *capital gain*, on which he pays no tax unless the security is sold, and even then the tax is only 25 percent. For people in a high income tax bracket, capital gains are much more advantageous than cash dividends.

c) Since World War II there has been a general expectation of a rising price level. Inflation has been in the air. Inflation raises profits, and this is reflected in higher stock prices. But the face value of a bond does not change. A man who puts $1,000 into a 20-year bond may find that the dollars he receives 20 years later buy only half as much as before. Had he bought a stock, its price might have advanced somewhat in proportion to the general price level, and the purchasing power of his capital would have been protected. Common stocks are thus "a hedge against inflation," in the popular phrase. When there is a strong expectation of inflation, money will rush into stocks, pushing their price up and their yield down, even to the point of disrupting the normal relation with bond yields.

d) Finally, stock prices and yields are influenced by speculative buying and selling in the hope of short-term gain, with no close relation to long-term values. Stock prices are apt to be abnormally high near the peak of a boom, and then to fall abnormally low during the subsequent recession.

Taking these things into account, it remains true that the expected yield on common stocks (including expected capital gains as well as dividend payments) is normally above bond yields. There is also wide variation in yield from one stock to another. When a stock has an unusually high yield, this often means a high risk that the yield may not continue.

Riskiness also influences the rates charged on bank loans. Small and little-known companies must pay a higher rate than national corporations with a top credit rating. Loans to individuals are considered riskier than business loans, and carry a higher interest rate on that account.

3. *Expense involved in the loan.* A further consideration in the case of small loans is the cost of making the loan and collecting the payments. It may take about as much paperwork to lend $1,000 to a farmer as to lend $100,000 to a manufacturing company. This means that the bank's costs *per dollar lent* are higher for small loans, and this warrants a higher interest charge.

4. *Competitiveness.* Small-town banks usually charge considerably higher rates than big-city banks, and small companies are charged more than large ones. The giant corporation with nationwide credit standing can often raise money for less than half the rate charged to a small company. This is due partly to different lending costs. But another reason why the large borrower fares better is that he can turn to alternative sources of supply, while the small borrower often cannot.

Banking is not a very competitive industry. Three quarters of the towns and cities in the United States which have banks have only one bank. The small businessman or farmer in these towns has little alternative but to borrow from the local bank on whatever terms it may set. Rarely are there more than 10 banks in the same city.[4] This means oligopoly, and usually of a cooperative kind. Banks in the same city normally agree to make the same service charges on checking accounts, pay the same interest rate on savings deposits, and charge the same rates for personal loans and mortgage loans. There cannot be an equally specific agreement on rates for business loans, because these vary with the size of the loan and the quality of the customer. But it is regarded as bad form for one bank to go after a regular customer of another bank, and particularly to do this by lending at a lower rate. "Shopping about" from one bank to another is discouraged, and the custom is for a business concern to deal with the same bank year in and year out.

The large national corporation is in a quite different situation. It can borrow in New York, or Chicago, or San Francisco. It may distribute its borrowings over several banks rather than tying itself to one. Because of these alternatives it can demand and get a lower interest rate than the small borrower. The rate charged by New York City banks to top-quality borrowers is the lowest rate in the country for business loans. Rates in smaller cities and towns shade upward from this, until one reaches the grocer in a small Montana town who has recourse only to one bank and pays perhaps double the rate which General Motors is paying in New York.

To sum up: the rate of interest increases with the *length* of the lender's commitment, the *riskiness* of the transaction, the *expense* associated with the loan, and the *market power* of the lending institution. Be-

---

[4] In 1949, only one fourth of 1 percent of all cities with banks had more than 10 banks. David A. Alhadeff, *Monopoly and Competition in Banking* (Berkeley, Calif.: University of California Press, 1954), p. 21.

cause of these factors, the highest money market rate is usually several times the lowest one.

Over the course of time, however, the pattern of rates moves up and down together. This sympathetic fluctuation stands out quite clearly in Figures 9–5 to 9–7. The reason is that the markets for different securities are linked by *possibilities of substitution* on both the lending and borrowing sides. A man can dispose of his savings through various types of intermediary or can put them directly into corporate or government securities. The financial intermediaries have a similar range of alternatives. Money can be put into common stocks, corporate bonds, government issues, or mortgages. Individuals and financial organizations are constantly looking around for securities offering the most desirable combination of yield and safety.[5]

Borrowers have a similar range of alternatives. The federal government can sell securities with a duration of anything from three months to 20 years. The large corporation can also raise money by selling various types of security. Even the small consumer may have several credit channels open. The art of debt management consists in exploiting these opportunities so as to get money at the lowest cost.

The efforts of borrowers and lenders to do the best they can for themselves meet in the money market, and establish demand and supply curves for each type of security; and these curves define an interrelated pattern of interest rates. The position of each rate depends on the position of all the others, and particularly on the level of certain key rates which are taken as market indicators, such as the Treasury bill rate and the prime loan rate in New York City. As these rates rise or fall, others are pulled along with them.

The best way to see why this must be so is to ask what would happen if it were not so. Suppose that, at a time when yields generally are falling, the yield on 20-year government bonds remains unchanged. What will happen? Buyers of securities, finding these bonds relatively more attractive than before, will shift funds toward them. The demand for 20-year governments will rise. On the supply side, the government will reduce its new issues of long-term bonds and increase its issues of shorter-term securities which can be put out at lower interest rates than before. This increase in demand and drop in supply will drive up the price of 20-year governments (which drives *down* their yield) until it is once more in proper relation to the general pattern. This shiftability on the part of

---

[5] This combination will of course vary from case to case. The conservative investor may prefer a small, safe return, while the speculator will take greater risks in the hope of larger income. But each investor, if he makes a rational calculation, will have a preference system on this matter. Market demand curves for different types of security are derived from these preference systems, just as demand curves for goods are derived from consumption preferences.

borrowers and lenders links the various submarkets into what amounts to a national money market.

A WORD ABOUT PROFIT

What Is Profit?

In discussing property incomes we have not yet mentioned the word "profit." Is profit a separate type of property income? What is it, and under what conditions does it arise?

We noted in Chapter 6 that the meaning of profit in economics differs from its meaning in accounting or business. The economic meaning of the term may be clarified by looking at a simple business organization, such as a grocery store. Mr. Greengage sets up a store and operates it for a year. At the end of the year, after paying all expenses, he has some money left over. Is this profit? Not necessarily. We must consider that if Mr. Greengage hadn't gone into business for himself he could have earned a salary working for someone else. He might have earned, say $10,000 a year as a store manager for A & P. So this amount must be charged against his own business as a *cost*—a salary which he pays, or should pay to himself. This is termed an *imputed* cost.

This is still not the end. Mr. Greengage had to spend, say, $50,000 to buy and furnish the store. If he had not put this money into the store, he could have put it into securities yielding a cash income. With care and prudence he might have realized a yield of 5 percent, or $2,500. So this $2,500 should also be set down as an imputed cost which must be covered if he is to break even on the year's operations.

He is only making a profit, in the economic sense of a net surplus, if he has left at the end of the year more than the $12,500 which he could have gotten anyway by hiring out his labor and money to somebody else. If he has $15,000 left at the year's end, his profit is $15,000 − $12,500 = $2,500. But if he has only $10,000 left, he has made a loss (a negative profit) of $2,500. He is $2,500 worse off than he would have been if he hadn't started the grocery store.

Profit, in short, is the net income from an enterprise after deducting all necessary expenses *including* imputed salary and interest costs, calculated at rates which could be obtained in alternative employments. Profit in this sense can be either positive or negative. *Whenever we use the term profit hereafter, it should be understood in this sense.* What is called profit in business usage will be referred to as *accounting profit*.

Why do we count imputed salary and interest as part of the cost of running a business? Because if a business owner cannot earn competitive returns on his labor and capital, he will presumably try to get out of the business and into something else. If profits in a competitive industry are negative, people will want to get out of the industry. As they do this, production will fall and prices will rise until the industry returns to a position of zero profits. Conversely, if profits are positive more people will enter this line of business. Output will rise and prices will fall until profits return to zero. Only at the zero profit level is the industry in equilibrium. This is the mechanism of competitive adjustment which was described in Chapter 6.

Competitive adjustments are not always rapid, particularly on the downside. Incomes may remain subnormal for a long time before producers are forced out of an overexpanded industry. The squeezing out of excess capacity from cotton textiles, bituminous coal, and other declining industries has been a slow and painful process.

One can count with more confidence on positive profits causing a rapid expansion of productive capacity, provided there is no barrier to people entering the industry. Under monopoly or oligopoly, of course, there may be barriers to entrance and positive profits may continue indefinitely.

How Important Is Profit?

The *possibility* of profit is central to the operation of a private enterprise economy. No one will put money into a certain line of production unless he expects to earn at least the going rate of interest. Typically, he will hope to do better than this. In many cases this hope is doomed to disappointment. But unless *some* businesses in the economy are yielding positive profit, the expectations of others will wither and the system will lose its vitality.

The *possibility* of profit for the efficient, the enterprising, or the lucky is not the same thing as the *existence* of positive profit on balance for the economy as a whole. In a fully competitive economy, one would expect that the profits of some would be about offset by the losses of others. Unusually efficient firms in an industry may be making positive profits, but firms of less than average efficiency will have negative profits. If demand is shifting toward a particular product, all producers may be making profit; but producers of substitute products which are suffering a fall in demand will be making losses. The entire economy is subject to swings of prosperity and depression; but the profits of boom years are offset by losses on the downswing. Thus taking an average for the entire economy over 10 or 20 years, one might expect profit to be approximately zero. If this is not so, one can surmise that the economy is not fully competitive.

The actual situation in the United States is not easy to determine. Statistics on accounting profit are available only for incorporated businesses, which leaves out most of retailing, service, and agriculture. Table 9–1, derived from business income tax returns, gives accounting profits for all business corporations since 1949. Losses of companies making losses have been deducted from the profits of the remainder, and corporate income taxes have also been deducted. The remainder is calculated as a percentage of total stockholders' equity, and as a percentage of net national product.

Let us accept these accounting figures, although a number of questions might be raised about them.[6] There remains the difficulty that we must deduct *imputed interest* on the stockholders' equity from accounting profit in order to see whether any economic profit is present. What interest rate should be used for this purpose? The pure rate of interest, as indicated by government bond yields, averaged about 3 percent during the fifties. The yield of top quality corporate bonds averaged about 4

Table 9–1

Net Accounting Profit, All Business Corporations, after Corporate Income Taxes, 1949–61*

Year	(1) Profit as a Percentage on Stockholders' Equity	(2) Profit as a Percentage of Net National Product
1949	8.9	6.6
1950	11.3	8.6
1951	9.0	6.4
1952	7.7	5.3
1953	7.5	5.3
1954	7.0	5.1
1955	8.5	6.3
1956	7.9	6.1
1957	7.1	5.5
1958		4.6
1959		5.5
1960		5.0
1961		4.9

* Sources: Col. 1: Bain, *op. cit.*
Col. 2: *Statistics of Income* and *Survey of Current Business.*

percent. Considering the greater risk attaching to stock ownership, it would perhaps be reasonable to take 5 percent as a competitive rate of return on stockholders equity.

Accounting profits since 1949 have averaged about 8 percent. Comparing this with our 5 percent norm, one might conclude that economic profit constituted about one third of accounting profit. Viewed from another standpoint, economic profits constituted perhaps 2 percent of net national product. Note that profits since 1956 have been appreciably lower than before 1956. This is associated with the low growth rate, high

---

[6] Notably the question whether depreciation allowances based on original cost were not too low to provide for replacement of equipment, considering the large rise of prices since 1939. To the extent that depreciation allowances are understated, true costs are understated and profits are overstated.

unemployment rate, and general sluggishness of the American economy since the mid-fifties.

There is wide variation in profit rates in different types of industry. Bain presents the following calculations for 1953:[7]

MAJOR SECTORS	AVERAGE ACCOUNTING PROFIT, AS A PERCENTAGE OF STOCKHOLDERS' EQUITY, AFTER INCOME TAX, ALL CORPORATIONS
Finance	10.1
Manufacturing	8.1
Construction	7.8
Services	5.9
Wholesale and retail trade	5.7
Public utilities	5.1
Mining and quarrying	4.5
Agriculture, forestry, fisheries	2.9
Average, all sectors	7.8
SUBSECTORS OF MANUFACTURING	
Motor vehicles and equipment	12.9
Electrical machinery and equipment	10.9
Chemicals	9.5
Tobacco manufactures	8.7
Primary metals	8.4
Beverages	7.2
Furniture and fixtures	6.5
Apparel and related products	3.2
Textile mill products	3.0
Average, all manufacturing	8.1

Note that profit is not spread evenly over the economy, but is concentrated in certain sectors. Thus finance, manufacturing, and construction yielded substantial profit. Public utilities, which are subject to government control and which include the depressed railroad industry, yielded about zero profit. The extractive industries had negative profits. Within the manufacturing sector, contrast the positive profits of the automobile, electrical, chemical, tobacco, and steel industries with the negative profits of the highly competitive clothing and textile industries.

Reasons for Profit

These statistical results confirm the theoretical conclusions of Chapter 7. Continuing profit is found mainly under conditions of *monopoly* and *oligopoly*, where prices may be held above the competitive level. Automobiles, heavy electrical equipment, cigarettes, chemicals, and

---

[7] Joe Bain, *Industrial Organization* (New York: John Wiley & Sons, Inc., 1956, pp. 384–85.

basic steel are all industries whose output is concentrated in the hands of a few major producers.

Profit may also occur in competitive industries for several reasons:

1. *Differences in company efficiency.* In theoretical reasoning about competition, we often assume equal cost levels for different producers in the same industry. Statistical studies have demonstrated repeatedly that this assumption is unwarranted. In any industry with many producers, one finds that costs per unit of output are lower for some firms than for others. The industry as a whole may show zero profit. But the most efficient firms will be earning substantial profit, while at the other extreme will be marginal producers with negative profits who are barely hanging on. The reasons for these cost differences are not well understood. Differences in the age and modernness of machinery, differences in plant layout, locational differences, differences in raw material costs, and differences in management skill not fully offset by salary differences are probably among the important factors.

2. *Favorable demand shifts.* When demand for a product rises, productive capacity will be expanded, but this takes time. During the period before the new plants come into production, established producers will earn positive profits.

3. *Innovation.* A company may develop a new or improved product, or a cheaper way of making some existing product. The innovation may yield a large profit for the time being. Unless there are restrictions on competition, however, other companies will copy the new development. As this happens, output expands, prices fall, and profit moves back toward zero.

Profit arises mainly from shifts in the "given conditions" of the competitive economy—demand and technology—plus the fact that adjustments in production take time. But competitive profit is a fleeting thing. It tends to disappear as soon as it has performed its economic function of drawing more resources into lines in which demand has risen or cost has fallen. If we could deduct monopoly and oligopoly profits from our statistical tables, profits in the American economy would probably come out close to the zero level which one would expect on theoretical grounds.

A Case against Profit?

As long as there are student political clubs and debating societies, there will continue to be argument over the merits of "the profit system." It is a good idea, however, to define one's target carefully before opening fire. Indiscriminate attacks on profit are likely to misfire; and those who think they are attacking profit are often at bottom attacking one or more of the following:

1. *Property income in general.* One can argue on ethical grounds that all income should be earned by personal effort, and that property income should be eliminated. There is no reason, however, to distinguish profit from any other form of property income. Most of what is called profit is in fact interest, and there is no logic in separating out profit for special attack.

2. Inequality of income. Property ownership is highly concentrated. Most property income is received by a small minority of the population, and this aggravates the overall inequality of income distribution. If inequality is the real target, the main line of attack lies through the tax system. The personal income, corporate income, and inheritance taxes already have a strong leveling effect. Whether more or less should be done in this direction is naturally a matter of political controversy.

3. Monopoly power. Most of the profit in the American economy arises in quasi-monopolistic industries. An attack on excess profits, then, is largely synonymous with an attack on business monopoly. This has been a traditional subject of political debate in the United States for a century or more.

The logic of these three lines of attack is quite different, and the practical remedies available are also different. Lumping them together in an omnibus attack on profit in general arouses a suspicion that the critic has not thought through his position.

SUMMARY

1. Money market transactions involve an *exchange of money against securities. Interest* is the price for parting with money.

2. Households are the main lenders or suppliers of funds. Business concerns and government agencies are the main borrowers or demanders of funds. Savings banks, life insurance companies, and other financial intermediaries serve as middlemen between lenders and borrowers.

3. The rate of return on business plant and equipment is the net addition which it makes to company revenues divided by its cost. A project will be undertaken only if its expected return exceeds the rate of interest on borrowed funds. The lower the interest rate, the more projects will be undertaken, and the greater the demand for funds.

4. The supply of funds is probably quite inelastic, i.e., savings habits at any time are rather rigid. Intersection of the supply and demand curves determines the quantity of funds exchanged and the market rate of interest.

5. In a growing economy both the demand and supply curves are shifting to the right. The long-term trend of interest rates depends on which shifts more rapidly. In the United States, interest rates have fallen moderately over the last century.

6. The rate of interest varies directly with the *length* of the lender's commitment, the *riskiness* of the transaction, the *expense* associated with the loan, and the *market power* of the lending institution.

7. Profit is the net income of an enterprise after deducting all costs, *including imputed salary and interest costs.*

8. The *possibility* of profit from particular projects is essential to the momentum of a private enterprise economy. But this is quite compatible with zero *realized* profits for the economy as a whole.

9. Actual profits in the United States, after allowing for imputed interest, are a very small part of national income. Profit occurs mainly in industries marked by monopoly and oligopoly.

Competition, Planning, and Economic Efficiency

I advocate a semi-revolution.
The trouble with a total revolution
(Ask any reputable Rosicrucian)
Is that it brings the same class up on top.
Executives of skillful execution
Will therefore plan to go halfway and stop.
Yes, revolutions are the only salves,
But they're one thing that should be done by halves.

ROBERT FROST

PART ONE BEGAN by sketching two patterns of economic organization: a centrally planned economy on the Soviet model, and an economy coordinated through a network of competitive markets. The analysis of a market economy was then elaborated by looking more closely at particular kinds of market, beginning with product markets and going on to markets for productive resources. We want now to stand back and look again at the market economy as a whole, this time from the standpoint of judging its performance. How good a system is it? What are its main strengths and weaknesses?

The same questions may be asked about the planned economy. We are apt to assume that central planning must be inefficient just as the Russians assume that capitalism is inefficient. Yet the national output of the U.S.S.R. has risen rapidly since 1950. Perhaps planning works better than we think. At any rate we should make a systematic effort to find out.

THE MEANING OF ECONOMIC EFFICIENCY

We are concerned here with *static efficiency*, or *efficiency at a point of time*. This has some bearing on economic growth over time, but we are not concerned directly with growth at the present stage.

An economy is statically efficient if it meets four main tests:

1. *Resource supplies should correspond to individual preferences.* Workers should be able to choose where to work and how much work to do. With somewhat less confidence one can argue that the level of saving in the economy should correspond to household preferences.

2. *Resources should be fully employed.* If this is not so, the economy is clearly working below capacity.

3. *Resources should be efficiently combined.* Each producing unit should be using those methods which, given the state of technology and the prices of labor and capital, yield lowest cost per unit of output. In constructing the cost curves of Chapter 6 we simply *assumed* that this was true, that managers were doing the best possible job of management. But this condition may or may not be met in practice.

4. *Resources should be properly allocated.* As a first approximation, this means that output of each product should be carried to the point at which price equals marginal cost. Price measures the value consumers attach to an additional unit of product A. Marginal cost, in its basic meaning of opportunity cost, measures the value they attach to the other things which would have to be sacrificed to make possible an extra unit of product A. When these two things are in balance, output of product A is just right.

If these conditions are satisfied the economy has reached an efficient position, that is, *a position in which it is impossible to make any individual better off without making someone else worse off*. We can always make Mr. A better off by firing Mr. B from his vice-president's job and putting Mr. A in his place. Or Mr. A can be made better off by taking income from Mr. B and handing it over to Mr. A. But we cannot determine whether such changes will increase total satisfaction in the community. We take the agnostic position that we cannot know what happens inside people's heads, hence we cannot add or compare their satisfactions. Only if we can benefit Mr. A without injuring anyone else can we say definitely that total welfare has risen. This is the reason for the rather complicated definition given in the first sentence.

Note that this definition of economic efficiency leaves a good many things on the side. It does not take account of public services which cannot be sold in the market, and to which the test of price equals marginal cost can accordingly not be applied. It does not solve the problem of personal income distribution, which we take as settled by some sort of political consensus in the community. It takes the state of technology as given, and does not ask where technical improvements come from or whether they will come faster under one form of economic organization than another.

The definition of static efficiency, in short, while it appears quite sweeping, remains a limited definition. Comprehensive evaluation of an economy would have to take account of its performance on these other fronts as well.

EFFICIENCY UNDER PLANNING

We can scarcely undertake here a full evaluation of Soviet economic performance. Much of the necessary information is not available, and in any event space limitations would prevent an adequate treatment. There is room only for a few comments and suggestions.

Resource Supplies

Labor supplies in the U.S.S.R. are determined largely by personal preference. The most serious restriction on labor mobility is perhaps the housing shortage, which leads people to remain in jobs where they have assured housing. In one other respect, however, job choices are freer than in most other countries. Anyone capable enough to be accepted for higher education receives a state scholarship. The financial barrier to entering the higher occupations has been removed.

The supply of capital equipment is decided centrally by government, and it is well known that a higher proportion of productive resources has been devoted to capital goods and a smaller proportion to consumer goods than is true in most Western countries. Soviet leaders have deliberately sacrificed the present to the future. They have restricted living standards today to make possible higher living standards, plus greater industrial and military might, tomorrow.

If one holds that the division of national output between capital goods and consumer goods should be based on household preferences, the Soviet system is open to criticism. Soviet citizens would almost certainly have preferred to consume more in the present and make less provision for the future. Their preferences on this point have been violated.

Against this one can argue that the present generation is naturally shortsighted, that people give too much weight to their desire for immediate consumption and too little to the welfare of their grandchildren. Is it not a legitimate function of government to offset this shortsightedness and to take a long view of the community's interest? Soviet leaders may have gone too far in this respect. But who is to say, and how would one go about proving it?

The Level of Employment

On this score the Soviet economy deserves good marks. There are errors in planning which cause some plants to work temporarily below capacity. But there is no general insufficiency of demand—rather the reverse. Production is usually pressing hard against capacity. Labor is scarce, and anyone wanting to change jobs finds a new one without difficulty. The economy is not subject to the frequent recessions and underemployment which occur in the United States.

Resource Combination and Management Efficiency

We now enter an area in which Soviet performance is usually thought to be well below that of the capitalist countries. But this is a treacherous area, in which statistical evidence is hard to find and interpret.

Output per man-hour, industry by industry, is typically lower in the U.S.S.R. than in the U.S.A., but the meaning of this is unclear. A notable feature of the Soviet economy, compared with the United States, is that labor is relatively plentiful and capital relatively scarce. One would thus expect Soviet production methods to be more labor-intensive, i.e., to use more labor and less capital per unit of output, than is true of the same industry in the United States. It follows that Soviet industry should show *lower* output per man-hour of labor and *higher* output per unit of capital equipment than is true in this country.[1] Such a result would not necessarily indicate lower overall efficiency in the U.S.S.R.

There are, however, significant indications of inefficiency in the management of Soviet enterprises. The gamesmanship between enterprise directors and higher officials in formulating production plans, the multiplicity of targets and controls to which the enterprise is subject, and the emphasis on sheer physical output have several unfortunate effects. Enterprise directors have an incentive to conceal their production capacity from higher authorities, thus securing a low production target which is easily reached. There may also be a tendency to hold back and not exceed planned output by too much, since this would be a sure way to get the plant's target raised for the following year. Large total output may be attained at the expense of a proper assortment of output. Too much of some things may be produced and not enough of others. Quality may be neglected or deliberately reduced to turn out as many units as possible. Finally, output may be produced at excessive cost. Plant cost records do not seem to be scrutinized too carefully if the output record is satisfactory.

There are also indications of waste and delay at higher levels of administration. The continued centralization of key decisions in Moscow

---

[1] Example: Suppose the United States uses 75 men and 2 automatic coal cutters to produce 150 tons of coal a day, and suppose that the U.S.S.R. attains the same output with 150 men and 1 automatic cutter. Then labor and capital productivities would compare as follows:

	LABOR (Tons per Man)	CAPITAL (Tons per Machine)
U.S.A.	2	75
U.S.S.R.	1	150

means a large administrative machine reaching down through the republics and sovnarkhozy, a vast amount of record-keeping and paperwork, and considerable delay in reaching decisions. Transportation is slow, and needless crosshauling of materials seems to be common. Supplies will be in transit from the Ukraine to the Urals, while at the same time similar products are shuttling in the opposite direction. Delivery delays and material shortages are a serious obstacle to production, and a whole class of "pushers" or expediters has grown up alongside the official procurement machinery. Campbell comments that "in both trade and industry . . . Soviet enterprises require much bigger inventories relative to a given flow than American firms do. This slow turnover of inventories in the Soviet economy means the immobilization of a very large amount of resources that might be put to more productive use. Presumably, poor Soviet performance in this respect is caused by such factors as slow transportation, the hoarding instincts of managers, the existence of goods that are unsalable, and a slow production cycle in some branches of manufacturing."[2]

These qualitative indications are confirmed by productivity measurements.[3] Output per man-hour is not just moderately lower in Soviet industry, as one might expect, but averages only about half of the American level. There are wide differences among industries in this respect. In some, labor productivity is almost at the U.S. level, while in others it is less than one tenth as great. Nor is lower labor productivity offset consistently by higher capital productivity. One can find cases, notably rail transportation and pig iron production, in which the U.S.S.R. does use capital more intensively and gets greater output per unit of equipment. But there are many cases in which the reverse is true. Soviet industry also usually requires more raw materials per unit of output than is true in U.S. industry. All in all, then, Soviet production is considerably more expensive in terms of inputs per unit of output.

The sector which shows up worst in this respect is agriculture. Soviet agriculture is extremely inefficient by U.S. standards. Yields per acre for most major crops are less than half as great. Eggs per hen, milk per cow, meat yield per beef animal, are far below U.S. levels. And labor requirements are much higher. It takes three times as many farm workers in the U.S.S.R. to produce the same amount of milk, five times as many to produce a given quantity of potatoes, and seven times as many to produce the same amount of grain. One reason is the lower level of mechanization in Soviet agriculture—only one fifth as many trucks and tractors, only one quarter as much electric power as on American farms. The result is to tie up in agriculture about 40 percent of the Soviet labor force, compared with our 7 or 8 percent.

---

[2] Robert W. Campbell, *Soviet Economic Power* (Boston: Houghton Mifflin Co., 1960), p. 78.

[3] For a review of available evidence, see R. W. Campbell, *op. cit.*, chap. 4.

The variability of Russian productivity from one area of the economy to another, as Campbell points out, "suggests imbalance and unevenness in planning. It seems a clear conclusion that the Russians have been slower to take advantage of technological progress and organizational improvements in some branches than in others, and that the Soviet system of incentives and controls has been much more effective in some sectors of the economy than in others in getting managers and planners to improve performance. There is also an implication here that capital investment planning has been faulty. One suspects that the planners have not always directed their investment to the areas where it would have the greatest effect in raising labor productivity and reducing manpower requirements."[4]

Resource Allocation

Efficiency in this respect requires that money costs of production be an accurate measure of social or opportunity costs, and that price equal marginal cost in each line of production. In the Soviet economy neither of these things is true. Cost of production in Soviet usage covers labor, materials, and depreciation of equipment. But it does not include interest on the capital used in the enterprise, which is treated as a gift from the state. To this extent production costs are understated, and the degree of understatement varies from industry to industry. The cost of goods requiring much capital equipment comes out relatively too low, while the cost of goods with a high labor content is relatively too high. This bias in the costing system works against rational allocation of resources.

Moreover, prices are not related to costs in a systematic way. This is true particularly of consumer goods prices. Consumer goods, in addition to costs of production and marketing, carry a substantial mark-up in the form of a "turnover tax"; and this tax varies widely from one product to the next. Product A may carry a tax of 50 percent, while product B is taxed 150 percent. No one knows how these decisions are made. But one can surmise that they reflect partly planners' judgments of essentiality, more essential goods carrying lower tax rates, and partly the capacity to produce a particular item. The tax is set to produce a price at which consumers will just purchase the planned output, as explained in Chapter 5.

The result is similar to the result of monopolistic restriction, and may be illustrated by Figure 10–1. Take two products, A and B, which we assume to have similar demand curves and the same unit production cost OC. In a market economy, these products would be priced at OC and the same quantity of each (OQ) would be produced. In the Soviet production plan for 1964, however, the quantity of product A is set at OA, the quantity of B at OB. In order to "clear the market," A must be priced

---

[4] *Op. cit.*, p. 80.

at OP_A, which means adding a large turnover tax CP_A to production costs. Product B must be priced at OP_B, which will mean adding the lower tax rate CP_B.

This involves misallocation of resources in terms of satisfying consumer preferences. Product A is being (relatively) underproduced while Product B is (relatively) overproduced. The value which consumers

FIGURE 10–1

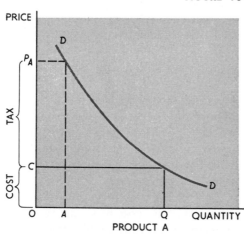

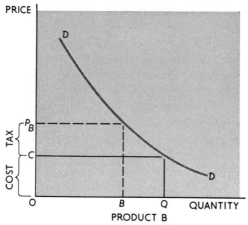

Both products have the same unit cost of production and the same demand schedule. The planners, however, decide to produce only OA of the first and OB of the second. Turnover taxes are set so that just these quantities can be sold.

place on an additional unit of A is shown by OP_A, while the value placed on the last unit of B is is shown by the much lower figure OP_B. Consumer satisfaction could be increased by shifting resources from B to A, since consumers would value the extra output of A more than the amount of B which they would have to give up. How serious this misallocation is in practice we do not know, since we have no list of turnover tax rates; but it is probably a serious defect of the system.

A Concluding Question

We come out of this brief survey with mixed findings. The Soviet economy seems efficient in some respects, inefficient in others. The most serious criticisms are perhaps that it fails to get maximum output from the available resources, and that planning of consumer goods output is not geared systematically to consumer preferences. Whether the high percentage of resources devoted to capital goods production should also be considered a defect depends on how far one feels that household savings preferences should be binding on the national economy.

We conclude with a puzzle: In terms of static efficiency, the Soviet economy does not seem to deserve an A grade. Yet its growth rate is one of the highest in the world. Since 1950 Soviet national output has grown at 6 to 8 percent a year, compared with a long-term average of about 3 percent for the United States. Why this contrast between static and dynamic efficiency? How can an economy with so many structural defects continue to expand so rapidly? We shall return to these tantalizing questions in Part Four.

EFFICIENCY UNDER PLANNING: SOME POSSIBILITIES OF IMPROVEMENT

Soviet economic organization is not fixed and unchanging. Soviet officials have shown a capacity to learn from past mistakes, and to apply Western economic ideas to planning problems. Major changes in economic organization were announced in 1957 and 1962, and smaller changes are being made constantly.

What more might be done to increase the efficiency of resource allocation and use in the Soviet economy? Several possibilities come to mind:

1. Closer attention might be given to consumer preference in planning consumer goods output. Soviet planners should learn and use the demand curve concept. Instead of arbitrary and variable rates of turnover tax, it would be preferable to work toward an equal tax on all consumer products. If gloves are taxed 75 percent, the same rate should be levied on shirts, stockings, tables, washing machines, and motor scooters. (Food might be exempted, as it often is under state sales taxes in the United States.) Then prices, while not *equal* to cost as in a market economy, would be proportionate to cost, which can be defended as a "next best" basis for pricing. Consumers would still be getting less of everything than they would like, but they would feel the pinch equally across the board. Quantities produced would be guided by consumer preferences as shown in demand curves, rather than by planners' ideas about what consumers want or should be given.

Changes might also be made in retailing practices. There is chronic complaint from Soviet consumers about the monotony, poor styling, and poor quality of consumer products. Since all goods are scarce, manufacturers have the whip hand. They unload what they choose to produce on the state retail outlets, which must then unload the goods on consumers. The retailing organizations might be given more authority to bargain with manufacturers over design and quality, and even to stop buying from factories which fail to meet reasonable standards. This would involve some idle capacity and apparent waste in the short run. But if it succeeded in breaking the mentality of a sellers' market it could bring great advantages to consumers over a longer period.

2. The Soviet government has already gone some distance in raising farm prices and putting them on a regular commercial basis. But why not go the whole way? Why shouldn't the state trading organizations which buy food for city consumers have to depend entirely on offering sufficiently attractive prices to get the deliveries they want? And why shouldn't each collective farm be left free to plan its output so as to make most money in view of prevailing prices for various products? This would offer greater incentive for agricultural efficiency. It would also induce each farm to specialize in products for which it has greatest natural advantage, something which has not been true of Soviet agriculture in the past. Each farm should also have more latitude than it now has to reach independent decisions on quantity and type of machinery to be purchased, use of fertilizers, crop rotation, and other problems of farm management.

3. Industrial enterprises are subject to a multiplicity of targets and controls. The manager is told in detail what to produce, and how much labor, materials, and other inputs he may use. Targets are set for unit costs, man-hour output, machine utilization, and many other things. Different targets may conflict, diverting effort into wasteful directions.

Couldn't the control system be streamlined to advantage by substituting a single criterion of success, the yearly profit of the enterprise? Tell the manager to go ahead and make money, but don't try to tell him how. Leave it to him to juggle inputs so as to achieve lowest production costs, and to arrange his output pattern to get greatest sales revenue. Then, assuming that product and factor prices have been set correctly, he will be making best use of the resources committed to his care. A good profit showing could be rewarded through both profit sharing and promotion.

A more drastic departure would be to allow enterprises to reach their own decisions about expansion, and to bid for the necessary funds on a competitive basis. Suppose the government decided to set aside for investment an amount of money equal to 25 percent of GNP, and put this up for auction at a 5 percent interest rate. It might turn out that at this rate the amount enterprises were willing to borrow was considerably higher than the amount available. Then for next year the investment quota would have to be increased, or the interest rate would have to be raised, or both. But it should be possible by experiment to set an equilibrium rate of interest just sufficient to balance the demand and supply of funds. Any enterprise contemplating expansion could then apply for money at the going rate of interest. If management could present satisfactory evidence of enough demand for its products so that the proposed investment would pay off, loans would be made on regular banking principles. Capital allocation would be determined by competition rather than by arbitrary planning decisions, and funds would flow to points in the economy at which demand was rising or new technical improvements were being introduced.

Yugoslavia has experimented with this blend of public ownership and decentralized economic control, with interesting results. The U.S.S.R. and other communist countries, however, still consider this approach unorthodox and dangerous. The reasons are at least partly political. Enterprise managers who were given this degree of independence and authority might become powerful enough to challenge the government leadership. Only a very secure and self-confident government could risk this much relaxation of central control.

4. Without going as far as has just been suggested, greater use could be made of the interest rate concept. The idea of a percentage return on capital could be a useful guide in two respects:

a) For allocation of investment funds among sectors of the economy. This is a major power of the central planners at present. One can scarcely expect them to sacrifice this and substitute slavish obedience to interest yields. But they might usefully estimate the yield of capital in various fields before reaching final decisions. Then if they decide to go contrary to the interest criterion, they are at least making a deliberate rather than an ignorant decision. Over the past 20 years, the marginal yield of investment in agriculture, transportation, and housing has probably been *much* higher than in most other fields. There is little evidence that planners were even aware of this fact.

b) For choice of production methods. The key men here are the engineers in charge of designing new plant and equipment, the so-called "project makers." Many of these men have rediscovered the interest concept and use it as a common-sense guide to decisions. Suppose one design involves spending $100,000 more on plant, but yields a saving of $10,000 a year in labor and other operating expenses. Then the extra capital expenditure will pay for itself over a 10-year period, usually termed in Russia the *period of recoupment*. This is obviously the reciprocal of the yield on the project. A pay-out period of 10 years means an annual yield of $\frac{1}{10} = 10$ percent.

Whether a project will pay for itself in 6, or 8, or 10 years is often used as a test of its worthwhileness by Soviet engineers. The calculations are quite similar to those made in a capitalist business. Interest, having been chased out the front door, has come in at the rear. The use of these methods is somewhat shamefaced, however, and is subject to periodic criticism by orthodox Marxists. It would be a good idea to accept these techniques more openly and to have critical discussion of their usefulness. At present, the pay-out period used as a criterion varies widely from industry to industry, with the consequence that use of capital is pushed more intensively in some fields than in others. There is need for greater standardization of these criteria throughout the economy, so as to reach something like an equal marginal yield of capital in all uses.

THE EFFICIENCY OF A MARKET ECONOMY

Most of what needs to be said on this subject already has been said in earlier chapters, but the main points may now be drawn together and summarized.

Resource Supplies

The supply of labor is determined mainly through individual choice by each member of the labor force, but occupational choices are not entirely free. The most serious restriction is the cost of higher education, which limits entrance to the professional and executive occupations.

The supply of capital is heavily influenced by household decisions about saving, but this is not the only influence at work. A sizable part of business profits never reaches the stockholders, but is saved and reinvested directly. Corporation executives may save more in this way than the stockholders would choose to do if they had the money in their own pockets. Moreover, the amount saved in the economy depends on demand as well as supply. If demand for funds is low, there will be recession and a drop in income; and though people might *like* to save a certain amount, their incomes will not permit them to do so. We shall go into this thoroughly in Part Three. Meanwhile, one should be cautious about asserting that the level of saving is *determined* by household decisions.

The Level of Employment

A common and justified criticism of the market economy is that it does not operate continuously at full capacity. Looking at the records for the United States over the past century, one notes frequent declines in economic activity. Our record on this has been better since World War II than during the thirties. But over the past decade the economy has frequently been operating 10 percent or more below capacity. In addition to the insecurity and hardship which this causes for the workers who happen to be unemployed, it is wasteful from an overall economic standpoint.

On the positive side, one can say that the American economy does not *need* to perform as sluggishly as it has been doing in recent years. We know a good deal about what might be done to raise the level of activity, and the difficulty in taking the necessary steps is more political than economic.

Resource Combination and Managerial Efficiency

On this front the market economy deserves a good score. Under pure competition, each producer must operate as efficiently as others are doing. Otherwise he will find that his cost per unit of output is higher than the market price, and he will eventually be eliminated from the industry. Under monopoly and oligopoly, the outcome is less certain. There is still an incentive to reach maximum efficiency, because reducing costs will always increase profits. But the lure of a little more profit may be less effective than the fear of failure, which always hangs over the head of the competitive producer.

Resource Allocation

Here, too, the market economy rates higher than the planned economy. While one can point to some distortions in labor markets and money markets, broadly speaking, productive resources are correctly priced. Money costs of production correspond reasonably well to opportunity costs. Moreover, under pure competition price equals marginal cost, so that the correct amount of each product is being produced. We need not repeat the demonstration of this in Chapters 4 and 6.

The widespread existence of imperfect or monopolistic competition is not very upsetting to this optimistic conclusion. Monopoly and oligopoly are upsetting, and are also quite common. Monopoly typically leads to too little of the monopolized product being produced. Oligopoly can also lead to this result, and in addition it can lead to the wastes of idle plant capacity and excessive selling expenditures.

Weighing these things together, it appears that the market economy meets the tests of static efficiency quite well, or at least better than the centrally planned economies have done to date. One is restrained from wholehearted enthusiasm mainly by the existence of business cycles and underemployment, and by the frequency of monopoly and oligopoly in product markets.

GOVERNMENT ACTION OUTSIDE THE MARKET MECHANISM

Admirers of the market mechanism have sometimes carried their admiration to the point of asserting that it can solve virtually all economic problems, and that government intervention is usually unnecessary or harmful. Before concluding this chapter, therefore, we should remind ourselves that: (1) Static efficiency isn't everything. There are a variety of other problems which have to be solved outside, or at least alongside, the market mechanism. (2) An ideal system of competitive markets will not spring up and persist of its own accord. Government action is often needed to establish markets or improve their operation. A review of these possibilities for constructive government action provides a good transition to our analysis of policy issues in Part Two.

Economic Growth

The market mechanism answers the question of how to distribute a *given* amount of productive resources among various lines of production. It is less clear that it provides a satisfactory answer to the question of how fast these resources should *grow* over the course of time.

The growth of the nation's stock of capital equipment is heavily influenced by household decisions about saving and consumption. But on what ground can one say that these decisions are *correct* from an overall standpoint? Why should the preferences of the present generation be taken as decisive for the level of investment, which will affect the welfare of many generations to come? If this generation is shortsighted in some measure, why should the national economy be similarly shortsighted?

These questions are important even in prosperous industrial countries. They are even more important in the less developed countries, where voluntary household savings are typically small. Suppose the government of one of these countries decides that development should be accelerated and that more of the country's resources should be diverted to capital goods at the expense of current consumption. Can one say that this interference with private decisions is necessarily wrong?

Economic growth depends also on *the rate of technological process*. In reasoning about static efficiency, the state of technology is always taken as given. But where does technology come from? Can a private market economy be counted on to produce a rapid flow of new inventions? Or are there things which government can usefully do in this connection?

Economic Stability

However good the market system may be for allocating economic resources *at full employment*, it does not solve the problem of how to achieve and maintain full employment. One can construct on paper an ideal market economy which could not deviate far from full employment, and in which deviations would be quickly corrected. But this is not the world in which we live. There is nothing in actual market economies which insures them against waves of depression, or for that matter against chronic underemployment. Maintenance of near-capacity operation requires deliberate stabilizing actions which only government is in a position to take.

Public Services

It has always been recognized that there are community needs which cannot be met through individual choice in the market place. National defense cannot be sold to the citizens in small pieces. It must be produced by government and financed through a system of taxation.

This raises several questions: (1) *What types* of production fall properly within the public sector? Police protection and national defense are clear cases. Public education and public highways are generally accepted. As one gets into such things as health, housing, and social insurance the degree of controversy increases. Where should the boundary be drawn?

2. *How much* of each public service should government produce? What is a proper level of expenditure on defense, education, highways, and the rest? It is difficult to apply the test of marginal cost = price because these services are usually not sold at a price. What principles can we find as a substitute?

3. How should the *tax burden* be distributed? This is closely related to the issue of personal income distribution. By tilting the tax scales in one direction or another, government can make the distribution of income after taxes more equal or less equal than before.

The theory of prices and markets does not answer these questions, and we are forced to reach beyond it for other bases of decision.

Income Distribution

In a competitive economy individuals are paid according to their contribution to production. One can argue that this is a fair and proper basis for income distribution, but then one is talking philosophy as well as economics. If someone else argues on ethical grounds that the talented and efficient should be taxed to support their weaker brethren, one cannot prove him wrong by appealing to economic theory. Income distribution is bound to be a subject of political struggle, in which the results of the market will be modified to some extent.

The struggle is partly over the pattern of *resource ownership*, on which the market distribution of income basically depends. In reasoning about static efficiency, resource ownership is always taken as given. But this does not render it immune to criticism at a more fundamental level. Property ownership in the United States is still concentrated in a minority of families. Should these families be allowed to pass on their holdings intact to their descendants? Or should property be taxed away at death and each generation obliged to start afresh in the economic race?

Similiar questions arise with respect to the distribution of personal skills and capacities. These are partly inherited, but they depend also on training and education. The set-up of higher education is especially strategic in determining how many people, and which people, can qualify to become accountants, dentists, architects, or electrical engineers. Government can affect the outcome by its expenditures on educational facilities, teaching salaries, and scholarship or loan funds. This amounts to changing the institutional structure within which people compete for a livelihood. It is a change in one of the givens of the competitive problem.

GOVERNENT ACTION TO IMPROVE THE MARKET MECHANISM

The argument that a system of private competitive enterprise leads to maximum efficiency rests on an idealized picture of the system, in which everyone is perfectly informed and all markets are purely competitive. But these conditions are not feasible in all sectors of the economy, and even where they are feasible, competitive markets will not spring up and persist of their own accord.

There are numerous industries in which atomistic competition is not feasible. In the area of public utilities, it would be inconvenient and expensive to have more than one producer in the same territory. In many other industries there is room for only a few producers, because the optimum scale of plant is large relative to total demand. The consequence is oligopoly, and it is difficult to make members of an oligopoly group behave competitively in the sense of following independent price and production policies.

In these cases the regulatory force of competition is not operative. What can be put in its place? The possibilities include informal supervision and pressure on the industry, regulation of prices and service by a government board, and government operation. In any event there would be widespread agreement that unchecked exercise of monopoly power cannot be permitted.

Even where competitive markets are feasible, they will not necessarily arise, persist, and operate effectively. Government action may be needed to make effective competition possible. Such action, while sometimes criticized as meddlesome intervention, is fundamentally pro-private enterprise.

Government can sometimes *create markets* where they would not otherwise exist. A good example is the local offices of the state employment services. These are not used by workers and employers as fully as they might be. But to the extent that they are used, they enable each employer to find out what labor is available and each worker to find out what job vacancies exist in the area. This permits a more effective matching of unemployed workers and available jobs.

The effectiveness of competition can often be improved by *provision of information*. It is often argued with some reason that consumers are so ignorant and misinformed that their preferences provide only a dubious guide to production decisions. But one need not conclude that consumer choice should be supplanted, or that a wise and benevolent government should give people what is *really* good for them. The moral is rather that government should provide information on the basis of which consumers can pursue their interests more effectively. Information activity includes setting objective grades and standards, as is done for many food and drug products, so that buyers can determine more accurately what they are getting. It includes the efforts of the Federal Trade Commission and other agencies to prevent false advertising statements. It includes the testing of products and distribution of facts about performance by such private groups as Consumers Union and Consumers Research.

A special case of this sort is provision of technical and market information to *small business* concerns. There are numerous industries in which production can be carried on efficiently by small independent units. But small producers cannot afford to set up large research and development laboratories, or to make elaborate market surveys and economic forecasts. These activities need to be organized on a larger scale, and their results made generally available. The classic case in American experience is agriculture, where small private producers have been aided effectively by an elaborate network of government research, education, marketing, credit, and advisory services. Many lines of industry and trade could benefit from this same sort of cooperative effort.

Even though competition may be more efficient, collusion to set prices and regulate production is usually more profitable. So government is called on to *prevent collusive action* and to protect competitive markets. The work of the Department of Justice and other federal agencies on this front will be examined in the next chapter.

The argument for competitive industry usually assumes that *money costs of production are an accurate measure of social costs*. While this is broadly true, one can find instances in which it will not be true. If a factory pollutes a stream in which people would like to fish or swim, or if it sends out dense clouds of smoke which deposit soot for miles around, there are costs to the community which will not be counted as costs by the company concerned. If a company works its employees hard to the age of 50 and then lays them off to be supported on relief, it is imposing a cost on the community which should be (but will not be) covered by the price of its products. Such discrepancies between private and social cost can often be corrected by government action.

This is one example of a broader economic phenomenon which has been termed *neighborhood or external effects*. Competitive economic theory is ultraindividualistic in assuming that the satisfactions of each individual in the system are independent of the behavior and satisfactions of other people. This is clearly not true. If my neighbor keeps a barking dog, or gives noisy parties, or drives his car very badly, this has an effect on me. On a broader plane, if other citizens are free not to educate their children beyond the fourth grade or to go about in public with communicable diseases, this affects me and my family. These neighborhood effects justify police protection, compulsory education, health regulation, and other things which restrict freedom of individual choice.

An important case of interdependence among economic units involves the *external economies* discussed in Chapter 6. The costs of one company or industry may depend on those of related companies or industries. Simultaneous expansion of several related industries may lower costs for all of them. It will be worthwhile from an overall standpoint to stimulate such expansion, even though it would not pay any one company to go ahead on its own. This is an especially important consideration for countries in the early stages of industrialization.

WHAT REMAINS OF THE COMPETITIVE CASE?

The emphasis on government action in the last few pages may seem to have undermined the confidence in competitive markets which we developed in earlier chapters. So it should be re-emphasized in conclusion that these qualifications do not destroy the presumption in favor of competitive markets wherever they can be established. Where it is feasible to have something approaching atomistic competition, there is reason to expect that free markets will yield better economic results than any alternative arrangement. Moreover, despite marked monopoly power in some sectors of the economy, the competitive prescription remains applicable to perhaps two thirds of private production in the United States, comprising most of agriculture, trade, services, building construction, and light manufacturing.

What the preceding section mainly demonstrates is not that the argument for competition is *wrong*, but that it is *incomplete*. It demonstrates the mistake of thinking that a competitive economy implies a do-nothing government. And it underlines the legitimate and necessary functions of government in a capitalist system.

SUMMARY

1. The static efficiency of an economy can be judged by whether (*a*) resource supplies correspond to individual preferences; (*b*) resources are fully employed; (*c*) resources are efficiently combined; and (*d*) resources are properly allocated. If these conditions are met, the economy has reached a position of maximum welfare.

2. The Soviet economy ranks high on the first two tests, not very high on the last two. But in spite of this failure to achieve static efficiency, national output has been rising faster in the U.S.S.R. than in most other countries.

3. The efficiency of the Soviet economy could be improved by taking demand schedules as a guide in planning consumer goods output, by allowing more freedom of decision to enterprise and collective farm managers, by substituting price and profit incentives for detailed physical controls, and by making greater use of the interest rate concept.

4. The market economy generally rates higher than the centrally planned economy in terms of static efficiency. Its main defects are failure to achieve full employment of resources, and some distortion of resource allocation due to monopoly and oligopoly.

5. General reliance on the market mechanism does not imply a do-nothing government. Government action *outside* the market system is needed to achieve full use of resources, a high rate of capital formation, rapid technological

progress, an adequate supply of public services, and an acceptable distribution of personal income.

6. Government action is needed also to maintain and improve the system of competitive markets. Actions in this category include creating markets, providing improved information, aiding small producers with research and other services which must be organized on a large scale, preventing private price fixing, taking account of neighborhood effects in consumption and protection, and controlling the operation of industries where monopoly power is unavoidable.

PART | TWO

GOVERNMENT AND THE MARKET ECONOMY

That man's the true conservative
Who lops the mouldered branch away.

ALFRED LORD TENNYSON

Every boy and every gel
That's born into this world alive
Is either a little Liberal
Or else a little Conservative.

W. S. GILBERT

When we reflect how difficult it is to move or deflect the great machine of society, how impossible to advance the notions of a whole people suddenly to ideal right, we see the wisdom of Solon's remark, that no more good must be attempted than the nation can bear.

THOMAS JEFFERSON

ONE CAN construct on paper a purely private economy, watched over by a caretaker state; but no one has ever actually seen such an economy. In all capitalist countries government performs important economic functions, and these functions have been gradually increasing. This has led to acrimonious political debate. To some, government is a beneficent instrument for promoting the general welfare. To others, government action spells creeping socialism and suppression of private initiative.

Debating this issue at the level of general principle usually leads to an exchange of political insults—"reactionary," "do-gooder," "socialist," and so on—which seems almost completely sterile. It is more profitable to look at government economic activities piece by piece, and to evaluate each on its own merits. This pragmatic approach reveals good reasons for most of what government is doing, reasons that stem from the limitations of the market system described in Chapter 10. Government action is designed for the most part to develop and sustain the network of private markets, or to do things that the market mechanism is inherently incapable of doing.

The market mechanism by itself does not ensure a stable level of economic activity, or a rapid rate of technical progress, or an optimum level of investment and capital accumulation, or an unassailably just distribution of personal income. Action on these matters must be taken in some measure *outside* the market system. Government action is needed also to create and maintain the basic framework of competitive markets, which will not necessarily persist of its own accord. Finally, government must carry on production outside the market system to meet community needs that the citizens have decided, through political channels, can best be served in this way. The citizens may be wrong in so deciding, but one cannot prove them wrong by appealing to economic theory.

While most economic activities of modern governments seem legitimate in principle, this leaves wide room for debate. Is the scale of a particular program too large or too small? Is it well designed to achieve the objectives at which it is aimed? Are there new lines of activity that government might usefully pursue? These economic issues are the core of modern politics. In Part Two we run the gamut of these issues and ask what we can learn by applying economic analysis to them. The sequence of discussion is as follows:

1. We can all agree that competition is a fine thing. But how competitive is the American economy in practice? Is the trend toward freer competition or toward greater concentration of market power? What is government now doing, and what more can it do, to enforce competitive behavior? (Chapter 11)

2. In some sectors of the economy, competition has deliberately been limited or abandoned. Public utilities are unavoidably monopolistic, and

their prices are regulated by government commissions. About half of agricultural production is covered by guaranteed minimum prices, accompanied in some cases by production controls. Retail competition in some products has been significantly restricted by resale price maintenance laws. What is the effect of these policies, and to what extent should they be continued? (Chapter 12)

3. Turning to factor markets, we consider first the supply and pricing of labor. What do trade unions try to get from employers and how do they go about it? How does collective bargaining affect wage rates, labor supply, hours of work, and labor productivity. Does an overall evaluation of unionism indicate benefit or harm to the economy? What can be done to reduce the likelihood of crippling strikes, particularly in industries whose continuous operation is important to public safety and convenience? (Chapter 13)

4. Inequality in personal income distribution is sometimes considered a shortcoming of a competitive economy. How unequal is income distribution in the United States, and is inequality increasing or decreasing over the course of time? How far should leveling of personal incomes be a deliberate object of government policy? What is the effect of taxes and transfer payments on income distribution at present? (Chapter 14)

5. After examining the organization of private production, we turn to the public economy. How much is presently spent on providing public services? Do we have too much of these services or too little? We usually cannot apply the test of price = marginal cost. Is there anything which can be put in its place? What kinds of tax are levied to cover the cost of public services? Who pays each type of tax, and how does this add up for the revenue system as a whole? It turns out that the overall tax burden is unevenly distributed, by income level and by region of the country. Is the present distribution of the burden desirable and, if not, what changes can be suggested? (Chapter 15)

6. Thus far the discussion has been confined to a single country. What about competition across national boundaries? What determines the products a country exports and imports? If free competition within a country has desirable effects, can the same be said of free international trade? Is there any justification for protective tariffs and other types of trade restriction? (Chapter 16)

Part Two, in sum, covers the *microeconomic* issues of government policy, applying to them the analytical tools developed in Part One. *Macroeconomic* problems of monetary control, fiscal policy, and other policies to promote economic stability and growth are left to a later stage, since they require concepts that will not be developed until Part Three.

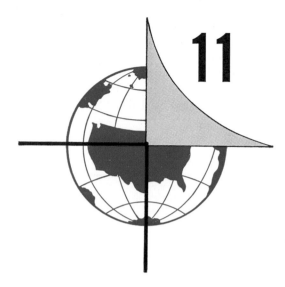

Promoting Competition

> Monopolies are odious, contrary to the spirit of free government and the principles of commerce, and ought not to be suffered.
>
> MARYLAND DECLARATION OF 1776

THE MAIN TRADITION of economic thought in the United States is one of competitive private enterprise. There is wide agreement that competitive organization produces better results than either private or public monopoly.

But is competitive enterprise a feasible objective? It is often argued that there is so little competition left in the American economy that we cannot rely on it as an organizing principle. So we must begin by inquiring whether this is true. How competitive is the American economy? Is the trend toward freer competition or the reverse? Will efforts to preserve competition be frustrated by the march of history?

THE IMPORTANCE OF MARKET POWER

It would be nice if one could toss industries into boxes labeled "monopoly," "oligopoly," and "atomistic competition." One difficulty with this is that oligopoly is a matter of degree. Oligopoly can mean that three companies produce all the industry's output. But it can also mean that there are twenty important producers plus a fringe of smaller competitors. The price-output results will probably be closer to those of

231

atomistic competition in the twenty-company case than in the three-company case. Where does "strong oligopoly" leave off and "weak oligopoly" begin?

One can learn something, however, by looking at the proportion of a market which is occupied by a few producers. The situation in *manufacturing* is suggested by Table 11–1. In one third of all manufacturing in-

TABLE 11–1

Industrial Concentration in Manufacturing, 1954

Percent of Industry Shipments Supplied by the Largest Four Firms	Number of Industries	Percent of Industries	Percent of All Manufacturing Shipments
75–100	40	9.2	8
50– 75	101	23.3	17
25– 50	157	36.2	35
0– 25	136	31.3	40
	434	100.0	100.0

Source: Joe Bain, *Industrial Organization* (New York: John Wiley & Sons, Inc., 1959), p. 120.

dustries, producing one quarter of manufacturing output, the four leading companies turned out half or more of the industry output. These are situations of strong oligopoly. At the opposite extreme, another third of the industries, producing 40 percent of manufacturing output, had less than 25 percent of their output controlled by the four leading companies. These are situations of weak oligopoly or atomistic competition. A middle third of industries had between 25 and 50 percent of their output controlled by the top four companies. It must be emphasized, however, that the operation of an industry depends on relations among the leading companies, on the number of smaller companies, and on the ease with which new companies can enter the industry. Two industries with the same percentage of output controlled by the top four companies may show quite different economic behavior.

Turning to other sectors of the economy, *public utilities* are typically monopolies subject to public regulation of prices and service. This sector includes electric power, gas and water supply, local street transportation, and telephone and telegraph service. Freight and passenger *transportation* typically shows a high degree of seller concentration. The number of railroads, truck or bus companies, and airlines serving the same route is usually small. Radio and television broadcasting, motion picture production, and magazine and newspaper publishing are also highly concentrated industries.

The situation in *mining* is variable. Metallic mining, including iron, copper, aluminum, lead, and zinc, usually shows high concentration. Stone, sand, clay, and gravel have numerous small producers. Bituminous coal is marked by atomistic competition, and so is crude petroleum production except for output controls imposed by legislatures.

Agriculture is atomistically competitive in the sense that there are millions of producers, none of whom supplies a significant part of total output. Within the last generation the working of competition has been modified by government control legislation. But about half of farm output continues uncontrolled, and even where controls exist, farmers react to them in atomistic fashion. The *forestry* and *fishery* industries show a low degree of concentration.

The situation in *retail distribution* varies with the size of the city, large cities having more sellers of a particular product than small towns. It varies also with the type of retailing. There are more groceries and clothing stores than there are building material dealers, new car dealers, or fluid milk distributors. On the whole, retailing is less concentrated than manufacturing, and something approaching atomistic competition is quite frequent.

Local *service* industries present a similarly diversified picture. They range from moderately high concentration in some lines (hotels, motion pictures) to something close to atomistic competition in laundry and dry cleaning, household service, and other areas. In general, this group of industries lies toward the atomistic pole.

The construction industry is really a group of related industries. For commercial and industrial buildings, apartment houses, highways, and other large projects there are usually only a few companies in each area. The number of house builders is much larger, and they compete in essentially atomistic fashion. The same is true of the subcontractors who do painting, plumbing, electrical, and other types of building work.

How does this add up for the economy as a whole? The highest degree of seller concentration is found in public utilities, transportation, communications, metal mining, large contract construction, and heavy manufacturing. At the other pole, conditions approaching atomistic competition are found in agriculture, forestry, and fisheries; housebuilding and subcontracting; coal mining and nonmetallic mining; most of the service industries; and a large proportion of retail markets. In between one finds every possible shading of weak, moderate, and strong oligopoly. At a rough estimate, one might say that two thirds of private output in the United States is produced under conditions of reasonably effective competition, while one third is produced under severe restrictions on competition.

TRENDS IN INDUSTRIAL CONCENTRATION

In addition to looking at the current situation, one must consider long-run tendencies. Has industrial concentration been increasing or decreasing? Does this provide any clue to what may be expected in the decades ahead?

In any economy one finds forces working in both directions, some making for a decrease in industrial concentration, others for an increase. The outcome is not pre-ordained, but depends on the balance of forces at a particular time; and it will be different in different lines of production. The forces making for *greater* industrial concentration are discussed below:

1. Technical developments usually increase the economies of large-scale production, and hence the optimum size of producing units. The feasible number of competitors in a particular market depends partly on the optimum size of plant relative to total demand. If technical progress raises the optimum size of plant faster than demand rises, industrial concentration will tend to increase.

2. In addition to factors increasing the most efficient size of *plant*, there may be factors increasing the most efficient size of *company*. The difficulty of managing a very large enterprise is supposed to set natural limits to the growth of companies. But modern communications systems, developments in organizational theory, and improved business education may be relaxing these limits quite rapidly. It may be as easy to manage an enterprise with one hundred thousand workers today as it was to manage one with five thousand workers 50 years ago.

3. Even though efficiency is not increased, monopoly profit can be gained by merging competing companies to achieve control of prices and production. Businessmen may be expected to take advantage of such opportunities where the legal situation permits.

4. Financiers who promote the merger of competing concerns can also make substantial profits. How? Simple enough. Buy up the old companies for $300 million and sell $400 million worth of stock in the new merged company to the general public. This then leaves $100 million for company officials, investment bankers, lawyers, and other insiders. This was a big factor in the growth of the early railroad empires, the many manufacturing mergers in the period 1880–1910, and the mushrooming of public utility holding companies in the 1920's. Controls over stock flotation are tighter now than they were before 1929, but there is still plenty of money to be made from arranging mergers.

5. The increasingly expensive advertising of branded products makes it harder than it used to be for a new company to break into an industry. The new venture must be backed by a large advertising budget; and if the effort to penetrate the market fails, this money will be lost. A well-established concern is in a better position to take such a gamble than a new enterprise, and even so it may not succeed. The Ford Motor Company is reported to have spent $350 million in developing and promoting the Edsel car, which failed to win market acceptance and was discontinued after a short time.

What forces are working in the opposite direction to reduce industrial concentration?

1. The markets for most products have grown through general economic expansion. If the total output of an industry is growing, industrial concentration will decline unless the leading companies grow at least as rapidly. One might expect that established companies, having an inside track, would at least keep pace with the growth of total demand. But there are many cases in which they have not. In a number of the famous early "trusts"—steel, tobacco, oil refining, aluminum, farm machinery—the proportion of output controlled by the leading companies today is considerably smaller than it was 50 years ago.

2. Transportation has improved and become cheaper. Where transportation is expensive, local producers are sheltered from the competition of those in other localities. In the early nineteenth century the local grist mill, sawmill, cobbler, and so on had a monopoly in their immediate area. The railroad brought products of one area into competition with those of another, and gradually created regional or national markets for most consumer goods. The automobile has had a similar effect as regards retailing and service industries. When one can jump into one's car and shop anywhere in a 20-mile radius, the number of dealers who are in competition with each other is much greater than if one had to go about on foot or by streetcar.

3. While we think of technical change as making for larger production units, this is not always true. Improvements in electric transmission and the development of portable generating units, for example, have made it possible to set up groups of power-driven machines almost anywhere. No longer must the textile mill be built near a waterfall, and built large enough to take full advantage of the power installation. The mill may now be built almost anywhere and may be larger or smaller without much difference in operating efficiency.

4. The rapid pace of technical progress in recent decades has also increased competition *across industry lines*. An established product may find itself undercut and eliminated by a development in another area of the economy. With the discovery of synthetic yarns, chemical companies found themselves in the textile business. Television sets undercut motion pictures. There is a growing tendency for companies well established in one industry to spread out in other directions, increasing the severity of competition in the areas which they enter.

5. The growth of large *buyers* in many markets, while it does not reduce the concentration of sellers, does offset and reduce their market power. The outstanding example is the rise of the large retail chains and their price struggles with the manufacturers.

6. Government policy can cut in either direction. A lowering of tariff barriers exposes domestic producers to more severe competition from producers abroad, and this has been the tendency in the United States since the mid-thirties. But tariffs can also be raised, with restrictive effects on competition. Vigorous antitrust enforcement can reduce industrial con-

centration, while lax enforcement will work in the opposite direction. Government can restrict competition by regulating farm prices, crude oil production, or other matters; or it can decline to intervene in these ways.

These conflicting tendencies will balance out differently in different industries. One will find sellers' market power increasing in some sectors of the economy while at the same time it is decreasing in others. In adding things up for the economy as a whole there is a further complication, the changing importance or *weight* of various sectors. Agriculture is a much smaller part of the American economy than it was a hundred years ago. Transportation, communications, and public utilities are relatively larger. Such changes alter the mix of monopoly and competition in the economy, apart from what is happening *within* each sector.

How have things worked out in the United States over the past century? It is a safe guess that the American economy in 1870 was more atomistic than it has been at any time since. Agriculture was still the dominant industry. Manufacturing produced only 16 percent of total output, and most production was on a small scale. Big business meant the railroads and not much else.

Between this time and 1905 there was a significant increase in industrial concentration. The main development was a massive merger movement in manufacturing, which at the same time became a more prominent part of the total economy. Between 1880 and 1904 there were over three hundred major industrial combinations. These absorbed about 5,200 separate plants, and by the close of the period controlled about 40 percent of the manufacturing capital of the country. Among these combinations, 78 controlled 50 percent or more of the output of their industries. Market domination by a single large company reached an all-time high in manufacturing around 1905, from which it has since receded somewhat.

Between 1905 and 1935 the most important development was the growing importance of the public utility sector and the combination of utilities into giant holding companies. There was also increased concentration in retail distribution. In 1905, there were only two major grocery chains controlling about 2 percent of national sales. By 1935 the five largest chains controlled one quarter of grocery sales. Similar trends were evident in other retail fields. But the growth of large retailers may well have intensified competition in retail markets. It serves also to offset manufacturers' market power and can produce a lower level of manufacturers' prices and profits.

Within the manufacturing sector, there was little change in concentration between 1905 and 1935. In some new industries, such as automobiles and tires, concentration increased as producers were weeded out through bankruptcy. In older industries, on the other hand, concentration tended to decline from the peak reached at the end of the merger movement. Increased vigor of antitrust enforcement after 1910 may have been partly responsible.

It is noteworthy that there has been no tendency toward further increase of industrial concentration since about 1935. Concentration in the utility sector has declined through the growth of smaller companies and the breaking up of the largest holding companies under federal legislation passed in the New Deal period. There has been no significant trend one way or the other in manufacturing and other sectors. In manufacturing, the growth of large companies plus occasional mergers has been offset by the enormous expansion of the total national market over the past 30 years. The atomistic agricultural sector has continued to decline in relative importance. But the retailing and service industries, which also tend in an atomistic direction, have increased in importance. Thus the economy seems for the time being to have settled down on a plateau, with little movement in either a competitive or monopolistic direction. The two hundred largest nonfinancial corporations, which owned more than half of all corporate assets in 1935, held a somewhat smaller percentage in 1955.

We can conclude that there is no convincing evidence of an inevitable decline of competition. Any tendency in this direction over the past century has been gradual and intermittent, and there have been strong forces working in the opposite direction. There is no firm basis for asserting that efforts to strengthen the forces of competition in the economy are foredoomed to failure.

The general desirability of competition, and the unlawfulness of efforts to restrict it, were laid down in the Sherman Act of 1890 and the Clayton Act and the Federal Trade Commission Act of 1914. These statutes, usually termed "the antitrust laws," remain the cornerstone of our policy concerning competitive markets. To explain their meaning and practical effect is the main purpose of this chapter.

THE LAW AGAINST COLLUSIVE AGREEMENTS

Section 1 of the Sherman Act provides that "every contract, combination . . . or conspiracy, in restraint of trade or commerce among the several States, or with foreign nations, is hereby declared to be illegal."

How has the Supreme Court interpreted and applied this provision over the years since 1890? Some things are clear. A direct agreement on prices among rival sellers (or buyers) is illegal. So is any agreement which would have the effect of raising prices or reducing output. An agreement that each company in an industry will produce only so much per month, or that no one will build new productive capacity, or that existing capacity will be shut down or destroyed, would be illegal. The law also bans any agreement to share the total market by allocating customers or territories, or by each company accepting a fixed percentage of total industry output.

It is important to note that *existence* of a collusive agreement is illegal, regardless of the economic consequences. The courts have assumed that the effects will be harmful. The Justice Department does not have to prove that prices have actually been raised or that profits are exorbitant. Nor will it do the industry any good to argue that the market power secured by the agreement has been used in a responsible manner. The existence of such market power is itself unlawful.

As one goes beyond simple price or output agreements, one gets into more doubtful territory. Industry-wide trade associations, perfectly legal in themselves, often carry on activities which verge on restriction of competition. These activities include:

1. Promotion of uniform accounting methods for calculating production costs. From this it is a short step to trying to ensure that the costs of different companies will come out at about the same level, and from this to adding on a "reasonable" profit margin. This could lead to a standard price schedule which all companies would be urged to observe under penalty of being considered "uncooperative" or "unethical." To go this far would doubtless be illegal, but one can stop a step or two short and leave people to draw their own conclusions.

2. Price-filing or bid-filing systems, under which members send the association full information on new prices. Building contractors in an area may agree to file with the secretary of the association their proposed bids on a particular contract. This makes it possible to put pressure on low bidders to come up to the general level. The group may even agree that a certain contract shall go to a particular company, in which case other contractors will be instructed to file higher bids. In a manufacturers' association, each company may agree to give 30 days' advance notice of a price change. If a company proposes a price cut which would be unwelcome to its colleagues, the association secretary has 30 days in which to talk the company out of it.

3. Preparation of statistics on production, inventories, sales, and future demand. One association, for example, sent its members each month an estimate of prospective demand for the industry's product in the following month. Each company president had in his desk drawer a figure showing his company's "normal" percentage of the industry's output. Multiplying this percentage by the association total gave him his production schedule for the month. This simple device succeeded in controlling total industry output, sharing it among the member companies on an agreed basis, and protecting prices at a profitable level. There was never any *direct* price agreement, but the arrangement was nevertheless attacked by the Justice Department and was disbanded.

Strong oligopoly poses difficult problems. Suppose three or four companies control three quarters of an industry's output. Once these companies get used to each other's way of doing business, they need scarcely talk to each other to maintain effective control of prices. If they do talk to each other, no one is going to know about it. Discussions will be on the telephone or over the luncheon table, with no records kept and no evidence of agreement. Price leadership can be used to announce price changes, other companies simply following any move by the leader. The antitrust sleuth finds it hard to pick up the trail of such arrangements. Even if he does, what kind of court order can he secure? Can members of an industry be forbidden to speak to each other socially? Can companies be forbidden to sell at the same price?

The crime defined by the Sherman Act is one of "conspiracy," and the courts have been reluctant to act unless collusion can be proved. At the same time they have been worried by oligopoly situations and the ease with which prices can be manipulated under them. There has been some tendency to move in the direction of holding that "conscious parallelism of action" is an offense under the law, even when agreement cannot be proved. Simple price leadership will normally not be held unlawful. But if the companies also maintain an elaborate similarity of policy on other terms of sale such as quantity discounts, price differentials between various qualities and types of produce, and freight charges or delivered price arrangements, the courts may find a breach of the law. It is unlikely that "all that much parallelism" could occur without intimate cooperation among the companies.

What can be done about a proven case of illegal price fixing? The Antitrust Division of the Department of Justice, which has main responsibility for prosecuting these cases, can use either or both of two procedures. First, it can file a criminal action under which the companies and the executives responsible, if convicted, are liable to fines of not more than $50,000 and imprisonment for not more than one year. This is not as forbidding as it may sound. The respectable business executives who appear in these cases do not look like criminals, and juries have been reluctant to convict them on criminal charges. But the potential effectiveness of criminal procedures should not be written off. In 1961 several high officials of the major electrical manufacturing companies were fined and sent to jail for agreeing to fix prices of heavy electrical equipment. The companies, in addition to fines, had to pay large damages to the government agencies and private utilities to whom they had sold this equipment. They suffered damaging publicity, and were ordered to desist from price agreement in the future.

The other possibility is a civil suit, which may be filed alone or along with a criminal action. If the defendants are found guilty in a civil suit, the judge normally issues an *injunction*, a "don't do it again" kind of order, forbidding continuation of the unlawful practices. If the companies violate the injunction, they can be fined for contempt of court. This achieves much the same result as a criminal suit, but without the stigma of a criminal conviction.

How much effect has the prohibition of collusive agreements had on the American economy? The law has certainly checked the development of the industrial cartels which flourish in many other countries. In view of the acknowledged deadening effect of cartels on competition and efficiency, this is an important accomplishment. In addition, the law has doubtless reduced the number of price-fixing agreements and understandings. It has not entirely eliminated them; but the possibility of prosecution has an intimidating effect, just as every speeder does not have to be picked up to discourage speeding. The most serious loophole in the law is the difficulty of detecting friendly cooperation among large oligopolists.

An incidental and unintended effect of the law has been to stimulate outright merger of competing companies. Competition among rival concerns can be restricted either through agreement or by absorbing the rival concerns into a larger company. While the Sherman Act made agreement illegal, mergers were more loosely controlled, and the urge to suppress competition was thus diverted in the latter direction. The campaign against collusion intensified the problem of monopoly. This leads us to the second main facet of the antitrust laws.

THE LAW AGAINST MONOPOLIZING

Section 2 of the Sherman Act states that "every person who shall monopolize, or attempt to monopolize, or combine or conspire . . . to monopolize any part of the trade or commerce among the several states, or with foreign nations, shall be deemed guilty of a misdemeanor. . . ." The primary thrust of this section is against *exclusion* of competitors from an industry. The Clayton Act goes further in listing specific exclusionary practices:

1. A common device of the early "trusts" was predatory price-cutting. A new competitor would be greeted by severe price cuts in his area of operation, the trust's losses on these sales being made up by its profits in other areas. The competing concern could thus be driven into bankruptcy and forced to sell out or come to terms with the trust. Section 2 of the Clayton Act, which prohibits price discrimination where the effect may be to lessen competition, was intended to strike at this practice.

2. Another early device was the "tying contract," under which the buyer of company A's product agreed not to buy from any competing company. If company A was the dominant producer, and buyers had to be sure of getting its products, they might be forced into tying contracts which effectively prevented any new producer from gaining a foothold. Such contracts are forbidden by Section 3 of the Clayton Act.

3. Section 7 of the Clayton Act, as amended and strengthened in 1950, prohibits mergers where the effect "may be substantially to lessen competition, or to tend to create a monopoly."

What does the law mean? The offense under the Sherman Act is *monopolizing*, rather than a *monopoly*—a kind of activity, rather than a state of being. One element of the offense is clear. There must be either a single company or a small group of companies occupying a predominant position in a particular market, a position such that one can make a case that competitors have been eliminated or potential competitors prevented from entering. How large a share of the market must the monopolist or the oligopoly group occupy in order to become suspect? The courts have never been willing to say, but some clues can be drawn from past decisions. A company occupying 90 percent of a market, as Alcoa did in the aluminum ingot market at the time of the antitrust suit against it in 1945, is certainly vulnerable. A few companies occupying two thirds or more of a market would probably be subject to attack. If the share held by the top four or five companies fell below 50 percent, antitrust prosecution would probably not be successful. There can be a good deal of market power in the economic sense without monopolization in the judicial sense.

Given concentration of an industry in a few hands, there are at least three standards which might be used to determine whether there has been an offense against the Sherman Act:

1. On the most lenient interpretation, the monopolist or oligopoly group would have to be found guilty of deliberately and effectively excluding competitors from the industry. Further, the methods used would have to go beyond the bounds of ethical business practice, to the point where they might be regarded as predatory and unfair.

2. On a stricter interpretation, exclusion of competitors even by normal and legitimate business methods might be considered unlawful. Thus a company or group of companies which always expanded ahead of demand, leaving no possible loophole for new rivals, or which bought up all available sources of raw material for a product, or cornered all available patents, or put other obstacles in the way of potential producers, might be found guilty.

3. The above interpretations rest on the *conduct* of the parties. A more severe interpretation would rest on the *structure* of the market, and would make mere possession of undue market power unlawful, regardless of how it had been acquired or maintained. This would go in the direction of forbidding *monopoly* in the economic sense—a state of affairs, without reference to specific actions which might be construed as monopolization.

For many years the courts held mainly to the first interpretation. The oil and tobacco trusts were dissolved by the courts, not just because they were big, but because they had used unfair tactics against competitors. A group which could keep out competition by gentlemanly methods was safe. The dictum that "mere size is no offense" was frequently reiterated. The government failed to win a conviction in the steel case of 1920, even though U.S. Steel alone produced half of the nation's basic steel at this time and the top eight companies produced about 70 percent.

Since the New Deal period, however, antitrust enforcement has been more vigorous and the tone of judicial opinion has shifted. Court decisions have veered toward the second interpretation above: exclusion of competitors by a group which has "too much" of the market is unlawful, even if it is accomplished by fair and normal business methods. The Supreme Court has not yet been willing, however, to go all the way to the third interpretation that mere possession of undue market power is unlawful. It came almost to this point in the Aluminum Company decision of 1945, which involved a long-standing case of market power; but since then the Court seems to have drawn back from this advanced position.

STRONG OLIGOPOLY: THE "TOUGH NUT" FOR ANTITRUST

It remains doubtful, therefore, whether one can get at gentlemanly and well-behaved oligopoly under the present antitrust laws. What to do about steel, copper, aluminum, oil refining, automobiles, heavy machinery, electrical equipment, cigarettes, and the rest? Parallel action is achieved without overt agreement, so that it is difficult to invoke the ban on collusion. Exclusion of competitors is so discreet—indeed, usually requires no positive action because of the heavy costs of entry in these industries—that the courts hesitate to support a finding of monopolization. There is considerable agreement that uncontrolled market power in these industries can have harmful effects. There is little agreement as to what, if anything, might be done about it.

Some students of the problem have suggested a legal limit on the size of companies. This could be either an absolute limit on size of assets or number of employees, or a provision that no company may supply more than a specified percentage of output in a particular market. The feasibility of such proposals is doubtful. A uniform limit on absolute size would be meaninglessly high for small-scale industries but might be unduly restrictive where large-scale plants are essential. A 25 percent share of a particular market might be innocuous under some circumstances, quite dangerous in others. Most companies, too, make a variety of products. Which one would be used in testing whether a company's market share is too large? Exercise of judgment on such points would be necessary no matter how the law might be written.

Most experts, therefore, favor continuation of a case-by-case approach under the Sherman Act, involving examination of each industry on its merits. The most powerful remedy available under the Sherman Act is dissolution, the breaking up of a company into several smaller companies. The remedy has been employed sparingly, the courts being almost as reluctant to impose capital punishment on a corporation as on an individual. The old Standard Oil and American Tobacco trusts were divided in 1911 into a number of successor companies, and a few other dissolutions decrees have been issued since that time. If it were desired to use this device for a real drive on oligopoly, it might be necessary to amend and clarify this portion of the Sherman Act. Two leading authorities have suggested[1] that Section 2 of the Act be amended so that (*a*) "unreasonable

---

[1] Carl Kaysen and Donald F. Turner, *Antitrust Policy, A Legal and Economic Analysis* (Cambridge, Mass.: Harvard University Press, 1959). Professor Joe Bain has added the weight of his authority to this suggestion in *Industrial Organization* (New York: John Wiley & Sons, Inc., 1959), pp. 608–9.

market power" would itself be made unlawful, with no need to prove nefarious conduct by the companies concerned; (*b*) the courts would be instructed to dissolve the companies, provided no lesser remedy appeared adequate and provided that dissolution would not unduly reduce efficiency.

There are two main types of dissolution procedure: (1) *horizontal* dissolution, under which a company owning several plants producing the same kind of product is ordered to dissolve and set up several smaller companies; and (2) *vertical* dissolution, in which a company controlling successive stages of a production cycle—say, everything from mining bauxite ore to producing aluminum pots and pans—is required to get out of some of these stages.

Horizontal Dissolution

Horizontal dissolution was applied in the early oil and tobacco cases. It clearly could be applied to many of the present highly concentrated industries if this seemed expedient. The three major cigarette producers could be divided into 10 or more companies, since each has several plants. The basic steel producing operations of U.S. Steel could be divided into at least three clusters, centered on Pittsburgh, Gary, and Birmingham. Altogether, one could probably make 20 or more efficient-sized steel companies out of the present half-dozen leading producers. In the window glass industry there are only four companies but about 20 plants, which could form the basis of separate companies. American Can, which produces more than half of all tin cans in the country, has about 60 plants, which could be reorganized into a number of new companies. These illustrations are not intended as advocacy, but simply to suggest technical possibilities.

Wouldn't breaking up large corporations in this way reduce industrial efficiency? This involves our earlier distinction between the efficiency of large *plants* and the efficiency of adding similar plants together into a large *company*. The first question is not involved here, since no one proposes to dismember individual plants; but it is worth noting that the efficiency of mammoth plant units is often exaggerated. In most manufacturing industries, the optimum scale of plant is small enough relative to the size of the market so that the industry could accommodate at least 10 to 20 efficient-sized plants, and often many more than this. In a study of 20 manufacturing industries, Bain found only two (automobiles and typewriters) which had what he termed "very important" economies of plant size, i.e., the optimum plant size exceeded 10 percent of market capacity, and unit costs would be raised by 5 percent or more at half this size.[2] On the basis of one plant per company, then, one could usually get enough companies to produce reasonably effective competition.

But are there not important gains in efficiency from having a num-

[2] *Op. cit.,* p. 348.

ber of plants organized under common management? One must distinguish between bargaining advantages and genuine economies. A giant corporation may be able to drive a harder bargain with material suppliers, bankers, and others from whom it buys; and it can often manipulate product prices to advantage. But these are not gains from the standpoint of the economy as a whole. Genuine economies would have to come mainly from the following sources:

1. A large company may be able to hire unusually capable managers, who then have a chance to use their talents over a wide range of production. Against this must be set the possibility that large-scale organization may lead to excessive paperwork and red tape, delayed decisions, internal intrigue, and other types of bureaucratic inefficiency.

2. Selling costs per unit may be reduced by being spread over a large volume of output, even though production costs are no lower.

3. In industries which rest on complicated scientific techniques, large-scale organization of research and development may produce better results than could be obtained from a number of smaller laboratories. This is not certain, however, and there is no reason why a large research organization must be supported and accompanied by a giant production organization. Government agencies, universities, trade associations, private consulting laboratories, and other groups are active in the research field and provide possible alternatives to the one-company research center.

The extent to which there are genuine economies from multiplant organization is unclear. Bain obtained estimates from management people on this point in 12 of the 20 manufacturing industries which he studied, with the following results: "For six of the twelve . . . the existence of any significant multi-plant economies was denied, even though in three of these six industries the larger firms had attained substantial multi-plant development. For the remaining six of the twelve cases, some multi-plant economies were claimed to exist to the extent that a firm with three to ten plants would be more efficient than a one-plant firm. But the extent of cost reduction . . . was generally estimated as 'small,' 'slight,' or not exceeding 2 or 3 percent."[3]

In some cases, then, horizontal dissolution might involve loss of efficiency. On the other hand, the public would benefit from the more competitive behavior which would result from having 20 companies in the industry instead of three or four.

Vertical Dissolution

Many of our economic giants derive their strength in part from vertical integration, from controlling an entire production cycle. The leading steel companies produce everything from iron ore to tacks and nails. The major oil companies own oil wells, pipe lines and tanker fleets, oil re-

---

[3] *Op. cit.*, p. 351.

fineries, and chains of retail gas stations. There may be some gain in efficiency from this adding together of successive production processes, though the gains are harder to visualize than in the case of horizontal integration. What is clear is that vertical integration confers great bargaining advantages, and may enable the integrated company to put an economic squeeze on its smaller competitors.

The Aluminum Company of America, for example, was for 50 years the sole producer of aluminum metal in the United States. In addition, the company produced a wide variety of finished aluminum products. A number of smaller companies bought aluminum from Alcoa and fabricated it into various end products. Alcoa, because of its dominant position at each level of the industry, could determine the prices of both aluminum metal and finished aluminum products, and thus determine the "spread" available to cover manufacturing costs. This spread could be varied to make things easier or harder for the little fellows in the industry. Suppose Alcoa raised the price of primary aluminum without raising the price of finished products. This made no difference to its own profits, since the price it charged itself for aluminum was purely a matter of internal bookkeeping. It made a great difference to the profits of the small producers, however, and could obviously be used to drive them out of existence.

To prevent this sort of economic pressure, the Antitrust Division has sometimes sought a dissolution decree restricting the major companies to a specified level of operation. The major motion picture producers, for example, were ordered to get out of theater operations, because the court judged that this gave them an unfair competitive advantage over picture producers who did not own theaters. New companies were set up to take over theater operation, and these companies bought the theaters from the producing companies at a negotiated price. A leading student of the oil industry has proposed that the major refining companies be ordered to get out of both the pipe-line business and the filling-station business.[4] This would give the small independent refiners a freer hand in buying and transporting crude oil and in disposing of their products through retail outlets.

Other Approaches to the Oligopoly Problem

While dissolution is the most direct and effective approach to the problem of strong market power, several other techniques deserve mention:

1. Something can be accomplished through investigation and publicity. Government agencies can spell out clearer standards of good economic performance for an industry, analyze the operation of our closely

---

[4] Eugene V. Rostow, *A National Policy for the Oil Industry* (New Haven, Conn.: Yale University Press, 1948). This proposal was violently attacked in the press as, among other things, "socialistic." Actually, the proposal was aimed at stronger competition and freer private enterprise.

controlled industries in the light of these standards, and publicize the results. The industries concerned typically resist even this mild form of public surveillance as "snooping" into private business affairs. But these industries, by virtue of their importance in the economy and the fact that they are not subject to the usual discipline of competitive markets, become "vested with a public interest." Adequate knowledge of their operations is necessary as a basis for wise public policy.

Some would go further. Those who fear that the ease with which prices can be raised under strong oligopoly may contribute to chronic price inflation have suggested that wage and price increases in these industries be made subject to approval by a government board. The missing check of market competition would be replaced by government regulation. The wisdom of such proposals is doubtful. Government price control has not worked very well in the public utility industries, for reasons which will be explained in the next chapter. It seems unlikely that it would work any better in steel, oil, or copper. If one dislikes the prospect of direct controls, however, the logical alternative is to make the structure of these industries as competitive as possible through the dissolution technique. Some sort of control over private market power there must be. If we are unwilling to institute competitive controls, it seems likely that events will move toward the opposite pole of government regulation.

2. The prospects for competition are improved by the fact that the market for most products is growing. If one could ensure that most of the growth would come either through new companies or the expansion of smaller existing companies, the market domination of our present industrial giants would gradually diminish. Over a period of 40 or 50 years one could achieve considerable decentralization without actually dissolving existing companies. There seems in any event to be some tendency for older companies to expand less rapidly than smaller or newer companies. United States Steel had about two thirds of the basic steel producing capacity of the country when it was formed in 1901. Today its proportion has fallen to about 30 percent. Another classic case is the International Harvester Company whose share of the farm machinery market fell from three quarters in 1911 to less than one quarter today.

Government can aid this tendency in a variety of ways. The sale of aluminum plants built with government funds during World War II to two new producers, Kaiser and Reynolds, provided Aloca with its first serious competition. Wherever there is a choice in disposing of government-owned facilities or in placing government contracts, this could be used to build up efficient small producers. As a minimum, there should be a clear policy of not favoring the largest producers and not increasing industrial concentration through government sales and purchases. The federal Small Business Administration is active in this area, and is helping in particular to meet the capital needs of small business. A company with assets below $5 million and annual net income below $2.5 million, and which has been unable to secure a regular bank loan, can apply to the SBA. Approved loans are typically repayable over a period of 5 to 10 years, and carry interest rates ranging from 4 to 6 percent. The SBA also helps to finance intermediary organizations, termed small-business investment companies, which then advance funds to small concerns. The SBA is presently authorized to lend up to a total of $1.2 billion, but this ceiling can presumably be raised when demand warrants.

3. It is important also to prevent the formation of new industrial giants through merger of competing firms. A vigilant pro-competitive policy could have prevented the formation of U.S. Steel and other companies whose market power constitutes a continuing problem. Certainly such agglomerations should be prevented in the future.

Until 1950 the check on mergers was weak. But section 7 of the Clayton Act was amended in 1950 to forbid one company to acquire either stock or the physical assets of another company in the same type of industry where the effect "may be substantially to lessen competition" or where the merger would "tend to create a monopoly." How far the courts will go in forbidding mergers under this section has still to be determined on a case-by-case basis. Assuming vigorous enforcement by the Antitrust Division, the law appears strong enough to check encroachment on competition by this route.

4. Where a monopoly or oligopoly has been aided by tariff protection, the tariff can be lowered to give consumers the benefit of competition from other countries. We shall argue in Chapter 16 that the tariff is a dubious device, which can be justified only in exceptional cases. It is especially dubious where it serves to protect, not competitive private enterprise, but private monopoly power.

To sum up: it is sometimes argued that we can do *nothing* about concentrated market power. This is surely incorrect. It would be fair to say that we cannot do anything very spectacular very quickly, or by relying entirely on one approach. We must try a variety of approaches—checking further concentration through merger, dissolving large concerns here and there, strengthening the competitive power of small enterprise, analyzing and publicizing the economic performance of concentrated industries—with a view to making gradual progress over the course of decades. General intent, sense of direction, and vigor of action are the main things.

EXCEPTIONS TO ANTITRUST

While the antitrust laws remain our basic charter in the matter of monopoly and competition, a variety of exceptions have grown up over the years. Two of the most important, agricultural price controls and retail price fixing, are examined in Chapter 12; but several others will be reviewed briefly here.

Patent Protection

Anyone who believes he has developed an original product or production method can take it to the Patent Office in Washington and apply for a patent. Something like 50,000 applications are filed every year. An overworked staff of patent clerks spends a few hours searching the files to see whether any similar device has been patented in the past. If they can find none, and if the new device doesn't seem too ridiculous, a patent will be issued. This gives the patent owner exclusive right to the product or process for 17 years. Anyone else who makes anything too similar to it can be sued for patent infringement and, if found guilty, will have to pay damages.

A patent is a legal grant of monopoly, immune from question or prosecution under the antitrust laws. The original purpose of the patent system was to reward the lone wolf inventor by protecting the use of his discovery for a long enough period to yield him some financial return. Large returns for successful inventions would supposedly spur more people to tinker and experiment, and would increase the amount of inventive activity. In modern times, however, an inventor is more likely to sell his patent to a corporation than to exploit it himself; and an increasing proportion of inventions are made in corporation laboratories by salaried research workers. The main present-day argument for patents, then, is that the system is necessary to induce companies to spend large amounts on research and development. Why should a company maintain an elaborate research organization if discoveries are immediately thrown open to all its competitors? Protected use of the discovery for 17 years enables the company to recover the money which has been sunk in developing it.

There is doubtless good reason for some degree of patent protection, but many students of the patent system feel that its original intent has been distorted over the course of time and that it now offers unreasonable protection to monopolistic activities. Common criticisms include:

1. Patent law is complicated, patent lawyers are high priced, and patent suits are long and expensive. The threat of patent litigation has thus become an important weapon of intercorporate warfare. A large company has sometimes gone to a smaller competitor and said in effect: "Your product encroaches on certain patents which we own. We propose to sue you. Stop it, or else." The charge of patent infringement may or may not be warranted. What matters in such a situation is not the merit of your patent but the size of your purse. The small company, faced with ruinous legal expenses, must usually accept the terms laid down by the larger one. It may be forced to pay royalties to the big company under a patent license, or to accept a merger, or to go out of business.

2. A patent can be used to hold a new product or process off the market instead of putting it on the market. There are cases in which application of a new technique has been long delayed because it would have

upset existing production methods and reduced the value of present plant and equipment.

3. A company which wants to produce under a patent belonging to another company can do so by getting a license from the patent holder, which usually involves paying a royalty of so much per unit produced. Large companies which own overlapping patents in the same area will often issue licenses to each other to avoid any threat of patent suits, an arrangement known as *cross-licensing*. Or all patents in an industry may be turned over to a trade association or a special company set up for the purpose, which then issues licenses to each of the participating companies. This is known as a *patent pool*.

Licensing arrangements can operate in a way which liberates and strengthens competition. The automobile industry has long had a patent pool under which patents owned by one company are available to all other companies without restriction and without charge. But licensing systems can also be used to restrict and suppress competition. The companies in a cross-licensing agreement or a patent pool may refuse to license any newcomer, thus barring new companies from the industry. Or the licensing arrangements may be used to divide up the market, with each company retaining a monopoly in a specified field.

Patent licenses have also been used to limit the amount of a product which can be manufactured and the price at which it can be sold. One of the most elaborate arrangements of this sort was developed by the Hartford-Empire Glass Company, which held the key patents on machinery used in glass bottle manufacturing. A bottle manufacturer was given a license to produce under these patents only on condition that he produce a certain kind of bottle, in specified quantities, sell only within a certain geographic area, and at a specified price. The entire national market for many types of bottle was thus subdivided and controlled. Anyone who questioned or violated the prescribed arrangements was simply put out of business by withdrawing his license. This arrangement was eventually broken up by court order after the Justice Department brought suit under the antitrust laws.

These criticisms have been accompanied by proposals for reform of the patent system, with a view to retaining essential protective features while minimizing harmful effects on competition. Some of the main suggestions which have been made are:

1. The validity of disputed patents might be submitted to a special patent court, with all expenses being borne by the government to remove any disadvantage of weaker companies.

2. It could be spelled out clearly in law that patent licensing may not be used to fix product prices, set output quotas, divide up markets, and impose other restraints on competition. Such restraints have already been held illegal in the Hartford-Empire case and other cases, but the law might be made more explicit on this point.

3. It might be provided that a patent owner must issue a license to any other producer on payment of reasonable royalties.

4. Since World War II most of the money spent on scientific research has come from the federal government, either through its own laboratories, or through grants to universities and research institutes, or through paying the research expenses of business concerns. Yet the inventions resulting from this research are often patented by companies or individuals. Where invention has been financed by government, it would seem that the resulting patents should belong to government and should be made available to all comers.

Union Activity in Product Markets

In considering the economic consequences of unionism one must distinguish between (*a*) bargaining with employers over wages and other terms of employment in the *labor market*, which we leave for analysis in Chapter 13; and (*b*) intervention to fix prices or restrain competition in the *product market*, which falls logically within the scope of this chapter.

Unions have a direct interest in product prices, since it is price which gives the employer the wherewithal to meet his wage bill. An employer in a small-scale, competitive industry may sometimes find his selling price reduced to the point where he feels compelled to cut wages or go out of business. A union in such an industry has a practical interest in "stabilizing" prices (which always means raising them!) in order to remove pressure on the wage level, and the union can sometimes control prices more effectively than the employers.

Suppose the dry cleaning industry in a city is "menaced" by price competition. Companies undercut each other on prices, profits are low and uncertain, efforts to reach a price agreement are unavailing. To the rescue rides the International Brotherhood of Teamsters. It organizes the delivery truck drivers and perhaps the plant employees as well, and signs a wage agreement with each company. But it does more than this. It organizes a price-fixing agreement among the employers and undertakes to police the agreement. A company which cuts prices now finds its labor supply cut off and is quickly forced back into line. Dave Beck, originally West Coast head of the Teamsters and later International President, perfected and applied this technique to numerous retailing and service industries in Seattle, and was awarded every sort of civic honor by grateful businessmen. It has since been extended to many other areas of the country.

This sort of union-employer combine flourishes also in building construction. The building contractors in a city form an association, one purpose of which is to present agreed bids on public contracts and to divide the available business on a controlled basis. They agree with the local building trades unions that they will employ only union members, and the unions agree that their men will work only for members of the contractors' association. This forces all contractors to join the association and observe the price-fixing agreement, on penalty of getting no labor. Part of the arrangement may be a cash pay-off by the companies to key union officials, but this is petty larceny compared with the grand larceny which the contractors perpetrate on the public.

In other cases a union has acted on its own to shut off competition. Local 3 of the International Brotherhood of Electrical Workers in New York City has long had a rule that switchboards and other electrical apparatus shipped into New York from outside must be disassembled and rewired by members of the Local. This effectively excludes outside manufacturers from the New York market.

There is a curious anomaly in the antitrust laws at this point. If *employers alone* conspire to fix prices or restrict competition, they are breaking the law. If *employers and unions* together do the same thing, the scheme is still illegal. But *if the union acts alone*, without visibly conspiring with employers, it can impose any restraints on pricing and competition which it may choose. The Clayton Act provides that "labor is not an article of commerce," and this has been interpreted by the courts as meaning that independent actions of a labor organization cannot be prosecuted under the antitrust laws. A union can strike against a price-cutting employer, refuse to work for a new company, impose a ban on products from outside the area—all quite legally so long as no one can prove that employers are involved in the scheme.

This situation is illogical. It seems desirable to amend the law so as to distinguish between matters of *labor relations* and matters of *commercial competition* in product markets. As regards the latter, anything which would be unlawful for business concerns to do in the product market should be equally unlawful for trade unions. To hold otherwise is to open a large gap in the antitrust system, through which price agreements can ride intact so long as employer participation cannot be proved.

Transactions within a State

The antitrust laws cover only activities affecting interstate commerce. A good deal of local retailing, service, and construction activity does not cross state lines and is immune to federal regulation. Many states have their own antitrust laws, but there is usually no provision for enforcement and the statute remains a dead letter.

The general tenor of state and municipal regulation is in fact highly anticompetitive. State and local governments are more vulnerable than the federal government to concentrated pressure by business groups, demanding legislation to restrict competition in their particular bailiwick; and the inert majority of consumers which is hurt by such legislation puts up no effective defense.

Most states have laws which discriminate against out-of-state producers. There is an almost incredible variety of such restrictions. Many states maintain their own plant quarantine systems, which are designed partly to protect local nurserymen. "Fresh eggs" are sometimes defined as eggs laid within the state, "fresh fruits and vegetables" as state-grown produce. Some states discriminate against trucks which come in loaded as against those which come in empty. Most states have laws requiring preference for residents in making state purchases or awarding contracts, and many cities do the same. Dairy farmers cannot ship milk to a particular city unless their farms have been inspected and approved by state or local health authorities; simple refusal to inspect farms outside the state is sufficient to bar them from the market. Most states prohibit transportation of alcoholic beverages into the state except by authorized dealers. This does not promote temperance, but it does protect dealers' margins.

There is point in Wilcox's comment: "These measures have the same defects as do barriers to international trade. In fact, they may be more harmful, since the area they leave open to competition is a smaller one. As we move from 'Buy American' through 'Buy Indianan' and 'Buy Middletown' to 'Buy Main Street,' the consequences differ, not in kind, but in degree."[5] Carried to their logical conclusion they would carve up the vast free trade area of the United States, a major source of our economic efficiency, into hundreds of Balkan principalities surrounded by high trade barriers.

Similar observations may be made on state licensing requirements for various occupations. These are doubtless legitimate for professions which require long training and which involve public health and safety, such as medicine, dentistry, and law. But state licensing systems have been extended far beyond these proper boundaries. Wilcox points out that "there are as many as 75 trades where entry is restricted by law . . . most states license barbers, beauticians, chiropractors, funeral directors, surveyors, and salesmen of insurance and real estate. A number of states also license such tradesmen as plumbers, dry cleaners, horseshoers, tree surgeons, automobile salesmen, and photographers. Altogether, there are more than 1,200 occupational license laws, averaging 25 per state."[6]

Administration of these laws is usually entrusted to a board composed entirely of members of the occupation. A group of plumbers decides what is a proper examination for a plumbers' license, administers the examination, and decides who has passed and who hasn't. Since the members of any occupation have a direct interest in holding down the number admitted to it, it would be surprising if these laws were not administered with restrictive intent. Supervision by state government officials is usually nominal and often entirely lacking.

These two types of law are restrictive and antisocial. Many of them are thinly disguised "grabs" by small groups in the economy. They

---

[5] Clair Wilcox, *Public Policies toward Business* (rev. ed.; Homewood, Ill.: Richard D. Irwin, Inc., 1960), p. 348.

[6] *Ibid.*, p. 348.

persist because the public doesn't know about them, and because each one seems to take only a small bite out of the consumer. One can hope that citizens of each state and community will gradually become better informed about what goes on in their own backyards and take greater interest in preserving free occupational choice and free competition.

A WORD ON ENFORCEMENT

The achievements of the antitrust laws to date are certainly substantial. Direct price-fixing agreements have been driven underground, and their scope and effectiveness severely limited. Business concerns have been warned off any close approach to single-firm monopoly. Unfair and predatory tactics against smaller competitors have been ruled out of bounds. Companies have been given reason to worry about standing out on the landscape as "too big" in their respective industries. One reason why some oligopolists have cheerfully watched their market share shrink is the consolation of greater immunity to antitrust prosecution.

How much can we expect to make of the antitrust approach in the future? This depends on what we want to make of it, and particularly on how much money and manpower we devote to enforcing the law. The effectiveness of any piece of economic legislation can be predicted by looking at the budget of the enforcing agency. The statute books are cluttered with impressive-looking laws which mean nothing because no one is doing anything about them. Lobbyists and legislators know well that the best way to fight legislation is not to oppose its passage but simply to cut off funds for enforcement.

This was essentially the fate of the antitrust laws from 1890 to 1935. The annual budget of the Antitrust Division of the Department of Justice never rose above $200,000, and the number of lawyers employed was never more than 25. This small group was supposed to preserve competition through the whole of American industry! Considering the discrepancy between the enormous resources of business corporations and the tiny resources of government, it is amazing that the antitrust laws had any effect whatever. The number of prosecutions started by the Antitrust Division was less than 10 per year until 1906, and typically between 10 and 20 per year from 1906 to 1939.

The antitrust laws began to be enforced more seriously during the late New Deal period. Between 1934 and 1942 the budget of the Antitrust Division rose from $154,000 to $2,325,000; the number of lawyers employed rose above two hundred, and the number of cases started per year began to exceed 50. After some slackening during the war years, antitrust activity revived after the war and has continued on a higher plateau under both Republican and Democratic administrations, with an average of close to 50 cases being started each year.

If the policy of promoting competition is to be taken seriously in the future, there is need for further enlargement of the staff and budget of the Antitrust Division. The Division is still much smaller than the police force of the District of Columbia, and tiny compared with the number of companies and the volume of activity which it is responsible for monitoring.

There should also be a shift in the emphasis of enforcement activities. About half of the antitrust actions initiated since 1890 have involved three groups of industries: food processing and distribution, building materials production and distribution, and the service trades. By contrast, there has been little activity in steel, nonferrous metals, chemicals, machinery, electrical equipment, and other branches of manufacturing.

The main thrust of the law has clearly been against collusive agreement in small-scale industry rather than against monopoly and oligopoly in large-scale industry. There are practical reasons for this. In terms of winning public support for antitrust, it is expedient to concentrate enforcement on industries which are widely distributed throughout the country and which come into direct contact with consumers. The food processing, service, and building construction industries meet this requirement; basic steel, chemicals, and electric turbines do not. Moreover, the state of the law and the outlook of the courts must be considered. The Antitrust Division knows it can win a case against outright collusion by little business, but it is not sure how far the courts will support it in moving against tacit collusion by big business. Since the enforcement budget is so small, it seems sensible to concentrate it on cases where the chances of success are highest.

One would not want to suggest that the Antitrust Division should act less vigorously against outright collusion than it has in the past. But it might well act more vigorously against concentrated oligopoly, and shift the emphasis of enforcement toward heavy manufacturing. The difficulties in doing this are obvious. The Sherman Act might have to be amended in certain respects. Larger enforcement funds would be needed. Political opposition would be intense. This brings us back to the basic question of how far we mean what we say about the desirability of competitive markets. If we do mean it, positive movement in a competitive direction is not going to be achieved painlessly.

SUMMARY

1. At a rough estimate, two thirds of private output in the United States is produced under conditions of reasonably effective competition, one third under monopoly or strong oligopoly.

2. Certain forces in the economy are always making for greater industrial concentration, while others are working in the opposite direction. Over the last 30 years the two sets of forces seem to have just about offset each other.

3. The Sherman Act of 1890, and the Clayton Act and Federal Trade Commission Act of 1914, are usually known collectively as "the antitrust laws." They prohibit open agreement among competitors to fix prices or control production, and such agreements have been largely prevented; but tacit collusion among a few large companies has not been checked.

4. The antitrust laws also forbid *monopolizing*, that is, action by one or more dominant companies to exclude competitors from an industry. But the courts have not yet gone so far as to hold that mere *existence* of market power is itself unlawful.

5. The most difficult problem under antitrust is strong oligopoly, where a few large companies are able to regulate prices by tacit agreement. One approach is through dissolution of large companies into smaller ones, which could sometimes be done with little or no loss in efficiency. But this is a drastic remedy which the courts have hesitated to apply.

6. Other lines of approach include investigation and publicity, support for new enterprises and small enterprises, prevention of further concentration through mergers, and tariff reductions to permit foreign competition.

7. The antitrust system could be strengthened by changes in patent legislation, by preventing unions as well as business concerns from restricting competition in product markets, and by eliminating state laws which restrict competition.

8. The Antitrust Division of the Department of Justice needs a substantially larger staff and budget. This would permit more vigorous activity in oligopolistic industries which thus far have been largely neglected.

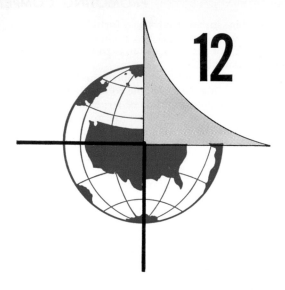

Restricting Competition

"It seems to me that th' on'y thing to do is to keep pollyticians an' businessmen part. They seem to have a bad inflooence on each other. Whiniver I see an aldherman an' a banker walkin' down th' street together I know th' Recordin' Angel will have to ordher another bottle iv ink."

FINLEY PETER DUNNE

THE POLICY OF CONTROLLING industry through competitive markets has never been applied to every sector of the economy. Public utilities have been accepted as inevitably monopolistic, and have been made subject to government regulation. In other industries, atomistic in structure and competitive by tradition, it has been charged that competition works unfairly and government should intervene to ensure fair prices for producers. The outstanding case is agriculture, which has been subject to extensive regulation of prices and production since the early thirties.

NATURAL MONOPOLY: REGULATION OF PUBLIC UTILITIES

This group of industries includes electric power, gas, telephone and telegraph communication, railroading, local street transportation, and a number of others. The characteristic feature of a public utility is that optimum scale is very large, so that long-run marginal cost continues to fall with increasing size. This makes it efficient to have only one company operating in a particular area. So consumers must depend for an essential service on a monopoly which, left to itself, might fail to provide adequate service or might charge unreasonable prices. The public can be protected only by giving a public body power to control prices and service.

Regulatory agencies have been set up both at state and federal levels. Electricity and gas service, telephone service, and other services within a single state are usually regulated by a state agency, usually termed the public utility commission or public service commission. Interstate distribution of electricity, rail transportation, and other activities reaching across state lines are regulated by a galaxy of federal commissions, including the Interstate Commerce Commission, the Civil Aeronautics Board, the Federal Power Commission, and the Federal Communications Commission.

The existence of these agencies is certainly essential, but their record of performance is unimpressive. There are several reasons for this:

1. Although some outstanding people have served on these commissions, the average caliber of commission members is not high. No special qualifications or experience are required. Many appointments are frankly political. Low salary levels make it difficult to attract or keep capable people.

2. Staffs are too small to do an adequate job. The budgets of the state utility commissions average less than a half-million dollars per year. A single utility company may spend much more than that on legal and accounting talent. Regulation is essentially a battle between public and private experts, but the scales are heavily weighted in favor of the latter.

3. The powers of the regulatory commissions are mainly negative rather than positive. They can forbid a utility to raise prices, but they are not equally well equipped to bring about price reductions.

4. Because regulation of profits affects property values, utility companies can appeal commission decisions to the courts under the Fourteenth Amendment. This makes utility regulation somewhat cumbersome, expensive, and uncertain.

5. The economic issues involved in utility regulation are complex and difficult. An understanding of the unsatisfactory results of utility regulation to date requires a brief review of these underlying issues and problems.

SOME ECONOMIC ISSUES IN REGULATION

It seems simple enough to say to a private monopoly, "You must sell your product at a fair price," and to set up a board charged with enforcing this edict. This approach is often advocated, not only for public utilities, but for highly concentrated manufacturing industries such as basic steel. If an industry is raising prices too fast or making too much money, why not set up a board to regulate its prices? A century of experience in utility regulation reveals the host of difficulties involved in such an attempt. Only the most important of these can be outlined here.

"Fair Return on Fair Value"

The courts have ruled that the owners of utilities are entitled to a fair rate of return on a fair valuation of the property. But they have not been willing to lay down definite principles for determining either fair value or fair return. The meaning of these terms is argued out afresh in each case.

One major issue involves the difference between the original cost of a plant and the cost of building the same plant today. Consider a steam generating plant built by an electric power company for $10 million at the depressed price levels of 1935. To build the same plant today might cost $25 million. Which is the "fair value" of the property? Should the company be allowed to earn 6 percent on original cost, which would mean $600,000, or 6 percent on reproduction cost, which would be $1,500,000? During a long upswing of prices, the companies will be strongly in favor of reproduction cost, while the commissions will usually favor original cost. During a downswing of prices, the positions are reversed. The courts have usually given the not very helpful advice that "both principles must be given due consideration."

Another difficulty is that the 1935 plant will be partly worn out by 1960. How much should be deducted from its value on this account? There are various possible ways of calculating depreciation, and much room for argument concerning them.

After the value of the company's property has been decided, the next question is how high a return the company should be allowed to earn on this value. The yield of an investment, as we saw in Chapter 9, normally includes the pure rate of interest plus a risk premium which varies with the riskiness of the enterprise. There is not much risk involved in operating a public utility, since it usually controls an essential service with a stable or expanding market. The rate of return on public utility property, therefore, should presumably be not very far above the rate on a long-term, riskless government bond. But precisely what rate should be allowed depends on the judgment of a particular commission. The permitted rate has usually been between 5½ and 8 percent, toward the low end of this range during the thirties and forties when all interest rates were low, higher during the fifties when money rates generally were higher.

Control of Operating Costs

If price to the public is to be fair, not only must profits be reasonable but operating costs should be held to a minimum. Production costs, however, result from decisions of private management. The utility commissions, while they usually have legal authority to investigate operating costs and disallow specific items, actually do so only in cases of flagrant abuse. A lax management can allow costs to creep up higher than necessary, and then apply to the commission for higher rates which will enable it to earn the customary return on these inflated costs.

The argument is not that executives of public utilities are less efficient than executives in other lines of industry. This may or may not be true, and a factual test would be difficult. The point is simply that they *can* be inefficient and still survive. There is no automatic check on inefficiency such as exists in a competitive industry. Nor is there a strong financial incentive to improve efficiency over the course of time.

Government price regulation falls short of being a satisfactory substitute for competition partly because it does not exert strong pressure for maximum efficiency.

Negative Control versus Positive Initiative

Proper economic performance by an industry is a positive concept. It requires that plants in the industry be of optimum scale and be managed with maximum efficiency. It requires that output be increased so long as it can be sold at a price which will cover marginal cost. It requires aggressive expansion of plant capacity where necessary to meet this production objective.

FIGURE 12–1

Different Output Policies for a Utility

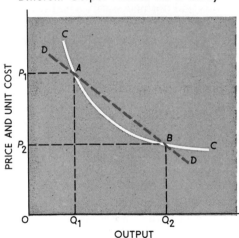

CC is the long-run average total cost curve. The company can earn a normal profit at *either* A or B. A cautious management operating at A may decide to stay there, even though expansion would be in the public interest.

If the things are to be done, however, they must be done through management initiative. The commission can scarcely compel them. Its powers are essentially negative, to prevent exorbitant prices and profits.

The inability of a utility commission to take positive steps toward desirable economic performance may be illustrated by Figure 12–1. CC is the long-run average total cost curve for a particular utility. It shows the unit cost of producing various quantities of output after allowing time for construction of new plant capacity. It includes whatever return on capital is allowed by the controlling commission. DD is the product demand curve. Suppose the utility is presently operating at A, with price OP_1 and output OQ_1, and earning just the rate of return which the commission allows. On the surface everything seems all right, but it really isn't. If demand is as shown, the company could afford to build new plant capacity and expand to B, where it would be selling output OQ_2 at price OP_2. Here it would still be covering costs and earning the allowable rate of return, while consumers would be getting more of the product at a lower price.

To move from A toward B requires positive action. Management must gamble that the demand curve is as elastic as shown and that larger outputs can be sold at a profitable price. But since the company is already earning satisfactory profits at A, it may decide to sit tight and not take the risks of expansion. Managers of monopolies seem often to underestimate the elasticity of their demand curves, and to follow a conservative policy of low output and high prices. If they can be forced to cut prices, this turns out to be profitable. But they have to be forced, and the typical public utility commission is reluctant to do this.

The Possibility of Net Losses

A utility commission is supposed to set a price which covers average total cost including a fair profit. But this will not necessarily yield the best price and output from a community standpoint. We concluded in Part One that output of each product in the economy should be expanded to the point at which price equals *marginal cost*. But this will not always yield a reasonable profit to the company, and may involve losses.

Consider the situation sketched in Figure 12–2. Here we have an enterprise with a large plant and heavy overhead costs. As output is expanded, average total cost falls steadily, and for a long time marginal cost lies below average cost. The standard illustration is a main-line railroad. Buying and building the right of way, laying the rails, and maintaining the roadbed involves heavy fixed costs. But once the road is there, the more tons of freight are run over it, the lower will be the average cost per ton. Eventually marginal cost and finally average cost will turn upward, presumably because the railroad gets overcrowded with trains. But this point may lie far to the right of the actual rate of operation, as in the case shown.

What price policy should be followed in this case? Ordinary principles of utility regulation might lead to operation at A, where the enterprise can earn just a normal profit with price OP_1 and output OQ_1. Our standard of economic efficiency, however, requires that output be expanded so long as price is above marginal cost. This would lead to operation at B, with price OP_2 and output OQ_2. At this point, however, the company cannot break even. Price is below average total cost by the distance *BC*. Since the commission cannot order a company to accept an unprofitable price, it cannot enforce such a policy. The price OP_2 would be feasible only with public subsidy or public operation of the industry.[1]

FIGURE 12–2

Alternative Pricing Criteria

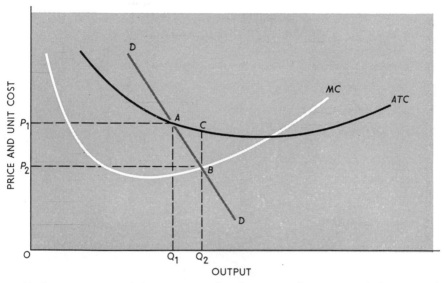

In this situation a public utility commission might order a price of OP_1, since with this price and output OQ_1 the company will just cover average total costs. It is economically desirable that output be increased to OQ_2, that is, to the point at which price equals marginal cost. But this would mean a loss to the company, so will not be done.

Declining Demand and Vanishing Industries

There are other cases in which losses are inevitable and price regulation may provide no workable solution. Consider a utility whose demand curve is falling over the years. Railroad passenger service, the New York subway system, and city bus systems are good illustrations. The rapid growth of private auto travel has meant a downward shift in demand curves for these types of public transportation.

Suppose such an industry in its heyday enjoys the demand *DD* in Figure 12–3. It operates at *A*, gets full use of its facilities at a low price, earns reasonable profits, and all is well. *DD* now begins to shift downward. Volume declines and unit cost rises. The company and the public utility commission will see only one answer: raise prices to cover the

---

[1] There has been considerable discussion among economic theorists over whether a government enterprise *should* necessarily equate price and marginal costs, and over what form of taxation should be used to make up the losses resulting from such a policy. The discussion is mainly academic rather than practical. Boards of publicly owned monopolies are about as conservative as those of private monopolies. They are usually ordered by law to cover all costs of their operation, and thus tend in the direction of point *A* rather than point *B*.

higher costs. The industry travels up ATC to the left. This can go on until demand has fallen to D_1D_1. Here the utility can still break even by operating at B, with considerably higher prices and lower volume than at the outset.

But suppose demand falls farther to D_2D_2. Now the remedy of raising prices breaks down. There is no longer *any* price which will cover average total cost. Either service must be abandoned, or a government subsidy provided, or government must take over the enterprise and run it at a loss. One can find examples of all three developments. The public bus systems have been abandoned in some American cities and replaced by jitney taxi service or by nothing at all. State and city governments

FIGURE 12–3

The Vanishing Industry Case

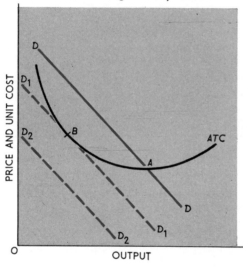

If this utility's demand curve falls below D_1D_1, there is no longer any price which will cover average total cost. Either service must be abandoned or losses must be subsidized by government.

have granted subsidies to support railroad commuter service into New York City and other East Coast communities. In other cases, declining industries have been unloaded on the government and turned into public corporations.

Transportation: Competition among Monopolists

Although we have been regulating transportation for several generations, public policy remains ill-defined and ill-coordinated. The railroads were regulated originally to prevent their charging exorbitant rates for passenger and freight transportation, of which they had a monopoly except for limited competition from the waterways. As road and air transport have increased in importance, however, the problem has become one of equalizing competitive opportunities among the various transport media, so that each can perform the functions in which its relative efficiency is greatest.

We are not within sight of this objective at present. Most types of transportation are subsidized by the public, but the subsidies vary erratically from one type to another. The railroads, while they received large land subsidies in the nineteenth century, have received little since that time. Trucks and buses contribute to highway costs through taxes on motor vehicles, tires, and gasoline; but they are still subsidized to some extent. Air and water carriers receive free use of the air and waterways, and large public contributions to the cost of shipbuilding, harbors, and airport construction. There is some reason for the railroads' complaint that the scales of competition are tilted against them, and that this is one reason for the steady decline in their percentage of the transportation business.

The orientation of regulatory policy is restrictive and anticompetitive. There is no positive drive to promote cheap, efficient transportation by whatever medium proves best suited to a particular task. The tendency is rather to protect vested interests, to restrict competition among the various media, to keep everyone in business somehow, and to prevent newcomers from getting a foothold if this will inconvenience established companies. New airlines cannot be established, and existing airlines cannot fly new routes, without CAB approval. New trucking concerns must apply for a license, and this is generally refused if it appears that the new concern would cut into the business of existing truckers or of the railroads. Instead of setting only maximum rates on freight transport, the I.C.C. now sets minimum rates for both railroads and truckers, to control competition and regulate the amount of business going to each carrier. The railroads maintain that this prevents them from moving promptly to meet trucking competition.

These policies may keep everyone alive, but they certainly don't keep everyone efficient. Part of the difficulty is that no one agency is responsible for taking an overall view of transportation policy. The Bureau of Public Roads goes merrily ahead sponsoring roads and highways, the I.C.C. regulates railroading and trucking, the Civil Aeronautics Board handles air transport, and the Maritime Commission subsidizes shipping. No one has the job of thinking about rational policy for transportation as a whole. There are probably few sectors of the economy which stand to gain more from thorough review and a fresh approach.

PUBLIC OWNERSHIP AS AN ALTERNATIVE

Private management combined with public regulation is only one answer to the utility problem. The main alternative is public ownership and operation of natural monopolies. This alternative has been widely employed in Britain, the British Commonwealth countries, Western Europe, and many of the less-developed countries—in fact, almost everywhere outside the United States.

The relative advantages of private and public operation have been argued for decades. Some of the points most commonly made in favor of public ownership are:

1. It simplifies the structure and responsibilities of management. The American pattern of public utility regulation involves two-decker management. There is a full-fledged private management responsible for decisions on business policy. But on top of this is placed a public board responsible for supervising what private management is doing. If the public utility commission is to do its job effectively, it must have a large staff of experts and technicians paralleling the staffs of the companies it regulates. This is expensive, time consuming, and apt to be mutually frustrating. Under government operation these two layers are merged into a unified management, responsible for operating the enterprise in the public interest.

2. It establishes public service as the criterion of successful performance, and allows this criterion to be applied in a positive way. Management can devote its full attention to defining economic policies which will serve the public interest, and to putting them into operation. A management responsible to private stockholders is bound to be biased toward policies which yield maximum profit.

3. It reduces the financial restrictions on management decisions. Government does not go bankrupt, while business concerns do. A private corporation cannot afford losses over any extended period. Yet there may be circumstances, as noted in the previous section, in which it is desirable to provide a public service at a price below full cost. This can be done by handing over government money to a private company to cover its losses, as we now do for passenger airlines and merchant shipping; but this procedure is obviously subject to abuse. If an enterprise is unlikely to be profitable in the foreseeable future, there is much to be said for nationalizing it and bearing the costs directly rather than indirectly.

The main considerations against public ownership are suggested by the battle cry of "politics and bureaucracy." Specifically, it is charged that:

1. A government enterprise is under irresistible public pressure to make uneconomic decisions. The unions will expect a government agency to be a model employer, and to give in with good grace to wage demands. At the same time consumers and politicians will object to raising product prices enough to cover the higher costs. Particular areas of the country will work through political channels to get plants and facilities located there, whether or not the location makes sense from a cost standpoint. This political pulling and hauling may lead to losses which will have to be met from general tax revenues.

2. Political intervention in appointments may make it difficult to recruit management officials on a merit basis. Salary restrictions on public officials make it hard to compete with private business for top talent. The result may be mediocre and unimaginative leadership of public enterprises.

3. The management of a government monopoly may be characterized by rigid procedural rules, elaborate paperwork, and skilled buck-passing. This can cause serious delay in decisions, poor service, and arbitrary treatment of customers. The seriousness of this risk depends a good deal on how the public industry is organized. Bureaucratic tendencies are more likely to develop in a regular government department than in an independent public corporation such as the British Railways or the Tennessee Valley Authority. One must remember also that bureaucracy is not unknown in private business. The management procedures of our railroads have a charmingly antiquated character which would do credit to any government bureau.

There is no magic in public ownership which will automatically solve the economic problems of an industry. Naïve socialists have sometimes imagined that nationalizing a private industry would usher in the new Jerusalem. Production would now be "for use, not for profit," whatever that may mean. Wages could be raised and prices lowered, managers would immediately become efficient and public spirited, the union lion would lie down with the management lamb. They have been quite surprised to find that on the morning after nationalization everything remains much as before. It is still hard to figure out how fast capacity should be expanded, what prices should be charged, whether operating losses are justifiable, and so on. It is hard to mediate the conflicting pressures from workers, consumers, legislators, and others. Good day-to-day management continues to be a hard, unremitting task, never perfectly performed.

EXCESSIVE COMPETITION: THE CASE OF AGRICULTURE

To this point we have been considering industries in which competitive organization is impossible, and in which the regulatory force of competition must be replaced by public control. We now turn completely around to consider cases in which competition not merely exists but it is claimed that competition is excessive and harmful. The most important industry in this category is agriculture.

An initial difficulty is that there is no single agricultural problem for which one might be able to find a single solution. There are several distinct problems, of which the most important are chronic overexpansion of productive capacity, high sensitivity of farm prices to shifts in demand or supply, and poverty among the marginal fringe of the farm population. These problems must be explained before considering possible remedies.

BASIC ECONOMIC PROBLEMS OF AGRICULTURE

Chronic Overcapacity

Many countries of the world have difficulty feeding their population from their own production. The American problem is precisely the reverse—a problem of plenty rather than want. American agriculture is geared to turn out more produce than the market will take at acceptable prices.

What is the evidence for this assertion? How can one tell whether an industry is overexpanded relative to others in a market economy? If the market mechanism is working effectively, the marginal productivity of labor and capital employed in each line of industry will be approximately equal. The money return to a factor of production is a rough measure of its marginal productivity. Thus one should find that labor of the same skill and quality earns roughly the same wage at different points in the economy. If labor in particular industry earns substantially less than comparable labor in other industries, this indicates some blockage in the market mechanism. There is too much labor, and probably too much of other resources, engaged in the low-wage industry.

There is abundant evidence of low earnings in agriculture relative to urban industries. Hired farm labor has never in modern times earned even half as much as unskilled factory labor, and the ratio has usually been closer to one third. The incomes of farm operators, including the value of farm produce consumed at home, are typically less than half those of semiskilled factory operatives. Considering that farming involves considerable skill, versatility, and independent judgment, that the farmer works a longer week and year than the factory worker, and that his income includes some return on his capital, this is an odd situation. The farmer is apparently right in claiming that competition has been working to his disadvantage.

How did American agriculture get into this situation? Through a chronic tendency over the past 50 years for the supply of farm products to rise more rapidly that the demand for them. These demand and supply trends are deep-seated and require a word of explanation.

The *demand* for foodstuffs depends basically on the number of mouths to be fed. The rate of population growth in the United States fell off considerably from 1914 to 1940 because of the cessation of mass immigration and a considerable drop in birth rates. This had a depressing effect on agricultural demand. Since 1940 birth rates have risen once more, and the U.S. population has been increasing at about $1\frac{1}{2}$ percent per year. This bulge in the population curve will be quite helpful to agriculture, as the babies of the fifties grow up into adolescents with voracious appetites during the sixties. It is uncertain, however, whether population growth will continue at the same rate or will taper off again.

Most products can depend, not only on growth of population, but on the rise of people's incomes and living standards. Even if population were stationary, producers of household appliances, restaurant meals, and vacation trips could count on a rising sales volume. Agriculture, however, benefits less from rising incomes than do other industries. Food is a basic necessity and, while people eat somewhat better as they become better off, their spending on food rises much less rapidly than their incomes. Professor Theodore Schultz has estimated that, at present U.S. income levels, an increase of 10 percent in people's incomes produces an increase of something like 2½ percent in demand for food. (The *income elasticity of demand* for food, in other words, is about 0.25 percent.) The main thing which happens as people's incomes rise is not that they buy more food, but that they shift to more expensive foods—less beans and more sirloin steak. They also demand more service with their food—more processing, fancier packaging, freezing, and so on. But this means increased demand in manufacturing and retailing rather than in agriculture.

Suppose population continues to increase at around 1½ percent per year, and that personal income per capita rises at the long-term average of a bit under 3 percent. This would mean an increase in total personal income of around 4 percent per year. With an income elasticity of 0.25, the demand for farm products would rise about 1 percent per year over the long run. If supply rises faster than this, there will be downward pressure on farm prices. Since agriculture is already overexpanded, farm output should rise *less* than 1 percent per year over the next decade or two to redress the supply-demand balance.

The actual tendency of agricultural output is to increase a good deal faster than this. Farm output in 1960 was 50 percent higher than in 1940, an increase of about 2 percent per year. This happened even though acreage planted declined slightly and the farm population fell by almost one third, from 30.5 million to 21 million. How could output rise so much when the number of farms and farm workers was falling? The answer lies in a sensational rise of agricultural productivity. Output per worker in agriculture in 1960 was more than double that in 1940, a much higher rate of productivity increase than in the economy as a whole. Farmers now use much more mechanical equipment than they did a generation ago. Capital per farm worker, measured in constant dollars, almost doubled between 1940 and 1960. Chemical fertilizers are used more intensively and effectively. Hybrid corn and other improvements in seed, improved control of plant diseases, improved breeds of livestock, and many other developments have contributed to higher productivity. There has been an increase in average size of farms in some regions, as the more successful farmers have bought out people retiring or moving to the city; and this has enabled machinery to be used more effectively. There is no indication that the possibilities in these directions are being exhausted or that the rise of farm productivity is slackening.

This rapid increase in productive capacity, combined with a slower rate of increase in demand, accounts for the present overexpansion of agriculture. Overexpansion is particularly serious in cotton, which has suffered from the competition of synthetic fibers and from loss of export markets; and in wheat, where domestic demand is sluggish and a world wheat surplus available at low prices hampers our export position. There is less overcapacity in dairy products, fruit and vegetables, and cattle raising, where demand trends are more favorable and export markets are not important. There is thus a dual problem of cutting back total agricultural capacity and of redistributing the remaining capacity among products, getting more of it into lines for which demand is expanding and leaving less in products such as wheat and cotton where demand is especially weak.

The problem of overcapacity is aggravated by the low price elasticity of demand. For many manufactured goods, a 10 percent increase in output might mean only a 10 percent drop in price. But in the case of agriculture, a 10 percent increase in output may mean a 30 to 40 percent drop in price. This means that a *small* excess production of a particular crop has a *large* depressing effect on the growers' incomes. The amount of overcapacity in agriculture is not large—probably of the order of 5 to 10 percent of total agricultural production. Yet this small output surplus would, if prices were left completely free, drive them down to a level which farmers would regard as intolerable.

Short-Term Instability of Farm Prices

Inelasticity of demand, combined with fluctuating and uncontrolled production, tends to produce large year-to-year swings in farm prices

FIGURE 12–4

Fluctuations in Wheat Prices

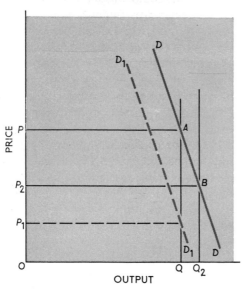

Starting from demand DD and price OP, *either* a decline in demand to D_1D_1 *or* a bumper crop which raises output to OQ_2 will cause a sharp drop in wheat prices.

and incomes. Farm prices are much more vulnerable than most other prices to the ups and downs of the business cycle. Suppose that in a year of normal prosperity wheat production is OQ, demand is DD, and price is OP (Figure 12–4). Now a depression sets in. Demand falls to D_1D_1.

Oligopolists in a manufacturing industry would probably react to this by cutting output in order to hold up prices. But farmers cannot control production in this way. There are too many of them, and it is not to the interest of one farmer to reduce his wheat acreage unless others do the same. They are likely, then, to keep right on producing OQ, and this (unless the government intervenes through price supports) will mean a drastic drop in wheat prices to OP_1.

The accident of an unusually good crop is also likely to cut farmers' incomes. This follows directly from inelasticity of demand, which means that larger quantities produce less revenue. Suppose that because of unusually favorable weather the wheat crop is OQ_2 instead of the normal OQ. With demand unchanged at DD, price will drop from OP to OP_2. The "good year" turns out not to be so good after all, for wheat growers' total income (OQ_2BP_2) is a good deal smaller than the income in a normal year $(OQAP)$.

These wide swings in prices not only involve personal hardship but also make it harder for farmers to make a rational choice among alternative lines of production. There is widespread agreement that government should try to smooth out these price fluctuations.

The Marginal Farmer and Rural Poverty

The *average* income of farm families is a misleading figure, because it conceals great variation among them. The wheat farmer with 5,000 acres of good cropland, or the rancher with 10,000 head of beef cattle, is at one end of the scale. At the other is the family with 50 acres of worn-out land, barely able to feed itself and to buy a few necessities in town. These are all farm families, but they are worlds apart.

There are about four and a half million so-called "farm units" in the United States. But only two million of these have market sales of $2,500 or more per year.[2] These are the core of our farming industry, and produce more than 90 percent of marketed farm output. They are clearly capable of producing as much as the national market can absorb at reasonable prices. The remaining farm units may thus be regarded as surplus.

Where and what are the remaining farm units? Many of them should not be called farms at all. One and a half million are classified by the census as "part-time and residential farms." The people who live on them usually get most of their income from nonfarm sources, and are not really part of the farm problem.

This leaves upwards of a million full-time commercial farms with annual sales of less than $2,500. Almost half a million have cash sales of less than $1,200. After deducting costs of farm operation, this leaves too little for decent family living. The low earnings of these families reflect

---

[2] The top 3 percent of our farms, each with annual sales of $25,000 or more, produce about one third of total commercial output.

low productivity, due to a number of causes: too little acreage to employ the full time of the farmer and his family; land which is eroded, depleted of fertility, or unproductive for other reasons; inadequate equipment and poor farming methods; and tenancy arrangements which sometimes give the tenant little incentive for productivity. The greatest concentration of such families is found in the old cotton areas of the Southeast, but they are found also in the cut-over areas of the Lake States, on the fringes of forest regions, and on dry land near the western edge of the Great Plains.

These families constitute a special problem. Raising farm prices doesn't help them much, because they have little to sell. The general answer to their problem is clear: they shouldn't be where they are. They should be on better land or larger farms in other locations, or they should be out of agriculture altogether. But it is not easy to accomplish this in a society which believes in free choice of occupation and residence, and where people can use their freedom to make mistakes.

THE POLICY OF FARM PRICE SUPPORTS

With this background, let us look briefly at the poultices which we have been applying to our agricultural ailments over the past 30 years. Many things have been done about agriculture, but the policy which has gradually assumed central importance is that of price supports. Not all agricultural products are covered by the system. The products which must be supported by law are: cotton, wheat, corn, dairy products, tobacco, rice, peanuts, wool, mohair, tung nuts, and honey. Certain others may be supported if the Secretary of Agriculture so decides. Under this optional provision support prices have been established for soybeans, cottonseed, oats, barley, rye, flaxseed, beans, and sorghum grain. The products under price support make up about half of total agricultural output, while the remaining half is still sold at free market prices.

A price support is a guaranteed minimum price. If the market establishes a still higher price, well and good. Price is free to fluctuate upward, but it may not fall below the support level. How is the support price calculated? A central concept here is *parity*, which means essentially that the price a farmer receives for his product should bear the same relation to the price he pays for industrial products as it did in some base period. Crudely, "If a bushel of wheat bought a cotton shirt in 1950, it should buy the same shirt today." *Example:* Suppose that in 1950 the price of wheat was $2.00 per bushel. Instead of shirts we should use some average of all goods purchased and the government does calculate each month an index of "prices paid by farmers." Suppose that in 1950 this index stood at 100. By 1960 it has risen to 120, an increase of 20 percent. The parity price of wheat in 1960, then, is 20 percent higher than in 1950, or $2.40 per bushel.[3]

---

[3] The actual calculation of parity prices is considerably more complicated than this example suggests. Different base periods have been used for different products,

The parity price is an arbitrary figure. Take the question of what year or years should be chosen as the base period for parity calculations. There is no scientific answer to this question. The tendency has been to select a base period during which farm prices were unusually high relative to nonfarm prices, in order to get the highest possible parity price. Moreover, there is no reason why the price of wheat should rise at the same rate as prices of other products for all time to come. Divergent price movements in the economy are normal, reflecting mainly the differing rates of productivity increase in different industries. Carried to its logical conclusion, the parity concept would mean that all prices in the economy must march along forever in lock-step. The parity price, despite its pseudo-scientific appearance, is actually a piece of "political arithmetic."

But there is more political arithmetic to come. How close should the government come to full parity? Should the minimum guaranteed price be 50 percent of parity, or 75 percent, or 100 percent? This is a central issue in political battles over farm legislation. While the decision is partly arbitrary, the state of demand for farm products can be found lurking in the background. During World War II demand was very strong and farm prices were allowed to rise to 110 percent of parity before ceilings could be imposed. Postwar needs abroad plus the Korean War kept demand strong through the early fifties, and support prices were typically set at 90 percent of parity. As demand receded toward more normal levels, the administration fought for and secured from Congress a flexible system under which the Secretary of Agriculture could set prices for basic products anywhere between 75 and 90 percent of parity, depending on the supply-demand situation for a particular product. Support prices for corn, wheat, cotton, and other basic products in recent years have been close to the 75 percent minimum, while dairy products and others defined by law as nonbasic have been supported at rates down to 60 percent of parity. The price support system thus makes some concession to economic realities.

How does the government make good on its commitment to support the price of cotton at, say, 32 cents per pound? By standing ready to buy any quantity which may be offered on the market at this price. If demand is good or the crop small so that the market equilibrium is above 32 cents, all is well and the government need do nothing. But if the market weakens and the price threatens to fall below 32 cents, the government is bound to start buying and to buy as much as necessary to maintain the price. The lower private demand falls, the more government must buy. In recent years government has held something like a full year's crop of

---

usually with a view to getting the highest possible support price for each! Recently, an effort has been made to shift over to a moving base, which would be an average of prices received and paid in the most recent 10-year period. Thus parity prices for 1963 would rest on a base of 1953–62. This has advantages over a fixed base, which tends to get more and more obsolete as it recedes into the past.

wheat, corn, and cotton, stored in warehouses all over the country at considerable expense.

The fact that the system rests on government purchase and storage explains why it has been confined to nonperishable products. Livestock producers have occasionally descended on Washington to demand support prices for meat, but have invariably been turned down. The deep-freeze lockers of the country are not adequate to hold the meat surplus which would accumulate under a support system. Where supports have been used for products which do not store very well, the result has been a fiasco. Some years ago the large holdings of potatoes in government warehouses began to sprout at an embarrassing rate. Part of the supply was dyed black and disposed of as cattle feed, part was simply destroyed. Potatoes have been out from under supports since that time.

Who gains and who loses under a price support arrangement? The main effects can be explained by a demand-supply diagram (Figure 12–5). *DD* and *SS* are the demand and supply curves for cotton or wheat,

FIGURE 12–5

Operation of Agricultural Price Supports

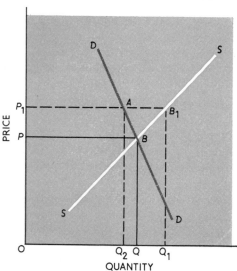

Supporting price at OP_1 instead of the equilibrium *OP* reduces consumption and leads to a surplus of $AB_1 = Q_2Q_1$. Consumers pay more both as food buyers and taxpayers, and this money is transferred to farmers.

or whatever. *OP* and *OQ* are the equilibrium price and output which would result in a free market. In the absence of government intervention, buyers would pay and producers would receive *OPBQ*. Instead of this, government undertakes to support prices at OP_1. Immediately a gap opens up between the amount which buyers are willing to take off the market (OQ_2) and the amount which farmers want to produce at the support price (OQ_1). The "surplus," $OQ_1 - OQ_2$, must be purchased and stored by government. The consequences are:

1. Farmers' incomes are increased to $OP_1B_1Q_1$. Only part of this income comes from private buyers (OP_1AQ_2). The remainder comes from the government in return for government purchases ($Q_2AB_1Q_1$).

2. Consumers get less of the product than before, but pay more money for this reduced amount.

3. In their capacity as citizens, consumers are taxed an amount $Q_2AB_1Q_1$, which the government turns over to the farmers in return for the "surplus" produce.

The most embarrassing feature of the system is the tendency for ever-larger quantities of unsold produce to accumulate in government warehouses. Is there any way to avoid this? What about restriction of production? If farmers could be limited to producing OQ_2 instead of OQ_1, then the system would be in balance after a fashion. Present farm legislation provides for production controls on the six basic commodities. After a referendum of growers, in which the control proposal must get a two-thirds majority, the Secretary of Agriculture is empowered to impose production controls. He can say, for example, that only so many million acres may be planted to winter wheat in 1964, and can allocate this total by states, by counties, and by individual farms. The acreage that is planted to wheat, corn, and cotton has been restricted since the early fifties.

This has still not prevented the accumulation of large surpluses. What happens when a farmer is told that he must cut his wheat acreage by one third? First, the acres which he takes out of production are the least productive acres. The best land continues to be used for wheat. Second, the farmer concentrates fertilizer, labor, and equipment on these remaining acres, works them more intensively than before, and raises the yield per acre. A cut of 20 or 30 percent in acreage, then, may yield little or no reduction in output. The logical response would be for the government to cut acreage still further; but this could lead eventually to a situation in which each farm was only one third utilized, and the foolishness of the system would become transparent.

Thus the accumulation of surpluses continues. Government holdings of commodities acquired through price support operations now total more than $5 billion. In addition to the money tied up in these products, much of which will eventually be lost through spoilage or cut-rate sales, there are heavy warehousing expenses. The only outlet for any considerable part of this surplus lies in foreign countries.

There may have been a case for price supports as a temporary measure under the depressed conditions of the thirties. But as so often happens, what began as a palliative has hardened into a permanent policy. This policy does not get at the basic agricultural problems and has in fact retarded the search for fundamental remedies. The most important defects of the price support program are:

1. It has laid a heavy tax on the nonfarm population, both directly to provide money for government purchase and storage, and indirectly through higher food prices. Nor is this clearly a transfer from higher-income urban groups to lower-income rural groups in the population. There are many millions of low-income families in the cities, and food is a large item in their budgets. On the receiving end, the benefits of price supports go mainly to the larger farmers who market most of the farm produce.

2. The program has made little contribution to the problem of rural poverty. The poorest million farms in the country bring little produce to market, so higher market prices cannot add much to their incomes. The larger and more productive a commercial farm, and the less it really needs price supports, the more it benefits from the present program.

3. The program has aggravated the overcapacity which constitutes the basic problem of American agriculture. Guaranteed high prices have kept farms in production which might otherwise have been withdrawn from production, and have stimulated expansion of output when contraction was in order. High prices have also choked off demand and made it harder to find market outlets for our productive capacity. This is particularly serious as regards wheat and cotton. U.S. cotton prices are so far above the world level that we are almost out of the export market, which has been taken over increasingly by Brazil, Mexico, Egypt, and other producers. In the domestic market, high cotton prices make it easy for producers of synthetic fibers to undersell cotton and take over more and more of the clothing business. U.S. wheat prices are out of line with those of Canada, Argentina, and other major producers, and our export position has suffered accordingly. A policy of pricing farm products out of the market is not in the long-run interest of the farm population.

4. The logical outcome of guaranteed prices is production control through quotas reaching down to the individual farm. Such a system is clearly undesirable. It keeps all existing farms in operation, but allows each to be operated at only a fraction of its full capacity. Land, equipment, and the farmer's time are all underutilized. Moreover, the pattern of production becomes frozen. Production of each crop must continue on the same farms, in the same states, in perpetuity. New producers cannot break in, and established producers will not shift to other crops because they would lose their valuable quota privileges. Shifts of production which may be desirable because of changing markets and technology are effectively prevented.

SOME POSSIBLE DIRECTIONS FOR FARM POLICY

This is not the place to develop a comprehensive policy for American agriculture. The issues are complicated and even lifetime students of agriculture are not in full agreement. But one could probably get widespread agreement on the following propositions:

1. The key to a solution of agriculture's problems lies partly outside agriculture, in a rapid and sustained growth of nonagricultural industries. A rapid rise in consumers' incomes raises the demand for farm products. An abundance of urban job opportunities pulls labor off the land and helps hold farm production within bounds. Thus general economic growth is helpful on both the demand and supply sides. Schultz has estimated that (in the United States) urban industries must expand three to four times as rapidly as agricultural production for agriculture to remain in a healthy condition.[4]

2. Elimination of overcapacity requires that a substantial acreage be permanently retired from agriculture. The percentage reduction in acreage must be larger than the desired reduction in output, because of the tendency for the remaining acres to be worked more intensively. During the late fifties the federal government moved in this direction through the "soil bank" program, but the deposits in the bank were neither large nor permanent enough to meet the need. An effective program should incorporate the following characteristics:

a) The retirement of land from agriculture should be permanent rather than temporary. This amounts to government buying the land rather than renting it, as under the soil bank program.

b) Emphasis should be on retirement of whole farms rather than parts of farms. In this case the farm operator would probably retire or move to town. If only part of a farm is taken out of production, the farmer will stay on the land and be underemployed.

c) Priority should be given to retirement of marginal, low-income farms. This would reduce rural poverty as well as farm production.

d) The program should probably be several times the size of the original soil bank program. This would mean a large initial cost to the government. But it would be a once-for-all cost, and would remove the need to buy up large surpluses in future years.

3. If land and labor are to be taken out of agriculture and without hardship to the people involved, ways should be found to ease the transition of ex-farmers to urban employment. The first essential is to have enough jobs available through a vigorous full-employment program. The state employment services could help to advise people in rural areas as to where the job outlook is most promising. It might also be desirable to advance moving costs to farm families leaving for the city, to be repaid over a reasonable period in the future.

4. Pricing of farm products should be returned as rapidly as possible to the free market, keeping only the safeguards against depression to be described in a moment. With the scaling down of farm capacity already suggested, market prices should yield adequate incomes to the efficient family-sized farm. Reliance on market pricing would eliminate the problem of burdensome surpluses and the need for production controls. Market

---

[4] Theodore W. Schultz, *Agriculture in an Unstable Economy* (New York: McGraw-Hill Book Co., Inc., 1945).

prices would also perform their traditional function of shifting land and other resources toward farm products whose demand is rising away from products where demand is declining.

5. There remains the problem of sharp drops in farm income in depression years. A depression which produces little decline in industrial prices can produce a drop of 20 or 30 percent in farm prices. This degree of instability is more than farmers can reasonably be asked to bear, and there is a good case for some form of protection against it.

A possible approach to the problem has been suggested by Professor Schultz. During prosperity there would be no effort to raise farm prices or incomes above market levels. At the onset of depression, however, a support program would go into action. Government could announce that a depression exists when full-time unemployment rises above some specified percentage of the labor force, or when total national output falls by a specified amount. This announcement would set in motion remedial measures designed, not to support farm *prices*, but to support farm *incomes* through direct cash payments.

Suppose that the price of wheat just before the depression began was $2.00 per bushel. There would be no effort to hold the price of wheat at this level. On the contrary, it would be allowed to fall to whatever extent might be necessary to clear the market. But at the same time government would guarantee the farmer cash payments based on a specified percentage of the pre-depression price. This percentage could be generous or niggardly. If it were established at 85 percent, wheat farmers would be guaranteed an income of $1.70 per bushel sold. As soon as the market price fell below $1.70, the government would begin cash payments to make up the difference. If at the bottom of the depression the price of wheat had fallen to $1.20, government would be paying farmers a direct subsidy of 50 cents a bushel. Subsidy payments would continue until *either* the market price climbed back above $1.70 *or* the depression was officially declared over.

This would provide depression protection for farmers, similar to the unemployment compensation system for wage earners. It can be justified both as disaster protection for farmers and as a way of sustaining purchasing power during depression. Its merit, indeed, is that it *is* strictly a depression measure. It would not require subsidies to farmers in good years, nor would it involve perpetuating obsolete price levels. There would be a new "parity level" at the peak of each prosperity period.

EXCESSIVE COMPETITION: THE RETAILING REVOLUTION

Until well into the twentieth century the small, owner-operated retail shop was the order of the day. The corner grocer, the druggist, the hardwareman, and the lumberyard operator were key figures in the community. They sold on credit as well as for cash, waited on the customer, ran the packages around to his home if required, and provided a highly personalized retailing service.

Beginning about 1920, the position of the small merchant was challenged by a rapid increase of large retail units, usually linked in chains covering a region or even the entire country. This tendency was particularly strong in grocery, drug, auto accessory, and general or department stores. These mass distributors often bought directly from the manufacturer, eliminating the wholesaler on whom the small merchant had traditionally relied. By large orders, hard bargaining, and eliminating the wholesalers' margin they were able to buy cheaper than the small retailer. In terms of store operations, it turned out that the optimum-sized retail unit was much larger than had previously been realized. The mass distributors were able to handle merchandise at substantially lower unit costs than their smaller competitors. Finally, the chains operated on a cash-and-carry basis. Self-service instead of the hovering sales clerk, elimination of expensive delivery systems, and abolition of credit with its accompaniment of collection costs and bad debts, reduced retailing costs and made possible lower prices.

For these reasons drug and grocery chains could undersell the small retailer by 10 percent or more and still make handsome profits. To most people this price advantage more than offset the loss of credit and delivery services. Customers flocked to the large retailers and their share of the national market rose rapidly. This was essentially a technological revolution, involving displacement of high-cost retailing methods by lower-cost methods.

But while consumers rejoiced, the small merchant was panicked. The mortality rate of retail shops has always been high. But the rise of mass distributors accelerated the demise of small merchants and the survivors found their profits severely squeezed. Cries of outrage soon reached Congress and the state legislatures, accompanied by demands that something be done.

Three main things were done. Many of the states passed laws levying a license fee on retail stores, the size of the fee rising steeply with the number of stores operating under common ownership. This gambit was not very effective. The states did not dare levy high enough taxes to offset the cost advantages of chains and put them out of business. Moreover, the taxes were obviously discriminatory and were held unconstitutional by many state supreme courts. These laws have now generally been repealed.

At the federal level, the Robinson-Patman Act of 1936 provided that price discrimination by a seller which might injure competition among his buyers was illegal unless the seller could prove that the price difference was justified by a difference in costs. This was intended to hamper the mass distributor in bargaining with manufacturers, and to prevent him from getting goods at much lower prices than his small competitors. This objective was only partially attained. Chains were able to get around the act by contracting for a manufacturer's total output, or by setting up their own manufacturing facilities.

A third device was the state "fair trade" or "resale price maintenance" laws. These laws permit a manufacturer of a branded article to specify a fixed retail price below which no retailer may sell his product. The technique is for the manufacturer to sign a contract with one or more dealers under which they promise, as a condition of receiving his product, that they will not sell it for less than a specified price. Thus far the restriction is not serious, for some retailers might refuse to sign and it would take the manufacturer a long time to line up all dealers in a state. But resale price maintenance laws commonly provide that, when a price-fixing contract has been signed with one dealer, it becomes binding on *every* retailer in the state, whether or not he has signed it or even heard of it. Any retailer who violates the fixed price is punishable under state law. The result is a monopolist's dream—legalized *private* price fixing, with no public control or standards of reasonableness, but with public enforcement of the fixed price.

The purpose of these laws is to provide a generous guaranteed margin between the retailer's buying price from the manufacturer and his selling price to the consumer. They are promoted mainly by associations of independent retailers in various fields, particularly drugs and cosmetics, liquor, books, photographic equipment, and electrical appliances. The prescribed margins are based on the costs of the small retailer and are intended to prevent the more efficient mass distributors from selling at lower prices and expanding their share of the market. Consider, for example, a drug item on which the manufacturers' price is $1.00. A small pharmacist might retail this at $2.50 to cover his costs and earn what he considers a reasonable profit. A large drug chain with lower costs and mark-ups could retail the item profitably at $1.75. In a free market, the retail price would tend toward $1.75. The small man's profits would be squeezed and he might be forced to the wall. Under resale price maintenance, the small dealers see to it that the minimum price of the article is set at $2.50 or better, and the large chain must observe this price. The chain is thus prevented from passing on its lower costs to the public and winning more customers through lower prices.

It is sometimes argued that retail price fixing benefits the manufacturer as well as the merchant. The manufacturer, it is said, has a valuable asset in his brand name. This value is likely to be impaired by price cutting, since the public tends to reason that low price indicates low quality. There may be a little to this, but not very much. On the whole, manufacturers have little to gain from retail price fixing. Political pressure for this type of legislation comes mainly from retailers' associations. Once a resale price maintenance law has been passed, the association sets to work to "persuade" manufacturers to set high fixed prices on their products. If a manufacturer is reluctant, he is brought into line by a threat to boycott his products unless he signs up. Most manufacturers find it prudent to go along with the system, but this does not prove that they are convinced of its merit or that they would try to control retail prices if given free choice.

The immediate effect of a resale price maintenance law is to raise prices of the products covered by it. A number of research studies have found that the effect on prices is substantial. But the matter does not stop there. Guaranteed retail margins encourage various kinds of economic waste. Merchants who are forbidden to compete with each other in price will try to compete through lavish store layouts, delivery facilities, credit terms, advertising, premiums, and the like. Selling costs are needlessly inflated. Moreover, attractive profits combined with inability to control entrance leads to multiplication of retail units. The available business is split up finer and finer, each store operates below capacity, and retailing costs per unit of goods sold are higher than they need be. Retailers can then argue that, since their costs are so high, they must have the protection of resale price maintenance in order to survive. Thus the wheel comes full circle.

There is little doubt that resale price maintenance laws are undesirable. Fortunately, the consequences have been less harmful than might have been expected. The products which lend themselves well to price maintenance comprise only about 10 percent of all retail sales. Food and clothing, where prices fluctuate considerably and brand names are of minor importance, have been little affected. Chain and department stores have gotten around the legislation by introducing their own brand names, which they are free to price as they choose, and which are typically priced below the national brands. Finally, there is widespread violation of the fixed resale prices by discount houses and other retail outlets. This is difficult to police, partly because of the number of outlets involved, partly because of doubts about the constitutionality of the price maintenance laws, and partly because manufacturers are lukewarm toward the system. But the fact that price maintenance laws are only partially effective does not justify them. Outright repeal of these laws would be preferable.

SUMMARY

1. Public utility industries are inherently monopolistic, and this has led to regulation of price and service by state and federal agencies.

2. Public regulation, while it protects against exorbitant profits, does not ensure maximum operating efficiency, adequate expansion of plant capacity, or an equating of price with marginal cost. The control boards are hampered by the negative nature of their powers as well as by inadequate staffing.

3. Most countries outside the United States prefer public ownership and operation of utility industries. The question of private versus public operation is a technical one, to be decided in each case on grounds of economic efficiency rather than general principle.

4. The basic problems of American agriculture are chronic overexpansion

of productive capacity, short-term instability of farm prices, and low productivity and incomes for the bottom quarter or so of the farm population.

5. Government agricultural policies, which involve guaranteed minimum prices for about half of farm output, have not attacked these problems successfully. The price support system has laid a substantial tax on consumers, benefited mainly the larger farmers who need it least, aggravated the problem of overcapacity, and led toward detailed government control of farm operations.

6. Policy should now be oriented toward reducing farm acreage substantially and permanently, restoring free pricing and free choice by farmers of what to produce, and maintaining farm incomes during depression.

7. Over the past 50 years there has been a gradual displacement of small independent retailers by large chain stores. One way in which the independents have tried to fight back is by sponsoring "fair trade laws" which permit retail price fixing. These laws maintain a needlessly high level of prices, lead to wasteful selling expenditures, and encourage an inefficiently large number of retail units.

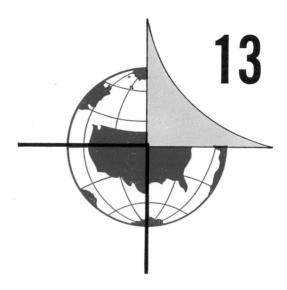

Trade Unionism and Collective Bargaining

"Well, it's too bad that th' golden days has passed, Hinnissy. Capital still pats Labor on th' back, but on'y with an axe. Labor rayfuses to be threated as a frind. It wants to be threated as an inimy. It thinks it gets more that way. What do I think iv it all? Ah, sure, I don't know. I belong to th' onfarchnit middle class. I wurruk hard, an' I have no money . . . No man iver sthrikes in sympathy with me."

"They ought to get together," said Mr. Hennessy.

"How cud they get anny closer together thin their prisint clinch?" asked Mr. Dooley, "They're so close together now that those that are between them are crushed to death."

Finley Peter Dunne

The last two chapters were concerned with public policy toward monopoly and competition in product markets. When we turn to the labor market, we encounter the charge that trade unions exert strong and undesirable monopoly power over the price of labor. To this unionists retort that without unionism the employer has the whip hand and can enforce substandard wages and conditions for which the market provides no ready corrective. So we must examine the economic impact of union operations, the kinds of government control which already exist, and proposals for additional or different kinds of control.

Space does not permit discussion of the history and structure of trade unionism in the United States. But the reader should be reminded that there are three main levels of union organization: the *local union* of workers in a particular plant or locality; the *national union*, such as the United Automobile Workers or the International Brotherhood of Electrical Workers, which is a federation of many local unions in the same trade or industry; and the *national federation*, such as the American Federation of Labor and Congress of Industrial Organizations, whose membership includes most national unions in the country.

The AFL-CIO is an educational, organizing, and political body. It represents labor on issues pending before Congress and takes an active interest in elections. But negotiation with employers over economic issues, usually termed *collective bargaining*, is the responsibility of the national and local unions in each industry, with the national union gradually assuming a predominant role.

THE FRAMEWORK OF COLLECTIVE BARGAINING

The first objective of a union is to win recognition from the employer and the right to bargain with him over conditions of employment. In earlier years this often involved calling a strike to force the employer's hand. The National Labor Relations Act of 1935, however, established an election procedure for winning recognition. A union which claims a majority of the workers in a plant can apply to the nearest office of the National Labor Relations Board for certification of its right to represent the workers in question. If the evidence is unclear, or if the employer contests the claim, the Board calls an election by secret ballot. If two or more rival unions claim representation rights, their names all appear on the ballot and workers also have the option of voting for no union. A union winning a majority in such an election is certified by the N.L.R.B. as bargaining representative for all employees in the plant,[1] and the employer is then legally bound to bargain "in good faith" with this union. This procedure has largely eliminated the old-style organizing strike.

The commonest sort of bargaining is between officials of a single company and officials of the local union which has bargaining rights in that company. But the scope of bargaining tends to expand to cover all companies which compete closely in the same product market. There is a simple reason for this. If the carpenters' union in Milwaukee charges Contractor A $4.00 an hour for carpenters' labor but allows Contractor B to hire labor for $3.00, B can consistently underbid A for construction contracts. So unions typically try to enforce the principle of *the standard rate*. The simplest way to enforce it is for the union to drive a single bargain with the whole group of competing employers.

---

[1] Strictly speaking, all employees in the *bargaining unit* in question. Several bargaining units may exist in a single plant—for example, certain groups of skilled workers may be allowed to bargain separately from the main body of employees. There are occasions, too, in which several companies competing in the same industry have been included in a single bargaining unit. The N.L.R.B. has authority to determine the proper boundaries of the bargaining unit in each case.

In some industries competition is confined to a single city. This is typically the case in house building, newspaper printing, local trucking, cleaning and dyeing, and other service industries. Here one usually finds a local union bargaining with an association representing employers throughout the area. The teamsters bargain with the local trucking association, the typographical union with all the newspaper publishers, the carpenters or plumbers with the local building contractors' association, and so on. When an agreement is reached, it becomes binding on all unionized employers in the area.

In manufacturing, competition among employers is usually on a regional or national basis. The logical outcome would be a single bargain between the national union and a national employers' association for the industry. But in a country as large as the United States this is not always easy to arrange, and many employers object to it on principle or because they think they can drive a better bargain through independent action. Thus one finds a wide variety of arrangements, of which the commonest are:

1. *Industry-wide bargaining*, in which a union bargains with a national employers' association or with several regional associations. This is found in railroading, coal mining, hosiery, pottery, men's and women's clothing, merchant shipping, over-the-road trucking, and a number of other industries.

2. *Pattern bargaining*, in which the union singles out one or a few leading companies in the industry as its point of attack. The terms secured from these companies set the pattern for the year, and an effort is made to bring other companies into line under threat of strike. This comes close to industry-wide bargaining, but is not quite the same thing, since there is scope for different terms if a particular company can make a case for exceptional treatment. This approach is used in automobiles, where the union usually selects either Ford or General Motors as its prime target; in basic steel, where U.S. Steel has been the traditional point of attack; and in electrical equipment, where the union tries to set an initial pattern in either General Electric or Westinghouse.

3. *Company-by-company bargaining.* Here local union officials play a more prominent role, while in the first two cases national officials bear the brunt of negotiations. Even where local bargaining prevails, the national union tries to ensure some consistency in wage and other terms of employment. The national convention or the executive board may specify standard demands which each local is expected to put forward in a particular year. National field representatives usually sit in as advisers on local negotiations, and can object to serious deviations from national policy. In many unions, too, local agreements are not effective until they have been approved by national headquarters. The object is to bring an industry-wide perspective to bear on local negotiations, and to see that no employer gains a competitive advantage over his rivals.

The outcome of collective bargaining is a written agreement, often termed a *union contract*. But this kind of contract is not enforced by going to court. It is observed voluntarily because both sides find it to their interest to observe it. It is perhaps better termed a *collective agreement*—collective because it covers a number of workers and frequently a number of employers as well. The agreement usually runs for a year, though some unions negotiate two-year or three-year agreements. Some time before the agreement expires the two sides choose representatives, formulate demands, and begin negotiations over terms of the next agreement. If they are unable to settle their differences before the old agreement expires, a strike usually follows. But more than 99 percent of the agreements which expire each year are renewed successfully without a strike.

The signing of an agreement does not end all differences of opinion between union and management. The wording of the document is never perfectly clear. The union may contend that clause 12 of the agreement should be interpreted in a certain way, while management views it as meaning something quite different. There may also be disputes over facts. The agreement says that a worker may be fired for drinking on duty. A foreman fires John Jones for drinking, but Jones says the foreman is wrong and appeals the case. Should Jones stay fired or shouldn't he? If peace is to be maintained in the shop from day to day, there is need for judicial machinery to decide issues of fact and interpretation arising during the life of the agreement. Without this, the union would either have to accept all management decisions during the year or would have to strike frequently over small grievances.

This need is normally met by a *grievance procedure*, which is a standard feature of collective agreements. It provides that an aggrieved worker may take his case to his union representative, who will discuss the matter with the foreman. If the matter is not adjusted at this level, it is passed up to successively higher levels of union and management, perhaps culminating in discussions between a national union official and the company's vice-president in charge of industrial relations. If agreement cannot be reached even at the top, the case is usually referred to a neutral arbitrator from the outside, and both sides agree to accept his decision.

ECONOMIC ISSUES: WAGES

"Money isn't everything," an employer once remarked, "it's only 90 percent." Certainly money matters are the most visible, dramatic, and comprehensible issues in collective bargaining. It is on the wage front, too, that the impact of unionism is most readily appraised in terms of the economic concepts developed in Part One.

Collective bargaining affects the wage structure at several levels. It affects the relative wages paid by different companies in the same industry. It may change the entire wage level of one industry relative to other industries. It may even alter the wage level of the economy as a whole. These different kinds of influence need to be sorted out and explored.

Intercompany Differences within an Industry

We noted in Chapter 8 that the labor market is not very effective in equalizing the rates paid by different employers for the same type of labor. Under nonunion conditions it is not uncommon to find some companies in an industry paying 30 or 40 percent more than other companies. These differences may be partly fictitious, because the high-wage companies are probably getting more productive workers than the low-wage companies. But even if one could correct for labor quality, the remaining wage differences are wider than one would expect to find in a highly competitive market. They arise partly because companies differ in efficiency and wage-paying ability. Some have newer and more modern equipment, or a better location, or better management, or some other cost advantage. Another important consideration is that there are normally more people looking for work than there are jobs available. Full employment is an unusual situation in the labor market. Low-wage companies can thus continue to get labor by drawing on the pool of unemployed.

As an industry becomes unionized, the union will try to establish a uniform wage level for competing companies. In practice, this means leveling *up* intercompany differences rather than leveling down. Suppose that before unionization companies in the industry were paying common labor at rates varying from $1.00 to $1.60 per hour. The union may try in the first instance for a standard rate of $1.50 throughout the industry. But the union scale is not applied inflexibly. If a company can convince the union that paying the standard rate would put it out of business, it may be allowed to pay less. Unless a company is hopelessly inefficient, the union hesitates to push it over the cliff and throw people out of work. At the upper end of the scale, companies already paying above the standard rate will not be allowed to level down; but they may be allowed to mark time while the rest of the industry catches up with them. The union's strategy is gradually to herd companies in the direction of a common wage level, with full equalization as an ultimate ideal.

Efficient, high-wage companies will not be hurt by this policy. But the less efficient companies are put under pressure to raise their efficiency or perish. Some sources of inefficiency, such as obsolete equipment or poor location, may turn out to be irremovable. But if the main difficulty is poor administration, management may be able to offset the higher wage level by working harder. Union wage pressure can be a powerful stimulus to management effort and efficiency.

Unions argue that the principle of the standard rate is fair and natural. If a loomfixer is worth so much per hour to one textile mill, he should be worth the same amount to another. In a purely competitive labor market, workers of the same skill and efficiency would receive the same wage. The union is simply trying to offset the deficiencies of actual labor markets and to duplicate the results of pure competition. A further argument is that the standard rate "puts a floor under competition," and prevents any company from gaining an unfair competitive advantage by underpaying its workers.

These arguments are persuasive for companies in the same geographical area. Some question may be raised, however, about the wisdom of leveling up plants in different areas. Suppose a shirt factory in Chicago is competing with a shirt factory in a small Wisconsin town where living costs are 10 percent lower. It can be argued that the Wisconsin plant, instead of being forced to the Chicago level, should be allowed to pay 10 percent less, which would still give its workers the same living standard as the Chicago workers. One consideration is whether it is desirable, as a matter of social policy, to encourage decentralization of industry from metropolitan areas to smaller centers. Leaving a gap between small-town and big-city wage rates will encourage decentralization, while complete leveling will discourage it. A similar problem arises as regards the Southern states, which have traditionally had somewhat lower living costs and considerably lower wage rates than the Northern states. The wage gap has encouraged industrialization of the South, and closing this gap would probably retard the rate of industrialization. Which course is desirable is not just a question of equity to wage earners but also a question of national policy on industrial location.

Wage Differences among Industries

Those who fear union monopoly power often have in mind the possibility that unions may raise wages more energetically in some industries than in others. The demand for labor is a derived demand, which follows the principles noted in Chapter 5. Industry demand curves for labor differ in shape and inelasticity. So if unions behaved like monopolists in product markets, they would push wages up rapidly where demand is very inelastic and follow a more moderate policy where elasticity is greater. In consequence, some kinds of labor would be overpriced and others underpriced compared with what would happen in competitive markets.

How do unions actually behave in this respect? How do the leaders of a national union decide how much to demand in their industry year by year? They appear to be influenced by three main considerations: the expectations and attitudes of their members, the movement of wages in related industries, and the business outlook in their own industry.

Workers always regard a wage cut as a defeat, and union leaders are bound to fight against any wage reduction. If prices are rising, workers expect wages to rise at least proportionately. The movement of the consumer price index over the past year thus becomes a key factor in wage negotiations. Other elements in the workers' recent experience may also be significant. If the union has customarily delivered increases of 10 cents an hour in past years, workers will expect something like the same amount this year.

Some importance attaches to the movement of wages in neighboring industries. Leaders of the steelworkers watch the increases being won by the auto workers, the electrical workers, and other unions in heavy industry. The West Coast longshoremen watch the increases of East Coast longshoremen, and also the wages of warehousemen, truckers, and merchant seamen. Leaders of one union do not want to appear less aggressive and successful than those of other unions which might be considered comparable. On the community level, workers' wives gossip over the back fence about their husbands' earnings. When several plants in a city have given increases, word begins to spread that "everybody in town is getting 8 cents this year," and this exerts pressure on other companies and unions.

A third factor is the sales and profit outlook for the industry. If plants are operating at capacity, there is a large backlog of orders, prices are firm and profits high, the union will set more ambitious targets than if the opposite circumstances prevail. Unions keep well informed about the economic position of their industry through the work of their research departments, published business information, and unofficial "leaks" from company office staffs. But there is always some uncertainty in interpreting the economic outlook. Employers are naturally cautious about the future and try to hedge against the possibility that business may turn down during the coming year. The union has a vested interest in optimism, in predicting continued high profits which would justify a higher wage level. In addition to tactical maneuvering, there are often genuine differences of opinion about how much the industry can safely afford to pay, differences which may lead to a bargaining deadlock.

The first two factors, attention to living costs and to the movement of wages in other industries, make for a uniform upward movement of wages in all industries. The third factor, concentration on profits and ability to pay in a particular industry, makes for different rates of movement. Since the profitability of different industries varies considerably at any time, some unions will be in a position to raise wages faster than others. So it can be argued that a strong union which finds itself in a favorable economic environment will tend to push its wage level more and more out of line with wages in other industries.

Is this a real danger in practice, and how serious is it? Solid evidence is hard to come by. One approach is to compare the rate of wage increase in strongly unionized, weakly unionized, and nonunion industries over some period of time, say 1940 to 1960. The difficulty here is to disentangle the influence of unionism from that of other forces bearing on wage rates. Wherever a union exists it will claim full credit for any wage increase in its industry. But this claim cannot be taken at face value. Wages in the industry would have risen anyway because of rising wages in other parts of the economy and because of labor market competition. How much more they may have risen as a result of union pressure can never be determined precisely.

Another approach is to take the pattern of wage rates as of 1960 and try to pick out groups which seem overpaid for the kind of work they are doing. If one found a correspondence between overpaid workers and powerful trade unions, this would be significant. But who is to say what is a fair or normal return for a certain kind of labor? Suppose the locomotive engineer does earn three times as much as a shop laborer. Perhaps his work takes so long to learn, and requires so much skill and effort, that it is worth that much more. Perhaps the high hourly wage of the coal miner is justified by the danger and unpleasantness of his work. Without a precise yardstick for measuring the worth of a particular job, statements that one group is overpaid can never be more than informed judgments.[2]

Interindustry wage differences in the American economy do not look as wide as one might expect if each union behaved like a rational monopolist. This may be partly because some union leaders are "lazy monopolists," and settle for less than the maximum which they could extract. Union power is also countered by employer resistance. Employers do not want to see the wage and price level of their industry pushed high enough to cause a serious drop of sales. In some industries, too, a union which pushes wages too high may be undercut by the growth of non-union companies operating at lower wage levels. This is especially likely in atomistically competitive industries where entrance is easy and average plant size is small.

One can nevertheless detect groups which seem to be receiving more than a competitive return for their labor. Workers in the building trades, the printing trades, and the railroad running trades may be somewhat overpaid, even considering their superior skill. In the manufacturing sphere steelworkers, auto workers, and oil refinery workers seem high relative to textile, clothing, and food processing workers. There seems no reason why milk delivery men should receive as much as they do, and some other trucking groups may be out of line.

A union is in the best position to enforce out-of-line wage rates where: (1) the workers involved are in a strategic position and can stop production by walking out, as is true of truckers or building tradesmen;

---

[2] Such judgments can be made more precise, however, through a procedure known as *job evaluation*, under which jobs are rated on the basis of learning time, skill, pleasantness, responsibility, and so on, and these ratings are added to give a total point score for each job. Job evaluation is usually used only within a single plant. In Holland, however, an ambitious effort has been made to apply it throughout the economy so as to determine "proper" relative wage rates for all important jobs. This does not eliminate the possibility of argument, but it makes arguments more precise by shifting them to the issue of whether the scoring system used is complete and reasonable.

(2) the group does not cost too much to buy off, i.e., its wages form a small percentage of production costs; (3) product prices are controlled through monopoly or oligopoly arrangements, so that wage increases are readily passed on; (4) industry profits are high because of rapid technical progress or a rapid rate of increase in demand. In short, an inelastic and rapidly rising demand curve for labor is favorable to abnormally large wage increases.

The General Level of Wages

We saw in Chapter 8 that the general level of real wages rises over the long run at a rate governed mainly by increases in the physical productivity of labor.[3] If productivity is rising 3 percent a year, then money wages can rise at this rate without any increase in unit production costs or product prices. With constant prices, a 3 percent money wage increase means a 3 percent real wage increase as well.

Can strong unionism force the real wage level up faster than it would rise anyway on productivity grounds? The chances of doing this by squeezing business profits are not good, because employers have an escape hatch in the form of higher prices. Suppose that next year, while productivity is rising 3 percent, all unions in the country demand and secure wage increases of 6 percent. What will happen? Unit production costs are now higher than before. In industries where prices are subject to monopoly or oligopoly control, employers will probably raise prices promptly to offset the higher costs. Prices will rise also in competitive industries because of higher demand resulting from the larger amount of money in workers' hands. When things settle down one may well find prices up by 3 percent, money wages up 6 percent, and hence real wages up by only the 3 percent which they would have risen anyway. The main result is a higher price level rather than a gain in real wages.

A price increase of this sort is usually termed *cost inflation* or *sellers inflation*. There is little doubt that this sequence of events *can* occur. How far unionism actually has been responsible for rising prices in the United States is a hotly disputed issue, to which we shall return in Chapter 19.

In any event one can conclude that, if unionism is to affect the real wage level materially, it must do so by changing the *supply* of labor or the *productivity* of labor, which we saw in Chapter 8 to be the basic wage determinants. Unionism has certainly decreased labor supply over the past half century by establishing shorter hours of work and more holidays and vacations, by supporting strict restrictions on immigration from other countries, and by urging earlier retirement of workers from the labor

---

[3] Productivity is a slippery concept, with numerous possible interpretations. We use it here in the sense of net labor productivity, after deducting the cost of the other factors which cooperate with labor. Strictly speaking, it is *marginal net* productivity of labor which is pertinent for wage determination. The available statistics usually refer to average rather than marginal productivity. But while average and marginal productivity differ in absolute level at a particular time, their rate of increase over the course of time may not differ materially.

force. This reduction of supply must have raised the price of each man-hour of labor.

The effects on productivity run in both directions. One can argue that unions have increased productivity by putting pressure on employers for better production and personnel management. On the other side one can find cases in which unions have enforced the hiring of unnecessary workers or the use of obsolete and inefficient production methods. The net effect is uncertain and doubtless varies from one industry to another.

Public Policy toward Wage Bargaining

On the wage front, the record of unionism is a mixed one. Some of the effects appear good in the sense of contributing to a more rational and equitable wage structure. Other effects—overpricing of some types of labor, possible acceleration of inflationary tendencies, possible adverse effects on productivity—may be considered economically undesirable. There are substantial differences of opinion among economists as to whether the good effects outweigh the bad or vice versa.

Even if one concludes that the net effect is undesirable, it is hard to find a remedy which would not be worse than the disease. It is sometimes suggested that a union be forbidden to bargain with more than one employer. This seems to be the concrete meaning of proposals to "apply the antitrust laws to labor." It would weaken if not destroy national union organization, and shift the balance of power in collective bargaining in favor of the employer.

Such proposals imply an adverse judgment on unionism as a whole, including its noneconomic as well as its economic consequences. Most students of labor relations would not go this far. They are impressed with the positive contribution of unionism in protecting the worker's tenure of his job, improving working conditions in small ways as well as large, and processing day-to-day disagreements through the grievance procedure. They consider that unionism is on the whole a useful and desirable institution. But this opinion rests partly on personal experience and political preference, and cannot be supported scientifically against anyone holding the contrary opinion.

Another common proposal is that bargained wage rates be made subject to review and approval by a government board. This was done as part of the effort to control inflation and to prevent damaging strikes during World War II. Both bargained wage increases and voluntary increases by nonunion employers required approval by the National War Labor Board before becoming effective. The result was that genuine bargaining over wages and other issues almost ceased. After some preliminary sparring, one side or the other was usually happy to pass on a dispute to the Board in the hope of a favorable decision; and Board rulings came to have a decisive effect on terms of employment throughout the country.

Detailed government control of wages may be tolerable for short periods of war emergency, but over a longer period the effects would almost certainly be undesirable. In any event, both unions and employers are so strongly opposed to this approach that it is not a serious possibility.

Without going this far, government can and does exercise persuasion in key wage bargains. The Kennedy administration's successful effort in the fall of 1961 to persuade the United Steelworkers to accept a smaller increase than in preceding years is a case in point. The 1962 Report of the Council of Economic Advisers to the President attempted to set out general criteria for judging the reasonableness of wage increases. Such efforts may have both educational influence and practical effect over the long run. In any case, education and persuasion seem the most feasible course at this stage.

ECONOMIC ISSUES: HOURS OF WORK

One of the most striking trends in American industry is the great reduction in the work week over the past century. The early New England textile mills worked an incredible 72-hour week. Today the five or five and a half day week, with 35 to 40 hours of working time, is the general practice. In addition to this reduction of weekly hours, there has been a considerable reduction in *annual* hours of work through the spread of paid holidays and vacations. Long-service employees now generally receive from two to four weeks vacation, and most companies provide from six to ten paid holidays during the year.

Unions have taken the lead in pushing for reduction of working hours. The rise of productivity and real wages over the past century would doubtless have brought some reduction in any event. With rising hourly wages, a rational worker would use part of his larger income to "buy" more leisure. It is not easy, however, for the worker to make his preferences effective. He cannot bargain with the employer for an individual hours reduction as he can for an individual wage increase. Everyone in the plant must work the same schedule, and so reduction of hours requires an institutional decision. Employers have been slow to make such decisions and unions have had to nudge the employer again and again.

Until recently reduction of the work week probably added to national output. Experimental studies have shown that reducing hours from, say, 60 to 54 typically increases weekly output per worker. Reducing hours again from 54 to 48 will probably still bring output gains. The shorter week means that workers are more thoroughly rested, less subject to illness and accidents, able to work harder and to turn out more per hour. But as hours are shortened this effect tapers off. Eventually the increase in output per hour will no longer outweigh the reduction in hours, so that weekly output must fall. Just where this point is depends on the kind of work, and particularly on how much muscular effort and fatigue is involved. For most kinds of work it seems likely that a reduction of hours from 40 to 30 would mean a drop, though not a proportionate drop, in weekly output.

We have thus reached the point at which hours reduction is beginning to cost something in terms of output and real income. Unions in the future will be increasingly in the position where to cut hours will mean giving up some income which their members might have enjoyed. This does not mean that hours should not be cut, for workers may consider the increased leisure worth what it costs. But the choice needs to be put clearly before union members so that they can reach an informed decision.

Union leaders probably tend to overshoot the mark, and to press for shorter hours than the members would choose if they were in possession of all the facts. Straight thinking is beclouded particularly by the fallacious notion that shorter hours are a remedy for unemployment. Whenever there is serious unemployment in an industry or in the economy at large, unions argue that unemployment could be eliminated by reducing the work week. Suppose there are a million workers attached to the automobile industry. With current demand for cars and modern production methods, only 750,000 workers are needed while the remaining 250,000 are unemployed. Could this situation not be corrected by reducing the work week from 40 hours to 30? A million workers employed 30 hours a week would provide the same number of man-hours to the industry as 750,000 working 40 hours a week; and if we overlook the possibility that output per man-hour might change in the process, the whole million could now be hired.

But employment in the proper sense of man-hours worked has not been increased by this change. What has happened is that unemployment, instead of being concentrated on certain workers, has been spread evenly over the whole labor force. *Full-time* unemployment has disappeared, but this is paid for by the fact that everyone now gets less work and income than before. This sort of work-sharing may be appropriate to tide over a temporary slump. It is not an appropriate way of meeting a permanent decline in an industry's demand for labor. The only genuine remedy for the situation is to create enough job opportunities elsewhere in the economy so that the 250,000 surplus automobile workers can move out of that industry into others.

In the same way one can show that cutting hours is not an appropriate remedy for general depression. It does nothing to create additional employment, but simply spreads a low volume of employment more evenly over the available labor force. The proper approach is to raise total demand for labor.

ISSUES OF PERSONAL RIGHTS: THE UNION SHOP

In matters of labor relations economics carries one only so far. Some of the issues which get bargained about and which arouse strong feeling are not directly economic. Yet these issues are important and cannot be neglected in any discussion of collective bargaining. One of the oldest and hottest issues is how much pressure can legitimately be put on workers to join unions and stay in them.

A union is naturally concerned with protecting and strengthening its organization—against employer efforts to weaken or oust it, against raids on the membership by rival unions, even against the members' lethargy and reluctance to pay dues. Unions have accordingly developed a number of protective devices which they strive to get written into union contracts.

The strongest of these is the *closed shop*, under which the employer may hire only workers who are already union members. This is often accompanied by an arrangement under which employers notify the union office of vacancies and recruit new workers through the union. This type of provision was outlawed by the Taft-Hartley Act of 1947, on the ground that it interferes with the right of all workers to seek employment and unduly restricts the employer's freedom of choice. It continues on a "bootleg" basis, however, in printing, building construction, and certain other industries where unions and employers have been accustomed to it for generations.

The commonest type of union security provision is the *union shop*, which is found in about two thirds of all collective agreements. This does not limit the employer's freedom of hiring or the right of any worker to seek a job. But once a man has been hired, and if he survives the probationary period, he must join and remain in the union as a condition of continued employment. This means basically that he must pay dues, which in most unions run between 1 and 2 percent of workers' monthly earnings. Beyond this he is free to take as much or as little part as he chooses in union affairs. The union shop is usually accompanied by a *check-off* clause, under which union dues are deducted from the worker's paycheck along with social security and other deductions, and are turned over directly to the union by the employer.

The union shop is legal under federal law, but has been banned by state law in a number of Southern and Western states. The basic argument for the union shop is that, since the union bargains for all workers in the plant, all workers should contribute to its support. We do not allow residents of a town to decide whether or not to pay taxes in return for the educational, police, and other services which the town provides. Why should any worker be allowed to get a "free ride," receiving all the benefits of the union contract and the grievance machinery, but contributing nothing to the cost of these services? A supplementary argument is that a union whose security is guaranteed can afford to be more reasonable and constructive in collective bargaining. If people can drop out at will, the union must engage constantly in selling itself to the workers. The simplest way to do this is to denounce the employer and keep stirring up grievances against him. Only a secure union can admit that the employer is sometimes right and settle issues in ways which all members may not approve.

Against the union shop, it is often argued that it interferes with the right to work. The state anti-union shop laws are usually termed "right-to-work laws." This rests on a misunderstanding. Except for a few unions which exclude Negroes, women, or other categories of worker from membership, the union shop does not prevent anyone from getting a job or the employer from hiring anyone he chooses. (These discriminatory membership provisions are of course undesirable and should be eliminated.) The effect of a union shop is to bar *the right to work at a particular company without paying union dues*. The burden imposed on workers is mainly financial. A few workers may have conscientious objections to unionism and may feel compulsory membership as a violation of personal freedom; but these cases are rare. It is usually the worker's pocketbook which is hurting, not his conscience.

The central issue is whether workers gain enough from a strong union to warrant taxing all employees for its support. One's opinion on this is bound to depend on one's assessment of how much workers gain through collective bargaining. Those who feel that workers would do about as well for themselves without a union should logically oppose the union shop. Those who believe that workers benefit materially from unionism will be inclined to support it. There is thus no demonstrably right answer to the union shop debate even at an objective level, and certainly not in the hurly-burly of bargaining, where the divergent interests of union and management typically lead them to take opposite sides.

ISSUES OF PERSONAL RIGHTS:
DEMOCRATIC CONTROL OF THE UNION

One purpose of unionism is to protect the worker against being pushed around by the employer. But it is often asserted that workers in pursuing this objective have created a juggernaut which they are powerless to control, and that they now need protection against the union as well as the employer.

Most union constitutions are admirably democratic in form. The local union is usually governed by a membership meeting, in which all members have equal voice and vote. The national union is governed by a national convention, which usually meets every year or every two years, and to which the locals send elected delegates. National union officials are elected by the convention and are responsible to it.

Yet despite these procedural safeguards, power usually gravitates to a small minority. Few union members attend meetings consistently. A strike vote, a vote on acceptance of new contract terms, or some other crisis may draw a large turnout. But in between crises attendance at union meetings usually averages 10 percent or less of the membership. A few wheelhorses attend regularly, elect each other to office, and control union policy. Minority control is, of course, a general characteristic of private associations. In what political party, women's garden club, or university faculty does the majority actually shape the course of events?

At the national level, the same officers tend to be re-elected with monotonous regularity. Some national union presidents, such as Lewis of the Mine Workers and Tobin of the Teamsters, held the top office for 30 to 40 years. The reasons for this are complicated. In part, it reflects satisfaction with the job which the leader has done in the past, a feeling that experienced leadership is preferable to inexperience, and a desire to avoid factional conflict within the union. Further, there is no place for an ex-union leader to go, no other employment to which he can readily turn. Convention delegates have their share of human sympathy, and hesitate to turn the old horse out to grass. Union officers also work hard to keep themselves in office by the normal devices of machine politics. They use their power of appointment to union jobs to reward followers, punish critics, or sidetrack dangerous rivals. They stage-manage the national convention to keep themselves in the limelight and others out. Strong-arm tactics against opponents have not been unknown in the Mine Workers, Teamsters, and certain other unions.

Is all this democratic? This depends on what one means by democracy. If one means, "Do the members determine union policy?" the answer is largely "No." Union policy is shaped by the national leaders and to some extent by local leaders, though the members' attitudes and expectations are always a factor in policy decisions. But if one asks, "Are unions operated in the interest of their members?" the answer is predominantly "Yes." Union leaders prefer to do a good job for their members rather than a poor job, and this makes sense in political terms. It keeps the leader popular and smooths his path to re-election and continued control.

Still another question is, "Can the members get rid of leaders who act contrary to their interests?" The answer to this is "No and yes." It is not easy to launch a frontal attack on an entrenched machine, and efforts to do so frequently fail. But if the leaders of a national union do act contrary to the interests of the members, several things may happen to them. The AFL-CIO may move onto the scene, as it did in expelling the Teamsters' and Longshoremen's unions for misbehavior, and this weakens the leadership though it does not necessarily remove it. There may be an internal revolt in the union, spearheaded by rival office-seekers. Another possibility is that local unions may secede and join a different national organization, or even form a new one. Finally, a union which is sufficiently mismanaged may simply dwindle and die. Over the long run, then, the power of national union leaders is less arbitrary than it may seem at first glance.

One does find cases in which union officers have abused their power for personal enrichment. This occurs especially in small-scale, competitive industries such as building construction, local trucking, cleaning and dyeing, the fur and garment industries, and longshoring. And it centers mainly in the larger cities, notably New York and Chicago. In some cases professional criminals move into control of local unions, oust the regular officers, and maintain their control by force of arms. In other cases legitimate union officers have discovered ways of collecting personal tribute from employers or the union treasury. Union racketeering is usually carried on with the support of local political organizations and the local police force, and employers in the industry often go along willingly in order to buy labor peace.

In an effort to check such malpractices, legal controls have been imposed on internal union affairs. The Landrum-Griffin Act of 1959, passed after heated Congressional debate, provided among other things that unions shall file an annual financial report and other specified information with the Secretary of Labor; that officers of a labor organization shall not receive money or other benefits, directly or indirectly, from employers with whom they are dealing; that they shall not embezzle union funds, under penalty of fine or imprisonment; that they shall not borrow money from the union in excess of $2,000; that no one who has been a member of the Communist Party or who has been convicted of a felony may serve as a union officer; that local union officers must be elected at least every three years and national officers at least every five years; that election of local officers and of delegates to national conventions must be by secret ballot; that the Secretary of Labor may set aside any election in which these provisions have not been observed and order a new election; and that no union member may be fined, expelled, or otherwise disciplined without a full and fair trial.

Union leaders accept some of these provisions as reasonable, but oppose others. Many employers and conservative legislators feel that the present law does not go far enough. The struggle is certain to be renewed in future sessions of Congress and the trend appears to be toward increasingly detailed government regulation of union affairs.

STRIKES AND STRIKE PREVENTION

An incidental discomfort of collective bargaining is the occasional shutting down of production through strikes. This leads one to wonder whether strikes could not be prevented by developing government machinery for peaceable settlement of labor disputes.

The loss of production through strikes should not be exaggerated. With rare exceptions such as 1946, time lost per year through strikes averages less than 1 percent of the man-days worked in unionized industries, or considerably less than the time lost through illness, accidents, and absenteeism. Nor is this 1 percent necessarily a net loss. In an industry where all plants are operating at full capacity, a strike will reduce total output. But this is an unusual situation. More commonly there is some slack in the industry, and business lost by one company through a strike may go to a competing company. If the UAW strikes General Motors,

Ford will sell more cars and its workers will earn more money. Many industries also have seasonal ups and downs. If the United Mine Workers goes on strike for two or three months of the year, it can make up the loss by putting in more time in the remaining nine months.

Still there is often some loss of production. Is there any way by which such losses might be avoided? One could provide that, where a company and union cannot agree on the terms of a new contract, production shall continue while the issues in dispute are decided by a government board. But a little thought reveals that this solution has disadvantages. It is mainly the threat of a strike which causes the parties to compromise their divergent demands and reach an agreement. If a strike occurs, the mounting losses to both sides continue to exert pressure for agreement, and when the losses become heavy enough the strike will be settled. Viewed from this standpoint, a strike is *one route toward eventual agreement*.

If both sides knew in advance that a strike was impossible, the pressure to compromise and reach agreement would be much reduced. Each side would tend to make extreme demands, stand pat on them, pass responsibility for decision to the government board, and hope for a better result than it could have attained by direct action. This tendency became quite strong during World War II under the National War Labor Board. Genuine private bargaining declined in importance, and Board decisions came to dominate the provisions of union contracts.

Prohibiting strikes, then, would tend to eliminate private collective bargaining and to substitute government regulation of wages and working conditions. This would be a drastic change in our system of industrial relations. Almost all union and management officials, and most students of labor matters, would be opposed to such a change.

Disputes in Essential Industries

While some strikes do little harm, there are certain industries in which continuous operation is essential. A railroad strike has a disruptive effect on the national economy. So does a long strike in basic steel. Strikes in local transportation, police or fire protection, electric light and power, deliveries of food and fuel, or provision of hospital services can endanger public health and safety.

A number of devices, none of them wholly satisfactory, have been developed to deal with disputes in essential industries:

1. A *compulsory waiting period*. The President, Governor, or other appropriate official may require the parties to a dispute to maintain the status quo for a specified period of time. This is often termed a cooling-off period. But it may equally well be a heating-up period! It does not settle the dispute, and a strike at the end of the period is both legal and likely.

2. A *board of inquiry*. A waiting period is of little use unless some-

thing positive is done during the period. So it is sometimes provided that the President or Governor may convoke a board of neutral persons, with authority to investigate the disputed issues and make recommendations concerning them. The board typically has no authority to compel either party to accept its recommendations. This leaves a probability that one or both sides will reject the suggested terms and a strike will result.

3. *Plant seizure.* This was frequently used by the federal government during World War II to ensure compliance with decisions of the National War Labor Board. But the constitutionality of government seizure in peacetime is doubtful. Apart from this, the procedure raises practical problems. Who is responsible for managing a company which has been taken over by the government—the existing management, or a new and perhaps inexperienced government official? Who is entitled to profits earned during the period of government operation? Can the government operators sign a contract with the union, and is this binding after the company is turned back to private management? At most, seizure is a stalling device which allows time for negotiations looking toward a genuine settlement.

4. *The choice of procedures approach.* The most original state law in this field is a Massachusetts law worked out by a committee headed by the late Professor Sumner Slichter. It permits the Governor to choose in each case among a variety of alternatives, ranging from informal mediation to plant seizure, or to use several of these devices in succession. The underlying philosophy is that in the end the parties will have to work out terms which they are willing to accept and live with. Until they do this, the dispute remains essentially unsettled. The best way to put pressure on them to settle is to keep them guessing about what the Governor may do if they fail to agree. The law has already been applied in a number of cases and seems to have yielded satisfactory results.

5. *The special status approach.* This approach, also suggested by Professor Slichter, has not been adopted anywhere but remains an interesting possibility. It involves abolition of the right to strike in a specified list of essential industries, backed by severe penalties against any union calling a strike. This would reduce the economic power of unions in these industries, and by itself would constitute government intervention on the side of management. As an offset, therefore, Slichter suggested that workers in these industries be given special guarantees similar to those applying to civil service employees. It might be provided, for example, that their wages would rise at least as rapidly as the average of all other wages in the economy. They might also be guaranteed seniority protection, pension rights, and other benefits.

None of these procedures is fully satisfactory, and handling of emergency disputes will doubtless continue to be one of the most difficult areas in industrial relations.

SUMMARY

1. Trade unionism has decreased wage differences among rival companies in the same industry; perhaps led to wider differences between industries; raised the real wage level, mainly by reducing labor supply; and perhaps contributed to chronic upward pressure on the price level.

2. While one may deplore certain aspects of wage behavior under collective bargaining, there is no clearly preferable alternative. Neither proposals to break up national unionism nor proposals for government wage regulation command much public (or expert) support.

3. Trade unionism has played an important role in the great reduction of working hours over the past century. This reduction was desirable even on output grounds. But we have now reached a stage at which further reduction of hours means lower output and incomes, and so the desirability of further reductions should be weighed carefully. In particular, one must reject the notion that cutting hours is an appropriate remedy for unemployment, either in a single industry or in the whole economy.

4. The union shop issue does not involve the right to work, but rather the question whether all employees should be obliged to pay dues to a union which has a majority in the plant. This is essentially a power struggle between union and management organizations, with no objectively correct answer.

5. Trade unions, like other private associations, are typically governed by a minority; but there is effective pressure on this minority to govern in the interest of the general membership. In some industries, however, union leaders have abused their power for personal gain; and this has led to increasingly detailed government control of internal union affairs.

6. Loss of output through strikes is not a serious problem in most industries; but it is serious where continuous operation is important to public health, safety, or convenience. Procedures which have been applied or discussed for such industries include a compulsory waiting period, a board of inquiry, plant seizure and operation by government, the choice of procedures approach, and the special status approach. None of these is as yet fully adequate to cope with the problem.

Income Inequality and Public Policy

Some people's money is merited,/And other people's is inherited,
But wherever it comes from,/They talk about it as if it were something you
    got pink gums from.
This may well be,/But if so, why do they not relieve themselves of the
    burden by transferring it to the deserving poor or to me?
. . . .
The only incurable troubles of the rich are the troubles that money can't cure,
Which is a kind of trouble that is even more troublesome if you are poor.
Certainly there are a lot of things in life that money won't buy, but it's very
    funny—
Have you ever tried to buy them without money?

OGDEN NASH

Distribution should undo excess/And each man have enough.
WILLIAM SHAKESPEARE, *King Lear*

A STANDARD CRITICISM of capitalist economies is that, while the average
level of income may be high, this income is unequally distributed. There
are extremes of wealth and poverty. So we must look further into who
gets how much in the United States, whether income distribution has been
growing more equal or less equal over the course of time, what government has been doing about it, and what we may need to do in the future.

HOUSEHOLD INCOMES IN THE UNITED STATES
The bare facts of income distribution were set out in Chapter 2. But
now we must try to explain why the distribution looks as it does.

300

There are close to 50 million families in the United States, plus more than 10 million individuals living by themselves. The median income of unattached individuals is surprisingly low—only about $2,700 in 1960. The reason is that these are mainly young people who have not yet developed substantial earning power, or handicapped people unable to hold a regular job, or older people dependent on modest pensions. Older people, in particular, have serious income problems. For most purposes, however, it is best to concentrate on the family units which include 95 percent of the population.

The distribution of family incomes in the United States in 1960 is shown in Table 14–1.[1] The median income for all families in this year

TABLE 14–1

Distribution of Families by Annual Income, 1960*

Annual Income (Before Income Taxes)	Number of Families (000)	Percent of Families	Aggregate Income Received	
			Millions	Percent
Under $2,000	3,287	7.2	3,987	1.1
2,000– 2,999	3,006	6.6	7,583	2.2
3,000– 3,999	4,155	9.2	14,645	4.2
4,000– 4,999	5,095	11.2	22,973	6.6
5,000– 5,999	5,320	11.7	29,253	8.4
6,000– 7,499	7,499	16.6	50,448	14.4
7,500– 9,999	7,973	17.6	68,522	19.6
10,000–14,999	5,690	12.5	67,931	19.5
15,000 and over	3,345	7.4	83,824	24.0
Total	45,370	100.0	349,166	100.0

* Source: Survey of Current Business, April, 1962.

was a bit under $6,500, that is, half the families in the country had less than this while the other half had more. The figures in Table 14–1 refer to income *before* federal income taxes, and would be substantially lower after taxes. At the bottom of the scale, about one seventh of all families were living on incomes of less than $3,000 per year. At the upper end, one fifth of all families had incomes above $10,000. This top group received 43.5 percent of all money income.

Is the present distribution of income fair or unfair, desirable or undesirable? How might it be changed if we wanted to change it? Before tackling these questions we must ask why the present distribution looks as it does. The following factors seem particularly important:

Occupational wage differences. We saw in Chapter 8 that the labor market establishes widely differing wage rates for different occupations, from floor sweepers and farm laborers at the bottom to surgeons and corporation presidents at the top.

---

[1] This table, and other figures cited in this section, come from sample surveys conducted by the U.S. Bureau of the Census.

Availability of employment. There is wide variation of incomes *within* each occupational group. One important reason is variation in the amount of work done during the year. A skilled man worth $3.00 an hour, if he works a 2,000-hour year, will come out at the end of the year with $6,000. But suppose that, for health or other reasons, he prefers to work only part time. Or suppose there is a recession and he is laid off for part of the year. In this event he may work only 1,000 hours and will show up in the income table at the $3,000 level.

This produces shifts in income distribution over the business cycle. During a depression many people are laid off or forced into part-time work, and drop into the lower income brackets. Inequality of incomes increases. During prosperity these people are re-employed, their annual incomes rise, and inequality is reduced.

Number of wage earners per family. No longer can we assume that family income comes entirely from the man of the house. Almost half of the women in the United States between 20 and 65 are in the labor force. The proportion of working wives is rising rapidly. Grown sons and daughters often remain at home until marriage and contribute to family income. The 1956 survey showed that 45 percent of all households had more than one income earner. The ratio was only 19 percent for families with incomes below $1,000, but 69 percent for families in the $10,000–$15,000 range. Thus an important reason why some families have higher incomes than others is that more people are contributing to the income.

Distribution of property ownership. About 20 percent of personal income in the United States comes from interest, dividends, and other returns to property ownership; and distribution of property is highly unequal. Most income-yielding property is held by a small minority of the population. The top 5 percent of income recipients in the United States receive more than two thirds of the dividend payments and about half of all property income. The concentration of property incomes is much greater than that of incomes from work. The top 5 percent of income recipients get only about 10 percent of total wage and salary payments.

The upper income groups do not consist mainly of idle coupon clippers. It is unfashionable in America to live without working. In 1956, only 2 percent of families with incomes above $15,000 were living solely on property income. About two thirds of these household heads held salaried jobs, while almost all the remainder were self-employed. The high-income family usually combines property income with substantial income from work. The property element, however, makes the overall income distribution more unequal than it would be otherwise.

Lack or loss of productive ability. While property income helps to explain the upper reaches of the income distribution, this factor provides the main explanation of the lower end of the distribution. In 1960 there were still three million families and more than four million unattached individuals with incomes below $2,000 per year. How can this be? Low wages can be ruled out at once, since few people today earn less than $1.00 an hour. The largest group consists of households with no member in the labor force. Many of these people may have worked at one time, but have been disabled by accident or disease. Many are older people who can no longer hold a steady job. There are many broken homes, in which the wife cannot look after the children and hold a job, and has to get along on public or private charity.

The other main element in the lowest-income group are the marginal farmers, whose situation was explained in Chapter 12. They are handicapped by small acreage, poor soil, adverse weather conditions, or disability of the farm operator. But since they can usually provide their own food and shelter, they have some advantage over relief clients in the city.

The basic factor in the lowest incomes, then, is inability to hold a job or to perform effectively on the job. This is worth stressing because it cannot be corrected simply by higher wages. The normal increase in the national wage level year by year leaves the hard core of poverty largely untouched.

Supplementary income payments. People who cannot earn income may still receive income payments outside the production process. These are usually called *transfer payments.* They include private pension payments, public pensions under the social security system, government payments to farmers, unemployment compensation, aid to special groups such as the blind and dependent children in broken homes, and general public relief. Such payments raise many of the poorest families above where they otherwise would be, and thus reduce the inequality of incomes.

RECENT TRENDS IN INCOME DISTRIBUTION

So much for the present. What of the past and the future? What has been happening to income distribution over the past several decades, and what may we reasonably expect in the decades ahead?

In order to talk about trends in income distribution, we need a more precise measure of this concept. One common measure is illustrated in Figure 14–1. On the horizontal axis we measure percentages of household units, while the vertical axis shows percentages of total personal income. If income distribution were perfectly equal, then the first 20 percent of households would receive 20 percent of total income, the first 40 percent of households would receive 40 percent of income, and so on. Income distribution would be represented by points along the straight line OY.

We may imagine also the opposite extreme of perfect inequality.

Suppose one household received all income in the economy, while the other 99.999 percent received nothing at all. Income distribution would then follow the path *OXY*.

Any actual income distribution will fall between these extremes. Suppose a particular country in a particular year has the distribution shown by the dotted line in Figure 14–1. This is called a Lorenz curve, after its originator. The curve shown represents a moderately unequal distribution. The lowest 40 percent of families receive only 20 percent of total income, while the top 10 percent receive 25 percent of income. If we call the area above the dotted line *A*, and the area below the line *B*, we can get a numerical measure of inequality by calculating $A/A + B$. This

FIGURE 14–1

The Lorenz Measure of Income Distribution

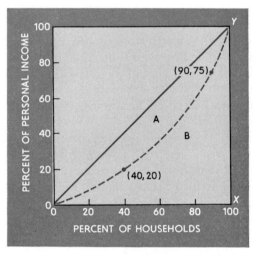

Each point on the dotted line shows the percentage of income received by a certain percentage of household units. The shallower the line, the more equal the distribution of income. A numerical measure of income inequality can be obtained by calculating $A/A + B$.

is sometimes termed the *Gini coefficient*. It can have any value between 0 (complete equality) and 1 (complete inequality).

A movement toward greater income equality is shown by a shallower Lorenz curve and a drop in the Gini coefficient. A move toward inequality means a bending outward of the Lorenz curve and a rise in the Gini coefficient.

The course of events in the United States since the midthirties is shown in Table 14–2 and Figure 14–2. The years 1935, 1950, and 1960 have been selected for comparison. Table 14–2 shows the mean income of the lowest 20 percent of families, the next 20 percent, and so on in each year, adjusted to dollars of comparable purchasing power. It shows also the percentage of all personal income received by the lowest 20 percent, the next 20 percent, and so on. The corresponding Lorenz curves for 1935 and 1960 are charted in Figure 14–2.

There has clearly been a shift toward greater income equality. The shift occurred mainly between 1935 and 1950—actually, between

1935 and 1945. From 1945 to the present there has been little change in the pattern of distribution.

To understand the reduction of inequality between 1935 and 1945 we must look back to the six basic factors already described. We shall find

TABLE 14–2

Distribution of Family Personal Income, before Federal Income Taxes 1935–36, 1950, 1960*

	INCOME BEFORE TAXES					
QUINTILES (20 Percent Groups)	Mean Annual Income (1960 Dollars)			Share of All Personal Income (Percent)		
	1935–36	1950	1960	1935–36	1950	1960
Lowest	827	1,299	1,576	4.2	4.8	4.6
Second	1,840	2,976	3,758	9.3	10.9	11.0
Third	2,803	4,405	5,581	14.2	16.1	16.3
Fourth	4,206	6,045	7,721	20.8	22.1	22.6
Highest	10,161	12,622	15,585	51.5	46.1	45.5
Total	3,951	5,469	6,845	100.0	100.0	100.0

* Sources:
  1935–36: L. G. Reynolds, *Labor Economics and Labor Relations*, p. 535.
  1950: *U.S. Income and Output*, 1958, p. 161.
  1960: *Survey of Current Business*, April, 1962, p. 14.
  Figures are adjusted to 1960 dollars using Consumer Price Index (1947–49 = 100) revalued to 1960 = 100.

that they were all working in an equalizing direction over this period.

There was a marked reduction in occupational wage differentials from 1935 to 1945. Wages of manual workers rose relative to white collar

FIGURE 14–2

Distribution of Household Income before Federal Income Tax, United States, 1935–36 and 1960

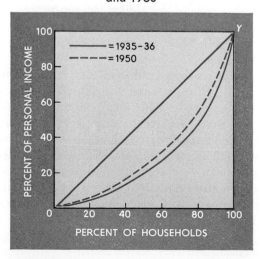

salaries, and laborers' wages rose relative to those of skilled workers. The reasons for this were explained in Chapter 8.

Employment opportunities were much more plentiful during the forties than during the thirties. The many low incomes in 1935 reflected partly the heavy unemployment at that time. After 1940 these people were reabsorbed into employment, with a consequent increase in their annual incomes.

Another particularly depressed group during the 1930's was the farm population. During and after World War II the high demand for food raised farm prices and brought a relative improvement of the farmer's position. This narrowed the income distribution for the nation as a whole.

Property income has been a declining proportion of total personal income. Business profit rates have not fallen appreciably. But the proportion of profits *paid out as dividends* has dropped, mainly because of increases in the corporate income tax. Rent, interest, and dividends, which formed 22 percent of personal income in 1929, had fallen to 13 percent by 1961. Since these types of income are received mainly by the wealthier groups, the result has been to pull their incomes down closer to the national average.

In addition to the reduced importance of property income, there are indications that property income became more equally distributed between the 1920's and the 1940's. Kuznets has calculated that during the 1920's the top 5 percent of income recipients got more than 80 percent of dividend payments and more than 55 percent of all property income. By the late forties, however, they were getting only 70 percent of the dividends and about 40 percent of all property income.[2] Income-yielding property is more widely dispersed among the population than it was a generation ago.

Finally, the New Deal era brought a marked increase in transfer payments to low-income groups, including old age pensions and assistance, unemployment compensation, veterans benefits, aid to dependent children, and general relief. These payments helped to raise the bottom of the income distribution.

Since the late forties these tendencies have slowed down and in some cases been reversed. There has been little further shrinkage of occupational wage differences, and in some industries differentials have widened. Rising interest rates have checked the drop in the relative importance of property income. Studies by Professor Lampman for the National Bureau of Economic Research suggest that the distribution of property ownership has become less equal in recent years. Increases in pension rates, unemployment compensation rates, and other transfer payments have done little more than keep pace with price inflation. On balance, the distribu-

---

[2] Simon Kuznets, *Share of Upper-Income Groups in Income and Savings* (New York: National Bureau of Economic Research, 1953).

tion of household incomes shows no marked trend toward either greater or less inequality; and barring war or other catastrophes, this stability seems likely to continue for the foreseeable future.

INCOME REDISTRIBUTION: THE MARKET APPROACH

The present distribution of income is not necessarily ideal. And there are things which can be done about it. We can and do alter income distribution through the tax structure, through transfer payments, and in other ways. What government should do in this respect is a classic political issue.

We must distinguish first between measures which affect income distribution *through* the market mechanism and measures which operate *outside* the market. On the former there is little disagreement in principle, while the second is more controversial.

We noted in earlier chapters that one source of inequality is limited access to the higher occupations. Doctors, lawyers, engineers, and business executives have substantial incomes because there are too few of them, relative to the market demand. Earnings of laborers and farmers are depressed because there are too many of them. There are barriers to movement up the occupational ladder.

This suggests that important gains can be made by enabling people to shift from low-productivity occupations to others where their productivity and earnings would be higher. If a factory laborer worth $4,000 a year can be converted into a doctor worth $15,000 a year, this is a step forward both for him and for the community. The man has more interesting work and larger income, and he is contributing more to national output.

It is hard for people of mature age to make large occupational shifts. Most of the shifting has to be accomplished by enabling young people to enter the managerial and professional occupations. The main obstacle is the cost of higher education for these occupations. The average cost of a B.A. degree in the United States is now close to $10,000. An M.D. may represent a cash outlay of $25,000 or more. (Moreover, the income which a person gives up by going to college for several years when he might have been working must be counted as a cost of his training.) Many families in the United States cannot consider an investment of this size. Despite the tradition of "working your way through college," many able young people are barred from higher education on financial grounds. This is injustice to the individual and economic waste to the community.

There are at least two ways of breaking this financial bottleneck: through *loans*, and through *scholarships*. One can argue that, since the individual benefits from professional training through higher income, he should be required to pay the training costs. This would mean setting up a loan fund from which students could borrow up to some maximum amount, with repayment spread over a period of years after graduation.

The student himself would have to estimate whether the prospective gain in income from added training would be sufficient to repay the loan and leave some margin of advantage.[3] College vocational advisers could give the student information on prospective earnings in various occupations, and also give tests which would help him to gauge his own abilities. Since ability is not subject to precise measurement, and since earnings in the higher occupations vary widely with ability, each student would still be gambling somewhat. But it would be *his* gamble. Lack of initial capital would be removed as a barrier to free choice. The question of how many people should be educated for each occupation, and who they should be, would be left to individual decision.

Many colleges and universities have modest loan funds, and the record of repayments has been good. A fund of adequate size, however, might have to be underwritten by government. It seems odd that we have large federal agencies to make loans to farmers, home owners, small businessmen, veterans, and even foreign governments. Yet we have no credit agency to back capable young people who want to invest in higher education. There is an opportunity for social engineering in constructing such an Educational Finance Authority.

A second possibility is scholarship grants from public funds. This is common practice in many countries. In Britain the great majority of university students hold government scholarships. The number of students, however, is much smaller relative to population than in the United States. In Russia students admitted to universities and training institutes automatically receive a living allowance as well as free tuition. The allowance is meagre and parents still have to contribute something if the student is to live well, but the bulk of the cost is borne by the state.

We have gone some distance in this direction in the United States. Private colleges often have substantial scholarship funds. State colleges and universities provide free or low-cost tuition. We have had one experience with federal grants covering both living costs and tuition—the "GI program" for veterans of World War II and the Korean War. This seems to have operated well from the standpoint of both the students and the universities. More recently, federal money has been allocated for graduate fellowships in engineering, science, and mathematics under the National Defense Education Act of 1958. Science and engineering were selected on the politically appealing ground that "the Russians are doing it" and that these occupations have special significance for national de-

---

[3] This is essentially the calculation which a business manager must make in deciding whether to buy an item of capital equipment (Chapter 9). The student should count as a cost not only his educational expenses but the income which he might have earned by going to work after high school instead of entering college. These costs would be accumulated forward to graduation day at an appropriate rate of interest. On the income side, one would have to estimate future income over the student's lifetime *in excess* of what he could have earned without the advanced training; and this gain in income would be discounted back to graduation. An excess of gain over cost would indicate that the training is worthwhile.

fense. But one could make a case for putting other types of professional training on a scholarship basis.

The economic difference between the loan and scholarship systems is illustrated in Figure 14–3. *DD* and *SS* are the demand and supply curves

FIGURE 14–3

Economics of Loans and Scholarships

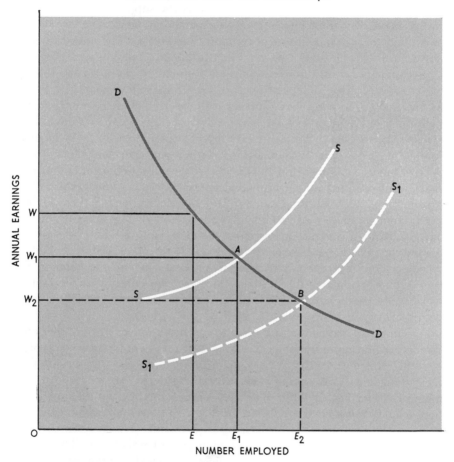

SS and DD are supply and demand curves for medical service. We suppose that the number of doctors is limited to OE by restricted access to training. With a loan system, SS becomes operative, the number in the profession rises to OE_1 and incomes fall to OW_1. With a scholarship system, supply increases to S_1S_1, numbers increase to OE_2 and incomes fall to OW_2.

for, say, medical service. We suppose, however, that the supply of doctors is restricted artifically to *OE* because only this number can finance the cost of medical training from their own resources. Employment in the profession is thus limited to *OE* and doctors' incomes settle at *OW*.

Suppose we set up a loan system which allows anyone to enter medical school if he believes that future income will cover the cost of the loan. The true supply curve *SS* now becomes operative and *A* emerges as the equilibrium position. The number of doctors increases to OE_1 and their annual incomes fall to OW_1. This is a loss to the doctors who were previously earning OW. But it benefits the new doctors who are now able to get into the profession; and it enables the public to buy more medical service at a competitive price.

Suppose we go farther and give each medical student a scholarship which covers all costs of his training. This operates like a reduction in production costs of a commodity, and shifts the supply curve of doctors rightward to S_1S_1. For a given level of expected income, more people will be willing to undertake medical training than before. The long-run equilibrium is now at B, with OE_2 doctors earning an annual income of OW_2.

Compared with the previous equilibrium at A, there are the following effects: (1) Doctors trained before the scholarship system went in lose by the change, for they have already paid the cost of their education but will now receive incomes lower than they had expected. (This could conceivably be met by a lump-sum payment to these doctors.) (2) Doctors trained after the new system begins neither gain nor lose. Their prospective income is lower, but this is offset by the reduction in educational costs. (3) Consumers of medical services benefit from a lower price. OW_2 is in fact a subsidized price, since it does not cover the full cost (including training expenses) of providing the service. (4) This subsidy, the annual scholarship budget, comes from the taxpaying public. If the people paying the taxes are a different group from those who receive the medical services, there is an income transfer from the former to the latter. If the two groups coincide, there is no transfer; but consumers of medical services are then paying a hidden tax cost in addition to the visible price which they pay in the market.

The scholarship system is open to objection on the ground that consumers are getting more medical service than they would choose at a price covering full cost, and that they are paying more for this service than they think they are paying. On the other side, it can be argued that medical service has neighborhood effects extending beyond the individual, that people *should* get more of it than they would pay for voluntarily, and that interference with market pricing is justifiable. This is essentially the argument for free elementary and high school education. The public would certainly take less of these services if given the option of paying a full-cost price or going without. How far this line of reasoning should be extended to health and other services is a problem of political choice for the community.

This case has been developed at length because education probably offers widest scope for altering income distribution through the market mechanism. But there are other possibilities as well. Government can help marginal farmers to transfer to other occupations. To the extent that this reduces excess agricultural capacity and enables the remaining farmers to earn equilibrium incomes, the effects are favorable. Government can also help to accelerate movement from depressed areas to expanding regions of the country. Such programs have favorable income effects while involving minimum interference with market allocation and voluntary choice.

INCOME REDISTRIBUTION OUTSIDE THE MARKET: GENERAL CONSIDERATIONS

Government can also alter income distribution by superseding the market. Public services which benefit everyone may be financed by taxes which weigh most heavily on the well-to-do. Government can make cash payments to certain groups in the population out of tax revenues. Such transfers are typically in an equalizing direction, from higher brackets to lower brackets.

FIGURE 14–4

A Simple Argument for Income Equalization

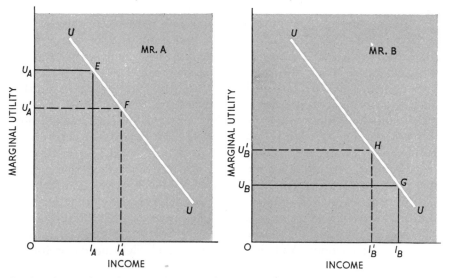

Mr. A and Mr. B have the same capacity to derive satisfaction from income, shown by *UU*. But B's income of OI_B is much larger than A's income of OI_A. Hence the marginal utility of income to B (OU_B) is much smaller than to A (OU_A). Transferring income to A will add to his satisfaction more than it reduces B's satisfaction, so total satisfaction will be increased.

How far government should go in equalizing incomes is a classic political issue. At one time economists believed that they could give a scientific answer to this question. The answer was that a transfer of income from richer to poorer people would increase total satisfaction. The reasoning can be explained with the aid of Figure 14–4. Consider a simple community consisting of two men, Mr. A and Mr. B. We suppose that their capacity for deriving satisfaction from income is identical, and that for each man the satisfaction derived from an additional dollar of income decreases continuously as his income rises. Money is used to buy goods, and consuming additional goods yields decreasing marginal utility as explained in Chapter 5.

These assumptions are sketched in Figure 14–4. Mr. A and Mr. B have identical marginal utility curves, UU, which fall steadily from left to right. But they have different incomes. B is a well-to-do fellow with an income of OI_B, while A's income of OI_A is only about one quarter as large. So the marginal utility of income to B (OU_B) is much less than to A (OU_A). It thus seems that the *combined* satisfaction of the two men could be increased by shifting some income from B to A. Suppose we levy a tax on B which reduces his income to OI'_B, and give this money to A, raising his income to OI'_A. The satisfaction lost by B as we move up his utility curve from G to H is clearly less than that gained by A in moving from E to F. Thus total satisfaction has been increased. Indeed, since OU'_A is still greater than U'_B, it would pay to transfer some more income from B to A, and to continue this process until the incomes of the two men are equal.

People who advocate greater equality have this reasoning in the back of their minds. They feel that an extra dollar means a lot to the poor, while to the rich man it means very little. But the argument has been undermined by economic theorists, who point out that its assumptions are dubious and cannot be verified by observation. How do we know that marginal utility curves slope steadily downward? Perhaps appetite grows with eating, and utility curves may slope upward for a while. And how do we know that different people have the same capacity to derive satisfaction from income? Perhaps the well-to-do man, whose income has allowed him to cultivate expensive tastes, has a much higher utility curve than the poor man. Perhaps he derives just as much satisfaction from his last dollar as the poor man does from his. This aristocratic line of argument may seem unconvincing, but can one prove that it is wrong? There is no way to get inside the skins of Mr. A and Mr. B, or to compare their subjective satisfactions. And this weakens the classical argument for income equality.

But even if one concludes that utility is unmeasurable, there are other arguments favoring greater equality of income:

1. Inequality reduces satisfaction because of the necessity of "keeping up with the Joneses." Whatever my income may be, there is always someone around with twice as much, and I feel under pressure to emulate his standards. (There is also someone around with only half as much as I have, but the satisfaction I get from looking down on this fellow is less than the discontent I feel from looking at the man above me.) Without changing my income, my satisfaction could be increased by reducing the gap between me and those higher up. Since everyone except the top man in the income distribution presumably feels this way, general satisfaction could be increased by a reduction of inequality.

2. In a democracy where people are legally and politically equal, how can one justify large differences in income and consumption levels? Doesn't inequality undermine democracy by giving the wealthy a disproportionate influence in political affairs? One need not believe that there is a direct telephone line from Wall Street to the White House to sense some incompatibility between inequality of incomes and our professions of equality in other spheres.

3. The case for greater equality can be argued also on religious and ethical grounds. If people will not voluntarily follow the Biblical injunction to "sell what thou hast and give to the poor," perhaps their consciences should be aided by the tax collector.

4. Property income is sometimes regarded as particularly open to ethical criticism. "Unearned income" from property is considered inferior to wage and salary income. Since property income goes mainly to the higher brackets, one can argue that it is right to redistribute some of it through taxation.

5. An important economic argument relates to maintenance of full employment. There is chronic danger, it is argued, that money savings will exceed the amount which businessmen and others are willing to borrow. When this happens there is a deficiency of spending in the economy and production and employment fall. Thus anything which reduces the level of savings in the economy will reduce the likelihood of unemployment. Since wealthy people save a large proportion of their incomes while poor people save very little, transfer of income from rich to poor will reduce saving and increase consumer spending.

The difficulty is that these arguments can be countered by an equal number on the other side. Those who believe government should not set out to redistribute income contend that:

1. Wage and salary income, which makes up four fifths of personal income, is received for services performed. It is unjustifiable to take away from people what they have earned through their own efforts.

2. There is also an ethical basis for property income. Property is simply congealed labor, the result of *past* effort plus saving. The state is no more entitled to take away the fruits of past labor than of present labor.

3. To the argument that inequality arouses envy and discontent, one can retort that envy may stimulate productive effort. One can try to keep up with the Joneses by working harder or climbing to a higher occupational level. Conversely, if income differences become too small, no one may consider it worthwhile to undertake skilled and difficult work. The wage and salary differences which emerge in a competitive labor market ensure an adequate supply of labor to costly, strenuous, or unpleasant jobs.

4. Taxation may have other harmful consequences. A heavy income tax may make people decide to work fewer hours and spend more time on the beach. Taxation of business profits, by reducing the return on invest-

ment, may cause less investment to occur. This will mean slower growth in productive capacity and national output. One can argue that what the country needs is more saving rather than less saving, and that heavy taxation of large incomes and business profits reduces saving to an undesirably low level.

It is clear even from this brief listing that economic analysis can never determine what is a correct income distribution. This remains at bottom a matter of ethical conviction and political preference. A man of one opinion cannot hope to convince a man of different mind by sheer weight of evidence. Like many problems in political economy, this issue is essentially one of *degree*. Scarcely anyone would advocate *complete* equality of incomes. At the other extreme, few people today would defend the degree of inequality which existed in Britain around 1800, or which exists today in some of the less developed countries of the world. The practical question is always *how much* equality is feasible and desirable at a particular time.

The trend of economic policy in Western industrial countries during this century has been toward greater income equality. But this does not prove that the policy is right in any absolute sense. It may merely prove, as embittered aristocrats contend, that there are more voters in the lower brackets!

REDISTRIBUTION OUTSIDE THE MARKET: U.S. EXPERIENCE

How far have we already carried the tendency toward equalization of incomes through the government budget? In a general way, we know that the fiscal system operates in an equalizing direction. Most of the transfer payments go to people in the brackets below $5,000 a year, while the federal personal income tax falls heavily on the brackets above $5,000.

But any effort to be more precise than this runs into two kinds of difficulty. First, who actually pays various types of tax? Does the corporation income tax fall entirely on the stockholders, or is some of it added on to product prices? What about sales and excise taxes, social security taxes, and the rest?

Second, who benefits from the provision of government services? In some cases the benefits can be traced to a particular group. School expenditures benefit people who have children, agricultural research and extension benefits farmers, and so on. But it is difficult to allocate military expenditures, foreign aid, and general government overhead. The simplest assumption is that each citizen benefits equally from these expenditures, but they could also be allocated on the basis of income or property ownership.

For these reasons an analysis of how government operations change the distribution of real income involves many assumptions and much hard statistical labor. One effort of this sort is shown in Table 14–3.[4] Though the results are necessarily rough, they suggest a substantial redistribution of income. Comparing the final distribution after taking account of government operations with the initial distribution, one finds that the percentage share of the lowest bracket has more than tripled, rising from 1.4 to 5.0 percent. The top bracket, on the other hand, has fallen from 26 percent to 18 percent. The amount of income which has been redistributed downwards works out at almost 17 billion dollars, or about 9 percent of total personal income.

TABLE 14–3

Government Impact on Income Distribution,
United States, 1950

Money Income Class (Based on Initial Income)	Distribution of Spending Units (Percent)	Initial Income Billions	Initial Income Percent	Final Income Adjusted for Taxes, Transfers, and Government Services Billions	Final Income Adjusted for Taxes, Transfers, and Government Services Percent
Less than $1,000	14	2.804	1.43	9.736	5.0
1,000–1,999	19	16.188	8.23	21.860	11.3
2,000–2,999	21	28.466	14.47	31.734	16.4
3,000–3,999	19	33.750	17.16	34.790	18.0
4,000–4,999	11	27.438	13.95	26.211	13.6
5,000–7,499	11	36.370	18.49	33.968	17.6
7,500 and over	5	51.687	26.28	34.747	18.0
Total	100	196.703	100.00	193.046	100.0

While the fiscal system has a marked equalizing effect, it falls far short of full equalization. Even in the final distribution, average income per spending unit is $13,364 in the highest bracket compared with $1,337 in the lowest bracket. It would have been necessary to redistribute an additional 43 billion dollars to bring about equal income per spending unit. The fiscal system of 1950, therefore, resulted in moving the initial in-

[4] Data for this Table and for Figure 14–5 are adapted from Alfred H. Conrad, "Redistribution Through Government Budgets in the United States, 1950," in Alan T. Peacock (ed.), *Income Redistribution and Social Policy* (London: Jonathan Cape, 1954), pp. 178–268.

The initial income in the first two columns includes only income from work or property, exclusive of transfer payments. It may be regarded as the "pure" or "original" distribution which is later modified by government action.

The main steps in going from this distribution to the final distribution at the right-hand side of the table were: (1) transfer payments were added in; (2) federal, state, and local taxes were deducted, using specific assumptions about who pays various types of tax; (3) the value of free government services, taken as equal to their cost, was allocated among the various income brackets. For defense and other general services of government, it was assumed that each citizen shares equally in the benefits. The assumptions and procedures used are spelled out in detail in the original source.

come distribution about 28 percent of the way toward full equality (which is taken as simply a measuring rod, not necessarily a desirable objective.)

The leveling effect of fiscal operations is shown graphically in Figure 14–5. Note the substantial difference between the Lorenz curves representing initial and final distributions.

FIGURE 14–5

The Government Impact on Income Distribution, 1950

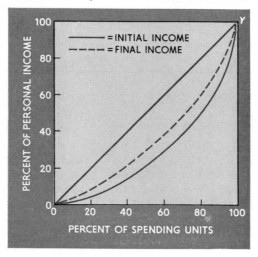

ELIMINATING POVERTY

We cannot expect agreement on the wisdom of transferring income from people with $25,000 a year to those with $5,000 a year. But one might get agreement on the desirability of eliminating really substandard conditions. For the first time in human history, it is now technically feasible to eliminate poverty over a vast area such as the United States. It would be gratifying if the United States could be the first large nation to accomplish this task. If we do not, we can be fairly certain that the U.S.S.R. will have accomplished it within the next generation. Competition in abolishing poverty should not be less challenging than competition in armaments or space rockets.

How many people in the United States can be regarded as living in poverty? There is no precise answer, because standards of living are conventional and change over time. What was acceptable in 1850 is considered substandard today. If we take as our standard the "American way of life" depicted in the slick-paper magazines, most Americans are impoverished. But this is unrealistic. The definition of poverty must be constructed with an eye to how most people are actually living. If the target is set too high, it becomes useless as an objective.

The Bureau of Labor Statistics computes regularly the cost of a "city worker's family budget." This is designed to provide a modest living for a family of four, something above mere subsistence but below the level of genuine comfort. The cost of this budget at present varies between $4,000 and $5,000 a year, depending on size of community and region of the country.

A rough definition of poverty might be as follows: (1) single individuals with an annual income below $1,000; (2) married couples with less than $2,000; (3) families of four with less than $3,000; (4) families of six or more with less than $4,000. This definition is not easy to apply, because it is hard to get a cross-classification of households by annual income and size of family. Making the best estimate one can, it appears that something like 25 million people in the United States are still living below the poverty line. For this group the much-heralded affluent society remains a mirage.

Who are these people? They include upwards of a million marginal farm families, mainly in the Southern states; several million people over 65 who are unable to work and have inadequate income from other sources; upwards of a million other families where the husband is disabled or absent; and a substantial number of families headed by low-skilled workers, who are toward the bottom of the wage ladder and are particularly subject to irregular employment.

Poverty is no longer mainly a wage problem. Most of these people are not wage earners. The wage-earners in the poverty group are there mainly because of irregular employment, which may reflect low work capacity, rather than because of low hourly wages. Hourly wage rates have now risen to the point where almost every wage earner can enjoy a modest livelihood *provided* he is able to work a full 2,000-hour year. This is encouraging from one standpoint, but discouraging from another. It means that such poverty as remains cannot be eliminated by the normal increase of wage levels in the years ahead.

We are faced now with enclaves of poverty in a generally prosperous economy. Poverty is localized in groups which for one reason or another have been unable to find a firm foothold in the wage system. It must accordingly be attacked by rifle-shot measures aimed at particular groups, rather than a shotgun approach designed to raise incomes in general. The main lines of attack include:

Agricultural Policy. Nothing need be added here to what was said in Chapter 11. It was argued there that policy should be oriented toward removing low-productivity land from production and transferring a sizable portion of the farm population to other industries.

Social Insurance. People who normally work and earn adequate incomes may fall into the poverty group through temporary or permanent loss of earning power. Most workers suffer unemployment at one time or another. Everyone who lives long enough eventually becomes unable to work through old age. Even before this, a worker may be disabled by acci-

dent or disease. His earnings may be interrupted by illness, which also involves extra costs for medical care. If he dies prematurely, his family may
be left with no means of support.

The chances of these things happening can be estimated, just as one
can estimate the probability of a house burning down or a car being involved in an accident. This makes it possible to apply the principle of insurance and to make advance provision through reserve funds. Most
countries now have social insurance funds to which the worker and his
employer contribute while he is working, and from which he is entitled to
draw specified amounts when unable to work. This may not involve
much transfer of income to wage-earners from other groups in the population. The worker contributes part of the cost himself. The remainder
comes mainly from payroll taxes on the employer which, according to
best guesses about tax incidence, are either shifted back to the worker in
lower wages or shifted forward in higher prices to consumers, of whom
workers form a large proportion. The main transfer of income, then, occurs *within* the wage-earning population, and is a transfer between periods of working and not working. The result is to level out the worker's
lifetime income, and to prevent his falling into poverty because of the
normal hazards of industrial life.

Minimum Wage Systems. We have said that poverty is not mainly
a wage problem. This is true in two senses. Wage rates in the United
States have now reached a level at which the great majority of workers
can attain a decent livelihood *provided* that they are regularly employed.
Moreover, the general wage level cannot be raised appreciably by exhortation or government decree, since it depends mainly on the advance of
labor productivity.

But this argument should not be pushed too far. The labor market is
an imperfect instrument, and there are at any time some wage rates lower
than they need be. There are groups of workers whose bargaining position
is poor and whom the employer can hire for less than their productivity.
Examples are workers in isolated locations where alternative job openings
are scarce, or minority groups which are discriminated against in hiring.
There are also companies which, because they can hire labor cheaply, fail
to use it efficiently. They are paying the worker his productivity, but
productivity is low because of poor management.

A legal minimum wage can serve the useful purpose of bringing a
small minority of lagging wage rates up to the standard which has been
found feasible by the majority of employers. If one finds, for example, that
only 5 percent of workers at a particular time are earning less than
$1.25 an hour, there is little danger and considerable benefit in bringing
everyone up to this level. Not the least important benefit is that some
employers, when forced to pay higher wages, will work harder to find
ways of increasing plant efficiency. Higher wages need not come out of

profit, but may come partly from a forced-draft increase in productivity.

The United States has a federal minimum wage of $1.25 per hour for workers in interstate commerce. The industrial states of the northeast typically have state minimum wage laws covering retailing, service, and other intrastate industries. State minimum wages are typically below the federal level, reflecting partly the fact that trade and service workers are worth less in the market than the manufacturing workers who are the main "customers" of the federal Act, and partly the greater timidity and conservatism of state legislatures as compared with Congress. Most states in the South and Midwest still lack effective minimum wage legislation.

Family Size and Living Costs. Two cannot live as cheaply as one, and six certainly can't live as cheaply as two. An income which is adequate for a man and wife may be very skimpy when it has to cover three or four children as well. But wage schedules are based on the job rather than the man. A carpenter receives the same amount whether he is a bachelor or has a family of ten.

Most industrial countries except the United States have now established family allowance systems. These involve monthly payments of so much per child, independent of the father's wage or other family income. They are *social* payments, not *relief* payments. The bank president receives the same monthly allowance for his child as the street sweeper. The allowance is considerably less than the cost of rearing the child, but it goes some distance in that direction.

The kind of income transfer involved depends on how the payments are financed. If they are financed from special payroll taxes, as in France, there is little *vertical* transfer among income brackets. The operation is mainly a *horizontal* transfer from bachelors and childless couples to families with children. If general government revenues are involved, there is likely to be some vertical transfer as well because of the heavy reliance of most governments on income taxation.

Is it a good idea for the government to transfer income from people without children to those with children? This is a question of social equity on which economics has little to say. The arguments in favor of family allowances tend to focus on the child, while the contrary arguments focus on the parents. On the positive side, it can be argued that society has an interest in seeing that the next generation is reared under decent conditions. It is not the child's fault if he is born into a ten-child family rather than a two-child family; and he should not be penalized severely in terms of living space, nourishment, health, and education.

On the other hand, bachelors and curmudgeons may argue that child-rearing is a personal responsibility with which society should have no concern. A family which has many children must be prepared to bear the financial consequences. It is sometimes argued also that family allowances will encourage families to have more children than otherwise, thus imposing a population burden on the economy, and that the system encourages large families among the poorest groups in the population, which may have inferior hereditary qualities. But there is little evidence that family allowances actually have any influence on family size.

Depressed Areas. Geographical pockets of poverty can arise from high specialization of a region in one line of production. A drop in demand for the product, or a locational shift of the industry to another region, may leave a stranded population which has difficulty in converting to other employments. The sharp drop in coal mining employment over the past generation has left islands of unemployment in the mine towns of Pennsylvania, West Virginia, and Kentucky. The shift of cotton textile manufacturing to the South created pockets of unemployment in New England.

There are two lines of adaptation in such cases. Some people will move out of the area, and younger people are especially likely to move as they find few job opportunities at home. In addition, new industries may move into the area to take advantage of the plentiful labor supply. How rapidly this second tendency operates depends on such things as: the locational advantages of the area for other lines of production; the quality and trainability of the labor force; whether the traditional wage level of the area is high or low; the effectiveness with which community leaders mobilize to attract new industry; and the general level of employment in the economy.

These tendencies toward out-migration of labor and in-migration of industry might wipe out regional unemployment "in the long run." But both tendencies operate slowly, and there is a good case for public action to accelerate the process. Out-migration can be speeded by retraining of workers in new skills, by the placement activities of the state employment services, and by loans or grants to cover family moving costs. Inward movement of industry can be accelerated by studying and publicizing the area's locational advantages, by assistance with building programs and credit facilities, by tax concessions, and in other ways. Vigorous activity in these directions is more constructive, and in the end less expensive, than simply keeping the population of a depressed area alive through relief payments.

General Relief. We come finally to straight cash hand-outs which serve only to keep people alive at a minimum level. This is the most demeaning and undesirable form of public support. The strategy of an attack on poverty should be to reduce direct relief to the smallest possible role. Families which contain at least one employable member should be prevented from falling onto the relief rolls through a combination of full employment policies, social insurance, family allowances, and the other measures described above. But there will always be the unemployable, the barely employable, the people who never work regularly enough to come within the orbit of the wage system and social security programs. For these people general relief is a last resort. The argument for it is purely humanitarian. The only argument against it is that it takes tax money. By and large, relief does not "keep people from working," since there are few employable people in the relief population.

These comments suggest the protean nature of poverty. One must whittle away at the problem from all sides by coordinated use of these various devices. And this strategy must rest on the solid base of a productive, fully employed, and growing economy. Raising the real incomes of the poorest groups in the population means in the last analysis getting more *goods and services* to them, and these goods can come only from the efforts of the employed part of the population.

SUMMARY

1. Distribution of personal income in the United States is quite unequal. The reasons include different wage and salary levels for different occupations, irregularity of employment, differing numbers of wage earners per family, unequal distribution of property ownership, and lack or loss of productive ability.

2. Between 1935 and 1945 income distribution became considerably more equal, but there has been little change from 1945 to the present.

3. Government can act to change the distribution of income either *through* the market mechanism or *outside* the market mechanism. The most important example of the first type is steps to reduce the financial barrier to higher education through loan or scholarship systems.

4. Government also shifts income outside the market system through taxes and transfer payments. There is at present a substantial downward transfer from richer to poorer groups. Whether we are doing too much or not enough in this direction is a highly controversial question. There are economic arguments on both sides, but economics alone cannot provide a definite answer.

5. While income equality *per se* remains debatable, steps to eliminate poverty command a greater measure of agreement. Policy measures in this area include: transfer of marginal farmers to other occupations, adequate social insurance systems, a legal minimum wage, family allowances, special attention to geographical pockets of unemployment, and overall measures to achieve high employment and rapid economic growth.

The Public Economy

"It was as true," said Mr. Barkis, "as taxes is. And nothing's truer than them."

CHARLES DICKENS

To tax and to please, no more than to love and to be wise, is not given to men.

EDMUND BURKE

MOST OF THE THINGS I consume are bought from private sellers at a market price. How much of each article I get depends on my ability and willingness to pay the price. For the nation, the amount of each article produced depends on the balancing of consumer preferences and production possibilities explained in Part One.

Alongside this private economy there exists a public economy operated on quite different lines. I cannot go to the store and buy a certain quantity of national defense. I do not pay a price for sending my child to the local public school or driving my car over the state highway. Public services have two distinguishing characteristics: they are usually provided without charge to the individual recipient, and they are available equally to all comers. I cannot choose to go without national defense and consume a great deal of public education, while my neighbor makes the opposite choice. The principles of choice, market pricing, and resource allocation which apply in the private economy no longer apply in the public sphere.

But the government has no magic power to commandeer resources or make something out of nothing. The resources needed to build highways, operate schools, and maintain the defense establishment must be bought and paid for. The money comes from taxes levied on the citizens. Here is where trouble starts. We all enjoy using government services, particularly when we can view them as falling from the sky without cost. But we hate to pay the taxes which lurk in the background.

What kinds of good and service are typically provided through public channels? Why not others as well? Where should we draw the line between the private economy and the public economy? How can we judge whether the government is producing too little or too much of a particular service? Is there anything in the public economy which corresponds to the rule of price = marginal cost in the private economy?

Who should pay the taxes required to finance public services? What types of tax do we use at present, and who pays them? What problems arise from the fact that services are provided and taxes levied by several layers of government? These issues are the focus of this chapter.

THREE FUNCTIONS OF GOVERNMENT BUDGETS

Government budgets perform three main functions:[1] (1) The *allocation* function. A tax reduces the amount of money which people have available for spending on privately produced goods and services, and this frees resources in the private economy. As government spends the tax money, however, government use of resources increases in a way which offsets the drop in private use. An increase in the level of taxes and expenditures *re-allocates* resources from the private to the public economy. This re-allocation is accompanied by changes in the structure of production and employment, since the things on which government spends money will differ from the things on which consumers would spend the same money in the private economy.

2. The *distribution* function. Government may levy just enough taxes to cover the cost of public services. But it may also levy taxes on some people in the economy in order to transfer the proceeds to other people, who then have this money available for private spending. This does not alter the level of government services or affect the allocation of resources between the private and public sectors. It is a transfer of private purchasing power, and these payments are accordingly called *transfer payments*. The question of how far government should go in this direction was examined in Chapter 14.

3. The *stabilization* function. During the past generation it has been realized increasingly that the government budget can be used to correct extremes of inflation or deflation. The prescription for a countercyclical

---

[1] The terminology used here follows the analysis of Richard A. Musgrave, *The Theory of Public Finance* (New York: McGraw-Hill Book Co., Inc., 1959), especially Part I.

budget policy is easily stated, though it is not easy to apply. If the economy is fully employed and prices are rising, total spending is excessive and should be reduced. One way of doing this is to have the government take in more money than it spends, that is, run a budget surplus. Conversely, during an unemployment period when more spending is needed, one possible policy is for the government to spend more than it takes in, or run a deficit. The practical difficulties of designing and applying such a policy will be examined in Part Three.

In this chapter we assume that functions (2) and (3) are being performed satisfactorily. The economy is in a state of full employment with stable prices. Some community consensus has been reached on what constitutes a proper distribution of income, and the appropriate transfers are being made through the government budget. Leaving these matters aside, we focus here on function (1), on the *management of the public household*. What services should be provided by government? In what quantity should they be provided? How should the costs be divided among the taxpaying public?

PUBLIC EXPENDITURE: QUESTIONS OF PRINCIPLE

Scope of the Public Sector

With some exceptions such as the post office, public services are usually provided without charge. The fact that a service is *provided* by government does not mean that all the ingredients need be *produced* by government. All national defense equipment could conceivably be produced in government arsenals and shipyards. In practice, the great bulk of military equipment is purchased from business concerns. Government pays the cost of building new schools and highways, but the building job is normally contracted out to private construction companies. Direct government production is thus considerably smaller in scope than government provision.

There are several reasons why a service may be provided without charge. The most important reason, the hallmark of a *public good*, is that it is impossible to exclude individuals from enjoyment of the service. The national defense establishment protects us all willy-nilly. If a city sets up a smog control system, all residents benefit from the purer air. It is not feasible to let some people use the city streets and not others. Thus if one tried to finance these services on a price basis the attempt would surely fail. No one would pay the price, because he could continue to enjoy the service without paying. The *principle of exclusion*, which applies in private markets, cannot be applied here.

There is a second class of cases in which a price system is conceivable but would not be very workable. It would be awkward to put all the highways of the country on a toll basis, though we achieve something like this by financing them mainly from gasoline taxes and other charges on highway users. It would be hard to run a fire department to put out fires only in buildings which had paid for this service. City collection of trash and garbage could be put on a fee basis, but there are health reasons for not giving each family free choice on garbage disposal.

This suggests a third type of case, where a price system would be workable but where we choose to supersede the price system as a matter of social policy. The outstanding case is education. It would be possible to finance education by tuition fees from first grade through to college graduation. But we decided long ago that there is a public interest in a literate, enlightened citizenry, and that this warrants a system of tax-supported public schools. Such cases involve what Musgrave calls *merit wants*.[2] They are cases in which we interfere with individual choice on either or both of two grounds: (1) one person's consumption of a service has repercussions on others in the community. It is important to me and my children that my neighbor's children be educated. (2) Inadequacies of consumer knowledge and foresight may cause people to underbuy even in terms of their own self-interest. This is notoriously true of both education and preventive medical care.

These three situations—where a price system is impossible, where it is administratively difficult, and where it would restrict consumption below the socially desirable level—define the normal scope of the public sector in a private economy. Controversy centers mainly on the third case, on how far one should push the concept of merit wants. Economic individualists would restrict it narrowly. Some economists have argued that all education should be put on a price basis. People of opposite political bent would extend public provision to cover vocational and professional training, medical and health services, subsidized housing, and other things. Either position can obviously be pushed too far. Reliance on government to give people "what is good for them" can be carried to totalitarian lengths. But extreme individualism can lead to low standards of health, housing, and education, accompanied by high consumption of comic books and patent medicines.

The Level of Public Expenditure

Establishing the proper *scope* of the public sector does not determine the proper *level* of public expenditures. Any government service can be provided on a meager or lavish scale. How much of each type of service should government undertake to provide? For the private sector we concluded that production should be expanded so long as price covers marginal cost. Is there a corresponding principle which can be applied in the public sector?

There are cases in which a project yields measurable benefits, and by comparing these with estimated costs one can judge whether the project

---

[2] *Op. cit.*, pp. 13–14.

is worthwhile. Consider a multiple-purpose river development project, which produces a combination of electric power, flood prevention, irrigation, and improved navigation. For power output, one can estimate the price at which the power can be sold on a commercial basis. The value of flood prevention can be judged by the property damage resulting from past floods. As regards irrigation, one can compare the cash value of crop production on irrigated land with production on the same land before irrigation. For navigation benefits, one can estimate the probable increase in tonnage carried by water, and how much it would have cost to move this tonnage by rail or other methods. Adding these things, one gets an estimate of total benefits from the project which can be compared with the probable cost. This type of calculation is used by the Army Corps of Engineers, the Bureau of Reclamation, and other agencies concerned with river development.[3]

But these cases are the happy exception. In most cases there is no objective measure of the benefit from a public service. What can we do then? An economist might approach the problem as follows: people get satisfaction from public services, just as they do from privately sold goods and services. They must therefore be presumed to want public services, to have a demand for them. It should be possible then, to construct Mr. Jones' demand curve for highway services just as we construct his demand for food or clothing. He would probably pay a good deal for a two-lane highway to drive to work from his home in the suburbs. If the highway were made wider and better it would yield some additional benefit, and so would additional highways linking him with other communities. These benefits taper off, however, and Mr. Jones' demand curve would fall from left to right in the usual way.

Suppose we got demand curves for highway service from everybody in the country and added them together to get a total demand curve. The cost of building increasingly fancy highway systems can be estimated, giving a supply curve for highway services. By noting the intersection of the demand and supply curves, could we not read off the proper level of highway expenditure?

This would be a nice solution. But there are two major difficulties. First, there is no objective way of discovering the demand curves of the citizens. For privately marketed goods, buyers reveal their preferences by their behavior in the market. In the case of public services, however, people have an incentive to conceal and understate their preferences. Expressing a high preference could lead to paying higher taxes. Expressing a low preference costs you nothing, since you know that you will have equal access to whatever level of service the government decides to provide. Sec-

---

[3] The problems of calculation are of course more complicated than this sketch suggests. For a good analysis of the theoretical and practical difficulties, see Otto Eckstein, *Water Resource Development* (Cambridge, Mass.: Harvard University Press, 1958).

ond, there are problems in adding up preferences. The people who benefit from a particular service are not exactly the same people who pay the corresponding taxes. Provision of the service thus involves a transfer of income from one group to the other. A decision to provide a certain level of service is also a decision that a certain income distribution is desirable, and there is no scientific basis for reaching decisions about income distribution.

This leaves us with no clear guide to the proper level of expenditure on public services. There seems no alternative but to accept the results which emerge from the political process. Political decision making is admittedly imperfect. It is not feasible to submit every expenditure decision to a popular referendum. And when legislative representatives take action on spending bills, it is not clear just whom or what they are representing. A voter choosing among alternative candidates is probably not much influenced by the candidate's views on particular spending programs. He may be influenced by whether the candidate or his party is identified with "high spending" or "low spending." But he is apt to be vulnerable to the candidate who promises simultaneously to raise expenditures, reduce taxes, and balance the budget.

How does the political process work out? Does it contain any inherent bias toward "overspending" or "underspending"? Does it lead to a higher or lower level of public services than the citizens would prefer on the basis of full information and rational reflection? There are wide differences of opinion on this point. One school of thought maintains that government is biased toward overspending. The voters, it is argued, have an optical illusion on this matter. They regard public services as free goods and fail to realize that they must be covered by taxes. Thus they press for more service than they would do if the costs were clearly visualized. In the legislative lobby, groups urging new spending are likely to be better organized than those urging tax reductions. Spending programs usually benefit a specific group, which will therefore press hard for them. Tax reductions benefit the citizens at large, whose interest in them is consequently diffuse and ill organized. This school of thought relies also on the spectre of the power-hungry bureaucrat, eager to expand his empire in accordance with Parkinson's Law.

An opposing school maintains that we have been seriously underspending on public services. The media of mass communication, it is argued, assiduously promote the idea that private production is "good," while government functions are "bad" or at least suspect. Taxes are of course "bad," since they are extracted by force from a groaning citizenry. But spending by these same citizens on the products of private business is "good." The public is urged constantly by high-pressure advertising to buy more and fancier consumer goods. No similar advertising campaign is conducted on behalf of better schools and hospitals, urban redevelopment, natural resource conservation, and other public goods. As a result, too much effort goes into producing private consumption goods, while too little goes into providing public services. We pack our plastic dishes into our nylon picnic bag and climb into our chrome-ornamented car. We then drive our undereducated children through smog-filled air on an overcrowded highway to lunch in a weed-ridden park beside a polluted stream.

Which school of thought is more nearly correct? There is no objective way of deciding. They are free to tackle each other in the political arena, and we are bound by the result. At a technical level, however, there may be ways of increasing the rationality of tax and expenditure decisions. In particular, one might find ways of relating the two kinds of decision more clearly in the public mind and in the legislative process.

One other noncontroversial statement can be made. After it has been decided what amount of a public service is to be provided, this should be done in the most efficient way. Overstaffing should be avoided, and other costs held to a minimum. The standard techniques of scientific management are being applied increasingly to government operations.

PUBLIC EXPENDITURE: TYPES AND TRENDS

There is a cliché to the effect that the American economy is characterized by "big business," "big labor," and "big government." Government expenditures, it is said, have been rising disproportionately fast in recent decades and have now reached alarming proportions. This suggests several quantitative questions: How does one measure the economic importance of government relative to the private economy? How rapidly has the relative importance of government been rising, and why? What are the major purposes of public expenditure? What is the distribution of functions among different levels of government?

There are several possible measures of the significance of government operations: (1) *total government expenditure* indicates roughly how much is being collected each year in taxes. But this total includes a large volume of transfer payments which go right back to the citizens. Thus it is a good deal larger than: (2) *the cost of providing public services.* This indicates the proportion of our productive resources which is being devoted to satisfying community wants, or the proportion of national output organized on a tax-supported rather than a private market basis. Most of the materials required for public services, however, are purchased from private business concerns. In 1961, business sales to government amounted to a bit more than $58 billion. If we deduct this amount we get a still smaller total, (3) *the cost of direct government production.* This includes only goods and services produced by government agencies, not those which are simply *purchased and distributed* by government. Basically, it is the public payroll.

These three totals compared as follows in the calendar year 1961: total government expenditure, including transfer payments, was $149.3

billion. The cost of providing public services was $109.1 billion. Output produced directly by government came to $50.8 billion. One can pick and choose among these figures, depending on the purpose in mind. In terms of resource use, the second and third totals are most significant and we shall concentrate on them here.

Direct Government Production

One approach to the importance of government is to ask what proportion of national output is produced by government agencies or, thinking in terms of inputs, what proportion of our resources is used in direct government production? The most important input is labor, and we have reliable figures of public and private employment. Table 15–1 and Figure 15–1 show government employment as a percentage of total employ-

TABLE 15–1

Government Employment as a Percentage of
Total Employment, United States, 1900–1960*

	1900	1910	1920	1930	1940	1950	1960
Federal							
Military	0.5	0.4	0.8	0.5	1.1	2.8	3.6
Nonmilitary	1.1	1.2	1.7	1.4	2.2	3.5	3.3
State	0.3	0.3	0.5	0.7	1.1	1.8	2.3
Local	3.1	3.4	4.0	5.4	5.9	5.4	6.7
Total	5.0	5.3	7.0	8.0	10.3	13.5	15.9

* Figures through 1940 are adapted from S. Fabricant, *Trend of Government Activity since 1900* (New York: National Bureau of Economic Research, 1952). The 1960 data are from U.S. Department of Labor, *Employment and Earnings*, June, 1962. All school employees are classified as local through 1940. For later years they are distributed between local and state governments in proper proportion. The federal figure for 1940 excludes emergency relief workers.

ment at intervals from 1900 to 1960, and also the division of employment among the federal, state, and local governments.

Judged by the employment yardstick, government has almost tripled in relative importance since 1900. Civilian employees of the government were 4.5 percent of all workers in 1900, 12.3 percent in 1960. If members of the armed forces are added, almost one sixth of all employed workers were working for various levels of government in 1960.

Contrary to popular impression, the federal government is not the largest producer of ordinary or nondefense services. The state and local governments have more than twice as many civilian employees as the federal government. Local government alone provides more than half of all civilian public employment, mainly because of the great size of the school system. The federal government's share of civilian public employment has risen only slightly since 1900. It is mainly the military establishment which makes the federal government loom so large on the budget scene.

The share of the nation's capital resources used by government has also risen. Fabricant estimates that in 1900 the government owned about one sixteenth of the nonmilitary capital assets of the country. By the late forties, government owned about one fifth of all nonmilitary assets, with an estimated value of more than $50 billion. If military items were also included, government's share would be even higher. Most of this increase

FIGURE 15–1

Government Employment as a Percentage of
Total Employment, United States, 1900–1958

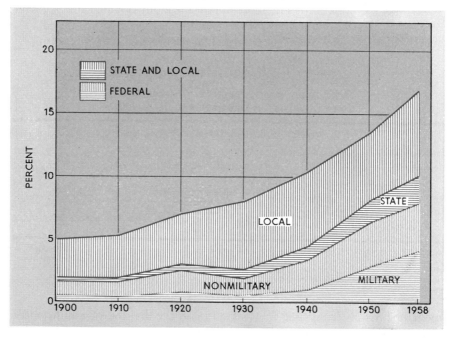

occurred during the years 1929–46. Because of the depression of the thirties, followed by unavailability of materials during World War II, private investment was *negative* over this period, while there was heavy government investment in both military and nonmilitary items.

Cost of Public Services

In addition to the public payroll, government buys large amounts of goods and services from private industry. This includes the work of contractors in building new schools, highways, airports, and other facilities; the cost of military aircraft, missiles, and other defense products; and a great variety of supplies for the daily operation of government agencies. By adding government purchases to government payrolls we get the *cost of providing public services* or, what amounts to the same thing, *government expenditures exclusive of transfer payments*. By calculating this total as a percentage of GNP we can see how much of our national output is being channeled through government rather than through private markets.

Table 15–2 shows the situation in selected years since 1900. Expendi-

TABLE 15–2

Government Payrolls and Purchases as Percentage
of Gross National Product, 1903–61*

Federal	1903	1913	1929	1939	1949	1954	1961
Military	0.8	0.6 ⎫		1.4	5.3	11.3	9.4
Nonmilitary	1.1	1.3 ⎭	1.3	2.2	3.4	1.8	1.6
State and local	4.5	5.2	6.9	9.0	6.9	7.6	9.7
Total	6.4	7.1	8.2	12.6	15.6	20.7	20.7

* Data on government payrolls and purchases were derived as follows:
1903–13: S. Fabricant, *op. cit.*, Tables D-1 through D-4, pp. 225–234.
1929–61: *Survey of Current Business*, July, 1962, pp. 6–7.

ture trends have been broadly similar to the employment trends shown in Table 15–1. The proportion of national output absorbed by government has more than tripled, from a bit over 6 percent near the beginning of the century to about 21 percent at present. Local and state governments are the main providers of civilian services, being about six times as important in this respect as the federal government. At the federal level, the most dramatic development has been the sharp increase in military expenditures. Before 1940 these typically formed only one tenth of all government spending and around 1 percent of GNP. Today military spending is about half of the total cost of public services and about 10 percent of GNP.

Where Does the Money Go?

One fifth of our national product is a lot of output. What concrete form does this take? What are the main types of service provided by each level of government? Figures 15–2a, 2b, and 2c show the situation as of 1961.

The federal government provides basically national defense. This may be news to businessmen who find themselves regulated by the ICC, FTC, SEC, FPC, FCC, CAB, and other alphabetical agencies. These activities are important, but they cost little in money and manpower. If we include the foreign aid and atomic energy programs as part of the defense effort, national defense absorbs about three quarters of the cost of federal services. Everything else has to fit into the remaining quarter.

At the state level, education and highways form more than half of all costs. Educational expenditures include grants to localities for the public school system plus the cost of the state universities and other institutions of higher education. The states have traditionally borne the main burden of highway construction, though increasing support is now being received from the federal government. Other important state services include health and hospital care, natural resource conservation, and law enforcement. Relief expenditures are also important, but these are transfer payments and consequently do not appear in Figure 15–2*b*.

The main local service has always been the public school system.

FIGURE 15–2a

Cost Distribution by Level of Government and Type of Service,
United States, 1958 (Percent)

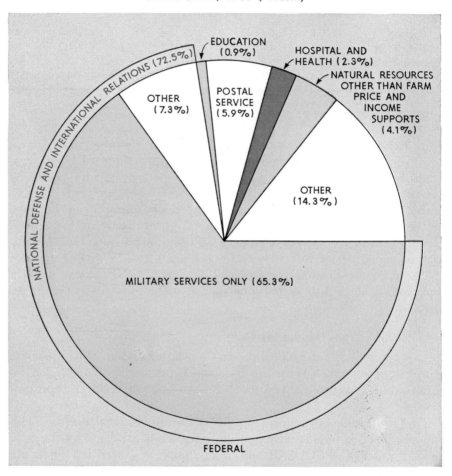

Since 1945 school expenditures have risen unusually fast because of the population upsurge, which has greatly increased the number of children to be trained. Today local governments devote about half their resources to education. The next largest item is streets and roads, which includes county roads in rural areas as well as streets and sidewalks in the cities. Other sizable items are police protection, fire protection, water supply, trash and garbage collection, hospitals, and libraries. There are also important transfer payments in the form of cash relief.

FIGURE 15–2b

Cost Distribution by Level of Government and Type of Service,
United States, 1958 (Percent)

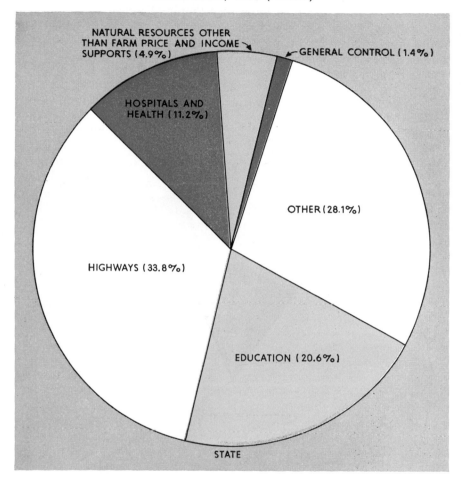

NATURAL RESOURCES OTHER
THAN FARM PRICE AND INCOME
SUPPORTS (4.9%)

GENERAL CONTROL (1.4%)

HOSPITALS AND
HEALTH (11.2%)

OTHER (28.1%)

HIGHWAYS (33.8%)

EDUCATION (20.6%)

STATE

Altogether, then, three quarters of the cost of public services in the
United States goes for four items: national defense; education; roads,
streets, and highways; and police, fire, and health services. General government administration, the "swollen bureaucracy," takes only a small
percentage. It is an illusion to think that large amounts of money can be
cut from government budgets without also cutting the level of service provided.

Behind the Uptrend

This analysis of the content of public services makes it easier to visualize what lies behind the long-term rise in government expenditures.
Particularly important have been:

1. *The changed international situation.* The United States in 1900 still stood on the fringes of world politics. The game was being played out in Europe among the traditional great powers—Britain, France, Germany, Russia, and the Austro-Hungarian Empire. Fascinating as the game was, no one expected it to erupt in major wars, the last of which had ended almost a century before with the downfall of Napoleon. In these circumstances our military establishment of a hundred thousand men was an inexpensive sideshow.

FIGURE 15–2c

Cost Distribution by Level of Government and Type of Service,
United States, 1958 (Percent)

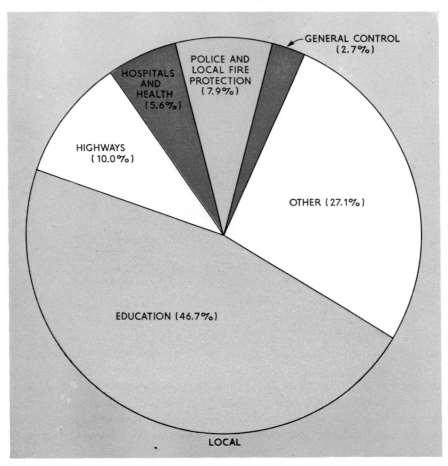

No one need be reminded of the very different circumstances of the 1960's. After two destructive world wars, which have left their residue of expense, the United States and the U.S.S.R. have emerged as super-powers in a world torn by dissension. Tension between these powers and their adherents seems likely to continue for many years. This necessitates a larger military establishment than existed before 1940, while at the same time the cost of modern weapons has greatly increased. It is a far cry from the machine guns and field artillery of 1918 to the long-range missiles and atomic submarines of today.

2. *Urbanization of the population.* In 1900 only 40 percent of the American people lived in towns and cities. Today the proportion of town-dwellers is two thirds and still rising. City people consume more public services per head than country people. The farmer draws water from his own well, disposes of his own trash and garbage, protects his property as best he can from fire and theft, needs no streets, sewers, or public parks. In the city these functions are provided at public expense. The resulting network of municipal services, while counted as part of national output, should perhaps be considered an unavoidable cost of complex, congested urban living.

3. *Rising real incomes.* Real income per capita in the United States almost tripled between 1900 and 1960. Higher incomes increase the demand for almost everything, but for some things more than others. Food and other necessities show a low income elasticity of demand. Most services, on the contrary, show a high income elasticity. Thus as real incomes rise, production of services rises a good deal faster than production of commodities. This is true of such privately produced services as travel, entertainment, vacation resorts, medical care, and beauty care. It is true also of public services. As living standards rise, people demand longer and better schooling, fancier highways, faster postal service, more adequate police and fire protection.

Not only does the volume of public services rise for these reasons, but these services become relatively more expensive to provide. They are essentially labor services, and in our economy the price of labor rises steeply over the long run. Nor is there the same opportunity to substitute capital for labor which one finds in commodity production. A doubling of auto workers' wages over 20 years will not double the price of an automobile, because of the possibility of substituting machinery for labor and making improvements in production methods. But a doubling of policemen's salaries will come close to doubling the cost of police protection. The radio patrol car, to be sure, covers more ground than the foot patrolman, and the eye of the television tube is now peering over the shoulder of the school teacher. But the possibilities of capital substitution are still limited, and both public and private services seem bound to become more expensive over the course of time.

4. *Rising educational standards.* Education deserves special mention because it absorbs such a large part of state and local budgets and because demand for education has risen so spectacularly. For every thousand pupils enrolled in Grade 5 in 1910, only 139 graduated from high school and only 23 succeeded in finishing college. High school graduates

were a small aristocracy. Today high school graduation proves mainly that one has lived to the age of 18, and even college graduation is so common that it gives no assurance of a high income job. Out of a thousand fifth grade pupils in 1952, 581 graduated from high school and 301 went on for at least some college training. The ratios in the sixties will doubtless be higher still.

This educational revolution is due partly to the higher income level of the country. Rising incomes make it less necessary for youngsters to begin contributing to the family budget at an early age. Rising incomes also provide taxable capacity to cover the cost of educating people for longer periods. Added to these economic factors is the traditional American belief that "education is good for you." It will help you adjust to adult life, find a wife or husband, get a better job, and derive greater enjoyment from your leisure time.

At any event, enrollment has risen substantially since 1900. Enrollment in colleges and universities has increased more than tenfold, from 237 thousand in 1900 to almost four million in 1961, a number which is expected to double by 1970. When one considers also the increased variety and complexity of the subjects taught, improvements in the style of classrooms and dormitories, and the great increase in teachers' salary levels, it is clear why educational expenditures have increased not only absolutely but as a percentage of national income.

5. *The car and the highway.* The inventor of the internal combustion engine unwittingly launched a huge increase in future public expenditures. The passenger car has now largely replaced rail travel as well as local subway and bus systems. The truck has cut deeply into railroad freight traffic. The auto and truck manufacturers, however, do not provide roads on which their vehicles can run. This remains a public responsibility. As the number and speed of vehicles has increased, standards and costs of highway construction have risen steadily. The costs have gotten beyond the fiscal capacity of the states and increasing federal subsidies have become necessary. The 41,000-mile interstate network of superhighways, started in 1958 and expected at that time to cost about $25 billion, is being financed to the extent of 90 percent from federal funds. The federal government also contributes to support of the older national and state highway systems.

Cars and highways are complementary goods, but one falls in the private and the other in the public sector. Private decisions to buy cars and trucks compel public decisions to allocate more resources to road building. Thus an item which bulked small before 1900 has become a major object of public expenditure.

The growth of public expenditure, then, reflects a long-term increase in demand for public services, based on rising incomes, urbanization, and other growth trends in the economy. One should expect that public expenditures will continue to absorb at least the present proportion of our productive resources and probably a gradually rising proportion. The only possibility of sizable reductions lies in the military sphere, but this would require favorable developments in the international situation which are not now in sight.

PUBLIC REVENUE: TYPES OF TAX

While government raises some money through borrowing, most of what is spent comes from taxation. Table 15–3 shows the main sources of

TABLE 15–3

Sources of Tax Revenue, Fiscal Year 1960–61*

Type of Tax	Federal Collections $ Million	Percent	State Collections $ Million	Percent	Local Collections $ Million	Percent	Total Collections $ Million	Percent
Personal income	41,338	53.3	2,355	12.4	258	1.3	43,951	37.8
Corporate income	20,954	27.1	1,266	6.6	...	...	22,220	19.1
Property	...	...	631	3.3	17,370	87.8	18,001	15.5
Sales taxes, excises, and customs	(12,649)	(16.3)	(11,031)	(57.9)	1,432	7.2	25,112	21.6
General	...	...	4,510	23.7				
Motor fuel	2,333	3.0	3,431	18.0				
Alcohol and tobacco	5,110	6.6	1,689	9.0				
Other	5,206	6.7	1,401	7.2				
Other taxes, including licenses	2,529	3.3	3,774†	19.8	744	3.7	7,047	6.0
Total	77,470	100.0	19,057	100.0	19,804	100.0	116,331	100.0

* U.S. Bureau of the Census, *Governmental Finances, 1961*, October, 1962.
† Of which motor vehicle and operators' licenses provided 1,641 million or 8.6 percent of state revenues.

general tax revenue at each level of government in a recent fiscal year. The table does not include every type of government income. For example, it does not include revenues from commercial sales by government enterprises, such as sale of electric power by TVA or sale of subway services by the New York City system. Nor does it include the payroll taxes levied to support the old age pension and unemployment compensation systems. This money goes into separate trust funds earmarked for pensions and unemployment benefits. The government runs a large insurance business as it were, alongside its other operations. But there is no need to mix this into our picture of how general government services are financed.

The amount of tax revenue *collected* at each level of government does not correspond with the amount *spent* at that level. The federal government makes cash grants to the states for various purposes, and the states in turn make grants to local governments. The emphasis of Table 15–3 is on tax *collections* rather than on where the money is eventually spent.

The tax sources used by different levels of government overlap considerably. While the federal government is the main recipient of income taxes, some states also tax personal and corporate income. The states join the federal government in taxing alcohol, tobacco, and motor fuels. Both state and local governments use sales taxes, and a few localities even levy income taxes. A half century ago, the revenue sources of each level of government were quite distinct. As expenditure needs have grown, however, each level has tried to tap more and more sources. This has produced a complicated overlapping network of taxation. Whether the present structure could be simplified to advantage by federal-state agreement is an important practical problem.

While tax structures overlap, the "center of gravity" differs for each level of government. Four fifths of federal revenue comes from income taxes on individuals and corporations, and excise taxes provide almost all the remainder. The main sources of state revenue are gasoline and motor vehicle taxes, general sales taxes, and personal and corporate income taxes. These provide about 70 percent of state tax collections. At the local level, the general property tax is still of overwhelming importance, providing more than 85 percent of tax revenues.

These differences in center of gravity are important for discussion of whether certain services should be provided by the federal government or at lower levels. This is often debated as a matter of high principle, of political centralism versus "states rights." But it is also a matter of hard cash. To say that something should be done by the federal government amounts to saying that it should be financed from income taxes. To push it down to the state level means that the funds will come largely from sales and excise taxes. Local responsibility means reliance on the general property tax. Since different people pay these various types of tax, this is a pocketbook issue which can generate heated argument.

The Personal Income Tax

This tax has been the outstanding fiscal development of the twentieth century. Along with its twin, the corporate income tax, it gives the federal revenue system great elasticity and enables Washington to collect enough to both cover federal expenditures and part of state and local expenditures.

The 1962 level of personal income tax rates is shown in Table 15–4. The tax rises by steps or "brackets," only a few of which are shown here, with each increment of income subject to a higher rate than the one before. The *marginal* tax rate, the rate on the last increment in an income of given size, is shown in column (4). Beginning at 20 percent, it rises to a ceiling of 91 percent on all income over $400,000.

The *average* rate, the percentage of the whole income which must be paid in taxes, is shown in column (6). For an income of $20,000, for example, the marginal tax rate is 34 percent, but the average rate is only a bit over 20 percent. At the $100,000 level, the marginal rate is 72 percent, the average rate about 51 percent. The average tax rate is always less than the marginal rate. It is "dragged down," as it were, by the lower marginal rates on earlier increments of income.

If, as one goes from lower to higher income brackets, a tax takes an *increasing* proportion of people's incomes, the tax is said to be *progressive*. A tax which takes the *same percentage* at each level of income is a *proportional* tax. A tax which takes a decreasing percentage from the higher incomes is termed *regressive*—it bears most heavily on the lowest income groups in the population. By this test the U.S. personal income tax is steeply progressive.

TABLE 15–4

Tax Rates on Personal Income, United States, 1962*
(Married Couple, Two Dependents)

Gross Income (1)	Deductions and Exemptions (2)	Taxable Income (3)	Marginal Rate of Tax (4)	Tax (5)	Average Rate of Tax (6)	Income after Tax (7)
$ 1,000	$2,500	$ 0	20%	$ 0	0.00%	$ 1,000
2,000	2,600	0	20%	0	0.00%	2,000
5,000	2,900	2,100	20%	420	8.50%	4,580
10,000	3,400	6,600	22%	1,372	13.72%	8,628
15,000	3,400	11,600	26%	2,616	17.31%	12,384
20,000	3,400	16,600	34%	4,124	20.62%	15,876
25,000	3,400	21,600	38%	5,888	23.55%	19,112
50,000	3,400	46,600	59%	18,294	36.59%	31,706
100,000	3,400	96,600	72%	51,192	51.19%	48,808
200,000	3,400	196,600	87%	131,682	65.84%	68,318
300,000	3,400	296,600	89%	220,614	73.54%	79,386
400,000	3,400	396,600	90%	310,580	77.65%	89,420
500,000	3,400	496,600	91%	401,546	80.31%	98,454

* The actual tax schedule contains many more steps in Column (1), with the marginal tax rate rising gradually from step to step. This simplified version is intended merely to indicate the general nature of the system. It assumes that only the standard deductions are taken. Larger deductions would of course reduce the tax paid.

In practice, the progression is less steep than Table 15–4 would suggest. Few people actually pay more than about half their income in taxes. Figures published by the Treasury Department show that in 1958 taxpayers reporting gross income of between $50,000 and $100,000 paid on the average 34.7 percent of this income in taxes, instead of the 45 percent or so suggested by Table 15–4. People with incomes between $200,000 and $500,000 paid 46.5 percent of their income in taxes, whereas Table 15–4 suggests an average of around 75 percent.[4]

Why do actual tax rates work out lower than the rates in the official schedule? The reason is partly that there are numerous deductions from gross income before the income tax is computed. These include charitable contributions, taxes paid to state and local governments, and medical expenses above a certain level. Interest on certain types of security, notably state and municipal bonds, is exempt from federal taxation. People

[4] *Statistical Abstract of the United States*, 1961, p. 380.

in the top income brackets have a strong incentive to invest in tax-exempt securities.

There are also ways of reducing one's income for tax purposes a good deal below one's true income. These methods are termed tax *avoidance*, to distinguish them from illegal *evasion* of taxes by simply not reporting income received. One method, widely used in business, is to take part of one's compensation in the form of an expense account rather than in salary payments. Or part of an executive's compensation may be put into a prepaid retirement annuity which is not counted as income until he begins drawing pension payments. Or he may be given the right to purchase company stock at a reduced price (a "stock option"). The higher

TABLE 15–5

Individual Income Tax Returns with Income
by Adjusted Gross Income Classes, 1958
(Number of Returns in Thousands,
Income in Millions of Dollars)

ADJUSTED GROSS INCOME CLASS	No. OF RETURNS (1)	ADJUSTED GROSS INCOME (2)	INCOME TAX AFTER CREDITS (3)	PERCENT OF ALL TAX COLLECTION (4)
Under $1,000	7,010	3,724	38	0.1
$ 1,000–$ 1,999	7,691	11,369	496	1.4
$ 2,000–$ 2,999	7,413	18,537	1,139	3.3
$ 3,000–$ 3,999	7,472	26,150	1,998	5.8
$ 4,000–$ 4,999	7,385	33,191	2,945	8.6
$ 5,000–$ 9,999	17,904	121,384	13,389	39.0
$ 10,000–$ 14,999	2,488	29,214	4,291	12.5
$ 15,000–$ 19,999	588	10,055	1,757	5.1
$ 20,000–$ 49,000	635	18,209	4,270	12.4
$ 50,000–$100,000	92	6,050	2,107	6.1
$100,000–$199,999	18	2,310	981	2.9
$200,000–$499,999	4	1,115	516	1.5
$500,000–$999,999	1	360	175	0.5
$1,000,000 and over	*	499	233	0.8
Total	58,701	282,166	34,336	100.0

* Less than 500.
Source: *Statistical Abstract of the United States*, 1961, p. 379.

the marginal rate of tax, the greater the incentive to tax avoidance. This has become a highly developed art, to the great benefit of the legal and accounting professions.

Although large incomes are charged the highest rates, they do not provide the bulk of tax collections. About 60 percent of personal income tax receipts come from incomes below $10,000, because that is where most of the personal income of the country is concentrated (Table 15–5). People with incomes of $100,000 and over provide only about 5 percent of tax payments. Large incomes are conspicuous, but there aren't many of them; and the amount of taxes which they pay is reduced by the possibilities of avoidance just described. The main reason for levying high marginal rates on large incomes is not that they yield much revenue but rather that they gratify a widespread sentiment against income inequality.

There has been much controversy over the indirect effects of the personal income tax on the supply of labor and capital. On a common-sense basis, one might argue that if the government takes away a sizable percentage of each hour's earnings, people will not work as many hours as they would otherwise. But the income tax cuts in two directions, which tend to offset each other. On one side, it amounts to lowering the real wage rate per hour of effort. An individual dividing his time between work and leisure finds work less rewarding than before. To put the same point in reverse, he finds that leisure has become less expensive. So according to the normal principles of substitution he will choose less work and more leisure.

But the tax also reduces the individual's weekly income. Unless income is of no account to him, he will feel some inclination to work *more* hours to regain his former income and scale of living. This *income* effect works in the opposite direction from the *substitution* effect, and there is no firm basis for predicting which will predominate. The outcome will depend on the shape of individual preferences for income and leisure, the distribution of personal incomes, and the steepness of the tax progression.

It is difficult to investigate this matter statistically. There have been a few studies of independent professional men who can work a longer or shorter week, and can retire at an earlier or later stage of their careers. The results are inconclusive. It typically appears that some members of the group have adjusted to the tax structure by working more, others have decided to work less, and the net effect on labor supply has been small.[5]

More significant may be the effects on the supply of capital. One cannot be sure how far the upper income groups react to heavy taxation by cutting consumption and how far by reducing saving, but the effect on saving must be substantial. Nor is this reduction of private saving offset by an increase in government saving, since the tax revenue is used mainly for current government expenses. There is thus a reduction in saving for the economy as a whole. Whether this should be viewed as good or bad depends on whether one thinks that "undersaving" or "oversaving" is a more serious danger in our type of economy, a problem which will be explored in Part Three.

In addition to an overall reduction in capital supply, there may be an especially sharp reduction in the supply of equity capital for new or

[5] See in particular George Break, "Income Taxes and Incentives to Work: An Empirical Study," *American Economic Review*, September, 1957, pp. 529–49.

risky enterprises. Venture capital on a large scale used to come mainly from wealthy individuals, while the low- and medium-income groups have always tended toward savings accounts, annuities, and fixed-income investments.

The Corporate Income Tax

This is on the surface a remarkably simple tax. The first $25,000 of profits is taxed at a rate of 30 percent, and everything over that at a rate of 52 percent. The object of this gradation is to aid small enterprises which, because they cannot tap the general capital market, must grow mainly through reinvestment of earnings. This degree of aid, however, is probably too small to have much practical effect.

While this tax is simple in principle, it is complicated in practice by the fact that "profit" is such a slippery concept. Determining a company's profit for the year requires the determination of its costs. One thorny problem is the size of depreciation charges on plant and equipment. Suppose a company buys a $100,000 piece of equipment which is expected to have a service life of 20 years. A simple straight-line formula yields annual depreciation of $5,000, which is entered as a cost item. But if the company were allowed to write off the item over a five-year period, as has sometimes been done as a special incentive to companies in defense production, the annual depreciation charge would be $20,000. Cost would be higher, profit lower, and the company would pay less income tax. After the end of the five-year period, the situation is reversed. The company will be paying *more* income tax than if it had spread out the depreciation over a longer period. But meanwhile it has staved off the evil day. And a rapidly expanding company can stay ahead of the game for a long time.

Who pays the corporate income tax? The traditional answer has been the corporation, which means the common stockholders. The reasoning behind this conclusion is simple: under either monopoly or competition, the intelligent business manager will adjust his production and selling price to make maximum profit. It will not pay him to alter this adjustment, even though the government decides to take away half his profit in taxes. Even with a tax, it can never pay to make *less* profit than you were making before.

This line of argument seems broadly correct. In some cases, however, a monopolist or oligopolist may not be charging prices high enough to maximize profits. Possible reasons for this sort of behavior were described in Chapter 7. In such cases imposition of an income tax might cause the company to raise prices closer to the maximum-profit level, thus regaining part of the income lost through the tax. Part of the burden of the tax would be shifted forward to buyers of the product.

One can perhaps conclude that *most* of the corporate income tax is borne by stockholders, but that a minor part is shifted forward to the consuming public. Since stock ownership is concentrated in the higher income brackets, the corporate income tax is a *progressive* tax.

The corporate income tax doubtless reduces the funds available for new investment. Part of the money taken by the tax would otherwise have remained in the enterprise and been reinvested directly. Of the remainder paid out in dividends, some would have been saved and put back into the capital market. This is a particularly serious matter for new enterprises whose main hope of expansion lies in making large profits and plowing them back into the business. When taxes take half of any profit, the growth prospects of the small enterprise are materially reduced.

The corporate income tax reduces the demand for funds as well as the supply. It means that a new investment which is expected to yield a return of 10 percent will actually yield, after taxes, only 5 percent. This makes the venture less attractive and reduces the likelihood of its being undertaken. The demand curve for funds is shifted downward to the left. The volume of investment is reduced and, depending on how drastically supply has been curtailed, the rate of return on capital may also be reduced.

The Excise Tax

The venerable history of this tax is attested by the Scotch ballad, "The de'il's awa' wi' th' exciseman," a sentiment warmly echoed by later generations. It is a tax on the production or sale of a commodity, usually a necessity with inelastic demand which can be counted on to produce a dependable revenue. Salt and matches have been favorite objects of taxation in many countries. Today alcohol and tobacco are usually mainstays of the excise tax system. This is sometimes justified on the moral ground that heavy taxes, which means high prices, will discourage the use of these harmful articles. But people cling to tobacco and alcohol with remarkable tenacity. There is not much discouragement of consumption, but for precisely this reason there is a tax yield which delights the treasury authorities.

During World War II in the United States, the need to increase federal revenue and discourage private consumption led to a great multiplication of excise taxes. Excises were imposed or raised on automobiles, trucks, tires, gasoline, passenger travel, telephone and telegraph bills, theater admissions, night club entertainment, and a wide variety of allegedly "luxury" products, including jewelry, furs, luggage, radio sets, cameras, sporting goods, and musical instruments. This was justified as a temporary way of meeting the war emergency. But temporary taxes have a way of becoming permanent, and most of these excises are still with us. Sellers of these goods chronically protest the taxes as discriminatory, but the Treasury's firm assertion that "we need the money" has thus far been conclusive with Congress.

Federal excise taxes now yield over $10 billion a year. More than four fifths of this comes from five items: alcohol, tobacco, cars and accessories, gasoline, and telephone bills. Many of the other items are little more than nuisance taxes which could be repealed with small loss of revenue.

An excise tax is levied on the supplier of a good or service, but part or all of the tax is typically shifted forward to the buyer. Consider a product produced at constant long-run cost and sold under competitive conditions (Figure 15–3). *DD* is the demand curve and *PS* the long-run

FIGURE 15–3

Excise Taxes in Competitive, Constant-Cost Industry

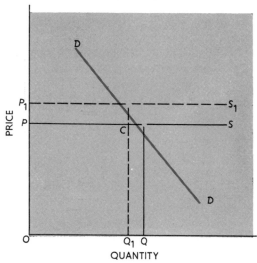

DD is the demand curve and PS the long-run supply curve. Imposing an excise tax of PP_1 raises the price of the product from OP to OP_1, and reduces the quantity produced from OQ to OQ_1.

supply curve. Equilibrium price will be *OP* and output *OQ*. Now an excise tax of PP_1 is placed on each unit produced. This addition to costs raises the supply curve to P_1S_1, and leads to a new equilibrium with price OP_1 and output OQ_1. (The excise tax could be treated also as a deduction from the producers' income, that is, a downward shift of *DD*. The result would be the same.)

These are long-run results and take time to work themselves out. After the dust has settled, however, it turns out that:

1. Output of the product is permanently reduced. The extent of the reduction depends on the elasticity of demand.

2. The price of the product to consumers is raised by the full amount of the tax. The entire tax has been shifted forward. Note that this result depends on the assumption of constant costs. If the supply curve were forward sloping, indicating an increasing cost industry, the price rise would be less than the amount of the tax.

3. The result depends also on the assumption of a competitive industry. If the product were sold by a monopolist, and if he were maximizing profit before the excise was imposed, he could not avoid bearing part of the tax through reduced profits. Consumers would still bear part through higher prices and reduced consumption.

In all cases, then, at least part of the tax is shifted forward, the price of the product is raised, and output is reduced. The main burden of the tax typically falls on the consumer.

The items which provide most of the excise tax revenue are articles of mass consumption. A family with $5,000 a year spends a larger *percentage of its income* on cars and accessories, gasoline, tobacco, alcohol, and telephone service than does a family with $20,000 a year. The low-income family consequently pays a higher percentage of its income in excise taxes than does the high-income family. Excise taxes are *regressive*. They take about 5 percent of the income of the poorest group in the community. This drops to less than 2 percent for those with incomes above $10,000 a year.

The Sales Tax

This is basically a state tax. State expenditures on highways, education, and other items have risen rapidly since 1945 and are still shooting upward. On the revenue side, the states are squeezed between the general property tax, where they must defer to the localities, and the income tax, where they cannot compete too heavily with the federal government. So they have turned to the general sales tax, which promises a large yield with low collection costs. About two thirds of the states now have sales taxes, at rates ranging mostly between 2 and 4 percent. The tax is assessed at the retail level and normally applies to all commodities but not to services. A number of states exempt food, which reduces the tax burden on the poorest families, and a few exempt medical and health supplies.

Retailers are usually required to compute the tax separately from the price of goods sold, and to show it as a separate item on the customer's bill. The intent is that the buyer shall pay the tax, and we can take it that this result is largely achieved. It follows that a general sales tax is regressive. As one goes up the income scale, the percentage of income spent declines and the percentage saved rises. The percentage of family spending which goes for services rather than goods also rises with increasing incomes. Thus the *percentage of income spent on goods only*, which is the basis of the sales tax, must go down with rising income. Calculations made some years ago for the state of Illinois indicated that in the $1,000–2,000 range, 80 percent of family income was spent on items subject to tax. But families with incomes above $10,000 spent only 45 percent of their income on taxable items, hence were taxed only about half as heavily as the poorest groups.

The Property Tax

This is the mainstay of town and city finance, and is well known to every householder. Each May, I receive a bill stating the assessed value of my house and lot, the tax rate for the year, and, by simple multiplication, the amount which I owe the city. It is quite clear who pays this tax. I do. So do my neighbors. So do farmers and landowners in general. The only possibility of significant shifting is in the case of office and commercial buildings, residential apartments, and other buildings constructed for rent. Over the long run people will not put money into building projects unless they yield as much as other types of investment. Property taxes will have to be counted as a cost, along with maintenance and other operating costs, and will be passed on to the tenants in rent charges.

The property tax is moderately regressive, though not so strongly as sales and excise taxes. It takes close to 5 percent of incomes below $2,000, but only 3½ percent of incomes above $10,000 a year. The property tax may be regarded as inequitable since it falls on only one type of asset. And it is an inflexible revenue source because changes in assessments lag well behind price changes.

THE IMPACT OF TAXATION

How do these taxes add up in terms of the total impact of the tax structure? Musgrave's estimates, shown in Table 15–6, rest on detailed

TABLE 15–6

Distribution of Tax Revenue by Income Class, United States, 1954*
(Percent of Adjusted Money Income Paid in Tax)

INCOME CLASS	PERSONAL INCOME TAX	CORPORATE INCOME TAX	EXCISE AND SALES TAX	PROPERTY TAX	ALL TAXES
Under 2,000	3.1	3.9	10.7	4.8	22.8
2,000– 3,000	5.4	4.0	9.6	4.3	23.5
3,000– 4,000	7.3	3.4	8.7	4.1	23.8
4,000– 5,000	8.6	3.3	8.3	4.1	24.7
5,000– 7,500	11.9	3.8	7.8	3.8	27.4
7,500–10,000	14.7	4.3	7.1	3.6	29.9
Over 10,000	15.4	14.7	4.1	3.4	39.5
All incomes	11.1	6.5	7.3	3.8	29.4

* Derived from Tables A–2, A–4, and 2 of Richard A. Musgrave, "The Incidence of the Tax Structure and its Effects on Consumption," in Joint Committee on the Economic Report, *Federal Tax Policy for Economic Growth and Stability;* papers submitted by panelists appearing before the subcommittee on tax policy, November 9, 1955.

assumptions about shifting which are described in the original source. The 1954 data are now some distance in the past, but there have been no major changes in the tax structure which would change the general drift of the conclusions.

The total impact of the U.S. tax structure in this year was mildly progressive as regards the brackets below $10,000 a year, in which the great bulk of the population was concentrated. Families with incomes of less than $2,000 a year paid about 23 percent of their incomes in taxes, while families between $7,500 and $10,000 paid about 30 percent. The progressive effect of the personal and corporate income taxes slightly outweighed the regressive effect of sales, excise, and property taxes.

Above $10,000 a year, income taxes dominate the scene increasingly and give a sharper progressive tilt to tax payments. The average of 40 percent tax payments for all families above $10,000 is not very revealing because it covers such a wide range of incomes. A more detailed breakdown would show progression all the way up the scale, with the highest brackets paying something above 50 percent of the income in taxes.

THE TAX SYSTEM: SOME UNSETTLED ISSUES

Who Should Pay the Taxes?

The previous section provides a factual background for discussion of tax policy. But it is only a background. We cannot conclude that "whatever is, is right." Many people believe that the present tax system has grave defects. Scholars have been seeking correct principles of taxation for centuries, so far without much success. The themes which recur most frequently in the literature are the "benefit principle" and the "principle of ability to pay."

The benefit principle. Taxes are levied to provide public services which benefit the recipients. Is it not reasonable, then, that each person should pay taxes proportionate to the benefits which he receives? On this view, the taxpayer is "buying" public services with his tax payments, much as he buys goods and services in private markets.

This principle is useful where a public service benefits a clearly defined segment of the population and where there is some basis for assessing the amount of the benefit. People who use the highways benefit from highway construction, and their consumption of gasoline is a rough measure of how much they drive. Hence it makes sense to tax gasoline and earmark the proceeds for highway construction. This is carried even further in state turnpike systems where motorists are charged a toll proportionate to the number of miles driven.

Another illustration is multiple-purpose river development. Irrigation water has a cash value, and farmers can be charged for the water received. Flood control benefits cities and farmland along the river, and this provides a basis for assessing part of the project cost against state and local governments. Electric power generated by such projects can be priced and sold on a commercial basis.

But what about general government services, of which national defense is the classic example? Who benefits from defense expenditure, and in what measure? One approach starts from the proposition that all citizens are free and equal. Protecting Mr. A against foreign invasion is worth precisely as much as protecting Messrs. B, C, D, and the rest. On this reasoning, each individual should contribute the same absolute amount. Another approach, however, stresses the fact that it is mainly the *property* of

Messrs. A, B, C, and D which is being protected. Or perhaps it is their accustomed way of life, which is linked with income level. On this basis, it
would be legitimate to charge each household according to its property
holdings or current income. There is no objective basis for choosing
among these or other possible alternatives. Thus the benefit principle
trails off into a maze of philosophical uncertainties.

The principle of ability to pay. Another ancient maxim is that
people should contribute to the public treasury "according as they are
able." This referred originally to inherent personal faculties. The mighty
warrior or the clever merchant could contribute more than the village
idiot. In modern times, it has generally been interpreted in terms of
wealth or income. The nineteenth century British economists used the
doctrine of decreasing marginal utility to justify progressive taxation, on
the ground that a dollar taken in taxation means less loss of satisfaction to
the rich than to the poor. More recently, however, this application of marginal utility has become suspect for the reasons outlined in Chapter 14.
One can still have a personal preference for this line of reasoning, but
this is different from claiming scientific validity for it.

The search for indisputable principles of taxation thus leads into a
dead end. Decisions about tax levies, like those about public expenditure,
emerge from a political process which is our only guide to the preferences
of the electorate. Differing schools of thought may try to sway citizens
and legislators. But in a democratic community all elements must accept
the results of the political process—at least until the next election.

Neutrality in Taxation

It is generally accepted as desirable that a tax system should interfere
as little as possible with individual choice in the private sector of the
economy. Public expenditure necessarily means a diversion of resources
from private consumption and investment. The private economy must
"move over" to make room for the public economy. In doing this, however, there should be minimum distortion of the choices which people
are still free to make between private goods and services, between saving
and consumption, between work and leisure, and so on. The ideal tax system should be *neutral* as regards these choices.

The concept of tax neutrality has been used particularly as an argument against excise taxation. Consider a simple community in which consumers have a choice between product A and product B, at market prices
determined in the usual way. The government now finds that it needs
to raise a million dollars more in taxes. One way to do this is to put an excise tax on A. This raises the price of A and tilts the balance of consumer choice against it. People find themselves consuming less of A and
more of B than they preferred in the first instance. It is usually argued
that consumer satisfaction would be increased if the government, instead
of taxing A, simply deducted a million dollars from people's incomes and

left them free to choose between A and B at the old prices. Precise demonstration of this point requires an indifference diagram and the usual simplifying assumptions. But even on a commonsense basis, it seems reasonable that consumers will be worse off if government goes around the economy attaching arbitrary penalties to consumption of particular products. Unless there is some social reason why people *should* be discouraged from using a particular product, one cannot justify the discrimination involved in excise taxes.

The difficulty is that income taxes, sales taxes, and most other general taxes involve their own type of distortion. An income tax influences the choice between work and leisure, and may cause people to do either less or more work than they "really prefer." It also influences choice among occupations by reducing the relative income (after taxes) of the higher-paid jobs. A general sales tax amounts to a tax on spending and tilts the balance in favor of saving as against consumption. Most actual sales taxes apply to goods only, and thus tilt the balance of consumer choice against goods in favor of services. The only truly neutral tax is a poll tax—so much per head, regardless of income or anything else. But this is a very regressive tax which has little to commend it on other grounds.

Even if full neutrality is unfeasible, one can perhaps think in terms of degrees of neutrality. An income tax is more nearly neutral than excises on specific commodities. A general tax on spending is more neutral than a sales tax limited to certain types of good, and so on. The broader the base of the tax, and the fewer the possibilities of substitution which it leaves uncovered, the more nearly does it meet the criterion of neutrality.

Relations among Levels of Government

The size of the United States, and the provision of public services by several layers of government, raises complicated fiscal problems. There is the obvious problem of achieving a reasonable division between the tax sources tapped, and the functions performed, by different levels of government. There is also a more subtle problem of maintaining a balance between resources and responsibilities at each level over the long run.

We have seen that the state and local governments are the main providers of peacetime public services. The states and localities have borne the brunt of the tremendous increase in demand for education, highways, and municipal facilities over the past 20 years; and these demands show no sign of slackening in the years ahead.

But the main sources of state and local revenue are inelastic. (We define as *inelastic* a tax whose yield rises less than proportionately to increase in national income. Conversely, a tax whose yield rises more than proportionately to growth of national income may be termed *elastic*.) The sales tax, bulwark of state finances, is inelastic. Why? Because as national income rises, the percentage devoted to purchase of goods declines, while the percentage spent on services rises. The property tax, on which town and city governments so largely depend, is also inelastic. But the personal income tax is elastic, because as incomes rise more and more people are pushed up into higher brackets where they are taxed at higher rates. Lucky federal government! How can it lose over the long run?

The lower levels of government are trapped between rapidly rising needs and restricted tax sources. Eckstein has estimated that, on the basis of tax levels and expenditure trends in the late fifties, the state and local governments will by 1968 have a combined deficit of about $3.5 billion.[6] But the federal government, on the basis of "medium" assumptions about federal expenditure, will have a budget surplus by 1968 of $7.5 billion. The federal government thus seems in danger of having too much money, while other levels of government have too little.[7]

What might be done to correct this imbalance? There are several possibilities: (1) The federal government might take over functions now being performed by the states and localities, thus lightening their expenditures and increasing its own. (2) Without any change in the present division of functions, the federal government might share more heavily in the *cost* of certain functions through larger grants to the states. The federal government has already assumed a larger share of highway expenditures, and many are urging larger federal contributions to school construction costs and other educational expenditures. (3) Federal tax rates might be lowered and the space left in family budgets might be filled at least partially by increases in state and local taxation. This could keep both groups of budgets in balance without any change in the present division of expenditures.

Which of these courses should be chosen raises questions of political philosophy. Advocates of local autonomy are not going to agree with advocates of centralized federal responsibility. The *economic* stakes involved in the choice are of two kinds. First, what degree of progression do we want in the total tax structure of the country? If one favors a high degree of progression, this leads to a preference for the personal income tax, which in turn leads to a preference for federal spending. People of this mind should logically favor alternatives (1) or (2). If one wants less progression than at present, this indicates heavier reliance on sales, excise, and other regressive taxes, which means a preference for state and local taxation. This leads logically to a preference for alternative (3).

Second, how far should the federal budget be used to equalize the level of public services in different parts of the country? Equalization of service is an accepted principle within each state. State highways do not suddenly deteriorate when they pass through a low-income area, then pick up again when they come to a prosperous district. State grants to the lo-

---

[6] Otto Eckstein, *Trends in Public Expenditures in the Next Decade* (New York: Committee on Economic Development, 1959), p. 9.

[7] This was written before one could foresee how far the Kennedy administration's 1963 push for tax reduction would be successful.

calities for education help to reduce disparities of educational opportunity.

But what about differences among the states? There are wide differences in per capita income and taxable capacity. The state with highest per capita income in 1959 (Delaware, $2,946) was almost three times as well off as the lowest state (Mississippi, $1,162). The poorer states tax their citizens just as heavily *relative to their incomes* as do the richer states. Indeed, the percentage of personal income collected in state and local taxes is somewhat higher in the three groups of Southern states than in the industrial Northeast. But because these high rates are applied to a small income base, the tax yield is disappointing.

Left to their own devices, the poorer states would have to get along with lower levels of roads, education, health, and other public services. The most direct way of reducing these disparities is through cash grants to the poorer states from the federal budget. Federal revenues come in disproportionate measure from the wealthier states. The Middle Atlantic and East North Central regions had 45 percent of U.S. personal income in 1957, but contributed almost 58 percent of federal tax revenues. The reason is the predominance of income taxation in the federal system. The use of cash grants-in-aid thus means that federal revenues drawn in good measure from the wealthier states are being used to support public services in the poorer states. There is a *geographical* transfer of income as well as a transfer from higher to lower income brackets.

Those who approve this transfer will exclaim, "Why of course! This is a basic advantage of our federal union. We are Americans first and citizens of Alabama second. Any American, wherever he lives, is entitled to a decent basic level of public service. If New York and Connecticut have to be milked to make this possible, so be it." But colorful rhetoric could also be employed on the other side. Having raised the issue, we leave it to the reader's own reflection.

SUMMARY

1. Government budgets perform an *allocation* function, a *distribution* function, and a *stabilization* function. This chapter is concerned mainly with the allocation function.

2. Certain services are provided by government because they cannot be sold at a price, or because market pricing would be administratively difficult, or because market pricing would not lead to a socially desirable allocation of resources.

3. There is usually no objective basis for judging *how much* of a particular public service should be provided. This decision is made through the political process.

4. Production of government services has tripled in relative importance since 1900, and now forms about one fifth of national output. Federal expenditures are primarily for defense. State and local expenditures are mainly for education, streets and highways, and police, fire, and other protective services.

5. The main reasons for the relative increase in government services are the deterioration of international relations, urbanization of the population,

rising real incomes, rising educational standards, and the highway demands created by the automobile.

6. A *progressive* tax is one which takes an increasing proportion of income as one goes up the income scale. A *regressive* tax is one which takes a decreasing proportion of the higher incomes.

7. The federal government relies mainly on the personal and corporate income taxes, which are progressive. States rely mainly on sales taxes and local governments on property taxes, which are regressive. The overall impact of the U.S. tax system is mildly progressive in the brackets below $10,000, more steeply progressive above that level.

8. Some tax authorities have argued that taxes should be assessed on the basis of benefits received, while others have emphasized ability to pay. Economics provides no clear basis for choice between these principles.

9. It is generally accepted that a good tax should be *neutral*, that is, should not interfere with individual choice in the private sector of the economy. But since none of the leading types of tax is neutral, one is faced in practice with a choice of evils.

10. Federal revenues tend to rise more rapidly than national income over the course of time, while state and local revenues tend to rise less rapidly. This squeeze on state and local finances might be met by (1) the federal government taking over more functions, or (2) the federal government making larger cash grants to the states, or (3) reducing federal tax rates and raising state and local tax rates.

11. The choice among these approaches is a political choice, depending partly on how one feels about income redistribution between income brackets and between geographical regions. The greater the reliance on the federal budget, the more of both kinds of redistribution will occur.

The International Economy

> Our interest will be to throw open the doors of commerce, and to knock off its shackles, giving perfect freedom to all persons for the vent of whatever they may choose to bring into our ports, and asking the same in theirs.
>
> THOMAS JEFFERSON
>
> Free trade, one of the greatest blessings which a government can confer on a people, is in almost every country unpopular.
>
> THOMAS BABINGTON MACAULAY

EVEN THOSE WHO BELIEVE in free competition within a country often question the extension of this principle to international trade. Competition among American business concerns may be all right, but let's not admit foreigners to the game. Let's "buy American" and "keep American dollars at home." There is something about foreign trade which seems mysterious and different.

One difference is that prices of foreign goods are quoted in foreign currency. In the Galeries Lafayette in Paris I see a bottle of perfume priced at 50 francs. What will this cost me in dollars? I cannot tell until I know the *rate of exchange* between francs and dollars. An exchange rate is a special kind of price, the price of one national currency in terms of another. Like any other price, it is influenced by demand and supply pressures operating in a market; and it can be fixed above or below the free market equilibrium by government controls. This requires some explanation before we go on to the principles underlying international trade.

EXCHANGE MARKETS AND THE EXCHANGE RATE

The Mechanism of International Payments

How do buyers of goods in one country manage to pay the sellers of goods in other countries? How do dollars get converted into pounds, lira, francs, and other currencies?

Consider an American importer who buys bicycles from a British exporter. The importer sells these to customers in the United States and receives dollars in return. But the British exporter, who bought the bicycles from a British manufacturer, has to pay for them in pounds. How is the importer, who has dollars, going to pay the exporter, who needs pounds?

The answer is that there are other people in these countries who are in the opposite situation. There are importers in Britain who have pounds, which they need to change into dollars to pay exporters in the United States. Suppose a British importer has bought raw cotton from an American exporter, and suppose that the value of the cotton happens to equal that of the bicycles. Then the four parties could get together and work out the clearing arrangement shown in Figure 16–1.[1] The American ex-

FIGURE 16–1

Direct Clearing of International Payments

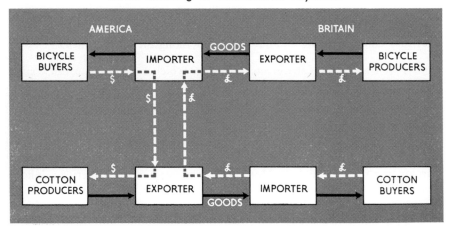

porter can receive pounds from his British customer, trade these for dollars to the American importer, who then uses them to pay off the British exporter. (Or the clearing could be done in Britain with dollars crossing the ocean instead of pounds.) Now everyone has been paid off, and everyone is happy. American exports have paid for American imports, al-

---

[1] Figures 16–1 and 16–2 are adapted from similar diagrams in T. C. Schelling, *International Economics* (Boston: Allyn and Bacon, Inc., 1958), pp. 5–7.

most as though the cotton had been traded off against the bicycles in a single deal.

It would be awkward if each time an American importer needed a thousand pounds he had to hunt up an exporter who had exactly a thousand pounds. Foreign transactions occur at different times and in varying amounts. The logical solution is to set up a clearing house which will undertake to buy or sell dollars or pounds in any amount to all comers. The nature of such a clearing house is shown in Figure 16–2. As in the previous

FIGURE 16–2

A Clearing House for International Payments

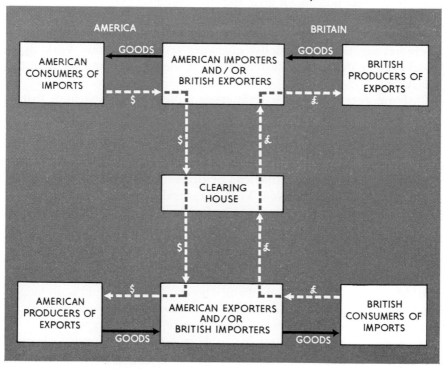

diagram, solid lines indicate movements of goods, broken lines show movements of money. The clearing house trades pounds for dollars at the top of the diagram, and dollars for pounds at the bottom. As long as the two flows remain in balance, they cancel out and the system works smoothly. Actually, there will be difference in the flows from day to day, and the clearing house needs some pounds and dollars of its own to tide over short periods of imbalance.

Note that it does not matter whether it is the American importer or his colleague the British exporter who buys pounds in exchange for dollars. They share a common interest. They are on the *same side* of the foreign exchange market. The American importer and the American exporter, on the other hand, are on *opposite* sides of the market, one selling dollars and the other buying them. The requirement for balance in the market is that American exports and imports should be equal in value, in which case they cancel out or "pay for each other."

In practice, there is no single clearing house for foreign exchange. The main dealers in foreign exchange are banks, chiefly banks in leading financial centers such as New York and London. The large New York banks keep checking accounts (in pounds) at the principal London banks. (The London banks have similar dollar accounts in New York, but it will be clearest to look at the process from the American end.) When a New York bank "sells pounds," it gives the customer a claim of so many pounds on its London checking account, taking his dollars in return. When it "buys pounds," these are added to its balance in London, and it pays off by increasing the seller's dollar checking account in New York. It is checks rather than actual currency which shuttle back and forth across the Atlantic.

How does this work out? Suppose a New York bank finds that it has more customers wanting to buy pounds than to sell them. As a result, the bank's checking account in London will decline. Up to a point, the bank may simply let this happen. But if the account becomes dangerously low, the bank will have to replenish it by buying pounds somewhere. It may buy from another American or British bank. Or it may go to the Federal Reserve Bank of New York, a central bank or "bankers' bank," where it has a checking account. The Federal Reserve has an account at the British central bank, the Bank of England. It can sell the New York bank pounds from this account, deducting the dollar cost from the bank's account with it. If the Federal Reserve's own account at the Bank of England falls too low, it can replenish it by shipping gold to London and getting credit in pounds on the Bank's books. Although gold is no longer used as currency by private parties, it remains the ultimate method of settling differences between a country's receipts and payments.

The foreign exchange market, in short, is an interconnected network of private and central banks, which have checking accounts with each other and can shift funds back and forth as needed. The mechanism is basically the same as that through which checks are cleared between different regions of the United States.

Thus far we have considered only exchange dealings between Britain and the United States. But the clearing house principle which works for two countries can be extended to cover a larger group of trading nations. In this case it is no longer necessary for United States imports from a particular country to be balanced by exports *to the same country*. It is sufficient if U.S. exports to *all countries* equal its imports from all countries. If this is true for each country in the group, the system is in balance and the clearing house mechanism will work. An extreme case is shown

TABLE 16–1

A Simple Export-Import System

	IMPORTS			
	A	B	C	TOTAL IMPORTS
A		100		100
B			100	100
C	100			100
Total Exports	100	100	100	300

EXPORTS (row label beside the A, B, C rows)

in Table 16–1. Country A exports only to B, B only to C, and C only to A. No country is in balance with any other single country, but each is in overall balance, with its exports equal to its imports. This recalls the famous "triangular trade" of the eighteenth century, in which the British West Indies shipped sugar to New England, which shipped rum to Britain, which shipped cloth to the West Indies.

The Balance of Payments

Now what determines how many pounds I can get for an American dollar? An exchange rate is a price, and so it is influenced by supply and demand. An import of goods to the United States, which is sold in the United States for dollars, creates a supply of dollars available for conversion into foreign currency. Conversely, an export from the United States creates a *demand* for dollars, since the foreign buyer must get dollars to pay for the goods. Thus an increase in U.S. exports raises the demand for dollars, while an increase in U.S. imports raises the supply. In a free exchange market, the first development would raise the price of dollars in terms of other currencies, while the second would lower it. The principles are the same as those applying in commodity markets.

Exports and imports are only one type of international dealing. Other transactions also affect the demand for and supply of dollars. Any transaction which obligates someone in the United States (an individual, business concern, or government agency) to make payment to someone abroad creates a *supply* of dollars. Conversely, anything which obligates foreigners to make payment to Americans creates a *demand* for dollars.

The main kinds of transaction which create a *supply* of dollars are:

1. *U.S. imports of merchandise.*

2. *U.S. imports of services.* The main items under this heading are U.S. tourist expenditures abroad and payments to foreign ship lines for shipping services.

3. *U.S. military expenditures abroad.* These include expenditures by U.S. military personnel stationed abroad, purchases by our armed

forces for their own use, and "offshore procurement" (purchase of equipment abroad for delivery to other countries under military assistance programs).

4. *Interest and dividend payments* to foreign owners of U.S. securities.

5. *Unilateral transfers and gifts* by Americans to other countries. It has long been customary for immigrants to the United States to send back money to relatives and others in their home countries. But today the largest item under this heading is U.S. government grants to other countries under our international aid programs.

6. *Long-term loans and investments* by Americans to other countries. This includes U.S. government loans to other countries. On the private side, it includes purchase of plants and facilities abroad by U.S. businesses, and purchase of foreign securities by Americans. These transactions are sometimes summed up as *capital exports*. (It seems odd at first that a capital export has the same effect on the foreign exchange market as a merchandise import. One way to remember this is to realize that an *export* of capital funds is an *import* of securities or titles of ownership, for which we are obliged to pay foreigners in dollars.)

7. *Net short-term investment or lending* abroad by Americans. This covers any increase in U.S. holdings of promissory notes or other short-term assets, including an increase in our holdings of bank balances in foreign countries. These are capital exports, though they are subject to collection or transfer on short notice.

8. *Inflow of monetary gold.* The foreign country shipping the gold receives a corresponding dollar credit on the books of the Federal Reserve Bank of New York. Thus the supply of dollars is increased.

If any of these transactions seems mysterious or difficult, look at it carefully. You will find that it meets the original test of obligating someone in the United States to pay dollars to someone abroad.

Each of these items has its counterpart on the other side of the balance sheet. The *demand* for dollars is increased by United States exports of goods or services, by foreign long-term investments in the United States, and by any other transactions which obligate foreigners to make payment to us.

Putting the two sides of the picture together, we get a statement known as the *balance of payments*. The U.S. balance of payments for 1960 is summarized in Table 16–2. Note that in this year we shipped abroad almost $5 billion more goods than we imported and also cleared a couple of billion dollars on other current items. How did other countries get the $7 billions necessary to close this gap? The answer must be that we were providing dollars to the rest of the world on a large scale. And so we were. We spent about $3 billion abroad for military purposes. We gave away almost $2 billion in economic assistance. Government and private long-term loans abroad totaled nearly $3 billion. In fact, we did such a

TABLE 16-2

Balance of Payments of the United States, 1960*
(Millions of Dollars)

Item	U.S. Receipts (Demand for Dollars)	U.S. Payments (Supply of Dollars)	Net Balance
Merchandise shipments	19,409	14,722	4,687
Tourist travel	968	1,744	−776
Transportation	1,816	1,942	−126
Military expenditures	335	3,048	−2,713
Interest and dividends	3,205	929	2,276
Other current items	1,567	942	625
Unilateral transfers:			
Government grants		1,641	−1,641
Private remittances and			
pensions		848	−848
Long-term loans and investments:			
Government		582	−582
Private	200	2,544	−2,344
Net errors and omissions		648	−648
Short-term loans and credits:			
Government	2,227	527	388
Private		1,312	
Gold inflow or outflow	1,702		1,702
Total	31,429	31,429	0

* *Source:* Economic Report of the President, January, 1962, p. 295.

good job of providing dollars that we came out about $2 billion *behind* on the year's operations. The deficit was closed by shipping almost $2 billion of gold abroad, and by some increase in our short-term debt to other countries.

A striking feature of the balance of payments is that it always balances. The two columns add up to the same amount and the net balances total to zero. Every item above the dotted line in the payments column may be regarded as a purchase—of goods, services, or securities. These purchases must be paid for in one way or another. They are paid for largely by the reverse flow of goods, services, and securities above the line in the receipts column. If receipts are insufficient to cover payments, the United States must either have run up bills in other countries or paid off in gold. The items below the dotted line, then, are *balancing items.* When they are included the circle is closed and the table must balance.

The fact that a bookkeeping statement balances does not mean that the balance shown is satisfactory. A company's yearly profit and loss statement always balances, but the balancing item may be a large loss. Similarly, a payments statement such as Table 16–2 may reveal a "balance of payments problem." For example, a country importing much more than it exports must ask itself how long it can continue to make up the difference by borrowing. When borrowing capacity has been exhausted, creditors will have to be paid off in gold. Continued drain of gold from a country is a sign that remedial measures are in order. What form these measures take will depend on how the foreign exchange market is organized.

Exchange Rates: The Free Market

Having examined the factors determining supply and demand for foreign exchange, we now ask how these forces influence the price of one currency in terms of another. This price can be quoted in either of two ways. We can say that the price of a pound (in dollars) is $2.80, or that the price of a dollar (in pounds) is £.357. The two come to the same thing. It will be least confusing to Americans to use the first method, and to ask what determines the price of a pound in terms of dollars.

In a free exchange market, the answer would depend on supply and demand curves of the usual sort (Figure 16–3). But we must pause to ask what these curves mean and why we are justified in giving them this shape. Why will we try to get more pounds if the dollar price of pounds is lower? The answer lies in the fact that a reduction in the price of pounds reduces the dollar price of everything which Britain has to sell. A bicycle selling in Britain for £20 will cost me $100 if the price of pounds is $5. But if the price of pounds falls to $3 the bicycle costs me only $60, and if pounds fell to $1 the bicycle would be a very attractive buy at $20.

Each cut in the price of pounds, then, makes British goods cheaper to Americans and stimulates British exports to the United States. This increases the demand for pounds to pay for these exports. The same is true for other transactions in the balance of payments table. Cheaper pounds will encourage American tourists to travel in Britain and to do more shopping there. It will stimulate the use of British shipping for ocean transport. Thus the demand for pounds will increase right down the line.

The supply of pounds behaves in the opposite way, and for the same reason. A drop in the dollar price of the pound makes American goods *more expensive* to Britishers. If the pound is worth $5, a $3,000 American car costs £600 in Britain. If the pound falls to $2, the same car costs £1,500, and far fewer will be bought. A drop in the price of the pound, then, tends to reduce British imports from the United States and thus to reduce the supply of pounds. Thus the pound supply curve, *SS*, will normally slope upward to the right.

If the demand and supply situation were as shown in Figure 16–3, the price of pounds would settle at $2.80, and £35 million per month would be bought and sold at this rate. Similar diagrams could be constructed for other currencies, and we could discover the dollar price of French francs, German marks, Italian lira, Norwegian kroner, and so on. All these rates

FIGURE 16-3

Demand and Supply for Pounds

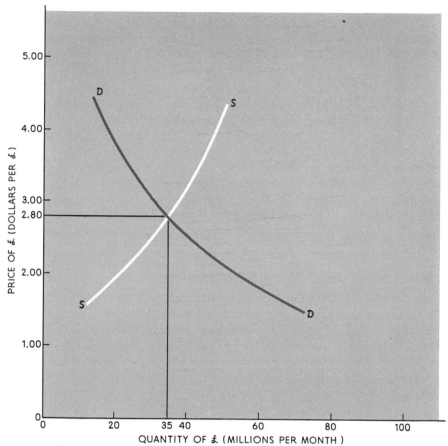

must be mutually consistent. If a pound is worth $2.80, and if a dollar is worth 5 francs, then a pound will have to be worth about 2.80 x 5 = 14 francs. (Suppose instead that the pound was worth only 10 francs. Figure out how you could make a lot of money by exchanging francs into pounds, pounds into dollars, and dollars back into francs.) If there is any discrepancy in these *cross rates* foreign exchange dealers will hasten to take advantage of it, and this will quickly bring rates back into line.

Any shift in supply or demand conditions alters the market equilibrium. Suppose U.S. imports from Britain begin to rise, with no increase in our exports or other offsetting items. This shifts the pound demand curve in Figure 16-3 to the right, and the price of the pound will rise. But this rise in the price of the pound, as we have seen, tends to discourage imports and all other items in the payments column of Table 16-2, while it stimulates exports and other items in the receipts column. A freely fluctuating exchange rate thus helps to keep total receipts and payments in balance.

Complete freedom of exchange rates, however, has practical disadvantages. It increases the uncertainty involved in international transaction. A British importer who places an order for delivery of American cars three months from now cannot be sure how he will come out on the deal, since he cannot tell how many pounds it may cost him to cover the dollar price. The longer the period for which future commitments are made, the greater is the risk of unforeseen shifts in exchange rates. Fluctuations in prices on a free exchange market may also be exaggerated by speculative activity. If the dollar price of pounds begins to fall, this may be taken as a sign that it will fall further, and that one can make money by selling pounds now and buying them back later. If enough people do this, the price *will* fall further and will continue to fall as long as dealers continue in this state of mind. Thus the price fluctuations which occur in any free market may be intensified and this may cause hardship to those who need foreign exchange at a particular time to meet business commitments.[2]

Exchange Rates: The Stabilized Market

For these reasons most governments undertake to stabilize the value of their currencies in terms of foreign currencies—not necessarily forever, but at least for some years at a time. They do this just as the United States government stabilizes the price of wheat, by a standing offer to buy or sell any quantity of foreign exchange at the pegged price. The British government, for example, undertakes to hold the dollar price of pounds within a narrow range in the vicinity of $2.80. If the price is tending to rise above this range, the government through the Bank of England comes into the market and sells pounds in whatever amount is required to hold the price down. Conversely, if the price of pounds is sagging the government intervenes to buy pounds (provide dollars) in any necessary amount.

It is easy enough to see how this works on the upside. Since governments can manufacture their own currency at will, there is no difficulty about providing as many pounds as necessary to hold the price *down*. But what about the reverse situation, where the government must provide dollars to hold the pound price *up?* Where do the dollars come from, and how long can the process continue? There are several possibilities. The British government normally holds substantial bank balances and other short-term assets in New York, and it can draw on these *dollar re-*

---

[2] This is not to say that speculative activity need always have this effect. Speculation may be either stabilizing or destabilizing, depending on circumstances too technical to be detailed here. Proponents of free exchange markets argue that the effects will normally be in a stabilizing direction, but the possibility that they might be destabilizing cannot be ruled out.

serves. It could conceivably borrow additional sums in New York. It could borrow from the International Monetary Fund, which owns large amounts of the main national currencies and can lend these up to specified limits. Finally, it could ship gold to New York and get dollar credits at the Federal Reserve.

But these steps are palliatives, not remedies. If the pound continues weak, this indicates a continued imbalance between British receipts and British payments, and corrective measures must be taken. These may include restrictions on imports, restrictions on travel and other expenditures by Britishers, efforts to stimulate exports, increases in British interest rates which may lead foreign investors to shift funds to London, and various other things. Stabilizing the exchanges by borrowing or using up reserves simply provides a breathing space during which such measures can be worked out and begin to produce their effects. If the proper measures are not taken, or if they do not work, the government will eventually come to the end of its reserves and will face the more drastic step of devaluing its currency.

Devaluation is a lowering of the stabilized price which the government undertakes to maintain. Britain did this in 1949, when the dollar price of the pound was reduced from about $4.00 to $2.80. (The opposite step of *raising* the value of a nation's currency is also possible but is rare in practice.) A sufficient devaluation will correct a balance of payments problem through the stimulus which it gives to exports and other receipts items, and the curb which it puts on payments items. But since it is a drastic step, and since there is danger of its becoming habitual, responsible governments try to do it as rarely as possible. When devaluation is inevitable, they try to do it at one blow and to set a new rate which can be maintained for quite a few years to come. Almost all European countries joined Britain in reducing the dollar values of their currencies in 1949; there have been few changes since that time. But some of the Latin American countries have devaluations every few years.

A stabilized exchange market is thus not too different from a free exchange market. It enables a government to prevent moderate fluctuations on either side of what the long-term equilibrium would be in a free market. But it does not permit the government permanently to maintain a stabilized rate much higher than the market would establish. If Figure 16–3 represents the normal supply-demand situations for pounds during the 1950's, with a market equilibrium in the neighborhood of $2.80, then government can offset moderate shifts of the SS and DD curves over short periods. But it would not have been feasible for the British government to maintain a stabilized price of, say, $4.00 for the pound. At this price there would have been a consistent excess supply of pounds (excess demand for dollars), the government would have had to provide dollars year in and year out, its dollar and gold reserves would have been exhausted, and it would have had to devalue—which is what it actually did.

Exchange Rates: Exchange Control

A country can maintain the price of its currency permanently above the free market price, however, by direct rationing of foreign exchange. Remember the explanation in Chapter 5 of how government can set the price of a commodity below the market equilibrium provided it is willing to ration the commodity. Setting the price of a country's currency *above* the market equilibrium means setting the price of foreign currencies *below* the equilibrium level. Foreign currencies thus become "scarce" and must be rationed.

Suppose the free market rate for Brazilian cruzeiro is 1,000 cruzeiros to the dollar. The Brazilian government, however, decides to peg the cruzeiro at 500 to the dollar). This is an overvaluation of the cruzeiro, an undervaluation of the dollar. What will happen? The overvaluation of the cruzeiro acts as a stimulus to imports and a penalty on exports. There will be serious imbalance in the balance of payments—perhaps $20 million per month available from export sales, but $40 million demanded by eager importers. Pretty soon dollars will be changing hands under the table at rates above the official price.

But the government can prevent this as follows: All exporters can be required to turn over the dollar exchange they receive to a government agency in return for cruzeiros at the legal rate. The government then resells these dollars to importers for cruzeiros at the same rate. Since importers want $40 million a month and there are only $20 million a month available, a basis must be found for rationing dollars among the surplus of applicants. This involves a judgment of national needs. A country which is bent on industrialization, for example, may give priority to imports of machinery and raw materials, while discriminating against consumer goods and particularly against luxury products.

Maintenance of artificial currency values through exchange control is thus a feasible procedure. Its desirability is another matter. It entrusts great discretion to administrative officials, slows down the handling of foreign exchange, increases the uncertainty of export and import dealings, and provides ample opportunity for favoritism and abuse. It also interferes with freedom of international trade. For these reasons the International Monetary Fund and other international economic bodies have discouraged its use. But countries committed to some measure of economic planning, and particularly countries with large development programs, insist that it is a desirable and necessary instrument for their purposes.

THE BASIS FOR INTERNATIONAL TRADE

Trade in One Commodity

In international trade, just as in national trade, goods tend to be bought where they are cheap and sold where they are expensive. If the price of a commodity in two locations differs by more than the cost of shipment, and if there are no other barriers to trade, the commodity will be bought in the cheaper market and shipped to the other.

The principle may be illustrated for one commodity by Figure 16–4. The supply and demand curves for aluminum in the United States are shown at the left-hand side of the diagram, while the corresponding curves for Britain are shown on the right-hand side. The vertical scales

FIGURE 16–4

International Trade in One Commodity

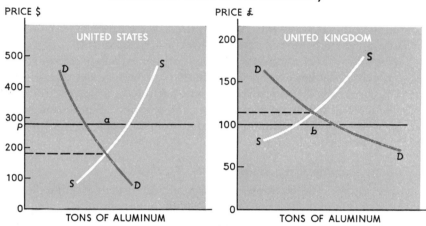

In the absence of trade, the market price is much lower in the United States than in the United Kingdom. This makes it profitable to export aluminum from the United States to the United Kingdom. With free trade, an equilibrium will be reached in which price is the same in the two countries, and exports (a) from the United States equal imports (b) to the United Kingdom.

are drawn on the assumption that the exchange rate is £1 = $2.80. On this basis, the dollar and pound scales are identical, and we can work back and forth across the diagram at will.

The price which would prevail in each country in the absence of trade is shown by the dotted lines. The price is much lower in the United States—under $200 a ton, compared with more than $300 a ton in Britain. This makes it profitable to export aluminum to Britain to take advantage of the price spread. (Shipping will cost something, but we ignore this since it makes little difference to the argument.) The export of aluminum reduces the supply available in the United States, thus raising the American price, and adds to the supply in Britain, which lowers the British price. If we ignore transport costs, this process will go on until the price of aluminum is equal in both countries at OP, shown by the solid lines in the diagram. Why OP rather than some other price? Because at this price the quantity available for export from the United States, shown by the distance a, just equals the quantity which the British are willing to import, shown by b. At any higher price, potential exports would exceed imports, while at a lower price exports would fall short of desired imports. Only at

OP does the combined demand of the two countries precisely equal their combined production. The equilibrium price, therefore, must be *OP*.

Trade in this case has the following effects: (1) production of aluminum is expanded in the cheaper location (United States), and reduced in the more expensive location (United Kingdom). (2) Prices rise in the United States and fall in the United Kingdom, coming to equality at a new intermediate level. (3) Aluminum is exported from United States to United Kingdom.

Note that price has risen a good deal more in the United States than it has fallen in the United Kingdom. This is because we have shown the U.S. demand and supply curves rising a good deal more steeply than those in the United Kingdom. If the situation were reversed, it would be the British who would undergo the main price adjustment.

Note also that the argument depends on the exchange rate of £1 = $2.80, which we suppose has been established in the way described in the previous section. A different exchange rate would alter the vertical scales and produce a different flow of imports and exports. (Figure out an exchange rate at which aluminum would move from Britain to the United States rather than vice versa.)

Many Commodities: What Will Be Traded?

The actual trade situation is more complicated than this. Trade cannot move only in one direction, as in our aluminum case. Many commodi-

TABLE 16–3

Comparative Prices, United States and United Kingdom

Commodity	U.S. Price (Dollars)	U.K. Price (Pounds)	Price Ratio (Dollars/ Pounds)
Radio tubes (dozen)	1	1	1
Wheat (bushel)	2.50	1	2.5
Coal (ton)	30	10	3
Wool cloth (100 yards)	150	30	5
Shoes (dozen pairs)	280	40	7
Bicycles (each)	90	10	9

ties are produced in each country and are available to be traded. What determines which products a country will export and which it will import? The broad answer is comparative cheapness. A country exports goods which are comparatively cheap at home compared with prices abroad, and imports goods which are comparatively cheap in other countries.

The principle of comparative cheapness can be illustrated by the hypothetical figures in Table 16–3. The table shows for each product the U.S. price in dollars, the British price in pounds, and the ratio of the dollar price to the pound price. Note that we cannot say whether any product is actually cheaper in the United States or in Britain. This depends on the rate of exchange, which we do not yet know. But even without this we can say something about *comparative* cheapness. Looking at the right-hand column, we see that the ratio of the dollar price to the pound price varies greatly. Items toward the top of the table are comparatively cheap in the United States. Items toward the bottom are comparatively expensive in the United States, and comparatively cheap in Britain. We get the same result by looking down each of the first two columns. In the United States a bicycle is worth 90 times as much as a dozen radio tubes, while in Britain it is worth only 10 times as much. Again, we reach the conclusion that bicycles must be comparatively cheaper in Britain.

Given these relative prices, which we suppose are based on production costs, the movement of trade depends on the rate of exchange. Suppose the rate were £1 = $10. Then everything would be absolutely cheaper in the United States, and all six items would be exported to Britain. But this could not continue. There would be a great supply of pounds and no demand, and the price of pounds would fall. Conversely, suppose the rate were £1 = $0.50. This would make everything cheaper in Britain, trade would move solely from Britain to the United States, and so this also turns out to be an unfeasible exchange rate.

Some intermediate exchange rate, however, will be feasible in the sense of balancing the flow of trade. At a rate of £1 = $4, for example, it would pay to ship the top three items in the table from the United States to Britain, and to ship the bottom three items from Britain to the United States. (A little arithmetic on each product will show why this is true.) The rate of exchange slices through the middle of the list of price ratios in Table 16–3. Products above the line move in one direction, those below the line in the opposite direction.

This analysis helps to dispose of an argument which often arises in discussions of international trade. One looks at another country, say Japan, and observes that the wages of Japanese workers are much below those of American workers. Surely, then, every kind of product must be cheaper in Japan. Unless we protect ourselves by high tariff walls, U.S. markets will be flooded with Japanese goods. All trade will be moving from Japan to the United States; nothing will be moving in the other direction.

There are two errors in this argument. First, it is comparative *prices* that matter, not comparative wage rates. Price is related to cost, and the cost of producing an article depends on productivity as well as on wage rates. It is quite possible for one country to have higher wages than another in a particular industry and yet turn out goods at lower cost because of greater productivity. Moreover, price includes capital, management, and material costs, and lower labor costs may be offset by higher costs for these other items. The fact that hourly wage rates are lower in Japan than in the United States, then, says nothing about relative prices. Studies during the 1950's indicated that Japan was still at a price disadvantage in world markets in numerous industries, including metals, machinery, and heavy electrical equipment.

But suppose an extreme case. Suppose that the dollar price of every product works out lower in Japan than in the United States. (This is equivalent to our British case with an exchange rate of £1 = $0.50.) This would not prove that two-way trade is unfeasible. It would prove merely that the exchange rate is seriously out of line, with the yen undervalued relative to the dollar. Such a situation could not continue. The dollar price of the yen would have to rise until the exchange rate once more sliced through the middle of the price table instead of falling entirely outside it.

Comparative Advantage: Some Domestic Examples

We have argued that trade depends on the comparative cheapness of products in different countries. But on what does cheapness depend? If goods are produced under competitive conditions in each country, prices will reflect money costs; and these costs reflect quantities of land, labor, capital, and other resources used in production. If radio tubes are relatively cheap in the United States, this means basically that they are cheap *in terms of the physical resources required to produce them.* To put the matter in reverse, American productive resources are particularly well adapted to production of radio tubes, more so (still following Table 16–3) than they are to production of bicycles. The United States has a *comparative advantage* in radio tube production, while Britain has a *comparative advantage* in bicycle production.

This does not tell us, and we need not know, anything about *absolute* levels of productive efficiency in the two countries. U.S. productive resources may have higher productivity in each and every line of production. Now if the United States were exactly twice as productive as Britain in every line of activity, there would be no basis for trade and no trade would occur. (The ratios in the right-hand column of Table 16–3 would all be the same.) But in actuality our productivity advantage is *uneven*—much greater in some lines than in others. So it pays us to concentrate on products in which our productivity advantage is greatest, in which we have a *comparative advantage*, and to import those in which our advantage is least.

The notion of comparative advantage is sufficiently important that it will be worthwhile to illustrate it from various points of view. The principle applies within countries as well as between countries, and so we can begin with a domestic illustration. Consider five farms, each of which has the option of feeding beef cattle for market or of growing corn and fattening hogs. The amount of beef which each farm could produce if it concentrated on beef is shown in the first column of Table 16–4, the amount of pork which could be produced by concentrating on pork

TABLE 16–4

Comparative Advantage in Farming

FARM	POTENTIAL BEEF PRODUCTION (TONS PER ACRE)	POTENTIAL PORK PRODUCTION (TONS PER ACRE)	BEEF/PORK RATIO
A	5	50	0.1
B	40	200	0.2
C	50	150	0.33
D	30	75	0.4
E	30	60	0.5

production appears in the second column and the ratio of potential beef output to pork output appears in the right-hand column.

What will each farm produce? We cannot tell without knowing the prices of beef and pork. A farm will produce beef if its prospective receipts are greater in that line, that is, if beef production × price of beef > pork production × price of pork. This is the same as saying

$$\frac{\text{beef production}}{\text{pork production}} > \frac{\text{price of pork}}{\text{price of beef}}$$

Suppose beef is selling at \$1.00 a pound and pork at 30 cents, so that the second ratio is 0.3. Then farms C, D, and E, whose beef/pork production ratio is greater than this, will produce beef. Farms A and B will find themselves better off producing pork. The price ratio slices through the middle of the table just as the exchange rate did in our earlier case, and determines the most profitable line of production for each farm.

Note that the farms specializing in each product need not be those which are *absolutely* best in that line. Farm A is the poorest pork producer in the group. Yet it will cling to pork production longer than anyone else, even if pork prices are only a little more than one tenth of beef prices. The reason is that, while farm A is a poor pork producer, it is an even worse beef producer. Comparative advantage can mean *either* that one is particularly good at the product in question or particularly bad at other things. The fact that certain desert areas in Nevada concentrate on sheep grazing doesn't mean that these areas are absolutely best for this purpose, but since their productivity in other lines would be close to zero, they have a *comparative advantage* in sheep production.[3]

This suggests a second illustration, involving trade between regions of the United States. Why doesn't each region produce everything it

---

[3] This illustration serves also to amplify a point made during the discussion of agricultural policy in Chapter 11: agricultural resources will be allocated most effectively if prices are left free to indicate the state of demand and if farmers are left free to switch from one product to another on the basis of comparative advantage. Government price and production controls interfere with the operation of comparative advantage and thus with location of production in the best areas for each product. This reduces the efficiency of the agricultural sector.

needs? Why not "keep New England money at home"? Why are some kinds of production located mainly in one region, others mainly in another?

Regional specialization arises because a product can usually be produced more efficiently in some parts of the country than in others. For primary products this may be due to climate, soil fertility, or natural resources. In manufacturing it may be due to a highly skilled labor force, development of subsidiary industries supporting the main industry, long managerial experience, closeness to materials, or closeness to markets.

Suppose Texas and New England were separate countries, with no trade between them; and suppose that the productivity situation was as shown in Table 16–5. We use labor input as a shorthand device for in-

TABLE 16–5

A Case of Interregional Trade

	BEEF PRODUCTION (Lbs. per Day of Labor)	SHOE PRODUCTION (Pairs per Day of Labor)	PRICE RATIO BEEF/SHOES
Texas	200	40	5
New England	40	20	2

put of resources in general, and suppose that within each region products will exchange according to the ratio of labor input. Then in New England a pair of shoes will exchange for two pounds of beef. In Texas, however, the "beef price" of a pair of shoes will be much higher—five pounds of beef instead of two.

Suppose now that trade is opened up between these "countries." Surely it will occur to some New Englander to ship shoes to Texas, where their "beef price" is higher than at home, and to ship beef in the opposite direction. Ship 200 pairs of shoes to Texas, where they can be exchanged for 1,000 pounds of beef, bring this back to New England and trade it for 500 pairs of shoes, export these to Texas and get 2,500 pounds of beef, and so onward to riches. But as our trader and his friends get to work, the price of shoes will begin to rise in New England and fall in Texas, just as in the aluminum case. Overlooking transportation costs, the price ratio will eventually become the same in both regions.

Table 16–5 does not tell us where the price ratio will settle down. To discover this, we would have to know the demand and supply curves for each product in each region. Suppose the price settles at 4:1, four pounds of beef exchanging for a pair of shoes. Then each region has gained from the opening up of trade. By concentrating on shoe production and importing beef, the New Englanders now get for a day's labor 80 pounds of beef (= 20 pairs of shoes). Without trade they could have gotten only 40 pounds. The Texans also gain by concentrating on beef production and importing shoes. For a day's labor they can now obtain 50 pairs of shoes

(= 200 pounds of beef), whereas formerly they could have gotten only 40 pairs. It appears that Texas has gained less than New England, but this is because we chose 4:1 as the new price ratio. If the ratio settled at a level more favorable to Texas, say 3:1, the Texans would gain more and the New Englanders less. *The division of the gains depends on the terms of trade.* But at anything between the original price ratios of 2:1 and 5:1, each region will gain something.

Note one curious thing about this case. Texas has greater productive capacity than New England in both products. One's first thought, then, might be that Texas will do best by producing everything for itself. Yet Texas actually gains by importing shoes and shipping beef in return. Texas has an *absolute* advantage in everything; but it has a *comparative* advantage in beef, where its absolute advantage is greatest. New England has a *comparative* advantage in shoes, where its absolute disadvantage is least.

This is not quite the end of the story. If economic resources are more productive in Texas in every line of endeavor, people in Texas will enjoy a higher standard of living. *Real* wage rates, which are based on absolute productivity, will be higher in Texas than in New England. If people respond to economic advantage, and if movement between the two regions is easy, one should see a migration of New Englanders to Texas to take advantage of the higher wage levels there; and there should also be an outward movement of capital from New England to take advantage of higher profit rates. The movement of labor and capital should continue until productivity levels and income levels have been brought close to equality in the two regions. We shall see in Chapter 26 that something like this has actually been happening in the United States over the past several generations.

The results of this case may be summarized as follows:

1. Where two regions are linked by trade, each will export the products in which it has *comparative* advantage. This is true regardless of absolute productivity levels in the two regions.

2. The gain from trade is the increase in total output which results from each region specializing in the products in which it has comparative advantage.

3. The division of this gain between the regions depends on the price ratio which is established for the products exchanged. (In international dealings this is called *the terms of trade*, defined most simply as the ratio between the prices which a country pays for its imports and the prices it receives for its exports.) At least one of the regions must gain, and usually both will gain.

4. Over long periods, differences in *absolute* productivity levels among regions tend to be eliminated by movement of labor and other resources toward the high-productivity regions.

Comparative Advantage: The International Case

Suppose we revised the side headings in Table 16–5 to read "France, Norway," and the column headings to read "herring, perfume." Would the conclusions be changed? In most respects, no. In international trade, as in interregional trade, each country tends to export products in which it has a comparative advantage. Even the poorest country can find some things in which it is "least bad." Where trade occurs, both countries usually gain; and the division of the gain depends on the terms of trade.

Conclusion (4), however, does not apply on a world scale. The main reason is that the richer countries will not allow large-scale immigration from the poorer countries. The economic incentive for movement is there, but immigration laws prevent it from becoming effective. Movement of capital from one country to another is easier, but there are obstacles on this front as well. Countries with a high absolute level of productivity can thus maintain a permanent superiority in living standards, with no tendency for this to be eroded through transfer of productive resources. The difference in living standards between "developed" and "underdeveloped" countries has actually been widening over the past century.

It is instructive to know that comparative advantage underlies the main currents of international trade. But what lies back of comparative advantage? A country's natural resource endowment is important. Only countries within certain climatic limits can grow bananas, coffee, cocoa, rubber, and other tropical crops. Wheat and corn require soil of a certain composition, moderate rainfall, moderate temperatures, and an adequate growing season. Only a few large tracts of land in the world meet these requirements. Mining and oil extraction depend on the occurrence of mineral and oil deposits in certain locations.

Whether a country has a large labor supply relative to its capital stock or whether the reverse situation prevails has an important bearing on the development of secondary industries. A country in which labor is abundant and therefore relatively cheap will normally have comparative advantage in labor-intensive industries. Thus Japan has comparative advantage in radios, cameras, bicycles, and other manufacturing industries which require a heavy input of labor. Puerto Rico has comparative advantage in clothing production. It is of course not enough for a country to have large numbers of illiterate peasants. People must be recruited and trained for industrial employment, moved from country to city, and motivated to work regularly and efficiently.

Some industries require large amounts of capital and relatively small amounts of labor. Oil refining, basic chemicals, metal refining and fabrication, machinery production, and automobile and truck production are examples. It is not surprising, therefore, to find these industries concentrated in the capital-rich areas of North America, Western Europe, and the U.S.S.R. The sheer size of a country is important in this connection. A small country, unless it can join with its neighbors in a common market scheme, may not have a large enough market to support an optimum-sized steel mill or auto assembly plant.

There are other less tangible but important types of productive resource. A country with long experience in a particular industry has an accumulated stock of technological know-how which for the time being gives it a lead over less experienced countries. A country in which scientific and engineering research is highly developed will come up with more ideas for new products and processes than a country without such facilities. This is particularly important in industries with a strong scientific orientation, such as chemicals and electronics. The existence of a large and enterprising business class confers an advantage, not only in the industries in which a country is presently engaged, but in moving into new types of industry.

These intangible resources of management skill, scientific capacity, and technological know-how are to some extent transferable among countries, and the rate of transfer can be speeded by deliberate action. Japan borrowed heavily from the West during the critical phase of its industrialization between 1870 and 1900, and Russia borrowed heavily during the first half of this century. Know-how does not confer a *permanent* advantage in the same sense as size, climate, or natural resources.

Depending on the configuration of productive resources in a country at a particular time, it will export certain products and import others. The size of the export sector relative to production for home use depends partly on the size of the country. Size and internal diversity make for greater self-sufficiency. Thus exports are only a few percent of total output in the U.S.A. and the U.S.S.R. In Denmark and Norway, on the other hand, exports are a high percentage of output and the trade position is vital to national prosperity. Trade is also an important percentage of output in Britain, the West European countries, Canada, Australia, and most of the Latin American countries.

The possibility of trade breaks the close linkage which would otherwise prevail between production and consumption in each country. Trade makes it possible for consumers to enjoy a wide variety of products which could not be produced efficiently, or perhaps not at all, in the home country. It also becomes possible to produce export commodities in amounts much greater than could be absorbed by the home market, the excess being traded off against imports. Particularly in small countries, the pattern of production may look quite different from the pattern of consumption.

Trade may also increase the *specialization* of production in a country, i.e., cause it to concentrate on a narrower range of products than it would do in the absence of trade. But this depends on circumstances, and cannot be laid down as a general rule. If Malaya were not able to export rubber and tin, the population would probably concentrate largely on subsistence agriculture. In this case trade makes for greater diversity of production rather than the reverse.

BARRIERS TO TRADE: THE TARIFF CONTROVERSY

If two regions or countries have differing resource endowments leading to different comparative advantages, trade between them will be mutually beneficial. It follows that barriers to trade will be harmful.

Building a tariff wall between Texas and New England would hurt consumers on both sides of the wall.

Why, then, do most countries have tariff systems and other restrictions on free movement of trade? Are political leaders simply irrational? Did they not study elementary economics? The broad answer is that restriction of imports, while rarely in the interest of the population as a whole, is often in the interest of specific industries which are subject to import competition. These industries work hard to restrict imports, while the general public is apt to remain apathetic. Moreover, the arguments for trade restriction are easily intermingled with patriotic sentiment. It is easier to get the public aroused about protecting American labor and capital against foreign competition than it would be to whip up sentiment for "protecting Illinois labor and capital" against "Alabama competition," though the logic of the two cases is similar.

There are numerous types of trade restriction,[4] but the import tariff is historically the most important and we shall concentrate on it here. Further, we shall concentrate on the protective aspects of the tariff rather than on the revenue which it yields. During the 1850's about 90 percent of federal revenue came from customs duties. During the 1950's, however, less than 1 percent of federal revenue came from this source. Arguments over the tariff today thus turn mainly on its price and production effects rather than on its revenue effect.

A tariff is a tax on imports. The importer is required to pay either a certain percentage of the value of the imported article (an *ad valorem* duty), or so many dollars and cents per physical unit imported (a *specific* duty). The effect of imposing a tariff on a product which is produced both in the United States and abroad may be illustrated by Figure 16–5. DD and SS are the demand and supply curves for the product in the United States. OP is the "world price," the price at which the article can be imported from other countries. Under free trade, this price will prevail in the United States as well. By seeing where the price line intersects the U.S. supply curve we discover that OQ of the product will be produced in the United States. QQ_3 will be imported and total American consumption will be OQ_3.

Now suppose the United States imposes a specific duty of PP_1 per unit. Importers must now pay the world price plus the tariff and will have to sell the product in the United States for OP_1. Going across to DD, we see that U.S. consumption of the product will decline from OQ_3 to OQ_2.

---

[4] A type which has been particularly important since the 1930's is the *import quota*. Here a country specifies how much of a particular commodity may be imported from abroad, and perhaps even how much may be imported from particular countries. This goes naturally with a system of exchange control, which requires importers to come to the government for their foreign exchange requirements. Exchange controls and import quotas are found particularly in the less developed countries of Asia and Latin America. But the United States also uses quota restrictions on oil, copper, lead, zinc, and certain agricultural products.

FIGURE 16–5

Effect of a Tariff on Imports

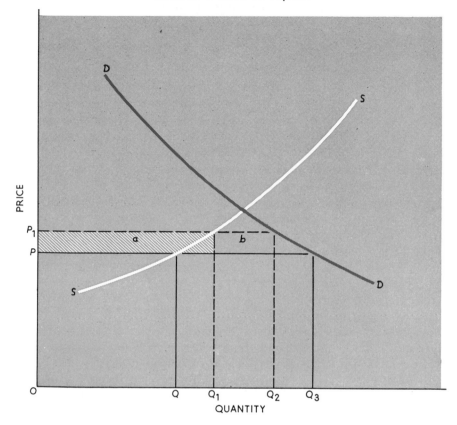

With free trade (solid lines) the product sells in the United States at the world price *OP*. U.S. production is *OQ*, imports *QQ₃*, and consumption *OQ₃*. A tariff of *PP₁* per unit (dotted lines) raises the price to *OP₁*. Consumption falls to *OQ₂*, imports fall to *Q₁Q₂*, and home production increases to *OQ₁*.

U.S. production, however, will increase from *OQ* to *OQ₁*, which was presumably the point of putting on the tariff. With U.S. production up but consumption down, imports will fall to *Q₁Q₂*.

Who gains and who loses from the tariff? The direct effects are:

1. There is a *revenue* effect, an increase in the customs receipts of the government. This is equal to the rectangle *b* (*Q₁Q₂* units of imports × *PP₁* tax per unit). This is of course not a gain from a national standpoint, since the customs revenues are paid by buyers of the product.

2. There is a *protective* effect, shown by the increase in domestic production from *OQ* to *OQ₁*. Some American producers who would not have been able to cover costs and survive at a price of *OP* are able to keep going at *OP₁*.

3. There is a *redistribution* effect, a transfer of income from con-

sumers to companies in the industry. The marginal producer, located right at Q_1, has production costs of OP_1 and is just able to survive with the tariff protection. But everyone else in the industry is receiving more than he needs. The increased profit to the industry is shown by the part of the shaded area a lying to the *left* of ss.

4. There is likely also to be an *export* effect. Putting a United States tariff on some item coming from Italy will probably lead the Italians to retaliate by higher duties against U.S. exports to that country. Even if there is no direct retaliation, a drop in U.S. payments for imports must be offset by a change in other items in the balance of payments statement. Unless we are willing to lend or give away more abroad, our exports will have to fall, because other countries have fewer dollars with which to buy them. Thus, against the increase in employment and profits in the protected industry one must set a drop in employment and profits in other U.S. industries which send part of their product abroad. Nor is this an even exchange from a national point of view. The export industries which are hurt are presumably those in which we have comparative advantage, while the protected industry presumably does not have comparative advantage in the world market. If it did, it would need no protection.

The effects may be summarized as follows: The industry which receives the tariff protection is benefited; other American industries engaged in export trade are hurt; total national output is reduced by a diversion of resources from products in which the United States has comparative advantage to products in which it does not; and consumers of the protected product get less of it at higher prices.

These effects are unfavorable on balance. Why, then, is tariff protection so widely practiced? Surely there must be some arguments in its favor. In reasoning about this one must distinguish carefully between the interests of a particular industry and the interests of the national economy. A tariff is normally beneficial to producers of the protected product and the higher the tariff the better, up to the point at which imports are excluded entirely. Tariff increases enable the domestic industry to produce more, charge higher prices, earn more money, and employ more people. So it is not surprising that industries subject to import competition should lobby energetically for tariff protection.

Specious reasoning begins when an industry sets out to prove that "what's good for us is good for the country." This is typically done by focusing solely on benefits to the industry while ignoring or denying the injury to consumers and exporters. The argument is often supported by pseudo-scientific reasoning. It is argued, for example, that it is fair to impose a tariff sufficient to equalize costs of production at home and abroad. If an item costs 40 cents to produce in the United States and can be bought abroad for 20 cents, then there should be a 20 cent tariff to "maintain fair competition between American and foreign producers."

This so-called "scientific" tariff principle has actually been written into law in some cases. Consider its implications. What is the standard for determining cost of production in the United States? Should one take the costs of the most efficient existing producer, or of the least efficient producer? Should one consider the potential costs of new producers who might be able to survive at a higher price? A glance at Figure 16–5 shows that by going up the supply curve far enough one can justify any tariff one wants to, including a tariff high enough to exclude imports completely. In effect, the "scientific tariff" advocates are saying that whenever foreign producers can undersell *any* American company in *any* product, their advantage should immediately be canceled out by tariff duties. Whatever else this may be, it certainly is not scientific. It denies the principle of comparative advantage, and in fact denies the possibility of any profitable trade among nations.

If one-industry arguments are to be discounted, what about the national interest? Are there circumstances in which tariff protection can be justified on national grounds? There are several:

1. *National defense.* Adam Smith, pioneer advocate of freer trade, nevertheless asserted that "defense is of more importance than opulence." The United States would be ill-advised to import long-range missiles or missile components. It can be argued that we need to preserve some watch production because watchmakers' skills are readily transferable to fuses and other military items. But one must not stretch the national defense argument too far. Everything which we might want to use in wartime need not be made within the United States in peacetime. Some stockpiling is feasible, and some foreign sources are reasonably secure. Maintaining an adequate number of watchmakers does not necessarily involve maintaining a large watch industry. We have many millions of trained military reservists, although only a fraction of this number are under arms at any one time. It shouldn't be any harder to organize a "watchmakers' reserve" than a naval air reserve.

2. *Infant industries.* This famous argument for protection, expounded in Alexander Hamilton's *Report on Manufactures*, has always been popular in countries in the early stages of industrialization. The argument is that a new industry may be relatively inefficient in its early years, while plants are being expanded to optimum size, labor and management skills developed, and market connections established. During this period it is vulnerable to low-cost competition from more experienced foreign producers. If it can be sheltered for a time by tariff barriers, however, efficiency can be raised to the point where it can compete with foreign producers on a free basis. The "infant" will have grown up and the protective walls can be dismantled. This argument was used to justify protecting American manufactures against foreign (primary British) competition during the early nineteenth century. It is widely used today by

the countries of Asia, Africa, and Latin America which are trying to push industrialization in the face of competition from more advanced industrial countries.

This is an argument for *temporary* or transitional protection for industries which, when fully developed, will turn out to have comparative advantage in the countries concerned. It is not an argument for *permanent* protection. It is not applicable to industries which will never be able to attain a competitive position in world markets. Its application in a particular case, therefore, requires careful investigation of prospective costs and revenues.

Even in valid cases there is the practical difficulty that the infants often refuse stubbornly to grow up and be cut loose from the apron strings. They get used to the high prices and profits guaranteed by the tariff wall and fight against its removal, even when fully capable of standing on their own feet. Protection which was supposed to be temporary thus often turns out to be permanent after all. Tariffs with a terminal date, or tariffs shrinking at a specified rate, might provide an answer to this problem.

3. *Terms of trade.* A country which is a large buyer of a certain product can sometimes alter the price to its advantage by imposing an import duty. Suppose the United States is the sole importer of coffee and Brazil the sole exporter. Suppose further that coffee supply in Brazil is completely inelastic. Coffee growers bring the same amount to market regardless of price. If the United States now imposes an import tax of 10 cents a pound, this will lower the price received by Brazilian producers by 10 cents while leaving the price to U.S. consumers unchanged. The Brazilians bear the full brunt of the duty while the U.S. Treasury gets the revenue. (Verify this if you wish by sketching a supply-demand diagram.)

Even if conditions were not this extreme—the United States simply the major importer, Brazil the major supplier, supply highly inelastic rather than completely inelastic—the United States could gain something from this sort of maneuver. This would not be regarded as a gentlemanly act by the Brazilians, however, and might lead to economic retaliation. It can scarcely be advocated as good national policy, particularly for an economically powerful nation such as the United States.

4. *Antidepression measures.* It will be shown in Part Three that, if the United States were suffering from depression, and if it could cut its imports without anything happening to its exports, the result would be a rise in U.S. production and employment. On a commonsense basis, "money which was being spent abroad will now be spent at home." Demand for domestic products will rise, and employment will rise with them. This works hardship on other countries, of course, since the reduction of imports by the United States will throw people out of work abroad. For this reason it is often termed a "beggar my neighbor" policy. It is doubtful also whether the policy is feasible for any length of time. Other countries

would certainly retaliate to cut their imports from the United States, so that any advantage we might gain would be of short duration.

5. *Making haste slowly*. On a different plane stand arguments which relate, not to imposing a tariff in the first instance, but to removing it where it has been long established. Lowering a tariff amounts to forcing down product prices, and may have a disruptive effect on the industry concerned. Plants may be closed down, and workers faced with the necessity of moving to other jobs. These resource transfers are painful, and the economists' argument that it is all for the general good is likely to be received with ill grace. This is not a positive argument for tariffs, or an argument for inaction in lowering them. It is simply an argument for gradualism. Tariffs should be lowered gradually and judiciously—preferably during prosperity rather than depression, with due notice to all concerned, and with advance planning to help plants and labor to convert to new uses.

What does this boil down to? In the United States case, imposing import restrictions to solve temporary depression problems or to lower the prices which we pay to other countries seems shortsighted and inadvisable. The infant industry argument, whatever merit it may have possessed in 1820, is surely no longer applicable to the world's leading industrial nation. This leaves national defense as the only argument for protecting U.S. production of items which are in fact closely related to national security and which cannot survive without such protection.

AMERICAN TRADE AND TRADE POLICY

The Pattern of Trade

The American economy is relatively self-sufficient. Imports and exports typically form less than 5 percent of GNP. But United States imports of $15 billion or so a year are large relative to the productive capacity of other countries and the total volume of world trade. The U.S. purchasing power, and changes in U.S. tariff regulations, are matters of world-wide concern.

Our closest trading relations are with Canada and the Latin American countries, which provide about half of our imports and take better than 40 percent of our exports. European countries account for about one third of our imports and exports, and Asia about 20 percent.

Manufactured goods form about three quarters of American exports, while foodstuffs and raw materials form only one quarter. (This is a great change from the nineteenth century, during which the United States exported mainly food and raw materials and took manufactures in return.) On the import side, foodstuffs and raw materials make up about half of the total. This is partly an inflow of tropical crops not grown in the United States—coffee, cocoa, palm oil, bananas, crude rubber, cane sugar—and partly a flow of metals, petroleum, and other raw materials needed to supplement our own production. Finished and semifinished manufactures make up the remaining half of United States imports. To a considerable extent then, our foreign trade is now an exchange of manufactures against (different types of) manufactures. The detailed list of the manufactures which we export and import reflects the operation of comparative advantage.

More than half of our commodity imports enter the United States free of duty. This category consists mainly of foods and raw materials not produced in the United States. A tariff on these products would have no protective effect and would be resented as an effort to tax foreign producers and exporters. Even as regards dutiable imports, the tariff has little protective effect in about half the cases. These are products which are either not produced in the United States or in which abolition of tariffs would have little effect on the volume of imports. Examples of the latter sort are petroleum, cut diamonds, lumber, and nickel. For only about one quarter of our import volume, then, does the tariff offer significant protection to American producers. Congressional battles over tariff policy are focused on this quarter of our import trade.

A striking feature of the U.S. balance of payments is that merchandise exports typically exceed merchandise imports by several billion dollars a year. This is normally offset by an outward movement of American capital—private investment abroad, plus U.S. government loans and grants to other countries. We lend or give other countries the dollars needed to buy our export surplus. Any remaining imbalance in the accounts is offset by gold movements, which have sometimes attained substantial volume. During the late thirties, for example, capital was flowing *to* the United States rather than from it as nervous European investors tried to hedge against the impending war by shifting funds to New York. In addition, we maintained our customary export surplus. The result was an increase in U.S. holdings of gold from about $4 billion in 1933 to $22 billion in 1940. In the late fifties and early sixties, on the other hand, we were making foreign loans and grants at a rate considerably above our surplus of merchandise exports. Partly in consequence of this the U.S. gold stock fell during the years 1958–62 from about $23 billion to $16 billion. This gold drain aroused serious concern and led to corrective measures which will be examined in Chapter 24.

The Trend of Trade Policy

The United States was for many years a strongly protectionist country. During the early nineteenth century protective tariffs were erected as a way of nurturing new manufacturing industries and enabling them to withstand the competition of British manufactures. But these infant industries declined to grow up; and tariff protection, instead of being a transitional device, became a permanent feature of national policy. The center of protectionist sentiment was the industrial Northeast and the

Republican party. Support for freer trade came mainly from export industries, which at this time meant principally agriculture. Free trade sentiment was particularly strong in the South, with its interest in cotton exports. The Republican party dominated national politics from the Civil War until 1930, and the protectionist forces usually came out on top. The peak of this movement was reached with the Smoot-Hawley Act of 1930, which raised tariffs to an all-time high and led to retaliatory action by many other countries.

The Democratic victory of 1932 brought a sharp shift toward freer trade accompanied by a transfer of tariff-making authority from Congress to the Executive branch. The Trade Agreements Act of 1934 authorized the President to negotiate with other countries for a reciprocal lowering of tariff barriers, reductions by the United States to be matched by concessions of equal value by the other party. No tariff, however, could be cut below 50 percent of the 1934 level. This grant of authority to the President was subsequently renewed by extending the Trade Agreements Act each time it expired. Particularly significant was the renewal of 1945, which authorized the President to reduce tariffs by 50 percent of the rates in effect *on January 1, 1945.* Thus duties which had already been cut 50 percent under the original act could be reduced by another 50 percent, or to 25 percent of the 1934 level.

Between 1934 and 1948 trade agreements were negotiated with 29 countries, including all our important trading partners. Duties were cut on about 90 percent of all dutiable imports. In over three quarters of these cases, the rate of duty was reduced by 45 percent or more, and a quarter of our imports experienced tariff reductions of 66 to 75 percent.

The amount collected in tariff duties fell from 47 percent of the value of dutiable imports in 1934 to 28 percent in 1945 and 12 percent in 1953.[5] About half of this decline seems to have been due to tariff reductions under the Trade Agreements Act. The remaining half was due to the great rise of prices between 1934 and 1952, which automatically reduces the restrictiveness of a *specific* duty (though not of an *ad valorem* duty). *Example:* A tariff of $1.00 each is imposed on a certain grade of cotton shirt. If the import price of the shirt is $2.00, this is a 50 percent duty. But if the price doubles to $4.00 and the tariff is not changed, the rate has fallen to 25 percent.

Thus in about 15 years the United States was transformed from a high-tariff country to a moderate-to-low tariff country. Tariff rates today, which are not very different from those in effect in 1950, lie mainly between 10 percent and 20 percent of the value of imported products. These rates are not negligible, but in few cases are they high enough to be prohibitive.

---

[5] Howard S. Piquet, *The Trade Agreements Act and the National Interest* (Washington, D.C.: The Brookings Institution, 1958), p. 25.

During the fifties the movement toward tariff reduction lost momentum. Congress continued to renew the Trade Agreements Act, but grudgingly, and with limitations which made it easier for American producers to campaign against proposed tariff reductions by appealing to the U.S. Tariff Commission or the Office of Defense Mobilization.

The drive toward freer trade was resumed by the Kennedy administration in 1962. The immediate occasion was the rapid progress of the European Economic Community or "Common Market," which includes France, West Germany, Italy, Belgium, Holland, and Luxembourg. The treaty establishing the Community provides for gradual reduction of tariff barriers among the member nations, and reduction is actually proceeding ahead of schedule. It provides also for freer movement of labor and capital, and a variety of other steps which together come close to full economic union. Many Europeans hope that economic integration will provide a favorable setting for closer political ties.

But while tariffs are being reduced within the Community, they remain up against the outside world. This raised the possibility that the United States might gradually be frozen out of its largest foreign market. The Kennedy administration argued that the best way to avoid this was to give the President power to bargain with the E.E.C. for a lowering of their external tariff in return for reductions in our own. Public support for the proposal was strong, and protectionist sentiment seemed weaker than in previous years. The outcome was the Trade Expansion Act of 1962, passed by substantial majorities in both House and Senate.

The new Act runs for a period of 5 years. It permits the U.S. government to bargain for reductions of up to 50 percent in most existing tariffs, and to negotiate on broad categories of goods rather than on individual items. Tariffs which are already below 5 percent can be eliminated entirely. A novel provision is that, for products in which the United States and the E.E.C. countries together account for 80 percent of world trade, we can bargain with the E.E.C. for complete abolition of tariffs.

The Act also provides transitional assistance to companies and workers hit by foreign competition resulting from tariff reductions. Companies may receive tax relief, government loans, and technical aid in converting facilities to different products. Displaced workers may receive cash payments of up to $61 per week for a maximum period of 78 weeks. These benefits are considerably more generous than those provided by the state unemployment compensation systems. There is provision also for retraining programs to help workers learn new skills which are in active demand.

SUMMARY

1. International trading and financial relations require a *foreign exchange market*, in which the currency of one country can be converted into that of another. The chief operators in this market are large private banks and central (government) banks. An *exchange rate* is the price of one currency in terms of another.

2. A country's foreign transactions are summarized in its *balance of payments*. When changes in gold holdings and in short-term credits are included as balancing items, receipts and payments must always be equal. But the fact that the statement balances says nothing about whether the balance is satisfactory.

3. In a free exchange market, the price of (say) pounds in terms of dollars would be determined by supply and demand in the usual way and would vary from day to day. But since frequent variation is inconvenient, governments usually undertake to *stabilize* the price of their currency. They do this just as the U.S. government stabilizes the price of wheat—by a standing offer to buy or sell at a fixed price. The stabilized price, however, should be near the equilibrium level which would exist in a free market. If the price is too high, the country will have a balance of payments deficit, lose gold, and may have to *devalue*, that is, lower the price of its currency.

4. A country can maintain the price of its currency permanently above the free market price, however, by rationing foreign exchange. Such *exchange control* has dubious consequences, but is nonetheless widely used in the less developed countries.

5. A country normally exports products which are comparatively cheap at home compared with prices abroad, and imports goods which are comparatively cheap in other countries. Underlying comparative cheapness of a good *in terms of money* is comparative cheapness *in terms of the physical resources required to produce it*. This is usually termed *comparative advantage*. So we end up with the proposition that a country exports products for which it has a comparative (though not necessarily an *absolute*) advantage.

6. Specialization based on comparative advantage leads to larger total output than if each country (or region) produced all its own requirements. This economic gain is usually divided between the trading partners, the exact division depending on the price ratio or *terms of trade* between their products.

7. A tariff is a tax on imports. It benefits the protected industry by enabling it to sell more goods at a higher price. But consumers are injured, and so are export industries which suffer retaliation by foreign countries.

8. Most arguments for the desirability of tariffs are fallacious. But one can justify temporary protection for promising *infant industries*, and continuing protection for industries which are essential to *national defense*. It is also reasonable that, where a tariff has long existed, it should be withdrawn gradually rather than suddenly; and that the plants and workers which suffer from the change should be assisted in transferring to new activities.

9. Until 1930 the United States was a high-tariff country. But under the Trade Agreements Act of 1934, as subsequently renewed and extended, tariffs were more than cut in half by 1950. During the fifties Congress was grudging in approving further tariff reductions. The Trade Expansion Act of 1962, however, portends a new period of tariff cutting and perhaps an approach to free trade within the North Atlantic community.

PART | THREE

THE ECONOMICS
OF INCOME AND EMPLOYMENT

Bell, book, and candle shall not drive me back,
When gold and silver becks me to come on.
WILLIAM SHAKESPEARE, *King John*

WE HAVE now reached a turning point in the course. Parts One and Two focused on particular industries and markets. They raised questions of this sort: Supposing that national output in 1963 is $600 billion, how much of this output will consist of breakfast cereals, automobiles, potatoes, cement, and so on? What will be the market price of each product? How much cash income will go to each individual in the economy?

Throughout this discussion we took the general level of economic activity for granted. We assumed that the economy runs along quietly at capacity year after year. But everyone knows that this is not true. Sometimes the system operates well below capacity. Plants are partly idle and many workers are unemployed. At other times production shoots up and unemployment shrinks. We know also that the price level fluctuates widely. These price swings can be quite upsetting, and we need to understand why they occur.

In Part Three, therefore, we focus on forces affecting the economy as a whole, on what is usually termed *aggregative economics* or *macroeconomics*. This analysis is related, of course, to the microeconomic analysis of Part One. The whole is the sum of its parts. But macroeconomics involves a different emphasis and point of view. We ask, not what determines the demand for television sets, but what determines *total demand* in the economy; not what determines the price of new cars, but what determines the *average level of all prices;* not why a particular industry is expanding, but why *most industries* are expanding at one time and contracting at another. This effort to explore the central heart beat of the

FIGURE 1

Production and Unemployment, 1918–62

economy requires new concepts, and a more thorough analysis of money supply, spending, and saving.

A good way to introduce these issues is to look at the behavior of the American economy since World War I. The red line in Figure 1 shows changes in the physical output of the economy. The white line shows the percentage of the labor force that was completely unemployed. The unemployment figure, naturally enough, moves in an opposite direction to the production figure.

Note the jittery movement of production and employment, and the frequent reversals of course. After the postwar depression of 1920–22, production rose quite strongly until 1929. Then occurred the catastrophic decline of 1929–33. This depression shook the economy to its foundations, and led to the wave of New Deal legislation. Despite government efforts to promote recovery, unemployment remained unusually high and production unusually low until the onset of World War II. During the war production rose to unprecedented heights and unemployment almost vanished.

Most economists, smarting from the Great Depression and still nervous about the future, predicted a serious depression after World War II. It came as a pleasant surprise that the drop of production in 1946 was brief and mild. The economy then set off on a period of sustained expansion, broken only by mild recessions in 1948–49, 1953–54, 1957–58, and 1960–61. During the late forties consumers and business concerns were catching up on things they had been unable to buy during World War II; and after 1950 the Korean War gave a new stimulus to demand and production. Since the mid-fifties, however, the rate of expansion has slackened. Unemployment has increased gradually, and there has been a good deal of unused plant capacity. The obvious slack in the economy, and the fact that our output has risen more slowly than that of most other industrial countries, has aroused widespread debate over causes and possible cures.

The historical record raises several major questions. Why do we have these ups and downs of production? The downswings since 1945 have been mild, but they are still annoying. Must we put up with these interruptions of progress every three or four years? What can be done to immunize the economy against declines and to accelerate its upward movement? Why has the rate of expansion slackened since the mid-fifties? Is there any reason why our production per head should be rising only 1½ per cent a year, while in Italy, Germany, Japan, and the U.S.S.R. it is rising 5 to 7 per cent a year?

Now look at Figure 2, which shows changes in the average level of prices. The depression after World War I brought a sharp break in prices, which then remained almost stable through the prosperous years 1922–29. The 1929–33 depression brought another sharp price decline—the nickel hamburger, the $500 new car, the restaurants advertising "all you can eat for 60 cents." Prices rose again during the partial recovery of the thirties, and advanced more sharply during and immediately after World War II. There was a smaller spurt of prices during the first year of the Korean War.

Since the Korean War ended in 1953, the trend of prices has been mildly upward. Prices have not fallen during recession and have usually risen during prosperity. Wages have risen substantially in bad years as well as good. This has led to predictions that our economy has entered an era in which prices will move in only one direction—up.

FIGURE 2

Wholesale Price Index, 1918–62

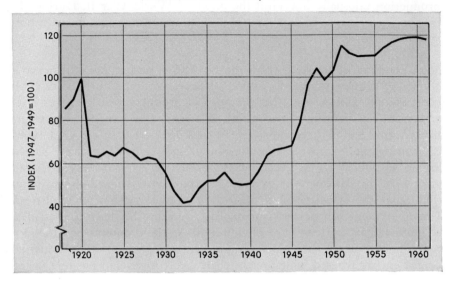

Is this prediction correct? If so, who is responsible? Business groups blame unduly large wage increases. Union leaders retort by blaming business for demanding exorbitant profit margins. Is a continued mild uptrend in prices harmful to the economy, or can it be exhilarating? If it is harmful, can anything be done about it? Can we have *both* a high level of spending, leading to capacity production and full employment, *and* a stable level of prices?

These are very practical questions, and many people feel strongly about them. Economists are by no means agreed on the answers. But if we cannot always provide answers, we can at least explain what the shooting is about and help the reader to formulate his own views intelligently rather than emotionally.

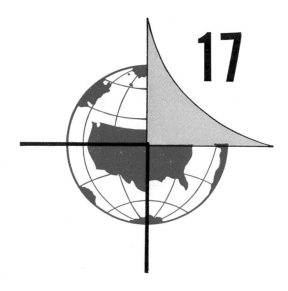

National Income: Meaning and Measurement

Never ask of money spent
Where the spender thinks it went.
Nobody was ever meant
To remember or invent
What he did with every cent.

ROBERT FROST

IN ORDER TO TALK about the total output of an economy, as we propose to do in Parts Three and Four, we need some way of defining and measuring this output. We shall be speaking frequently of Gross National Product, National Income, and similar quantities. Where do they come from? How are they estimated? What assurance have we that the estimates are reliable? To find out, we must explore a subject usually known as *national income accounting*.

While the effort to measure national output goes back for centuries, national income accounting is a recent development. Detailed and comparable estimates for the United States go back only to 1929. A few other countries were preparing national estimates before World War II. Since 1945 this kind of work has been accelerated by the Statistics Division of the United Nations, which has assisted member countries to set up national income measurements and publishes annual statistics for most countries of the world.

A few years ago the writer encountered in London an economist

389

friend who is a leading authority on national income. He had just gotten off a plane from India and was about to board one for Brazil. On being asked how he managed to get around the world so much, he explained, "After all, old man, *every* country has a national income." He was quite right. There are national income estimates for Kenya and Jamaica, for Burma and Iran. If there aren't figures for Togoland and the Fiji Islands,[1] there soon will be.

National income accounting is now the central framework for describing and analyzing a national economy. If one asks what is going on in a particular economy, whether it is advancing or declining, or how its internal structure is changing over the course of time, the answers run in terms of national income tables. So it is necessary to get this measurement system clearly in mind. Having done this, we can use the system to explore short-term fluctuations of national income in Part Three, and long-term economic growth in Part Four.

A PRODUCTION STATEMENT FOR ONE COMPANY

Our problem is to add up all the productive activity going on in an economy during a certain period. Production is carried on mainly in business units, of which there are several million in the United States. Let us first consider, therefore, how we might picture the activities of a single company over a year's time. If we can do this for each company, we can then add up the activities of all companies to get a picture for the nation as a whole.

Table 17–1 shows the X Manufacturing Company's operations during 1961. It is adapted from the ordinary income statement or "profit and loss" statement. It is constructed according to the principles of double entry bookkeeping. In old-fashioned physics, at least, "whatever goes up must come down." In accounting, "whatever comes in must go out." Every dollar which the company receives has to end up somewhere. If it is not paid out for materials, labor, taxes, or other expenses, it must have stayed in the company and will show up as profit. The right-hand side of the table shows the value of what the company produced during the year. The left-hand side shows where the money went, including how much of it stayed behind in the company's hands. And the two sides must always balance.

Sources of Funds: "Value Added"

Table 17–1 deserves careful study. Look first at the right-hand side. The company has manufactured and sold to its various customers $1,550 thousand worth of goods. It has also produced $100 thousand worth of goods which were not sold during the year but are sitting in the ware-

---

[1] As a matter of fact, there *are* estimates for the Fiji Islands. They were collected by an enterprising British economist who traveled from island to island by sailboat, busily counting piles of copra in every port.

TABLE 17–1

Production Statement for the X Manufacturing Company, 1961
(Thousands of Dollars)

ALLOCATIONS		SOURCES	
Depreciation	80	Sales to Company A	300
Taxes other than corporate profit taxes	30	Sales to Company B	600
Wages and salaries	680	Sales to Company C	450
Social insurance contributions	25	Other sales	200
Net interest	10	Inventory increase	100
Corporate profit tax	59.5	Total value of production	1,650
Net dividends	30		
Undistributed profits	35.5	Minus: Goods and services purchased from other producers	700
Total allocations of value added	950	Total value added	950

house as increased inventory. Since what we are after is total production during the year, this amount must be added. (The inventory figure might have been negative instead of positive. The company might have sold more than it produced, and thus reduced inventories.) Thus we come out with total production of $1,650 thousand.

But did the X Company itself produce this much? It used up during the year $700 thousand worth of materials and service purchased from other companies—raw materials, electric power, trucking and freight services, office supplies, and so on. This $700 thousand constitutes production by these other companies, not by the X Company. What the X Company has really produced is the *difference* between the value of the ingredients purchased from other companies and the value of its own finished product. This difference of $950 thousand dollars is termed *value added* and is considered the true production of the X Company for the year.

The importance of calculating in this way becomes clear when we try to add different companies' production together into a national total. Consider what would happen otherwise. Wheat worth $100 is sold to a miller who grinds it into flour worth $150, after which it is baked into bread worth $300, and finally retailed to consumers for a total of $450. How much has been produced in the process? Is it $100 + $150 + $300 +$450 = $1,000? No, it is not. Total production is only $450, the amount which consumers pay for the final product. Where is the catch? The catch is that in the $1,000 total the value of the original wheat is counted *four* times, the value added by the miller is counted *three* times, and the value added by the baker is counted *twice*. The only way to eliminate this double counting is to deduct, at each stage of production, the materials purchased from people at earlier stages and to count only value added at that stage as true production. In this example, value added is $100 for the wheat farmer, $50 for the miller, $150 for the baker, and $150 for the grocer: $100 + $50 + $150 + $150 = $450, which is the right answer.

Allocations or Uses of Funds

Where does the money go? Every dollar's worth of production must be accompanied by a dollar's worth of expense or profit. How does this work out on the left-hand side of Table 17–1?

The first item, *depreciation*, is money set aside to cover wear and tear on buildings and equipment and to replace them when they are worn out. Suppose a machine costs $50,000 and is expected to wear out at the end of 10 years. Then according to the simplest ("straight line") depreciation formula, the company will put aside $5,000 each year. At the end of the 10 years it will have the $50,000 necessary to buy a new machine. Depreciation charges are a necessary cost of production. Unless they are set aside, the company is "living on its capital." Its equipment will eventually wear out and there will be no money available to replace it.

The next item is mainly *property taxes* paid to the city or county, plus *excise or sales taxes* which the state and federal governments collect on some products. *Wages and salaries*, a large item in most companies, needs no explanation. Most employers must also contribute a certain percentage of payrolls to finance the state unemployment compensation and federal old age pension systems—hence *social insurance contributions*. The company may also have to pay *interest* to bondholders or to banks which have lent it money.

These items, plus purchased materials which have already been deducted on the right-hand side of the account, make up all the *costs* of running the enterprise. What's left, if anything, is an accounting *profit*. The X Company did well in 1961 and came up with a profit of $125 thousand. This gets split three ways, shown by the last three items on the left-hand side. A large share goes to the federal government under the corporate profit tax. The remainder may be paid out to the stockholders in dividends or held back to expand the business. Different companies follow different policies on this point. Some customarily give a large "payout" of earnings, others a small payout. The X Company in this year made roughly a 50–50 split.

Thus we have managed to account for $950 thousand, which must and does equal the value of production on the right-hand side. Note that all the items on the left-hand side represent *income* to somebody, while the items on the right-hand side represent value of *product*. The table may thus be regarded *either* as an income statement or a product statement. We shall see that the same is true of production statements for the economy as a whole. This is why one finds the terms *national income* and *na-*

tional product used interchangeably. They can be interchanged freely, because their size must be identical.

A PRODUCTION STATEMENT FOR THE ECONOMY

Now let's see what is involved in adding up the activities of all production units in the economy. Most production comes from business corporations, and we have already seen how to handle them. Provided we are careful to eliminate double counting by deducting purchased materials at each stage, we can add the figures for all companies in the country and come out with a statement looking just like Table 17–1, though the totals now run in billions instead of thousands. On the right-hand side this will show *total value added* by the productive activities of all companies. This can be viewed also as *total production for final use*, since production of materials by one company for sale to other companies has been eliminated in the totaling. On the left-hand side, our consolidated statement shows the *total income* resulting from corporate activities, including corporate tax payments and business profits. Total income must equal total product, just as for a single company.

There is no difficulty either in adding the production of the several million farmers, grocery storekeepers, and other small producers whose businesses are not set up as companies. Their production statements are actually simpler than the one we set up for the X Company. The farmer pays for his purchased materials, pays his property taxes, and perhaps pays a little interest to the local banker. What's left over is his net income for the year. We may say, if we like, that part of this income is really wages for his labor, part is interest on his investment in the farm, and part may be profit. But it's all income, and it's all his. The same is true for grocery store operators, professional practitioners, and other individual proprietors. In the U.S. national income accounts, the incomes of all such people are lumped together as *income of unincorporated enterprises*.

What else remains to be added? The federal, state, and local governments hire a lot of people and spend a lot of money. So they must be producing something. Government production, as we saw in Chapter 15, mainly takes the form of services; and these services are usually not sold in the market for a price. So what value can we attach to them?

National income estimators have adopted a simple rule on this point: government services are worth what they cost. The value of government's product equals the money spent to provide it. This assumes that the citizens know what they are doing. If they don't think a particular public service is worth its cost, they can get after their elected representatives to have it reduced or eliminated. But there is no way to *prove* that government production is worth precisely this much and no more. To anyone who questions the soundness of the present rule, all one can say is "Go find a better one."

With government, as with other producing units, we must avoid double counting. Suppose the cost of all government services in 1961 was $150 billion. Of this amount, $50 billion was paid to government employees while $100 billion was paid to business concerns for goods and services—everything from missiles and space vehicles to carbon paper for Washington offices. Can we say that the value added by government was $150 billion? Obviously not. The $100 billion of government purchases has already been counted as part of the output of private industry and cannot be counted again. We are left with $50 billion, which leads to a simple rule: *value added by government equals the government payroll*. This $50 billion goes into the value of national product on the right-hand side of the sheet, and the same $50 billion goes into the wage and salary item on the left-hand side. The statement continues to balance.

Have we now finished adding up the national income? Not quite. There are a few other things which do not enter the market place and are not sold at a price, but which it seems legitimate to count as part of national income. We call these *imputed income*, to indicate that no cash transaction is involved. The largest items are: (1) The value of farm produce consumed on the farm. This is usually valued at the price which the farmer could get by selling it rather than at the retail price he would have to pay if he were buying it. It can be argued that this value is too low, and that this is one reason why farm incomes always look so low compared with city incomes. (2) The rental value of owner-occupied houses. If a tenant pays rent to a landlord, we say that this measures the services yielded by the house, and should therefore be counted as part of national product. Suppose now the tenant buys the house. There is no longer any monthly rent. Yet the house yields the same service as before, and it would seem odd not to continue counting it as part of national product. We estimate, therefore, what the homeowners of the country would have to pay for the services of their houses if they were renting them, and this is added to both sides of the national production statement.

Imputation could be carried even farther, and there are nice questions about how far it should be carried. Johnny's haircut by the neighborhood barber adds $1.50 to national product. Johnny's haircut at home by the porridge-bowl method adds nothing to national product. What about housewives' labor put into cooking, cleaning, and household management? Valued at the cost of a hired housekeeper, this would add a large amount to national product. But national income statisticians have not been this daring, and production within the household is not counted.

The result of this adding-up is shown in Table 17–2. The figures are now billions instead of thousands. They are still hypothetical, though not very different from the actual U.S. figures for 1961. Table 17–2 bears a strong resemblance to Table 17–1, but a few changes should be noted. On the sources side, we have added government production and imputed production. And sales by private producers have been broken down by *type of purchaser*, to show how much output went to consumers, how much to business concerns, and how much to government.

TABLE 17–2

Production Statement for the Economy, 1961
(Billions of Dollars)

ALLOCATIONS		SOURCES	
Depreciation	45	Value added in the market economy	430
Taxes other than corporate profits		Sales to consumers	295
taxes	50	Sales to business	70
Wages and salaries	280	Sales to government	60
Social insurance contributions	22	Increase in inventories	5
Income of unincorporated enterprises	48	Value added by government	50
Rental income of persons	12	Other nonmarket (imputed)	
Net interest	20	production	40
Corporate profits taxes	22		
Net dividends	15		
Undistributed profits	8		
Current surplus of government enter-			
prises	−2		
Gross national income	520	Gross national product	520

One thing looks odd in the table: how can there be any "sales to business" by other businesses? Didn't we wash these out in the totaling process? We did wash out all transfers of materials and services *to be used up in current production.* The "sales to business" shown in Table 17–2 include only plant construction, machinery, and other capital goods destined to last beyond the current year. They are *final sales,* and as such stand on the same basis as final sales for consumer use or government use. This item, which will turn out to be important in our later discussion, is usually termed *plant and equipment investment* or *private fixed investment.*

There are a few additions also on the allocations or income side of the table. *Income of unincorporated enterprises* has been added to include the earnings of farmers, small unincorporated businesses, independent professional men, and the like. Some government enterprises, such as the TVA, do sell their products for a price. The profits or losses of these enterprises appear under *current surplus of government enterprises. Rental income of persons* includes not only cash rents paid by tenants but the imputed rent of owner-occupied houses. With these additions, the table is just like Table 17–1, and once more the two sides must balance. Gross national product and gross national income are the same thing looked at from different standpoints.

U.S. GROSS NATIONAL PRODUCT IN 1961

The national income accounts prepared by the U.S. Department of Commerce look a bit different from Table 17–2. It will be a good idea to examine the official figures for 1961, partly so that you will recognize this kind of table when you meet it, partly to illustrate the varying ways in which such tables may be constructed. Table 17–3 gives the Department of Commerce data for 1961, with only slight rearrangement.

The right-hand side of the table, as before, shows the value of final production during the year, including government production and imputed production. Output is now subdivided, however, on the basis of *who bought it.* This reflects the strong interest of economists in business cycle analysis during the crucial period when our national income ac-

TABLE 17–3

U.S. National Income and Product, 1961*
(Millions of Dollars)

Compensation of employees:	302,174	Personal consumption expenditures	338,058
Wages and salaries	278,821		
Supplements	23,353	Gross private domestic investment	69,257
Income of unincorporated enterprises	47,832	Government purchases of goods and services	107,430
Rental income of persons	12,259		
Net interest	20,027	Net foreign investment	3,980
Corporate profits:	45,537		
Corporate profit tax	22,251		
Dividends	15,018		
Undistributed profits	8,284		
Inventory valuation adjustment	−16		
National income	427,829		
Indirect business taxes	48,187		
Business transfer payments	2,132		
Statistical discrepancy	−3,086		
Less: Subsidies minus current surpluses of government enterprises	−1,676		
Net national product	473,386		
Capital consumption allowances (depreciation)	45,339		
Gross national product	518,725	Gross national product	518,725

* Source: *Survey of Current Business,* July, 1962, p. 6.

counts were taking shape. Consumer spending, business spending, and government spending behave differently during the business cycle, and so it was considered important to separate them out. But this kind of breakdown is also significant for other purposes.

It is easy to see how the items in Table 17–3 are derived from those in Table 17–2. *Personal consumption expenditures* is the sum of sales to consumers and imputed production. *Gross private domestic investment* is the sum of capital goods sold to business and increase in inventories, the latter being counted as a type of investment. *Government purchases of goods and services* is the sum of business sales to government and the government payroll. *Net foreign investment* is a new item, arising from the fact that we sell goods and services abroad and buy things from abroad. Roughly, this item is exports minus imports. If the United States sends abroad more than it gets back from abroad, it must be engaging in lending or foreign investment.

On the left-hand side of Table 17–3, almost all the items are familiar from previous tables, though their order has been slightly reshuffled. The main newcomers are *inventory valuation adjustment*, a technical adjustment which need concern only the specialist,[2] and *statistical discrepancy*, which needs a word of explanation. We must now break down and confess that the national income division of the Department of Commerce does not actually collect income statements for every producer in the economy and add these up as we have supposed. Figures to fill in the different totals in Table 17–3 are collected from a wide variety of sources, and most of them are estimates of varying degrees of reliability. When all the spade-work has been done and the two sides of the table have been added up, they should logically balance. But unhappily they don't, because of gaps and errors in the basic information. "Statistical discrepancy" is simply an item put in to *make* the table balance. It may be positive or negative, and amounts to saying, "We slipped up somewhere."

THE GRAND TOTAL AND SOME SMALLER TOTALS

We have been explaining how a lot of building blocks are piled on top of each other to arrive at gross national product. Now let's see how the blocks can be taken apart to get smaller totals which are interesting for various purposes. We start at the top with the biggest figure, and work down to smaller and smaller subtotals.

1. *Gross national product.* This is the most global of national income concepts. GNP professes to total up all of the productive activity in a particular country during a certain period of time. It is the best single answer to the question, "What did we turn out in the United States in 1961?"

But this seemingly solid figure is no stronger than the rules by which it is constructed. It depends on what we agree at the beginning shall be considered production. Marxists include only *material* production; and so the GNP totals for Russia, Poland, and other communist countries do not include the services of teachers, doctors, civil servants, entertainers, and the like. They leave out part of what we would consider to be national output. The United States figures include some kinds of imputed income

---

[2] The reason for this is that part of the increase (or decrease) in value of inventories shown on the right-hand side of the table may have resulted from a change in price levels rather than a change in quantity of inventories held. Since the object of Table 17–3 is to get at physical quantity of output during the year, we want to take out of the inventory total any change resulting from price movements. The inventory valuation adjustment is an effort to do this, and may be either positive or negative depending on which way prices have moved.

but leave out others, notably household production. Thus the total can be increased or decreased by changing the rules of the game.

Two other misunderstandings should be avoided. First, *GNP is not a measure of consumer welfare*. An increase in GNP from one year to the next may mean an increase in output of consumer goods, or it may not. Part of the increase, or conceivably the whole of it, may be in business investment or in government activity. The tremendous increase of GNP during World War II was accompanied by a reduction of civilian consumption.

Second, *GNP is not a measure of productive efficiency*. In mechanics, efficiency is the ratio of work done to force exerted. In economics, efficiency is the ratio of output to input. If a country's output rises 5 percent in a particular year *with no increase* in the use of labor, capital, land, and other inputs, this is a 5 percent increase in efficiency. But if inputs have also risen 5 percent, there has been no change in efficiency. The economy is simply bigger, not more efficient. The GNP figure tells us nothing about inputs, and therefore says nothing about efficiency.

2. Net national product.   Another possible criticism of GNP is that it overstates how much has been produced during the year, since it fails to take account of the wearing out of factories, machinery, office buildings, houses, and other capital goods. Part of the year's output must be devoted to replacing this depreciation, which is also termed *capital consumption*. Only after providing for replacement can one tell how much of the 1961 product is available for use *without eating into capital*. This remainder, GNP minus capital consumption, is termed *net national product* or NNP. Table 17–3 shows that in 1961 GNP was $518.7 billion, capital consumption was $45.3 billion, and NNP was consequently $473.4 billion.

The terms *gross* and *net* have this meaning wherever one meets them. Thus *gross business investment* is the amount of new plant and equipment built during the year, plus additions to inventories. But some plant and equipment wore out during the year, indicated by the size of depreciation allowances. By deducting depreciation from gross investment we get *net business investment*, or the net increase in the stock of productive equipment.

A serious difficulty with NNP is that the capital consumption allowance on which it rests is one of the more uncertain figures in the national income table. The main ingredient in estimated capital consumption is the amount put aside for depreciation by business concerns. The Department of Commerce is forced to take these business estimates at face value. But how do we know that they precisely measure the wearing out of capital during the year? Some companies may overdepreciate, others may underdepreciate, and the net result is unclear. Since capital consumption is rather a guess, NNP is a guess also. So, having explained what it means, we shall make little use of it in later chapters. In discussing ups and downs in total production, we shall usually fall back on the more solid GNP figure.

3. *National income.* Suppose we stop looking at Table 17–3 as a total of *production* and look at it as a total of *incomes*. We ask now how much income workers, investors, and other suppliers of the factors of production have earned in the course of the year's activities. This is useful in calculating labor and capital shares in national income.

The sales value of the year's output, after providing for depreciation, is NNP. Isn't this the figure we are seeking? Not quite. Everything which producing units receive in return for goods sold is *not* available for the factors of production. Business concerns must pay sales taxes, excise taxes, property taxes, and various other fees and licenses. These are shown in Table 17–3 as *indirect taxes*, to distinguish them from the direct tax on corporate profits. After deducting indirect taxes and a few smaller items, we see that *national income*, the total earnings of the factors of production, amounted in 1961 to $427.8 billion.

4. *Personal income.* Not all the income which Table 17–3 shows as belonging to the factors of production actually reaches them. This is notably true of profit income. The government takes close to half through the corporate income tax, and boards of directors vote to hold back part of the remainder. Thus the stockholders may end up getting a quarter or less of "their" profits. There are also deductions from labor income. The amount which a worker pays into social security and private pension funds, as well as what the employer contributes on his behalf, is counted as belonging to him, but he never sees it.

On the positive side, people receive some income which has not been earned in the course of current production. Veterans receive various cash benefits, farmers receive government checks for land taken out of production, workers receive unemployment compensation payments and old age pensions, relief cases receive checks from the city, and so on. All these government *transfer payments* are counted as part of personal income. There is also a small volume of business transfer payments through pensions and other private welfare plans. In 1961, transfer payments of every sort totaled $33.4 billion.

Personal income, then, is income actually received from every source, including transfer payments, before payment of personal income taxes.

5. *Disposable income.* This is simply personal income *after* payment of income taxes. It is how much money people finally have left to spend or to save. It is an interesting figure for retailers and consumer goods manufacturers, since it indicates the size of the consumer market. If disposable income is rising, most businesses can expect to find their sales rising as well.

We can summarize this section by listing the magnitude of these various totals in 1961, as derived from Table 17–3:

	MILLIONS OF DOLLARS
Gross national product	518,725
Minus: Capital consumption allowances	45,339
Equals Net national product	473,386
Minus: Indirect business taxes	48,187
Plus: Other minor items	2,630
Equals National income	427,829
Minus: Corporate profits taxes	22,251
Undistributed profits	8,284
Corporate inventory valuation adjustment	−16
Social security contributions	21,620
Plus: Government transfer payments	31,269
Net interest paid by government	7,341
Business transfer payments,	2,132
Equals Personal income	416,432
Minus: Personal income taxes	52,784
Equals Disposable income	363,648
Consumption	338,058
Savings	25,590

USES OF NATIONAL INCOME: COMPARISONS OVER TIME

Learning these concepts may have seemed tedious, but they greatly increase one's ability to analyze economic events. We shall suggest a few of their main uses, and indicate some pitfalls which await the unwary user.

One use of national income figures is for historical analysis of how a country's output has changed over long periods of time. Has U.S. national output risen steadily or intermittently? At what rate, on the average? Are we getting richer by 2 percent a year or 5 percent?

The first difficulty in tackling these questions is that we are working with a rubber yardstick. All our figures of national output are expressed in dollars. But a dollar sometimes measures a larger quantity of physical goods and sometimes a smaller quantity, depending on changes in prices. When prices rise, our yardstick shrinks—a dollar equals less goods than before; and when prices fall, the yardstick expands again.

The technique of adjusting for price changes is termed *deflation*, and was described in Chapter 1. Its accuracy depends on the accuracy of the price indexes which are used in the process. Since price indexes are never perfect, the deflated or *constant dollar* figures which result are never completely reliable.

The difference made by adjustment for price changes is illustrated in Figure 17–1. Since prices have gone up over the long run, GNP in constant dollars rises more slowly than GNP in current dollars. It is a sound rule never to use current dollar figures for comparisons over any extended period of time.

FIGURE 17–1

U.S. Gross National Product, 1929–61

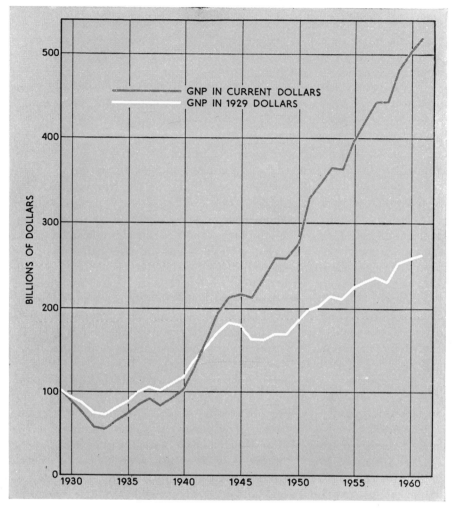

Even after the price experts have done their best, we are far from being out of the woods. Here are a few brain teasers:

1. The deflation procedure assumes that we are dealing with unchanging products. Prices may vary up and down, but the products being priced are supposed to remain constant. But in practice product quality is always changing, usually for the better. The 1960 Ford is not the 1935 Ford. The dacron and cotton shirt of 1960 is not the same as the cotton broadcloth shirt of 1940. Quality can sometimes be measured. One can discover how many thousand miles a four-ply tire will run before the tread is gone. If a tire costs 20 percent more in 1960 than in 1950, but if it will also run 20 percent more miles, there has been no increase in the price

per thousand miles of use. But in many cases no such measurement is possible.

One of the writer's colleagues argues persuasively that there was no real increase in consumer prices between 1950 and 1960, although the Consumer Price Index showed a rise of about 25 percent. His argument is as follows: Give a family a 1950 Sears Roebuck catalog and a 1960 Sears catalog. Give them $1,000 and allow them to make up an order list from *either* the 1950 or 1960 catalog, but not from both. If the family decides to use the 1960 catalog, which he believes most people would do, this must mean that they consider the higher 1960 prices more than offset by improved quality.

Quality improvements, whether measurable or not, are certainly important. To the extent that they are not allowed for in our price indexes, the rise in price levels is overstated and the rise in real GNP is consequently understated.

2. This difficulty becomes even more serious if some goods disappear completely from the shopping list and new articles take their place. How does one compare the price of a horse and carriage in 1890 with the price of a "horseless carriage" in 1940? Or the cost of traveling a thousand miles by Pullman car in 1910 with first-class jet air fare for the same distance in 1960? What about products which don't replace anything, because nothing like them existed before? Television sets, vitamin pills, sulfa drugs, electronic computers, isotopes, and many other things now included in our national "market basket" are recent developments. They had no price in 1930 because they didn't exist.

Price indexes and GNP totals are not well adapted to covering drastic changes in the items going into national output. Over short periods during which people's way of life stays much the same, our measurements work reasonably well. But as we stretch out the period covered, we run into increasing difficulty. How much does it mean to calculate that the average American lives 3.2 times as well in 1960 as he did in 1870? The truth is that he lives very *differently*. By present standards, he seems to be living much better. But it is a bold man who would attach an exact percentage figure to the improvement.

There is a similar difficulty, as we shall see, when we try to make comparisons between countries with very different ways of life. Does an average American family live twice as well as an average Russian family? Three times as well? Certainly the *pattern* of life is very different. How much more one can say is open to question.

3. For judging increases in consumer welfare it is important to look at the *makeup* of GNP as well as its size. Nobody eats GNP. We must focus on that part of GNP which is destined for consumer use. And perhaps not all of that. The New York executive spends a good deal on railroad tickets for commuting from his home in the suburbs. This counts as part of the national product which he "enjoys." But does it add to his

satisfaction? On the contrary, it is a time-consuming nuisance. The more money he spends in this way, the *worse* off he is.

Simon Kuznets, a leading authority on national income, argues that many things which we count as part of national output should be considered *costs* rather than *products*. The costs involved in sustaining enormous metropolitan areas—travel costs to and within the area, subway systems, high rents arising from urban crowding, police protection, and other overhead expenses—should be deducted from national output. Similarly, Kuznets maintains that national defense costs should not be counted as part of national product. Since these types of expense have been increasing with disproportionate speed, we may not be getting better off as rapidly as the GNP totals suggest.

4. GNP measures outputs, not inputs. It says nothing about how much effort was needed to produce a certain output. Here we can strike an optimistic note, for the amount of effort going into the national product has been declining for at least a century. Our grandfathers worked a 60-hour week, our fathers a 48-hour one. Our children will probably work no more than 30 hours a week, and have a couple of months vacation besides. If we include this gain in leisure time, welfare has been rising faster than the output figures indicate.

5. The rules about imputed output affect the behavior of GNP over the course of time. Before 1900 housewives in the United States did most of the baking, clothes making, laundry, and other household services. Since these things were done at home without pay, they didn't count as part of national output. Since 1900, more and more of this work has been shifted outside the home. We have pre-packaged and pre-cooked foods, commercial bakeries, garment factories, commercial laundries and dry-cleaning establishments, repair shops of every description. The output of these establishments is bought and sold, hence *is* counted in GNP. Thus even if people consumed no more food or clothing than before, it would *look* as though GNP had increased. The actual increase in consumer goods production since 1900 is doubtless somewhat less than the apparent increase for this reason.

Despite these doubts and qualifications, we shall go boldly ahead in later chapters to compare GNP figures for a hundred years and more. But the reader has been warned to keep tongue in cheek and not to take the figures more seriously than they deserve.

USES OF NATIONAL INCOME: COMPARISONS OVER SPACE

In this international age, people want to make income comparisons among countries. The United Nations has to do this for the practical reason that member nations are supposed to contribute to the U.N. budget in proportion to their national incomes. No wonder every government has to have a national income estimater! People interested in the comparative strength of capitalist and communist economies want to compare GNP in Britain, the United States, or Japan with GNP in Russia, Poland, or China. People interested in the less developed countries want some measure of how badly off these countries are. Is GNP per head higher in Mexico than in India? Is Indonesia better off than Ghana?

The problems involved in international comparisons are similar to those involved in comparisons over time for the same country. First, there is the problem of currency units. Japanese GNP is in billions of yen, while U.S. GNP is in billions of dollars. How do we get from dollars to yen, or marks, or rupees?

One simple expedient is to use the official exchange rate between the two currencies. A U.S. dollar at present exchanges for about 5 Indian rupees. So we can take the GNP of India, divide by 5, and say that the result represents Indian GNP "converted to U.S. dollars." The trouble with this is that official exchange rates may not correspond closely to the actual buying power of the two currencies in their home countries. Anyone traveling in England in the early fifties could observe that a British pound would buy at least as much as four dollars would buy in the United States. The official exchange rate, however, was £1 = $2.80. The pound was undervalued. Similarly, the Japanese yen was undervalued in the late fifties, and visitors to Japan came home laden with radios, cameras, and pearls. South American currencies, on the other hand, are usually overvalued. They will not buy as much as the corresponding amounts of U.S. money would buy at home, and so tourists find few bargains in Latin America.

Suppose we forget official rates and set out to find the proper ratio between the dollar and the yen. We could make up a shopping list of consumer goods, see what the whole list would cost in the United States in dollars, and then what it would cost in Japan in yen. If the U.S. cost is 100 dollars and the Japanese cost 20,000 yen, one might say that 1 dollar = 200 yen is a proper conversion factor. But how do we get our shopping list in the first place? Japanese consumption habits are different from those in the United States. If we start with a "Japanese market basket" and price these items in both countries we shall get one result, while if we start with a "U.S. market basket" we shall get a different result. A common compromise is to try both procedures, get two exchange ratios, and then average them.

Suppose we have handled the currency conversion problem in one way or another. GNP totals for other countries of the world have been converted into dollars. We next divide each country's GNP by its population, to get national output *per capita*. We can then make up a comparative listing such as that shown in Table 17–4.

Any table of this sort deserves a hard look. It seems to say that the average American is living 30 or 40 times as well as the average Burmese or Indonesian. Unfortunately, it just isn't so. I am not living 40 times as well as the people in Bali. Nor am I living 10 times as well as the average

Japanese. Something seems to have gone wrong with the arithmetic. What is it?

At least four things have gone wrong. First, we are comparing an overwhelmingly rural population living largely on a subsistence basis, in Burma or Indonesia, with a dominantly urban population living in a cash economy in the United States. It might make some sense to compare farmers living in the mountains of Java with hillbillies in the southern Appalachians. But it makes little sense to compare the Javanese farmer with people in New York City or Chicago.

TABLE 17–4
Gross National Product per Capita, Selected Countries, 1957*

COUNTRY	GNP PER CAPITA (U.S. Dollars)	COUNTRY	GNP PER CAPITA (U.S. Dollars)
United States	2,577	Greece	340
Canada	1,947	Japan	306
Sweden	1,380	Brazil	293
Australia	1,316	Mexico	262
New Zealand	1,310	Turkey	220
Great Britain	1,189	Peru	179
France	943	Egypt	142
West Germany	927	India	73
Venezuela†	648	Pakistan	70
Italy	516	Burma	57
Argentina	490		

* M. Usui and E. E. Hagen, *World Income 1957* (Cambridge, Mass.: M.I.T. Center for International Studies, 1959).
† Average of 1952 and 1953.

Second, we are comparing very different patterns of life. The Japanese middle-class house, with its sliding wooden panels, simple furniture, absence of central heating, secluded and beautiful garden, and staff of low-paid servants, involves much less cash outlay than the more elaborate and mechanized middle-class household in the United States. But if the Japanese family spends one quarter as much, does this mean it is living only one quarter as well? From some philosophical standpoints, it may be living better. The problem is similar to that of comparing Americans in 1960 with Americans in 1860.

A third problem is the great importance of nonmarket production in the poorer countries. The rural household in these countries does almost everything for itself. Food growing, cooking, clothes making, laundering, barbering and other personal services, manufacture of simple household furniture and utensils, gathering of fuel, and many other things are done in the home. The national income statistician is apt to overlook these things except for food production, and even food is typically undervalued by being taken at the farm price rather than the retail price. No wonder the output figures for these countries come out so low. It would be interesting to see how different the results would look if everything done by the Indian housewife were revalued on a cash basis.

Finally, consumption is important only in relation to need, and need is relative to climate and other things. The fact that people in the northern United States have to build solid houses, spend money on heating, and change to warm winter clothing is not a *gain* in their standard of living. It is a *cost* of living in a cold climate.

This is not to say that we shouldn't make intercountry comparisons; but until the bases of comparison have been improved, the figures should not be taken too seriously. The *ranking* of countries shown in Tables 17–4 may be roughly correct. Consumption levels in Canada and the United States are somewhat above those in Western Europe, most West European countries are above the Latin American group, and Latin America is generally above the Asian countries with the exception of Japan. But Table 17–4 exaggerates the *distance* between countries on the list, and makes the rich countries look richer than they actually are.

SUMMARY

1. For a single production unit, total *output produced* equals total *income created.*

2. The same principle applies when the output of individual units is added to get totals for the national economy. *National product equals national income.*

3. In making this addition one must avoid double counting by deducting the cost of materials purchased by a production unit, and showing as its output only the *value added* in production.

4. One must include also the value of services produced by government, which is taken as equal to the government payroll; and certain items of imputed income, of which the most important are farm produce consumed on the farm and the imputed rent of owner-occupied dwellings.

5. Review the relations between *gross national product, net national product, national income, personal income,* and *disposable income* by studying the summary listing at the end of that section.

6. In tracing changes in a country's GNP over the course of time, one must first correct for price changes to get *real GNP* or *GNP in constant dollars.* Even after this has been done there remain logical difficulties arising from changes in quality of products; disappearance of some products and appearance of others; the fact that some items consumed in a complex urban society can be regarded as costs rather than additions to income; changes in the input of effort required to produce a certain output; and shifts of production from the household to the market or vice versa.

7. For these reasons GNP comparisons become less meaningful as one extends the period covered. Comparisons over 10 years are reasonably precise. The meaning of comparisons over a century is much less clear.

8. Similar problems arise in GNP comparisons among countries at the same time. Such comparisons are complicated by differences in patterns of life, rural versus urban residence, importance of nonmarket production, and the needs imposed by climate and geography. This prevents any precise measurement of the income gap between the richer and poorer nations, but the gap is certainly less wide than it appears in the usual statistical comparisons.

The Level of National Income

> We first survey the plot, then draw the model;
> Then must we rate the cost of the erection;
> Which if we find outweighs ability,
> What do we then but draw anew the model.
>   WILLIAM SHAKESPEARE, *King Henry IV* (*Part II*)

THE NATIONAL INCOME concepts of Chapter 17 help us to measure and describe changes in the economy. But they do not *explain* these changes. Why was United States GNP in 1962 about $550 billion? Why wasn't it higher or lower? Production cannot rise above the capacity of the economy, which is limited by available supplies of labor, capital, and other resources. But there is no law which prescribes that the economy must operate at full capacity. Why does the American economy operate close to capacity in some years and a good deal below capacity in others?

A related question is what determines the level of prices. Suppose all prices had been twice as high in 1962. Then the money value of GNP would have been about $1,100 billion. Why weren't prices twice as high, or half as high? What determines the price level anyway?

In Part One we learned how to analyze the operation of a particular market. The forces operating in a market can be summarized in supply and demand curves, which determine the quantity and price of the goods exchanged. Can the same sort of reasoning be applied to the economy as a whole? Are there forces working systematically to determine the *total* production of goods and services and the *general* level of prices? And can these forces be summarized in a way similar to the supply-demand diagrams of Part One?

It is a challenging task to explain the great tidal movements of the economy. It is also a task of great practical importance. Every so often the economy turns downward into recession. Unemployment mounts and cries of alarm fill the air. Many remedies are offered to check the decline and set the economy back on the upward path. Which of these proposals are useful, which are ineffectual, and which may be positively harmful? One cannot judge without understanding why production and employment move up or down.

Another practical question: Over the past 10 years the American economy has operated considerably below capacity *even in years of peak prosperity*. Unemployment has remained continuously higher than most people consider desirable, and has crept up gradually over the course of time. The yearly rate of increase in United States GNP has been below that of most other industrial countries. Why this sluggishness in the economy? What steps could be taken to move output up closer to capacity? This has become a matter of public concern and political debate.

Until the 1930's most economists maintained that a capitalist economy tends naturally to operate at full capacity. A depression was only a temporary setback, which did not require corrective action by government. If economic forces were left to work themselves out, they would automatically check the slump and restore prosperity. This view was severely shaken by the Great Depression. In 1940, after 11 years of below-capacity operation, about 15 percent of the American labor force was still unemployed. This does not look like a self-adjusting economy. Eleven years is a long time to wait for economic forces to operate. In the end, capacity operation was restored by World War II rather than by natural recovery.

Alongside the orthodox view there were always economic heretics such as John Hobson, William T. Foster, Waddill Catchings, and Major Douglas, founder of the "Social Credit" movement. These men maintained that there is a fatal flaw in the economy which prevents it from operating at a stable level. The economy, it was argued, turns out a steadily increasing flow of goods, but does not provide enough purchasing power to take these goods off the market. Every so often a shortage of purchasing power develops. Then goods pile up in the stores, businesses reduce production, and workers are unemployed.

In this bald form the argument is surely incorrect. Think back to the logic of national income accounting. The two sides of the account always balance. For every dollar of goods put on the market, there is a dollar of income created. This is received by somebody and is available for spending. There is no built-in leakage of income from the system which would mean an *unavoidable* shortage of purchasing power. True, income may go to households or businesses which choose not to spend it. But this is a different matter. It depends on human decisions, and human decisions can be changed.

So we must discard both of the older views—the view that the economy tends naturally toward capacity operation, and the view that it must suffer frequent relapses because of a structural defect. In a particular economy at a particular time, there are forces operating to determine an equilibrium level of production and employment. But this equilibrium will not necessarily be at the level of capacity operation. It may by good fortune just be at that level; but it may also be above or below it.

What are the basic economic forces at work? How do they determine an equilibrium level of output, and where will this be? This chapter and the next are aimed at answering these questions.

INCOME AND SPENDING

Everyone would agree that the level of demand affects the level of production, and that demand involves spending. Most discussions of prosperity and depression take spending as a point of departure. Consider the following commonsense "explanation" of depression: "Why is business bad? Because there is not enough spending. Why isn't there enough spending? Because people's incomes are low. Why are people's incomes low? Because business is bad." This sort of circular reasoning cannot explain anything. Yet one hears it repeatedly in popular discussion.

Autonomous and Induced Spending

How can we get out of this circle and onto a useful method of analysis? The clue is that, while spending is heavily influenced by income, it does not depend *solely* on income. With the same level of income, people may decide to save more and spend less or vice versa. We have also developed credit and borrowing, which makes it possible to spend more than you have.

With no change in income, then, any economic unit can suddenly decide to spend more or to spend less. This is termed an *autonomous* change in spending. But if income changes first and spending changes simply as a consequence, this is termed an *induced* change.

This difference may be illustrated as follows: Consumer income this month is $100 billion, of which $90 billion is spent and $10 billion is saved. Suppose consumer income next month rises to $101 billion, and that consumers continue to divide their incomes between spending and saving in the same proportion. Then next month consumer spending will be $90.9 billion, and saving will be $10.1 billion. There has been an *induced* increase of $0.9 billion in consumer spending. But this cannot be used to explain anything, because it is simply a result of the $1 billion increase in income. We did not explain where this $1 billion came from. We simply supposed it. This leaves us in the position of the Greek who maintained that Atlas was supporting the earth but could not answer the question, "Who is supporting Atlas?"

Suppose instead that consumer income next month remains unchanged at $100 billion, but that consumers reduce their saving ratio. They decide next month to spend $91 billion instead of the previous $90. This *autonomous* increase of $1 billion in spending *can* be regarded as a prime mover. It will lead to an increase in retail sales, which in turn will stimulate output and employment.

Now we seem to be on the right track. An autonomous increase in spending anywhere in the economy will have an expansionary effect. It will certainly cause an increase in sales, probably an increase in production and employment, and possibly an increase in prices. An autonomous decrease in spending will have opposite effects.

Types of Spender

To see how autonomous changes in spending can occur, let's go back to the classification of customers for national output used in Chapter 17. We saw that the whole of national output must be sold to consumers, business concerns, government agencies, or foreign buyers. Let us look briefly at each of these groups.

Consumers are the largest customers for national output. Yet this is the sector in which surprises are least likely to occur. American consumers as a whole behave rather consistently, saving 7 or 8 percent of disposable income and spending the remainder. Changes in consumer spending are mainly induced by income changes. Large autonomous changes occur only in unusual circumstances, such as war or threat of war. In 1941–42 and again in 1950–51 millions of families rushed to the stores to stock up on key items "before the hoarders got all the goods."

The *business* spending which is significant here is what we called in Chapter 17 *business investment*, or final sales to business. Its main components are investment in plant and equipment, investment in inventories, and residential construction. Each of these has an autonomous element and is rather volatile. They rise rapidly at some times and drop at others, with a consequent impact on total spending.

Businesses also normally save part of their profits. A change of policy on this point will affect total spending. A decision to distribute a larger share of profits to stockholders (= a reduction in business saving) will raise spending, while the reverse decision will lower it.

Government agencies now buy about 20 percent of national output. An increase in government purchases raises total spending, while a cut in purchases lowers it. Taxation works in the opposite direction. An *increase* in taxation *reduces* spending, since it leaves consumers with less income than before. A cut in taxation leaves people with more money in their pockets and thus raises spending.

Foreign buyers provide part of the demand for our goods and services. An increase in foreign spending on our products has the same stimulating effect as an increase in domestic spending. Exports of goods and services will rise, and U.S. production and employment will increase.

But we buy abroad as well as sell abroad. An increase in our imports from other countries has a depressing effect. Why is this? Because more goods are available for sale on the American market, but no new domestic purchasing power has been created to absorb these goods. The truism that "for every dollar of goods produced there is a dollar of income created" no longer works if the income has been created *abroad* while the goods are shipped for sale *here*. Put another way, an increase in the amount of U.S. income spent on foreign goods leaves less available for purchase of domestic production.

A Check-list of Forces

We can now list the autonomous changes which may raise or lower the level of spending; and we can be sure that this is a *complete* list, because of the completeness of the national income accounts on which it is based. Anything which affects the level of national income must do so through one of these channels.

Sector	Autonomous Changes Producing Expansion	Autonomous Changes Producing Contraction
Consumer	Increase in consumption expenditure	Decrease in consumption expenditure
Business	Increase in plant and equipment investment	Decrease in plant and equipment investment
	Increase in inventory investment	Decrease in inventory investment
	Increase in residential construction	Decrease in residential construction
	Decrease in business saving	Increase in business saving
Government	Decrease in tax rates	Increase in tax rates
	Increase in expenditure programs	Decrease in expenditure programs
Foreign	Increase in exports	Decrease in exports
	Decrease in imports	Increase in imports

This list is useful in several ways. First, it provides a test of alleged causes of economic expansion or contraction. If someone argues that a certain development will raise national income, one can ask: Which of the expansionist channels is it going to affect? How do we know? Can we be sure that there will not be offsetting (depressing) effects on other items in the table?

Second, it provides a rudimentary basis for economic forecasting.

One can go down the list and ask what will probably happen to each of these quantities over the next year and so build up an estimate of national income. This is a rather primitive technique, but some professional forecasters do little more than this.

Third, it provides a framework for discussion of public policy. Suppose the economy is in depression and the problem is how to get out. One can begin by asking what it might be feasible to do to each item in the expansion column. There may be several levers which can be manipulated with some prospect of success. Having analyzed each of these, one can go on to the problem of choosing which levers to pull.

The problem is not always too little spending. Occasionally in the United States, and more frequently in some other countries, there has been a problem of too much spending, leading to price inflation. The contraction column of the table then becomes pertinent, and one must look down it for ways of reducing spending.

AGGREGATE ECONOMIC EQUILIBRIUM

In Part One we become familiar with the concept of equilibrium in a particular market. In equilibrium, the amount of a product which people are willing to buy at the prevailing price equals the amount which sellers are willing to supply. A similar approach can be used for the economy as a whole. *Aggregate demand* is total spending from all the sources listed above—spending by consumers, businesses, government, and foreign buyers. *Aggregate supply* is the total value of goods and services being produced in the economy. The economy will be in equilibrium, with no tendency to expand or contract, only if aggregate demand and aggregate supply are equal.

If aggregate demand exceeds aggregate supply, an expansion is set in motion. If the economy is operating well below capacity, this will be mainly an increase in production and employment. But as expansion proceeds, some industries approach capacity and their prices begin to rise. Eventually one may reach a stage at which the whole economy is operating at capacity and output increases are no longer possible. If aggregate demand still exceeds aggregate supply, the only effect will be a rise in the price level.

If aggregate demand falls short of aggregate supply, a contraction is set in motion. This could take the form of a drop in prices, or a drop in output, or some mixture of the two. In the present American economy most prices are hard to reduce, partly because it is not feasible to cut wage rates which form the bulk of production costs. Insufficient demand, then, leads mainly to a drop in production and employment.

There is an important difference, however, between reasoning about overall economic equilibrium and reasoning about equilibrium in one market. In dealing with a single market, one can safely assume that *supply and demand are independent.* An increase in production of potatoes will not increase the demand for potatoes. But in analyzing the national economy, the assumption of independence no longer holds. An increase in total output *will* raise incomes, which will lead to an induced rise in spending. Aggregate supply and aggregate demand are interrelated.

A Basic National Income Identity

Let us explore this interrelation by looking at an economy in which business concerns must finance any new investment by borrowing from households. There is no business saving. Government is included, and can run either a budget surplus or a deficit. We ignore foreign trade for the time being, since this would complicate the story without adding anything essential.

Gross national product can be viewed either as total *output* or as total *income*. Thinking first in terms of output, all output must go either into consumption (C), business investment (I), or government purchases (G). Hence we see that

$$GNP \equiv C + I + G$$

The identity sign $\equiv$ is used to indicate a statement which must be true by definition.

Turn now to the income side and consider all the places where income can go. All the income generated in the course of production is paid over to government in taxes (T), or is saved by households (S), or is spent on consumption (C). So from this standpoint

$$GNP \equiv C + S + T$$

But since things which are equal to the same thing are equal to one another

$$C + S + T \equiv C + I + G$$

Canceling out C and shifting T to the right side, we arrive at

$$S \equiv I + (G - T)$$

Saving equals investment plus the government deficit. This is often termed the *basic national income identity*.

The Condition of Aggregate Equilibrium

But if the economy always balances out in this way, how can it ever be out of equilibrium? How can there ever be an expansion or contraction in national income?

The answer lies in a simple but vital distinction between *past transactions* and *future plans*. Our national accounting measurements always refer to a completed period in the past. We close the books at the end of the year and total up consumption, saving, and other key items. We then find that the identities just listed hold good. They *must* be true by the nature of the accounting system, as was explained in Chapter 17.

But suppose that instead of the past we are looking forward to the future. Here we stand on January 1, 1964, considering the movement of the economy over the year ahead. Now instead of *completed investment* we are interested in *planned or intended investment*. Similarly, it is *planned saving, consumption, and government budgets* which are pertinent.

For the rest of this chapter, whenever we use one of the standard national income concepts, we shall use it in its *future or intended* sense. S means *intended saving*, I means *intended investment*, and so on. It is important to grasp and remember this point, since the whole analysis depends upon it.

Can we now continue to maintain that (planned)

$$S = I + (G - T)?$$

By no means. Consider that savings and consumption decisions are made by some 50 million households, with no central coordination. Investment plans are made separately by many thousands of large businesses and millions of smaller ones. Budget plans are made by thousands of state and local units as well as the federal government. These decisions could conceivably add up in such a way that the amount households are planning to save just equals the amount which business concerns and governments are planning to borrow. But this would be no more than an accident, and is in fact very unlikely.

But suppose this accident does occur, and that (planned)

$$S = I + (G - T)$$

What does this mean? The left-hand side shows the amount which households are planning to pull out of the income stream through saving. The right-hand side shows the amount which business and government units are planning to add to the stream by spending beyond their current incomes. Consider the present level of national income as the water level in a tank. Then if the outflow of water through the "savings pipe" is just balanced by the amount pumped in through the "investment pump," the level of the tank will remain unchanged. The system is in equilibrium.

This basic condition for aggregate equilibrium can be met in a variety of ways. Suppose that at the present level of national income households wish to save $100 billion. Thus the equilibrium condition becomes

$$100 = I + (G - T)$$

A little figuring reveals that the economy could be in balance with investment of $100 billion and a balanced government budget; or with investment of $120 billion and a budget surplus of $20 billion; or with investment of $80 billion and a budget deficit of $20 billion; or with any other combination which adds up correctly. Some of these combinations may be considered preferable to others, but they are similar in that any of them would maintain the current level of income unchanged.

Now what happens if the multitude of spending plans do not add up in this way? Suppose that (planned)

$$S > I + (G - T)$$

This means that the amount leaking out through the savings pipe is greater than the amount being added by the investment pump. There is a deficiency of total spending, and the level of income must fall. This means, incidentally, that households will not actually be able to save as much as they had intended, because their incomes will be lower than they expected. This brings out an important principle: If there is a divergence of plans on the two sides of the equation, *the gap is closed by a change in the level of income.*

Suppose the gap is in the other direction. Suppose that (planned)

$$S < I + (G - T)$$

The amount pumped in by business investment and government deficits exceeds the amount drawn off in savings. (Where do business and government get this extra money? From the banking system, as we shall see in Chapters 21–22). In this case the level of national income will move upward. As incomes rise, people will save more than they had intended originally. Once more the gap in plans sets up a movement of national income in a direction which tends to close the gap.

In sum,

If $S = I + (G - T)$, the level of income will remain unchanged.
If $S > I + (G - T)$, the level of income will fall.
If $S < I + (G - T)$, the level of income will rise.

THE LEVEL OF NATIONAL INCOME

So far so good. We have seen how a divergence in spending plans can raise or lower the level of national income. But we still have no way of defining what the equilibrium level of income will be at a particular time.

A clarification is necessary here to avoid misunderstanding. In the last chapter we drew a careful distinction between Gross National Product, Net National Product, and national income. Precise definition of this last term is important if one is really interested in income, and in the division of income into labor and property shares.

But when the man in the street, or even the man in Washington, speaks of "national income," he usually *means* Gross National Product. This is the significant total if one is interested in changes in national output and employment. At any rate, it is the total with which we are concerned here. What we want is a way of defining the equilibrium level of GNP. But we shall use the term national income as interchangeable with GNP, bowing on this point to popular usage.

A useful approach to the problem is illustrated in Figure 18–1. On

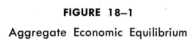

FIGURE 18–1

Aggregate Economic Equilibrium

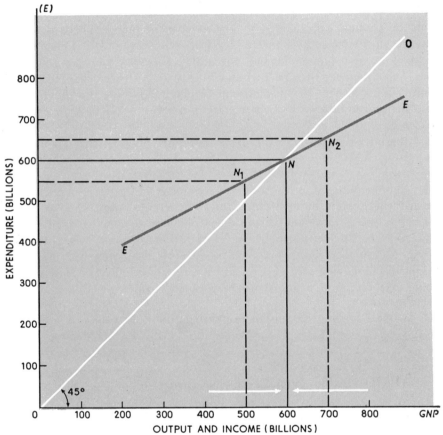

At any point on OO expenditure and output are equal. So any equilibrium position must lie on OO. The expenditure schedule EE shows planned spending at each level of income. Note that spending rises with income, but less rapidly. The intersection of EE and OO at N defines the equilibrium level of income, which is $600 billion.

the horizontal axis we lay out GNP, or national output. On the vertical axis we lay out total spending on national output by consumers, businesses, and government.

Now what is the meaning of aggregate equilibrium? It means that producers are able to sell just what they are producing, so that they have no incentive to produce either more or less. The requirement for equilibrium is that *expenditure on national output must equal the cost of na-*

tional output (including the "normal" profit with which we became familiar in Part One.) So let's lay out a line, *OO*, running up from the origin at an angle of 45 degrees. At any point on this line, total output and total expenditure are equal. Thus *any position of aggregate equilibrium must lie on OO.* One can regard *OO* as a kind of supply curve, since it shows the conditions under which various levels of production would be forthcoming. If expenditure were $400 billion, then $400 billion of output would be forthcoming on a sustained basis. If instead of this, expenditure were $500 billion, then $500 billion would be produced; and so on up to the output capacity of the economy. (What happens if demand rises above capacity we leave until the next chapter.)

We set against this on the demand side the expenditure schedule, *EE*. This shows the amount which all spending units will desire to spend at various levels of national income. It refers to *planned* or *intended* spending. *EE* shows planned spending rising as income rises, which seems logical. But note that *spending rises less rapidly than income*, because saving is also increasing. The reasons for drawing *EE* in this way will be explained in a moment.

The logic of *EE* is exactly the same as that of the demand curves in Part One. It is an "iffy" or hypothetical construction, a snapshot of spenders' intentions at a moment of time. It says that *if* at this moment national income were $500 billion, then households, businesses, and governments would want to spend $550 billion. *If*, on the other hand, income were to be $700 billion, spenders would want to spend $650 billion. Since only one such possibility can be realized, only one point on *EE* is pertinent at a particular time.

In constructing *EE*, just as in constructing a demand curve, we assume that certain things are known and constant. For each level of income, we must assume some distribution of personal income among households. (Rich families typically save more than poor ones.) Each household is supposed to know definitely how much it would spend and save at various income levels. Similarly, each business concern and government unit is supposed to have definite spending plans for the period ahead. Monetary conditions and interest rates must be taken as given, since they will affect spending plans. The price level must also be taken as given, so that we can work with "constant dollars." What happens when some of these given conditions change will be explored in later chapters.

Once we know the location of *EE*, we can determine the equilibrium level of national income. The equilibrium is defined by the intersection of *OO* and *EE* at *N*. At this point total spending is $600 billion, and the volume of goods being produced is also $600 billion. So producers can find a market for their current output. Everything will go along smoothly so long as the underlying conditions remain unchanged.

The fact that *N* is an equilibrium position can be shown also by supposing that output is at some other level and asking what will happen. Suppose output were running at only $500 billion per year (N_1). Looking across to the expenditure axis, we see that planned expenditure at this income level would be $550 billion, well above the level of current production. This excess demand would give businesses an incentive to expand production, and the system would move to the right toward N.

Suppose on the other hand that production somehow reached a level of $700 billion (N_2). Could this level be sustained? No, it could not, because total expenditure would be only $650 billion. There would be a shortage of demand, unsold goods would pile up, and production would be cut back.

The small arrows on the horizontal axis of Figure 18–1 indicate that, if actual output is anywhere below the equilibrium level of $600 billion, output will tend to rise. Conversely, if output is above the equilibrium level, it will tend to fall.

Three cautions should be added:

1. There is nothing particularly *good* about equilibrium. It is a position of rest, but not necessarily a desirable position. Point N in Figure 18–1 might turn out to be a long way below the capacity of an economy. Only by a stroke of luck would it coincide with the point of full employment.

2. The fact that the economy at any moment may be regarded as *moving toward* an equilibrium position such as N does not mean that it will actually get there. Long before this has happened EE will have changed its location, which means that N has also shifted, and the economy then sets off after this new will-of-the-wisp.

3. In a sense, we are not interested in equilibrium positions at all. The main usefulness of Figure 18–1 is to help in analyzing conditions of *change*. Take the "business cycle." What happens during a recession is that EE starts to drop, pulling production down after it. After a while it hits bottom and begins moving upward again. *Question:* How can this wavy up-and-down dance of EE be made less violent than it has been in the past?

Those who complain of the sluggishness of the American economy since about 1955 are saying that even in the best years N has been considerably below full capacity. *Question:* What could be done to raise EE so that it would intersect OO at a higher level, a level corresponding to full employment? These are problems of change, but we need an equilibrium diagram to get at them effectively.

COMPONENTS OF SPENDING: CONSUMPTION

We have now gotten ahead of the game by drawing a schedule for total spending without saying anything about the behavior of different types of spenders. So we must backtrack and look at what determines consumer spending, business investment, and the rest. We continue for the moment with our simplified economy, in which all saving is done by households and all investment by business concerns. And we leave government on the sidelines, to be brought in at a later stage.

The Short-Run Consumption Schedule

Let's look first at consumers. How will consumer spending behave as national income moves up and down? What is the shape of the *consumption schedule* relating various levels of national income to consumer spending at each level?

The main things which determine the answer are:

1. *The thriftiness of individual families.* Each household has its own spending schedule, indicating how it would behave at various levels of family income. These schedules have a characteristic shape. Even if income is low, a family will continue to spend some minimum amount on the basic necessities of life. If necessary, it can spend beyond its income for a while by not paying bills and by borrowing. This is called *dissaving* or *negative saving*.

The consumption schedule of the Jewkes family is shown in Figure 18–2. Note that to the left of B the family is dissaving. At B, where its income has risen to $6,000 a year, it is just breaking even. Above this level, it begins to make positive savings, shown by the widening gap between CC and the 45 degree line.

The break-even point above which savings begin can be taken as a measure of the family's thriftiness. The household shown by C_1C_1, which breaks even only at $10,000 a year, is less thrifty than the Jewkes family. Now the national consumption schedule is the sum of all family schedules in the country. If most families begin to save at a low level of income, this will produce a low break-even point on the national consumption schedule. The less thrifty the population, the higher the break-even point will be.

There are substantial differences among countries in this respect. Japanese families are considerably more thrifty than American families at the same relative income level. This is one reason why Japan's national savings rate is higher than ours.

2. *The short-run flexibility of spending plans.* The break-even point gives us one interesting fact about a household's consumption schedule. The other interesting thing is the *slope* of the schedule, which shows how the family reacts to a *change* in its income. The slope of CC indicates how a change in income will be divided between spending and saving.

Lord Keynes devised a famous term in this connection, *the marginal propensity to consume*. If a family, on receiving an additional $100, increases its spending by $75, its marginal propensity to consume is $3/4$. There is a twin concept, *the marginal propensity to save*, which in this case would be $25/100 = 1/4$. Since all income must be either saved or spent, the two propensities must add up to 1.

FIGURE 18–2

Consumption Schedule for the Jewkes Family

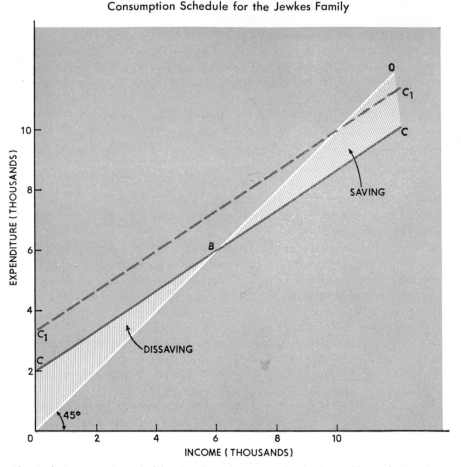

The Jewkes' consumption schedule, CC, shows how much the family would spend at various levels of annual income. To the left of B, that is, below $6,000 a year, they spend more than they receive. To the right of B, spending is below income and there is positive saving. C_1C_1 is the consumption schedule for another family, which begins to save only at the $10,000 level.

The consumption schedule for the Jewkes family was drawn to show a marginal propensity to consume of $\frac{2}{3}$. An increase of $1,000 in income brings increased spending of $667 and increased saving of $333. And we assumed that the m.p.c. remained constant for all levels of income, so that CC is a straight line.

How will actual families react to income changes in the real world? One can imagine two extreme possibilities: A family might be completely "set in its ways." It is used to living in a certain way and is determined to go on living that way. If income falls, consumption expenditure will remain unchanged, and the difference will be made up by cutting savings or (if necessary) by dissaving. If income rises, consumption spending will again remain unchanged, so that all the extra income is added to savings. For a family behaving in this way, *CC* would be a *horizontal straight line*, indicating an m.p.c. = 0.

The opposite extreme is that of a family living always "from hand to mouth." If it gets more income, it immediately finds ways of spending this on increased consumption. If income falls, consumption is cut back correspondingly. In this case, *CC* would coincide with the 45 degree line, indicating an m.p.c. = 1.

Most families' reactions are doubtless somewhere between these extremes. If income rises, spending will also rise, but not as much as income. Similarly for a fall in income.

The consumption schedule resembles a demand curve in that its shape depends on *how much time is allowed for adjustment*. If a family's income suddenly rises, it may not find anything to do with the extra money next day or next week. But by next month it will probably have increased its spending; and by next year, if the higher income level is expected to continue, it may have found ways of spending practically all of the increase. *The longer the adjustment period, the steeper the slope of CC*, i.e., the higher the m.p.c.

3. *The distribution of income among households.* Thus far we have spoken only of consumption schedules for particular families. But we are really interested in the *national* consumption schedule, showing how much consumer spending we can expect at various levels of national income.

In working up from family consumption schedules to the national schedule, there is a large missing link. We can't say how much of a $500 billion national income will be spent unless we know *who gets the $500 billion*. We must know the distribution of this income among families in the country. Then we can look at each family's consumption schedule, see how much it will spend, and total up.

An important and controversial question is how the national consumption schedule is affected by the degree of inequality in household incomes. Suppose we start from the income distribution shown in Chapter 14. Now a band of Robin Hoods descend on the country and start taking from the rich and give to the poor. Income distribution becomes more equal. How will this affect consumer spending? One's first thought is that the poor man receiving an extra dollar will spend a larger proportion of it than the rich man who lost it would have done, and this is probably right.[2]

But the matter is more complicated than this. How much family A spends depends partly on the living standards of other families in the community. If there are families much better off, and whose living standards

---

[2] See in this connection M. Bronfenbrenner, T. Yamane, and C. H. Lee, "A Study in Redistribution and Consumption," *Review of Economics and Statistics*, May, 1955, pp. 153 ff. This study shows the m.p.c. falling from 0.98 for families with incomes of $2,000–$3,000 to 0.60 for families with incomes above $7,500.

family A would like to imitate, this may raise family A's consumption schedule. This is the familiar "keeping up with the Joneses." If incomes in the community become more equal, this reduces the pressure for competitive consumption and may lower the consumption schedule. This could

FIGURE 18–3

The National Consumption Schedule

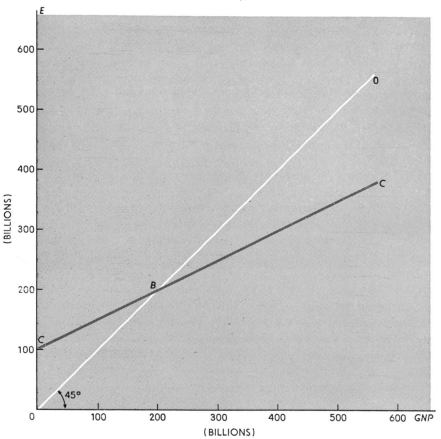

The national consumption schedule, CC, shows how much all households in the country would plan to spend at each level of GNP. As in the case of the Jewkes family schedule, there is negative saving to the left of *B*, positive saving to the right of *B*.

conceivably be important enough to outweigh the direct effect of income transfers.

It is clear in any case that income distribution is important, and that in constructing the national consumption schedule we must take distribution as given.

A possible national consumption schedule is shown in Figure 18–3. It resembles the household consumption schedule of Figure 18–2, except that we are now dealing with billions of dollars instead of thousands. To the left of B, total saving is negative. At B it is zero, and to the right of B it is positive by an increasing amount.

The region to the left of B is of little importance. It does not mean much to say that consumer spending would still be $100 billion even if GNP were zero, because the system would presumably have collapsed before this. The only modern instance of negative saving occurred at the bottom of the Great Depression of the 1930's.

What we want mainly to learn from the consumption schedule is how the economy behaves to the right of B. If GNP rises $50 billion, what will happen to consumption? Conversely, if a recession sets in and GNP drops $30 billion, how much will consumption go down? The answer which we read off from CC is that consumption will rise by one half of any increase in GNP, and will fall by one half of any decline.

Consumption Behavior in the Long Run

We come now to a puzzling feature of the national consumption schedule. As a family gets richer, the percentage of its income which is saved rises substantially. Figure 18–3 implies that the same is true for the nation. As national income rises, the "savings gap" between CC and OO widens. A little arithmetic reveals that the percentage of income saved is 0 at $300 billion, 0.166 at $600 billion, 0.222 at $900 billion, and so on. Since U.S. national income has more than doubled over the past several decades, one would expect the savings ratio to have risen.

When one looks at the statistics, however, one gets a surprise. Data for the years 1950–60 are shown in Figure 18–4. Since government is not yet in the picture, we show on the horizontal axis *privately available income*, while the vertical axis shows consumption expenditure. Each point shows the data for a particular year. The straight line $C_L C_L$ (L for long-run) provides a close fit to these points, and the equation of this line turns out to be $C = 0.81Y$. This says that, *regardless of the level of income*, about four fifths will be spent on consumption and the other fifth will be saved. The proportion of income saved does not rise as the nation grows richer.

This seems to contradict our previous conclusion. Yet it must be accepted as historical fact. Indeed, Professor Kuznets' studies indicate that this has been true over a much longer period. He finds that the proportion of national income saved has not changed materially since 1870, though real national income has risen several fold since then.

How can we explain this apparent paradox? The explanation lies in the distinction we drew earlier between short-run reactions and long-run behavior. CC in Figure 18–3 showed the short-run impact of a change in income. Over a few months or calendar quarters, the response of consumption to income changes is quite sluggish.

Given a longer period for adjustment, however, people are quite capable of finding ways to use additional income. Former luxuries come to be

FIGURE 18–4

Relation of Consumption to Income, 1950–60

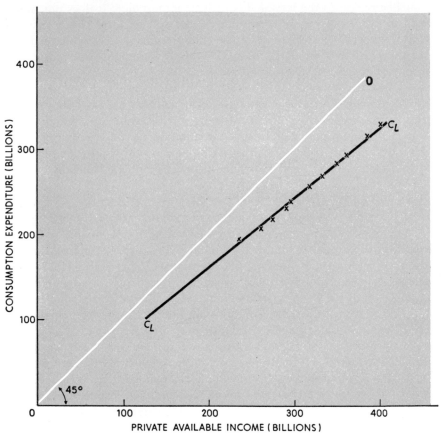

$C_L C_L$ summarizes the actual relation of consumer expenditure to privately available income over the years 1950–60. Each point on the chart shows the data for a particular year, and $C_L C_L$ is a line of best fit to these points.

regarded as necessities, and new products appear to stimulate consumer demand. This gradual increase of living standards in response to rising incomes may be viewed as an *upward shift* of the short-run consumption schedule (Figure 18–5). The schedule rises from CC to $C_1 C_1$, then to $C_2 C_2$, and so on into the future. The small circles may be regarded as representing the normal level of income at periods 10 years apart, so that $C_3 C_3$ carries a date 30 years later than CC. When these are linked up, they form the *historical expenditure schedule* $C_L C_L$, which resembles the curve fitted to actual data in Figure 18–4.

Why should CC shift upward over the course of time? One hypothesis is that a family's spending depends, not on its *absolute* income, but on its income *relative* to that of other families within its horizon. If the income of every family rises by 20 percent, but they keep the same standing relative to each other, there is no reason why any family should change the distribution of its income between saving and consumption. This competitive aspect of consumption was stressed long ago by Veblen, and has been given more precise form by Duesenberry and others.

FIGURE 18–5

Long-run Shifts of the Consumption Schedule

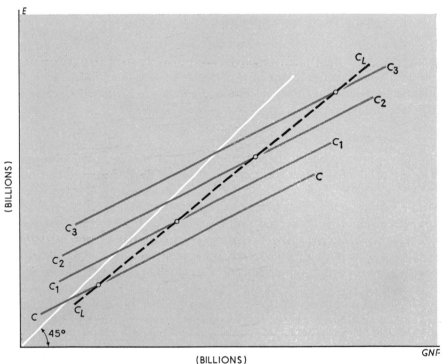

CC shows short-run consumption reactions at a particular time. C_1C_1 shows the same reactions ten years later, when people are habituated to higher living standards; and so on. Because of continued upward shifting of the short-run schedule, consumption over the long run follows the path shown by C_LC_L.

The appearance of new products which open up different patterns of consumption is perhaps an important factor. If Americans had their present incomes but could spend these only on 1890 products (an impossible and self-contradictory hypothesis), they would probably spend a smaller percentage of their incomes than they actually do. Adding more and more horse carriages, kerosene lamps, overstuffed furniture, and ice cream sodas to the family budget would eventually seem unsatisfying. But the ranch-style suburban home, the automobile, aviation, electric appliances, radio and television, and other things have completely transformed consumption standards. The new way of life may or may not be more satisfying than the old. It certainly requires more money and helps sustain the propensity to consume.

The advertising fraternity may be partly responsible for American devotion to consumption. Without the constant whipping up of consumers' appetites by television commercials and other methods, people might spend less than they actually do. (Banks and other savings institutions try to redress the balance by counter-advertising against consumption!) But the inventors and engineers who keep the stream of new products flowing must carry the main responsibility.

COMPONENTS OF SPENDING: INVESTMENT

In addition to consumer demand, there is a demand from business concerns for a new plant, equipment, and other capital goods. So we must ask what determines the level of *planned or intended investment.* The main influences appear to be technology, the level of national income, and the rate of interest.

Invention

Investment consists partly of building more capacity to produce familiar products by familiar methods. A great deal of investment, however, arises from invention and technical development. These may be *product* discoveries, or they may be *process* discoveries, which enable an existing product to be turned out at a lower cost. They may be *major* inventions such as the railroad, electric power, or the automobile, which lead to a great burst of investment lasting for decades. Or they may be *minor* inventions and improvements, individually small, but adding up to a substantial total.

The level of planned investment depends partly on how many such inventions have been turned up by scientists and engineers in the recent past. At some times there may be many good ideas lying about waiting to be put into production. At other times, usable inventions may be scarcer, and investment will accordingly be lower. The fact that major inventions are irregular and unpredictable produces substantial variation in the level of investment.

The Level of Income

It is reasonable to expect that the higher the level of income, the greater will be the volume of planned investment. There are several reasons for this. First, at a higher level of income more industries will be producing close to capacity; and this raises the question whether it would not be wise to increase capacity. If a company fails to expand at the right time, or at the same rate as competitors in the industry, it may lose in competitive position over the long run. Second, a rising level of sales tends to be projected into the future. High demand generates an atmosphere of optimism and a willingness to take major investment decisions. Conversely, at low levels of national income businessmen turn pessimistic and postpone investment projects. Third, as national income rises business profits also rise, and profits are a major source of funds for investment. As profits rise and businesses have more money to spend, they are more willing to increase their investment plans.

The Rate of Interest

While a good deal of investment is financed from profits, some is normally financed by borrowing. This is true particularly of residential and commercial construction, and of public utility investments. In these cases the cost of borrowing may influence the investment decision.

The method of calculating the prospective return from an investment project was explained in Chapter 9. Suppose a company has carried out these calculations for a particular project. It finds that the expected rate of return is 5 percent per year. Should it go ahead with the project or drop it? If it has full confidence in the certainty of the returns,[3] the decision can be made by *comparing the rate of return with the market rate of interest*. If the market rate is 4 percent, it will pay to go ahead with the project. The company can borrow money at 4 percent, use it to earn a return of 5 percent, and pocket the difference. But if the market rate were 7 percent, it would not pay to undertake the project.

At any time business concerns throughout the economy are considering a multitude of possible investment projects. Some of these are so good that they would yield a return of 15 or 20 percent on their cost. Below these are others which might yield only 10 percent; and still lower down are projects yielding only 8, 6, or 4 percent. How far down the list companies decide to go is influenced by the cost of borrowing. They will borrow and invest more at a low rate of interest than at a high one. In short *the lower the rate of interest, the higher will be the investment schedule*.

The probable shape of the investment schedule is shown by *II* in the bottom panel of Figure 18–6. Its height above the horizontal axis depends mainly on the technical opportunities for investment open at a particular time, and is influenced also by interest rates and availability of credit. The upward "tilt" of the schedule depends on the responsiveness of investment to higher levels of national income.

EQUILIBRIUM IN THE NO-GOVERNMENT ECONOMY

In our simplified economy, the consumption schedule and the investment schedule provide all the information we need to determine the equilibrium level of national income. This can be explained in either of

---

[3] This is an important qualification. The economic future is never entirely certain. Long before a plant or machine has served out its physical lifetime, it may be rendered obsolete by new inventions, or consumer demand may shift away from the product to something else, or new competitors may come in and oversupply the market. Because of these uncertainties, business concerns will usually invest only if the expected return is considerably higher than they would demand in a completely certain world.

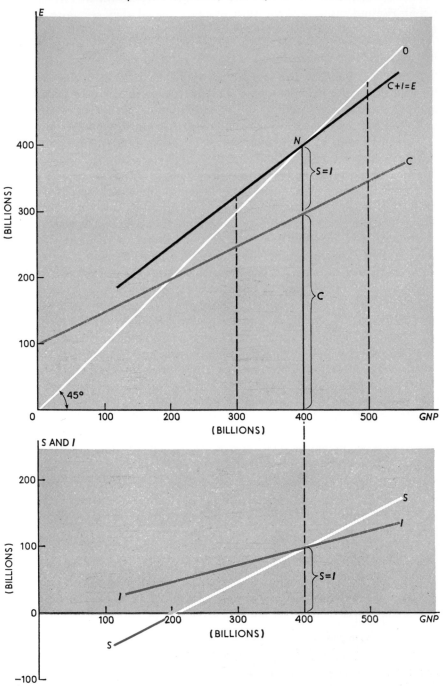

FIGURE 18–6

Consumption, Investment, and Equilibrium Income

The *lower* panel shows the level of planned investment and intended saving at various levels of income. The economy can be in equilibrium only when these two quantities are equal, that is, at $400 billion. In the *upper* panel we add planned investment to consumption to get the total expenditure schedule, *E*. The intersection of *E* with OO at *N* defines the equilibrium level of income, which must of course be the same as that derived by the other method.

two ways, which come to the same thing, and are sketched in the upper and lower panels of Figure 18–6.

The upper panel is laid out in the same way as Figure 18–1. The horizontal axis shows total output. The vertical axis shows total expenditure, which consists of consumer spending and investment spending. First we draw in the national consumption schedule from Figure 18–3. Now add on top of this the amount which business concerns will plan to invest at each level of income. This gives us the *C + I* line, which shows how much will be spent on consumption and investment together.

By the reasoning used for Figure 18–1, equilibrium income is defined by point *N*. Only at this point will total spending just cover the cost of the goods and services being produced. If output were either higher or lower, one can show that the system is not in balance and will move back toward *N*.

The same information is shown from a different viewpoint in the lower panel of Figure 18–6. Instead of the consumption schedule, we draw here its twin, the saving schedule *SS*. Note that the point of zero saving in the lower panel lies directly below the break-even point of the consumption schedule in the upper panel. To the left of this point, saving is negative, and to the right it is positive.

Now draw in the investment schedule *II*, showing planned investment at each level of national income. Note that the height of this schedule above the horizontal axis in the lower panel is equal to the distance between *C* and *C + I* in the upper panel.

In this simple economy without government, the requirement for aggregate equilibrium is that (planned)

$$I = S$$

Thus the equilibrium income level is defined by the intersection of *SS* and *II*, which occurs at $400 billion. This is the same result reached in the upper panel, and this must be so, since the two diagrams rest on the same basic data.

In equilibrium, then, output = $400 billion, consumption = $300 billion, and saving = investment = $100 billion. The savings drain is exactly matched by the volume of planned investment, and all is in order.

COMPLETING THE PICTURE: THE IMPACT OF GOVERNMENT

All spending in the economy is not private spending. The federal, state, and local governments are also large spenders. The kind of spending which is pertinent here is *government purchases of goods and services.* Transfer payments are not included. (Why not? Because transfer payments do not constitute a claim by government against current production.) Government purchases of goods and services now run over $100 billion a year, which is enough to have a large impact on the economy.

Government spending is planned well in advance—in the case of the federal government, 12 to 18 months in advance. It can be taken as independent of short-run fluctuations in national income. When we add it on top of consumer spending and investment spending, as in Figure 18–7, we get a new total expenditure line $(C + I + G)$. This runs parallel to

FIGURE 18–7

Equilibrium Income with Government Included

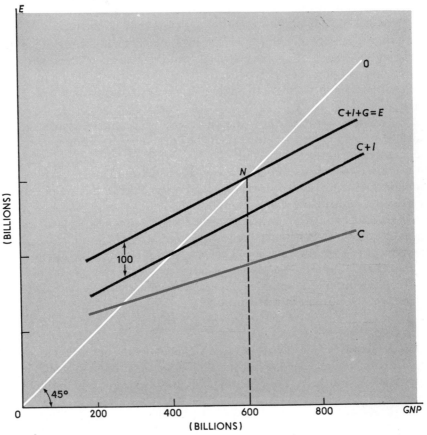

In this diagram we bring in government for the first time, by adding a constant $100 billion of government spending on top of consumption and investment expenditure. When we do this, we must remember that taxes are now being taken out of consumers' incomes. So CC will be lower and flatter than before.

the $(C + I)$ line, the vertical distance of $100 billion between them representing the constant volume of government expenditure.

What about the other side of the coin? What about taxes? Taxation reduces consumers' incomes, so they have less to spend and save than they would have otherwise. *Taxation changes the location and shape of the consumption schedule.*[4] Not only is the consumption schedule lowered, but its slope is reduced. Why is this? It arises from the progressive struc-

---

[4] It doubtless also affects the investment schedule; but the effects depend on the kind of taxes used, and an exploration of them would delay us at this point.

ture of the income tax, on which the federal government now depends so heavily. As income rises, the tax "bite" increases not only absolutely but as a percentage of income. This reduces the slope of *CC*.

Government spending thus *raises* the level of total spending, while taxation *reduces* it. The net effect depends partly on whether tax revenues typically exceed expenditures, or whether budget deficits are the general rule. It depends also on the absolute size of the government budget. Curiously enough, the effects of $1 billion of government spending and $1 billion of tax receipts do not just cancel out. Even a balanced government budget has an effect on the equilibrium level of national income. But an explanation of this puzzle must wait until Chapter 20.

The Expenditure Schedule Once More

Let's look back for a moment to see where we've been. At the outset, to explain the idea of aggregate equilibrium, we drew the expenditure schedule *EE* in Figure 18–1 out of thin air. The reader had to take its general slope on faith.

Now we have shown how the total expenditure schedule can be constructed by adding up the consumption, investment, and government expenditure schedules. The top line in Figure 18–7 is identical with *EE* in Figure 18–1. In later chapters we shall usually show only *EE* and ignore the components. But one should remember that they are lurking in the background and that, if any of them changes, *EE* will also change.

The expenditure schedule is a powerful organizing concept. Given the location of *EE* at a particular time, there is only one sustainable or equilibrium level of national income for the economy. If this level is unsatisfactory, one must operate on one or more of the components of *EE* —raising them if total spending is too low, lowering them if it is too high. When it pays to operate, and what instruments are most effective, will be considered in later chapters.

SUMMARY

1. An *induced* change in spending is one which occurs in response to a prior change in income. An *autonomous* change is independent of any change in income. Autonomous changes are of primary importance in explaining a rise or fall in national income.

2. Autonomous changes are particularly likely to occur in business spending on plant and equipment, inventions, and construction. But they can occur also in the consumer, government, or foreign trade sectors.

3. The economy is in equilibrium only if total spending from all sources equals the cost of the goods and services being produced. Canceling out consumption from both sides, we can show that equilibrium requires that

$$S = I + (G - T)$$

The amount being drained out of the income stream through saving must be offset by an equal amount pumped in through investment and/or a deficit in the government budget.

4. This condition is always satisfied for any *past* period, since the rules of national income accounting ensure that income and product will be equal. But

it is not necessarily satisfied if the terms are re-defined to mean *plans* for a future period.

5. If *planned*

wrong

$$S < I + (G - T)$$

there will be a deficiency of spending in the next period and national income will fall. So actual saving will be less than was planned, because incomes are lower. And investment may be larger than planned because unsold goods will pile up in inventories. The original divergence between plans on the two sides of the equation *is closed through a change in national income.*

6. Similarly, if *planned*

these are wrong

$$S > I + (G - T)$$

spending will exceed the value of current output, so output and/or prices will rise. There is an expansion of national income.

7. To define the equilibrium point precisely, we construct a diagram on which the vertical axis shows total (planned or intended) expenditure, and the horizontal axis shows Gross National Product. We lay out a line *OO* running up from the origin at an angle of 45 degrees, at any point on which total spending and total output are equal. Thus *any equilibrium position for the economy must lie on OO*. We also lay out an expenditure schedule *EE*, which shows the amount of planned expenditure at each level of national income. Since spending rises less rapidly than income, *EE* slopes upward less steeply than *OO*, hence must intersect it. *The intersection of EE and OO defines the equilibrium level of national income.*

8. The logical precautions which must be observed in constructing and using this diagram are precisely the same as for the supply-demand diagrams of Part One.

9. The expenditure schedule is made up of several components: a *consumption schedule*, an *investment schedule*, a *government expenditure schedule*, and a *net foreign trade schedule*. We omit the last as of minor importance for the United States.

10. The *national consumption schedule* depends on the consumption schedules of individual households and on the distribution of income among them. There has been considerable debate, but no final agreement, on whether greater equality of incomes raises or lowers the consumption schedule.

11. The fraction of any increase in income which goes into increased consumption is termed the *marginal propensity to consume*. The fraction going to increased saving is the *marginal propensity to save*. Since all income must be spent or saved, the m.p.c. and the m.p.s. total up to 1. The m.p.c. is the same thing as the slope of the consumption schedule. When we draw the consumption schedule as a straight line, we are assuming that the m.p.c. is constant for all levels of income.

12. The (short-run) consumption schedule, as usually drawn, shows the percentage of income saved increasing as income rises. Yet when we look at statistics over long periods we find that the percentage of income saved has remained roughly constant. Given time, people find ways of spending their larger incomes, and the national consumption schedule keeps shifting upward.

13. The *investment schedule* depends mainly on the rate of inventive activity, the level of national income, and the rate of interest.

14. *Government expenditure* raises the level of total spending. But taxation reduces spending by lowering the consumption and investment schedules. Even if government expenditures and tax receipts are equal, the effect on national income is not neutral. (See Chapter 20.)

Income Analysis: Extensions and Applications

Money, the life blood of the nation,
Corrupts and stagnates in the veins
Unless a proper circulation
Its motion and its heat maintains.

JONATHAN SWIFT (1720)

IN CHAPTER 18 we laid out the central ideas of modern income analysis. Now we must see how these ideas can be applied for various purposes.

In constructing the expenditure schedule, we assumed that the underlying schedules for consumption, investment, and government spending were known and constant. But actually they are jumping about all the time, and so the expenditure schedule is constantly shifting. What happens when the expenditure schedule moves up or down? How much, and how quickly, will this affect the equilibrium level of national income?

How do we judge whether a particular level of national income is desirable? It is usually said that output should be high enough to ensure full employment. What does this mean, and how do we know when we are there?

Little was said in Chapter 18 about the price level, except for the usual assumption that it remains constant. But we know that it actually doesn't remain constant. Most of the time since 1940 prices have been rising, which is usually termed *inflation*. What is inflation, how does it come about, what are its economic consequences?

CHANGES IN SPENDING: THE MULTIPLIER

To see why the expenditure schedule may shift, one need only refer to the list of spending decisions given early in Chapter 18. Any autonomous change in spending plans—in the consumer, business, government, or foreign sectors—will change the expenditure schedule. Such changes are occurring all the time, and so the expenditure schedule is constantly changing position.

What does this do to the equilibrium level of national income? Clearly, a rise in the expenditure schedule will tend to *raise* the level of income, while a drop in the schedule will *lower* it.

The effect is illustrated in Figure 19–1. The expenditure schedule EE is identical with that in Chapter 18. Suppose for one reason or another the schedule shifts upward by $50 billion to E_1E_1. It now intersects OO at a higher level, N_1. National income will begin to rise, and expansion will continue until a new equilibrium has been reached at $700 billion.

Now note a curious thing: the increase in spending which set off the process was only $50 billion. But the result is to raise the level of income by $100 billion. The original impact has been *multiplied* by 2 in the course of transmission. How did this happen? And why did the *multiplier* turn out to be 2 rather than some other figure?

In terms of geometry, the answer lies in the slope of EE. Both EE and E_1E_1 were drawn with a slope of 1:2. So a vertical distance of 40 units corresponds to a horizontal distance of 80. Experimenting with a pencil will convince you that if the slope of EE were steeper than this, the multiplier effect would be larger. Conversely, if the slope were smaller, the multiplier effect would also be smaller.

But what does the slope of EE mean in economic terms? It shows *the increase in spending which will accompany a specified increase in income.* Drawing EE with a slope of 1:2 means that a dollar (horizontal) increase in income is accompanied by a 50 cent (vertical) increase in spending. This ratio of increased spending to increased income is termed *the marginal propensity to spend;* and its size determines the size of the multiplier effect. A higher marginal propensity to spend, which would mean a steeper slope of EE, would produce a larger multiplier.

What determines the size of the marginal propensity to spend? Suppose an expansion of output generates an additional dollar of income. Will this whole dollar be re-spent on domestic production? No, it will not, because parts of the dollar will "leak away" in various directions. Part of it will be drained off by taxation, some will go into savings, and some will be spent on imported goods.

Let m.p.i. stand for the *marginal propensity to import*, i.e., the proportion of any increase in income which is spent on foreign goods.

FIGURE 19–1

Effect of a Shift in the Expenditure Schedule

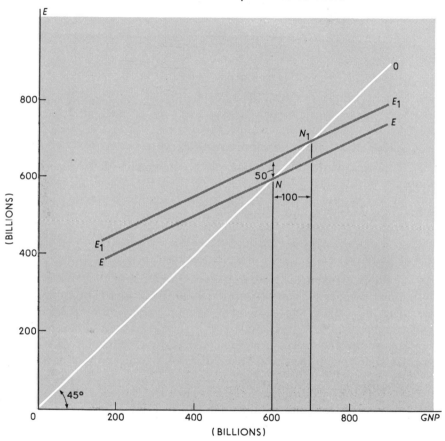

Here a rise of $50 billion in planned spending, from *EE* to *E₁E₁*, raises the equilibrium level of income by $100 billion. This is termed *the multiplier effect*. The size of the multiplier depends on the slope of *EE*, which is termed the *marginal propensity to spend*. The steeper the slope of *EE*, the larger the multiplier.

Let m.p.s. represent the *marginal propensity to save*. And let m.r.t. stand for the *marginal rate of taxation*, i.e., the proportion of any increase in income which is taken by government. Suppose in the present case that m.r.t. = 0.25, m.p.i. = 0.05, and m.p.s. = 0.20. Then out of an additional dollar of income there will be re-spent only

$$1 - (\text{m.r.t.} + \text{m.p.s.} + \text{m.p.i.})$$
$$= 1 - (0.25 + 0.20 + 0.05)$$
$$= 1 - 0.5$$
$$= 0.5$$

Thus the marginal propensity to spend is one half.

There is a simple relation between the size of the marginal propensity to spend and the size of the multiplier. If we indicate the multiplier by M, we find that

$$M = \frac{1}{1 - \text{marginal propensity to spend}}$$
$$= \frac{1}{\text{m.r.t.} + \text{m.p.s.} + \text{m.p.i.}}$$

The *larger* the "leakages" into savings, tax collections, and imports, the *smaller* will be the multiplier effect of an increase in spending.

ANOTHER VIEW OF THE MULTIPLIER

The logic of this may become clearer if we consider the multiplier as operating (as it actually does operate) *over the course of time*. Start with an equilibrium situation in which the economy is running along at an even level. Now suppose there is an autonomous rise in spending of $1 billion per calendar quarter because of, say, an increase in planned investment. If investment was previously running at $10 billion per quarter, it now becomes $11 billion. And suppose that the new level of $11 billion is maintained quarter after quarter into the future.

What happens next? The $1 billion is received by companies producing new plant and equipment, who pay out most of it to their workers, suppliers, and stockholders. But they may save some of it, and they pay something to the government in corporate income taxes. The workers and stockholders also spend part of what they get, save part, and pay part in taxes. Altogether, then, how much of the original $1 billion will come back into the market on the next round? If we continue with the illustrative figures used above, in which the marginal propensity to spend was one half, the answer is that there will be $0.5 billion of new spending.

This $0.5 billion goes from retailer to wholesaler to manufacturer, leads to production of additional goods, and finally gets passed out again as income. If the marginal propensity to spend has remained unchanged, on the next round there will be additional spending of half the $0.5 billion, or $.25 billion. This money then goes whizzing around the system and reappears as $0.25 billion of income on the next round. People proceed to spend half of this $0.25 billion, and so on and on.

How much income will finally result from the original $1 billion of new investment? The amount, in billions, is

$$1 + 0.5 + 0.5^2 + 0.5^3 + \ldots$$

By the formula for an infinite geometric progression, this sums up to

$$\frac{1}{1 - 0.5} = \frac{1}{0.5} = 2$$

Thus an autonomous increase of one dollar in spending eventually adds two dollars to national income. And a *permanent* rise of $1 billion in the level of planned spending raises the equilibrium level of national income by $2 billion.[1]

How long does the multiplier process take to work itself out? By adding $1 + 0.5 + 0.25 + 0.125 = 1.875$, we find that more than 90 percent of the impact will be felt during the first four rounds. But how long is a "round," in actual calendar time? This depends on how long it takes for money to travel the circuit from consumers through the business system and back to consumers again. In the United States, this period seems to be something like three months, so that it is roughly correct to take each round as equal to a calendar quarter. Most of the impact of an autonomous increase in spending will be felt within the first year after it occurs.

This version of the multiplier is illustrated in Figure 19–2, where the dotted lines trace the process of adjustment. The initial increase in spending, NA, goes chasing through the economy and reappears as an equal amount of income, AB. Half of this amount is re-spent, so there is a new wave of spending, $BC = \frac{1}{2} AB$. This goes through the circuit and comes out as a second round of new income, $CD = BC$. Half of this income is re-spent, and so on and on, bringing the economy closer on each round to the new equilibrium at N_1.

This analysis supposes that EE, after having shifted upward, sits quietly for a year or two while the economy adjusts to the new equilibrium. This is unlikely to happen in practice. Long before N_1 has been reached, the expenditure schedule will have shifted once more, and the economy will be off chasing its tail toward some new equilibrium. This method of reasoning is nevertheless useful. It tells us the *direction of movement* which will be induced by a shift in EE, and something about the size and speed of the movement.

The multiplier operates downward as well as upward. A drop in planned spending by consumers, business, or government will set off a more than proportionate decline in income. In the present illustration, income would fall by twice the initial drop in spending. This is part of the story of what happens in a business recession.

---

[1] Suppose that planned investment rose by $1 billion for only one quarter, and then returned to its previous level. What would happen? The income effect of this one-shot increase would gradually dwindle, and after a few rounds would have become insignificant. For the level of national income to be raised *permanently*, the increase in planned spending must also be permanent.

FIGURE 19–2

Operation of the Multiplier over Time

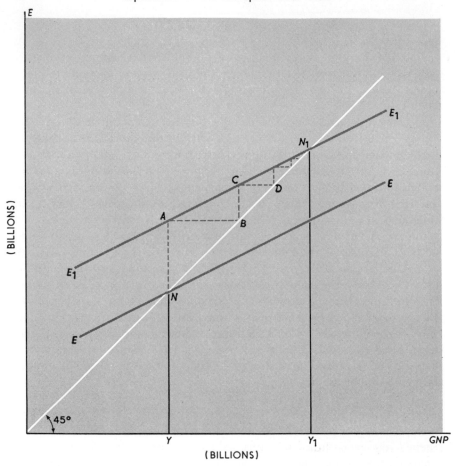

In practice the multiplier takes time to work out its effects. An increase in planned spending of NA this quarter generates increased income of AB next quarter, which leads to additional spending of BC in the following quarter; and so on. Thus the economy gradually approaches the new equilibrium at N_1.

EMPLOYMENT: FULL, LESS-THAN-FULL, AND OVER-FULL

So far we have not tried to appraise the equilibrium positions described in our diagrams. Equilibrium has been treated simply as a fact, as showing what is "in the cards" for the economy. But the outcome is not a matter of indifference. Some levels of national income are more desirable than others.

It is generally agreed that the economy should operate close to capacity. It should make full use of available supplies of labor, capital, and other resources. Since plant and equipment is diversified, it is hard to sum up this element in productive capacity. It is easier to add up the national labor supply, and so we tend to judge the use of our capacity by the percentage of the labor force employed. There is also a humanitarian reason for concentrating on utilization of human capacity. An idle machine may reduce national output, but the machine is not annoyed. An unemployed worker does suffer feelings of worthlessness, failure, and insecurity. Thus a high level of employment is a natural objective for any society.

How much employment do we want? "Full employment" is the standard phrase. But how full is "full"? It is not feasible for everyone in the country to be at work every day. We must allow for normal labor turnover—people laid off who must find new jobs elsewhere, people changing jobs of their own accord, and young people seeking work for the first time. Hunting jobs takes time, and so a certain proportion of the labor force is always "unemployed between jobs." This unavoidable minimum is usually termed *frictional unemployment.*

Frictional unemployment in the United States is usually estimated at about 3 percent of the labor force. Thus "full employment" would be reached when 97 percent of the labor force is at work. *NF* in Figure 19–3 indicates the output level corresponding to this volume of employment, which is assumed to be $600 billion.

Defining full employment, however, is a far cry from *attaining* it. Where the economy will actually operate depends on the position of the expenditure schedule. *EE* might intersect *OO* precisely at *N*, so that equilibrium would be reached at full employment. This would be a happy coincidence. But it is more likely that *EE* will lie above or below this ideal location.

Suppose the expenditure schedule is in the position E_1E_1. Then the economy cannot reach full employment. For at an output of $600 billion there would be spending of only $FA = 550 billion. There is a deficiency of $50 billion, shown by the distance *AN*. This is termed a *deflationary gap*, because it has a depressing or deflating effect on the economy. Note that although the deflationary gap is only $50 billion, the equilibrium level of income at N_1 is $100 billion below full employment. The multiplier effect is working against us here.

Does this mean that we must find $100 billion of additional spending to pull the system up to full employment? No, it does not. We need find only $50 billion, the amount of the deflationary gap. If E_1E_1 can be raised vertically by $50 billion, it will intersect *OO* at *N*. The multiplier effect will convert the initial impulse of $50 billion into a rise of $100 billion in national income.

Suppose instead that the spending schedule is located at E_2E_2. Now if producers turn out $600 billion of output, they will find that total spending adds up to $650 billion. There is excess demand of $NB = 50 billion.

FIGURE 19–3

Full Employment and Alternative Levels

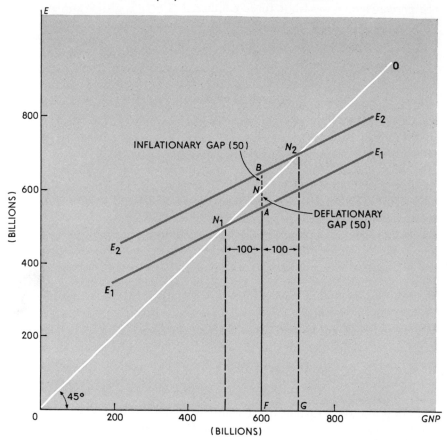

At OF, with GNP of $600 billion, there would be full employment. But if the expenditure schedule is in the position E_1E_1 there will be a spending deficiency or *deflationary gap* of $50 billion; and because of the multiplier effect the equilibrium level of income at N_1 will be $100 billion below full employment. Conversely, if the expenditure schedule is in the position E_2E_2, there will be excess demand or an *inflationary gap* of $50 billion and the price level will have to rise.

This is termed an *inflationary gap*. It makes life pleasant for anyone who has goods to sell, raises profits, and produces energetic efforts to expand output.

But how can this be? How can national income rise above the full-employment "ceiling"? The answer is that *physical* production cannot rise above the full-employment level or at least not much above it.[2] What

---

[2] In reality, capacity output is a zone rather than a single point. One can squeeze out more production by working men and machinery overtime, and by hiring people who would not ordinarily be considered employable. This "over-full employment" may add a few percentage points to national output. For simplicity, however, we often assume that there is a precise limit to employment and output, and that expansion of total spending beyond this will lead *only* to an increase in prices.

can happen, however, is a rise in prices for the same quantity of output. And if people demand more goods than business concerns are able to produce, prices will be marked up. Such a general increase in prices is usually termed *inflation*.

THRIFT: PRIVATE VIRTUE A PUBLIC VICE?

In the American tradition, saving is a Good Thing. This despite the constant effort of advertisers and finance companies to separate the consumer from his dollars and to encourage indebtedness.

Can what is good for the individual be bad for society? Two centuries ago Bernard de Mandeville, in his *Fable of the Bees*, asserted that the lavish spending of the French courtiers was socially valuable because it provided employment for great numbers of jewelers, perfumers, dressmakers, and wine producers. If the nobles ever learned to save their money, this employment would be lost and the French economy would fall into stagnation. More recently, many economists have been concerned about the possibility of "over-saving." If people save too much, it is said, there may be insufficient demand leading to general depression.

Who is right? Should saving be encouraged or discouraged? The nature of the problem can be explained by going back to the simplified private economy of the last chapter. The lower panel of Figure 18–6, Chapter 18, is reproduced here as Figure 19–4. *SS* shows the amount which would be saved at various levels of income. The income level corresponding to full employment is *OF*, and the amount which would be saved at full employment is *NF*.

Now, depending on the level of planned investment, this propensity to save may be either excessive or insufficient. Suppose the investment schedule is located at I_1I_1. If under these conditions people try to save *NF*, this is too much in the light of the planned investment of *HF*. As a matter of fact, they will not be able to save *NF*. If they try, planned saving will exceed planned investment. Output and income will fall, until the system reaches equilibrium at N_1. Because income is lower, actual savings will be only N_1D.

This underlines an important principle: How much people actually save does not depend just on how much they would like to save. If they try to save too much (relative to planned investment), national income will fall and they will end up saving less than they desired. This is sometimes called *the paradox of thrift*.

An opposite situation exists if the investment schedule is I_2I_2. Here there is under-saving in the sense that, at full employment, the amount saved (*NF*) falls short of what businessmen wish to invest (*GF*). This will mean an inflationary expansion of the economy, with rising prices but little increase in output. This can be prevented only by forcing down the investment schedule so that it intersects the savings schedule at *N*, or by raising the savings schedule so that it cuts the investment schedule at *G*.

FIGURE 19–4

The Economic Consequences of Thrift

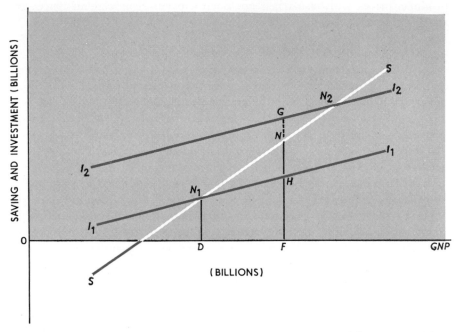

Suppose the saving schedule has the position *SS*, and that *OF* constitutes full employment. Then if the investment schedule is I_1I_1, the propensity to save is excessive. The level of income will be only *OD*, and people will actually be able to save only N_1D instead of the *NF* which they would like to save at full employment. Conversely, if the investment schedule is I_2I_2, the propensity to save is insufficient, and inflation will follow.

In this situation, increased saving would help to combat inflation and would benefit the economy as well as the individual.

The United States, Britain, and Western Europe seem to have been in this position frequently during the nineteenth century. Business investment plans often ran ahead of available savings, leading to complaints of a "shortage of capital." This doubtless helped to strengthen the belief that thrift is a civic as well as a personal virtue. Nor is this belief, and the circumstances which justified it, a matter of ancient history. Since World War II many of the western industrial nations have been chronically short of savings, not to mention the more acute shortages in the less developed countries.

Thus to the question "Would an increase in thrift help or hurt the economy?" one can only answer, "It all depends." It depends mainly on the level of planned investment at the time and place in question.

PRICE MOVEMENTS: CAUSES AND CONSEQUENCES

We must now face the problem of the price level. We avoided this in earlier sections by taking the price level as constant. A rise in the expenditure schedule produced a rise in output, while a drop in planned spending brought a drop in output. But through all this the price level remained unchanged.

This works reasonably well up to the capacity level OF, but it ceases to work above that level. Indeed, the part of the Y axis to the right of F in Figure 19–4 has no real meaning. It is a never-never land, a level of output which cannot be reached given the capacity limits of the economy. If people nevertheless insist on trying to buy more goods than can be produced, prices will have to rise. But how fast and how far? Will a new equilibrium be reached, and if so where will it be? The multiplier analysis doesn't really tell us. Beyond F we pass through the looking glass into a world where a different kind of analysis is required.

Sources of Inflation: Excess Demand

Look again at the position of E_2E_2 in Figure 19–3. What does this really mean? The quantity of goods that the various spending groups are trying to buy (BF) is greater than the quantity which can be produced $(NF = OF)$. There is $25 billion of *excess demand*, and the system is not in equilibrium. If production could be increased to OG, equilibrium could be re-established. But by saying that OF represents full capacity we have also said that production of OG is impossible. So that solution is out.

The only way to keep prices stable in this situation is to force E_2E_2 back down to a level where it intersects OO at N, so that demand and output are in balance. One way to do this would be for government to impose heavier taxes, and then lock up the money instead of spending it. Another possibility would be to ration the available goods, giving people only enough ration tickets to buy a total of NF, even though they still *want* to buy more. But rationing is an awkward and expensive device, hence is used mainly in war periods when there is great excess demand and the inflation threat is severe.

If neither of these things is done, prices will begin to rise. But how much? Why not by exactly $8\frac{1}{3}$ percent? Then the $600 billion worth of goods at the old price level, which is all the system can produce, will be *called* $650 billion worth of goods at the new price level. Thus people will be able to spend the $650 billion which they are apparently determined to spend, and all will be well.

But won't people soon realize that they have been tricked in this process? They are spending $650 billion all right, but because of the price increase they are *not getting as many goods as they originally intended to get*. What they wanted was $650 billion worth of goods *at the old prices* and they are not getting this much because their dollars now buy less than before.

They may possibly just sit back and take it.[3] But they don't have to,

---

[3] This would amount to saying that they are now satisfied with less goods than they thought they wanted, i.e., that E_2E_2 has fallen. This is one way by which equilibrium might be re-established, but not a very likely one.

and the chances are they won't. They are likely to react by trying to increase their spending, in the hope of still getting the things they originally desired. If the price of machinery has risen, businesses will raise their investment budgets. As cement, asphalt, and other elements in highway construction go up, government budgets will have to be raised. As prices of consumer goods rise, and housewives look reproachfully at their husbands, there will be a drive for wage increases.

Now the fat is in the fire. Business concerns, whose labor costs are higher than before, feel they have a legitimate case for further price increases; and, since spending is so high, they feel confident that their customers will pay the higher prices. But now workers come back and say, "Ah, living costs have risen some more, so we must have still higher wages." So it goes, round after round up the wage-price spiral, each group blaming the other and asserting its own innocence. And in a sense both are innocent, since the original cause was an unduly high level of aggregate demand for which no one is particularly to blame.

Where will it all end? It might never end. If each group can offset any increase in the price level by raising its own money income, and if all continue stubbornly to insist on getting more goods than the economy can produce, prices could go on rising year after year. If people become panicky enough, the rate of inflation can accelerate to the point where money becomes worthless. But in practice most inflations eventually slow down and reverse themselves, for reasons which we shall see in a moment.

Sources of Inflation: Sellers Inflation

The process we have been examining is usually called demand inflation. It is the traditional explanation of rising prices. There is another possibility, however, which some economists believe has been important in recent years. This hinges on autonomous increases in prices of the factors of production, including business profits. For this reason it is usually called *cost inflation* or *sellers' inflation*. Two examples:

1. Suppose that the economy is running along in equilibrium at full employment. But the steel industry decides that its profit margin is too low and decides to raise steel prices. Since steel is an important component of machinery, automobiles, commercial buildings, and many other things, producers of those things raise their prices to offset the increase in costs. These price increases stimulate wage demands and we are off, even though there was no excess demand in the economy to begin with.

2. The initial push can come from the labor cost side. Suppose again that the economy is in equilibrium at full employment. Productivity is rising at a rate which would permit wages to rise 3 percent per year without disturbing the price level. But since employment is high and the labor market is tight, unions and individual workers are in a strong bar-

gaining position. The unions demand, and the employers concede, wage increases averaging 5 percent. This raises labor cost per unit of output, so producers raise prices enough to cover the new costs and maintain normal profit margins. The monetary authorities, unwilling to check prosperity, permit the money supply to rise sufficiently to support the new price level. Everyone is happy, except those living on pensions or other fixed incomes.

How can one tell whether such a "cost push" has occurred in a particular case? It is not easy. The surface symptoms are similar to those resulting from excess demand. In both cases one finds money wages rising faster than productivity, and product prices are also rising. But where did the trouble start? It could have started from excess demand pulling up prices, then wages, then prices in spiral fashion. But it could also have started from unduly large wage demands which forced price increases, without any excess demand being present. What actually happened in a particular case may be very difficult to determine.

Perhaps the strongest evidence for some degree of "cost push" is the fact that in recent recessions the retail price level has often continued to rise, even though demand was declining. And wages have risen substantially despite the existence of unemployment. For example, wage increases in the recession year 1961 were almost as large as in the peak year 1960. This lends weight to the view that wage and price levels have behaved rather differently since 1945 than they used to do in earlier decades.

The Progress and End of Inflation

The theories which have been developed to analyze an inflation process are too complex for full treatment here, but we can suggest the kind of reasoning involved. Once an inflation is under way, almost anything may happen. The inflation may taper off and be followed by stable or declining prices. It may proceed at a regular rate round after round. It may speed up, leading conceivably to an astronomical rise of prices and a collapse of the monetary system such as occurred in Germany in 1923. Such horror stories are fortunately rare, and are usually associated with defeat in war.

Inflations in Western industrial countries typically slow down and reverse themselves after a while. There are several reasons for this:

1. While each group in the economy struggles to increase its money income to keep pace with the inflation, not everyone succeeds. Pensioners, bondholders, and other fixed-income groups can do nothing for the time being. White-collar salaries are typically sluggish and lag well behind price changes. Any group left behind in this way is of course being cheated. But this private misfortune is a public benefit. It slows down the rate of increase in money demand and thus has a braking effect.

2. The fact that we are used to seeing inflations slow down after

a while is a powerful reason why future inflations will probably follow this course. A marked rise in prices leads many people to feel that "prices are too high," that the trend will be reversed, and that it will be wise to wait and buy later. If this belief becomes strong enough, spending schedules will begin to drop; and when this happens, the inflation is over. An *expectation* of price stability is thus a powerful force *making* for price stability. If public attitudes changed so that price increases were expected to continue indefinitely, this brake would be removed and the economy would become more unstable than it now is.

3. Inflation can always be slowed down by a firm application of monetary controls. This mention of money should remind us that an important part of the inflation story has not yet been considered. If people keep on raising their incomes and their spending during an inflation, mustn't they be getting extra money from somewhere? How does this happen? Why do the banks and the Federal Reserve System permit the addition of this fuel to the fire? Couldn't the fire always be put out just by turning off the money tap? We shall be in a better position to consider these questions after examining the monetary mechanism in Chapters 21 and 22.

Some Disadvantages of Inflation

Inflation is normally a bad word in economic discussion. Why is this? Who gets hurt by inflation, and why should one worry about it? A steadily rising price level has several awkward consequences:

1. It reshuffles people's incomes in an unfair way. While total money income may keep up with the rise in prices, this is not true for every individual in the system. People living on pensions, bond interest, civil service salaries, and other fixed or sluggish incomes are unable to keep up. They can buy less than before, and so take a loss in real income. Many businessmen, on the other hand, get a windfall addition to profits. The value of their inventories is constantly rising. Raw materials bought at one price level are resold as finished goods at a higher price level. Strong unions may be able to appropriate part of these rising profits, and their members may keep ahead of the price level; but poorly organized groups of workers lag behind and lose out. The struggle of every group in the economy to keep up with the shifting price level produces much controversy and friction.

2. If the price increase is rapid, it creates conditions which may bring about a relapse in prices and production. Many businesses are surviving through windfall profits due to rising prices rather than through productive efficiency. If the price level stabilizes and this prop is removed, they come crashing down. The rise of business profits means more saving, and this is feasible only if planned investment is rising at the same rate. If investment slackens, disharmony appears at once. Moreover, as the price advance proceeds, people may begin to worry about the possibility of its

being reversed. An inflation can continue only so long as it is generally expected to continue. If the pace slackens, expectations of a price drop may become general, and this will actually bring on the drop.

3. Persistent inflation undermines the basis of long-term lending, on which a good deal of private investment and government financing depends. If prices are rising 5 percent a year, anyone who buys a 20-year 4 percent bond is completely foolish. He will be paid off eventually in dollars which are worth less than half as much as the dollars he loaned. Instead of getting a positive rate of interest on his money, he is getting a negative rate. Each year he receives his 4 percent interest, but meanwhile his bond has lost 5 percent in value. This is a poor bargain. If inflation continues, people will eventually catch on and stop buying bonds. Logically, they should also stop putting money into savings accounts and other assets with a fixed dollar value.

4. For countries heavily involved in international trade, there is another important consideration. A country which allows its prices to rise faster than those of competing export nations will find itself losing ground in foreign markets. The drop in exports will reduce spending and production at home. It will also lead toward an unfavorable balance of payments, with a consequent loss of gold or foreign exchange reserves, and the eventual necessity of taking corrective action.

Inflation is a matter of degree, and so are the inconveniences which flow from it. The above arguments tell more heavily against a 5 percent a year inflation than against a 1 percent a year inflation. Most economists, given free choice, would probably plump for a stable price level. But they differ in their willingness to tolerate departures from this ideal. If inflation reaches 1 percent a year, some will begin to worry and dig in their heels. At 2 percent, more would become concerned. At 5 percent a year, practically everybody would be down in the trenches asking what can be done to stem the tide.

It is thus unprofitable to argue the question, "Are you against inflation?" The relevant question is "*How much* inflation are you against?" And the choice is not actually free. Reducing the rate of inflation involves costs, and we must pause to examine why this is so.

The Trade-off between Inflation and Unemployment

It is easy to see that inflation is a matter of degree. It may not be so obvious that full employment is also a matter of degree. Production capacity is not completely fixed. Even when a plant is running at the capacity for which it was designed, one can still get more production by working overtime, adding more shifts, putting off maintenance and repairs, and so on. This may involve drawing into the labor force people who would not normally seek employment, but who are tempted by the sight of ample job opportunities. Under the pressure of high demand during World War II, we were able to stretch production capacity well beyond what most people would have considered possible in advance.

In drawing Figure 19–3, we put our finger on a figure which we defined as full employment. But in reality there is no such *full employment point*. Rather, there is a *full employment zone*, which may be fairly wide. When we say we are aiming at full employment, we really mean that we want a *desirable* level of employment.

This is not something which can be read off from a diagram. It is a matter of choice. We presumably want something better than the half-hearted prosperity of 1960 or 1962, which left 5 to 6 percent of the labor force totally unemployed and another 3 to 4 percent partially unemployed. Yet we do not want the frenetic activity of 1943–45, when unemployment was reduced to 1 percent at the cost of serious inflation. We want something in between.

The choice of a desirable level of employment is related to decisions about the rate of inflation. The unfortunate fact is that the higher up in the full employment zone we decide to operate, the stronger will be the upward pressure on prices. Pushing plants to the utmost raises marginal costs and forces up supply curves. Overtime work, third-shift work, new inexperienced workers—all involve higher costs per unit of output. Moreover, the higher the level of total demand, the greater the likelihood of "sellers' inflation." Thus forcing unemployment down to lower levels will involve larger price increases. Conversely, insistence on stable prices will require a higher unemployment rate than would be necessary otherwise.

The problem of choice is illustrated by the *possibility curve* in Figure 19–5.[4] Each point on this curve represents a feasible combination of unemployment rate and rate of price increase. With unemployment of 10 percent, prices would actually be falling 2 percent a year. At some lower level of unemployment, here estimated at 5 percent, prices would remain stable. If unemployment were forced down to 1 percent, prices would be rising 5 percent a year. The curve has been drawn convex upward to indicate that, as the rate of price increase is accelerated, this will produce smaller and smaller declines in unemployment. This seems a realistic supposition for our type of economy.

The shape of the possibility curve at a particular time is institutionally determined. For example, one reason why the U.S. economy now runs into rising prices during an upswing, even when output is well below capacity, is the aggressive policies of strong trade unions and quasi-monopolistic business concerns. With greater restraint by private monopolists, it might be possible to get unemployment down to 3 percent instead of 5 percent before encountering rising prices. The possibility curve

---

[4] This Figure is adapted from the ingenious discussion in A. C. L. Day and Sterie T. Beze, *Money and Income* (New York: Oxford University Press, 1960), pp. 400–402.

FIGURE 19–5

The Trade-off between Inflation and Unemployment

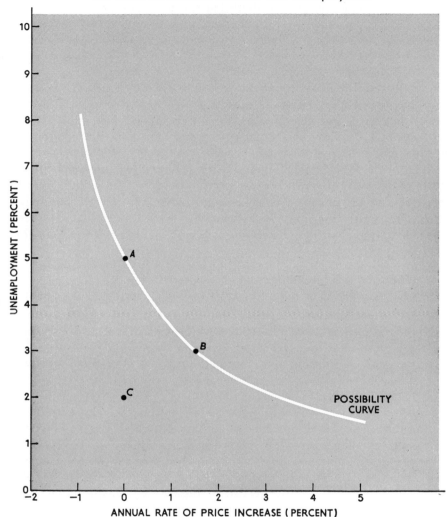

The possibility curve traces out all feasible combinations of unemployment level and rate of price increase. Thus one can have 5 percent unemployment with stable prices (A), or 3 percent unemployment with prices rising 1½ percent a year (B), or any other combination falling on the curve. Point C, on the other hand, while it is a preferable position, is not a feasible one.

would bend in more toward the origin. Anything that can be done in this direction obviously should be done.

Given the situation at a particular time, policy makers confront the problem of *selecting a point on the possibility curve*. Preferences on this are certain to differ. People who are particularly vulnerable to unemployment may prefer a point far to the right on the curve. People on fixed salaries who are in no danger of unemployment will prefer a point further to the left. Political liberals may want point B, while conservatives may prefer A. Everyone might agree that C, with low unemployment and stable prices, is best of all. But this is shadowboxing, since C is not a realistic possibility. In the end, there must be a choice of some point which does lie on the possibility curve and can be accepted as the least bad of feasible alternatives.

Without such a decision on objectives, one cannot decide what to do in a particular situation, nor can one appraise past policy actions. For example, the Federal Reserve System is frequently criticized as too tough in controlling business upswings. It is argued that interest rates are usually pushed up too fast and far so that borrowing and investment are unduly restricted. The underlying fact is that the System attaches greater weight to price stability and less weight to maximum employment than do many of its critics. Reflecting the conservative outlook of the banking community, it prefers a position rather high on the possibility curve. The critics are really saying that they would have chosen a lower position. This is the kind of issue on which no one can be "right" in any absolute sense.

The Outlook for Inflation

Expressing policy preferences is one thing. Making an objective forecast of future events is quite another. The most plausible forecast is for a gradual, intermittent creeping up of the price level. Since the end of the Korean War, the U.S. price level has risen at an average rate of about 1 percent per year. The rate of increase in most other Western Countries (Figure 19–6) has been somewhat greater.

There are several reasons for this tendency. Most governments now attach heavy weight to the objective of high employment. As soon as there is any sign of a let-down, steps are taken to check it. The objective is to keep production moving upward in line with the growing output capacity of the economy. But we have not yet found ways of maintaining a vigorous economic expansion with no increase in prices.

Looking back over the record of business cycles during the past century, one finds that there is usually a mild rise of prices on the upswing of the cycle. This is nothing new. What does seem to be new is the stubborn refusal of prices to fall during recessions. Wage cuts during recession have gone completely out of fashion. In fact, wages usually continue to rise, though less rapidly than in boom years. With a firm floor under wage rates and labor costs, the opportunity for price cuts is limited. The sensible thing, so it seems to businessmen, is to hold prices where they are and ride out the recession. Under atomistic competition, with demand falling, they would not be able to do this. But under monopoly or strong oligopoly it is quite easy.

The price floor held firmly during the U.S. recessions of 1953–54, 1957–58, and 1960–61. These were of course mild recessions, involving

FIGURE 19–6

Price Changes in Selected Western Countries, 1953–61
(1953 = 100)

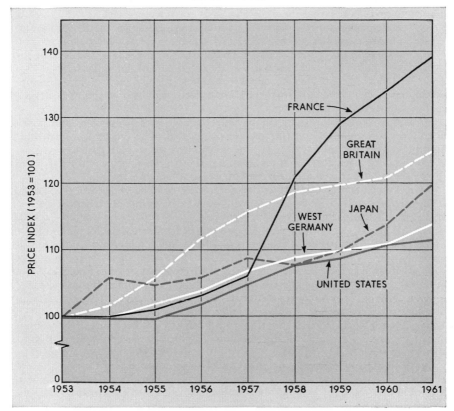

drops of only a few percent in total demand; and one can argue that a larger recession might force down the price level. But surely we don't want to bring on or tolerate a serious recession for the sake of knocking a few points off the price index.

The outlook, then, is for a *ratchet movement* of the price level— rising a bit during each prosperity period, leveling off during recession, and rising once more during the next boom. This means a slow upward drift of prices over the long run. Many economists would agree with this forecast, but they differ in how badly they feel about it. Some brush off the inconvenience of a rising price level as a minor cost of maintaining full employment. Others really worry about inflation and seek ways of preventing it, but thus far with limited success.

SUMMARY

1. An upward or downward shift of the expenditure schedule typically produces a larger change in the equilibrium level of national income. This is

termed *the multiplier effect*. If a rise of $1 billion in planned expenditure raises the equilibrium level of income by $2 billion, the *multiplier* has a value of 2.

2. The size of the multiplier depends on the *marginal propensity to spend*, that is, on the *slope of the expenditure schedule*. The greater the marginal propensity to spend, the larger the multiplier; and conversely.

3. The marginal propensity to spend depends on what fraction of any increase in income leaks away into *increased saving, increased tax payments*, and *increased spending on foreign goods*. The larger these leakages, the smaller the marginal propensity to spend, and the smaller the value of the multiplier.

4. The multiplier can be understood most readily by viewing it as operating *over the course of time*, through successive rounds of spending, enlarged incomes, and re-spending.

5. The *equilibrium level* of national income at a particular time is not necessarily the *desirable or full employment level*. The expenditure schedule may be so low that there is serious unemployment; or so high that demand exceeds the output capacity of the system, leading to rising prices. In the former case there is a *deflationary gap*, in the latter case an *inflationary* gap.

6. "Over-saving" is possible but not inevitable. The same level of planned saving may be either inadequate or excessive, depending on whether the investment schedule is high or low.

7. The price level may rise because the expenditure schedule is too high, i.e., because *EE* intersects *OO* to the right of the full employment point. This is termed *demand inflation*.

8. Even without excess demand, the price level may rise because of autonomous increases in prices of the factors of production, including business profits. This tendency, which is increased by strong unionism and by business monopoly, is usually termed *cost inflation* or *sellers' inflation*.

9. Once underway, an inflationary movement can become self-perpetuating. In economies of the U.S. type, however, a price rise usually tapers off after a short period.

10. A sizable inflation has several undesirable consequences: it redistributes personal income arbitrarily; it often leads to a relapse of prices and production; it undermines the basis of long-term lending; and it tends to worsen the country's balance of payments.

11. Full employment in practice is a zone rather than a single point. Moving higher within this zone involves stronger upward pressure on prices. Setting a national income goal means choosing a feasible combination of unemployment rate and rate of price increase. Preferences concerning the proper combination are bound to differ.

Taxes, Public Spending, and Fiscal Policy

Let us have the courage to stop borrowing to meet continuing deficits. Stop the deficits.

FRANKLIN D. ROOSEVELT (Speech, July 30, 1932)

Let us all be happy and live within our means, even if we have to borrow the money to do it with.

ARTEMUS WARD

ISN'T THERE a simple and straightforward way of holding total demand at the right level through the federal budget? If total spending threatens to be too high, can't it be reduced as much as necessary by levying heavier taxes? If on the other hand demand is too low and the economy is operating below capacity, can't this be corrected by increasing government spending, or by lowering taxes to permit more private spending? The use of government budgets to regulate total spending is usually called *fiscal policy*.

TAXES, PUBLIC SPENDING, AND NATIONAL INCOME

The way in which the government budget affects the level of spending was suggested in Chapter 18, but we must now go into this question more thoroughly.

A Few Preliminaries

When we speak of "the federal budget," just what do we mean? The *administrative budget*, which is submitted to Congress by the

President each January, is a legal document which follows conventional rules of government accounting. It includes all expenditures which require appropriations by Congress, and all revenues which go into the general funds of the Treasury. The surpluses and deficits which you see reported in the newspapers usually refer to the administrative budget. But the administrative budget does not fully reflect government's impact on the economy:

1. It excludes some important operations of government, notably the social security system. Each year government collects billions of dollars in payroll taxes under this system. The money goes into a trust fund, which is used to meet old age pension and unemployment compensation payments. In most years since the system began, more money has been going into the trust fund than has been coming out. Thus government cash receipts from the public are understated by the administrative budget, and any budget deficit (in cash terms) is correspondingly overstated. Another large trust fund not included in the administrative budget is the highway fund set up as part of the federal-state superhighway program which receives certain earmarked taxes on gasoline and motor vehicles.

2. It makes no distinction between government purchases of goods and services, transfer payments, and government lending operations. These are all treated equally as part of government expenditure. The economic effects of these transactions, however, are quite different.

In what follows, therefore, we shall use a different budget concept—*government transactions on income and product account*, or the government sector of the national income table. This includes only *transactions which give rise to current income*, thus omitting lending and similar operations. But it does include *all* current transactions, bringing in the social security system and the highway trust fund. It separates transfer payments from government purchases of goods and services. And it counts taxes as a deduction from income at the time they are incurred rather than when they are actually paid, which may be as much as a year later. This is a realistic procedure, since businesses and wealthy individuals do put aside money currently to meet later tax payments.

The "income and product budget" is calculated and published quarterly by the national income staff of the Department of Commerce. It typically shows a larger surplus (or smaller deficit) than the administrative budget. If the administrative budget is balanced, the income and product budget may show a surplus of several billion.

We shall follow another ground rule laid down in Chapter 15. *Government expenditure means government purchases of goods and services.* Remember that only government purchases of goods and services enter into the value of GNP. So when we want to add government spending to private spending, as we did in Chapter 18, we must use the term in this sense.

Transfer payments we shall regard as negative taxes. They increase the disposable income available for private spending, just as taxes reduce disposable income. When we speak of taxes, therefore, we shall mean *net taxes* or *tax receipts minus transfer payments.*

EXPANSIONIST EFFECT OF THE BUDGET

Government spending, as we saw in Chapter 18, counts as an addition to private spending. A dollar spent by government is as good as any other dollar in its direct effect on the flow of income. Taxes, on the other hand, reduce the disposable incomes of households and businesses and thus lower the level of private spending.

Suppose expenditures and tax receipts are equal, so that the budget is precisely balanced. One might then think that government is a neutral factor in the economy, and that the budget has no effect on the level of national income. But this turns out not to be true. *Even a balanced budget has an expansionist effect.* We shall try first to explain this proposition in words, and then give a graphical illustration.

Look at it this way: When government spends an additional dollar on goods and services, the full amount of this dollar enters the income stream. But when government collects an extra dollar in taxes, private spending is not reduced by a full dollar. It is reduced only by the amount which would have been spent out of this dollar, as shown by the marginal propensity to consume. The remainder of the tax comes from money which would have gone into private saving. The expansionist effect of the dollar spent thus exceeds the depressing effect of the dollar taxed, leaving a net addition to total spending and hence to the equilibrium level of national income.

Suppose the economy is operating below full employment. The President decides to give things a boost by spending an additional $50 billion on highways (or anything else you prefer). But he has a conservative Secretary of the Treasury, who insists that this expenditure must be covered by taxes. What will happen? The government takes away $50 billion of private income through the taxes. But at the same time it creates $50 billion of income which it pays out for the highway projects. Hence *private income remains unchanged.* Consumer spending and business investment can remain as high as before. But GNP has increased by the value of the highways built, or by $50 billion.

This is usually termed the *balanced budget theorem.* It asserts that an increase of x dollars in government spending, even if fully covered by an increase of x dollars in tax receipts, will raise the equilibrium level of national income by x dollars. Thus an economy with a government sector will have a higher equilibrium income than one without government.

To see whether there is any catch in this, let's do it over again with geometry (Figure 20–1). We start with the expenditure schedule in the

FIGURE 20–1

The Balanced Budget Theorem

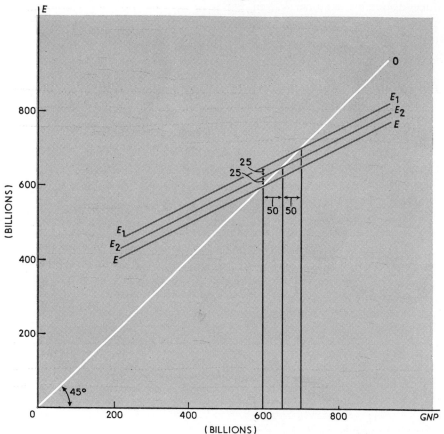

A $50 billion increase in government spending would by itself raise the expenditure schedule from EE to E_1E_1 and, through the multiplier effect, raise the equilibrium level of income by $100 billion. But if $50 of new taxes are imposed to balance the increased spending, this lowers the expenditure schedule to E_2E_2. The end result is that the equilibrium level of income rises by $50 billion, or just the amount of the (balanced) increase in the government budget.

position *EE*. The slope of this schedule, which is the marginal propensity to spend, is ½. The equilibrium level of income is $600 billion.

Now government enters the scene with its $50 billion highway program. This by itself would raise total spending $50 billion to E_1E_1, and the multiplier effect would raise national income to $700 billion.

But the Secretary of the Treasury insists on his $50 billion of taxes, People now have $50 billion less in their pockets than they had before the taxes were imposed. So they will spend less than before. How much less? The answer depends on the marginal propensity to spend, which we have assumed to be ½. If income drops by $50 billion, spending will drop $25 billion.

Thus the expenditure schedule drops by $25 billion, from E_1E_1 to E_2E_2. Why doesn't it drop all the way back to EE? Because part of the tax revenue comes out of saving rather than spending. So the new equilibrium level of national income, $650 billion, is higher than the level of $600 billion from which we started and it is higher by just the amount of the budget increase.

This argument is not watertight. It assumes that the basic propensities to consume and invest remain unaffected by an increase in the government budget, which would probably not be true in practice. Some kinds of government spending might frighten businessmen enough to cause a drop in private investment. But other kinds of spending, of which highways are a good example, will raise the profitability of many businesses and thus stimulate private investment. We have also assumed a rather odd kind of tax, which would yield the same $50 billion *regardless of the level of income*. Most actual taxes are not of this character.

Because of these and other considerations, one cannot assert that in practice a balanced increase of *x* dollars in the government budget will raise national income by precisely *x* dollars. The effect may be either larger or smaller, but there is little doubt that it will be in an expansionist direction.

THE IMPACT OF TAXATION

The federal tax structure in the United States has one outstanding characteristic: tax revenues rise sharply with an increase in national income and drop sharply when national income falls. The reasons lie in the nature of the personal and corporate income taxes, and in the importance of transfer payments.

1. *The personal income tax.* As national income rises, the incomes of most families in the country also rise. They move up into higher "tax brackets." As this happens, the *percentage* of their income taken in tax increases. So tax receipts rise, not just proportionately to income, but more than proportionately.

This can be explained by an illustration. Year 1 in Table 20–1 is a recession year in which incomes are at a low ebb. The economy now embarks on a boom, culminating in the prosperous Year 2. Between these two years each family's income rises by $1,000. We assume that the larger the income, the higher the percentage of income taken by taxation, as is true in our system.

Note what happens to tax receipts as income rises. The increase in personal income between Year 1 and Year 2 is 33.3 percent. But tax receipts rise by a whopping 57.5 percent. Of the $30,000 increase in income, $13,500 or 45 percent is drained off by an increase in tax payments. This will have a strong braking effect on any expansion of income.

It is instructive also to work the table in reverse. Suppose income falls from the level of Year 2 to the level of Year 1 as a result of recession.

TABLE 20-1

Effect of Progressive Income Taxation

	YEAR 1				YEAR 2			
ANNUAL INCOME	No. OF FAMI- LIES	TOTAL INCOME	AVER- AGE TAX RATE (%)	TAX RE- CEIPTS	ANNUAL INCOME	No. OF FAMI- LIES	TOTAL INCOME	AVER- AGE TAX RATE (%)	TAX RE- CEIPTS
2,000	10	20,000	20	4,000	2,000			20	
3,000	10	30,000	25	7,500	3,000	10	30,000	25	7,500
4,000	10	40,000	30	12,000	4,000	10	40,000	30	12,000
5,000			35		5,000	10	50,000	35	17,500
Total	30	90,000		23,500		30	120,000		37,000

Income *received* drops by $30,000. But personal income taxes also drop by $13,500. Thus the drop in *disposable* income is only $16,500, or 55 percent of the original decline in GNP. The braking effect works on the downswing of the cycle as well as the upswing.

2. The corporate income tax. The wide swings of business profits in our economy have already been mentioned. Profits rise faster than national income during a boom, and fall faster during a recession. About half of corporate profits go to the federal government in taxes. Because profits fluctuate so widely, the yield of the corporate income tax rises sharply in prosperity and drops sharply in recession. The braking effect on the economy is similar to that of the personal income tax.

3. Transfer payments. These payments rise substantially during recession and fall during prosperity. A recession means that more people are out of work, so unemployment compensation payments rise. Farm prices are likely to be falling, so government has to pay out more under price support schemes. Since jobs are hard to find, older people may decide to drop out of the labor market and begin drawing their pensions. During an upswing, these tendencies go into reverse and transfer payments shrink.

These changes in transfer payments work in the same direction as the swings in tax receipts. During recession, disposable income falls less than one might expect *both* because the tax "take" is reduced and because transfer payments are increased. During prosperity, the increase in the tax take *and the decline in transfer* payments slows down the rate of increase in disposable income.

The Built-in Stabilizer

On a commonsense basis one can see that this must have a stabilizing effect on the economy, tending to brake both expansions and contractions of national income. Moreover, the gyroscopic effect works automatically, with no need for diagnosis or deliberate action. This effect of the tax structure is usually referred to as the *built-in stabilizer*.

This commonsense impression can be pinned down by noting that taxation *reduces the slope of the consumption schedule*. In the no-government economy, this slope depends solely on the marginal pro-

FIGURE 20–2

Effect of Taxation on the Consumption Schedule

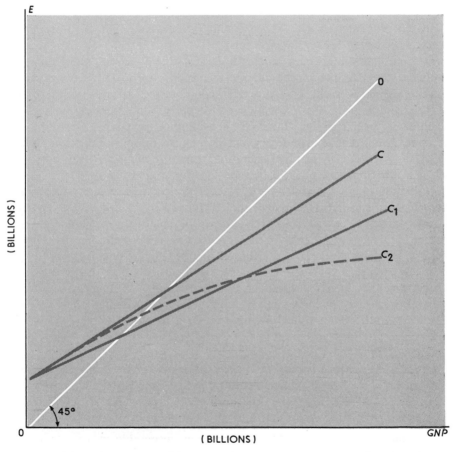

C is the untaxed consumption schedule. A proportionate tax on all income will rotate it downward to C_1. A progressive tax structure, under which rates rise as income increases, will give it a shape like C_2.

pensity to consume. But when taxation enters, an addition to personal income means less spending than before. Not only does some income go into saving but some is taken by taxation.

The shape of the revised consumption schedule depends on the tax structure. Two possibilities are illustrated in Figure 20–2. Let C be the original consumption schedule, with no taxation. Suppose a tax is introduced which is collected on all income received and is strictly proportional to income. This changes the consumption schedule to C_1. It remains a straight line, but with a reduced slope. The difference in slope between C and C_1 is equal to t, the marginal rate of taxation, which we have assumed to be constant.

Consider now a tax which exempts income below some minimum amount, say $2,000 per year. As a person's income rises above this minimum, the marginal rate of taxation also rises. This is a progressive income tax of the type used in the United States. It results in a consumption schedule such as C_2. This schedule is curved rather than straight, flattening out at higher income levels.

Since consumption is much the largest item in total expenditure, a reduced slope for the C schedule means a reduced slope for the expenditure schedule as well. The practical consequences of this fact are illustrated in Figure 20–3. Start with the expenditure schedule E, which includes a "primitive" or "untaxed" consumption schedule. The slope of E is steep and the multiplier is large. Suppose there is an autonomous drop of m dollars in planned spending, which lowers E to the position E_1. Then national income will fall all the way from Y to Y_1.

Suppose now that because of income taxation the consumption schedule, and therefore the expenditure schedule, has the reduced slope shown by E'. Then an autonomous drop of m dollars in spending will lower it to E'. Note that now the equilibrium level of income falls only to Y'_1. The tax system has cushioned the fall in income.

By working the diagram in the opposite direction one can show that the stabilizing effect works on the upswing as well. The tax structure reduces both the upper and lower limits within which the economy can fluctuate, and holds cyclical swings within a narrower range.

The strength of the built-in stabilizer depends mainly on two things:

1. *The income level at which taxation begins.* Almost all tax systems exempt incomes below a certain level, on the ground that it is unjust to tax the very poor. The higher the exemption, the smaller the stabilizing effect of the system. An exemption of $5,000 would produce less stabilization than an exemption of $2,000, since the proportion of personal income subject to tax would be much lower.

2. *The progressiveness of the rate structure.* If one wants to take away 30 percent of taxable income, this can be done in various ways. It can mean a proportionate 30 percent tax on all income above the exemption level. Or it can mean a schedule under which the marginal rate starts at 10 percent but rises to 90 percent on the largest incomes. The latter system will cause tax receipts to shoot up considerably faster than national income, and will consequently have a stronger stabilizing effect.

FIGURE 20–3

Effect of Taxation on Income Stability

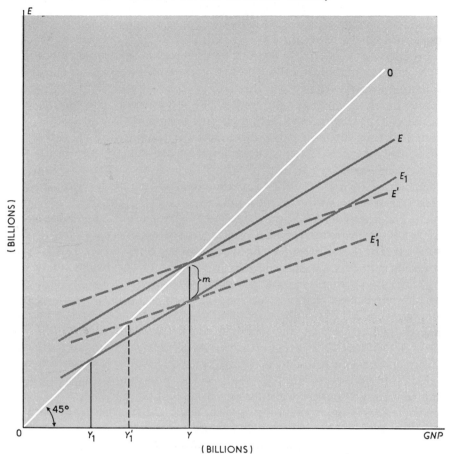

Suppose income taxation reduces the slope of the expenditure schedule from E to E'. Then the same drop of m dollars in planned expenditure will produce a smaller decline in GNP than would have occurred without taxation. Income falls only from Y to Y₁' instead of from Y to Y₁.

THE MEANING OF FISCAL POLICY

So far we have considered taxation and expenditure in isolation. We have seen that an *increase* in government expenditure *raises* the equilibrium level of national income, while a *cut* in expenditure *lowers* it. For taxation, the effects run in the reverse direction. An *increase* in tax rates *lowers* private spending and the equilibrium level of income, while a *cut* in tax rates *raises* the income level.

But in the real world taxes and spending go together. Actual budget making involves, or at least should involve, a careful adjustment of tax and expenditure levels relative to each other. The combination chosen for a particular year constitutes a *fiscal program*. *Fiscal policy is the choice of a fiscal program.*

Choosing a particular fiscal program involves choosing a certain size of budget surplus or deficit. It involves also an assumption about national income for the year ahead. The reason is that tax receipts depend heavily on the level of income. So without an assumption on this point one can have no idea of how the budget will come out.

Suppose government, on the basis of its best guess about next year's national income, chooses a program which just balances expenditures and tax receipts *at that income level*. This does not mean that the budget will actually come out balanced at the end of the year. If national income is higher than expected, there will be an automatic budget surplus. If it is lower, there will be a deficit. The large federal deficits which occur in recession years arise mainly from the abnormally low level of income rather than from deliberate decisions.

The meaning of fiscal policy may be clarified by looking at Figure 20–4.[1] A particular fiscal program is represented by a *budget line*, such as *A* in the diagram. At any point on this line, the level of federal spending and of tax rates is exactly the same. As one moves up to the right, however, the budget deficit decreases and eventually turns into a surplus. The main reason is that higher levels of national income yield larger revenues even at the same tax rates. The steepness of the budget line depends mainly on the marginal rate of taxation.

A different fiscal program is shown by line *B*. The difference between the programs is shown by the *vertical* distance between the two lines. Note that *at the same level of income*, program *B* involves a considerably larger deficit (or smaller surplus). This must mean that tax rates are lower or expenditures higher. Since either action will tend to raise national income, program *B* is more *expansionist* than program *A*.

The actual deficit or surplus in a particular year depends on two things: on the fiscal program, shown by the location of the budget line; *and* on the level of national income.

One paradoxical result is that a tax cut or an expenditure increase can *reduce* the federal deficit instead of increasing it. Either of these steps shifts the budget line downward. But it also, through the multiplier effect, raises the level of national income; and this tends to raise tax revenues and reduce transfer payments. If the multiplier is large and the budget line quite steep, the secondary effects might outweigh the original shift and produce a smaller deficit or even a surplus. This possibility is shown by a movement from position 1 on line *A* to position 2 on line *B*. Under these conditions we could quite literally "spend ourselves rich."

While this is a hypothetical possibility, it is not a realistic one for

---

[1] This is adapted from a similar diagram in the *Economic Report of the President*, January, 1962, p. 79.

FIGURE 20–4

Alternative Fiscal Programs

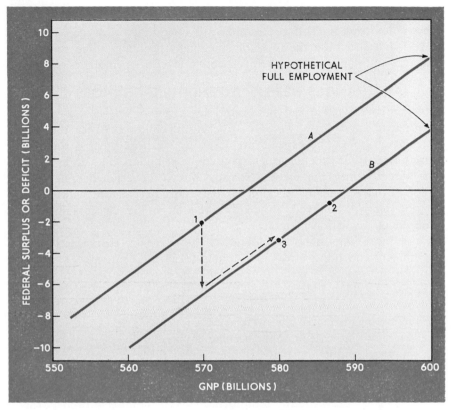

An unchanged fiscal program, such as line A, can produce either a surplus or deficit, depending on the level of GNP. Program B is more expansionist than A because, at the same GNP level, it involves a larger deficit or smaller surplus. Shifting from program A to program B involves an immediate increase of $5 billion in the deficit. But if the multiplier is 2 and the marginal rate of taxation is 30 percent, GNP will rise by $10 billion, leading to a $3 billion increase in tax collections. So one ends up at point 3, with a deficit only $2 billion larger than in the original position 1.

the American economy. Given the present structure of the economy, a more expansionist fiscal program will in fact produce a larger deficit—but not as much larger as one might think. Suppose the economy is operating below capacity and needs an expansionary push. Government decides to spend $5 billion more next year, leaving tax schedules unchanged. If the multiplier is 2, national income will rise by $10 billion. With present tax structures, about 30 percent of any increase in national income is drained off into federal revenues. Tax collections rise by $3 billion. So despite the original increase of $5 billion in spending, the deficit increases by only $2 billion. The economy moves from 1 on line A to 3 on line B. The drop in the budget line is partially offset by the fact that one is operating farther to the right in terms of national income.

In any event, the prospective surplus or deficit is not the decisive factor in budget making. The overriding consideration is the current and prospective level of national income, and how far this deviates from the full employment level. If the economy is operating below capacity and there is need to raise the level of spending, the budget line should be lowered; and conversely if the prospective level of spending is too high.

TAX CHANGES VERSUS EXPENDITURE CHANGES

The budget line can be altered by changing *either* tax rates or government expenditure. Is there anything to choose between these two types of change? The expenditure lever, as we have seen, is somewhat more powerful. If expenditures are raised by $1 billion, the whole amount goes directly into the income stream. But if government releases $1 billion of private income through tax cuts, only part of this will be spent and the rest will be saved. So it will take a larger tax cut to achieve the same effect on national income.

A more important consideration, however, is that taxation and government expenditure play different roles in the economy. *The function of government expenditure is to allocate resources to production of public services.* Expenditure should be set at a level which, *assuming full employment,* will divide national output between private and public production according to the preferences of the citizens. Under full employment, any increase in public services involves a diversion of resources from private production. If the public, acting through Congress, decides that it prefers to have an extra billion dollars worth of labor and materials devoted to national defense rather than to consumer goods, that is that. The task of Congress and the administration is to appraise and reflect these public preferences.

The implication is that government expenditures should not be varied to offset short-term fluctuations in national income. This is partly because it is difficult to vary public construction programs quickly, for reasons which will appear in Chapter 24. But more basically it is because the level of government services should be decided by long-term priorities. A new school or highway needed next year is presumably needed just as much whether the year happens to be a good one or a poor one. It is unnecessary to re-think the proper level of government activity every year because of business cycle swings.

If this is accepted, the burden of fiscal policy falls mainly on taxation (remembering always that transfer payments count as negative taxes). The *function of taxation is to regulate total spending so as to achieve a desired level of output and employment.* It is customary to state this objective as *full employment without inflation.* But this rather dodges the issue, as we saw in the last chapter. High employment and price stability are to some extent competitive, and one is forced to choose the best feasible combination of the two.

Once the objective is decided, and after there has been a forecast of total spending for the period ahead, one can say in which direction taxes need to be adjusted. If the level of spending threatens to be too high, leading to undue inflation, then tax rates should be raised to drain off this excess demand. But if the problem is insufficient demand, taxes should be lowered to raise private spending.

The latter course will involve a budget deficit, possibly a substantial deficit. People who dislike deficits will object that such a program is "inflationary." This depends on what one means by inflation. If one means simply a rise in the level of spending, then a budget deficit will have this effect. But if the level of total spending is too low, this is precisely what the economy needs. If one uses inflation in the proper sense of a rise in the price level, the effect of a budget deficit depends on the economic circumstances. If the economy is operating well below capacity, a deficit will mainly increase output and will have little effect on prices. Under these conditions the inflation objection is unwarranted.

If we treat expenditures and taxation as having quite different functions, what becomes of the historic connection between them? What becomes of the balanced budget? The answer is that under this approach *the budget surplus or deficit is not a direct object of public policy*. Expenditure levels and tax levels are determined independently on the basis of the function which each is expected to perform. Then we let the deficit or surplus fall where it may. Taxes and expenditures are planned, but the balance between them is not planned.

This approach to fiscal policy has been accepted by most economists for a generation. President Kennedy and other officials of the federal administration, expert bodies such as the Commission on Money and Credit, and numerous business groups have endorsed it. The President's 1963 recommendations to Congress for substantial tax reductions to stimulate the economy were based upon it. But there continues to be strong opposition from some groups in Congress and in the business community; and since tax powers are vested in Congress, it remains uncertain how rapidly the newer views will be incorporated in public policy.

Suppose Congress were persuaded to adapt this approach to the federal budget. How would it work out over the long run? Would budget surpluses in some years roughly balance deficits in other years? Or would deficits preponderate, leading to a gradual rise in the national debt? The answer depends on the strength of private spending, and particularly the level of business investment. In a period of active investment, such as 1945 to 1955, a correct use of fiscal policy would add little to national debt and might even reduce it. But during the 1930's, when private investment virtually collapsed, fiscal policy necessarily involved a preponderance of deficits. It is ironic that the quite small federal deficits of the New Deal era were widely assailed as leading to the downfall of the American economic system. With the benefit of hindsight, it seems clear that considerably larger deficits were called for.

OTHER IDEAS ABOUT THE BUDGET

1. *The annually balanced budget.* A traditional view in public finance has been that the budget should balance in each fiscal year. Whatever one can say for this principle at the state and local levels, as applied to the federal budget it has little merit. In fact, if taken seriously, it would have pernicious effects. It would mean *raising* tax rates during recession, to offset the natural decline in tax revenues, and *cutting* taxes during inflation to avoid a budget surplus. This is just the opposite of what should be done. Even exponents of "sound finance" rarely go this far. Deficits are accepted so long as they are unplanned and can be treated as nobody's fault, but proposals for deliberate deficits to stimulate the economy are strongly resisted.

The argument for annual balance in the federal budget is essentially a political argument. It rests on the view that there is a built-in tendency toward overspending. Self-interested groups of citizens are always eager to batten on the public purse. Power-hungry bureaucrats work constantly to expand their empires. Congressmen are too weak to resist these pressures. So the only remedy is to tie a ball and chain around government's ankle by saying, "If you want to spend, you've got to tax." How much there is to this line of reasoning you can judge as well as the next person.

2. *The balanced budget at full employment.* This idea comes closer to modern ideas about fiscal policy. It has been espoused by, among others, the Committee for Economic Development, a responsible and respected business group. Under this proposal, government expenditures would be determined independently on the basis of economic priorities. Next one would estimate how much the economy could produce at full employment. Finally, one would set tax rates so that, *if the full employment income were actually achieved*, tax receipts would just equal expenditures.[2] So long as the economy was below full employment, there would be an automatic deficit and the budget would be working in the right direction.

This is an optimistic program, since it implies that private consumption and investment will typically be high enough to maintain full employment without the further stimulus of a government deficit. This may or may not be true in practice. Most probably, it will be true at some

---

[2] The C.E.D. formulation is actually a bit more conservative than this. "It should be the policy of the government to set its expenditure programs and tax rates so that they would yield a constant, moderate surplus under conditions of high employment and price stability." (Committee for Economic Development, *Fiscal and Monetary Policy for High Employment*, New York, 1962, p. 26.)

times but not at others. It seems doubtful, therefore, that one can simply set a tax level and leave things to operate automatically thereafter. It is more likely that tax rates will need adjustment at frequent intervals, and one can imagine conditions in which it might be necessary to run a federal deficit for years on end to hold the economy near full employment.

/ 3. *Capital and current budgets.* An interesting type of budget system, developed in Sweden during the 1930's and since adopted by a number of other countries, distinguishes between the *current* expenditures of government and its *capital* expenditures. Most government expenditure falls in the current category—the civil service payroll, the pay and subsistence of the armed forces, purchase of materials for current use, interest on the public debt, and other transfer payments.

But there is also a large volume of expenditure on such things as schools, hospitals, post offices and other public buildings, superhighway systems, military installations, flood control, navigation, and reforestation projects. These are capital investments which will yield benefits to the public over a long period to come. There is no inherent reason why their full cost should be assessed against taxpayers in the particular year during which they are constructed. Why not finance them by issuing long-term bonds, and then assess interest charges against taxpayers who use the facilities in future years? If a private corporation builds a turnpike, it raises the money by selling bonds. If government builds the same turnpike, why shouldn't it finance it in the same way?

The difference, it may be said, is that the private corporation can charge tolls to pay interest on the bonds it has issued. But government can often do the same. It can charge for highway use, for power generated, for timber or grazing rights on public lands, for postal services, conceivably even for school and college education. If it seems unfeasible or unjust to charge those who actually use the facilities, the costs can be assessed against general tax revenues. The economic issue is whether the benefits which citizens derive from using a particular facility outweigh the social costs involved. If the answer is "yes," there is no ground for criticizing the use of debt financing.

Use of bond issues to finance public capital expenditures implies a continued growth of the public debt. But this is true also of private investment. Over the years 1930–58, the obligations of U.S. business corporations to their bondholders and stockholders increased from $156.5 billion to $260.5 billion. No one regards our business system as weaker on this account. The system is actually much stronger, because on the asset side of the balance sheet there is an equal accumulation of plant, machinery, office buildings, and other service-yielding property.

Similarly, a rise in public debt which is offset by an accumulation of service-yielding property might be regarded as normal. It has been estimated that the value of assets owned by state and local governments in the

United States increased from $8 billion in 1900 to $203 billion in 1958.[3] This increase in assets can be set against the increase of $55 billion in state and local indebtedness over the same period, and can be regarded as justifying or at least explaining the debt increase. The same is broadly true of *peacetime* increases in the federal debt.

THE QUESTION OF THE DEBT

There is still a widespread public feeling that increases in public debt are unsound and dangerous, and that reducing the debt should be a

TABLE 20–2

Public Debt in the United States, 1930–62
(Billions of dollars)

Year	Federal Government (End of fiscal year)	State and Local Governments	Year	Federal Government (End of fiscal year)	State and Local Governments
1930	16.2	18.5	1950	257.4	24.2
1931	16.8		1951	255.2	27.0
1932	19.5	19.2	1952	259.1	29.6
1933	22.5		1953	266.1	32.7
1934	27.1	18.9	1954	271.3	37.9
1935	28.7		1955	274.4	43.2
1936	33.8	19.5	1956	272.8	48.0
1937	36.4		1957	270.6	52.5
1938	37.2	19.4	1958	276.4	57.2
1939	40.4		1959	284.8	62.4
1940	43.0	20.2	1960	286.5	67.2
1941	49.0	20.2	1961	289.2	75.0
1942	72.4	19.7	1962	298.6	n.a.
1943	136.7	18.7			
1944	201.0	17.5			
1945	258.7	16.6			
1946	269.4	15.9			
1947	258.3	16.8			
1948	252.3	18.7			
1949	252.8	20.9			

Sources: *Historical Statistics of the United States*, pp. 728–30. *Statistical Abstract of the United States*, 1961. pp. 388–89. U.S. Department of Commerce, *Governmental Finances*, 1961.

major objective of fiscal policy. So we must look into this question before concluding.

The growth of public debt in the United States since 1930 is shown in Table 20–2. Most of the increase in federal debt occurred between 1941 and 1945. The rise of state and local debt, on the other hand, has

[3] Raymond W. Goldsmith and Robert E. Lipsey, *Studies in the National Balance Sheet*, National Bureau of Economic Research (forthcoming), Chap. 2.

occurred largely since 1945. It represents mainly school construction to educate the offspring of the "baby boom," and to a lesser extent the cost of highways and other public improvements.

But however acquired, doesn't this debt represent a burden on the population? How much of a burden, and for whom?

An important clue lies in the distinction between *real burdens* and *financial burdens*. The *real cost* of a public expenditure consists of resources which might otherwise have been put to some other use. It is an *opportunity cost*. This cost depends on the level of economic activity. In a period of heavy unemployment, one can argue that resources diverted to public use would otherwise be doing nothing. Their opportunity cost is zero. But if resources are fully employed, an increase in public production means an equivalent drop in production for private use. It is this drop which constitutes the real burden of the public expenditure.

At the height of World War II the American economy was operating beyond the point of normal full employment. Manpower, plant capacity, transportation, and other resources were stretched tight. Something like half of all resources was devoted to war production. If this had not been necessary, most of these resources would have been available for private consumption and investment. To the extent that resources were withdrawn from consumption, the population of the country "paid for the war" directly through a lowering of living standards. This cost could not be "passed on to future generations," since the future generations weren't around at the time!

There probably was some shifting of the war burden to future years, since resources were withdrawn from investment as well as consumption. Except for war plants and facilities, investment virtually ceased. Thus future periods were deprived of the flow of goods which might have resulted from investments which were in fact not made. But this argument is largely conjectural. It is possible that the low investment during the war contributed to an abnormally high rate of "catching-up" investment after the war, so that by 1960 our capital stock was as great as if the war had never occurred.[4]

Turning to the financial side, what is the significance of the fact that the national debt increased fivefold during the war years? The most obvious result is that more taxes must be raised each year to pay interest on the debt. The federal budget for 1963–64 included almost $10 billion for interest charges. The corresponding figure for 1939–40 was about $1 billion.

Is this an added burden on the people of the United States? It clearly would be if the U.S. government bonds were owned by residents

---

[4] This seems to have been true in Germany, Japan, and the U.S.S.R., where great wartime devastation was followed by very heavy postwar investment. There may be some underlying principle that "the farther you fall, the higher you bounce."

of Peru. In this case, our taxpayers would have to hand over each year $10 billion to the Peruvians for interest payments. This could not be done for long from our gold reserves, and the Peruvians might not even want that much gold. So eventually we would have to make payment by shipping goods of that value to Peru. This would reduce consumption levels in the United States and constitute a real burden on the population.

But the national debt is not held by Peruvians. It is held almost entirely by people and corporations within the United States. "We owe it to ourselves." So the taxes raised to pay interest on the debt come back into the pockets of people in this country. If the impact of the federal tax system were exactly the same as the ownership of the debt, this would amount merely to each person shifting money from one pocket to the other. To the extent that this is not true, the transfer affects the distribution of personal income. But it remains true that, for the population as a whole, the rights to receive interest balance off the obligations to pay interest. There is no burden of the debt in the sense that my house mortgage imposes a burden on me.

This does *not* mean that the size of the debt is unimportant. Paying interest on the debt requires tax levies, and levying taxes always harms the private economy to some extent. "There are no good taxes." Personal income taxes affect incentives to work; business taxes affect the ability and incentive to invest; excise taxes penalize consumption of certain products and distort the pattern of production. Even if the $100 which I pay the government in taxes comes right back to me as interest on government bonds which I own, I am worse off as a result of the transfer.

The inconvenience resulting from additional taxation is often termed *tax friction*. The tax friction resulting from the national debt can be measured by the percentage of national income which must be raised in taxes to pay interest on the debt. This depends on three things:

1. The size of the debt.
2. The rate of interest on the debt.
3. The size of the national income.

An increase in the size of the debt or the rate of interest increases the weight of the debt, while an increase in national income reduces it. If interest rates remain stable, the inconvenience of the debt increases only if it is growing faster than national income. If national income is rising 5 percent a year, the debt can also rise 5 percent a year without the economy being any worse off than before.

Table 20–3 shows interest payments on the federal debt, calculated as a percentage of GNP, at two-year intervals since 1929.

While the debt has risen from $17 billion in 1929 to about $300 billion at present, its economic significance has risen much less than this. In 1929, interest payments on the debt were 0.65 percent of GNP. Today they are higher, but not startlingly so, at a bit under 2 percent of GNP. Note also that the interest burden is somewhat *lower* today than it was

TABLE 20–3

Interest Payments on the Federal Debt, 1929–60

Calendar Year	GNP ($ Billions)	Interest Payments ($ Billions)	Interest Payments (Percent of GNP)
1929	104.4	0.678	0.65
1930	91.1	0.695	0.72
1932	58.5	0.599	1.02
1934	65.0	0.757	1.16
1936	82.7	0.749	0.91
1938	85.2	0.926	1.07
1940	100.6	1.041	1.03
1942	159.1	1.260	0.79
1944	211.4	2.609	1.23
1946	210.7	4.722	2.24
1948	259.4	5.211	2.01
1950	284.6	5.750	2.02
1952	347.0	5.859	1.69
1954	363.1	6.382	1.76
1956	419.2	6.787	1.62
1958	444.2	7.607	1.71
1960	503.2	9.179	1.82

Source: *Historical Statistics of the United States*, p. 139; and *Statistical Abstract of the United States*, 1961, pp. 301, 389.

at the end of World War II. The debt has continued to rise gradually, and interest rates have also risen, but this has been more than offset by the rate of increase in GNP.

The tax friction due to national debt typically falls during peacetime and rises sharply after major wars. It has been estimated that interest on the national debt of Great Britain amounted to 7.7 percent of GNP in 1818, soon after the end of the Napoleonic wars. During the peaceful nineteenth century, it fell substantially. But by the end of World War II, it was back up to 6.2 percent of GNP or about three times the U.S. level.

But are we not getting out of the problem too easily? What about the principal of the debt? Must we not repay this at some time in the future? The answer is emphatically "NO." Personal debts have to be repaid because people are mortal. My creditors want to make sure that I pay off my debts before I am gathered to my fathers. (Hence the length of time for which a bank will give a house mortgage decreases as the borrower's age increases!) But nations do not suffer from this human frailty. So there is no reason why national debt must be paid off, and in fact it never is. It may be reduced a bit in years of budget surplus. But for the most part, as old debts mature, the government simply "refunds" the debt by issuing new securities in place of the old.

All this is an accepted part of our financial system. Banks, insurance companies, colleges, and wealthy individuals hold large amounts of government securities in their portfolios. To them, these certificates of national debt appear as *assets*. And they are preferred assets because of the ease with which they can be converted into cash and the negligible risk of default. If the supply of such assets ever shrank materially through retirement of national debt, large investors would be embarrassed because they could not find such riskless assets elsewhere.

To sum up:

1. Public debt is primarily a residue of major wars. The growth of debt in peacetime is usually moderate.
2. Public debt owned within the country does not involve a financial burden in the same sense as private debt. It does involve the inconvenience of levying heavier taxes, usually termed tax friction.
3. It is not feasible or desirable to pay off any appreciable part of the debt carried over from past wars. The tax friction resulting from the debt, however, usually shrinks during peacetime because of the growth of national income.

In the first flush of enthusiasm for Keynesian analysis during the 1930's it became fashionable to say that the debt doesn't matter. This view is too extreme. The debt does matter, and a continued rise of national debt does have certain disadvantages.

On the other side of the ledger, however, must be set the costs of failing to take vigorous fiscal action to maintain high employment. The most obvious costs are the loss of current production and consumption resulting from below-capacity operation, the frustration and hardship inflicted on the unemployed, the rusting of work skills through disuse. But there is also the loss of reduced investment, a slower pace of economic growth, failure to keep up with other nations in the world-wide production race, and impaired morale of our citizens because of a feeling that the economy is not functioning as it could. How can it be seriously argued that these costs are outweighed by the friction associated with taxing and redistributing 2 percent of our GNP? The public fear of vigorous fiscal action is largely nonrational. Unless we become more rational on this point, as other nations are rapidly becoming, we shall find ourselves seriously handicapped in the future.

SUMMARY

1. In this chapter the *government budget* means government transactions on income and product account. *Expenditure* means government purchases of goods and services. *Taxation* means net taxes or tax receipts minus transfer payments.
2. Government expenditure by itself raises the equilibrium level of national income. Even if tax receipts are equal to expenditure, the budget has an expansionist effect. This is usually termed the *balanced budget theorem*.
3. Taxation by itself reduces private spending and lowers the equilibrium level of income.
4. The present U.S. tax structure is so constructed that tax receipts rise a

good deal faster than national income on the upswing, and fall faster on the downswing. This has an automatic braking effect on fluctuations in national income, usually termed the *built-in stabilizer*.

5. *Fiscal policy* is the deliberate adjustment of tax rates and government expenditure to achieve a desired level of national income. A specific combination of tax and expenditure levels constitutes a *fiscal program*.

6. The federal surplus or deficit in a particular year depends on two things: the fiscal program, and the level of national income. Because the latter is somewhat unpredictable, the budget result is often substantially different from what was intended.

7. The main consideration in choosing a fiscal program is the current and prospective level of national income relative to the output capacity of the economy. If the economy is operating below capacity, a more expansionist program is needed; and conversely if spending threatens to be excessive.

8. Short-run changes in the fiscal program should be brought about mainly by varying tax rates. Government expenditure should be set at a level which, *assuming full employment*, will allocate the nation's resources between private and public production according to the preferences of the citizens. These preferences presumably change rather slowly, and so it is not appropriate to vary expenditure to offset short-term fluctuations in national income.

9. A national debt owned within the country is not a burden in the sense that private debt constitutes a burden. It does, however, involve the inconvenience of raising more taxes to meet interest payments to bondholders. This *tax friction* can be measured by the size of interest payments as a percentage of GNP. It was about three times as high in 1946 as in 1929, because of the large debt increase during World War II. Since 1946, however, the tax friction arising from the debt has decreased slightly, i.e., interest payments have risen less rapidly than GNP.

10. There is no reason why national debt need be reduced over the long run. It is quite feasible for the Treasury to pay off old bonds and certificates as they mature by selling new securities of equivalent value. Federal securities are preferred assets for large institutional and private investors, and any substantial shrinkage of such assets would be inconvenient.

21

The Supply of Money

> Money is indeed the most important thing in the world; and all sound and successful personal and national morality should have this fact for its basis.
>
> GEORGE BERNARD SHAW

THERE IS a close relation between money and spending. The relation was put graphically by Sir Dennis Robertson, who called the amount of money in existence "money sitting," while spending was "money on the wing."

The fact that money exists doesn't tell us that it will be spent, or how rapidly it will be spent. This is why it seemed wise to start out in Chapters 18–20 by analyzing the basis for spending decisions, and what happens when these decisions change. But on the other hand money cannot be spent *unless* it exists, and an increase in the level of spending is apt to be accompanied by an increase in the quantity of money. So we need to understand where money comes from, the ways in which the quantity of money can be controlled, and the extent to which monetary controls can help in avoiding extremes of depression or inflation. These questions form the substance of Chapters 21 and 22.

THE NATURE OF MONEY

Money is as money does. Anything which members of a community are willing to accept in payment for goods or debts is money. Large round stones serve the purpose on the island of Yap. They can't be carried around in one's pocket. Indeed the happy inhabitants of this island don't have pockets. The stones remain immovable on hillsides throughout the island; but each stone has an owner, and ownership changes as payments are made. One large stone fell out of a boat years ago and lies in deep water some distance offshore. It is still wealth to its owner and counts as part of the island's money supply.

Among the Bantu tribes of East Africa, animals serve as a means of payment. A prospective bridegroom must pay the father of the bride so many cattle, sheep, or goats as a "bride price." Monetary systems have been based on cowrie shells, wampum, cloth, and beads. A prisoner of war camp during World War II developed an elaborate system of exchange in which cigarettes were accepted as currency.

Gold and other metals have always exercised a special fascination. They are durable, they can be fashioned into personal ornaments and art objects, and this commercial value reinforces their value as money. From Greek times until quite recently, money in the Western world meant metal coins which circulated partly by order of the sovereign but also by virtue of their metallic content.

The next stage in the development of modern monetary systems came with the rise of banking institutions in Europe during the fifteenth and sixteenth centuries. Banks gradually learned that they could issue paper notes which would be generally accepted as a means of payment. A. bank note meant originally that the banker had an equivalent amount of gold in his vaults, which he promised to pay to the holder of the note on demand. But so long as people had faith in the bank's soundness, there was no reason for them to demand payment. The notes passed freely from hand to hand because of the general belief that they were "as good as gold." After a time most payments came to be made in this way, and coins were reduced to serving as small change.

Still more recent is the practice of making payments by check. Businesses and individuals now hold most of their ready cash in the form of a checking account. One occasionally reads of an old lady with a passion for keeping bundles of bank notes in brown paper bags, but these stories make the headlines only because they are so rare. Most people regard a checking account as perfectly safe, and so it is. In the unlikely event that your bank should fail, deposits up to $10,000 are guaranteed through the Federal Deposit Insurance Corporation. Bankers refer to checking accounts as *demand deposits*, because the owner is entitled to withdraw them at any time on demand, without advance notice.

It may seem odd to regard checking accounts as money; but they meet the test of general acceptability. Checks written by a business concern, government agency, or other institution are normally accepted without question. So are personal checks with at most a quick glance at your driver's license. In addition, purchases are made increasingly on credit. When the bills roll in at the end of the month, how are they paid? By check, of course. This is much more convenient than going to the bank for paper money, and it also provides a ready record of what you have spent.

At the end of September, 1962, there was about $30 billion of coins and paper currency in circulation. Demand deposits in the hands of the public totaled about $115 billion. Thus demand deposits now form about four fifths of total money supply in the United States. Moreover, check money circulates faster than other kinds of money. More than 90 percent of all payments in the United States are made by check. So when we ask what determines the amount of money in existence, the main problem is what determines the amount of demand deposits.

We count checking accounts as money. Why do we not also count savings accounts? These are called *time deposits,* because the holder can be required to give a certain period of notice before withdrawing them. In normal times, most banks overlook this requirement and savings accounts can be withdrawn as freely as checking accounts. The total amount of time deposits in mid-1962 was $131 billion.

For that matter, why do we not count holdings of short-term government securities, which can be turned into cash without notice and with little risk? These resemble money in certain respects. They provide a safe way of holding reserve funds, and are counted as part of the liquid assets of businesses and individuals. Savings accounts and short-term government securities are often lumped together as *near money*.

But they are still not *quite* money. They are not directly and universally transferable. You can't go to the store and spend a savings account or a U.S. Treasury bill. They must first be converted into real money, which is then used as a means of payment. In the case of securities, the terms on which conversion can be effected are typically uncertain. A company knows that it can always sell its holdings of U.S. Treasury bills for cash; but the price of Treasury bills varies from day to day, and the outcome is uncertain until the bills are sold. Thus if I put a thousand dollars into securities, I cannot know how many dollars I will be able to realize in a year's time. The same thousand dollars put into a checking account will always be worth a thousand dollars. The difference is important. This is what one means by saying that money possesses *complete liquidity*.

The fact that we do not count near money as identical with true money does not mean that the amount of near money in existence is unimportant. Quite the contrary. If households and businesses have large holdings of savings accounts and government securities, this may make them more venturesome in spending their current incomes. For a couple of years after World War II, consumer spending almost equaled consumer income and personal savings dropped almost to zero. This was partly because consumers had accumulated many billions of savings during the war, which gave them a feeling of safety and increased their readiness to spend.

THE BUSINESS OF BANKING

There are banks and banks. Certain types of banks, important in their own right, lack the power to create demands deposits and hence are of no concern to us here. Examples are: (1) *Investment banks* or *underwriters*. These are securities merchants, who float new bond and stock issues on the general market. (2) *Savings banks*, whose business is to accept savings or time deposits. Money put into a savings account is usually left with the bank for a considerable period. This justifies the bank in putting the money into house mortgages, bonds, and other long-term securities. These securities earn interest, which constitutes the income of the bank. The bank pays interest at a lower rate to the depositors, covering its costs and hopefully making a profit from the spread.

The banks whose operations influence the money supply are called *commercial banks*. They are dealers in money or, if you prefer, dealers in loans. They also perform certain service functions. My bank receives my paycheck from my employer every month, allows me to draw checks on the account, sends me a statement at the end of the month and deducts a service charge for its trouble. But this is an unexciting and not very profitable operation. The lifeblood of commercial banking is sizing up would-be borrowers, advancing them money for a price, collecting the money when due, and re-lending the money on the next round.

Why is this sort of banking called *commercial?* Because in the early days most bank borrowers were engaged in commerce. Their need for loans is readily explained. A wholesaler buys a shipment of shoes from a manufacturer and must pay for it within 30 days. He will eventually re-sell the merchandise to retailers and collect for it, but this may take 90 days. How does he get the money to pay off the shoe manufacturer? If his business reputation and credit standing are satisfactory he can go to a bank and borrow the necessary money. The bank adds the amount of the loan to his checking account. He gives the bank a promissory note backed by the merchandise itself as *collateral*. (Collateral is something which the bank can lay hands on if the borrower fails to repay the loan. If I borrow money to buy a car, the bank can take over the car if I default on the payments. The car is collateral.)

Commercial bank lending is typically of this "tiding over" sort. A farmer needs money in the spring for seed, fertilizer, other farm costs, and living expenses. He must survive until the crop ripens in the fall, or until his cattle or hogs have been fattened and sold. The answer? A six-month bank loan, secured by animals or farm machinery as collateral. A manufacturer must buy raw materials and hire labor to work on products which may not be sold for months to come. He may need a bank loan to carry him through the intervening period.

A commercial bank provides *circulating capital* or *working capital*, which tides over the period between the beginning of a production process and the sale of the final product. This period is usually short. Hence commercial bank loans typically run between one and six months, with three months perhaps the commonest period. Commercial banks do not usually provide long-term money for plant construction. These *fixed capital* needs must be met by reinvesting profits or by selling new securities in the capital market.

The line between short-term and long-term lending is often unclear in practice. A company may never borrow for more than three months; but as one loan is repaid, and if the company continues to need money, the bank may immediately extend a new loan of the same amount. This can go on for years, provided the company continues to meet the bank's standards of financial soundness. In such cases the bank becomes a continuing partner in the enterprise, fortifying it with ready cash as needed, while on the other hand looking over management's shoulder and keeping an eye on the books. The company, so long as it continues to operate successfully, has a permanent source of working capital. But the fact that loans must be renewed every three months or six months enables the banker to bail out quickly if the business seems to be going downhill.

We can now see why the level of business borrowing moves up and down with the level of production. Suppose manufacturers believe an economic upswing is underway and decide to step up production schedules. They must immediately begin to lay out more money for payrolls, raw materials, and other operating expenses. Where will the money come from? Some companies may be able to draw on accumulated cash reserves, but others will go to the banks seeking larger loans.

Suppose the banks are willing to make additional loans. They can do so simply by adding the amount of the loans to the borrowers' checking accounts. Thus demand deposits rise. But demand deposits are money, the most important kind of money in the modern economy. So we reach an important conclusion: An increase in the level of economic activity is normally accompanied by an increase in the quantity of money. If banks are unable or unwilling to increase their loans, this acts as a brake on the expansion.

The converse is also true: A drop in economic activity is normally accompanied by a decline in demand deposits. If production is dropping businesses need less working capital than before and find themselves paying off old loans faster than they are requesting new ones. But how does a business (or an individual) pay off a loan? By allowing the bank to *deduct* the amount of the loan from its checking account. Repayment of loans thus means a drop in demand deposits.

This parallel movement of money supply and productive activity says nothing about causation. We are not asserting that changes in the quantity of money *cause* changes in the level of production, or vice versa. The interrelation is more complicated than this, as will appear in the next chapter.

BANK ASSETS: INCOME AND SECURITY

A good way to dig deeper into the nature of commercial banking is to look at the assets which banks hold and the liabilities which they owe. Instead of selecting a particular bank, let us look at the totals for all commercial banks in the United States at the beginning of 1962 (Table 21–1).

A central concern of any commercial bank is security and liquidity. The liability side of Table 21–1 shows that the banks of the country are obligated in theory to pay out fantastic amounts to depositors. Demand

TABLE 21–1

Consolidated Balance Sheet; All Commercial Banks
January 1, 1962

Assets (Billions)		Liabilities (Billions)	
Cash and interbank		Owners' capital	22,459
deposits	39,514	Time deposits	82,428
Balances with Federal		Demand deposits,	
Reserve Banks	16,918	including interbank	
U.S. government		deposits	166,261*
securities	66,578	Other	7,413
Other securities	23,937		
Loans	124,925		
Other	6,689		
Total	278,561	Total	278,561

* This figure is considerably larger than the $115 billion mentioned earlier as part of the money supply. The main reason is that it includes deposits held by one bank in another, and also government deposits, which are not considered part of money supply.

deposits can be withdrawn at once, and time deposits can be withdrawn on 30 days' notice. Thus it seems that households and businesses could descend on the banks and demand upwards of $200 billion in cash. They would not get very far, since there is only about $30 billion of cash in existence. This would amount to a general collapse of the banking system, which could happen only in extreme emergency. Something close to this did happen in early 1933 at the bottom of the Great Depression. Widespread public demand for cash led to the failure of many banks and finally to a "bank holiday," during which all banks were closed by government order until public confidence could be restored.

While a general "run" on the banks is unlikely, a particular bank may be faced with substantial and unexpected withdrawals. So it must stand ready to meet any demands for cash payment. The first three items on the asset side of Table 21–1—cash, balances with the Federal Reserve, and

U.S. securities—constitute successive lines of defense on which a bank can fall back to meet its obligations.

Cash

Banks normally hold some money in the till to meet depositors' requests for cash. Bills and coins are now a minor part of the monetary system, and the demand for cash is reasonably predictable. Moreover, while some customers are demanding cash from the bank others will be returning cash for deposit. Thus a bank can get along with a remarkably small amount of currency, usually only a few percent of its total liabilities.

Reserves

Should there be unusually heavy withdrawals of cash from a bank, it can fall back on its next line of defense—its checking account with the Federal Reserve Bank of its district. The Federal Reserve Banks, of which there are 12 in the United States, are *central banks* or *banker's banks*. They deal almost entirely with the commercial banks rather than with the general public. Their operations will be explained in the next chapter. Meanwhile we may note that commercial banks which are members of the system maintain substantial checking accounts, usually called *reserves*, with the Reserve Bank of their district. If a bank suddenly needs $50,000 of additional currency, the Federal Reserve ships it this amount of Federal Reserve notes, at the same time deducting $50,000 from the bank's checking account.

The minimum reserves which a commercial bank must carry are specified by law. A bank normally prefers to have reserves somewhat above the legal minimum, since it is only these "excess" or "free reserves" which can be drawn on for day-to-day operations. The drawback is that a checking account at the Federal Reserve earns no interest. It is an unproductive investment for the bank compared, say, with putting the same amount into government securities.

Government Securities

An important type of bank asset is short-term securities of the federal government. These earn interest and are readily salable should the bank run short of reserves. They are in fact often termed *secondary reserves*.

At the end of 1961 there was about $250 billion of U.S. securities in the hands of banks, business concerns, and individuals. (In addition, there were some $44 billion of special issues not available to the public, such as the securities held by the Old Age and Survivors Insurance system.) Commercial banks owned $67 billion, or about one quarter of the total. Their holdings were largely in the form of Treasury bills and certificates. These short-term securities are particularly attractive to the commercial banks, which dislike committing money for long periods.

The disadvantage of short-term federal securities is the low rate of interest which they carry. They typically pay something between 1 and 3 percent, whereas money put into business loans will yield 4 to 6 percent. On the other hand, government securities are safe and can readily be converted into cash.

Bank holdings of governments fluctuate in response to the demand for business loans. If the demand for loans is rising, the banks try to meet it both to keep the goodwill of their customers and to earn higher rates of interest. If necessary, they will sell some government securities and shift the money to loans. Conversely, in slack times when loans are being repaid faster than new loans are being demanded, the banks find themselves with idle resources which they can put back into securities. Earning 2 percent is better than earning nothing at all.

Loans

Commercial banks are basically lending institutions. Thus the largest category of bank assets is loans to businesses and households. We have already seen what happens when a loan is made. The borrower gives the bank a promise to pay, a piece of paper which counts as an asset. The bank gives the borrower an addition to his checking account, which increases the demand deposit item on the liability side of Table 21–1. The *loans* item on the asset side of Table 21–1 is the sum total of pieces of paper certifying that people owe the banks money. These are certificates of private indebtedness, just as a government bond is a certificate of public indebtedness. Commercial banks are in the business of buying certificates of indebtedness, public and private.

Bank loans include such things as: "commercial loans" in the old sense of loans to wholesalers, retailers, exporters, importers, and other merchants; working capital loans to manufacturers; agricultural loans to farmers (though a good deal of this is now handled by federal lending agencies); loans to consumers, where the commercial banks now offer vigorous competition to the personal finance companies; and mortgage loans for residential and commercial construction.

The volume of loans is only partly within the control of the commercial banks. It takes two to make a loan, and the borrower normally takes the initiative. The bank's influence is limited to being more or less receptive to loan applications and to varying the interest rate which it charges. No matter how receptive the banker may be, no matter how reasonable his terms, businessmen will not request loans unless they expect to earn a profit on the money. If the economy is in recession, loan applications will decline, and they will be revived only by an upturn in business activity.

BANK LIABILITIES: DEMAND DEPOSITS AND CREDIT CREATION

When I write a check for $100, this is an order to my bank to deduct $100 from my account and transfer it to the recipient of the check.

He then deposits it in his bank and gets the amount added to his balance. If we both have checking accounts in the same bank, the transaction is simple. The bank deducts $100 from my account and adds $100 to his. The bank's total deposits remain unchanged.

But suppose a check drawn on bank A is deposited in bank B. Bank A then owes bank B that much money and a transfer between the two banks is necessary. It is likely, however, that at the same time some checks drawn on bank B will have been deposited in bank A, so that the two debts will partially cancel each other. These cancellations are carried out through a central clearing-house in each city. Each morning every bank sends to the clearing-house all the checks which it has received drawn on other banks in the city. The totals are added up. A bank which has sent in more dollars worth of checks on other banks than others have sent in against it receives a payment of that amount. A bank which has an adverse balance must pay in that amount to the clearing-house. How does a bank "pay up" in such a case? By writing a check on its account with the Federal Reserve Bank of its district. Thus a bank which has more checks drawn against it than are being deposited with it suffers a reduction in its balance at the Federal Reserve.

If a check drawn in one city is deposited in another, the clearance procedure is more elaborate but not basically different. Again, the important thing to the individual bank is whether the total checks drawn against it are greater or less than the checks it is receiving drawn on other banks.

The term *demand deposits* is confusing. It suggests that to get a checking account I must *deposit* something in the bank. This idea seems so reasonable that it is hard to dislodge from one's mind. There is even an element of truth in the idea, for this is certainly one way to acquire a checking account. I can come into the First National Bank of Illyria and open a checking account by depositing either a check which I have received or a bundle of paper money. But note that *this does not alter the amount of money in the economy*. If I deposit a check, the increase in my checking account is exactly offset by a reduction in someone else's checking account. Total demand deposits remain unchanged. If I deposit cash, this increases the amount of demand deposits in existence, but it reduces cash in circulation by an equal amount. Total money supply remains unchanged.

How, then, can there ever be an increase or decrease in the supply of money? The answer is that there is a second way in which demand deposits can originate. Suppose I am a manufacturer with a growing business which requires more working capital. I ask my banker for a loan of $100,000 and, after looking into the soundness of the business, he approves the loan. What does he give me? Not a bale of $100 bills. He simply adds $100,000 to my checking account. In return, I give him a piece of paper promising to repay the money by a specified date. The transaction affects the bank's balance sheet as follows:

Assets		Liabilities	
Loans	+100,000	Demand deposits	+100,000

Here is an increase in demand deposits coming right out of the blue. My need for a loan has increased the money supply of the economy.

This apparent ability to create something out of nothing has subjected bankers to much criticism and complaint. There is a limitless supply of would-be borrowers, each very creditworthy in his own eyes. The banker, they feel, has only to agree. For can he not create new money at the stroke of a pen? If he declines to do so, is he not being mean and niggardly? "The monied interests," with their stubborn refusal to turn the money tap wide open, have been a favorite target of politicians, farm leaders, and others.

A banker hearing this kind of talk comes as close to foaming at the mouth as a banker ever could. He will maintain stoutly that his power to make new loans is strictly limited. He is likely to say, "Create money? Why, I can't do that. I can only lend out money which other people have first deposited with me."

What is the truth of the matter? Can the banks create money or can't they?

CREDIT CREATION: A MONOPOLY BANK

Suppose there is a single bank, with branches all over the country, which has a monopoly of the commercial banking business. This bank is required by law to maintain a balance with the Federal Reserve System equal to 20 percent of its demand deposits. And suppose that at the moment the bank is just meeting this requirement. Its Federal Reserve balance is exactly 20 percent of its demand deposits. It also has exactly the amount of till money which it considers necessary. In this situation the bank is indeed tied hand and foot. It is *loaned up*, as bankers say. If I approached it for a loan, it could only say "So sorry."

But help is on the way. Out of the hills comes a prospector who has found $1 million worth of gold nuggets in a canyon. Instead of gambling them away he turns them over to the bank, which credits his checking account. The bank then passes the gold on to the Federal Reserve, thereby increasing its balance at the Fed by $1 million. The effect on the bank's position is:

Assets		Liabilities	
Balance at Federal Reserve	+1,000,000	Demand deposits	+1,000,000

The bank's reserves have now been increased, so it can presumably increase its loans as well. By how much? The answer depends on the legal reserve ratio. If the ratio is 20 percent, the bank can make new loans of $4 million. Its balance sheet will then have changed as follows:

Assets		Liabilities	
Balance at Federal		Prospector's demand	
Reserve	+1,000,000	deposits	+1,000,000
Loans	+4,000,000	Borrowers' demand	
		deposits	+4,000,000

At this stage the bank has once more reached the limit of its lending capacity. Its extra $1 million of reserves will support the extra $5 million of demand deposits, but no more than this. It must now mark time until there is some further addition to its reserves.

In this simplified case one can conclude that:

1. There is a definite ceiling to the bank's lending capacity. This is determined by the size of its reserves and by the legal reserve requirement. If the legal ratio is 20 percent, it can lend only up to the point at which demand deposits are five times the reserves on hand. When the bank has reached this ceiling, it cannot increase loans without an addition to its reserves.

2. An addition to reserves enables the bank to increase its deposits by several times the amount of the addition. The degree of deposit expansion depends on the required reserve ratio. A reserve ratio of 20 percent will permit a fivefold expansion, as in our illustrative case. With a 10 percent ratio, deposits could be increased by 10 times the increase in reserves; and so on.

3. This principle operates equally in the opposite direction. A reduction in reserves will force a deposit reduction of several times that amount. Starting from a loaned up position, and with a 20 percent reserve ratio, a drop of $1 million in reserves would compel a reduction of $5 million in demand deposits.

The size of bank reserves is thus the central lever of the monetary system. An upward or downward movement in reserves has a multiple effect on the feasible level of demand deposits. This flexibility of the system permits the money supply to change rapidly in response to business requirements, but it is sometimes criticized as a source of instability and an aggravating factor in business cycles.

CREDIT CREATION: A MULTIPLE BANKING SYSTEM

How far do these principles apply to the United States banking system, which contains thousands of banks operating independently of each other? Let us consider this case, assuming again that all banks must keep legal reserves of 20 percent.

If all banks in the system are loaned up, the answer is the same as before. There can be no increase in loans without an addition to reserves. But here comes our helpful prospector once more. He must now choose a particular bank for his deposit, which we shall call Bank A. As before, the bank sends the gold to the Federal Reserve and receives a $1 million addition to its reserve balance.

How much can the bank lend on the basis of this increase in reserves? An inexperienced banker might reason as we did in the previous case: the $1 million of new reserves will support an additional $5 million of demand deposits. Demand deposits have already increased by the $1 million which was credited to the prospector's account. This leaves $4 million which the bank can lend.

In the present case, however, this answer would be wrong. The reason is that people do not borrow money to let it sit in the bank. They borrow it to spend. If a bank adds $4 million to checking accounts through new loans, the borrowers will immediately start writing checks against this amount. They are entitled to spend it all, and the only safe assumption is that they will spend it all in the near future.

In the previous case, where all checks drawn against the monopoly bank come back to branches of the same bank, this presents no problem. Money never leaves the bank, and the $5 million of new demand deposits will always remain covered by the $1 million addition to reserves.

In a multiple banking system, however, each bank must assume that the checks drawn on it will be deposited in *other* banks. If Bank A goes blithely ahead and lends $4 million dollars, it will soon find other banks descending on it *via* the clearing-house demanding payment of this $4 million. The bank has only $1 million of new reserves available to meet this obligation. So Bank A is in trouble, and the official who authorized the new loans is in disgrace.

How much *can* Bank A safely lend on the basis of its increased reserves? The answer in this case is $800,000. Why is this? Because even if this amount is checked out of Bank A at once, and the Bank has to pay over $800,000 of its new reserves to other banks, it still has $200,000 left to set against the prospector's demand deposit of $1 million. The 20 percent reserve requirement is satisfied and the bank is in balance.

This can be explained most clearly in balance-sheet terms. The first effect of the prospector's gold deposit on Bank A's balance sheet is as follows:

Assets		Liabilities	
Balance at Federal Reserve	+1,000,000	Demand deposits	+1,000,000

Bank A now lends $800,000 to customers. After the loans have been made, but before any of the money has been checked out, the Bank's books will look as follows:

Assets		Liabilities	
Balance at Federal Reserve	+1,000,000	Prospector's demand deposits	+1,000,000
Loans	+ 800,000	Borrowers' demand deposits	+ 800,000

Now the borrowers proceed to spend the full amount of their loans, and all the checks they write are deposited in other banks, which Bank A must repay by drawing on its account at the Federal Reserve. After this has happened, Bank A is left in the following position:

ASSETS		LIABILITIES	
Balance at Federal		Prospector's demand	
Reserve	+200,000	deposits	+1,000,000
Loans	+800,000		

Since the increase in reserves is 20 percent of the increase in demand deposits, the Bank is all right. But if it had tried to lend more than $800,000, its reserves would have been depleted to the point where it could no longer meet the legal reserve requirement.

This is the end of the story as far as Bank A is concerned, but it is not the end for the banking system as a whole. Other banks in the system have now gained $800,000 of reserves through the withdrawals from Bank A. Thus they are in a position to increase *their* loans, creating demand deposits in the process. How much can they lend? By the same reasoning used for Bank A, they will be able to lend $\frac{4}{5}$ of the increase in reserves, or $640,000.

This $640,000 is now checked out by the borrowers and deposited in still other banks, which gain reserves to this extent. These larger reserves will justify increased loans and demand deposits amounting to $\frac{4}{5}$ of $640,000; and so on and on.

When the process has worked itself out, demand deposits will have increased by

$$1,000,000 + 1,000,000(\tfrac{4}{5}) + 1,000,000(\tfrac{4}{5})^2 + \ldots\ldots 1,000,000(\tfrac{4}{5})^n$$

The sum of this series is:

$$1,000,000 \left(\frac{1}{1-\tfrac{4}{5}}\right) = 1,000,000 \left(\frac{1}{\tfrac{1}{5}}\right) = 5,000,000$$

The original increase in reserves has thus permitted a multiple expansion of demand deposits. The size of the expansion depends on the required reserve ratio. Since the reserve ratio was assumed to be one fifth, the increase in deposits is five times the increase in reserves.

What has happened here? The $1 million increase in reserves, which started out as a single lump in Bank A, has been spread around among a large number of banks through the drawing and deposit of checks. But none of it is extinguished. Wherever it ends up, it serves to support demand deposits of five times its own size. Thus *for the banking system as a whole* it is now possible to have $5 million more in demand deposits than it was possible to have previously. The conclusion reached in the discussion of a single monopoly bank holds in this case as well. The banking system *can* create money. It can lend several times the amount of any increase in reserves, the size of this leverage depending on the required reserve ratio.

If we look only at one bank, the "banker's reasoning" is quite correct. A bank which is already loaned up cannot lend anything more until it has had an increase in reserves, and it can lend no more than the amount of this increase. Indeed, it must lend somewhat less than this to remain in a safe position.

The banking system as a whole, however, can do something which no bank within it can do individually. It can pyramid an increase in reserves into a multiple expansion of deposits. At the end of the process, a consolidated balance sheet for all banks in the system will show the following changes:

ASSETS		LIABILITIES	
Balances with Federal		Prospector's demand	
Reserve	+1,000,000	deposits	+1,000,000
Loans	+4,000,000	Borrowers' demand	
		deposits	+4,000,000

This is exactly the result which we reached in the monopoly bank case.

CREDIT CREATION: SIMULTANEOUS EXPANSION IN A MULTIPLE SYSTEM

The case just examined is remote from real life. It is unlikely that an increase in reserves would go entirely to one bank, and that other banks would have to sit idly by while the reserves were gradually redistributed among them through successive rounds of depositing and re-lending.

The forces which increase or decrease bank reserves are examined in the next chapter. They include deposit and withdrawal of cash by the public, movements of gold into and out of the United States, actions of the U.S. Treasury, and actions of the Federal Reserve System. These forces are likely to hit many banks at about the same time and in the same direction.

Suppose, for simplicity, that all banks are receiving additions to their reserves at the same time and at the same rate. Then each bank is safe in lending more than it has received, *provided it keeps in step with other banks in the system*. Why? Because if each bank increases its demand deposits at the same rate as other banks, it can assume that the extra checks which are going to be drawn against it will be offset by extra checks drawn against other banks and deposited with it. It need no longer fear the loss of reserves which would follow if it were the only bank in the system making new loans. If all banks are expanding simultaneously, each can move directly and rapidly toward a 5 to 1 expansion of demand deposits on the basis of its new reserves. We are back, in effect, to the monopoly bank case.

Reality is never this simple. Changes in bank reserves do not hit all banks with equal force. During an expansion some banks will gain reserves faster than others, and part of their gains will be spread around to other banks as described in the previous section. On the whole, however, a model of simultaneous proportionate expansion of reserves and deposits is more realistic than any other.

It is worth noting that a *reduction* in the required reserve ratio has the same effect as an *increase* in reserves. Suppose that at a particular time there are $100 billion of demand deposits, which are just covered by $20 billion of reserves. The Federal Reserve decides to lower the reserve ratio from 20 percent to 15 percent, so that the banks need only $15 billion of legal reserves. This leaves them with $5 billion of *free or excess reserves,* which will permit an increase in demand deposits of $5 \times \dfrac{100}{15} = \$33.3$ billion.

All our illustrations have involved *increases* in bank reserves and deposits. The system is expanding most of the time, and positive arithmetic is easier to grasp than negative arithmetic. Everything which has been said about expansion, however, applies equally to contraction. If the banking system is loaned up, and if it then *loses* reserves (or the Federal Reserve raises reserve requirements), the banks will be obliged to reduce demand deposits by several times as much. How is this done as a practical matter? Mainly by making new loans at a slower rate than old loans are being repaid.

Does this sound confusing? What happens when a loan is repaid? A wholesaler has borrowed $50,000 from a bank on a three-month promissory note. At the end of the three months, unless the loan is extended or renewed, the bank automatically *deducts* $50,000 from the wholesaler's checking account. *Repayment of loans extinguishes demand deposits.* If the banks stopped making new loans completely, and simply waited for old loans to be paid off, demand deposits would fall quite fast. Actually, they need never go this far. By merely holding back, so that repayments run ahead of new loans, they can gradually reduce demand deposits to any desired level. This process is termed *credit contraction.*

SUMMARY

1. In the United States today, money consists largely of *checking accounts* or *demand deposits* at commercial banks.

2. The main business of a commercial bank is to make short-term loans to business concerns and households. *Making a loan creates a demand deposit.* Conversely, repaying a loan extinguishes a demand deposit. Thus the amount of "checking account money" in existence moves up and down with the volume of bank lending.

3. Partly because of business prudence, but mainly because of legal requirements, a commercial bank must hold a *reserve* equal to a specified percentage of its deposits. This takes the form of a checking account with the Federal Reserve Bank of its district.

4. If a bank's actual reserve percentage is just equal to the percentage re-

quired by law, it is said to be *loaned up*. It cannot increase its volume of loans unless it receives an addition to its reserves.

5. Under the U.S. system of many independent banks, a bank which receives an addition to its reserves cannot lend more than the amount of the addition—in fact, somewhat less. This is because it must assume that the loans will be spent rapidly, leading to deposit of checks in other banks and a consequent transfer of reserves from the first bank to these others.

6. But this transfer of reserves enables other banks to increase *their* loans; and so on through successive cycles. *For the banking system as a whole*, loans can rise eventually by several times the amount of the original increase in reserves. Review the last few pages of the chapter to make sure you understand just how this works.

7. Everything which is true of expansion is true also of contraction. If bank reserves fall, loans will have to fall by several times as much.

The Impact of Monetary Policy

> The force of the guinea you have in your pocket depends wholly on the default of a guinea in your neighbor's pocket. If he did not want it, it would be of no use to you.
>
> JOHN RUSKIN

PROSPECTORS FROM THE HILLS are not the main reason for changes in bank reserves, despite our example for chapter 21. What are the actual reasons why reserves may increase or decrease? What control powers does the Federal Reserve System have, and how are these powers used to influence the supply of money? And how does the supply of money influence interest rates, spending, and production?

We now think of the Fed mainly as a vehicle for controlling the availability and cost of money on a national scale, and for moderating the swings of the business cycle. But in the laissez-faire atmosphere of 50 years ago such a program would have seemed radical and impractical. The Federal Reserve System was created to serve limited and practical needs: to provide a rapid and effective system of check clearance; to provide a single fiscal agent for the federal government; to enforce rules of sound lending procedure on individual banks through periodic reports and visits by bank examiners; to provide a readily expansible supply of hand-to-hand currency; and to ward off "financial panics" (which had occurred with disastrous effect in 1873, 1884, 1893, and 1907) by creating a "lender of last resort" to which the commercial banks could turn in an emergency.

490

In the course of providing for these needs, however, the authors of the Act gave the Federal Reserve power to influence the level of bank reserves. Its powers were enlarged by a major revision of the Act in 1935, following the banking collapse of 1933. As the Fed has gained experience in using its powers, and as belief has grown that business cycles can be moderated by deliberate action, the emphasis of the System's operation has shifted toward overall monetary control. The original service functions remain important, but are now generally taken for granted.

STRUCTURE OF THE FEDERAL RESERVE SYSTEM

Most countries have a single central bank located in the national capital. Some of the European central banks are much older than our own. The Bank of Sweden dates from 1656, the Bank of England from 1694, and the Bank of France from 1800.

Because of the geographical diversity of the United States and the influence of sectional interests in Congress, it was decided in 1913 to create 12 Federal Reserve Banks with headquarters in commercial centers throughout the country. These banks are located in Boston, New York, Philadelphia, Richmond, Atlanta, Cleveland, Chicago, Minneapolis, St. Louis, Kansas City, Dallas, and San Francisco. Each bank has jurisdiction over a "Federal Reserve District," comprising states in its normal trading area.

All commercial banks with national charters must be members of the Federal Reserve System, and state banks may become members by meeting certain qualifications. Some 7,000 state banks either have not been able to qualify or have been unwilling to accept the controls and obligations of Federal Reserve membership. The 6,000 or so banks which are members, however, have about 85 percent of the demand deposits in the country; and many of the nonmember banks carry their reserves in member banks. The great bulk of banking activity thus falls within the orbit of the System.

The 12 Federal Reserve Banks are *central banks* or *bankers' banks*. This is true in a double sense. First, each of them is owned by the member banks in its district, which were required to put up 3 percent of their paid-in capital and surplus to provide initial capital for the central bank. The members receive dividends on this money, and elect six of the nine Federal Reserve directors in each district. Second, Federal Reserve dealings are almost entirely with the commercial banks and the U.S. Treasury.

Despite their private ownership, they are in a real sense *public banks*. Their main function is to influence the volume and cost of money in a way which will promote stable prosperity. They are not primarily profit-making institutions. After the member banks have received a guaranteed 6 percent return on their capital subscriptions, almost all remaining Federal Reserve profits are turned over voluntarily to the Treasury.

The System is directed by a seven-man Board of Governors, located in Washington. (When we speak loosely of "the Board" or "the Fed," it is usually this group that we have in mind.) Members of the Board are appointed for 14 year terms, one term expiring every two years. This protects the Board against domination by a particular administration and to some extent immunizes it against pressure from Congress. This vaunted independence of the Fed presents difficulties as well as advantages, and has given rise to considerable controversy.

The Board of Governors appoints three of the nine Directors of each Federal Reserve Bank. (Of the remaining members, three are expected to be commercial bankers, and three are chosen to represent industry, agriculture, and commerce. All six are elected by member banks in the district.) The chief officers of each bank, the president and first vice-president, must be approved by the Board of Governors. In addition, the Board of Governors dominates the strategic *Open Market Committee*, which decides on Federal Reserve purchases and sales of government securities. Thus despite the separation into 12 regional banks, the System approaches the centralization of authority found in the central banks of other countries.

The most important feature of the Federal Reserve System is its power to influence the size of bank reserves and the legal reserve requirement. The principal control powers are:

1. The System can lend to member banks at a specified rate of interest, which is called the *discount rate*. This rate is altered from time to time, reflecting Federal Reserve objectives and changing conditions in the money market.

2. The System can buy and sell federal securities in the open market, an activity known as *open market operations*. These transactions have a direct impact on member bank reserves, and are the main instrument of day-to-day monetary policy.

3. The System can alter within specified limits the percentage reserve which member banks must carry against their deposits. The outside limits within which the Board must operate, and the actual requirements in force in 1962, are shown in the following schedule:

	Minimum Reserve Percentage	Maximum Reserve Percentage	Actual Reserve Requirement, June 1, 1962
Demand deposits			
Central reserve cities (New York and Chicago)	10	22	16½
Reserve cities (other large and medium cities)	10	22	16½
Other member banks (smaller cities and towns)	7	14	12
Time deposits	3	6	5

TABLE 22–1

Consolidated Balance Sheet, Federal Reserve Banks

June 30, 1962

(Millions of Dollars)

Assets		Liabilities	
Gold certificates	16,158	Federal Reserve notes	28,658
U.S. government		Member bank reserves	17,206
securities	29,663	Other deposits	1,239
Loans, discounts, and		Deferred availability	
advances	136	cash items	3,245
Cash items in process of		Capital and surplus	1,439
collection	4,707	Other liabilities	65
Other assets	1,188		
Total	51,852	Total	51,852

Federal Reserve activities may be made more concrete by looking at a combined balance sheet for the 12 banks as of mid-1962 (Table 22–1). Let us examine some of the major items, starting on the asset side.

Gold Certificates

Gold has not circulated as money in the United States since 1933. Newly mined gold within the country, and gold coming into the United States from abroad, must be delivered to the Treasury at a price of about $35 per ounce. It is then interred in a vault at Fort Knox, thus completing its journey from underground to underground. The Treasury sells gold at the fixed price for jewelry, dental, and other requirements; and it stands ready to provide gold for shipment abroad in settlement of international transactions. For this purpose a ready reserve of gold bullion is kept in the vaults of the Federal Reserve Bank of New York, well guarded against enterprising members of the underworld.

When the Treasury buys a million dollars worth of gold, it hands over to the Federal Reserve a gold certificate for a million dollars. The certificate is a kind of warehouse receipt, indicating that there is that much actual gold around—in New York, in Fort Knox, or somewhere. The total of gold certificates in existence, then, roughly equals the amount of gold owned by the Treasury. This amount is influenced by international financial developments which are in some measure outside our control. During the late 1930's gold flowed in tremendous volume from strife-torn Europe to presumably safer havens in the United States. Treasury holdings rose from $4 billion in 1934 to $22 billion in 1941. From 1941 to 1958, the U.S. gold stock remained relatively constant in the range of $20–22 billion. Since 1959, however, there has been a considerable drain of gold out of the United States because of sizable deficits in our balance of payments.

Gold certificates are the basic assets of the Federal Reserve System and the main reserve against its various liabilities. The Fed is required by law to hold gold certificates equal to 25 percent of the total of Federal Reserve notes plus member bank reserves. In this limited sense gold is still the basis of our monetary system, and the gold stock sets the ultimate limit to expansion of currency and credit.

But this limit is flexible, and may even be regarded as fictitious, since it can be altered at any time by Congressional action. Until 1945 the requirement was a 40 percent gold reserve against Federal Reserve notes and 35 percent against member bank deposits. The circulation of currency rose so rapidly during World War II, however, that the gold reserves began to wear thin and it appeared that the Fed would soon be right up against the limit. At this point Congress obligingly lowered the reserve requirement to 25 percent. They would doubtless do so again if the present requirement threatened to become restrictive.

U.S. Government Securities

The Fed is a large holder of Federal securities, mostly of short duration, though it also holds several billion dollars' worth of issues running five years or longer. The System is in the market literally from day to day, buying or selling securities to raise or lower member bank reserves. These dealings are carried on between the Federal Reserve Bank of New York and a specialized group of 15 to 20 dealers in government securities. The effect of these open market operations will be examined in a moment.

Federal Reserve Notes

Turning to the liability side of Table 22–1, we find that the largest item consists of paper currency issued by the Federal Reserve System. In the early days of American banking, much of our paper money consisted of notes issued by individual commercial banks, backed only by the bank's promise to redeem them in coins or U.S. currency on demand. These notes passed freely from hand to hand so long as everyone had faith in the bank's promise. Quite often, however, this faith was misplaced. A bank issued notes too liberally, or made unsound loans, ending up in bankruptcy which left its notes worthless. The Federal Reserve Act provided, therefore, that notes could no longer be issued by individual banks but only by the Federal Reserve System.

If you take a bill from your wallet, you will probably find that it is a Federal Reserve note. The only other important kind of paper money now circulating is the U.S. Silver Certificate, issued in denominations of $1 to $10. Congressmen from the silver-mining states have promoted legislation compelling the Treasury to buy all silver offered to it at a fixed price. Some of this is reissued in the form of silver coins, but most of it remains in the Treasury and is represented by an equal value of bills issued to the public.

Issuance of Federal Reserve notes is a passive activity of the System. The amount in circulation depends on how much cash people want to carry in their pockets at a particular time. The amount goes up with rising incomes and has increased rapidly since 1940. Anyone with a checking account can go into his bank and say, "I want some cash." The bank will give him cash and reduce his account by that amount. If the bank runs short of till money, it can order some notes from the Federal Reserve bank of its district, which will send the notes and reduce the bank's reserve balance correspondingly. Where does the Federal Reserve bank get the notes? It gets them from a Treasury official in Washington, who gets them from the Government Printing Office where they are printed. In return the Fed must put up a deposit of the same amount, at least 25 percent of which must be in gold certificates, and the remainder either in gold certificates or government securities.

If people find that they need less cash, an opposite series of events occurs. Currency flows back to the banks for deposit, and the banks pass the excess currency on to the Federal Reserve and receive credit in their balances. The Federal Reserve can either stockpile the currency for the time being or pass it back to the Treasury. An inflow of currency from the public builds up checking accounts at each stage. An outflow of currency to the public reduces checking accounts all along the line.

Member Bank Reserves

These are the checking accounts which each member bank is required to maintain with the Federal Reserve Bank of its district. They are assets to the member banks and liabilities of the Federal Reserve System, which owes this amount to its members. The importance of member bank reserves has already been emphasized. They determine the amount of demand deposits which a particular bank may carry, and thus limit its lending power. The total of member bank reserves limits the lending power of the banks as a whole. Reserves are thus the focal point for control of the banking system. *Monetary policy* is essentially policy designed to affect the banks' ability to lend by altering the level of bank reserves.

THE TECHNIQUES OF MONETARY POLICY

Before describing how the Federal Reserve influences the supply and cost of money, we must note that there is another large operator in the money market. This is the United States Treasury, which is constantly issuing and retiring government securities in large volume, and which has a practical concern with the level of interest rates.

Treasury Financing Activities

The federal budget might be exactly in balance, with tax income just equaling expenditures on goods and services. In most years, however, the

Treasury has either a deficit which must be covered by selling securities or a surplus which can be used to retire securities.

Suppose there is a deficit of $5 billion in a particular year. The fact that government is putting $5 billion more into the income stream than it is withdrawing from the stream through taxation affects the level of spending in the economy. This *fiscal effect* of the deficit was analyzed in Chapter 20. In addition, depending on who buys the securities which are sold to finance the deficit, there may be an effect on the quantity of money. It is this *monetary effect* which interests us here.

Federal securities may be sold to individuals and corporations outside the banking system, or to commercial banks, or to the Federal Reserve Banks. These transactions have different monetary consequences.

1. If the Treasury sells $5 billion of bonds to investors outside the banking system, the quantity of money is not affected. The buyers pay by check, so their demand deposits are reduced by $5 billion. But as the Treasury spends the money, demand deposits are increased by the same amount.

2. Suppose the securities are sold to commercial banks, which pay by crediting the Treasury on their books. Then as the Treasury spends the money, demand deposits in the hands of the public rise by $5 billion without an offsetting decrease elsewhere in the system. Money supply has risen by $5 billion. The balance sheet effect is as follows:

MEMBER BANKS

Assets		Liabilities	
U.S. securities	+5 billion	Demand deposits	+5 billion

This assumes that the banks were not loaned up to begin with, and so had room for this increase in demand deposits.

3. The expansionary effect is even stronger if the securities are sold directly to the Federal Reserve System. In this case the Treasury's balance at the Federal Reserve is increased. As the Treasury spends the money, it issues checks on the Federal Reserve to private parties, who deposit them in their banks, which then present them to the Federal Reserve for credit. When the money has all been spent, the result is as follows:

MEMBER BANKS

Assets		Liabilities	
Reserves	+5 billion	Demand deposits	+5 billion

FEDERAL RESERVE BANKS

Assets		Liabilities	
U.S. securities	+5 billion	Member bank reserves	+5 billion

Not only has money supply risen by $5 billion, but member bank reserves have risen by $5 billion, which permits a further multiple expansion of the money supply.

Financing a Treasury deficit by selling securities to the banking system is not very different from financing the deficit by printing new money. The former procedure seems more respectable, possibly because it is harder to understand. It is also more expensive, since the Treasury pays interest on the securities which it would not have to pay on new currency issues. During World War II the Treasury covered its enormous deficits by selling $90 billion of securities to commercial banks and the Federal Reserve, in addition to the $105 billion which it was able to sell to private investors. The result was a great increase in the nation's money supply, which contributed to price inflation after the war.

The Treasury is heavily involved in the money market even when it is not running a surplus or deficit. The reason is that much of the public debt consists of short-term securities. In mid-1962 there was about $85 billion of outstanding issues with maturities of 1 year or less. Thus many billions of issues fall due each year and are normally *refunded* by issuing new securities. If the new issues are bought by precisely the same people who held the old securities, there is no monetary effect. But the Treasury may take advantage of the occasion to issue a different type of security aimed at a different group of investors. It may try, for example, to sell long-term bonds to nonbank investors and use the proceeds to pay off short-term issues held by the banking system. This would constitute a *lengthening of the debt*. By tracing through the balance-sheet effects in the usual way, we see that there will be a drop in demand deposits in the hands of the public and thus in the money supply.

Decisions about the length of new federal security issues, the market at which they should be aimed, and the rate of interest which must be offered to attract investors are made by a group of Treasury officials responsible for *debt management*. There is no need here to delve into this specialized and esoteric art. It is enough to say that debt management often involves switching of funds among different types of investors, and that this has monetary consequences.

The Problem of Monetary Control

If Federal Reserve policy were the only force acting on member bank reserves, the control problem would be considerably simplified. But this is not the case. Reserves are changing all the time because of currency movements into and out of the banks, gold movements into and out of the country, changes in Treasury cash balances, and other factors. Thus even if the Federal Reserve does nothing at all, member bank reserves will still fluctuate from day to day. A sizable research staff, mainly in the Federal Reserve Bank of New York, is engaged in keeping track of these movements and trying to predict them for the near future. These estimates are checked by higher officials in New York and Washington in the light of their experience and "feel" of the money market.

Suppose Federal Reserve officials conclude that, as things are going, member bank reserves will shrink over the next week by $200 million.

This will reduce the banks' lending ability and make for a tightening of credit. What should the Federal Reserve do? This depends on the objectives which the System is pursuing at the time. If Federal Reserve officials feel that credit restriction is in order, they may simply abstain and allow the prospective shrinkage of reserves to occur. Inaction does not necessarily indicate neutrality or indifference to monetary developments. It can be a matter of deliberate policy.

Suppose, however, that the Fed considers that member bank reserves are now at about the right level. In this event, it will act to raise member bank reserves by $200 million to offset the decline which would otherwise occur. Such action to offset an undesired movement of reserves is usually termed *defensive policy*. If the policy is successful, the statistical charts will show bank reserves moving along on an even level week after week. This does not mean that the Federal Reserve has been inactive, as might appear at first glance. On the contrary, it means that their action has been deft enough to offset fluctuations which would otherwise have occurred.

Finally, Federal Reserve officials may feel that monetary expansion is in order and that member bank reserves should be increased by, say, $300 million. In this case they will have to raise reserves by $500 million to offset the prospective decline of $200 million and still come out with the desired increase. These are the main permutations of Federal Reserve policy: abstaining and letting nature take its course; a defensive policy of "leaning against the wind" to offset undesirable changes; and an active policy aimed at reversing the prospective course of events.

Open Market Operations

Once the Federal Reserve has decided what to do, how does it go about doing it? The main instrument of day-to-day policy is purchase and sale of federal securities. Decisions on this front are made by the Federal Open Market Committee, consisting of the seven members of the Board of Governors, the president of the Federal Reserve Bank of New York, and four other presidents of Reserve banks. The Committee meets every three weeks. In addition, its members and key staff officials normally confer every morning over a telephone hook-up and arrive at decisions for the day. Actual trading is carried out through a trading desk in the Federal Reserve Bank of New York, since New York is the center for dealers specializing in government securities.

The impact of these operations is rapid and direct. When the System buys $100 million of securities it pays by check on the Federal Reserve Bank of New York. If the seller is a commercial bank, this check gives it an immediate addition to its reserve balance. If the seller is an individual or a nonbank corporation, it deposits the check in a commercial bank, which presents it to the Federal Reserve and receives credit. The balance sheet effect in this case is as follows:

MEMBER BANKS

ASSETS		LIABILITIES	
Reserve balances	+100	Demand deposits	+100

FEDERAL RESERVE BANKS

ASSETS		LIABILITIES	
U.S. securities	+100	Member bank reserves	+100

When the System sells securities, opposite effects occur. The buyer gives the Federal Reserve a check drawn on his commercial bank. The Fed deducts this amount from the bank's reserve balance. Thus member bank reserves shrink.

The principle involved is simple: Federal Reserve purchase of securities *raises* member bank reserves, while Federal Reserve sale of securities *lowers* reserves. The effect on bank reserves is almost instantaneous and its size is certain. This plus the fact that the size of security operations can be adjusted precisely to the supposed need makes them a natural choice for day-to-day use.

While the first impact of open market operations is on bank reserves, there are also important secondary effects. Suppose the Federal Reserve wants to tighten credit and consequently begins selling federal securities. This immediately lowers member bank reserves, which is a step in the desired direction. In addition, the increased supply of U.S. securities coming onto the market will lower their price. Now if the *price* of a fixed-interest security falls, its *yield* necessarily rises. Moreover, since the network of interest rates is interconnected, an increase in yield on one kind of security will tend to be transmitted to other securities. Thus there will be general upward pressure on interest rates, including rates charged on bank loans, and this will discourage borrowing. This is in line with the Federal Reserve's objective of restricting credit.

Member Bank Borrowing and the Discount Rate

A major complaint against the pre-1913 banking system was its inelasticity under pressure. There was no central reservoir of funds to which banks could resort in time of need. The authors of the Federal Reserve Act were at pains, therefore, to provide ways by which any solvent bank could draw on the virtually unlimited sources of the System to meet temporary emergencies.

A member bank can secure Federal Reserve funds and increase its reserve balance in either of two ways:

1. It may sell commercial paper to the Federal Reserve Bank of its district. This is known as *discounting*. *Example:* A bank brings to the Federal Reserve a promissory note from one of its customers for $100,000, due in three months' time. The discount rate at the time is 4 percent. The Federal Reserve discounts the note by deducting from its face value interest at 4 percent for three months, or $1,000. The remaining $99,000 is added to the member bank's reserve balance.

2. A simpler technique, and the one mainly used in practice, is a direct loan from the Federal Reserve to the member bank. The bank puts up either commercial paper or (more commonly) U.S. securities as collateral for the loan. The Federal Reserve charges interest on the loan at the existing discount rate.

The volume of member bank borrowing is not large. The banks dislike being in debt to the Federal Reserve, and try to work their way out of debt as quickly as possible. The Federal Reserve also looks with suspicion on any bank which draws too heavily on its borrowing privilege, and can if necessary cut off further credit. The possibility of borrowing, however, provides a breathing space for any bank which finds itself suddenly short of reserves. It gives a few weeks of grace during which the bank can make an orderly readjustment of its position.

The existence of this escape valve permits the other Federal Reserve powers to be used with greater assurance. Open market operations and changes in reserve requirements are general instruments, whose impact cannot be tailored to the situation of particular banks. Federal Reserve sale of securities reduces bank reserves in general, but it is impossible to say in advance which banks will be hit and how hard. Banks with sizable excess reserves may be little affected, while banks which are already loaned up may suddenly find themselves in a deficit position. The Federal Reserve is nevertheless free to push open market operations as vigorously as it wishes, for if the policy leaves a particular bank short of reserves it can always cover itself temporarily by borrowing. Over the longer run, of course, the bank will have to work its way back to a safe reserve position by going slow on loans and holding down its demand deposits. This is precisely the result at which the open market operations were aimed.

Each of the 12 Federal Reserve banks sets its own discount rate. The rates are usually the same, however, and policy for the whole System is coordinated through the Board of Governors. The discount rate is normally raised gradually during a business upswing, keeping more or less in step with the rise of other short-term interest rates. In a recession, the discount rate is usually cut substantially.

An increase in the discount rate has two effects. Since it increases the cost of borrowing from the Federal Reserve, it strengthens the member banks' unwillingness to remain in debt. More important, it serves as a signal to the banking community of the direction in which Federal Reserve policy is moving. A discount rate increase indicates that the Federal Reserve feels that expansion of loans should be slowed down, and that it intends to exert pressure toward that end. This usually encourages member banks to raise their own lending rates—a step which is bound to be unpopular with borrowers, but which can now be defended on the ground that "this is what the Fed wants us to do." Similarly, a lowering of the discount rate is a signal for more liberal lending policies and lower interest rates.

Member Bank Reserve Requirements

The ability to change reserve requirements is a powerful instrument. Profit considerations lead a commercial bank to keep its resources as fully invested as possible and to operate near the legal reserve minimum. Thus an increase in reserve requirements immediately throws many banks into a deficit position and forces them to restrict their lending. The weapon is in fact so powerful that it is not used for delicate adjustment of monetary conditions from week to week. For short-term purposes, the Fed relies on frequent open market operations, supported by occasional adjustments of the discount rate. Reserve requirements are changed less frequently, and mainly to offset substantial long-term movements in bank reserves.

During the 1930's, an enormous inflow of gold from abroad raised bank reserves sharply, while at the same time depressed business conditions prevented the banks from increasing their loans materially. The result was large excess reserves which for the time being put the commercial banks virtually beyond Federal Reserve control. In an effort to "mop up" these excess reserves, the Fed doubled reserve requirements between 1936 and 1938.

Since World War II, however, the banks' reserve position has been quite tight. Loans to businesses and consumers have grown steadily, reflecting rising production and price levels in the economy. But bank reserves have grown little, and were actually cut by the heavy gold outflow of 1958–61. The Federal Reserve has had to lower the legal requirements several times to keep the banks in a viable position. By 1962 the legal reserve ratios had been cut to 16½, 16½, and 12 percent, or about the middle of the range permitted by present legislation.

The Coordination of Policy Instruments

While the three control powers of the Federal Reserve System are legally separate, in practice they are used together to achieve the System's objectives of monetary restriction or monetary ease. The Fed will usually lead off with open market operations. This is particularly appropriate for defensive policy or where only small positive effects are desired. For larger adjustments, open market policy may be supported by changes in the discount rate. Changes in reserve requirements are made least frequently, and usually only when the Fed wants to produce a substantial easing of monetary conditions. Note that the lowering of reserve requirements since 1953 was concentrated in the recession years of 1954 and 1958.

The way in which these policy instruments are coordinated may be illustrated by the course of events during a business upswing. Suppose business loans and demand deposits have been rising for a couple of years. Production is nearing the physical capacity of the system. Price indexes are edging upward, arousing fears of inflation. The Fed decides that the time has come to put on the monetary brakes. It begins by selling off, say,

$500 million of short-term government securities. This lowers member bank reserves, and some banks find themselves below the legal minimum. These banks will probably tighten their lending policies. They may borrow from the Federal Reserve as a temporary expedient. They may also decide to sell some of their own holdings of government securities. These offerings, plus those of the Federal Reserve System, lower the market price of short-term government securities. This amounts to an increase in yield on governments, which makes for a general rise in short-term interest rates.

As interest rates rise, the Federal Reserve typically "follows the market upward" by raising its own discount rate. It does not like to get much ahead of the market, but neither does it lag materially behind it. The increase in the discount rate usually leads the member banks to raise the interest rate which they charge on business loans. This makes borrowing less attractive and helps to achieve the Federal Reserve objective of credit restriction.

These lines of policy will be pursued as long as the threat of over-expansion continues. Open market sales and discount rate increases will go on, hand over hand, for as long as necessary to achieve the desired braking effect.

ADVANTAGES AND LIMITATIONS OF MONETARY POLICY

The usefulness of monetary policy depends on whether the problem is to combat inflation or unemployment. Monetary policy is more effective on the former front than on the latter. "You can't push on a string," as the saying goes. During a recession the Federal Reserve can strengthen bank reserves, reduce interest rates, and establish an attractive atmosphere for borrowing. But it cannot directly affect the will to borrow. So long as business prospects seem poor, borrowers will hold off and the desired increase in loans and spending will not materialize.

It is toward the top of a boom which is threatening to pass over into inflation that monetary policy really comes into its own. As a technique for inflation control, monetary policy is alleged to have several advantages:

1. Decisions on monetary policy can be reached and applied rapidly, since power is concentrated in the Board of Governors. Fiscal policy, on the other hand, depends on the slower processes of Congressional approval and administrative action.

2. The effectiveness of monetary action is reasonably certain. By sufficiently vigorous action, interest rates can always be raised to a level at which the brakes take hold.

3. Monetary policy is an impersonal, thermostatic device, which produces its effects through the market mechanism. It is neutral as among individuals and groups in the economy. If the Federal Reserve succeeds in restricting credit, some would-be borrowers will be left unsatisfied. But the Federal Reserve does not presume to say which borrowers or which

projects shall be dropped from the list. This is left to negotiation between private borrowers and lenders.

But the effectiveness of monetary control should not be overstated. Monetary policy in practice is more complicated and less effective than appears from textbook examples. These difficulties and limitations deserve brief attention.

Conflicting Signals

What are the targets of monetary policy? How does the Federal Reserve decide whether tightening or loosening of credit is in order?

It is usually said that monetary policy should promote high employment and a stable price level. But these indicators sometimes point in different directions. Suppose the economy is coming out of a recession. Production and employment are rising but are still well below full capacity. Between 5 and 6 percent of the labor force remain unemployed. The price level, however, is rising at 2 percent a year. What should the Federal Reserve do? Should it follow a low-interest policy to stimulate further increases in production? Or should it tighten credit to hold down the price level?

Decisions about monetary policy are *not* automatic. They require judgment and the weighing of various objectives. Some critics of monetary policy feel that Federal Reserve officials, reflecting the outlook of the banking community, give too great weight to preventing inflation and too little weight to promoting production and employment. They err, it is argued, in the direction of chronic tightness of credit and an unduly high level of interest rates. Federal Reserve officials reply that they are doing no more than is necessary to check inflation, and that without a stable price level we cannot have sustained prosperity and rapid economic growth.

Prediction and Timing

Monetary action may be faster than most other policies, but it is far from instantaneous. It usually takes several months after an economic downturn or upturn before one can be sure of the direction of movement. There are cases in which appropriate Federal Reserve action was seriously delayed because the System misjudged the turning point.

Even after the Federal Reserve has decided to move, it takes considerable time for the effects to work themselves out. When credit is being restricted, it takes time for bank lending policies to be adjusted to a tighter reserve position, time for borrowers to react to higher interest rates, and time for financial decisions to be translated into production plans. Even after borrowers have decided to borrow less, it may be six to twelve months before this shows up in the level of spending.

"Slippage" in the Controls

If businesses and individuals could get funds only by borrowing from commercial banks, and if the banks could get increased reserves only at the option of the Federal Reserve System, the monetary authorities would have close control over the level of demand deposits. But this is not the case. Over the past half-century there has been a great increase in the importance of nonbank lenders, such as savings and loan associations, insurance companies, personal finance companies, and other *financial intermediaries*. Large corporations also have liquid funds which can be used to provide their customers with *trade credit* (an understanding that bills need not be paid for a specified period, such as 60 or 90 days). True, these intermediaries are dependent to some extent on bank loans, and a restriction of bank credit may force them to tighten their own credit terms. But monetary policy impinges on nonbank lenders only indirectly, and its impact is therefore less predictable.

Another important development since 1940 is that commercial banks and other business corporations have large holdings of government securities which can be sold off as needed. A company which cannot obtain more bank credit can still get money by selling securities. A bank which finds itself short of reserves can follow the same course, selling securities and using the proceeds to build up its reserves.

During the boom of 1954–57, when the Federal Reserve was trying to tighten credit, the commercial banks sold $10.9 billion of government securities, other financial institutions sold $3.7 billion, and nonfinancial corporations sold $3.6 billion. During the recession of 1957–58, when monetary controls were relaxed, the banks bought back $9.7 billion of securities and nonfinancial corporations bought $2.3 billion. This pattern of selling securities when money is tight and buying them back when money is easy has been rather consistent during the fifties and sixties.

It takes two to make a trade. Who was buying governments when banks and business concerns were selling? First, purchases by individual investors have moved in a reverse direction from those by business concerns. Individuals have bought when businesses were selling, and *vice versa*. Part of the answer, too, lies in the changing budget position of the federal government. During boom periods, when banks and other businesses want to sell securities, the Treasury may be running a surplus which enables it to buy up and retire its issues. During recession there is always a budget deficit. The Treasury finances the deficit by issuing additional securities, which are absorbed mainly by business concerns and the banking system.

Changes in the Velocity of Money

Monetary policy operates on the *quantity* of money in existence. Credit restriction during an upswing can slow down or prevent an increase in the money supply. But monetary policy cannot control the *uses* to which money is put. With enough ingenuity, people can find ways of making the same amount of money do more work than before. Warren Smith has commented that:

when credit conditions are tightened and the creation of new money through the banking system is restricted, pressures are automatically set up which cause the financial system to "hunt" for methods of mobilizing the existing money supply more effectively, thus permitting it to do part, or perhaps even most, of the work that would have been done by newly created money had credit conditions been easier.[1]

How much work money is doing can be measured by dividing the value of GNP by the money supply. The result is termed the *income velocity of money*. It shows how many dollars of production were financed by each dollar of money in existence. Income velocity has shown an upward tendency since World War II, rising from 2.09 in 1947 to 3.63 in 1961. Moreover, it tends to rise during boom periods and to fall during recession. These swings have often been considerably larger than the changes in the quantity of money. During the expansion of 1954–57, the quantity of money rose only 6 percent, but velocity rose 17 percent. During the recession of 1957–58, the quantity of money remained unchanged but velocity fell 3 percent. During the 1961–62 upswing, the quantity of money rose about 3 percent but velocity rose 5 percent.

Federal Reserve efforts at credit restriction on the upswing, then, are partially offset by increases in the effectiveness with which money is used. Households and business concerns adapt themselves to holding less money, relative to their incomes, than they did before. This permits the value of transactions to go on rising even without an increase in the money supply.

One can make a virtue of necessity by arguing that this provides a desirable degree of elasticity. Without this flexibility, the monetary brakes might take hold too hard and bring the economy grinding to a halt. But one cannot have it both ways. One cannot argue *both* that our financial system is quite flexible, which seems to be true, *and* that monetary controls are precise and predictable, which seems not to be true.

Possible Conflict with Treasury Objectives

All borrowers prefer low interest rates, but most of them can't do anything about it. There is one borrower, however, which can try to do something about it. This is the U.S. Treasury.

Interest on the national debt is now a large item in the federal budget, amounting to almost $10 billion in fiscal year 1964. A difference of 1 percent in the interest rate on federal securities makes a difference of close to $3 billion in cost to the government. Thus the Treasury Department has a natural interest in low rates, and its influence is apt to be exerted in this direction. It is particularly unhappy if the Federal Reserve is forcing down the price of federal securities and forcing up interest rates just

---

[1] *Staff Report on Employment, Growth, and Price Levels*, prepared for the Joint Economic Committee, 86th Cong., 1st sess. (Washington, D.C.: Government Printing Office, 1960), p. 344.

when the Treasury needs to float a large new issue. At such times there is likely to be discussion of the need for Federal Reserve "cooperation" with the Treasury. The implication is that the Federal Reserve should abandon its effort at monetary control for the time being, and help out the Treasury by keeping interest rates low.

Conflict of Internal and External Considerations

Measures which would be desirable for internal reasons may conflict with the country's international economic position. An excellent example of this occurred during the winter of 1960–61. The American economy was in recession and the Federal Reserve had taken the usual steps to reduce interest rates. Meanwhile the European economies were booming, and interest rates in most of them were well above the American level. This caused a large shift of funds from New York to England, West Germany, Switzerland, and other countries in search of higher yields. (National governments, central banks, and international business concerns have many billions of liquid funds, which they can invest temporarily in one country or another as they see fit. A substantial difference in short-term yields in different countries produces a movement of funds toward the high-interest locations.) This contributed to a heavy outflow of gold from the United States in 1960–61, and aroused fears of a "run on the dollar."

What should be done in such a situation? Some urged that American interest rates should be raised toward European levels to check the shifting of funds and the consequent outflow of gold. But to do this would discourage investment and interfere with recovery from recession. Should priority be given to internal recovery or to adjustment of the balance of payments? This sort of conflict adds one more complication to the life of Federal Reserve officials.

Uneven Impact of Monetary Policy

The assertion that monetary policy is neutral as among groups in the economy is questioned by some observers. True, the Federal Reserve does not set out deliberately to discriminate against certain types of business. But is not a restriction of bank credit inherently discriminatory? It is argued that this may be true in at least three respects:

a) Some companies have larger internal resources than others, and hence are less dependent on bank borrowing. Federal Reserve policy hits companies which depend heavily on the commercial banking system.

b) Some types of investment are more sensitive than others to changes in the rate of interest. A rise in interest rates may have little effect on manufacturing investment but may cut heavily into housebuilding and local government projects.

c) Some would-be borrowers have a higher credit rating and better banking connections than others. When the banks are forced to restrict loans, they will still try to accommodate the companies with top credit rating. Thus the impact of restriction may fall largely on smaller and newer businesses which are regarded as less creditworthy.

Statistical studies suggest that small concerns do suffer more than big ones during periods of tight money, both because of lower credit standing and smaller internal resources. But the evidence is not as clear-cut or striking as some of the complaints from small business might lead one to expect.

Defenders of monetary policy argue that these effects are not discriminatory in any meaningful sense. An increase in any price "discriminates" against people who can no longer pay the price and in favor of those who can. But one cannot conclude from this that no price should ever be raised. The rate of interest, it is argued, is no different from any other price in this respect.

WHAT DOES MONETARY POLICY ACCOMPLISH?

In earlier chapters we argued that the level of national income depends on the spending plans of consumers, business concerns, and government, which together make up the total expenditure schedule. If monetary policy affects the level of national income, it must do so by changing the plans of one or more of these groups. Is there reason to believe that it does have this effect, and how is the result produced? An approximate answer to this question can be given quite briefly. A more thorough analysis will be found in the Appendix.

Interest and the Level of Spending

1. *Monetary policy alters the supply of money.* The strength of this effect cannot be gauged simply by looking at monetary statistics. During a business upswing, the expansion of production and bank borrowings makes for a marked increase in demand deposits. A policy of monetary restraint shows up in the fact that demand deposits rise *less* than they would have risen in the absence of such a policy. But since one can never say "what would have happened if," the quantitative effect of monetary control is hard to estimate. On the downswing, demand deposits tend to fall as business declines. But the Federal Reserve can pump new money into the stream through security purchases, and may thus prevent the money supply from falling or even increase it.

2. *The supply of money affects the rate of interest.* We saw in Chapter 9 that the interest rate can be regarded as *the price of money.* From the lender's standpoint, it is the reward for giving up money, for "parting with liquidity." From the borrower's standpoint, it is the price which must be paid for increased cash in hand.

We can thus fall back on the familiar principle that an increase in the supply of anything will lower its price, and *vice versa.* An increase in the quantity of money leads, other things equal, to a fall in the rate of interest, while a reduction in the quantity of money will raise interest rates. One exception to this principle is explained in the Appendix, but it can be taken as a safe guide in most circumstances.

3. *The rate of interest affects the level of spending.* Looking first at consumers, a rise in interest rates may lower the consumption schedule by raising saving, or reducing borrowing, or both. It is usually said that saving is painful and that people have to be paid for doing it. The more they are paid, i.e., the higher the rate of interest, the more they will set aside out of current income. While this proposition has sometimes been questioned, it is probably dependable as a general rule.

Will a rise in interest rates cause families to borrow less for cars, furniture, electric appliances, and the like? Many consumers, of course, do not realize what rate of interest they are paying. They look only at the monthly payment, which depends on the purchase price of the article and the length of the loan as well as the rate of interest. If a rise in interest rates can be offset by a price reduction or a spreading out of payments, it may pass unnoticed. But usually a higher interest rate will mean larger monthly payments, and this should cause some reduction in consumer borrowing. It seems safe to conclude that a rise in interest rates will typically lower the consumption schedule.

Turning to business concerns, it is usually argued that a higher interest rate means less investment. As the cost of borrowing rises, more and more potential investment projects will appear unprofitable and will be abandoned or postponed. The logic of this is almost self-evident, and was explained in Chapter 18. But investment decisions are also influenced by the business outlook, risk considerations, profit levels, and other things. The cost of borrowing is only one factor, and may often be a minor factor, in investment decisions.

Factual studies suggest that the situation differs for different types of investment. Investment in inventories is probably not much affected by interest rate changes. Nor is plant and equipment investment by larger business concerns, where availability of internal financing is a dominant consideration. Even in public utility industries, where plant life is long and interest charges are important, there is little evidence of any appreciable effect of interest rate changes.

Interest rate changes do seem to have an impact on residential and commercial construction, on state and local government construction expenditures, and on investment by small businesses which cannot float securities on the national market and are heavily dependent on bank borrowing.[2]

As regards both the consumption and investment schedules, then, one can predict the *direction* of the effects induced by monetary policy. An increase in the rate of interest will lower the C and I schedules, and

---

[2] On this range of problems see Warren Smith, *op. cit.*, pp. 362–94.

hence the equilibrium level of national income. A decline in the interest rate tends to raise the C and I schedules, and thus to raise the level of income. But there is considerable difference of opinion about the *size* of these effects. Some believe that raising the interest rate 1 or 2 percent will reduce spending very little, while others think the effect will be substantial. These differences of opinion lead to differing judgments about the practical usefulness of monetary policy.

Credit Rationing and the Level of Spending

There is a second route by which monetary policy may alter the level of spending. Banks do not lend automatically to any company which is willing to pay the going rate of interest. They look into details of the borrower's business, including its ratio of current assets to current liabilities, its past earnings record and future prospects, the purposes for which the loan will be used, and the assurance that the loan can be repaid. After this appraisal the bank may decide to grant the loan in full, scale it down to a smaller amount, or reject it entirely. The volume of loans made always falls short of loan applications. The money market thus operates differently from a vegetable market, in which anyone with the price can get the goods.

The severity of the bank's appraisal is influenced by the state of its reserves. Toward the peak of a boom, would-be borrowers are pressing in from every side. Suppose the Federal Reserve now moves to cut bank reserves. The banks will respond, not only by raising the interest rate, but by imposing tougher requirements on prospective borrowers. They may decide to consider only applications of straight A quality, and A− or B+ propositions may go by the board. Conversely, if reserves are ample and the banks are eager for business, they can get more business by lowering their standards for loan applications. There is evidence that bank lending standards do vary in this way over the course of the business cycle.

Thus monetary policy produces effects through *lenders'* reactions as well as through *borrowers'* reactions, through changes in the *availability* of credit as well as the *cost* of credit. Even if borrowers are quite insensitive to interest rates, changes in the toughness of bank lending policies may raise or lower the expenditure schedule. Some economists would say that this effect is more important than the interest rate effect.

SUMMARY

1. Although the Federal Reserve System consists of 12 regional banks, important policy decisions are coordinated through the Board of Governors in Washington. And while in theory the Board is not subject to Presidential control, in practice it works closely with the Treasury and other agencies of government.

2. Monetary policy is directed at *member bank reserves*. The Fed operates by buying and selling securities in the *open market*, by varying the *discount rate* at which it will lend to member banks, and (less frequently) by altering the

reserve ratio which member banks must carry against their deposits. By co-ordinated use of these powers, the Fed can increase or decrease the amount of *free or excess reserves* in possession of the banks, and thus influence their ability and willingness to lend.

3. During a business upswing, the Fed typically restricts bank reserves by selling securities, and gradually raises the discount rate. This forces up private interest rates and also leads banks to ration credit more carefully. This lowers the consumption and investment schedules, which has a braking effect on the expansion.

4. During recession, the Fed bolsters bank reserves by selling securities, lowers the discount rate, and may lower reserve requirements. This brings lower bank interest rates and more liberal lending policies. But since the volume of loans depends also on the attitude of borrowers, and since borrowers are usually pessimistic during recession, monetary measures may not be sufficient to check the decline. Fiscal action is more dependable during a downswing.

5. While monetary control seems simple in principle, there are a number of practical complications, including: judgment in deciding when and how hard to apply the brakes on an expansion; the time-lag between policy decisions and the time at which these decisions begin to affect spending; slippage in the controls arising from the existence of financial intermediaries, and from large bank and business holdings of federal securities which can be sold as needed; the possibility that restrictions on the *quantity* of money may be offset by increases in the *velocity* of money; possible conflict between Treasury and Federal Reserve objectives; and possible conflict between internal stability considerations and external balance of payments considerations.

6. The linkage between our monetary discussion of Chapters 21–22 and the theory of income determination in Chapters 18–19 is as follows: Monetary policy alters the supply of money; the supply of money affects the rate of interest; the rate of interest (and variations in the liberality of credit rationing at this rate) affects the consumption and investment schedules; and this affects the equilibrium level of national income. The Appendix to this chapter provides a more complete synthesis of monetary analysis and income analysis.

APPENDIX: A SYNTHESIS OF MONETARY ANALYSIS AND INCOME ANALYSIS

The modern theory of income determination is a lineal descendant of earlier theoretical systems. Money played a large role in these systems, which usually went under the name of *monetary theory*. It will be useful to glance at some earlier ideas about money before considering its role in modern income analysis.

The Fisher Equation

Until quite recently economists thought of full employment as the normal condition of the economy, and of any deviation from full employment as temporary and self-correcting. Monetary forces, it was believed, reflected themselves mainly in movements of the *price level;* and attention was consequently focused on the relation between money and prices.

One line of reasoning was as follows: for every sale made in the economy, the number of dollars changing hands must equal the value of the goods sold. Thus the total amount of money spent in the country during a year must equal the total value of goods and services exchanged during that period.

Total spending may be thought of as the amount of money in existence, M, multiplied by the average number of times each dollar changes hands during the year. This second quantity, usually designated as V, is termed the *transactions velocity of money*. Total spending during the year, then, is MV.

The value of the goods and services exchanged may be thought of as the quantity of each good, T, multiplied by its price, P. Thus the total value of transactions during a year is PT, where P is an index of average prices of and T represents the physical quantity of goods exchanged.

Now total spending must equal the value of goods sold. They are simply different ways of looking at the same transactions, one from the standpoint of the buyers and the other from that of the sellers. It follows that

$$MV \equiv PT$$

This is the famous *quantity equation* or *equation of exchange*, often identified with Professor Irving Fisher of Yale.

On its face the equation is simply a truism. It resembles the $S = I$ formula in that it is true by definition for any past period. It does not necessarily say anything about causal relations in the economy.

With a few embellishments, however, the quantity *equation* can be turned into a quantity *theory* of money and prices. The velocity of money, it can be argued, depends on banking institutions and people's money-holding habits. These are reasonably stable over short periods, and so V can be taken as roughly constant. Moreover, if one regards full employment as the normal state of affairs, production cannot change much over short periods and T can also be taken as constant.

With V and T constant, and only M and P left to vary, the outcome is clear. An increase in M will produce a proportionate change in P. Double the quantity of money, and the price level will also double. Cut the quantity of money and prices will fall.

The simplicity of this theory, and the sweeping conclusions which could apparently be drawn from it, attracted a wide following. Most economists have gradually become convinced, however, that the theory is too good to be true. V turns out not to be very stable in the short run, tending to rise during business upswings and fall during downswings. More serious, T moves up and down over the course of the cycle. Indeed, it is these fluctuations in output in which we are mainly interested; but the quantity theory is not oriented toward fluctuations in T and does little to explain them.

The flexibility of V means that it is possible for spending to rise or fall with no change in the quantity of money. Moveover, under sellers' inflation the impetus to price increases comes from the cost side rather than the demand side. So one cannot regard money as the only prime mover in the economy. The quantity theory fails to highlight the forces behind the spending decisions on which total demand depends.

The Cambridge Equation

A different form of the quantity equation stems from the work of Professor Alfred Marshall of Cambridge, and is hence usually termed the *Cambridge equation*. It starts from the proposition that the quantity of money people wish to hold in cash or checking accounts is related to the size of their incomes. The fraction of their incomes which people choose to hold in money was designated by Marshall as k. Then the money holdings of any individual or business will be $m = ky$. *Example:* I have an income of $500 a month, and keep on the average $250 in my pocket and my checking account. Thus my k is 0.5, and my money holdings satisfy the condition

$$250 = 0.5 \, (500)$$

Since all the money in existence at a particular time must be held by somebody, we can sum up for the economy as a whole and conclude that

$$M = kY$$

where M is the average money stock over a certain period, Y is total money income during the period, and k is the ratio of money holdings to income.

Marshall's k is the same kind of creature as Fisher's V. Marshall thought that k could be regarded as roughly constant over short periods. He also supposed the economy to be fully employed, so that output does not change. Suppose now that the quantity of money increases. What will happen? People find that their money holdings are above the level, k, to which they are accustomed. They will try to get rid of the excess by spending it. Since output cannot rise, increased spending serves only to raise the price level. As prices rise, people's money incomes also rise. This expansion of income will continue until the ratio of money holdings to income has fallen to the normal level k. At this point people are once more willing to hold the enlarged money supply, and the system is in equilibrium.

A little calculation shows that this occurs when the price level has risen by the same percentage as the original increase in money supply. Thus we reach Fisher's conclusion by a different route: a change in the quantity of money leads to an equal proportionate change in the price level.

Marshall's system is subject to some of the same criticisms as Fisher's system. K does not remain constant over time, any more than V does. Nor does output remain constant over time. The Cambridge equation was nevertheless a substantial improvement. It focused attention on people's reasons for holding money balances, and on the relation of this to spending plans. It was a step toward the thoroughgoing analysis of spending which characterizes the modern approach.

MONEY AND INTEREST IN MODERN DRESS

Modern monetary theory starts from the observation that there are several reasons for holding money rather than just one reason, and that the amount of money held is related to the rate of interest as well as the level of income.

The demand for money may be divided into three parts:

1. *Transactions demand.* It is convenient to keep something in one's pocket and one's checking account to pay for current purchases. Given a certain income, the amount carried depends on personal habits and business practices. One could get by with a very small balance by buying entirely on credit and paying all bills by check on the first of the month. But most people pay bills intermittently over the month and also make cash purchases, which requires a sizable average balance. Business concerns also carry substantial cash balances to pay for current purchases.

These practices can be assumed to remain stable over short periods. Thus the transactions demand for money depends mainly on the number of transactions to be carried out, i.e., on the value of national output and income.[1] A larger national income means a proportionate increase in the transactions demand for money.

---

[1] In this Appendix, as in earlier chapters, we shall continue to use the term national income as equivalent to Gross National Product. And for convenience of notation, we shall use the letter Y instead of the more cumbersome GNP.

Transactions demand is probably little influenced by interest over the normal range of interest rates. If the interest rate becomes very high, however, people may try to economize on their cash balances so that they can put more into securities or savings accounts.

These suppositions are shown graphically in Figure 1a. The rate of interest is shown on the vertical axis, the quantity of money on the horizontal axis. Each Y line shows the transactions demand for money at a certain level of national income. It is completely unresponsive to the rate of interest over most of its length. If the interest rate becomes very high, however, people become willing to get along with less money for transactions purposes, so the demand curve bends to the left.

The demand curve Y_1 assumes a specified level of national income. Suppose instead that there is a higher income level. Then the transactions demand for money will be higher, say at Y_2, which lies to the right of Y_1. A still larger income will move the money demand rightward to Y_3 and so on.

FIGURE 1a

Transactions Demand for Money

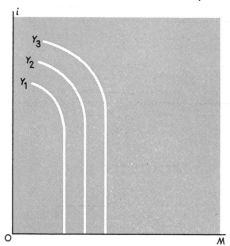

This kind of demand depends mainly on the level of income. Y_1, Y_2, and Y_3 show the demand at successively higher income levels. A diagram of the *precautionary* demand for money would look similar to this one.

2. *Precautionary demand.* If future receipts and expenditures were completely certain, the money carried for transactions purposes would cover all one's needs. But the future is never completely certain. A check which is supposed to arrive at a certain time may not arrive. I may have to make a business trip out of town on short notice. Before the invention of the credit card, this would have meant paying for the trip first and collecting from the boss later. A car accident or a sudden illness in the family may lead to unforeseen needs for cash.

Most people, therefore, will not be content to hold the bare minimum of cash needed to cover normal transactions. They will want a "rainy day" reserve in addition. This precautionary demand, like transactions demand, probably depends mainly on the size of incomes. As a man's income rises, he buys more safety as well as more of everything else.

The precautionary demand for money thus resembles the transactions demand curves shown in Figure 1a. There will be a different demand curve for each level of national income, and these curves will be unresponsive to interest except at very high rates. Because of this similarity, it has not seemed necessary to draw a separate diagram for precautionary demand.

3. *Speculative demand.* This type of demand affects investors, including business concerns as well as better-off individuals. While these people are a minority of the population, they hold large money balances; and the size of their holdings is related to the state of the securities markets.

Since speculative demand for money is a phenomenon of the securities markets, it has no direct connection with the level of production. Thus we have only one demand curve instead of a separate curve for each level of national income. What does this demand curve look like? In particular, how is the speculative demand for money related to the rate of interest?

It is helpful to recall that the rate of interest moves in the *opposite* direction from the price of bonds and other fixed-interest securities. To say that the interest rate is *rising* is the same as saying that security prices are *falling;* and vice versa. Now as security prices fall, more and more people will conclude

FIGURE 1b

Speculative Demand for Money

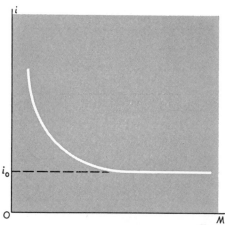

As the rate of interest falls (= securities prices rise), people will hold less securities and more money. At some minimum rate, i_0, any additional money will be held idle.

that prices are "too low," i.e. below their normal or long-run level, and that they will rise back toward this level at some later point. In an effort to "buy at the bottom," they will shift out of cash and into securities. Speculative holdings of money decline. Conversely, as security prices rise (= the interest rate falls), more and more people will conclude that prices are now "too high," and will shift out of securities into cash. The speculative demand for cash increases.

This produces the kind of demand curve shown in Figure 1b. *The speculative demand for money varies inversely with the rate of interest.* This amounts to saying that people will be more willing to hold securities the lower their prices.

Note one important feature of Figure 1b. At the interest rate i_0, the speculative demand curve for money becomes infinitely elastic. What does this mean? It means that at this level the yield on securities is so unattractive that investors will not increase their securities holdings at all. If additional money is pumped into the system, they will simply hold it in idle balances. This is usually termed the *liquidity trap.* The practical consequence is that *the monetary authorities cannot force the interest rate below* i_0. This limits the power of the central bank to take useful corrective action during a depression.

4. Total demand. The total demand for money, obtained by adding these three types of demand, will look as shown in Figure 1c. There are an infinite number of demand curves, each corresponding to a different level of national income, of which only three are shown here. Each curve slopes downward in response to lower interest rates until it reaches the critical minimum i_0, at which point it becomes infinitely elastic.

If we know the supply of money as well as the demand, we can determine the rate of interest. Suppose OM is the quantity of money in existence, so that MM is the money supply curve. And suppose that at the present level of income the demand curve for money is Y_1. Supply and demand must be equal,

FIGURE 1c

Total Money Demand and Interest Rate Determination

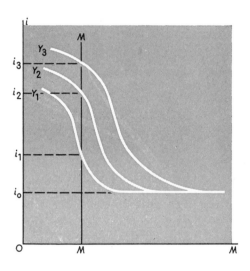

The total demand curves Y_1, Y_2, and Y_3 are a composite of the underlying demand curves in Figures 1a and 1b. Given such a demand curve, and given the supply of money, one can determine the rate of interest. Thus if demand is Y_1, and money supply is OM, the interest rate will be i_1.

since all the money in existence at a particular time must be held by somebody. Thus the rate of interest must be i_1, determined by the intersection of Y_1 and MM.

A higher national income Y_2, with the same quantity of money, will produce a higher interest rate i_2, defined by the intersection of Y_2 and MM. A still higher income Y_3 will result in the interest rate i_3, and so on. Thus we conclude that, given the money supply, *the interest rate varies directly with the level of national income.*

Suppose now that we take national income as fixed, say at Y_1, and make money supply the variable factor. Move MM to the left, indicating a smaller supply. The equilibrium rate of interest will be higher. Enlarge the money supply by moving MM to the right. The interest rate will be lower. This leads to a second proposition: *The interest rate varies inversely with the quantity of money.* (This holds good *until* one strikes the horizontal section of the demand curve, when the interest rate becomes unresponsive to further increases in money supply.)

INCOME DETERMINATION IN A MONETARY ECONOMY

We seem to have made a considerable step forward. In Chapter 18 we said that, in order to draw a consumption or investment schedule, one must assume some rate of interest. But this rate was pulled out of the air. Now we have shown how the interest rate itself is determined by the operation of the system.

But wait a moment. Are we as far ahead as we thought? All we have shown is that we can determine the rate of interest provided we know the supply of money *and the level of national income*. But in practice, of course, the level of national income is the great unknown. This is what we really want to determine in the end. So we seem to be going around in a circle.

The difficulty is that, having brought money into the picture, we have two equilibrium conditions to satisfy instead of one. These are:

1. *Equilibrium in Product Markets.* Total spending on goods and services must equal the cost of goods and services produced. We saw in Chapter 18 that this condition is satisfied when

$$S = I + (T - G)$$

or in the simplified no-government case,

$$S = I$$

2. *Equilibrium in the Money Market.* This requires that the amount of money people want to hold must equal the amount of money in existence. If we designate the former as L, and the latter as M, the condition is

$$L = M$$

Suppose we know the quantity of money in existence. (We have to take *something* as fixed in order to get anywhere at all!) But both national income (Y) and the rate of interest (i) are left free to vary. *Problem:* To find a combination of Y and i which will satisfy *both* of the equilibrium conditions simultaneously. If we can do this, we shall have a stable equilibrium for the economy, in which money supply, interest rate, and the total expenditure schedule will be mutually consistent.

Is this a soluble problem? Yes, it is. The solution can be shown in several different ways. The one chosen here requires effort to grasp; but it ties up a lot of things in a neat way.

Since we are now trying to determine Y and i simultaneously, our diagrams from here on will show Y on the horizontal axis and i on the vertical axis. The eventual solution, then, will be a *point* on this sort of diagram, a satisfactory pair of values for the two variables.

Start with the first condition of equilibrium, $S = I$, and look at Figure 2. Choose any rate of interest, i_1. Now, for this rate of interest there must be some level of national income which will make S equal to I. The rate of interest determines a certain amount of investment, so we must find a level of income at which people will choose to save just this amount. Suppose this turns out to be Y_1. Then point A on the diagram, with coordinates i_1, Y_1, is one point at which the $S = I$ condition is fulfilled.

But there are obviously many more such points. Choose a lower rate of interest, i_2. With lower interest, there will be a larger volume of investment. If the saving-investment equality is to hold, there must be more saving, and this will happen only at a higher level of income. The required level of income turns out to be Y_2. This gives us another point, B, which meets the $S = I$ condition. By repeating the same process we discover a third point, C; and so on.

FIGURE 2

Product Market Equilibrium

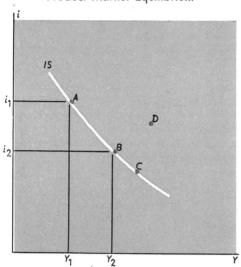

IS contains all combinations of national income (Y) and interest rate (i) which satisfy the conditions S = I. Thus A, B, and C are possible equilibrium positions for the economy, while D is not.

By linking together all such points, we derive the curve *IS*. This is the *locus of all combinations of* i *and* Y *which satisfy the* S = I *condition.* Wherever the economy may settle, then, it must be at some point along this line. Point *D*, for example, cannot be an equilibrium point because it does not satisfy one of the basic conditions.

Turn now to the second condition, $L = M$, and look at Figure 3. We proceed as before. Choose any rate of interest, i_1. Given this rate, the amount of money people wish to hold depends solely on the level of income (refer back, if you need to, to Figure 1c). But the quantity of money in existence is fixed. Thus we can find some income level at which people are just willing to hold this fixed amount of money. Suppose this turns out to be Y_1. Then point *D* gives us one combination of i and Y which satisfies the $L = M$ condition.

FIGURE 3

Money Market Equilibrium

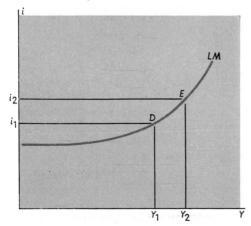

LM contains all combinations of Y and i which satisfy the condition L = M. Only points on this line, such as D and E, are possible equilibrium positions for the economy.

Choose another rate of interest, i_2. At this rate, it will take a different income level, Y_2, to equate L and M. This gives us a second point E. By discovering more and more such points and joining them up, we obtain the LM curve in Figure 3. This is *the locus of all combinations of i and Y which satisfy the* $L = M$ *condition.*

Why does LM slope upward to the right? As we move to the right, we are moving toward higher levels of income. People will thus want to hold larger money balances for transactions and precautionary purposes. But the amount of money in existence is fixed. So the larger transactions-precautionary demand can be satisfied only by persuading people to hold *smaller* balances for speculative purposes. This requires a rise in the rate of interest, since speculative balances vary inversely with interest. The rate of interest must rise enough to reduce the speculative demand for money by the same amount that the higher level of income has raised the transactions-precautionary de-

FIGURE 4

General Equilibrium:

Simultaneous Determination of Interest Rate
    and National Income

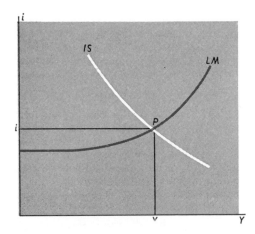

Any equilibrium position for the economy must lie on *both* IS and LM. The only point of which this true is the intersection point P. Hence the level of income will be Y and the interest rate *i*.

mand. Only in this way can the $L = M$ condition continue to be satisfied with a fixed amount of money.

Note, however, that the early section of LM has been drawn as a horizontal line. This corresponds to the horizontal section of the money demand curve in Figure 1c. This portion of Figure 1c, it will be remembered, indicates that at some (low) level of interest rates people will accumulate idle balances indefinitely instead of buying securities. This is the region of the liquidity trap. Starting from such a situation, as income rises the increased transactions-precautionary demand for money can be met for awhile by drawing off idle balances with no need for a rise in the interest rate. Eventually, however, the economy reaches a point at which further balances will be released only at a higher rate of interest. At this point LM turns upward.

Once the construction of the IS and LM curves has been grasped, the solution of our problem becomes simple. Look at Figure 4, where the two are brought together. Each curve shows a basic condition of equilibrium. For the economy to be in equilibrium, *both* conditions must be satisfied at once. The equilibrium combination of interest rate and national income *must* lie on *both* IS and LM. But this can happen only where the two curves intersect. The intersection at P, then, defines the general equilibrium of the system. The interest rate will settle at i and the level of national income at Y. And this will be a stable position so long as the underlying conditions—the expenditure schedule, the money demand curves, and the quantity of money—remain unchanged.

CHANGES IN THE LEVEL OF NATIONAL INCOME

In practice, the underlying conditions never do stay unchanged for long. The chief usefulness of the IS − LM diagram is as a tool for exploring the reactions which will be set up by any change in the basic conditions. Two examples will make the point.

AN INCREASE IN THE EXPENDITURE SCHEDULE

Suppose first that the IS curve shifts rightward to $(IS)_1$ (Figure 5). This means that, at each rate of interest, people are now willing to spend more than before. We need not ask why. An increase in planned spending by consumers, business concerns, or government might be responsible.

What reactions will be set up by this shift? The answer depends on the shape of LM. Three cases may be distinguished:

1. Suppose that $(IS)_1$ intersects LM somewhere in the range BC, over which LM slopes upward to the right. (This is probably the commonest case, and is the one illustrated in Figure 5.) Then equilibrium will be re-established at the intersection of $(IS)_1$ and LM. The rate of interest will rise from i to i_1, and national income will rise from Y to Y_1. The increase in spending will raise *both* national income and the rate of interest.

Note, however, that national income rises less than it did in the simple multiplier analysis of Chapter 19. The reason is that in Chapter 19 we assumed the interest rate to be unaffected by any shift in total demand. If this were so, and if the rise from IS to $(IS)_1$ left the interest rate unchanged at i, then the multiplier effect would push national income all the way out to Y_2. But in the present case the interest rate does rise. This acts as a brake on expansion and limits the rise in national income to Y_1.

2. There is a case, however, in which the simple multiplier analysis yields correct results. Suppose that both IS and $(IS)_1$ intersect LM in the range AB, i.e., the region of excess speculative balances. Then the rise in spending will not raise the rate of interest. Without the interest brake, the multiplier will be left to work out its full effect in terms of higher income.

This has been labeled the "Keynesian region" in Figure 5, because Lord Keynes called attention to this possibility and thought it was important in practice. In the abnormally depressed conditions of the 1930's interest rates may have reached the irreducible minimum which Keynes visualized, but this possibility has been of little practical importance since 1940.

3. A third possibility is indicated by the vertical section from C upward in Figure 5. At C the rate of interest is so high (security prices are so low) as to produce a general conviction that the movement will be reversed. Everyone has shifted into securities, and speculative holdings of money have fallen to zero. All the money in existence is being held for transactions and precautionary purposes. But we have assumed that these holdings are a constant proportion of income. Thus if the money supply is fixed, national income is fixed, and we can move no farther to the right on the diagram. The LM curve becomes vertical.

FIGURE 5

A Change in the Expenditure Schedule

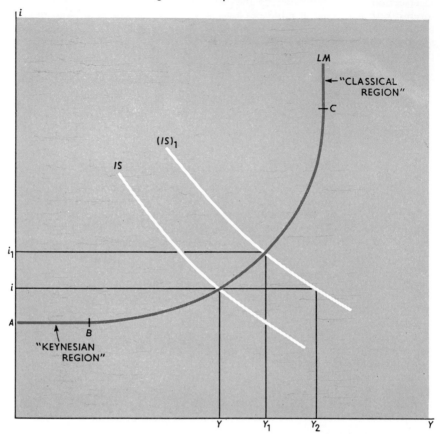

Over the upward-sloping region *BC*, a shift of *IS* will change *both* the interest rate and the level of income. Below *B*, the effect will be entirely on income; above *C*, it will be entirely on the rate of interest.

Suppose that the *IS* curve intersects *LM* at or above *C*. If *IS* rises still higher, the new intersection point will be immediately above the previous one. The only effect will be a rise in the interest rate, and there will be no effect on national income. This has been labeled the "classical region" in Figure 5, because these results correspond to those often assumed in economic theory before 1930.

"Real-life economies" are probably moving most of the time within the range *BC*, and the results which hold within that range are most likely to be of practical importance.

AN INCREASE IN MONEY SUPPLY

Consider now the effects of a change in the money market (Figure 6). The banks, influenced by Federal Reserve policy, have become willing to lend more than before at the same rate of interest. Thus *LM* moves rightward to the position $(LM)_1$. What will happen? The *IS* curve now intersects the monetary curve farther to the right, so that there is a new equilibrium level of interest and

FIGURE 6

A Change in the Supply of Money

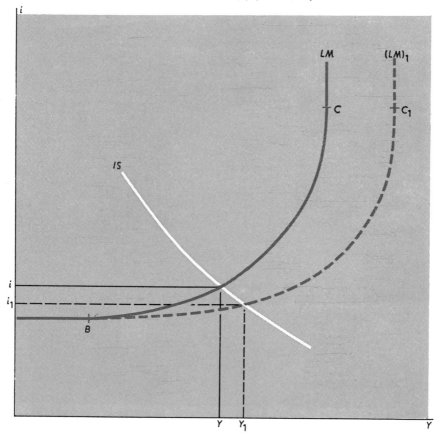

An increase in the supply of money shifts LM rightward, say to $(LM)_1$. The normal result will be a *rise* in national income and a *fall* in the rate of interest. But if IS intersects LM in the Keynesian region to the left of B, the increase in money supply will be ineffective.

national income. But note that these variables change in opposite directions. National income *rises* from Y to Y_1. The rate of interest *falls* from i to i_1. Moreover, a quick pencil test reveals that these results hold even if IS intersects LM in its vertical or "classical" region.

The relative size of the two effects depends on the slope of IS. Suppose IS is very steep, i.e., savings and investment decisions are little affected by changes in the rate of interest. Then an increase in money supply will mean a marked drop in the rate of interest, but only a small increase in national income. A very flat IS curve will lead to opposite results. The flatter the shape of IS, the greater the impact of an increase in money supply on national income.

This analysis helps to illustrate why equally good economists may reach different conclusions about the effects of monetary change, and thus come out with different policy recommendations. Such disagreements can often be put in the form of differences of opinion about the shape and location of the IS and LM functions. These are questions of fact. As continuing research throws more light upon them, the range for legitimate difference of opinion should gradually narrow.

23

Fluctuations in National Income

All Mathematics would suggest / A steady straight line as the best,
But left and right alternately / Is consonant with History.

W. H. AUDEN

The ebb will take off what the tide brings in.

THOMAS FULLER

THE NATIONAL INCOME DIAGRAMS in earlier chapters are still photographs
of the economy at a moment of time. They say that, if the expenditure
schedule is in a certain position, the economy will be tending toward a certain level of national income. If the expenditure schedule shifts, the equilibrium level of income will change.

We must now examine how the expenditure schedule actually does
shift over the course of time. It could conceivably go on rising steadily
year after year. But in practice it does not do this. Every few years there is
a setback, and expenditure and national income drop for a year or two before the upward climb is resumed. The task of this chapter is to follow
these movements with a movie camera, and to explore what determines
their timing and shape.

We shall concentrate on *description*, *explanation*, and *prediction* of
these swings in economic activity. What do they look like? What things
go up most rapidly during an expansion, and what things fall most in
recession? How can one explain the turning points in economic activity?

Why does an expansion always reverse itself after a while instead of going on upward forever? What progress has been made toward predicting future economic movements?

These questions are important. Elections are won or lost, businesses prosper or fail, people lose their jobs or find new jobs—all according to the swings of the business cycle.

DESCRIPTION

The nature of economic fluctuations can be judged from Figure 23–1, which is the chart shown in the introduction to Part Three. Note

FIGURE 23–1

Production and Unemployment, 1918–62

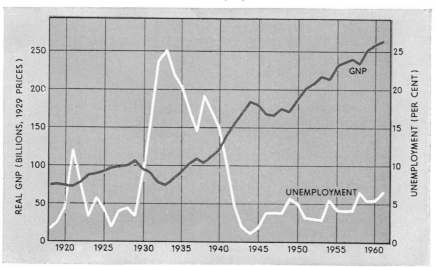

that every few years national output drops and unemployment rises. Then after a short time the movement is reversed. Output rises and unemployment falls.

These sawtooth movements are often called business cycles, but this can be misleading. "Cycle" suggests greater regularity than actually exists. If expansions and contractions followed each other at regular intervals, there would be no forecasting problem. The thing which keeps everyone sitting on the edge of his chair is uncertainty about when the next turn will come. Some economic expansions (1924–26, 1927–29, 1958–60) peter out after a couple of years. But one, the 1938–45 expansion associated with World War II, lasted almost seven years. The average duration of an upswing is something like three years. But an average is not an insurance policy.

The term "cycle" also connotes a strong similarity among different expansions and contractions. It suggests that we can find a single "business cycle theory" which will account for all of them. Few economists today would accept this view. There is a certain family resemblance among successive cycles. But each has individual characteristics, involving a combination of circumstances which will never recur in just the same form. Cycles differ in length, in size, in the combination of forces responsible for the upswing, in the reasons for ending of prosperity, and in the severity of the relapse.

It may be better, therefore, to speak of *economic fluctuations* or *fluctuations in national income*, which carries no implication of regularity or uniform causation.

One other problem of terminology: In popular usage, periods of economic expansion go by such varied names as "recovery," "prosperity," "boom." Periods of declining activity may be called "slumps," "recessions," "depressions." All this is rather confusing. Let us agree, therefore, to call a period of rising activity an *upswing*, and a period of declining activity a *downswing*. The point at which an upswing ceases and reverses itself we shall call the *upper turning point*. The end of a downswing is the *lower turning point*. A complete fluctuation, then, consists of a lower turning point, an upswing, an upper turning point, and a downswing. If this sounds less exciting than boom and slump, it has the advantage of saying exactly what we mean.

What goes on during one of these fluctuations? The most striking thing about them is the divergent movement of different elements in the economy. During a downswing some things fall a lot, others fall a little, while some go right on rising. In general, the things which fall most on the downswing also rise most on the upswing. It is necessary to say a bit about these differences in movement, since they provide some clues to why the fluctuations occur.

Some Things Fluctuate Widely

Among the items which show sizable fluctuations are:

1. *Business inventories* of raw materials, goods in process, and finished products. Businesses typically add substantially to inventories on the upswing and reduce them on the downswing.

2. *Machinery and equipment* expenditures also rise sharply on the upgrade and fall off during contraction. Because of the importance of investment, its main components have been charted in Figure 23–2. Note that residential and commercial construction showed little tendency to decline during the downswings of the fifties.

3. *Consumer spending on durable goods*, notably automobiles, furniture, and household appliances. These purchases are postponable and are financed partly by borrowing. During a period of economic uncertainty some families will be unwilling or unable to borrow, and will postpone their purchases to a more favorable time. Consumer spending on

FIGURE 23–2

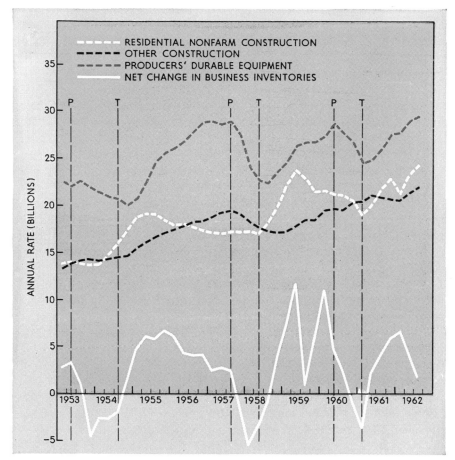

P indicates a cycle peak or upper turning point. T indicates a cycle trough or lower turning point. The dating is that used by the N.B.E.R.

food, clothing, and services, on the other hand, has not declined in any of the downswings since 1945.

4. *Production of durable goods.* With business spending on machinery and consumer spending on durable goods both falling, it stands to reason that output of durable goods must fall on the downswing. A downswing *is* mainly a decline in steel, metals, machinery, automobiles, and other durable goods industries. In recent downswings the total output of nondurable goods has dropped scarcely at all.

5. *Employment* rises and falls with production. On the downswing, several million people may be laid off completely and several million more reduced to working part-time.

6. *Business profits* may fall by 25 percent or so in even a mild down-

swing, then shoot up the same distance or more during the next upswing.

7. *Tax receipts* of the federal government fluctuate for the reasons noted in Chapter 20. Even the mild downswings of the fifties brought drops of $5 to $8 billion in federal revenues, mainly because of smaller receipts from the corporate income tax. The upswings of 1954–57 and 1958–60 brought increased revenues of close to $20 billion.

8. *Interest rates*, particularly short-term rates, move up and down substantially over the cycle. This is partly a natural result of fluctuations in the demand for money, partly a reflection of monetary policy.

Some Things Always Go Up

Among items which fluctuate little with general economic activity, we may note:

1. *Government purchases of goods and services.* State and local government expenditures have risen quite steeply since 1945, and the rise has continued right through the downswing periods. Federal expenditures have had a milder uptrend, and also show little relation to general economic activity.

2. *Consumer spending on nondurable goods and services.* This has risen sharply during upswings, leveled off a bit during downswings, but shows no period of actual decline.

3. *Wage rates.* Wages have risen in bad years and good. The rise has been slightly less rapid during downswings than during upswings, but the difference is not marked.

4. *The price level.* Both the wholesale price index and the consumer price index have edged up gradually over the past 10 years. The advance slows down and sometimes stops for a while during downswings; but except for a mild drop in prices during the downswing of 1948–49, there has been no general price decline in the United States since 1938.

Much more could be said about the behavior of the economy during periods of expansion and contraction.[1] But perhaps we have said enough to set the stage for an analysis of why these fluctuations occur.

EXPLANATION

It would be satisfying to discover a general cause of economic fluctuations, a single source of the uneven heartbeat of the economy. But it has gradually become apparent that there is no one prime mover. Each upturn and downturn is complex and to some extent unique. One needs an eclectic rather than a monocausal approach.

There are two main things to be explained. First, after the economy has started moving up or down, why does it build up momentum and

---

[1] The great center of research on this subject is the National Bureau of Economic Research in New York. Anyone who wants to delve into detail will find a wealth of publications by Wesley C. Mitchell, Arthur F. Burns, Geoffrey H. Moore, Solomon Fabricant, and other past and present members of the Bureau staff.

keep going in the same direction for a considerable time? Second and more difficult, why does the movement reverse itself after a while? After production has been rising for several years, the production index levels off and then starts to decline. Why doesn't expansion continue indefinitely?

The Mechanism of Expansion

Let us ask first how an upswing feeds on itself and develops enough momentum to continue for several years at a time. We break into the cycle just after the lower turning point. An upswing has begun and has continued long enough to convince the business community that recovery is underway. What happens from this point on?

1. The early stages of recovery are a good time to carry out investment plans. The banking system has excess reserves. Interest rates have tumbled during the downswing. Capital goods manufacturers have idle capacity, so that one can get prompt delivery of machinery and materials. Prices and wages are as low as they are likely to be in the foreseeable future. Labor is plentiful. Thus for anyone considering an investment project, the economic environment is unusually favorable.

2. Who is in a position to invest on the upswing? Young industries whose markets are growing at a rapid rate are particularly important. Such industries know that they must build new capacity, and the only question is when. They may hold back on the downswing until they can gauge its seriousness, and also in the hope of benefiting from lower costs at the bottom. But once the upswing is clearly underway, there is no longer any reason to delay. These industries will come strongly into the market for capital goods, and expansion projects initiated at this time may take two or three years to complete. The length of the physical *gestation period* on large construction jobs is one reason why activity keeps moving upward for a considerable time.

Even industries which are not increasing capacity must do considerable investment. Old equipment wears out or becomes obsolete as superior machinery is developed. New products may require different types of equipment. This replacement and modernization investment is timed with some reference to economic conditions. When profits are falling and the future is unclear, many companies follow a "wait and see" policy. They let old equipment wear out and do nothing about it, which for the time being intensifies the downswing. The longer the downswing continues, the more of this postponed replacement demand is built up for the future. Once the upswing is underway, this potential demand becomes effective and helps raise the level of investment.

3. Some industries have cycles of their own. Building construction seems to follow a cycle of 15 to 20 years in length. If an economic upswing occurs at a time when the building cycle is also on the upgrade, the vigor of construction activity adds momentum to the upswing. But if

the building cycle is in a contraction phase, this acts as a drag on the economy. It makes the general upswing shorter and weaker than it would be if building were also expanding.

4. Another feature of the early upswing is a rise in inventory investment. During the downswing, inventories are usually reduced to a minimum working level. As the lower turning point is passed and sales begin to rise, the first effect is to reduce inventories still further, because goods are being sold faster than they are being replaced. Quite quickly, however, companies will step up production schedules and increase their orders for parts and materials. There will be an effort to rebuild inventories and keep them in what is considered a normal ratio to the rising sales volume.

There is a further reason for a rise in inventory investment. In industries where raw materials are important and where material prices fluctuate widely, a manufacturer is unavoidably involved in price speculation. A tire company is partly a producer of tires, partly a speculator in rubber prices. So as soon as an upswing is underway many companies, reasoning that material prices are bound to rise, will order unusually large amounts in order to "beat the price rise."

5. With additional investment going on for these reasons, the upswing is clearly on solid ground. Part of the increased income generated in the capital goods industries is spent on consumer goods, thus raising demand and output in those industries. Increased employment in consumer goods production generates still more income, most of which is re-spent on the next round; and so on through the familiar multiplier process. Because of the large size of the consumer goods sector, the *absolute* increase in consumption during an upswing is typically larger than the increase in investment, even though it may have been investment which provided the initial push.

6. As the level of income rises, more and more industries find themselves operating close to capacity and begin to consider whether they shouldn't build new capacity. The rising cost of investment during a boom operates as a deterrent. But this is typically outweighed by the fact that the sales outlook is good, and that companies are making substantial profits which can be plowed back. There is also a competitive element at work. A company usually aims to keep at least its present share of sales in its industry, and preferably to gain a larger share. This means that its expansion plans must keep pace with those of rival companies. If demand for the industry's products is expected to be 20 percent higher five years from now than it is today, there will be a competitive scramble to see who can "get there fastest."

Thus we get *induced* investment, which occurs in response to rising consumer demand for existing products. Because of the high mechanization of many industries, the effect may be substantial. It may take a $50 million investment to raise annual output of a product by $10 million.

7. These processes have a cumulative, mutually reinforcing character, which readily explains why the pendulum continues swinging in the same direction for several years at a time. Autonomous increases in investment raise national income via the multiplier. As some industries near capacity, the continued rise in demand calls forth induced investment. This raises income still further, and so on. The process is both stimulated and fueled by rising profits which permit heavy reinvestment of earnings, and this is reinforced by injections of credit from the banking system. If the boom is strong enough to produce price increases, this also acts as a reinforcing factor. The fact that commodity prices are rising stimulates heavier buying to beat the increases. But this may cause prices to rise still faster, and so on.

So it is not hard to explain the cumulative nature of the upswing. The more difficult problem is why the upswing eventually slows down and reverses itself. Just when people have become confident about continued economic expansion, the rug is pulled from under them and the economy heads downward into recession.

Why is this? Must the boom come to an end? Couldn't a downturn be prevented, if only we were sufficiently clever? In the present state of knowledge the answer seems to be "No." To explain why is the next stage in our story.

The End of Prosperity

Various things *might* precipitate a downturn. A sharp drop in federal spending, unaccompanied by a corresponding cut in tax rates, could break the back of a boom. This was a factor in the downturn of 1953. As the Korean War came to a close, federal purchases of goods and services were cut by about $15 billion (at annual rates) between the first quarter of 1953 and the first quarter of 1954. But this was an unusual event. A sudden drop in the consumption schedule could also cause trouble, but this is of little importance in practice. Consumer spending and saving remain remarkably stable from year to year.

What typically happens is that business investment weakens after a time and stops advancing fast enough to keep the boom going. Note that steady economic expansion requires a *certain rate of increase in investment*, year after year. A high but constant level of investment is not sufficient. Why is this? If GNP rises year by year, then savings will also be rising. Unless planned investment rises at a sufficient rate to balance these higher savings, the expansion cannot continue. Maintaining an economic upswing is rather like racing a motorcycle up a steep slope. As soon as the machine loses momentum, it is in danger of toppling over.

What seems to happen on the upswing is that investment loses momentum and eventually falls below the required rate of increase. The reasons for an eventual slackening of investment are to some extent built into the pattern of the previous expansion. Several points deserve mention:

1. In the early stages of an upswing, there is usually heavy inventory investment to restore the normal ratio of inventories to sales. But once this has been accomplished, the rate of inventory investment slackens. Now if businessmen increased inventories this year by $10 billion, and if next year they increase them only $5 billion, this amounts to a *cut* of $5 billion a year in investment. A careful look at Figure 23–1 suggests that this typically happens during the last half of an upswing.

The same analysis applies to replacement and modernization of equipment. There is a tendency to delay this kind of investment on the downswing because of the uncertain business outlook. Thus the economy enters the upswing with a backlog of deferred demand. Once the upswing is underway, there is no longer any reason for delay. Businesses rush to make up for lost time. Orders for new equipment are placed at a rapid rate. The backlog of demand begins to shrink, and after a couple of years may be largely exhausted. This means a drop in demand for machinery and related items.

2. Another prominent feature of the upswing is a rush to increase plant capacity in industries with a strong uptrend of demand. But future movements of demand are always conjectural, and plant expansion may undershoot or overshoot the mark. Overshooting is especially likely in competitive industries where numerous firms are trying to estimate both the increase in total industry demand and the share of the market which they can hope to capture. If many firms are overoptimistic, total plant capacity can easily outrun the increase in demand. Since plant construction takes time, it may be several years before this becomes apparent. But as more and more plants come into operation and it becomes apparent that the industry is overexpanded, further plant construction will cease. This is an additional reason why investment, after rising for a few years, may weaken abruptly and unexpectedly.

3. Investment is a physical as well as a financial process. The feasible rate of investment is limited in the short run by the capacity of the capital goods industries, by the supply of metals, machinery, building materials, skilled construction labor, and so on. These industries enter the upswing with much idle capacity, and so for a while their production can expand rapidly. If the upswing carries to the point at which the capital goods industries are working to capacity, however, the rate of increase in investment must decline.

Capacity limitations do not compel an actual downturn of investment. But they can compel a drop in the rate of increase. This leveling off of investment must fairly quickly, after the multiplier has done its work, mean a leveling off of GNP. And this has awkward implications, as we shall see in a moment.

4. The upswing may or may not carry to the point at which there is upward pressure on the price level. If it does, another unstable and reversible element enters the scene. Part of consumer and business spending now becomes an effort to beat the next price increase. It depends on an expectation of further price increases in the future. If anything happens to shake this expectation, this "scare buying" will diminish or disappear; and the overbuying which was induced by fear of price increases will be offset by underbuying for some time.

5. How far have we gotten in demonstrating that the boom contains the seeds of its own destruction? We have shown that part of the investment on the upswing is of a sort which naturally goes into reverse after a while. Inventory investment, deferred replacement demand, and buying based on expectation of price increases are all of this character. Competitive overexpansion of particular industries during the upswing may lead, when it is eventually discovered, to a drop of investment in those industries. If the monetary authorities become concerned about rising prices and apply the credit brakes, this can also check the rise of investment.

Thus investment *may* level off or decline even before the capital goods industries are working at capacity. If the upswing carries these industries to capacity, investment *must* taper off for physical reasons. And this implies that the increase in GNP will also taper off.

But what is wrong with this? Why can't the economy taper off at a high level and move along a gently rising plateau? There are at least two reasons. First, a reduced rate of increase in consumer demand has a discouraging effect on induced investment. *Example:* Suppose it takes $2 million of investment to increase the annual production capacity of automobile plants by $1 million. Automobile demand has been rising $100 million a year. Thus the industry has been obliged to spend $200 million a year on new plants to keep up with demand. Now the annual rate of increase in demand drops to $50 million. This requires new plant investment of only $100 a year. Note that consumer demand is still rising. But the *decline in the rate of increase of demand means an absolute drop in investment.* The moral is that the economy must keep moving forward at a certain rate, or else it starts slipping back.

Second, most businessmen do not believe that the economy can hold indefinitely to a stable level of activity. They do not believe in "prosperity plateaus." They believe in cycles, having been conditioned to this by a century of economic history. As soon as an expansion begins to level off, many businessmen say "Ah! We are nearing the end of this upswing. The sensible thing now is to go slow on our investment plans and see what happens." As this impression spreads, it helps to bring on the downturn. And then everyone can say, "How clever we were. We knew it all the time."

Big Downswings and Little Ones

The growth of production and employment is interrupted every few years by a downturn. Since 1850 there has been no peacetime upswing which continued longer than about four years;[2] and many were cut short after two to three years. But some downswings are long and severe, while others are brief and mild. In the Great Depression of the thirties, GNP dropped by about 30 percent between 1929 and 1933, and full recovery was not achieved until the war boom of 1941–45. In the four downswings between 1946 and 1963, on the other hand, GNP never dropped more than 5 percent. This is sometimes taken as indicating that major downswings are no longer possible in the American economy.

What makes the difference between a small downswing and a large one? One important factor is the stage of the building cycle, which has its own slow-moving pattern cutting through the fluctuations of general business. If building construction is moving upward, one can count on a sizable volume of investment in good years and bad. Suppose all other investment dropped to zero. Then national income could drop only to the point at which saving equaled building investment (or, more realistically, building investment plus the federal deficit). This sets a floor to the downswing, and the higher the level of building activity the higher this floor will be.

But suppose the economy is in a downward phase of the building cycle. Then building activity provides less support, and downswings can go farther before hitting bottom. This was the situation in the 1930's. The building cycle reached a peak in 1925 and then turned down. By the time of the general downswing in 1929, building had fallen too low to provide much support. Throughout the fifties, on the other hand, building construction was high and rising. Each time a downturn occurred, the continued strength of building activity helped to arrest the downswing.

Another important factor is the uneven occurrence of major investment opportunities. Economists distinguish between *invention*, which is the use of scientific knowledge to develop a new product or method of production, and *innovation*, which is putting an invention to work in production. Invention is done mainly by scientists and engineers. Innovation requires a business decision to risk capital in a plant embodying the new technique. Only at this stage does the invention become economically important. Unless someone will back the idea with money, it gathers dust in the files of the U.S. Patent Office.

Invention and innovation are going on all the time. But there are

---

[2] Geoffrey H. Moore (ed.), *Business Cycle Indicators* (Princeton, N.J.: Princeton University Press, 1960), Vol. I, p. 670.

major and minor innovations. At one end of the scale is the small adjustment on a machine which increases its efficiency by 5 percent, and which earns someone a $100 prize from the company suggestion system. At the other extreme are the inventions which led to the railroad, electric power production, telephone communication, and the automobile.

A major innovation gives rise to a wave of capital investment. First a few pioneers demonstrate that the new technique is feasible, and that the public will take the product at profitable prices. After this imitators swarm into the new industry. Investment is heavy, plant capacity and output grow rapidly. This phase of rapid expansion may last for several decades. But eventually the potentialities of the new industry are fully exploited, output tapers off to a plateau, and investment falls.

To sustain the upward momentum of the economy one needs a series of major innovations, following each other at regular intervals, so that as the force of one new development tapers off there is something else to take its place. But this cannot be counted on. No matter how many well-financed research laboratories there may be, one cannot be sure of producing the equivalent of a new automobile industry every decade. Putting more money into scientific training and research should raise the *average rate* of invention, but it cannot make it completely regular. Significant discoveries cannot be turned out on the assembly line.

A major downswing could occur, then, because of a temporary lack of major inventions and innovations. It has been suggested that this may have happened after 1929. Heavy investment in electric power and automobiles helped to sustain prosperity during the twenties. But as these industries moved toward maturity, no new industries of equal importance appeared to maintain the momentum of investment. The downturn of the building cycle in 1925 served as an additional drag. Hence the severity of the 1929–33 downswing.

Contrast with this the situation during the fifties. By this time many important discoveries dating back to the thirties and forties were ripe for commercial application. The list includes automation in factory and office, computers and other electronic devices, applications of atomic energy, jet aviation and rocketry, major developments in chemicals and petrochemicals. These areas have generated a large volume of autonomous investment, oriented toward long-term development and largely independent of current demand. This flow of assured investment, plus the high level of construction activity, has sustained national income during the postwar period. Downswings have not been able to develop momentum. In each case the economy has hit bottom and rebounded after 9 to 12 months.

This can be illustrated by some arithmetic. The figures are pulled out of the air, but are not far from the mark for recent years. Suppose the pattern of investment at the upper turning point is as follows:

Residential construction	$20 billion (annual rate)
Autonomous business investment	25
Induced business investment*	25
Inventory change	5
Total investment	$75 billion (annual rate)

* This is gross investment, and includes all items which may be subject to short-term cyclical influences. It includes replacement and modernization of equipment as well as plant expansion based on expectations of rising demand. Our assumption that half of business investment is sensitive to short downturns and half is not is arbitrary. But it may be a reasonable estimate for this period.

Suppose that on the downswing the inventory figure drops to −5 billion, and that induced investment drops to 20 billion. Housebuilding and autonomous business investment remain unchanged. Thus total investment declines by 15 billion. If the marginal propensity to spend is 0.5, then the multiplier is 2 and GNP will fall by 30 billion. At present GNP levels, this would be a fall of about 5 percent.

Suppose on the other hand that housebuilding and autonomous business investment were declining year by year. This would lower the automatic "floor" under the economy, and permit deeper and longer declines in GNP. It is these two components of investment which really make the difference.

Concerning the probable behavior of the American economy during the sixties and seventies, one can only speculate. There is little evidence that private investment is inherently more stable than it used to be. The chief difference from earlier decades is the reduced value of the multiplier, due mainly to the greater importance of federal taxes and transfer payments. Recent estimates put the value of the multiplier in the neighborhood of 2, whereas pre-1940 estimates were usually between 3 and 4. Thus a $10 billion drop in investment now generates only a $20 billion decline in GNP instead of a $30 or $40 billion decline. This fact, plus the likelihood that any federal administration would move vigorously to combat a major downswing, warrants a belief that depressions on the 1929–33 scale are now impossible. But medium-sized downswings, larger than anything we have seen since 1940, are still within the bounds of possibility.

PREDICTION

What's going to happen next on the economic front? Everyone would like to know. Economic forecasting has become a favorite indoor sport of journalists, commentators, sales managers, and public officials. The quality of these forecasts varies greatly. Many are so vague or loaded with weasel words that the forecaster can hardly lose, but by the same token the user of the forecast can hardly benefit.

A good way to separate the men from the boys is to see whether a forecast uses numbers. Economics is a quantitative subject, and masses of current statistical information are now available. Unless an economic writer indicates a grasp of this material, and is willing to spell out his predictions in figures, he cannot be taken seriously.

The more reputable methods of prediction may be classified as: (1) barometric forecasting; (2) analytical forecasting using the GNP framework; (3) econometric forecasting, which is also analytical but quite complicated and for that reason is omitted here.

Barometric Forecasting

This method does not require any theorizing about the causes of economic fluctuations. It is purely inductive. It rests on the observation that things have happened in a certain way in the past, and a surmise that they may happen similarly in the future.

The best known example is the work of the National Bureau of Economic Research. Research workers at the Bureau have analyzed the movement of several hundred economic variables over a long period in the past, beginning in some cases as early as 1870. Particular attention has been paid to upper and lower turning points in each series, which presumably reflect the rhythm of overall economic fluctuations. From an examination of this material, the Bureau has established a precise year and month for each upturn and downturn in general economic activity. By comparing the turning points of a particular series with that for business in general, one can discover whether the series typically reverses itself earlier than general business, or at about the same time, or later.

On this basis, the series have been classified into three groups: (1) *Leading series*, which typically turn up and down in advance of general business. Included in this group are business failures, stock prices, new orders for durable goods, building contracts, average work week in manufacturing, new incorporations, and sensitive wholesale prices. (2) *Roughly coincident series*, which turn at about the same time as general business. This group includes employment, unemployment, industrial production, GNP, freight carloadings, corporate profits, and wholesale prices (except farm and food products). This amounts to saying that these are the series to which the Bureau attaches greatest weight in *defining* the turning points in general business, and also that these major indicators move quite closely together. (3) *Lagging series*, which move somewhat behind the swings of general business. Among this group are personal income, retail sales, consumer installment debt, manufacturers' inventories, and bank rates on business loans.

How can this kind of information be used by the economic forecaster? It is no use to look at the lagging series, because by the time they move the horse is already out of the barn. Even the coincident series do not help on prediction, though they can *confirm* a turning point two or three months after it has occurred. The only way to obtain an advance tip-off is to look at the leading series, which normally move ahead of general business. If five or six of these have already turned up or down, one can conclude that a turning point in economic activity is near.

Since particular interest attaches to leading series, their past performance is shown in Table 23–1. The figures in the first two columns show the *average* number of months by which each series has been ahead of general business at downturns and at upturns. These averages, unfortunately, conceal a good deal of variation from one cycle to the next. A series which shows an *average* lead of four months at the downturn may

TABLE 23–1

Average Timing of Selected Leading Series before 1957, and Their Timing in the 1960–61 Recession*

SERIES	FIRST YEAR COVERED	MEDIAN LEAD (−) OR LAG (+) IN MONTHS		LEAD OR LAG AT 1960–61	
		Peak	Trough	Peak	Trough
Liabilities of business failures†	1875	− 6.5	−7	− 12	−8
Industrial stock prices	1871	− 3.5	−6	− 10	−4
New order, durable goods	1920	− 5.5	−2	− 11	− 1
Residential building contracts	1915	−14	−6	− 17	−2
Commercial and industrial building contracts	1919	− 8	−2	no contraction	
Average work week, manufacturing	1920	− 6.5	−4	− 12	−2
New incorporations	1860	− 2	−6	0	−3
Sensitive wholesale prices	1892	− 2	−1	− 6	−2

* Data to 1957 are from R. A. Gordon, *Business Fluctuations* (2nd ed.; New York: Harper & Bros., 1961). They were compiled originally by Geoffrey H. Moore of the National Bureau. Leads for 1960–61 were calculated by the writer, using the Bureau's standard dates of May, 1960, for the upper turningpoint and February, 1961, for the lower turningpoint.

† This series is used in *inverted* form. Failures *rise* as business activity *falls*, and vice versa. Hence leads and lags refer to the inverted series.

vary all the way from a lead of twelve months to a lag of four months in different cycles. Blind reliance on any one indicator can be quite misleading. A particular series will sometimes "flash the signal" a good deal too early, while in other cases there may be no signal at all until after the fact.

There are two main reasons why a series may be a leading series: (1) It may measure something which foreshadows a change in productive activity. An increase in building contracts normally means a rise in construction work a few months later. A rise in new orders for durable goods leads directly to increased activity in the metals and machinery industries. An increase in incorporations means that the new businesses will shortly be spending money on plant and office facilities.

(2) A series may express the combined opinion of experienced observers about what lies immediately ahead. When large investors become convinced that a downswing is "bottoming out" and will soon end, they

will buy securities immediately to get in at the bottom. Thus the stock market will turn up before the upturn in physical production. The same is true of raw material prices and other items included in the "sensitive wholesale price" index.

The barometric approach rests on economic logic. There are good reasons why the leading series *are* leading series on the average. But the method also involves certain weaknesses:

a) The variability in the behavior of individual series has already been noted. A series which is "well-behaved" most of the time may deceive you in a particular case by reversing itself too early or too late.

b) Most economic series show small, irregular fluctuations from month to month. If an index declines in a particular month, one cannot tell immediately whether this is a real turning point or a minor variation which will be reversed next month. It may take two or three months to be reasonably sure, and this cuts into the forecaster's precious margin of time.

c) In addition, most series are not available to the public until two or three months after the period which they cover. This is one reason why business organizations often collect their own indexes, which may have limited coverage but can be gotten out faster than the official government figures.

Thus even if a leading series does genuinely lead in a particular case, the forecaster is bound to be several months behind in reaching a firm conclusion.

Note also that this method predicts only the turning points. With good luck it may predict a future downturn, or at least confirm the downturn soon after it has occurred. But it says nothing about the probable depth and duration of the downswing. Similarly for an upswing. Barometric methods are thus useful mainly for short periods of time in the vicinity of a turning point. At other times, which means most of the time, analytical methods will be found more useful.

The last two columns of Table 23–1 show how one would have fared by using this method to predict the business peak of May, 1960, and the trough of February, 1961. The indicators would not have been very helpful in anticipating the 1960 downturn. One of them never turned down at all. Most of the remaining series turned down about a year in advance of the general business decline. They gave the right signal, but a good deal too early. The indicators performed better on the upturn, most of them turning up one to three months ahead of the general business recovery.

Analytical Forecasting

This approach rests on the theory of income determination developed in Chapter 18. It starts from the components of total demand and the relations among them. It consists of estimating the components of demand, combining them into an estimate of GNP, and then cross-checking the results for consistency. The outcome is a detailed forecast of GNP and its main components, usually by calendar quarters, for a year or so ahead.

While the essence of the approach is easily stated, its application is more difficult. One difficulty is that "everything depends on everything else." Business investment in the next quarter will have some relation to consumer spending. But consumer spending depends on income, which depends partly on business investment. It seems that we cannot estimate any one component of GNP without already knowing the others.

There are two ways of breaking out of this circle. One way, quite important in econometric forecasting, is to use *lagged relationships*. If consumer spending in the *next quarter* depends on disposable income in *this quarter* (which we already know), we can make an independent estimate of this item. Similarly, if business investment next quarter can be related to business profits over the past four quarters (which we already know), we are on firm ground.

Another thing we can do is to take some components of GNP as independent of everything else, at least as a starting point. Obvious candidates include government spending, business investment, and exports. Let's see how far we can get by first estimating these items, then working back to consumer income and expenditure, and then cross-checking the results.

Look first at *government purchases of goods and services*. Each January the President sends Congress his proposed budget for the fiscal year running from July 1 of that year to July 1 of the following year. By midsummer, Congress has finished working over the items in the budget, and has determined the final figures. We are then on reasonably firm ground for four quarters ahead.

There is no central source of information on state and local government expenditures. But this item can safely be projected on the basis of past trends. Over the past decade it has risen consistently at about 10 percent per year.

The most important *investment* item is business expenditures on *plant and equipment*. This includes industrial construction, commercial construction, and machinery purchases. There are several indicators of future investment plans. Early each year the Department of Commerce and the Securities and Exchange Commission send a questionnaire to a large number of business concerns asking how much they expect to spend on plant and equipment during the year. The results are published in the March issue of the *Survey of Current Business*. The results of this survey typically come close to the amount actually spent during the year. The margin of error only averages about 3 percent, and in some years has been less than 1 percent. Information on recent business profits, on construction contracts awarded, and on new machinery orders serve as useful supplements to the Commerce-SEC results.

Residential construction moves more erratically. Efforts to predict its movement on the basis of consumers' incomes, surveys of consumers' intentions, and surveys of builders' plans have not been very successful. Availability of mortgage money, and the prevailing interest rate on mortgages, seem to be important factors. Construction contracts awarded provide some indications for the near future. Something can also be learned by analyzing basic factors affecting the demand and supply for new housing, such as the marriage rate, migration rates from country to city and city to suburbs, the existing supply of unsold new houses, the vacancy rate in apartment buildings, and the price of old houses.

Inventory change is an important component of investment but is also difficult to predict. Fortune magazine and Dun and Bradstreet make quarterly surveys of companies' inventory plans. One can also look at sales by manufacturers and retailers, the ratios of present inventories to sales, and how the current ratios compare with those which have been normal over the past. If the current inventory/sales ratio is considerably above normal, for example, there may be an effort to reduce it in the quarters ahead.

The Department of Commerce prepares forecasts of U.S. *exports and imports,* which are reported frequently in the *Survey of Current Business.* The International Monetary Fund and other international agencies also take an active interest in this field. Exports are inherently difficult to predict, since they depend on income levels throughout the world as well as our competitiveness in foreign markets. But this is a small item in our GNP accounts and moderate errors are not important.

After estimating each of these items, we add them up and find that the total comes to, say, $200 billion. The next step then is to incorporate this into a projection of total GNP, including consumer expenditures. We know that consumption is closely related to disposable income. Something like 92 percent of income is normally spent and the remainder is saved. We also know that disposable income is a good deal smaller than GNP. Government takes a large amount in taxes, though part of this comes back in transfer payments. Business savings are another substantial item. So we must examine probable tax receipts and transfer payments, corporate profits, and business savings. On the basis of this we conclude that disposable income will be, say, 70 percent of whatever GNP turns out to be.

From here on we proceed as follows:

$$\text{GNP} = \text{consumption} + \text{investment} + \text{government}$$
$$\text{expenditure} + (\text{exports} - \text{imports})$$
$$Y = C + I + G + (E - M)$$
$$\text{but } I + G + (E - M) = 200$$
$$\text{hence } Y = C + 200$$
$$\text{or } C = Y - 200 \tag{1}$$

We also know that $C = 0.92Y_d$, where Y_d is disposable income. And we know that disposable income is 0.70 of Y. Thus

$$C = 0.92Y_d$$
$$= 0.92(0.70Y)$$
$$= 0.644\,Y \tag{2}$$

Solving equations (1) and (2), we find that $Y = 561.8$ billion and $C = 361.8$ billion. This becomes our prelimininary estimate for the period we are considering.

This estimate still needs cross-checking and revision. It rests on economic relationships which, on the average, have held true in the past but which may need to be modified for the immediate future. In particular, it is wise to make an independent projection of consumer expenditure based on past trends, and to see how this compares with the total of 361.8 billions obtained above. Separate estimates are usually made for consumer expenditure on nondurable goods and services, which is a very stable item; and expenditure on durable goods, which is more volatile. Within the durable goods category, automobile purchases are so variable and important that they deserve a separate estimate.

An annual survey of consumers' buying plans conducted by the Survey Research Center of the University of Michigan, and a more recently developed survey by the Census Bureau, provide help on this front. Results of these surveys are published in the Federal Reserve Bulletin and have considerable predictive value. What consumers say they are planning to do about buying new cars, for example, yields a more accurate forecast of car sales than one would get by looking at consumer income alone.

There are also cross-checks of the "where is the money coming from" variety. Estimated business investment can be set against the funds available from depreciation allowances, retained earnings, and possible reduction of cash reserves. Any uncovered balance will have to be met by security sales to the public and bank borrowing. If the results indicate a substantial rise in business borrowing, this may push up interest rates, which may cause some lowering of investment plans.

It is useful to compare estimated government receipts and expenditures. Suppose the preliminary estimates indicate a large federal deficit. This suggests several possibilities: there may be something wrong with the estimates; or the estimates may be correct, but the size of the prospective deficit may lead to efforts to reduce it; or the deficit may actually materialize, in which case Treasury sale of securities to cover it will affect interest rates, bank reserves, and availability of credit to private borrowers.

After making these checks, one may want to revise some of the items in the preliminary estimate. The GNP equation must then be solved again to produce a new forecast, which can be checked by the same methods as the original estimate.

The results to this point are all in dollar terms. To judge the probable movement of physical output and employment, we must make a further estimate of changes in the price level.

It is helpful to examine the estimated level of GNP relative to the physical capacity of the economy. The closer the projected level of GNP is to full capacity, the more reason to expect that part of the rise will take the form of price increases rather than output increases. One can also see whether there have been recent price increases in metals, raw materials, and other basic products which will gradually work their way through to the finished goods level. It may make a difference whether important labor contracts are expiring and whether sizable wage increases are in prospect. Agricultural prices require a separate estimate, since they move differently from industrial prices.

Out of all this comes an estimate that the general price level will be, say, 2 percent higher a year from now than it is today. If the dollar value of GNP has been estimated at 5 percent higher, this means physical output will rise 3 percent over the year. Finally, the output estimate can be converted into an employment estimate on the basis of past relationships between volume of output and man-hours of labor required to produce this output.

SUMMARY

1. Fluctuations in national income are concentrated in the durable goods industries.

2. One important question is why, once the economy has started up or down, the movement gathers momentum and continues for some time in the same direction. Elements in the explanation include: the habitual instability of *inventory investment;* the fact that changes in consumer spending have a magnified effect on *plant and equipment investment;* and the importance of *expectations* in business decisions. When business concerns expect the economy to move in a certain direction, their reactions tend to produce the condition they expect.

3. A more difficult problem is to explain the *turning points*, particularly the upper turning point. Review the section on the end of prosperity for some clues on this matter.

4. Whether a downswing will be mild or severe depends partly on whether it occurs during a rising or falling phase of the longer cycle in building construction, and partly on whether there is a large and dependable volume of autonomous investment resulting from major innovations.

5. We need never expect another downswing as severe and prolonged as that of 1929–33, but we may well see sharper drops than those of 1946 to date.

6. A simple method of *barometric forecasting* involves the use of leading series which typically turn up or down in advance of general business. But this method is not entirely dependable; and at best it predicts only the *date* of turning points, not the *magnitude* of upward or downward movements.

7. A simple method of *analytical forecasting* involves the following steps: make an independent estimate of government spending, business investment, exports and imports; add in knowledge about the consumption function to get a consistent estimate of consumer spending and GNP; cross-check this projection in various ways and, if you discover weaknesses, go through the first two steps again; when you are satisfied with the forecast of *money* GNP, convert this to a forecast of *real* GNP by estimating the probable change in the price level.

Policies for Economic Stability

> The chief difficulty Alice found at first was with her flamingo: . . . generally, just as she had got its neck straightened out, and was going to give the hedgehog a blow with its head, it *would* twist itself round and look up in her face.
>
> *Alice's Adventures in Wonderland*

MUST WE CONTINUE to ride the swings of the business cycle? Must we look forward to periods when millions are unemployed against their will and the economy operates well below capacity? What can be done to maintain a higher and stabler level of output?

These have always been central issues of economic policy. And while the American economy today seems stabler than before 1940, it is not so stable that we can be complacent. Even a small downswing in the United States sends tremors through the world economy and strengthens Marxist predictions of the eventual doom of capitalism. We should not stabilize the American economy just to help other countries or to confute the communists. But these would be valuable by-products of an effort which is worthwhile for its own sake.

THE MULTIPLE OBJECTIVES OF POLICY

Policies aimed at capacity operation of the economy must take account of the fact that this is not the *only* objective. We are interested also in long-term economic growth, in price stability, in maintaining a decentralized market economy, and a variety of other things. These other objectives influence what it is wise to do on the stabilization front.

Economic Growth

We obviously do not want stable production *at the same level year after year*. With population and labor force rising, this would mean a steady increase in unemployment. We want stability *along a rising trend line*.

For the most part the objectives of capacity operation and rapid growth run in the same direction. A recession brings a drop in plant and equipment investment. This slows up the growth of capacity and drags down the long-run trend of production. Preventing recessions would mean a higher average level of investment and thus a faster growth of capacity over the long run.

It is possible, however, that policies adopted to promote stability could react unfavorably on growth. Since swings in business investment contribute so heavily to the business cycle, stability would be increased by *reducing* the share of investment in GNP. One could try to reduce corporate profits, to discourage household saving, and so on. But if these policies succeeded in reducing saving and investment, they would also reduce the growth rate, and we would be in danger of ending up with the stability of stagnation.

Price Stability

Here there is a real problem of choice. And one does not solve the problem by chanting the formula "we want full employment *and* stable prices." This is about as useful as spinning a Tibetan prayer wheel.

The nature of the problem was explained in Chapter 19. Capacity operation and price stability are both *matters of degree*. Employment may be more or less full. Prices may be more or less stable. And the two objectives are inversely related. Beyond some point, forcing down unemployment involves greater risk of price increase. Conversely, insistence on completely stable prices may require a considerable margin of unemployment.

This is such an awkward dilemma that everyone would like to find some way around it. Some of the favorite suggestions will be considered later in this chapter. But it is doubtful that there is any way around the problem given our present institutional setting.

It is also the kind of problem on which no one is really neutral. A good way to frame the problem in your own mind is as follows: (*a*) Who is hurt, and how much are they hurt, by operating the economy 5 to 10 percent below capacity? (This is what we have been doing most of the time since 1953.) (*b*) Who is hurt, and how much are they hurt, by a rise in the price level of, say, 2 percent per year? (This might well result from a vigorous full-capacity policy.) Where does the balance of advantage lie?

A Decentralized Market Economy

The stability problem would be much simpler if the key economic decisions were made on a centralized basis. If investment decisions were made by a central planning board, there would be no reason for investment to fluctuate sharply from year to year. If price and wage changes required approval from Washington, the upcreep of prices would be easier to handle. This is the way we do operate during war periods, and note that during such periods it has been possible to attain very high levels of production without any drastic rise in prices.

The preponderant opinion, however, is that we don't want to operate this way in peacetime. We feel there are economic and political advantages in having economic decisions made by millions of independent producing units. But while this is advantageous in most respects, it involves some costs. It is trickier to maintain high-level operation in this sort of economy than in a centrally planned economy.

THE OBJECTIVE OF CAPACITY OPERATION

Production below capacity constitutes economic waste. It means reduced investment and a lower rate of economic growth. It means reduced output of consumer goods and lower living standards. It means idleness and worry for many wage-earners, and frustration for business executives who find sales and profits falling despite their best efforts. Farmers, storekeepers, professional men, and dividend recipients feel the bite. Preventing depression is not simply an act of kindness to wage-earners. It benefits almost everyone and is one of the most widely accepted objectives of economic policy.

The objective of capacity operation is often described as *full employment*. A drop in employment of labor typically means a drop in the utilization of plant capacity and other resources. And from a statistical standpoint it is easier to add up units of labor than to add up plant capacity for a variety of heterogeneous products. The level of employment is a convenient thermometer reading of economic activity.

The objective of full employment does not imply that everyone in the economy will be able to keep his *present* job, in his *present* community, at his *present* wage rate. In an economy as large and dynamic as that of the United States, millions of jobs are bound to be disappearing every year. Old companies and jobs go out of existence for all the reasons outlined in Part One. New plants and new jobs appear, possibly across the street, possibly two thousand miles away.

A full employment policy involves an effort to sustain *total* demand at such a level that the number of new jobs appearing on the scene will at least equal the number disappearing. In a growing economy, the number of new jobs must be greater than this to absorb the annual increase in the labor force. For every worker losing a job or entering the labor force, there should be a vacant job somewhere in the system.

Because of the unavoidable turnover of the labor force, full employment does not mean that everybody in the system will be at work every day. It takes time for people to move from depressed areas to communities where employment is expanding. In seasonal industries such as agriculture, forestry, and construction, there is bound to be some loss of time in the slack season. Unemployment for such reasons is usually called *normal* or *frictional* unemployment. If actual unemployment is no higher than this, we say that full employment has been attained.

How large is this unavoidable minimum of unemployment? The answer varies with the size and diversity of the country, and with the efficiency of labor market institutions for helping workers transfer to new jobs. In the United States, something like 3 percent of the labor force is often taken as a reasonable estimate of frictional unemployment.[1] But in some of the smaller countries, such as Britain and Sweden, it seems possible to get along with between 1 and 2 percent.

While changes in the unemployment rate are a good indication of the direction in which the economy is moving, they are not a reliable guide to the gap between capacity operation of the economy and the actual level of operation. If the rate of full-time unemployment is 6 percent, and the frictional minimum is regarded as 3 percent, one cannot conclude that the economy is 3 percent below capacity. More likely, it is 8 to 10 percent below capacity.

The reason is partly that the number of full-time unemployed understates the supply of labor which would become available under conditions of adequate demand. As demand rises, full-time unemployed are rehired, people who have been reduced to part-time work against their will are able to get more work, some additional people are tempted into or (in the case of older people) retained in the labor force because of the ready availability of jobs, and scheduled work hours are apt to be lengthened somewhat. Thus the supply of man-hours can rise by considerably more than the 3 percent of excess labor which was apparently available at the start of the process. Moreover, an upswing usually brings a considerable increase in the man-hour output of workers already employed. The moral is that one should not be lulled into complacency by a small visible surplus of labor, and hence aim at an unduly low output target.

Can one in fact hope to hold the economy continuously near full capacity? In an economy as decentralized as ours, the answer seems to

---

[1] But note again that this implies a factual judgment and an expression of preference about the behavior of prices. During World War II we reduced unemployment to less than 1 percent by raising total demand to a quite inflationary level. Strictly, one should perhaps speak always of *desirable* employment rather than *full* employment.

be "No." A more realistic and feasible objective might be defined as follows:

a) To encourage vigorous upswings which will carry all the way to full employment. If an upswing threatens to overshoot the mark, which is not a danger in the American economy at most times, ways must be found to taper it off gracefully without provoking a drop in output.

b) To detect a downswing as early as possible, and to take steps which will break the force of the downswing and reverse it after a short time.

The instruments available for pursuit of this objective fall into three categories:

1. *Institutional reform*, which changes the structure of the economy so as to promote economic stability. The reform of commercial banking in 1913 through establishment of the Federal Reserve System is a good example.

2. *Built-in stability*, which operates automatically to check the momentum of upswings and downswings. The degree of built-in stability can be increased through tax legislation and other measures.

3. *Discretionary action*, which includes deliberate actions taken on an *ad hoc* basis after a downswing (or an undesirably strong upswing) has been detected. Monetary policy and fiscal policy are the prime candidates here; but there is often a question as to which should be used or in what proportions the two should be combined. This can be termed the problem of the *policy mix*.

INSTITUTIONAL REFORM

The favorite target of reform proposals is the monetary system. The fact that the banking system can lend several times the amount of its free reserves makes for expansion of demand deposits during an upswing. On the downswing, loans are repaid faster than new loans are issued, and the money supply shrinks. The credit structure expands and contracts like an accordion. It is argued that this aggravates economic fluctuations, making booms higher and depressions deeper than they would otherwise be.

Some economists have concluded that the remedy is to take the play out of the system by removing the banks' power to create money. One way to do this would be through a system of *100 percent reserves*, under which a bank would be required to hold a dollar of reserves against every dollar of demand deposits. If bank reserves rose by a billion dollars, demand deposits could rise by just that billion, not five billion or so as they can do at present. Since the Federal Reserve System can change bank reserves at will, it would have firm control over the money supply.

But what about the Federal Reserve System itself? The Board of Governors consists of fallible mortals. How can one be sure that they will do the right thing at the right time? Some proponents of monetary reform argue that Federal Reserve actions have often been misguided, and that the System has made little contribution to economic stability.

This leads to the suggestion that, instead of trusting to human judgment, one should bind the system to follow a definite "monetary rule." Suppose the output capacity of the economy is expected to increase by 4 percent a year. Then maintenance of price stability over the long run requires that total spending, the MV of the quantity equation, should rise at about the same rate. Assuming that V will remain reasonably stable, one might instruct the Federal Reserve to increase bank reserves (and thus the potential money supply) by precisely 4 percent, year in and year out.

This proposal has the attractiveness of any automatic device. No longer need the Board of Governors lie awake nights worrying about the next step in monetary policy. They need only follow the rule. But how effective would such a rule be? Whatever may be true in the long run, the velocity of money is certainly not stable in the short run. It shows a marked tendency to rise during business upswings and to fall during downswings. This amounts to saying that individuals and businesses have some latitude in their spending plans. Spending does *not* depend only on the amount of money in one's possession.

A smooth expansion of the money supply, then, would not necessarily produce a steady increase in spending. Nor would it prevent spending from dropping occasionally for the same reasons for which it drops at present. True, if spending dropped and the Federal Reserve continued doggedly to increase bank reserves according to the rule, there would be a rise in the lending capacity of the banking system. But this situation, while favorable to economic recovery, will not by itself initiate recovery. It takes borrowers as well as lenders to bring about an expansion of bank loans, and the presence of excess reserves does not directly affect the incentive to borrow.

These are limitations of *any* sort of monetary policy, whether discretionary or automatic. But it is not clear that an automatic formula gets around them more successfully than the present exercise of discretion by the Board of Governors. It is doubtful that there is any foolproof gyroscope which will relieve us of the necessity of using judgment and making occasional mistakes in monetary management.

STRENGTHENING THE BUILT-IN STABILIZERS

Built-in stabilizers have the great advantage that you don't have to think about them. It is not necessary to predict that a downswing is coming, in which case you may be wrong, or to wait until you are sure that a downswing is underway, in which case you may be several months too late. As soon as there is any drop in national income, the stabilizers operate immediately to brake the momentum of the decline.

It is important to underline that the stabilizers *operate in both directions*. We applaud them when they act to slow down a downswing. But we must not forget that they also act as brakes on an upswing and may stop it short of full employment. Starting from a position of under-employment, and with strong built-in stabilizers at work, it takes a larger initial push to propel the economy up to full employment than would be necessary otherwise. The system is more sluggish upward as well as downward.

The Budget as Stabilizer

This subject was explored in Chapter 20, and we need only underline the main points made there. A large public sector increases the stability of the economy for several reasons:

1. The existence of taxes means that disposable income rises less rapidly than national income during an upswing and falls less rapidly during a down-swing. Taxation reduces the value of the multiplier and thus makes the economy less responsive to any autonomous change in spending. This is true particularly of income taxes, but it is also true in lesser measure of sales taxes, excises, and most other taxes. Only a tax such as the poll tax, whose yield is independent of income, would fail to have any stabilizing effect.

2. Government purchases of goods and services are inherently stable. They do not respond appreciably to short-term fluctuations in national in-come. Thus the government budget has a stabilizing effect on the expenditure side as well as the tax side.

3. Transfer payments fluctuate in a stabilizing fashion over the cycle. Payments for unemployment compensation, pensions, relief, farm price sup-ports, and the like typically rise in recession and fall in prosperity, thus helping to offset swings in personal income.

One should not conclude that unemployment compensation rates should be raised, or that the level of public services should be higher, or that income taxation should be substituted increasingly for sales taxation *just* because these changes would increase economic stability. But one can say that the effect on economic stability is a *relevant consideration* in judging a proposed tax or expenditure change. A proposal which will in-crease stability should receive some bonus points on this score.

The changes which have occurred in federal taxes and expenditures since 1940 have been in a strongly stabilizing direction. Some interesting calculations on this point have been made by Duesenberry, Eckstein, and Fromm.[2] They work with a simulated model of the economy; but the model is designed to be realistic, and the results correspond closely to the actual course of events during the recession of 1957–58. One of their illus-trations assumes a moderate recession, set off by a drop of about $9 billion in autonomous demand (business plant and equipment expenditures, construction, and government purchases). This produces a drop of $7 bil-lion in the rate of inventory investment. Total investment falls by $16 billion. By the usual multiplier reasoning, one might expect a substantial drop in GNP. It turns out, however, that GNP falls only about $20 bil-

---

[2] James S. Duesenberry, Otto Eckstein, and Gary Fromm, "A Simulation of the United States Economy in Recession," *Econometrica*, October, 1960, pp. 749–810.

lion. Even more striking, personal consumption falls by only $4 billion, or a bit more than 1 percent.

What takes up the slack? The detailed calculations are shown in Table 24–1. The three most important stabilizers turn out to be: (1) a drop

TABLE 24–1

Hypothetical Behavior of the U.S. Economy in Mild Recession
(Billions of Dollars)

	PEAK QUARTER OF UPSWING	LOW QUARTER OF DOWNSWING
1. GNP	440.0	419.7
minus		
2. Depreciation	37.4	39.3
3. Indirect business taxes	37.1	37.1
4. Subsidies and statistical discrepancy	1.7	0.5
5. Corporate income taxes	20.9	16.4
6. Retained corporate earnings	7.4	4.1
7. Contributions to social insurance	14.6	13.8
plus		
8. Transfers	26.0	29.7
equals		
9. Personal income	346.9	338.2
minus		
10. Personal taxes	43.6	42.0
equals		
11. Disposable income	303.3	296.2
minus		
12. Personal saving	19.7	16.6
equals		
13. Consumption	283.6	279.6
plus		
14. Inventory change	plus 2.3	minus 5.3
plus		
15. Autonomous demand	154.1	145.4
equals		
16. GNP	440.0	419.7

of $4.5 billion in corporate income taxes, following from the sharp drop in corporate profits which typically occurs during recession; (2) a drop of $3.3 billion in business saving. This follows from the practice of holding dividend rates fairly stable through good years and bad, so that a drop in profit after taxes shows up almost entirely as a drop in retained earnings; (3) a rise of $3.7 billion in transfer payments, which adds to personal income.

The personal income tax also has a stabilizing effect, tax payments falling by $1.6 billion; but this is smaller than the three effects just listed. Why is this? It is because the three other stabilizers do such a good job that there is only a moderate drop in personal income. Most of the stabilizing effect, in other words, has occurred before one hits the safety net of the personal income tax. But if the drop of personal income were larger, the stabilizing effect of the income tax would be greater.

Strengthening the Budget Stabilizers

The most promising area for further progress on this front is probably the state unemployment compensation systems. In particular, it seems desirable to:

1. Raise the average level of benefit rates. The system was designed in the 1930's to offset half of the earnings lost by a worker during unemployment. Since that time wage levels have risen greatly and benefit rates have failed to keep pace. In many states at present the benefit payments offset 40 percent or less of the earnings loss. A general increase of benefit scales is desirable to restore at least the original 50 percent proportion.

2. Provide for a temporary lengthening of the benefit period during cycle downswings. In most states a worker can draw benefits for no more than 26 weeks. During both the 1957–58 and 1960–61 downswings, the federal government advanced money to the states to help them extend the period to 39 weeks for the duration of the recession. This was regarded as an emergency action, however, and required special legislation. It seems preferable to have standing legislation which would extend the benefit period automatically when unemployment reaches a certain level, and then reduce it again as unemployment shrinks.

These steps, in addition to their direct benefit to the unemployed, would put more money into circulation on the downswing and thus work in a stabilizing direction.

Greater Stability of Business Investment

Business investment is one of the less stable elements in the economy at present. Discussions of stabilization policy often accept wide swings of business investment as inevitable, and concentrate solely on ways of offsetting them. But we should not give up this easily. If ways could be found to reduce the instability of private investment, this would strike directly at the heart of the business cycle.

It is not useful to exhort business executives to regularize their investment for the sake of economic stability, if by so doing they would make less money for their companies. An effective program must make it *worthwhile* for companies to behave in a way which contributes to overall stability.

It might be possible to change the corporate income tax laws so as to do one or both of the following things:

1. *Smooth out the present wide fluctuations of profits after taxes.* This would even out companies' *ability* to invest, which might lead to greater stability in their investment spending.

One possiblity would be a liberal provision for *carry back of losses*. Suppose a company suffers a net loss in 1963 but had profits in the previous five years and paid full tax on them. The company could be allowed to re-open its tax returns for previous years, deduct the 1963 loss from the earlier profits, recalculate its tax liabilities, and claim a refund from the government. This procedure would raise companies' incomes and increase their ability to invest in poor years.

A second possibility would be systematic variation of the period over which companies are allowed to depreciate their plant and equipment. These periods are already closely controlled by rulings of the Internal Revenue Service, and these rulings could be altered according to the stage of the business cycle. During depression, depreciation periods could be shortened. This would raise the annual depreciation charge, which would reduce a company's calculated profits and its income tax liabilities, which would leave the company with more cash in hand. This should have a stimulating effect on investment. During periods of high prosperity, the Internal Revenue Service could be authorized to move in the opposite direction. It could lengthen depreciation periods, which would force companies to pay higher income taxes and leave them with less cash for investment.

This would actually be a clumsy way of varying the corporate income tax, raising it on the upswing and lowering it on the downswing. But it might be politically more palatable than a direct variation of the tax rate, because it seems more mysterious. Moreover, such a system would have greatest leverage on industries with large amounts of plant and equipment. These are presumably the best prospects for future investment in plant and equipment, and hence are the industries one wants to affect.

2. *Provide a direct inducement for companies to spread their investment more evenly over good years and bad.* One system, which is used in Sweden, permits companies to carry over part of their earnings in good years for investment during depression. The Swedish system provides that a company can earmark its profits, up to a specified maximum, as a special reserve for future investment. The incentive is that profits put into the reserve are exempt from corporate income tax. When unemployment figures reveal that a recession is on, the government announces that companies can take money from these reserves and invest it in plant and equipment. This policy is continued for as long as the recession continues. If a company does not use its reserve within a certain period of years, or if it uses it for purposes other than investment, it becomes liable for income tax on the amount involved.

DISCRETIONARY ACTION

The proposals made to this point would probably not be regarded as stabilization policy by the man in the street. If prices are rising too fast or unemployment is too high many people begin to ask, "Why doesn't the government do something?" By "doing something" they mean specific, *ad hoc* actions to check and reverse undesirable movements in the economy. The main measures which can be used are monetary controls, tax changes, and changes in government expenditure.

The weakness of discretionary action is that it requires discretion. Someone must detect an undesirable degree of inflation or deflation, figure out what might be done about it, and then try to do it. This raises problems of the *timing* of action and the *strength* of action.

The timing of action. If economic forecasting were an accurate science, it might be possible to diagnose potential trouble well in advance and have corrective measures waiting at the right time. But forecasting is not very accurate, and we are normally in the position of locking the barn door after the horse is some distance down the road.

There is loss of time for three reasons. First, it takes time to make sure that a turning point in the economy has actually occurred. Second, after trouble has been diagnosed, it takes time to work out corrective policies and get approval for them from the administration and from Congress. Third, discretionary actions require time to have their full impact on the economy.

There is thus an *information* lag, a *decision* lag, and an *impact* lag. The total of these can scarcely be less than a year. Considering the speed of economic events, this makes discretionary action a blunt instrument against the cycle. There is the awkward possibility that action taken at one stage of the cycle will come to fruition at a later stage when its effects will be in the wrong direction.

The strength of stabilizing action. Monetary and fiscal medicine can be given in larger or smaller doses. How does one decide what dosage is required at a particular time?

It might seem that one need look only at how far the economy is away from the desired target position. If the unemployment rate is 8 percent, one should take stronger action than if it is 6 percent. This is correct as far as it goes, but two other things must also be considered. One must look at *how long the disequilibrium has persisted*. Stronger action is necessary if 8 percent unemployment has existed for a year than if it has existed only three months. One must also consider the *direction of movement* in the economy. If the unemployment level is 8 percent and *falling*, this will indicate different actions than would be appropriate if unemployment were 8 percent and *rising*.

These considerations must be weighed together in determining how strong an expansionist or contractionist line the government should take.[3] Moreover, since each of these indicators is constantly changing, policy

---

[3] For an interesting discussion of this problem in terms of engineering control systems, see Day and Beza, *op. cit.*, Chap. 27.

must be under constant review and should be adjusted at frequent intervals. This argues in favor of measures which can be altered quickly and by small degrees, and against measures which take a long time to initiate.

MONETARY POLICY

Little need be added to what was said about monetary policy in Chapter 22. Monetary policy is a one-way street in the sense that it operates more effectively on the upswing than on the downswing. It is useful mainly in controlling a boom which is putting undue pressure on the price level. Here it has the advantage of being applicable in small doses. Credit can be tightened gradually through open market sales and interest rate increases. Carried far enough, credit tightening can always compel a reduction of bank lending and of investment. It can be argued also that monetary policy is neutral in the sense of not discriminating by name against specific borrowers or investment projects.

But monetary policy does not operate as promptly as is sometimes supposed. Changes in monetary policy are usually made some time *after* a turning point in economic activity. The new policy of credit ease or restriction is usually applied by small steps over a period of 6 to 12 months. And it takes considerable time for a change in credit terms to affect the volume of investment activity. In the case of credit loosening, it takes time for borrowers to react to the change in rates, time for new projects to be planned and initiated, and time for activity on these projects to reach peak proportions.[4]

The length of these lags is disconcerting. In the "twelve-month recessions" which have characterized the American economy since 1945, monetary policy can scarcely act fast enough to have much effect until *after* the tide has turned. In a two to three year expansion, monetary policy becomes effective mainly during the last half of the upswing. But there is danger that the restrictive effect exercised at this time will spill over into the subsequent recession when it is no longer appropriate.

The neutrality of monetary policy has also been questioned. Credit restriction bears harder on industries which depend on borrowing than on those which can use internal financing. It hits housing and state and local construction more heavily than manufacturing, and it hits small young companies harder than well-established concerns. Is it desirable that these particular activities, rather than others, be curtailed because total demand is too high? Complaints in Congress against "tight money" as a method of economic control may be partially misinformed, but they cannot be considered altogether unreasonable.

There is another long-range consideration. Monetary policy oper-

---

[4] Thomas Mayer, "The Inflexibility of Monetary Policy," *Review of Economics and Statistics*, Vol. XL, No. 4 (November, 1958), pp. 358–74. See, however, the critique of this article by Lloyd D. Orr, *Review of Economics and Statistics*, Vol. XLII, No. 3, Part I (August, 1960), pp. 329–31.

ates mainly by imposing periodic checks on the growth of private investment. In order to control total demand, the investment component of demand is restricted. Many people are concerned, however, because the growth rate of the United States economy since 1950 has been considerably lower than that of Western Europe, Japan, and most other industrial nations. This is attributed partly to a relatively low level of investment in the United States. If we need more investment over the long run, should we rely heavily on a policy instrument which operates by restricting investment? Might it not be preferable to stimulate investment through a low interest policy, and to use taxes to drain off any excess of demand at cycle peaks?

FISCAL POLICY

The automatic stabilizing effect of the government budget may need to be strengthened on occasion by deliberate action. The possibilities are clear: vary tax rates, vary transfer payments, vary public expenditures. What is the relative role of these three devices?

Varying Tax Rates

One can make a strong case that fiscal policy should rely *mainly* on tax changes rather than expenditure changes. This would mean lowering tax rates in periods of insufficient demand and raising rates when demand threatens to become excessive.

There are two reasons for preferring to rely mainly on tax changes. First, the tax structure is inherently more flexible. A change in personal income tax rates affects disposable income immediately because of the withholding system. A change in corporate income taxes affects income with only a short lag. Most of the expenditure budget, on the other hand, is quite rigid. Military expenditures, the regular government payroll, and interest payments on the national debt cannot be raised or lowered each time there is a turn in the business cycle. Even where expenditures can be varied, as on construction projects, it may take a year or more to produce a substantial change.

In addition to this argument of convenience, there is an argument of principle. The proper level of public services should be determined by long-run priorities, as explained in Chapter 15. If the decision has been made correctly, it will be little influenced by changing phases of the business cycle.

A depression involves a drop in private incomes, private spending, and consumer living standards. There is no reason to think that this makes people want a sudden increase in government services. What they mainly want is more money in their pockets so they can buy more of the things they were able to buy at the peak of prosperity. This desire can be met by reducing tax schedules, leaving people with more money to spend, and letting them spend it as they will.

The opposite policy of offsetting recessions by raising public expenditures contains obvious dangers. There is a danger of putting manpower and materials into things which the public does not particularly want, when by tax reductions the same resources could be channeled into things which people do want. There is also a danger of bringing about permanent increases in the scope of government activity accidentally rather than through deliberate choice. It is notoriously easier to expand government activities than to curtail them, and so decisions on this front should be based on long-run rather than cyclical considerations.

The prime candidate for a policy of tax variation is the personal income tax, which contributes such a high percentage of federal revenues. Fiscal experts have frequently advocated that the President be given power to vary income tax rates within prescribed limits, somewhat as the Federal Reserve System varies the discount rate. These changes could be geared to some indicator of economic activity. One could provide, for example, that for each 1 percent increase in the unemployment rate, the basic rate on the first bracket of taxable income would be reduced by 1 percent. Duesenberry, Eckstein, and Fromm (*op. cit.*) suggest a formula based on the percentage decline in GNP rather than the rise in the unemployment rate. They present illustrative calculations showing that this would have a substantial braking effect during recession. Alternatively, adjustments within the prescribed limits could be left to the discretion of the President.

A concrete proposal of this sort was submitted to Congress by President Kennedy in 1962. But Congress, jealous of its taxing power and anxious to receive credit for any tax reductions, has shown little willingness to approve such proposals.

Varying Transfer Payments

Fluctuations in transfer payments over the business cycle are largely automatic and should remain so. The stabilizing effect might be strengthened, however, by the changes already suggested in the unemployment compensation system. The extension of the benefit period to 39 weeks during the 1957–58 recession added about half a billion dollars to consumer incomes.

Another possibility is to speed up payment of money to which people are already entitled. When President Kennedy took office in 1961 during a mild downswing, a prominent economist was given a White House office and some simple instructions: "Get out the money." He was not expected to print money or to give it away without cause, but to expedite payments which would eventually be made anyway. For example, several million veterans were due to receive dividend payments on their wartime insurance policies. Through this man's activities, they received them in April rather than September. Refunds on 1960 income tax payments were expedited, and various other things were done. This acceleration of cash payments had a helpful effect on the recession.

Varying Public Expenditures

Government is involved year in and year out in spending on schools, hospitals, public buildings, streets and sewers, highways, irrigation and flood control projects, soil conservation and reforestation, slum control and urban redevelopment, atomic energy installations, and military facilities. These items add up to many billions each year—money which is going to be spent anyway, at one time or another. Could we not use this large volume of spending as a stabilizing influence, speeding it up during recession when private demand is low and cutting it back as the private economy recovers?

This seems like a sensible thing to do wherever feasible. In addition to its stabilizing effect, it might save the government money by bunching expenditures in slump periods when costs are relatively low. But one should not be overoptimistic about how much can actually be done. There are several difficulties:

1. Postponing work of high social priority during prosperity will cause a good deal of inconvenience. A nice type of depression project would be repairing pot holes in streets and highways. This is necessary work and uses a good deal of labor. It can be started up and tapered off rapidly, thus meeting the test of flexible timing. If one leaves all pot holes to be filled in the next depression, however, there will soon be a lot of broken springs and a great public outcry. Or consider the rapid increase in the need for school buildings since World War II. If we were willing to wait for a depression, many of the unemployed could usefully be put to work building schools. But meanwhile children would be sitting on each others' knees.

2. It takes time to get large construction projects in motion. Even after funds have been approved, sites must be acquired, specifications drawn, bids requested and contracts let, and the contractor must assemble the necessary work force and materials. On some projects one will get no expenditures during the first six months or even the first twelve months. It has been calculated that for public construction as a whole, only 32 per-cent of expenditures occur during the first year after authorization of the project, while subsequent expenditures may linger on for three or four years. Thus there is danger that projects initiated to check depression will get going just in time to add to inflation during the next boom.[5]

3. Countercyclical timing of public works requires budgets running beyond a single year. One needs an approved capital budget for several years ahead, with actual expenditures to be timed in the light of economic conditions. Congress has usually been reluctant to relax its year-to-year control over expenditures. Long-range approval was given, however, for

---

[5] Robert A. Dahl and Charles E. Lindblom, "Variation in Public Expenditure," in Max F. Millikan (ed.), *Income Stabilization for a Developing Democracy* (New Haven, Conn.: Yale University Press, 1953), pp. 347–96.

the federal-state superhighway program, which involves a prospective expenditure of more than $30 billion over a fifteen-year period. This made it possible to speed up highway construction during the slack years 1958 and 1961.

In addition to what can be done with normal public expenditures, there is sometimes pressure during recession to start extraordinary works programs. These include projects which are not of high priority by normal standards, but which will put people to work, get money in circulation, and yield some social benefit from resources presently unemployed. It seems unwise to undertake such projects for cyclical reasons alone, unless they are also considered to be worthwhile on a long-term basis. This is not the only way or the best way of getting unemployed resources back to work. Priority should be given to stimulating private consumption and investment through tax policy, and to shifting normal public works forward to an earlier date.

The Record of Fiscal Policy

As one looks back over the past 20 years, a striking conclusion emerges. Economists have been virtually unanimous that fiscal policy can be a powerful tool for economic stabilization. The learned journals have resounded with debate over just how the fiscal medicine should be applied. But has anyone been listening? The record reveals little use of discretionary fiscal action. Despite exhortation from the sidelines, the federal government seems to have been carrying on "business as usual."

Consider what happened during the recession of 1957–58. At the peak, in the third quarter of 1957, the federal budget surplus was running at an annual rate of $2.6 billion. At the bottom, in the second quarter of 1958, the government was running a deficit of $10.9 billion. This turnaround of $13.5 billion in the federal budget position certainly helped check the recession, but it was not brought about by discretionary action. There was no action at all on the tax side. Discretionary changes on the expenditure side are estimated at $1.5 billion—the special unemployment compensation program already mentioned, some acceleration of highway construction, some speed-up of other normal public works, and a few other items. The main factor was the operation of the automatic stabilizers —a drop of $6 billion in tax receipts and an increase of $3 billion in transfer payments under normal programs. There were also increases of several billion in defense and other regular government expenditures, but these increases had been planned before the recession and were unrelated to it.[6]

A study of the period 1945–59 concludes that "discretionary tax changes have not been employed even in the face of strong recessionary and inflationary developments throughout the economy." Sizable tax re-

---

[6] For a fuller account of this experience, see U.S. Bureau of the Budget, *Federal Fiscal Behavior During the Recession of 1957–58*, Washington, January, 1961 (mimeo).

ductions in 1948 and 1954 helped to moderate the recessions of 1949–50 and 1953–54, but this was accidental. The tax reductions were not made for that reason. On the expenditure side, the study concludes that "changes in the volume and character of Federal Government demand, particularly for defense purposes, have been an important source of economic instability." Changes in defense spending have been quite abrupt and, except during the Korean War, have not been accompanied by tax changes sufficient to offset their disturbing effect.[7]

Why has the federal government, and particularly the Congress, declined to do what economists prescribe? The answer is deeprooted in politics and administration. On the political side, it is difficult to separate debate over the *level* of taxation from debate over the *composition* of tax revenues. Suppose one could get agreement that federal revenues should be cut by $5 billion to stimulate economic recovery. The next question is *whose* taxes should be cut, and by how much? Each Congressman will have his favorite customers. Those who worry about the low-income groups may want to cut first-bracket tax rates or increase the exemption for dependents. Representatives from silk stocking districts may want to reduce the rates on higher brackets. Those who are concerned about business investment may suggest cutting the corporate income tax. Industries subject to excise taxes will launch a campaign to get these eliminated.

Thus any proposal to change the level of federal taxation leads to a struggle over who shall be benefited or penalized. Congressmen are unwilling to give up their right to engage in such struggles by turning over authority to the President. They are also unwilling to give up the political advantage of claiming credit for any tax changes which benefit important groups of voters.

The expenditure side of the budget is similarly enmeshed in politics. There are always members of Congress who feel that the level of public services is too low and that public expenditure should be increased as a matter of principle. During recession, when there is need for greater expenditure from *some* source, this argument is likely to be pushed with particular vigor. It may be presented as an antirecession argument, and as such it can be discounted. But at bottom the argument is that the long-term choices have *not* been correctly made, that the public sector is underdeveloped, and that "now is a good time to catch up." This is a legitimate political issue, and Congress will not forego its right to debate it each time from the ground up.

On the administrative side, a major weakness is the lack of central budget-making machinery in the Congress. The Executive branch has a "fiscal general staff" in the Bureau of the Budget, which is attached directly to the President's office. But Congress has no similar coordinating

---

[7] Joint Economic Committee, U.S. Congress, *Staff Report on Employment, Growth, and Price Levels*, Washington, 1959, pp. 215–16.

machinery. Both House and Senate get into the act. Within each chamber, revenues are considered by one committee while expenditures are considered by a host of subcommittees dealing with various agencies. Congress never considers the budget as a whole. No one plans the overall surplus or deficit. It "just happens," and often comes out a good distance from what the President originally recommended.

There are possible reforms which might improve this situation: an overall House-Senate committee on the budget, which would examine revenues and expenditures simultaneously, set overall expenditure goals, and give some guidance to the numerous appropriations subcommittees; a professional staff working under this Committee, and comparable to the Budget Bureau on the Executive side; and greater flexibility for the President to vary the expenditure of approved funds, instead of being tied to a rigid annual cycle under which each year's money must be spent by June thirtieth. But any proposal for greater centralization within Congress or greater discretion for the President reduces the influence of the individual Congressman over the spending of money. It is easy to see why such proposals face tough opposition in Congress and are slow to be adopted. But until more has been done in this direction, fiscal policy cannot begin to realize its potential usefulness as a stabilization instrument.

TWO SPECIAL PROBLEMS

This completes our general analysis of stabilization policy. But we must add a postscript on two special problems: coping with cost or sellers' inflation, and reconciling internal and external economic balance.

Sellers' Inflation

"Classical inflation" originates in an excess of money demand. The amount of money which consumers, businesses, and government wish to spend, at the current level of prices, exceeds the physical capacity of the economy. Something has to give, and this turns out to be the price level, which is pulled upward by the tug of excess demand.

Excess demand is not the only possible reason for a rising price level. Prices may also be pushed upward by spontaneous increases in costs, particularly labor costs. Suppose trade unions secure wage increases which exceed the average rate of productivity increase in the economy, so that labor cost per unit of output rises. Business concerns will reason that product prices should be raised to cover these higher costs; and in industries characterized by monopoly or cooperative oligopoly, they will be able to do this. Workers with their higher wages can afford to pay the higher prices, and all seems to be well.

But according to our reasoning about money in earlier chapters, the monetary circulation must also be increased. Otherwise interest rates will rise, spending will be reduced, and unemployment will develop. The monetary authorities must either accept responsibility for unemployment which they had no direct hand in creating, or increase the money supply sufficiently to finance capacity production at the higher price level. In a democratic community with a large labor vote, there will be strong pressure to choose the latter course. Thus the monetary brake on inflation may be removed, and the price level may come to depend largely on the size of wage increases.

The danger should not be exaggerated. Union leaders are not obsessed by money wage increases. Even if they were, occasional recessions plus the varying profits of particular companies and industries would impose some check on wage demands. Nor are most American industries fully unionized. Nor is monopoly and cooperative oligopoly the general rule in product markets. Nor are the monetary authorities entirely supine. Yet one cannot rule out the possibility that "cost push" may be an important factor in the economy at certain times.

What could be done to reduce the danger of this kind of inflationary pressure? The outlook is rather discouraging. The things which can be done are not clearly effective and the things which would be effective are undesirable or unlikely to be adopted. The commonest proposals include:

1. Government exhortation of union leaders to be reasonable in their wage demands, and also government exhortation of business executives to refrain from price increases. This cannot be dismissed as completely ineffective. In 1962, for example, the administration persuaded the United Steelworkers to accept a wage settlement lower than had been customary in previous years. When leading steel companies nonetheless announced a price increase, President Kennedy took a strong position against the increase and it was withdrawn. This sort of *ad hoc* intervention, however, can scarcely be recommended for everyday use.

2. Abolition of national unionism by providing that collective bargaining must be on a single-company basis. There is little chance of this proposal being seriously considered, and we argued in Chapter 13 that it is undesirable in principle.

3. Reducing business price fixing through vigorous antitrust action. While this is a desirable line of policy, one should not expect too much from it. Cooperative oligopoly is a particularly tough nut to crack.

4. Government control of wages and prices in key sectors of the economy. It would be hard, however, to reconcile any general yardstick for wage increases with the necessary and desirable diversity of wage movements in specific occupations and industries. In any event, Congress would scarcely authorize such controls in peacetime.

5. Upward pressure on wages and prices seems to originate in oligopolistic industries with considerable market power. So we may repeat the suggestion of Chapter 11 that such industries be kept under statistical surveillance by a government research organization. The facts about changes in wage rates, production costs, prices, and profits should

be determined and given wide publicity. The certainty of full publicity might exercise a cautionary effect on both unions and managements.

External Balance: The Problem in General

Most countries have extensive trading relations with other nations. In addition to maintaining internal balance between aggregate demand and aggregate supply, they must maintain balance between their foreign receipts and payments; and the interaction of these two requirements poses complex problems.

Suppose country A's imports show a persistent tendency to run ahead of its exports. What will happen? It is conceivable that the countries exporting to A may be willing to give away some of the goods. But trade relations are not normally conducted on a charity basis. The exporting countries may extend credit to A sufficient to cover the adverse trade balance, but there are limits to this process. If A continues to run an adverse trade balance year after year, it will eventually have to draw on its reserves of gold, dollars, pounds, or other "hard" (i.e., widely acceptable) currencies. As its reserves shrink, it must take corrective action to raise exports or cut imports. A prudent government will act well in advance of the danger point.

One might think that the reverse situation presents no difficulties. Suppose country B finds itself year after year exporting more than it imports. Is this a happy situation which can continue indefinitely? Not necessarily. For while the situation presents no difficulties for country B, it will raise difficulties for one or more other countries. If B is running a surplus, somebody else must be running a deficit. *All* countries cannot simultaneously export more than they import.

If B is willing to extend enough credit to cover its trade surplus, well and good. But if it insists on payment in hard cash, the game cannot continue forever. As other countries lose reserves, they will be forced to take corrective action, very likely by reducing their imports from B. If B is wise, it will forestall this by some adjustment of its own policies.

A good illustration is the recent position of West Germany. By holding down its price level more successfully than most other countries, and by effective salesmanship abroad, West Germany had succeeded by 1960 in building up a favorable export position. Exports were running substantially ahead of imports; and gold, dollars, and other currencies were flowing in at an almost embarrassing rate. But this meant a squeeze on other countries. The United States began to lose gold heavily, and Britain was also under serious pressure. So these countries suggested politely that Bonn change its policies. Bonn eventually agreed, though the adjustments were less drastic than other countries had requested.

Three main things were done in 1961: (1) The value of the German mark was *raised* relative to other currencies. This made German goods more expensive abroad and foreign goods cheaper in Germany, thus tending to cut German exports and raise imports. (2) Germany agreed to make substantial loans abroad, particularly to the less developed countries, thus financing part of the remaining export surplus.[8] (3) The tight money policy for which West Germany was famous during the fifties was relaxed. This was expected to produce a rise in the German price level, which would tend to raise imports and cut exports. Germany was thus sacrificing internal balance and permitting some inflation in the interest of a better external adjustment.

Let us go back to the unhappy position of a country with an unfavorable trade balance which cannot be allowed to continue. It must raise exports, or cut imports, or both. What to do? The possibilities include:

1. *Reduce the level of economic activity.* This will reduce domestic purchases of everything, including imports. This is an unpalatable remedy, particularly if the economy is already below full employment, and is unlikely to be adopted.

2. *Reduce domestic prices relative to foreign prices.* It is rarely possible to cut a country's price level. This would mean provoking a depression, and even then the fall in prices might be slight. But since the general trend of world prices is upward, a country may be able to hold back its price level sufficiently to secure a decline relative to levels in other countries. This is essentially what West Germany did during the fifties.

3. *Alter the rate of exchange.* The country can *depreciate*, i.e., reduce the value of its currency relative to those of other countries. This will make the country's products cheaper in other countries and thus increase the volume of exports. It also raises the domestic price of imported goods, which will reduce physical imports.

If this sounds tricky, reason it out with pencil and paper as we did in Chapter 16. Suppose that the dollar-pound exchange rate, presently at £1 = $2.80, were changed to £1 = $4.00. This would be a *depreciation* of the dollar, an *appreciation* of the pound. What would be the result? A British product worth £10, which formerly cost $28 in the United States, would now cost $40. People in the United States would buy less of it, and imports would fall. On the other hand, an American product worth $40, which previously cost £14.3 in Britain, would now cost only £10. Britishers would buy more of it, and U.S. exports to Britain would rise.[9]

---

[8] Before this point a curious thing had been happening. The United States has been providing billions of dollars to the less developed countries under the foreign aid program. These countries used part of this money to make cash purchases in West Germany, which offered lower prices on many items than the United States. West Germany ended up holding dollars, which could be used to draw gold from the United States as desired. It is not surprising that the American government eventually cried "No fair! If you want to export to the less developed countries, finance it yourself by lending them marks." This is what Bonn has in good measure now agreed to do.

[9] It is still not certain that the adverse balance of trade will be eliminated

4. *Seek long-term loans or grants.* If the balance of payments difficulties are regarded as temporary, and if the country's long-term borrowing power is strong, it may seek grants or loans to tide it over the emergency. The Marshall Plan grants to Britain and Western Europe after World War II helped to finance trade deficits which it was believed would be corrected, and which eventually were corrected, by the economic rehabilitation of these countries. At present it is mainly the less developed countries which are under chronic balance of payments pressure, and which are lined up at the lending windows of the developed countries.

5. *Impose direct controls on foreign trade.* Imports can always be reduced by sheer force. Tariffs can be raised to prohibitive levels. Alternatively, imports can be licensed or foreign exchange can be rationed according to some priority ranking of national needs. These direct interferences with freedom of trade are generally regarded as undesirable, but many of the less developed countries have resorted to them under pressure of necessity.

It is always possible by some combination of these measures to balance a country's external accounts. But these measures also affect the equilibrium level of income within the country. A country naturally gives first priority to full employment and economic development at home, and measures directed toward these objectives will sometimes work against the requirements of external balance. This complicates the problem of choosing a wise macroeconomic policy.

External Balance: The Recent U.S. Position

The United States has recently encountered two difficulties in its international economic relations. First, in each year since 1957 we have had a sizable deficit in our balance of payments. During 1958–60 this amounted to almost $4 billion a year, though it has now been considerably reduced. Second, New York has replaced London as the world's leading banking center. Foreigners hold about $25 billion of bank accounts and other short-term assets in the United States, which they can withdraw

---

Remember that the balance is calculated in money terms rather than in physical units. Even though our exports to Britain rise in physical terms, each item brings in fewer pounds than before because of the exchange revaluation. And though we buy fewer items from Britain, each costs more pounds than before for the same reason. Our balance of trade will be improved only if the favorable changes in physical terms are large enough to outweigh the adverse effect of the cheapening of our currency. The result depends, in short, on *elasticity of demand* in the two countries— elasticity of U.S. demand for British exports, and elasticity of British demand for U.S. exports. It can be shown that the trade balance will be improved only if the sum of the two elasticities is greater than one.

The actual size of export elasticities has been a subject of much debate. Students of international trade seem now to be of the opinion that exchange depreciation *will* improve the balance of trade position in most cases, but this cannot be laid down as a universal rule.

in gold whenever they choose. This poses a threat of a "run on the dollar" at some future time.

The balance of payments deficit does not arise from any weakness in our export position. On the contrary, our exports of civilian goods and services typically exceed our imports by $3–5 billion a year. But at the same time we have been turning over $7–8 billion a year to foreigners through our overseas military expenditures, government loans and grants under the foreign aid program, and foreign investment by U.S. business concerns. This means that foreigners' claims against us have been running considerably ahead of the counterclaims which we hold against them. This surplus of dollars they can either withdraw in gold or hold as bank accounts in New York. They usually do a bit of both. From the beginning of 1957 to the end of 1962, foreigners added about $10 billion to their holdings of short-term assets in the United States and also withdrew about $7 billion in gold.

A gold drain of this magnitude cannot continue indefinitely. Continued accumulation of foreign balances in New York is also worrisome, since the owners can demand payment in gold at any moment. We are still on the gold standard for international transactions. A U.S. bank depositor cannot come to his bank and ask to be paid off in gold. But a foreign depositor can do so, and the United States is obligated to make good.

What can be done to bring our international payments closer to balance? A number of possible steps can be ruled out: (1) An effort to devalue the dollar relative to other currencies would seriously damage our world position and would almost certainly not succeed, i.e., other countries would mark down their currencies to the same extent. (2) Nor can we suspend our obligation to pay off foreign creditors in gold on demand. Such an abandonment of the gold standard would be a body blow to the world monetary system. (3) We do not want to raise tariffs or impose other restrictions on imports from abroad. Apart from the general undesirability of trade restrictions, such a move would be self-defeating. Other countries would retaliate, and our exports would probably drop as much as our imports. (4) We do not want to cripple our foreign aid or overseas military programs. If these programs are desirable in themselves, they should not be abandoned simply for balance of payments reasons.

What possibilities of constructive action remain open? First, we can try to maintain and enlarge our trade surplus. This depends mainly on the efforts of U.S. business concerns to reduce costs through technical development, to improve product quality and design, and to sell effectively abroad. But government can make a contribution by discouraging increases in the U.S. price level, so that our sales prices will compare well with those of other industrial nations. Government tariff negotiators under the Trade Expansion Act of 1962 can also work to ensure our access to foreign markets on reasonable terms.

Second, we shall have to maintain short-term interest rates at a level reasonably comparable with Britain and Western Europe to discourage sudden shifts of short-term funds from New York to earn more abroad. This will sometimes conflict with a need to lower U.S. interest rates to stimulate recovery from recession, and a compromise will have to be struck. The seriousness of this conflict depends on how important short-term interest rates are as a factor in investment decisions, a matter on which there is wide difference of opinion.

Third, without abandoning our military and economic aid programs, these programs can be re-shaped to impose less strain on our payments position. Overseas military expenditures have already been reduced considerably, and can doubtless be reduced further by prudent management and by persuading our allies to assume a larger share of defense costs. Foreign economic aid can be tied, and already is largely tied, to shipments of American products. Alternatively, we can urge Britain, Germany, and other Western countries to give larger amounts of untied aid, some of which will be spent in the United States, so that the flow of payments will balance out.

In these and other ways it should be possible for us gradually to approach balance in our international accounts. The deficit in 1962 was already considerably smaller than in 1960, and the situation should improve further over the next year or two.

A more difficult and long-range problem arises from our position as the world's leading banking center. Banks, export and import houses, other business concerns, and wealthy individuals throughout the world want to hold sizable liquid reserves for working purposes. This need, usually termed the need for *international liquidity*, increases with the rising volume of world trade and production. The traditional and preferred form of reserve is gold. But the amount of gold is limited, and for a long time the world's gold stock has been rising less rapidly than the world's physical wealth and output. Thus to an increasing degree reserves are being held in the form of Swiss francs, German marks, British pounds, and other hard currencies. But above all reserves are held as dollar accounts in New York, accounts which can be converted into gold on demand, but which everyone trusts and expects will not be so converted.

The situation is similar to that faced by a U.S. commercial bank before the creation of the Federal Reserve System. The bank's depositors were entitled to come in and withdraw gold or currency whenever they wished. If they all tried to do this at the same time, the bank could not pay up. The system worked only because depositors, believing in the bank's soundness, were content *not* to withdraw their deposits. But occasionally a serious depression or some other event shook public confidence, people rushed in demanding cash, and many banks went under.

Similarly for foreign deposit holdings in the United States at present. These holdings now total close to $25 billion, and are still increasing. The U.S. gold stock, however, amounts to $16 billion, and $13 billion of this is earmarked as legal backing for Federal Reserve notes and deposits, so that our so-called *free gold reserve* is only $3 billion. If foreign depositors actually tried to convert their holdings into gold at the same time, the reserve would quickly be wiped out and we would have to suspend payment. The system rests on a delicate basis of confidence in the good intentions and good management of the U.S. monetary authorities. So long as this confidence lasts, the system works. But it is conceivable that future events (a continued shrinkage of our gold stock, a serious U.S. depression, a war scare) could produce a run on the dollar which would bring the structure tumbling down in disorder.

The solution to this problem on a national scale was a strong *central bank*, which became the ultimate repository of bank reserves, and had enough resources to rescue any bank which found itself in trouble. Professor Robert Triffin has argued eloquently that the solution on an international scale is to create a *world central bank*, a central bank *for* central banks. This world bank would become the main holder of gold and currency reserves, and deficits and surpluses in dealings between countries would be adjusted by transfers on the bank's books.[10]

Some tentative steps have been taken toward transforming the International Monetary Fund into this sort of institution. The leading hard-currency countries recently agreed to furnish the Fund on demand with substantial quantities of their own currencies. This central reserve pool, amounting potentially to between $5 and $10 billion, is available for lending to any country which finds itself under pressure through heavy withdrawal of deposits. This falls short of the more ambitious Triffin proposal, but is a step in the right direction. More steps in the same direction may follow, but this depends at bottom on maintenance of good economic and political relations among the Western powers.

SUMMARY

1. It is not feasible to eliminate fluctuations in national income completely. It should be feasible to detect and check downswings at an early stage, and to encourage vigorous recoveries.

2. The built-in stabilizing effect of government budgets could be strengthened by an increase in benefit levels under the state unemployment compensation systems, and by automatic lengthening of the benefit period at times of severe unemployment.

3. The corporate income tax system could be modified to reduce the present wide fluctuation of post-tax profits, and to give companies a financial inducement to spread their investment more evenly over good and bad years.

4. Monetary policy is effective mainly in controlling unduly strong upswings. But since it operates by checking investment, which may be considered undesirable from a growth standpoint, fiscal policy may be preferable even in boom periods. During recession main reliance must be placed on fiscal policy.

5. Fiscal policy should operate mainly through varying tax rates rather

---

[10] Robert Triffin, *Gold and the Dollar Crisis* (New Haven: Yale University Press, 1960).

than vaying public expenditures. This is partly because taxes can be changed more quickly, partly because decisions about the level of public services should be based on long-run rather than cyclical considerations. One possibility is to authorize the President to vary first-bracket personal income tax rates within prescribed limits, either according to a set formula or on a discretionary basis.

6. Something can also be done to accelerate normal public construction during recession periods, but the possibilities are limited because of the long time lags involved.

7. Despite the attractiveness of fiscal policy in principle, there has been little use of it in practice. The reasons are political and administrative, and seem likely to change only slowly.

8. It is recognized increasingly that a capitalist economy operating near capacity may be subject to *cost or sellers' inflation*. Opinions on the seriousness of this problem vary considerably, and in any event no satisfactory remedy is yet in sight.

9. An economy with extensive foreign trade may suffer imbalance in the form of a continuing balance of payments deficit, leading to a drain on its gold and other reserves, possibly resulting in trade restrictions or currency devaluation. The United States has been experiencing this problem since the late fifties. There is no single or easy answer to it. But it now appears that the U.S. problem is gradually being brought under control by a variety of measures, without the necessity of devaluation or severe restrictions on imports.

PART FOUR

THE ECONOMICS OF GROWTH

There's nothing constant in the universe
All ebb and flow, and every shape that's born
Bears in its womb the seeds of change.

OVID, *Metamorphoses*

Yet all experience is an arch where through
Gleams that untraveled world, whose margin fades
For ever and for ever, as we move.

ALFRED LORD TENNYSON

ONE OF THE great themes of economics concerns the growth of national output over the long run. This problem has been termed "the nature and causes of the wealth of nations" (Adam Smith), "the theory of economic development" (Joseph Schumpeter), "the conditions of economic progress" (Colin Clark). It is both more and less than the problem of economic history: more in that it strives for general principles, while the historian usually concentrates on the unique and particular; less in that it focuses on a few economic relationships and does not profess to explain the wealth of concrete experience.

If economic growth is so important, why have we left it to the end of the book? Partly because analysis of growth requires all the principles of microeconomics and macroeconomics developed in earlier chapters; and partly because it is a frontier problem of modern economics. Since one purpose of an introductory course is to carry students beyond the bounds of accepted knowledge into areas of uncertainty and debate, the growth problem forms a fitting climax to our discussion.

What is economic growth? It might be defined as the rate of increase in GNP. But if one is interested in the welfare of the population, it is more significant to look at changes in output *per capita*. Rising output per capita is the distinctive feature of modern economic progress; and the term economic growth will be used hereafter in this sense.

Economists do not assert that economic growth is "good," or that it makes people happier. It is quite possible that the average American of 1860 was happier than the average American of 1960. In this area, as in others, the role of economics is strictly instrumental. We do not consider whether a nation *should* aim at rapid material development. We focus rather on the question: *If a nation chooses this as an objective, what is the best way to go about it?* What conditions are favorable to economic progress and what are the main obstacles to be overcome?

Nor are economists simple minded enough to suppose that the rate of growth depends only on economic considerations. True, in the following chapters we shall concentrate on economic quantities, because they can be defined, measured, and reasoned about in a precise way. But this should not be misinterpreted as meaning that other things are unimportant. The political organization of a country, the system of property ownership, the relations among social classes, the pattern of family organization and child rearing, the values to which individuals are attached and the incentives to which they respond—all these have important consequences. But for most of these things we still have no satisfactory scheme of analysis; and in any event economists have no special competence in these areas.

Analysis of economic growth starts from the macroeconomic concepts of Part Three. We use the same apparatus of total demand, total supply, consumption and investment schedules, and so on. The national income approach provides an overall framework for measuring and analyzing economic change. But there is one fundamental difference. Until now we have taken the determinants of productive capacity as given—the labor supply, the stock of capital, the state of technical knowledge, forms of business organization, and so on. But as we shift to a telescopic view of change over decades and generations, all these things become variables. Labor supply is growing, the capital stock is increasing, the distribution of capital and labor among sectors of the economy is changing, technical change is producing drastic revision of products and methods of production. These things, instead of being taken for granted, must now be explained. This is what makes growth analysis both difficult and endlessly fascinating.

We do not at present have principles of economic growth applicable at all times and places. A few ideas have quite general usefulness (Chapter 25). But beyond these the growth problem looks quite different in the industrial capitalist countries (Chapter 26), the communist countries (Chapter 27), and the poorer agricultural countries (Chapters 28–29). The poor countries are given more space than the other two groups partly because there are more of them, partly because their efforts to shake off age-old poverty have attracted world-wide interest. The contributions that the richer countries are making to economic development, and the question of what the United States should do in this direction, are examined in Chapter 30.

In the Western industrial countries, economic growth can be taken for granted. Some of these economies have been expanding continuously for two centuries or more. Thus the main question becomes the *rate* at which growth will occur. National economies show substantial differences in growth rates, whether one looks backward for a century or whether one looks simply at experience since 1945. What are the reasons for these differences? Could the slowly growing countries accelerate their growth rate by changes in economic policy?

The growth rate of the same country also varies from time to time. Oak trees grow more slowly as they grow older. So do dogs, horses, and humans. What about national economies? It is sometimes asserted that the growth rate of a "mature economy" is bound to slow down gradually. On this basis it would be natural for the U.S. and U.K. to be growing currently at a less rapid rate than more recently industrialized countries such as Italy or Japan. But is the mature economy hypothesis correct? Does it rest on solid economic reasoning, or merely on a poetic analogy with biological processes?

In the communist countries, economic growth does not just happen through a myriad of independent decisions. The state planning commission sets output targets and imposes a program to achieve these targets. Communist leaders argue that this makes it possible to achieve higher growth rates than those prevailing in the capitalist world, and to do this consistently year after year.

For the U.S.S.R. there are production records reaching from 1928, when central planning was first applied, to the present time. These statistics have been thoroughly examined, revised, and analyzed by Western scholars. Thus we can usefully raise such questions as: What has been the rate of economic growth in the U.S.S.R., and how has it varied from time to time? What accounts for the relatively high Soviet growth rate? Does it really demonstrate the superior efficiency of central economic planning? Is the same rate of growth likely to be maintained in the future?

The poor countries of Asia, Africa, and Latin America present a third dimension of the growth problem. In most of these countries the institutional prerequisites for economic growth are not yet firmly established. Output per head is stationary, or rising slowly and precariously. In many countries hard-won increases in output threaten to be swamped by an even more rapid increase in population. The central problem is how to *initiate* a process of sustained growth rather than how to sustain or accelerate a well-established growth pattern.

Suppose a country is able to establish institutional conditions favorable to economic growth. What next? Strategic issues of development policy must be resolved in one direction or another. How severely should government squeeze consumers' living standards in order to raise the level of investment? Is industrialization the main key to economic progress? If so, what types of industry should be given priority? Can agriculture be taken for granted meanwhile, or is agricultural improvement an essential part of the development process? In countries with a large surplus of underemployed labor, how can this labor best be drawn into productive uses?

The wealthier capitalist and communist countries stand ready with advice and assistance. Each group urges the poor countries to choose its own path—the path of economic decentralization and limited government, or the path of one-party government and central economic planning. Each group provides a growing amount of loans and gifts to the poor countries, intended partly to influence them in its direction. This politico-economic competition is now the central fact in international relations. One must expect over the next half century a slow, inexorable, eventually decisive struggle of East and West for the allegiance of the countries of the South.

The Nature of Economic Growth

The rule is, jam tomorrow and jam yesterday—but never jam today.
Through the Looking Glass

"I wish you wouldn't squeeze so," said the Dormouse. "I can hardly breathe."
"I can't help it," said Alice, very meekly: "I'm growing."
Alice's Adventures in Wonderland

THERE IS at present no comprehensive and accepted theory of economic growth. This is partly because work on the subject has been renewed only recently after a long period of neglect. But it is also because of the variety of experience in different countries.

Most economies of Europe, North America, Australia, and Japan are growing and have been growing for a long time in the past. Economic growth has acquired a routine or built-in character. A growth theory for these economies involves, on the supply side, explaining how increases in labor supply, capital equipment, and productivity have cooperated to produce a sustained rise in productive capacity. On the demand side, the central problem is what behavior of aggregate demand is required over the long run to enable the rising output to be marketed on satisfactory terms.

In most parts of Asia, Africa, and Latin America, economic growth has not yet achieved this built-in character. Some of these economies have long been stagnant. Some seem to have grown appreciably in recent years, but there is no certainty that this will continue in the future. The common feature of these countries is that sustained growth cannot be taken for granted.

For these countries two additional questions are pertinent. First, what are the political and social preconditions of economic growth? What changes must take place in the society before there is any possibility of growth getting underway? Second, given these preconditions, what kind of impetus is required to set growth in motion? How did sustained growth begin in the older industrial countries? What kinds of deliberate push might be successful in the poorer countries today?

THE PRECONDITIONS OF GROWTH

It is all too easy to list conditions that may be desirable or even necessary for growth to begin. But one must be cautious. Some of the things put forward as preconditions are more properly regarded as consequences, or at least accompaniments, of economic growth. Doubtless some minimum set of circumstances are preconditions in the strict sense. But once economic growth has been set in motion, it calls forth political and social changes that make further growth still easier. Some characteristics of Western societies which we regard as favorable to growth, such as marked occupational and social mobility, a high level of education and technical training, a widespread habit of invention, and responsiveness to pecuniary incentives, are in large measure a *consequence* of economic progress.

Sticking to bare essentials, then, what does one find? First, there must be *economic unification* over a substantial area. A country inhabited by isolated tribes with no trade relations is not a country for economic purposes. There must be roads, a postal system, a common currency, and some development of regional or national markets. Only then can one begin to speak of *an economy* which may have the potentiality of progress.

There must be a *stable political authority*, capable of maintaining law and order, protecting property, and enforcing honesty in commercial relations. The government need not be democratic. In most of the older industrial countries, economic growth began before there was widespread popular participation in government. But the government must be interested in economic progress and willing to take measures to promote it. If the ruling group is interested mainly in military conquest, or in establishing certain theological principles, strong government may not lead to economic advance.

The top political leaders must be supported by a well-trained and reasonably honest *civil service*, capable of making government policy effective over a wide area. This may have been less necessary in earlier periods, when government was not the main engine of economic progress.

It is essential in today's poor countries, where governments are being called on to initiate and carry through complex development programs.

There must be a group of *business entrepreneurs*, able to launch new ventures and expand them over the course of time. In the older countries it seems often to have been the merchants who shifted over to being manufacturers. Landowners seem less likely to shift to business pursuits. A common hypothesis is that the entrepreneurs are often men who are psychologically alienated from their society, not integrated into the traditional culture, not fully accepted by the top social and political groups.[1] In support of this one can cite the business role of minority religious groups, such as the Methodists and other nonconformist groups in England, the Huguenots in France, the Parsees in India, the Jewish community in various countries. Note also the important role of immigrants, such as the Chinese throughout southeast Asia, the Indians in Africa, the Germans and other European immigrants in Latin America. Whatever the source, entrepreneurs must exist to permit the spawning of small enterprises, which is a characteristic feature of early economic growth.

There must be *reasonably free movement of products and factors of production*. This involves reduction of legal as well as physical barriers to movement. Goods must be able to move without heavy tolls, taxes, or restrictions on prices and production. People must be able to change jobs with some freedom. There must be legal and financial institutions for mobilizing capital funds. Without this it is impossible to channel productive resources in the direction of developing demands.

Finally, there must be *widespread responsiveness to material incentives*. Fortunately or unfortunately, the evidence suggests that this is not a major problem. Exposed to the temptation of modern consumer goods, the most primitive peoples become avid consumers in a remarkably short time.[2]

In the older industrial countries, these favorable conditions developed gradually over a long period. In Britain they existed by the eighteenth century, in most parts of Western Europe by the early nineteenth century. In the areas of overseas British settlement, where skills and institutions were imported from the mother country, favorable conditions for economic growth existed virtually from the beginning.

Must today's poor countries also go through a prolonged period in which the preconditions are gradually and painfully established? To what extent can the process be accelerated by effort within these countries and by prodding from the outside? No one really knows. But until these conditions are present one cannot expect more than halting and intermittent

---

[1] See in this connection Everett E. Hagen, *On the Theory of Social Change: How Economic Growth Begins* (Homewood, Ill.: The Dorsey Press, Inc.), 1962.

[2] For an astute discussion of the preconditions problem, see Gustav Ranis, "Economic Development: A Suggested Approach," *Kyklos*, Vol. XII, 1959, pp. 428–47.

growth. A favorable turn in export prices, or a large infusion of foreign capital, may raise per capita income in a country for a few years. But unless internal conditions are basically favorable, the pump will not catch, and the economy will relapse into stagnation.

THE PERIOD OF TESTING

The things just discussed are necessary, but not sufficient, conditions of growth. Even when they are present, some impetus is needed to kick off the growth process. What is this? How does growth usually begin? It is doubtful that there is a single answer. Government initiative can be important, as it was in Japan. Rising foreign demand for a major export product—textiles from England, lumber from Sweden, grain from the United States, raw silk from Japan—can be helpful. Technical progress in industry and agriculture may be of major consequence. Additional clues will be found in later chapters, where we recount what was going on in the United States, Western Europe, and Japan during the early phases of their economic growth.

An initial impetus, and a favorable response of the economy in terms of increased output, does not mean that growth is assured from that point on. The acceleration of output is typically gradual. It may be interrupted for shorter or longer periods. Eventually, if all goes well, one will notice a number of favorable symptoms: investment will be rising as a percentage of national income; the nation's capital supply will be rising at least as rapidly at the labor force; GNP will be rising faster than population. When these conditions have existed for a generation or more, one can usually conclude that growth has acquired a routine character and will continue indefinitely.[3]

This period of tentative and precarious growth has been given various names. Ranis, in the article cited previously, terms it the *breakout period*. Rostow has labeled it the *takeoff period*.[4] This term may be misleading, however, since it suggests a rate of acceleration faster than usually occurs in practice, and suggests also that movement is always in one direction. As a Burmese economist commented, "When we looked at our statistics for the early 'fifties, we concluded that we had taken off. Unfortunately, a short time later we landed again." There may be several such landings in the early years of growth. One is inclined to agree with the remark of a Yugoslav economist at a recent international conference: "Nations do not take off. They *creep over the threshold* of economic development."

---

[3] The dangers of generalization are illustrated, however, by the experience of Argentina. This economy, after growing at a good rate for several decades before 1930, was stopped dead in its tracks by the Great Depression of the 'thirties and by misgovernment and political turmoil during the 'forties and 'fifties. It is still unclear whether and when the upward march will be resumed.

[4] W. W. Rostow, "The Take-off into Self-sustained Growth," *Economic Journal*, Vol. LXVI, March, 1956.

From this point on we assume that sustained growth is already underway, and that we are examining the mechanics of a process whose origin we need not consider. But we shall revert occasionally to the special conditions of the poor countries which make it hard for them to creep over the threshold of development.

Looking at growth first from the supply side, productive capacity rises because of increases in factor supplies, notably the labor force and the capital stock; and in the efficiency with which these factors are used in production. Let us look at these things in turn.

ELEMENTS IN GROWTH: POPULATION

Growth of the labor force depends mainly on growth of population. True, there are gradual changes in the proportion of each age and sex group who engage in productive activity. But these can be neglected in a first approximation.

What determines the rate of population growth? Overlooking immigration and emigration, which are usually small because of political barriers, a country's natural increase depends on the excess of births over deaths. Birth and death rates are usually stated per thousand of population per year. A birth rate of 20 means *2 percent a year*.

There are natural limits to the variation of birth and death rates. In countries with good medical facilities and a normal age distribution of the population, the death rate is about 10 and cannot fall much lower. A birth rate of 50 seems to be about a physiological maximum. So one can assume that the rate of population increase will not exceed 40, or 4 percent a year. On the low side some countries, such as France and Ireland, have had virtually no population increase for decades at a time. An actual decline in population, while rare in modern times, is of course quite possible.

From this standpoint the countries of the world fall into two groups: industrial countries with low rates of population growth, and pre-industrial countries with rates which are high and rising. During the 1950's the population of Europe grew at about 1 percent a year, that of the United States at about 1½ percent. Most of the less-developed countries, on the other hand, had rates between 2 and 3 percent a year, and a few had pushed above the 3 percent level. And population increase in these countries is accelerating. Death rates are continuing to fall through the application of medical science, while birth rates remain near the physical maximum.

In the industrial countries, where economic growth has become routine, population growth does not seem to hamper the rise of per capita income. We shall present in the next chapter some calculations by Professor Simon Kuznets for eighteen countries over the past century. The rates of population increase varied quite widely, from near zero for France and Ireland to near 2 percent a year for Canada, the United States,

Australia, and New Zealand. Yet there is no visible relation between population increase and economic progress. Countries with a high rate of population growth enjoyed about the same rate of increase in *per capita output* as countries with lower population growth, which means that their rate of increase in *total output* was considerably higher.

Where the preconditions of growth already exist, rapid population increase can have positive advantages. On the demand side, it inspires a spirit of optimism to know that there will be 20 percent more people in the country 10 years ahead. Businessmen are less worried about overexpansion of capacity, because miscalculations will be rapidly corrected by population growth. Rising population compels a good deal of investment by both business and government, which helps to sustain aggregate demand. For the United States, Kuznets has shown a close relation between changes in the rate of population growth and changes in house building and (in earlier years) railroad construction. Rapid population growth probably also raises the consumption schedule. More children, more spending!

On the supply side, in the industrial countries the stock of capital equipment is increasing because of new investment, usually by 3 to 5 percent a year. If the labor force of the country were *not* increasing, this would soon present a problem of how to use all this capital effectively, that is, without a sharp decline in its marginal productivity. Population increase, by providing more workers to match the increasing supply of capital, helps to ward off this decline in productivity. If this seems unclear at the moment, it will be clarified a few pages along.

In the poor countries, on the other hand, rapid population growth is a decided disadvantage. Many of these countries already have a surplus of underutilized labor and a severe shortage of capital; and the rate of increase in capital is low. If the labor force could be held stationary for a time, while capital formation was accelerated, the labor surplus might gradually be absorbed. But if in fact the labor force is rising rapidly, underemployment will tend to increase over the course of time.

The ratio of labor to land is also high in some countries, and the marginal productivity of labor in agriculture is low. So population growth brings more mouths to feed without a proportionate increase in food output. During the nineteenth century, North America and Australasia avoided this dilemma by settling new land and by raising agricultural productivity. Britain and some of the European countries avoided it by building up enough export capacity in manufacturing to afford large imports of food. Neither avenue of escape is widely available to today's poor countries. There are few large tracts of uncultivated land; and the export capacity of these countries is too small to pay for large food imports.

Most serious of all, in many of these countries the preconditions of growth do not exist. Suppose population is rising 3 percent a year. Then just to keep from slipping backward GNP must also be raised by 3 percent. To make noticeable progress in living standards, GNP would have to rise 4 to 5 percent a year, something which few of the wealthier industrial nations have been able to achieve for any extended period. Most of the poor countries are not organized and prepared for this kind of national effort. So the prospect is that many of them will show little or no progress in per capita output.

ELEMENTS IN GROWTH: CAPITAL

A country's capital stock increases through investment, or *capital formation*. In physical terms, capital formation requires that part of the country's resources be devoted to producing capital goods rather than consumer goods and services. In financial terms, it requires that part of current income be saved and made available for investment. The institutional mechanisms through which this is accomplished include *household saving* out of income, *business saving* out of profits, and *government saving* out of tax revenues.

The relative importance of these channels varies from country to country. In communist countries, government saving is naturally the dominant form. In noncommunist countries, business and government saving together—*institutional saving*, if you will—normally provide most of the finance for capital formation. The United States is unusual in that houschold saving finances about 70 percent of net capital formation. In most other countries, personal saving accounts for less than half the total. In the poorer countries the ratio drops to about one quarter, with the remaining three quarters coming from institutional saving.

The Rate of Capital Formation

The percentage of national output which takes the form of capital goods is a key figure for any economy. The figure can be calculated by taking gross capital formation (GCF) as a percentage of GNP. Or, by deducting depreciation from both sides, we can get net capital formation (NCF) as a percentage of net national product (NNP).

In the United States in 1961, the relevant figures were as follows:

	(In Billions)
Gross national product (GNP)	518.7
Less capital consumption allowances	45.3
Equals net national product (NNP)	473.4
Gross capital formation (GCF)	71.7
Less capital consumption allowances	45.3
Equals net capital formation (NCF)	26.4

Thus the *gross capital formation rate* was GCF/GNP = 13.6 percent, while the *net capital formation rate* was NCF/NNP = 5.6 percent. The net figure is perhaps more significant, since it allows for capital used up during the year. But it is also less reliable, since estimates of depreciation are quite rough.

Capital formation rates vary widely throughout the world. They are typically highest in the communist countries, where gross capital formation often takes 25 to 30 percent of GNP. In the industrial capitalist countries, gross capital formation is usually between 15 and 25 percent, though Japan has at times reached the 30 percent level. In the poorer nonindustrial countries, gross capital formation is typically between 5 and 15 percent. After allowing for depreciation, net capital formation in these countries is often close to zero.

In the older industrial countries, the supply of capital typically rises faster than the supply of labor. Over the years 1870–1960, the net capital stock of the United States rose at an average rate of 3½ per cent per year. Since the labor force increased only 2 per cent per year, capital per worker was rising at 1½ percent. By 1960 each American was working with about 3½ times as much capital equipment as his predecessor in 1870.

The rate of capital formation accelerates during the early phases of economic growth. More rapid growth of output *requires* more capital and also *permits* a higher level of saving and capital formation. To detect this acceleration in the older industrial countries one has to go far back in history, before 1800 in the case of Great Britain, and before 1850 in the United States. But where rapid growth is more recent, we can get some indication from national income statistics. In Sweden GCF/GNP averaged 9.2 percent in 1861–70, 14.2 percent in 1911–20, and 20.5 percent in 1952–58. In Italy, the rate rose from 7.5 percent in 1861–70 to 15.2 percent in 1906–15 to 19.4 percent in 1952–58. In Japan, gross capital formation rose from 10.6 percent in 1892–1901 to 16.4 percent in 1922–31 and to 28.8 percent in 1952–58.[5]

The acceleration of investment is not a sharp spurt limited to a few decades. It is a gradual speed-up over two or three generations.

But acceleration does not continue indefinitely. The capital formation rate eventually levels off and moves along on a plateau. Sweden reached the 20 percent level in the 1920's and has remained near that level ever since. Britain had a gross capital formation rate of 13.6 percent in 1870–79, and has since not risen much above that level. The United States reached a rate of 20 percent soon after the Civil War and has never gone much above that.

Indeed, recent decades show some drop in the gross capital formation rate in both Britain and the United States; and there has been a substantial drop in the rate of net capital formation, because of the large amount of depreciation on a relatively old capital stock. This tendency

---

[5] Simon Kuznets, "Quantitative Aspects of the Economic Growth of Nations: VI. Long-term Trends in Capital Formation Proportions," *Economic Development and Cultural Change*, Vol. IX, No. 4, Part II, July, 1961.

has not yet appeared in the younger industrial nations of the West. But it may turn out to be a systematic feature of an aging economy.

This leveling off, and possible eventual decline, of the capital formation rate is surprising. Rich people save more than poor people. So as a country grows richer, why doesn't its savings rate keep on rising?

This is an intriguing question, to which we do not know the answer. But we can make some guesses about the United States. Farmers and small businessmen, who are heavy savers, have declined in relative importance over the past century. Wage and salary earners, who are less noted for thriftiness, have increased greatly in importance. The distribution of household incomes has become more equal, which may have reduced saving. The constant struggle to keep up with the Joneses, intensified by the vigor of American advertising, has kept the consumption schedule moving upward. The great increase in military expenditures since 1940, financed largely from income taxes, has reduced the possibilities of private saving. Finally, as we emphasized in Part Three, the level of saving depends on demand as well as supply. It depends on availability of investment opportunities as well as on the desire to save. There have been periods in this century when the investment outlook was not attractive, which reduced the level of national income and therefore of saving.

The Uses of Capital

What form does the new capital take? One thinks first of textile mills, steel works, automobile assembly lines, and other manufacturing equipment. This is part of the picture, but by no means all of it. Manufacturing typically takes only 20 percent or so of new investment; and all "modern" industries together take less than half. The remaining capital finds its way into every corner of the economy and takes a remarkable diversity of forms.

The stage of development of the country makes some difference to the allocation of capital, though not as much as one might think. Kuznet's calculations[6] in Table 25–1 show the percentage distribution of gross capital formation in the 'fifties.

Note that the poor countries give about the same relative attention to manufacturing and public utilities as the richer countries, and that they are equally generous in their construction of public buildings. But being mainly agricultural, they invest a higher proportion of their resources in this sector; and being poor, they invest less in houses, stores, office buildings, and service facilities.

We usually think of capital formation as a private process carried on by business concerns; but this is not entirely true. In the Western indus-

[6] Simon Kuznets, "Quantitative Aspects of the Economic Growth of Nations: V. Capital Formation Proportions: International Comparisons for Recent Years," *Economic Development and Cultural Change*, Vol. VIII, No. 4, Part II, July, 1960.

TABLE 25-1

Percentage Distribution of Gross Capital Formation in the 1950's

| | PERCENTAGE SHARE IN GROSS FIXED CAPITAL FORMATION | |
SECTOR	Average of Richest (Mainly Industrial) Countries	Average of Poorest (Mainly Agricultural) Countries
Agriculture, forestry, fishing	7.8	25.8
Mining, manufacturing, construction, power	30.0	28.1
Transportation and communication	14.9	15.3
Housing	21.5	13.9
Public administration	9.6	8.9
Other services	16.9	9.0

trial nations, government agencies and public corporations purchase about one third of all new capital equipment. In the less-developed countries, the government proportion rises to around 40 percent. In most countries public utilities are operated by public corporations, and account for 20 percent or so of investment. Public buildings and military installations take another 10 percent. And government frequently participates in housing, basic manufacturing, and other lines of investment.

A large part of capital formation consists in building physical structures—roads, dams, houses, factories, public buildings, stores, and offices. Construction activity typically accounts for about 55 percent of all investment; and this does not differ much as between richer and poorer countries. Machinery, railroad rolling stock, and other movable equipment typically forms about 35 percent of gross capital formation, while the remaining 10 percent consists of additions to inventories.

In physical terms, then, an acceleration of capital formation requires a massive build-up of personnel and facilities in the construction industries. Without this a poor country cannot get off the ground. And the ratio of construction to equipment does not decline appreciably as the economy matures.

CAPITAL, LABOR, AND OUTPUT

In a growing economy, labor supply and capital supply are rising. Since labor comes from population growth and capital from investment, there is no reason why their rates of increase should be at all similar. So what will be happening to output? This is a complicated question, and it is best to approach it in two stages.

Consider a situation in which *technical change* is completely absent. There are no improvements in products, methods of production, power sources, or anything else. The same products are produced in the same old way, year after year. Let's first analyze how output would behave under these conditions. Then we can bring in the influence of technical change as a second stage of the discussion.

It is desirable also to distinguish the situation of a poor country in the early stages of industrial development from that of an older industrial nation. The ratio of labor to capital is typically different in these two cases, so the problem of raising output is also different.

The Pre-Industrial Case

In the poor countries it is usually safe to assume that ample labor is available for industrial employment. In the cities, in addition to the visible unemployed, there are street vendors, rickshaw pullers, shoe-shine men, and others who produce and earn very little. In the countryside there are people who can be withdrawn from agriculture with little inconvenience. Rapid population growth is swelling the labor supply at an embarrassing rate. True, these people are not trained for work in modern industry. But this is a problem of personnel management, and not a highly difficult one. The main thing is that the people are there.

Under conditions of labor surplus, the rate of increase in the capital stock is of prime importance. As new industrial facilities are constructed, one can assume that the necessary manpower will be forthcoming to staff them. Labor is not a limiting factor.

Simple theorizing about growth in these countries often takes the further step of supposing that *the rate of increase in output will equal the rate of increase in capital.* In the absence of technical change, this seems a plausible proposition. Suppose the present capital stock of a country is worth $3 billion, and that with this capital the population produces an annual output of $1 billion. The *capital-output ratio*[7] is 3:1. Now suppose next year there is new capital formation of $150 million. Isn't it reasonable to suppose that this will lead to an output increase of ⅓ as much, or $50 million? If so, both capital stock and output will have risen *by 5 percent*, the proposition with which we began.

Under these conditions we can also calculate what rate of capital formation is necessary to achieve a specified rate of economic growth. In

---

[7] This slippery term must be treated with caution. The ratio of *total* capital stock to *total* output is the *average capital-output ratio.* The ratio between an *addition* to capital stock during the present period and the consequent *increase* in output in some subsequent period (say, a year later) is the *marginal capital-output* ratio. The latter concept is most commonly used in practice, because it is relevant for planning purposes, and because information on current additions to capital is more reliable than information on total size of the capital stock.

The marginal capital-output ratio can be defined on either a *gross* or a *net* basis. Conceptually, it is preferable to use the ratio of net capital formation to increases in net national product. But this involves estimates of depreciation which may be quite unreliable; and so statisticians and planners often relate gross capital formation to increases in GNP.

Quantitative information in this area is extremely crude. So while one often sees statements such as "the marginal capital-output ratio in underdeveloped countries is usually about 3:1," this is little more than a wild guess.

the above case, a 5 percent increase in output requires capital formation of 150,000,000/1,000,000,000 or 15 percent. The required investment rate turns out to be *the desired growth rate multiplied by the (marginal) capital-output ratio.* So a 3 percent a year rise in national output would call for $3 \times 3 = 9$ percent investment. A 7 percent growth rate would require $7 \times 3 = 21$ percent investment; and so on.

This kind of arithmetic is exciting at first glance. It seems simple and yet staggeringly important. And it is widely used in framing national development plans. One often finds planning boards reasoning essentially in this way: "Our population is rising 2 percent a year. To exceed this and make visible progress, GNP should rise 4 percent a year. Our best guess is that the capital-output ratio is $3:1$. Hence we must achieve a capital formation rate of 12 percent of GNP."

But such arithmetic is unreliable; and postaudits at the end of a plan period often reveal that the ratio of additional capital to additional output was quite different from the original forecast. There are several reasons for this. First, the output from a certain amount of capital depends very much on the *kind of industry* to which the capital is devoted. The capital-output ratio may be $10:1$ in housing, $5:1$ in electric power, $1:1$ in textile factories, and $0.5:1$ in agriculture. Unless these differences are taken into account, and unless the actual allocation of capital corresponds exactly with the planned allocation, the output results will differ from the original plan.

Second, the calculations assume that capital is installed and operated with some average or reasonable degree of efficiency. It is quite possible for capital to be wasted and for the output result to be zero. Third, in the important agricultural sector, output depends on weather, choice of crops, farm organization and management, and a variety of other things in addition to the amounts of capital used. So in this sector the assumption of a constant capital-output ratio is particularly implausible.

This is not to deny the critical importance of capital formation in poor countries, or the value of accurate information on capital stock, investment, and output. But there is need for caution in handling such information and for recognition of the necessarily wide margins of error.

The Industrial Case

In an advanced industrial economy one can no longer assume unlimited supplies of labor. On the contrary, we usually assume that the labor force is fully employed, and that additional labor can be obtained only through growth of population.

How does output behave in this case? This depends on what we assume about the way in which labor and capital combine in production. One possible assumption, that of *fixed factor proportions,* is that additional units of capital always require exactly the same amount of labor: ten new machines, ten new jobs—and no more. In this case output will grow at the rate of *the most slowly growing factor*. This will normally be labor. If the labor force is growing only 1 percent a year, then only 1 percent a year more capital can be used in production. If there is no technical change, and if there are constant returns to scale, output will also rise at 1 percent a year. This would be a gloomy world, in which consumption levels could be raised only by putting in more labor per head.

A more realistic assumption, which we used all through Part One, is that of *variable factor proportions*. This "treats capital as an abstract substance which can be shaped to absorb any size labor force . . . as putty with which any number can play."[8] Under these conditions the growth of output will be an average of the growth rates of the factors of production, but not a simple average. If labor supply is growing 2 percent a year and capital supply 4 percent, one cannot conclude that output will rise by 3 percent. In making up the average, we must weigh each factor by its relative importance in production, as indicated by the share of national income it receives.[9] In the American economy at present, labor receives about three quarters of national output, capital one quarter. So, if factor supplies were increasing as stated, one might expect the following result:

$$\text{Rate of increase of output} = \tfrac{3}{4} \text{ Rate of increase of labor} + \tfrac{1}{4} \text{ rate of increase of capital}$$
$$= (\tfrac{3}{4} \times 2) + (\tfrac{1}{4} \times 4)$$
$$= 2.5 \text{ percent per year.}$$

There are several interesting things about this result. It *is* possible now for output to rise faster than labor supply, and for living standards to increase over the course of time. The necessary condition is that capital should be increasing faster than labor, so that each man is working with more and more capital. But while output rises more rapidly than labor, it *rises less rapidly than capital*. So we can no longer assume a constant capital-output ratio. Here the ratio of capital to output will be rising or, the same thing in reverse, the marginal productivity of capital will be falling.

It may help to recall the discussion of Chapter 8. There we saw that if the supply of one factor increases with no increase in other factors, its marginal productivity will fall. By the same token, if one factor simply increases *faster* than other factors, its marginal productivity will likewise fall. So its price, which in a competitive system reflects its marginal productivity, will fall relative to those of other factors of production.

In the richer countries capital is typically increasing a good deal

---

[8] Edmund S. Phelps (ed.), *The Goal of Economic Growth* (New York: Norton, 1962), p. 97.

[9] This assumes a competitive economy in which each factor is paid according to its marginal productivity; it neglects the contribution of factors other than labor and capital.

faster than labor. So it is capital which faces the problem of a decline in its marginal productivity and rate of return. With no technical progress, continued accumulation of capital at a high rate will lower the rate of interest. The fall of interest rates relative to wage rates will of course encourage substitution of capital for labor; but since substitution possibilities are limited, this cannot entirely relieve the downward pressure.

Suppose this continues decade after decade. What will happen? The classical economists predicted that the result would be a *stationary state* of the economy. As capitalists continued to invest, the rate of interest would fall eventually to a level at which there was no longer any inducement to saving. Net saving and investment would then cease, and the nation's stock of capital equipment would remain constant. Population would also eventually become constant because of limitations on food supply; and (the Reverend Malthus added cheerfully) this constant population could live at no more than a subsistence level. Hence the label of the "dismal science," which economics carried for a century.

THE IMPACT OF TECHNICAL CHANGE

In reaching this gloomy conclusion we assumed away the possibility of *technical change or innovation*. When we bring this into the picture, we are immediately in a more hopeful position.

Technical change has two characteristics. First, it raises the productivity of resources in general. The same bundle of inputs now produces more output than before. If sheer increase of labor and capital would have raised output only 2 percent a year, innovation may make it possible for output to grow at 4 percent a year. The size of this plus factor we may call the *intensity of innovation*.

Second, technical change may raise the marginal productivities of the two factors *at different rates*. It may be of such a character as to raise the marginal productivity of labor more than that of capital, or vice versa. This property we may term the *factor biasedness of innovation*.

Here some definitions are in order. A *labor-saving innovation* is one which raises the marginal productivity of capital more than that of labor. *It acts like an increase in labor supply*. It provides opportunities to use additional capital without depressing its productivity. Mechanization and automation in manufacturing provide an abundance of illustrations.

A *capital-saving innovation* is one which raises the marginal productivity of labor more than that of capital. *It acts like an increase in capital supply*. Transmission of messages by radio instead of telegraph wires is an example of this sort. Another is the jet airplane, which can carry more trans-Atlantic passengers per week than a large steamship while costing considerably less to build.

A *neutral innovation* is the borderline case between these two.

Depending on which kind of innovation predominates at a particular time and place, one can say that technical change has a *labor-saving bias* or a *capital-saving bias*.

What kind of technical progress is desirable in practice? Should one prefer a labor-saving bias or a capital-saving bias? The answer depends on the supplies of labor and capital, and the rate of increase in these supplies, in the country in question.

In a poor country with surplus labor, the problem is to stretch a limited supply of capital, to give many workers a small bit of putty apiece. Here *capital-saving innovations* seem in order. Because Americans live in a country where capital is relatively abundant, we think of progress in terms of giving each man more capital to work with, a process usually termed *capital deepening*. But where labor is relatively abundant and capital scarce, one may need a deliberate policy of *capital shallowing*, that is, spreading the available capital more thinly over a larger number of workers. Up to a point, this will raise national output as well as provide more jobs. Such a shallowing seems actually to have occurred in Japan, one of the most successful examples of partially planned development, over the period 1880–1920.[10]

Return now to the situation of the richer industrial countries. In the last section we left them hanging onto the edge of the cliff—capital increasing faster than labor, marginal productivity of capital and the rate of interest falling, economic stagnation in the offing. To rescue them from this predicament we need a *labor-saving bias* in the process of technical change. If we can get this, the effect will be the same *as if the labor supply had risen faster than it actually did*. Technical change can serve as at least a partial corrective to the relative shortage of labor and abundance of capital which marks the growth process in the developed countries. It can prevent the marginal productivity of capital from falling as rapidly as it otherwise would, and thus stave off the day of doom foretold by the classical economists.

Has technical change in the industrial countries actually had a labor-saving bias over the past century? There are two reasons for an affirmative answer. First, there has been a strong incentive to labor-saving improvements. With labor becoming steadily more expensive, the problem of economizing labor has forced itself constantly on businessmen. It would be surprising if this were not reflected in the activities of inventors, engineers, and production managers. Some technical changes simply drop out of the blue as a by-product of basic scientific work; and there is no reason to expect that these *autonomous* inventions will have a bias in one direction or the other. But to the extent that inventions are *induced* by an effort to lower production costs, one would expect them to have a labor-saving bias.

The second piece of evidence is the behavior of profit and interest rates in the capitalist countries. True, these rates have fallen considerably relative to wage rates. The interest rate in the United States may even

---

[10] See on this point a forthcoming article by Gustav Ranis and John Fei in the *American Economic Review*.

have fallen absolutely over the past century, though the evidence is not conclusive. The main point, however, is that rates of return on capital *have not fallen as much as one would have expected* in view of the rapid increase of capital supply. What has sustained the yield on capital and prevented it from falling to a discouraging level? The most plausible explanation is a vigorous process of technical improvement with a marked labor-saving bias.[11]

A major uncertainty about the future of the industrial economies is whether this will continue to be true in the decades ahead. Who will forge ahead in the race between invention and capital accumulation? Will investment opportunities be worked out faster than they can be restored by technical discoveries? Will the return on capital drop sharply after all? If so, the outlook is discouraging. But one can hope for a more favorable outcome; and there are even some things which can be done about it.

TECHNICAL PROGRESS IN THE UNITED STATES

These ideas may be brought down to earth by looking briefly at growth experience in the United States. Studies at the National Bureau of Economic Research[12] indicate that, over the years 1890–1957, the number of man-hours worked in the United States rose at an average rate of 1.2 percent a year, while capital in use rose 2.5 percent a year. But output rose 3.6 percent a year, or about double the rate of increase of labor and capital combined. Technical progress was clearly a major factor.

Similar impressions result from calculations of labor productivity. Output per man-hour rose by 2.4 percent a year over this period. Some of this was due, of course, to the fact that capital was increasing more rapidly than labor, so that each man was working with more and more equipment. But less than half of the productivity increase—some writers would say less than one quarter[13]—can be explained on this ground. What explains the remainder?

When we say that the difference is explained by technical change, we are really making a confession of ignorance. For under this term we lump a variety of things, of which some are technical change in the strict sense and others are not; and about the relative importance of these things we know very little.

1. Technical change in the strict sense is undoubtedly important. This consists partly of improved methods of producing existing products. But even more important is the rise of new industries as a result of tech-

---

[11] See the persuasive analysis of this point in William J. Fellner, *Trends and Cycles in Economic Activity* (New York: Holt, 1956).

[12] See in particular Solomon Fabricant, *Basic Facts on Productivity Change* (New York, National Bureau of Economic Research, 1961); and John W. Kendrick, *Productivity Trends in the United States* (Princeton, N.J.: Princeton University Press, 1961).

[13] Robert M. Solow, "Technical Change and the Aggregate Production Function," *Review of Economics and Statistics*, August, 1957.

nical discoveries. One can list a long series of these over the past century —telephone and telegraph communication, oil refining, electric power, automobiles and trucks, radio and television, petrochemicals, plastics and other synthetics, electronics, and so on. The productivity of labor and capital in these new industries is typically higher than the previous average for the economy. So as these "high-powered industries" appear, and a larger share of the nation's resources is diverted into them, the average level of productivity rises.

While in principle one can distinguish the effect of an increasing *amount of capital* from the effect of *technical change*, this distinction is rather artificial in practice. For through technical change the growing capital stock takes on new and more productive forms. Further, it is only because of the profit opportunities opened up by technical change that capital accumulation proceeds as rapidly as it does. So scientific and technical discoveries are really responsible for much of the increase in national output which seems, in a superficial or statistical sense, to be due to increased capital supplies.

2. Labor and capital are not the only inputs to production. Part of the rise in their productivity, therefore, may come from using larger quantities of other resources. The amount of agricultural land in use in 1890 was considerably smaller than it is today. Our great oil fields, and many important mineral deposits, were unknown at that time. The potential of our rivers had not been harnessed for power production.

If we count organization and management as a separate factor of production, we can point to major improvements in this area. In 1890 management methods were still casual and traditional. The scientific management movement after 1900 brought major advances in production management. Developments in administrative organization have improved the overall coordination of large enterprises. More recently, mathematical methods have been applied with increasing success in management decision making.

3. Productivity calculations usually assume that labor and capital consist of identical units. A million man-hours worked in 1890 is taken as the equivalent of a million man-hours in 1960. This is clearly inaccurate. Americans of 1960 are better fed, healthier, larger, stronger than their grandfathers. They have on the average more than twice as much education. The level of skill and experience has risen. A much larger proportion of the labor force today consists of skilled craftsmen, white-collar workers, executives, and professional people.

There is an anomaly in our national income accounting on this point. We *define* investment as use of current resources to secure higher output in the future. But we *count* as investment only money spent on buildings, machines, and other forms of physical capital. Expenditures on health, education, vocational training, and other things which raise the productive capacity of human beings are not counted. This procedure is doubly unfortunate. It understates the level of investment in the economy, and it creates a bias in favor of material investment as against investment in human beings.

4. There is progress in machines as well as men. When a machine bought for $25,000 wears out and is replaced by another machine costing the same amount, we say that the country's capital stock has not increased. This is unrealistic. The new machine can usually do more work than the old. So the effectiveness of capital equipment rises faster than one would judge from the net capital formation figures alone.

5. The fact that the American economy increased tenfold in *economic size* between 1890 and 1960 must have had a favorable effect on productivity. The advantages of increasing size were underlined in Part One. It enables individual industries to build plants of optimum scale. It enables the country to support a diversified array of industries which reinforce each other, improvements in one industry reducing the costs of others. It enables the overhead cost of the nation's transport and communication network to be spread over an ever-larger volume of output. This reduces unit production costs independently of other favorable developments.

ECONOMIC GROWTH FROM THE DEMAND SIDE

So far we have asked only how larger quantities of output can be produced. For the classical economists, who assumed that any amount of production could find a market, this was the end of the subject. Growth of productive capacity was all that mattered.

The burden of Part Three, however, was that aggregate demand will not necessarily correspond with productive capacity. It may exceed capacity, or it may fall short. There *is* a demand problem as well as a supply problem.

The nature of the problem may be explained by Figure 25–1. This shows a simple no-government economy in which demand comes either from consumption or investment.[14] The short-run consumption schedule is CC. Production capacity when our story opens is OY_0. If this amount is produced, consumers will take C_0Y_0. Suppose planned investment just equals the intended saving of N_0C_0. Then the economy will be in equilibrium at full capacity. All is well for the time being.

But the story takes a new turn when we ask what is necessary for capacity operation to continue in the future. We must consider that *investment this year means greater productive capacity next year*. Suppose existing technology is such that $2.00 of new investment increases annual output capacity by $1.00. The capital-output ratio (strictly speaking, the *marginal* capital-output ratio) is 2:1. Then productive capacity next

---

[14] Figure 25–1 is adapted from Fellner, *op. cit.*, p. 112. The consumption schedule differs from that used by Professor Fellner, but the general line of analysis is the same.

year will be OY_1, the new capacity Y_0Y_1 being half the previous invest-ment N_0C_0.

If next year's capacity is to be fully utilized, investment next year must be N_1C_1, which with consumption of C_1Y_1 will provide a market for total output. The investment of N_1C_1, however, increases productive capacity for the year after next by Y_1Y_2 to a level of OY_2. In the year

FIGURE 25–1

The Demand Problem in a Growing Economy

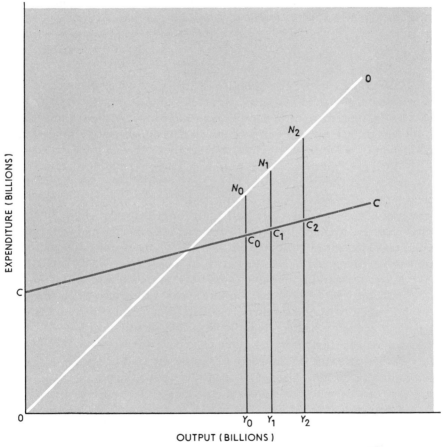

The full-employment capacity of this economy at the beginning is OY_0. If full employment is attained, consumption will be C_0Y_0 and investment N_0C_0. This investment creates new production capacity of Y_0Y_1. So next year the economy is operating on the line N_1Y_1, and investment must rise to N_1C_1 if full employment is to be maintained. And so on into the future.

after next, then, investment must rise to a level of N_2C_2 if full employment is to be maintained. And so on into the future.

Continued economic growth requires a rising level of investment. Investment must certainly increase in absolute terms. Must it also increase as a percentage of national income? Not necessarily. If CC remained in the position shown in Figure 25–1, the percentage of income saved would be rising year after year as we move out to the right. The investment percentage would have to rise correspondingly. But in practice, as we saw in Chapter 18, the consumption schedule seems to keep shifting upward so that the savings ratio does not rise materially. This reduces the burden on investment.

What happens if investment is not up to even this task? Suppose planned investment falls short of full-employment savings, not just for a year or two during a cycle downswing, but over a long period. Then two things will happen. First, actual investment being lower than it could be, the economy will move out more slowly along the Y-axis of Figure 25–1. The rate of growth in productive capacity is reduced. Second, even this smaller capacity will be underutilized most of the time. Booms will be short and weak, and recessions will be frequent.

One could explore the opposite situation, in which planned investment tends chronically to exceed the required amount. But this has not been a common situation in the Western industrial countries; and where it does occur, it is not difficult to control. It is unfortunately much easier to discourage investment than to encourage it.

What is likely to happen in practice? There is no logical reason why investment should rise at just the right rate over the long run. Yet it must have done something like this, for the industrial capitalist countries have grown at a rather steady rate with only brief setbacks. This favorable result must be attributed mainly to technical discoveries and innovations which have sustained the yield of capital and maintained the incentive for further investment.

Economists and businessmen got a bad scare during the Great Depression, when it seemed that opportunities for profitable investment had permanently declined. Some eminent economists asserted that the American economy had entered a new era of "secular stagnation." These fears almost vanished after 1940, but they have been reawakened by the sluggish performance of the economy since the mid-fifties. There is renewed debate over the danger of inadequate investment, and over what measures can be taken to stimulate it.

This is mainly a problem for the Western industrial countries. The communist countries can easily alleviate any problem of inadequate demand; and the underdeveloped countries can also assume in the aggregate that what they produce will be absorbed. So for most of the world the classical or supply-oriented approach to economic growth is still the more relevant one.

THE CHANGING COMPOSITION OF OUTPUT

Economic growth does not mean simply producing more and more of the same things. An economy cannot grow without changing the proportions of its outputs. There are several reasons for this.

Changes in the pattern of consumer expenditure. When people's incomes rise, they spend more on almost every kind of good. But there are differences in the *income elasticity of demand* for different products. Remember that income elasticity measures the relation between a small increase in consumer incomes and the resulting increase in consumer purchases. If, when consumer income rises 5 percent, purchases of men's shoes also rise 5 percent, the income elasticity of demand for shoes is 1.

In a poor country where most people are undernourished, the income elasticity of demand for food may be close to 1. But as the country becomes richer this figure will fall. People can eat only so much. In the United States, income elasticity of demand for farm products has been estimated at only 0.25. Income elasticity of demand for housing is higher than for food, but still typically below 1. For clothing, income elasticity in most countries lies between 1.0 and 1.5. This does not necessarily mean that people buy disproportionately *more* clothing as their incomes rise. But the kinds of clothing they buy are more varied, elaborate, and expensive. The items with highest income elasticity are services of a semi-luxury character: travel, entertainment, education, beauty care, and other personal services.[15]

Take a period, then, over which people's real incomes have doubled. This will *not* mean doubling of their consumption of every good and service. Food expenditure may have gone up 50 percent, clothing expenditure 100 percent, and spending on recreation and personal services 150 percent. The result is a shift in the makeup of family budgets. The dimensions of this shift in the United States between 1900 and 1950 are suggested by Table 25–2. Note the sharp drop in percentages spent on food and housing, and the sharp rise in the "sundries" category. "Transportation" means mainly the automobile, which has gotten its nose ever further into the tent and now takes about as much income as is spent on housing.

In a market economy, industry turns out what people are willing to buy. The changed distribution of consumer expenditures is reflected in the pattern of production. This accounts for the relative decline of manufacturing industries producing staple foods and clothing, the expansion of industries concerned with automobiles, gasoline, radios, and television, and the even more rapid expansion of the entertainment and service industries.

Differing productivity trends. The average rate of productivity increase in the economy conceals wide variations in particular sectors. Research workers at the National Bureau of Economic Research have calculated that, in the United States from 1889–1953, the productivity of labor and capital combined rose only 77 percent in the lumber industry;

[15] For an excellent review of the statistical evidence, see H. S. Houthakker, "An International Comparison of Household Expenditure Patterns," *Econometrica*, Vol. 25, 1957, pp. 532–51.

but it rose 259 percent in paper production and 778 percent in rubber goods. In the utilities group, productivity rose 207 percent in telephone service, but 1,664 percent in electric light and power.

Why should these differences lead to changes in the pattern of production? In a competitive market economy, product prices are closely related to production costs. If productivity is rising unusually fast in industry A, its unit cost of production will be falling unusually rapidly. This will be reflected in prices, and the products of industry A will become cheaper relative to other products. This will encourage consumers to buy more of A's products than before, and less of other things. The pattern of

TABLE 25–2

Distribution of Consumer Expenditures, U.S.A., 1901 and 1950*

	PERCENT OF TOTAL EXPENDITURE IN:	
	1901	1950
ITEM	(1)	(2)
Total	100.0	100.0
Food and beverages	43.1	32.5
Housing	18.1	10.6
Fuel, light, refrigeration	5.7	4.2
Clothing	13.0	11.5
Sundries:†	20.1	41.2
Transportation	2.9	13.8
House furnishings and household operations	6.8	11.0
Recreation, reading, education	3.4	5.8
Tobacco	1.2	2.0
Medical care	4.3	5.1
Personal care	0.9	2.3
Other	0.6	1.2

* U.S. Department of Labor, *How American Buying Habits Change*, Chap. ii, Tables 2–6.
† Detailed distribution of the sundries item in column 1 is for 1917–19; comparable figures for 1901 are not available. The sundries total of 20.1 per cent, however, is correct for 1901. There seems to have been little change in the sundries percentage between 1890 and 1920. The increase has come almost entirely since 1920.

consumption thus tends to shift *toward* products where productivity is rising very fast, and away from products where it is rising only slowly. The relative cheapening of electric power, for example, certainly has something to do with the phenomenal increase in power use since 1900.

New product development. Technical progress creates new products, which attract patronage by drawing demand away from older products. If a new product is a direct substitute for an older one, and if it is markedly superior or cheaper, the old product may vanish entirely. Horseshoes and carriages are virtually extinct in the United States. Demand shifts toward sectors of the economy in which new product development is particularly rapid, and away from those in which it is lagging.

This helps to explain a phenomenon which stands out in the industrial statistics. A new industry grows gradually in its experimental years, then enters a period of rapid growth which may last for several decades. This is the period during which the benefits of large-scale production are being reaped, costs and prices are being (relatively) reduced, and the new product is winning acceptance as a substitute for older goods. In time, however, the product achieves maximum penetration of its potential market. Meanwhile still newer products have appeared, which tend to displace this one. So growth tapers off and moves along on a plateau. The product may even "go over the hill" and head downward toward extinction.[16]

Yet despite this tapering off of individual industries, a country's *total* output can continue to grow at about the same rate decade after decade. The explanation lies in the continued appearance of new products which grow by partial displacement of older ones. Each new industry gives the economy a booster shot toward higher levels of total output.

What does a broker mean when he advises you to buy stock in a "growth industry"? What *is* a growth industry? It is an industry which has most or all of the following characteristics: the product is relatively new; productivity in the industry is rising faster than the national average; both price and income elasticity of demand for the product are high; and no dangerous competitors or substitutes are yet in sight. This is why you would have done well in 1920 by buying DuPont, General Motors, I.B.M., or A.T.&T.

Changing comparative advantage. We emphasized in Chapter 16 that a country need not produce everything for itself. It will do best by concentrating on products in which it has a *comparative advantage*. But comparative advantage is not a static thing. It changes with resource discoveries and technical developments. It changes also with *increases in the size of the economy*. In some industries the optimum scale of plant is very large. It is not feasible to build a pocket-size steel mill, or auto assembly plant, or aircraft factory. So in an economy with a GNP of $1 billion per year, it will not be sensible to produce these things.

But suppose the economy's output rises to $5 billion a year, then to $10 billion, and so on. The growth of the domestic market makes it feasible to introduce more and more types of manufacturing. First to appear will be industries in which the efficient scale of plant is relatively small, such as textiles, clothing, food processing, and other light consumer goods. As the economy continues to grow, it will become efficient to introduce more and more branches of heavy industry, until

---

[16] For confirmation of this as regards the United States, see the classic study by Arthur F. Burns, *Production Trends in the United States, Since 1870* (New York: National Bureau of Economic Research, 1934).

eventually the country may become largely self-sufficient in manufacturing. This process, usually called *import substitution*, has been important in the development of the United States, Canada, Japan, and other industrial countries. It will presumably be important also in the countries now embarking on the early stages of industrialization.

The nature of the process, however, must be properly understood. Economic planners in some of the poor countries seem to reason this way: "Rich countries produce a great deal of steel, automobiles, and machinery. So let us begin immediately to produce steel, automobiles, and machinery. Then we too will be rich." This reverses the causal sequence. The truth is that, *as a country becomes richer* (in ways which we have still to explore), the growth of large-scale industries becomes feasible. It is a result, or an accompanying characteristic, rather than a basic cause of economic development.

THE OVERALL RESULT: THE CHANGING PATTERN OF PRODUCTION

For all these reasons the makeup of GNP changes in a systematic way as economic growth proceeds. The direction of change can be tested in two ways. One can take a single country and examine what has happened to its production pattern over a long period of time. We shall do this for the United States in the next chapter. A second approach is to compare the present makeup of GNP in countries at different levels of per capita income. This approach is logically not the same as the first, but it yields similar results. It has the practical advantage of broader coverage, since the number of countries for which we have current information is much larger than the number for which we have solid historical data.

Kuznets has assembled information on about 40 countries and his results are summarized in Table 25–3. Category 1 includes North America, Australia and New Zealand, Britain, and the more prosperous countries of Western Europe. Those in category 2 are "middle-income" countries, including Japan, several from Latin America, and several from Southern Europe. Category 3 consists of underdeveloped countries at the bottom of the income scale.

Note what happens as we go from the poorest countries to the richest. The proportion of the labor force engaged in *agriculture* drops sharply. In the poorest countries this proportion may run as high as 70 to 80 percent. In the richer countries, it drops to between 10 and 20 percent. This is partly because of low income elasticity of demand for food. But another reason is major advances in agricultural productivity in the richer countries. In 1870 each farm family in the United States produced enough food for *two* families. Today, each farm family grows enough for *twelve* families. Rising productivity in agriculture is in fact a necessary condition for sustained economic growth.

The proportion of the labor force in *manufacturing* increases sharply with economic growth. In the poorer countries, the figure rarely exceeds 10 percent, and most of these are artisans rather than factory workers. In the industrialized countries, manufacturing typically employs around 30 percent of the labor force. When mining, construction, and public utilities are added, the figure rises to between 40 and 50 percent. This growth of urban industrial activities is in fact so characteristic that one is apt to see in it the prime mover of economic progress.

Table 25–3 indicates the changes through which the industrialized nations have passed and are still passing; for the underlying forces of change continue to operate, even at high income levels. And it fore-

TABLE 25–3

Industrial Structure of the Labor Force,
Countries Grouped by Product per Capita*

Category	1	2	3
Number of countries	13	10	15
Average percentage of labor force engaged in:			
Agriculture, forestry, fisheries	18.6	39.5	56.4
Manufacturing, mining, construction	37.8	25.5	17.6
Transportation and communication	8.1	5.2	3.4
Trade, banking, and finance	13.4	9.7	6.5
Other services (professional, personal, government)	22.2	20.1	16.1
Total	100.0	100.0	100.0

* *Source:* Simon Kuznets, "Quantitative Aspects of the Economic Growth of Nations: II. Industrial Distribution of National Product and Labor Force," *Economic Development and Cultural Change,* Supp. to Vol. V, No. 4 (July, 1957). For most countries. the data relate to the early 1950's.

shadows the structural changes which will occur in the poorer nations as they get started on a sustained path of economic growth.

SUMMARY

1. Sustained economic growth can get underway only under certain conditions. These include economic unification through transport and communications; a stable government with some interest in economic development; an adequate civil service; a group of potential business entrepreneurs; reasonably free movement of products and factors of production; and widespread responsiveness to material incentives.

2. Growth accelerates gradually in the early stages; and it is usually several decades before one can conclude that it has acquired a routine and continuing character.

3. In countries where growth has become routine, a rapid increase in population does not seem to hamper the rise of per capita income, and can even be advantageous. But in the underdeveloped countries, the present high rate of population growth is a handicap, and reduces the possibility of any improvement in living standards.

4. The rate of increase of capital in a country depends on its level of saving and investment. In most countries saving is now predominantly institutional rather than a matter of personal decision. Savings rates are typically highest in the communist countries, next highest in the industrial capitalist countries, and rather low in the poorer primary producing nations.

5. The growth of national output is related to the growth of labor and capital supplies. But the relation varies depending on whether one is talking about an industrial or a pre-industrial economy, and on whether technical change is brought into the picture.

6. In the pre-industrial case, it is plausible to take the increase of output as related mainly to the rate of increase in capital. The reason is that there is typically surplus labor in these economies which can be drawn on to man the new equipment. But it is unsafe to assume a fixed relation between increases in capital and increases in production. Capital can readily be misallocated or mismanaged; and in the predominant agricultural sector, weather and farm organization influence the level of output.

7. In the industrial case, assuming *no technical change* and *variable factor proportions*, the rate of increase in output will be a weighted average of the rates of increase of labor and capital. The rate of increase of capital in these economies is typically above that of labor. If there were no technical change, this would run the economy into a dead end. The marginal productivity of capital would fall, and so the rate of interest would fall, until there was no incentive for further saving. So the economy would settle into a *stationary state*.

8. Technical change makes possible more output from the same quantity of inputs. It now becomes possible for output to rise faster than *either* labor or capital supply.

9. Technical progress may also have the property of *factor biasedness*, that is, it may be predominantly of a *labor-saving* or predominantly of a *capital-saving* character. (Review the definition of these terms and make sure you understand their significance.)

10. In a pre-industrial economy with surplus labor, innovations should have a capital-saving bias, to spread the scarce capital, absorb underemployed labor, and maximize national output. But in an industrial economy one needs a labor-saving bias to offset the tendency of labor supply to grow more slowly than capital supply. If the labor saving bias is strong enough, it can keep the marginal productivity of capital from falling and ward off the stationary state.

11. The industrial countries have a demand problem as well as a supply problem. New investment raises the level of income, and hence the volume of desired saving, corresponding to full employment. So to maintain full employment year after year, *the level of investment must be rising at an appropriate rate*. Experience suggests, however, that it is not necessary for investment to rise *as a percentage of GNP*. The reason is that the consumption schedule keeps shifting upward, so that desired saving as a percentage of GNP does not increase.

12. The growth of national output is accompanied by systematic changes in the composition of output. The main reasons are: differing income elasticities of demand for varying types of product; differing productivity trends which lower the prices of some products relative to others; appearance of new or drastically improved products as a result of discovery and invention; and changing comparative advantage, which alters the country's pattern of imports and exports.

Growth in the American Economy

He was found by the Bureau of Statistics to be
One against whom there was no official complaint,
And all the reports on his conduct agree
That, in the modern sense of an old-fashioned word, he was a saint . . .
Both Producers Research and High-Grade Living declare
He was fully sensible to the advantages of the Instalment Plan
And had everything necessary to the Modern Man,
A phonograph, a radio, a car and a frigidaire.
Our researchers into Public Opinion are content
That he held the proper opinions for the time of year;
When there was peace, he was for peace; when there was war, he went . . .
Was he free? Was he happy? The question is absurd;
Had anything been wrong, we should certainly have heard.

W. H. Auden

IT IS IMPOSSIBLE in a few pages to do justice to the long-term growth of
the American economy. But we can sketch in the broad features of this
growth, and draw some comparisons with the experience of other Western
industrial countries.

THE ACCELERATION OF GROWTH: 1830–60

It is a truism that any country which embarks successfully on the
path of economic development goes through a period in which its growth
rate increases. If at one time GNP is rising 1 percent a year, and at a

later time it is rising 4 percent a year, there must have been a phase of acceleration in between.

The best evidence for the United States locates this phase at about 1830 to 1860. The indications are that output *per capita* rose little from 1800 to 1830, and some scholars doubt that there was any increase.[1] Beginning in the 1830's, however, the economic indexes move upward more rapidly. Shipments of goods by land more than doubled between 1830 and 1840, while shipments by water almost doubled. The first overall estimates of production date from 1839. Professor Gallman has estimated the increase of total commodity output as follows:[2]

TABLE 26–1
Annual Rates of Change
(Percent)

PERIOD	OUTPUT	POPULATION	OUTPUT PER CAPITA
1839–49	4.3	3.1	1.0
1849–54	5.4	3.1	2.2
1854–59	5.0	3.1	1.8
1859–69	2.1	2.4	−0.4
1869–79	5.0	2.3	2.6

Thus the annual increase in output during the 1840's was about 4½ percent, and the increase in per capita output was about 1 percent. The rate of growth accelerated further during the 1850's. The devastation of the Civil War brought a setback, and per capita output in 1869 was a bit below 1859. During the 1870's, however, the economy bounced back and the growth rate returned to the level of the 1850's. The economy was firmly embarked on an upward course.

There were several reasons for the acceleration of growth during these decades.

1. *Settlement of Western lands.* In 1830 the frontier ran roughly from Detroit to western Louisiana. By 1860 it had moved west of the Mississippi, and ran from northern Minnesota through Nebraska, Kansas, and Texas to the Rio Grande. Settlement involved substantial costs for clearing the land, building fences and farm buildings, and developing roads and schools. This was mainly a direct investment of labor by the settlers. The returns did not come immediately, since the market for farm prod-

---

[1] Some of the evidence is appraised in William N. Parker and Franklee Whartenby, "The Growth of Output Before 1840," in *Trends in the American Economy in the Nineteenth Century* (Princeton, N.J.: Princeton University Press, National Bureau of Economic Research, 1960), pp. 191–212. This source is referred to hereafter as *Trends*.

[2] *Trends*, p. 16.

ucts was still limited by transportation. But this land was so rich that there was great potential for expansion of production in later decades.

2. *Rapid growth of population.* The rate of population increase from 1830–60 was higher than it has ever been since that time, running at more than 3 percent per year. This rate means a doubling of population in about 22 years. Population grew through heavy immigration from Europe as well as a high rate of natural increase.

Considering that the United States in 1830 was thinly populated relative to its resource potential, the rapid growth of population was an advantage. Germans, Scandinavians, and other immigrant groups played a prominent role in Western settlement. Immigrants built the railroads in the West and flooded into the factories of the East. Rapid population growth also fed the belief in the irresistible momentum of America. It became an article of faith that everything would be "bigger and better" a few years ahead. This outlook is favorable to personal initiative and business investment.

3. *Railroading and the broadening of internal markets.* For a long time the only cheap transportation in the United States was coastwise shipping. East-West traffic had to move by wagon or pack animals at much higher cost. This slowed the pace of Western settlement, prevented the settlers from sending their produce East to market, and hampered economic unification of the country. Industry and population remained concentrated in Boston, New York, Philadelphia, Baltimore, and other coastal cities which were in touch with each other by water.

The canal building movement after 1810 did not solve the problem. Between 1810 and 1860 about $200 million, an enormous sum for those days, was spent on canals. About 70 percent of this came from government sources, primarily from state governments.[3] The Erie Canal and a few others made an economic contribution and were financial successes. (The Erie reduced freight costs between Buffalo and New York from 20 cents per ton mile to 2 cents.) But the geographical obstacles to canal building proved greater in the United States than in Britain or Europe, and most of the canals did not pay off.

A real solution of the transportation problem had to await the steam locomotive and the railroad. This development began in 1830, and by 1860, thirty thousand miles of track had already been constructed. Detroit, Chicago, St. Louis, New Orleans, and Memphis were linked with each other and with the East Coast. The impact of cheap mass transportation on the economy can scarcely be overstated. It opened to the Western farmers both the markets of the East Coast and export markets abroad. Eastern manufacturers, who could now distribute their products throughout the country, reaped economies of large-scale production. Mobility of

---

[3] Carter Goodrich, *Government Promotion of American Canals and Railroads,* 1800–1890 (New York: Columbia University Press, 1960).

labor was greatly increased. The rail network provided an indispensable framework for rapid economic growth.

While the railroads were particularly crucial during this early period, they continued throughout the nineteenth century to open up new areas of settlement, reduce transportation costs, knit together the internal market, and provide a major outlet for investment. Between 1870 and 1890 alone, 110,000 miles of new railroad track were built. No other industry has ever provided such a major source of investment demand over so long a period.

4. The first agricultural revolution. During the first half of the last century agricultural production managed to keep pace with population growth, but only by bringing new land under cultivation. Output per acre and per farm worker was probably not much higher in 1850 than it had been in 1800. But meanwhile a burst of technical development was setting the stage for a rapid rise in productivity after 1850.

The steel plow, essential for the heavy prairie soils, began to be used in the 1830's. Harrows and seed drills came into use in the 1840's, corn planters and cultivators in the 1850's. Cyrus McCormick patented his mechanical reaper in 1834, sold 50 machines in 1844, and a thousand in 1851. A practical threshing machine was used by the late 1840's. The first guano fertilizer from South America was put on sale in 1843, and the first chemical fertilizer in 1849.[4]

Farmers were given an incentive to take advantage of these improvements by two developments. During the 1850's there was a sharp increase in foreign demand for our farm products, following Britain's repeal of its import duty on wheat in 1846. During the 1860's the Civil War brought a sharp increase in domestic demand for food accompanied by a severe shortage of manpower, which made mechanization profitable. In 1870 the quantity of machinery and fertilizers purchased by American farmers was *five times* as large as in 1850. Thus the agricultural sector set off on a path of rising productivity which has continued ever since.

5. The "American system" of manufacturing. While the manufacturing sector was small before the Civil War, its rate of growth was high. Professor Gallman estimates that manufacturing production increased by *15 percent per year* from 1839 to 1849, and 10 percent per year from 1849 to 1859. In 1839 manufacturing provided only 17 percent of total commodity output. By 1859 this had risen to 32 percent.[5]

The rapid growth of population provided an insatiable market for consumer goods. The appearance of the stationary steam engine, which freed industry from dependence on "the old mill stream," was a major development. Another was the railroad, which made it economical to ship

---

[4] For a review of these and other developments, see Marvin W. Towne and Wayne D. Rasmussen, "Farm Gross Product and Investment in the Nineteenth Century," *Trends,* pp. 255–315.

[5] *Trends,* pp. 24–26.

manufactured goods over much greater distances. High protective tariffs prevented the "infant industries" of the United States from being swamped by imports from Britain and elsewhere. Profit rates, high by modern standards, provided both the incentive and the funds for expansion. Mass immigration provided a ready source of labor.

Another important development was standardized and interchangeable parts, pioneered by Eli Whitney and others. This was such a revolutionary idea at the time that European visitors referred to it as "the American system of manufacturing." Workers and tools could be made more productive by specializing on one part of a product instead of tailor-making the product as a whole. These early machine shops in the Connecticut Valley were the ancestors of the modern assembly line.

6. *Increased capital formation.* The higher rate of increase in national output after 1830 was accompanied by, and partly depended on, a higher level of saving and investment. There are no direct measures of saving during this period, but there are indirect indications in the production level of capital goods. Gallman estimates that capital goods production, as a percentage of total commodity output, rose from about 23 percent in 1839 to 27 percent in 1859 and 33 percent in 1869.[6] It then leveled off and fluctuated in the range of 30–33 percent for the remainder of the century. This conforms to the general observation that capital formation rates in the Western industrial countries have not continued to rise indefinitely. After an initial phase of acceleration, they seem to level off and move along on a plateau.

7. *The inflow of foreign capital.* Domestic savings were supplemented during this critical period by heavy foreign borrowing, particularly from Britain. The rapid inflow of foreign capital after 1830 confirms the increased rate of economic development. In 1830 our private and public indebtedness to foreigners was only $75 million, about the same as it had been in 1790. Between 1830 and 1840, however, our foreign indebtedness more than *tripled* to a level of $266 million. The figure dropped during the 1840's but shot up again during the 1850's, rising from $222 million in 1850 to $379 million in 1860.

During these years we were importing a good deal more than we were exporting. A large proportion of the rails, railroad rolling stock, industrial tools and machinery, and other things needed for our industrial build-up came from abroad. Not until after 1870 did we begin to approach self-sufficiency in capital goods production. We also imported substantial quantities of consumer goods while our own manufacturing industries were rising toward maturity.

How did we pay for these imports? Partly through exports of grain and other materials. Partly through the earnings of our merchant marine, which was then a large factor in world commerce. After the 1849 gold

---

[6] *Trends*, p. 38.

strike in California, we were able to ship large amounts of gold abroad. But all this was not enough, and so we balanced our accounts by borrowing. This process of running up debt continued throughout the nineteenth century.

We sometimes look skeptically at today's poor countries when they say that their own resources are inadequate and that they need loans to get them started on the path of development. We should remember that it is normal for countries to borrow in the early stages of building up their own industries. The United States itself was once a debtor and remained so for many decades.

A CENTURY OF PROGRESS: 1870 TO DATE

After the Civil War the United States entered a period of sustained growth which has now lasted for about a century. Thanks to progress in national income measurement, we can speak with some confidence about what has happened over this period. The bare bones of the record are set out in Table 26–2 and Figure 26–1. Note that the figures represent *decade averages* rather than single years. Thus the 1903 figure is an average for 1899–1908, the 1923 figure is an average for 1919–28, and so on. This procedure is intended to eliminate the short swings of the business cycle and throw long-term trends into sharper relief.

Growth has been well sustained over this whole period, with no sharp break except for the Great Depression of the 1930's. At the same time the pace of growth has been very gradual. The typical rate of increase in per capita output has been about 2 percent a year. But even a low rate of compound interest works wonders if you can keep it up long enough. A quantity growing at 2 percent a year will in a century have increased to six times its original value. And our GNP figures suggest that, as regards material consumption, the average American today is about six times as well off as his ancestor in 1870.

The rate of growth has varied considerably. In addition to the short business cycles analyzed in Chapter 23, there are longer and slower tides of economic activity—a period of 10 to 15 years in which growth is faster than usual, followed by an extended period of subnormal growth. These long swings have been investigated particularly by Abramovitz and Kuznets, and are often termed *Kuznets cycles*. They show up in the wavy shape of the trend lines in Figure 26–1.

Because of this irregularity of growth, it is unwise to draw sweeping conclusions about the economy from short periods of time. Popular writers are very subject to this myopia, and economists are not immune. A period of rapid growth (1921–29, 1946–57) sets up the cry of "permanent prosperity." A period of subnormal growth (1929–39, 1957–?) leads to predictions of economic stagnation. With the benefit of hindsight, these extremes of optimism and pessimism turn out to have been unwarranted.

An important question is whether the growth of the American

FIGURE 26–1

Real GNP and GNP per Capita, United States, 1869–1962 (1929 Prices)

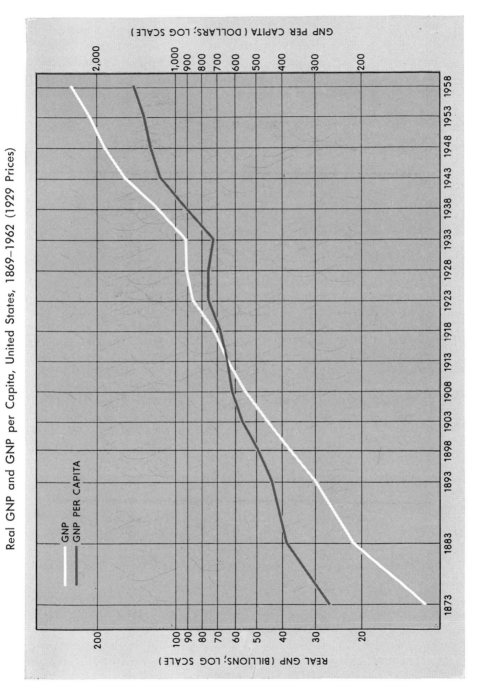

economy shows signs of slowing down over the long run. It is sometimes taken as natural that an old and rich country should grow less rapidly than it did at an earlier stage. What do the statistics suggest on this point?

One must distinguish between increase in *total output* and the rate of increase in *output per capita*. The growth of total output has slowed down materially, but this is mainly because the rate of population growth has dropped. From 1870 to 1914 the U.S. population grew at between 2

TABLE 26–2

Real GNP and GNP per Capita,* United States, 1869–1962
(1929 Prices)

	TOTAL GNP		GNP PER CAPITA	
DECADE CENTERED ON†	Decade Average (Billions)	Annual Rate of Change from Preceding Decade (Percent)	Decade Average (Dollars)	Annual Rate of Change from Preceding Decade (Percent)
1873	11.46	n.a.	263	n.a.
1883	21.05	6.3	384	3.9
1893	29.32	3.4	433	1.2
1898	36.28	n.a.	487	n.a.
1903	45.60	4.6	559	2.6
1908	54.51	4.2	607	2.2
1913	62.38	3.2	636	1.3
1918	70.93	2.7	673	1.0
1923	85.18	3.2	752	1.7
1928	90.53	2.5	752	1.1
1933	90.70	0.6	720	−0.4
1938	116.02	2.5	886	1.7
1943	154.30	5.5	1135	4.7
1948	181.76	4.6	1244	3.4
1953	208.68	3.1	1298	1.3
1958	243.17	3.0	1399	1.1

* Basic data from John W. Kendrick, *Productivity Trends in the United States* (Princeton, N.J.: Princeton University Press, 1961). Per capita figures are obtained by dividing GNP by "Total Population Residing in the United States," appearing in *Historical Statistics of the United States, Colonial Times to 1957*, p. 7, and *Statistical Abstract of the U.S.*, 1959, p. 5.

† Actually, decades are centered on the end point of the year named. Thus, the first decade is 1869–78, which centers on December 31, 1873; and so on. The figure for 1958 is an average for the nine years 1954–62.

n.a. = not available.

and 2.5 percent per year. Today our population is growing at only about 1.5 percent. This has been accompanied by a drop in the rate of increase of GNP.

The increase in output per capita provides a better index of consumer welfare and economic performance. Here too there has been something of a slowdown. The rate of increase was typically above 2 percent a year before 1914, but has been below that level for most of the time since. This is a bit puzzling. We saw in Chapter 25 that the growth in productivity of our labor and capital has not decreased in recent decades. On the contrary, productivity seems to be rising faster than ever before. Why, then, should output per capita be slowing down? The answer can only be that inputs per capita have fallen. Specifically, we aren't putting in as much labor per head as we did a half-century ago.

In 1914 the ten-hour day and the six-day week were standard practice except for a few groups of skilled craftsmen. By the mid-thirties the five-day, forty-hour week was firmly established. Since then hours worked per year have fallen further through the spread of paid holidays and longer vacations. The overall result is striking. Between 1910 and 1960 the number of people in the U.S. labor force doubled, but the man-hours used in production rose by only one third. Thus we should not be surprised that output per head isn't rising as fast as it used to. Except for the acceleration of productivity, the slowdown of output would be even more noticeable.

Leisure time has value in itself. The decline in working hours represents partly a choice of greater leisure over larger incomes. So we may still be getting "better off" as fast as we did in the palmy days before World War I. But in recent decades more of our rising welfare has taken the form of leisure, and less has appeared as increased material consumption, than was true at an earlier time.

THE UNITED STATES AND ITS NEIGHBORS: TYPICAL GROWTH RATES IN THE WEST

What is the long-term record of other industrialized capitalist countries? What constitutes par in growth rates?

For most of the industrial nations we now have national income estimates ranging over periods of fifty to a hundred years (Table 26–3).[7] Viewed with imagination, this table is rich in suggestions of the past. Note first the wide differences in rate of population growth. The highest rates are found in the United States and the British Commonwealth countries, while the European countries show much lower rates. Countries with more rapid population growth typically show also a more rapid rise in total output. Population increase does not seem to have been a handicap to nations whose institutions and resources were favorable to economic growth.

The rate of increase in output *per capita* shows no clear relation to population growth. Some countries with high population growth stand near the top of the table (United States, Canada, South Africa), but others are near the bottom (Australia, New Zealand). Some of the European countries with low population increase had high growth rates (Nor-

---

[7] Simon Kuznets, "Quantitative Aspects of the Economic Growth of Nations: I. Levels and Variability of Rates of Growth," *Economic Development and Cultural Change*, Vol. V, No. 1 (October, 1956), Tables 1 and 2.

way, Sweden), but others had much slower growth (Italy, Spain, Hungary).

Western economic growth has been gradual. Half the countries in Table 26–3 fall in the range of 1 to 2 percent a year as regards growth of per capita output. It is the steady and sustained character of the growth, rather than its speed, which has brought these countries to their present high level of output. The U.S. record compares well with that of other in-

TABLE 26–3

Long-term Growth of Population, Output, and
Output per Capita, Selected Countries
(Ranked in order of growth in output per capita)

				Annual Percentage Change in		
Country	Initial Period	Terminal Period	Decades Included	Output per Capita	Population	Total Output
1. Sweden	1861–68	1950–54	8.75	2.5	0.6	3.1
2. Japan	1878–87	1950–54	6.95	2.4	1.2	3.6
3. South Africa	1911–12	1949/50–1952/53	3.95	2.2	1.9	4.1
4. Norway	1900–1908	1950–54	4.8	2.1	0.8	3.0
5. United States	1869–78	1950–54	7.85	1.9	1.6	3.5
6. Canada	1870–79	1950–54	7.75	1.8	1.7	3.5
7. Ireland and Eire	1860–69	1949–53	8.65	1.6	−0.4	1.2
8. Denmark	1870–79	1950–54	7.8	1.6	1.0	2.6
9. Switzerland	1890–99	1949–53	5.65	1.4	0.7	2.2
10. Germany	1860–69	1950–54	8.75	1.4	1.0	2.5
11. France	1841–50	1949–53	10.55	1.3	0.1	1.4
12. United Kingdom	1860–69	1949–53	8.65	1.2	0.8	2.0
13. New Zealand	1901	1949/50–1953/54	5.025	1.1	1.7	2.9
14. Italy	1862–68	1950–54	8.7	1.0	0.7	1.7
15. Australia	1898–1903	1949/50–1953/54	5.1	0.9	1.6	2.6
16. Netherlands	1900–1908	1950–54	4.8	0.9	1.3	2.2
17. Hungary	1899–1901	1949	4.9	0.8	0.6	1.5
18. Spain	1906–13	1949–53	4.15	0.5	0.8	1.4

dustrial countries over the long run. But we have not been the fastest-growing country, as we are sometimes prone to think. Several other countries, notably Japan and Sweden, have outdone us in this respect.

Is there any tendency for the growth rate of industrial countries to slow down over the long run? Professor Kuznets concludes that there is. His tabulations[8] split the growth record of each country into a pre-1914 and a post-1914 period. Some of the younger industrial countries (Swe-

---

[8] Simon Kuznets, *Six Lectures on Economic Growth* (Glencoe, Ill.: Free Press of Glencoe, Inc., 1959), Lecture II.

den, Japan, Italy, Russia) show an acceleration of growth since 1914. In most countries, however, per capita output has risen less rapidly since 1914 than it did before. For the European countries, which suffered widespread devastation in two world wars, this is perhaps not surprising. It is more surprising for the United States, Canada, and other overseas areas.

Kuznets concludes that countries pass through three phases: a phase in which the growth rate accelerates markedly, a phase of more or less constant growth, and finally a phase of retarded growth. He finds the reason for the eventual retardation on the side of demand rather than supply: ". . . there are no inherently *compelling* reasons for the rate of growth of per capita product to decline . . . technological and other limitations on the *supply* side can hardly be viewed as an important factor. The major reason would therefore lie on the demand side. A long-term rise in real income per capita would make leisure an increasingly preferred good, as is clearly evidenced by the marked reduction in the working week in freely organized, nonauthoritarian advanced countries. One could argue that after a high level of per capita income is attained, the pressure on the demand side for further increases is likely to slacken."[9]

One is cautioned against premature generalization, however, by the fact that most of these countries have experienced a remarkable spurt of growth since World War II. Japan and West Germany raised their GNP at almost 10 percent a year during the 1950's, apparently exceeding even the U.S.S.R. in this respect. The average for the European common market area was better than 5 percent. It is too early to say whether this marks a genuine new era, or whether these growth rates will taper off during the 1960's and 1970's.

TRANSFORMATION OF THE STRUCTURE OF PRODUCTION

From this detour into general Western experience we return to the American story. National output has not grown through everything increasing in the same proportion. Growth and structural change are inseparable, for reasons given in Chapter 25.

The changes in the pattern of American output since 1870 are shown in Table 26–4. The main trends are familiar to any reader of American history. Note first the decline in the relative importance of agriculture, from a quarter of national output in 1870 to less than 5 percent today. Farm production has continued to grow in absolute terms, otherwise we should all be on short rations. But GNP has grown so much faster that agriculture's share has fallen drastically.

The reverse of the coin is the rise of manufacturing from 15 percent of production in 1870 to around 30 percent at present. The manufacturing share has been leveling off, however, and seems unlikely to increase much further.

The trade sector shows surprising stability over the long run. True,

---

[9] *Ibid.*, p. 38.

employment in trade has risen relative to other sectors. But in terms of *value added,* trade has fluctuated between 15 and 17 percent with no upward trend.

Government production has risen from 5 percent of GNP at the turn of the century to more than 12 percent at the present time. The reasons for this were analyzed in Chapter 15. A major factor is the much higher level of military expenditure.

There has been no appreciable change since 1900 in the relative importance of the service industries. But this is misleading because the figures include domestic service, which is a sharply declining industry. (The

TABLE 26–4

Distribution of National Income by Industrial Origin, United States,* 1869–1959
(Percent)

	Agri-culture†	Manufac-turing and Mining‡	Con-struc-tion	Trade	Finance, Insur-ance, Real Estate, and Other§	Transpor-tation, Commu-nication, and Public Utilities	Services	Govern-ment and Rest of World
1869	23.1	16.8	5.9	15.8	8.0	11.3	14.8	4.1
1879	19.9	16.1	5.2	16.9	8.4	13.5	15.9	4.1
1889	15.1	22.4	6.3	17.9	8.3	11.9	13.3	4.8
1899	19.9	21.2	4.4	17.5	8.2	10.8	11.8	6.5
1909	21.0	22.5	4.6	17.0	8.8	11.1	10.0	5.1
1919	21.0	26.9	2.7	15.1	7.9	10.7	7.4	8.3
1929	11.6	27.2	4.3	15.2	10.5	11.8	11.2	8.3
1929	9.4	27.2	4.3	15.2	14.5	10.9	11.8	6.7
1939	8.2	26.7	3.2	17.1	10.9	10.3	11.4	12.1
1949	7.8	30.8	4.8	18.6	9.2	8.5	9.8	10.6
1959	4.2	31.3	5.4	16.7	10.1	8.2	11.3	12.7

* Sources: 1869–1929: NICB, *Enterprise and Social Progress,* 1939, pp. 84, 95. 1929–59; *U.S. Income and Output, 1958,* p. 130; and Survey of Current Business, July, 1960.
† Figures for 1929–59 include forestry and fisheries.
‡ Figures for 1869–1929 include quarrying.
§ Figures for 1869–1929 are sum of "Finance" and unallocated "Other." Figures for 1929–59 are for "Finance, Insurance and Real Estate."

disappearance of servants is recognized throughout the world as one of the best indicators of economic development!) If this were separated out, production of services outside the home would show a considerable increase.

The sectors used in Table 26–4 are very broad. If we dig more deeply into any of them, we find more detailed crosscurrents. The make-up of the manufacturing sector, for example, has changed a great deal. A few important gainers and losers may be found in Table 26–5.

These trends are not surprising. In a capital-using economy, it is natural that production of capital goods should grow in importance. In addition to our own requirements, we export substantial amounts of chemicals, metals, machinery, automobiles, trucks, and tractors to other countries. In consumer goods we are dependent mainly on home demand; and some of these industries, notably textiles, are being invaded by foreign producers who have a comparative advantage in light manufacturing.

How far will past trends continue in the future? If we could extend Table 26–4 to the year 2000, what would it look like? Some of the past trends will doubtless slow down. The percentage of GNP coming from agriculture is already so low that it cannot fall much further. The manufacturing percentage will rise little if any. Overall, one can predict that the industries concerned with *physical production* will shrink gradually in terms of the percentage of GNP which they produce and the proportion of the labor force which they employ. The industries producing *intangible services* (trade, finance, the service industries, and government) will

TABLE 26–5

	PERCENTAGE OF MANUFACTURING OUTPUT	
INDUSTRY	1929	1959
Decreases		
Lumber and furniture products	7.0	4.5
Food products	9.8	8.4
Textiles	8.2	3.9
Clothing	5.8	4.0
Leather and leather products	2.8	1.3
Increases		
Automobiles and automobile equipment	4.3	6.3
Transportation equipment except automobiles	1.4	5.9
Electrical machinery	4.8	8.0
Machinery, except electrical	8.6	10.5
Chemicals	5.2	7.7

grow in relative importance. These industries already provide more than half the employment in the economy. This figure may rise above 60 percent by the end of the century.

There are two reasons why this is a safe prediction: income elasticity of demand for services is typically higher than for commodities, and production of services is less susceptible to mechanization. So, as consumers demand more and more services, this is bound to mean more employment. In manufacturing, on the other hand, it is often possible to meet rising demand with fewer workers through continued progress in mechanization and automation.

This is not to the credit of the service industries—rather the reverse. If more and more people are employed in these industries, and if the possibility of raising their productivity through mechanization is slight, this will slow down the overall rate of productivity increase in the economy.

REGIONAL DIFFERENCES IN OUTPUT AND INCOME

Most of us are concerned, not with national averages, but with what is happening in our own state and community; and what is happening economically may be quite different in Bangor, Richmond, Vincennes, and El Paso.

Industrial growth is usually concentrated at the outset. It settles into a country at some focal point where there is a clustering of population, transportation facilities, and other favorable circumstances. The industrial midlands in Britain, the Rhineland in Germany, the Montreal-Toronto-Windsor axis in Canada, and the state of São Paulo in Brazil exemplify this tendency. So it was in the United States. The coastal strip from Boston to Baltimore was the cradle of American industry. In 1860 there was still little industry south of Baltimore or west of the Alleghanies.

How does economic expansion in the industrial center affect the outlying regions? Economists have usually taken it for granted that the effects will be favorable, assuming that center and periphery are linked by an efficient transportation network. Higher incomes generated in the industrial centers will then get spread around the country in several ways: (1) The growth of population and industry in the center provides a growing market for foodstuffs and raw materials produced in the outlying regions, enabling the latter to increase their cash income. (2) Rising productivity in the center means higher wages there. This will induce people from outlying areas to migrate to the cities in the hope of higher incomes. As this happens, labor will become scarcer in the periphery, and wages there will also be forced upwards. (3) To the extent that wages remain depressed in the outlying regions, this provides an incentive for industry to migrate to those regions in search of cheaper labor. With capital flowing toward the periphery, and labor moving toward the center, factor returns will gradually become equalized throughout the country.

This optimistic view was adopted with enthusiasm by people in the early industrial centers. Bostonians, New Yorkers, and Philadelphians had little doubt that what was good for them was good for the country. But there were always mutterings of dissent from the West and South. The great fortunes, it seemed, were being made in the industrial centers. The rest of the country was reduced to providing these centers with raw materials and a market, and was forced to pay off to Eastern capital in high freight rates, high interest rates, and other ways.

At a more academic level, some economists have pointed out that the favorable or "spread" effects of industrial progress may be offset by "backwash" effects which are harmful to the nonindustrial regions:

1. While the peripheral areas can sell more food and raw materials to industrial areas, they may be able to do so only at unfavorable prices, i.e., prices which are falling relative to the prices of manufactured goods. Farmers are smaller and less well organized than manufacturers, and income

elasticity of demand for their products is relatively low.

2. Migrants to the industrial centers are likely to be young people with more than average energy and intelligence. The periphery is left with the least productive groups, and its human resources run downhill.

3. There are marked advantages to a new company in locating where others are already located. There they find a concentration of workers, suppliers, and customers; many bankers, accountants, management consultants, and other purveyors of business services; and rapid communication with the rest of the business community. These external economies may outweigh the pull of lower wages in the hinterland, and industry may continue indefinitely to cluster in a few areas. These "pessimists" also have less faith than the "optimists" in the actual prevalence of competition and in the efficiency of commodity and factor markets.

What has actually happened in the United States? Professor Easterlin's measurements (Table 26–6)[10] suggest that, at least since 1880, the

TABLE 26–6

Regional Differences in Personal Income per Capita, 1880–1950

	INCOME PER CAPITA AS A PERCENTAGE OF THE NATIONAL LEVEL				
REGION	1880	1900	1920	1930	1950
New England	141	134	124	126	108
Middle Atlantic	141	139	134	137	118
East North Central	102	106	108	115	112
West North Central	90	97	87	82	95
South Atlantic	45	45	59	55	71
East South Central	51	49	52	50	61
West South Central	60	61	72	62	81
Mountain	168	139	100	82	95
Pacific	204	163	135	128	120

Source: Richard A. Easterlin, *Trends*, pp. 139–40.

trend has been toward greater equality of income levels throughout the country. By 1880 the United States had two nuclei of economic growth. The traditional industrial centers of the East remained predominant, with an income level 40 percent above the national average. But a new area of high incomes and rapid growth had sprung up on the Pacific Coast. With its rich resources of land, gold, minerals, and timber, this region had incomes double the national average. It made good sense to go West, if you went far enough. The Southern states, on the other hand, stood at the bottom of the list, with incomes only half the national average.

An observer at this time might well have wondered whether these stark differences were part of the natural order of things, and whether

---

[10] Richard A. Easterlin, "Interregional Differences in Per Capita Income, Population, and Total Income, 1840–1950," in *Trends*, pp. 73–140.

they would continue indefinitely. The answer is now clear. They did not continue. From 1900 on, the Southern states gradually improved their relative position, and their progress was accelerated by World War II and the postwar boom. They are still below average, but not so far below. The Pacific Coast and Middle Atlantic regions have continued at the top, but their relative advantage has diminished. New England has declined to the point at which it is little more than average in income terms.

What accounts for this gradual reduction of regional differences? A major factor has been the more even diffusion of industry throughout the nation. The Midwest has always had a substantial blend of industry along with its agriculture, and the Pacific Coast has developed industries to serve its fast growing regional market. But now the Southern and Southwestern states have also become major centers for textiles, clothing, pulp and pa-

TABLE 26–7

Regional Differences in Degree of Industrialization,* 1880–1950

	LABOR FORCE INDUSTRIALIZATION AS PERCENTAGE OF THE NATIONAL LEVEL				
REGION	1880	1900	1920	1930	1950
New England	155	142	125	120	110
Middle Atlantic	150	140	125	120	110
East North Central	98	108	110	109	104
West North Central	77	82	86	85	86
South Atlantic	51	61	73	80	93
East South Central	45	53	62	67	83
West South Central	49	52	70	76	92
Mountain	145	111	90	88	94
Pacific	137	118	110	109	105

Source: Richard A. Easterlin, *Trends*, pp. 139–40.

* "Industrialization" was defined by the percentage of the labor force employed outside agriculture. For a particular date, this percentage was calculated for each region and for the country as a whole. Each region's percentage was then divided by the average for the country as a whole to yield the figures shown in the table. In 1880, for example, the proportion of the South Atlantic region's labor force employed outside agriculture was only half as high as for the nation as a whole. The Middle Atlantic region's proportion, however, was 50 percent above the national average.

per, furniture, chemicals, oil, aircraft, atomic energy, and space installations. Texas matches California's reputation as a state of permanent boom.

The statistics of this process are shown in Table 26–7. Industrialization is measured here by the division of the labor force between agricultural and nonagricultural pursuits. Note that in 1880 the Southern states were only about one third as industrial as the East Coast and Pacific Coast regions. But this eventually began to change, gradually up to 1930, more rapidly during the enormous expansion after 1940. By 1950 there was much less difference among regions in the proportion of the population engaged in agriculture.

Why does this lead to a leveling up of per capita incomes? Because per capita income in agriculture has typically been less than half of the level in industry. Thus the higher the percentage of a state's population engaged in agriculture, the more this drags down its average income. As the percentage engaged in agriculture becomes more nearly equal throughout the country, this reason for income differences decreases in importance. There has also been considerable leveling of incomes *within* the agricultural and *within* the industrial sector. In 1880 the average incomes of industrial workers in the richest (Pacific Coast) region were more than double the level of the poorest (South Atlantic) region. By 1950, the Pacific Coast was only about 40 percent higher. Within agriculture, where regional differences have always been large, income per head on the Pacific Coast in 1880 was 3½ times the level of the South Atlantic states. By 1950 this had dropped to 2½ times.

Another significant development is a more even spread of property income throughout the country. In 1880 the "propertied interests" were clustered along the east and west coasts. Property income per capita in the three Southern regions was only *one quarter* as high as in the New England, Middle Atlantic, and Pacific regions. By 1950, the South Atlantic and West South Central regions were drawing *half* as much property income per head as the richest regions. Ownership of businesses and securities is now spread more evenly around the country than it used to be.

These trends support the view that in a market economy the benefits of economic progress will penetrate to all corners of the nation, though not with perfect equality or lightning speed. The United States has experienced a vast migration of labor from low-income to high-income regions, and a large movement of capital in the opposite direction. One should not conclude, however, that reduction of regional inequalities has been due entirely to market forces. The leveling of industrial earnings has been hastened by minimum wage legislation and trade union pressure. Government price support programs have raised the relative level of farm incomes. The T.V.A. and other federal power developments have changed the face of large regions. Since 1940 government policy has influenced the location of military facilities and of plants engaged in military production, and these locational decisions have been oriented heavily toward the West and South.

OUR CHANGING INTERNATIONAL POSITION

We may conclude with a word on our changing economic relations with other countries. The changes are interesting, not only for their own sake, but because they are often thought to represent the stages through which any young industrial country must pass as it moves toward maturity.

Before the Civil War we typically imported more goods than we exported. But from the early 1870's onward, we normally had an export surplus. We were gradually becoming more self-sufficient in manufactures, while the opening of the West and the cheapening of rail and ocean transport were swelling our agricultural exports to Europe. For another generation, however, our export surplus was not sufficient to cover our other commitments. We had to pay interest and dividends to foreigners on the money they had loaned us, this figure running upwards of $100 million in most years. The era of free-spending American tourists had begun, and tourist expenditures rose rapidly toward the $100 million mark. So we were usually in deficit on an overall basis. Our indebtedness to foreigners continued to creep up, reaching a peak of about $3.5 billion in the late 1890's.

In 1897 our exports for the first time passed the billion dollar mark. In 1898 we had an unprecedented export surplus of $600 million. From that time on, we began to repay our indebtedness. In the normal course of events, we would doubtless have moved gradually from a net debtor to a net creditor position.

Our emergence as a creditor nation was greatly accelerated by the two world wars. During both wars we were the great arsenal of production for our allies. We shipped large quantities of foodstuffs, fuels, weapons, and other war materials, while receiving hardly any goods in return. How were they to pay for these supplies? First, by liquidating their holdings of U.S. securities and other assets, so that our foreign indebtedness vanished. Second, by running up large debts to us. During World War II the amounts involved were so staggering that they were mostly written off as part of our contribution to the war. But the Western allies did what they could in the way of payment. Thus they emerged in 1945 stripped of their asset holdings in the United States, while we emerged as the one great creditor nation.

At this stage we might have settled back to "live on our capital," drawing a large amount each year in interest and dividend payments on our foreign assets. Since other countries must basically make payment in goods, we would have had to run a trade deficit, consistently importing more than we export. This is usually termed a *mature creditor position*, and corresponds to the actual situation of Great Britain in the half century before 1914.

But we have not actually followed this course since 1945. Instead, we have continued to invest several billion abroad each year, partly through private and partly through government channels. These new investments have exceeded the interest and dividends due us from other countries, so there has been a continuing net outflow of capital. To finance this outflow, as well as our foreign military expenditures and other current items, we have had to maintain a sizable export surplus. When the surplus has not been sufficient, we have encountered gold losses and the other difficulties described in Chapter 24.

This process will doubtless continue for some time to come. But as our foreign assets rise, our annual interest and dividend receipts from abroad will also rise. In time this inflow of interest payments may exceed the outflow of new capital, so that we shall finally reach a mature creditor position. If and when this occurs, we should be prepared to adjust gracefully to a net surplus of imports. This kind of "unfavorable" balance of trade is really a favorable balance, for the nation is getting an increase in real income without any current effort.

What about detailed changes in the make-up of our foreign trade over the past century? The changes in *kinds of good traded* (Tables 26–8 and 26–9) are about what one would expect in a country making the

TABLE 26–8

Structure of U.S. Exports, 1850–1960
(Percent of Total)

Period	Crude Materials	Crude Foodstuffs	Manufactured Foodstuffs	Semi-Manufactures	Finished Manufactures
1851–60	61.7	6.6	15.4	4.0	12.3
1881–90	35.9	18.0	25.3	5.2	15.6
1901–10	31.0	10.6	20.1	12.8	25.6
1921–30	26.0	8.5	11.8	13.3	40.8
1951–55	13.0	7.1	5.6	11.6	62.7
1959–61	12.0	8.5	5.8	15.8	57.9

Source: *Historical Statistics of the United States; Survey of Current Business,* July, 1962.

TABLE 26–9

Structure of U.S. Imports, 1850–1960
(Percent of Total)

Period	Crude Materials	Crude Foodstuffs	Manufactured Foodstuffs	Semi-Manufactures	Finished Manufactures
1851–60	9.6	11.7	15.4	12.5	40.5
1881–90	21.3	15.4	17.8	14.8	30.8
1901–10	34.0	11.9	12.1	17.2	24.8
1921–30	37.1	11.8	11.4	18.2	21.4
1951–55	26.3	19.5	10.1	27.7	20.4
1959–61	20.9	11.9	10.8	21.4	35.0

Source: *Historical Statistics of the United States; Survey of Current Business,* July, 1962.

transition from an agricultural economy to the world's leading industrial nation. Before 1900 food products, minerals, and other raw materials were dominant in our exports. Around 1900, however, our manufacturing industries reached the stage at which exports of manufactured goods began to exceed food exports; and this trend has continued. Today, three quarters of our exports consist of manufactured products, and we sell more manufactures abroad than any other country. This contradicts the view that our high wage level puts us at a *general* disadvantage in competing with the manufacturers of other nations.

One fifth of our imports consist of tropical food products such as coffee, tea, cocoa, sugar, and bananas. Another quarter of our imports are minerals, oil, rubber, and other raw materials needed to feed our giant industrial machine. Rather surprisingly, more than half of our imports are manufactured goods; and these come mainly from Japan, Canada, Britain, and Western Europe. Yet we also export a large volume of manufactures to these countries. Why do the rich countries of the world take in each

TABLE 26–10

U.S. Exports by Destination, 1860–1960
(Percent of total)

Period	Europe	Canada	South America	Central America	Asia	Africa and Oceania
1860	74.8	6.9	4.7	8.8	2.4	2.5
1871–75	80.2	6.4	4.0	7.2	1.0	1.2
1891–95	79.5	5.5	3.7	6.8	2.3	2.2
1911–15	64.0	14.2	5.2	7.7	5.6	3.3
1931–35	47.4	14.8	7.0	8.0	17.3	5.5
1951–55	23.4	18.8	15.1	10.9	13.7	5.3
1959–61	32.4	20.8	11.8	9.2	19.4	6.4

TABLE 26–11

U.S. Imports by Source, 1860–1960
(Percent of total)

Period	Europe	Canada	South America	Central America	Asia	Africa and Oceania
1860	61.3	6.7	9.9	12.5	8.3	1.3
1871–75	55.6	5.9	11.0	16.6	9.7	1.3
1891–95	50.6	4.6	14.9	16.3	10.8	2.7
1911–15	46.6	7.7	12.8	14.5	15.8	2.5
1931–35	30.1	13.8	14.3	10.3	28.7	2.8
1951–55	20.2	22.5	21.2	12.0	16.3	7.7
1959–61	29.2	20.7	16.2	10.1	17.7	6.1

other's washing in this way? The answer lies in the principle of comparative advantage analyzed in Chapter 16. For some manufactured goods, the United States is the lowest-cost location in the world. For other types, Japan or Britain or Italy may be the most efficient location. Thus all can gain by exchanging their particular specialties.

This casts an interesting sidelight on the dilemma: what happens when the whole world becomes industrialized? In the past, much of world trade has consisted in the underdeveloped countries shipping food and raw materials to Europe and North America, taking manufactures in return.

But now every country wants to industrialize and produce its own manufactures. So what happens? Won't the basis for world trade dry up and disappear? On the basis of trade relations among the present industrial nations, the answer seems to be "no." Development of manufacturing in all countries will not eliminate comparative advantage. West Africa may end up as the world's leading textile producer, Japan as the largest ship-builder, India as one of the lowest-cost steel centers. Each nation can continue to exchange its specialties, and the volume of world trade may rise rather than fall. But this depends on the course of world politics more than on economic considerations. World trade *could* flourish in the peaceable international community which is not yet in sight.

As regards the direction of our foreign trade (Tables 26–10 and 26–11), the most striking feature is growing *diversification* over the course of time. The other countries of North and South America have grown in importance to the point where they now account for almost half our imports and exports. Asia has also grown in relative importance, mainly because of the remarkable expansion of the Japanese economy. Our trade with Europe, which was of dominant importance before 1914 has now dropped to about one third of the total. But it is still large in absolute terms, and the phenomenal growth of Western Europe since 1950 means that it will continue to be a major trade partner in the future.

SUMMARY

1. The United States growth rate accelerated materially in the period 1830–60. This was associated with westward expansion, very rapid population increase, establishment of a railroad network, marked technical developments in both agriculture and industry, a rise in the rate of domestic saving, and large-scale borrowing from abroad.

2. Over the years since 1870, U.S. output per capita has advanced at an average rate of about 2 percent a year. The rate of growth has been uneven, however, and there was one major setback during the 1930's. *Total output* has grown more slowly since 1914 than before 1914, due mainly to slower growth of population. The growth of *output per capita* has also slowed down a bit in recent decades, mainly because of a marked drop in hours worked per year by members of the labor force. If leisure were counted as part of national output, one might conclude that the rate of progress has not declined.

3. A few other Western industrial countries have grown faster than the United States over the past century, but most have grown more slowly. There is no apparent relation between rate of population growth and rate of increase in output per capita. Most countries show the same slowing down of growth after 1914 observed in the United States. But Japan and Western Europe have once more grown very rapidly since 1945. It is too early to say whether this acceleration will continue.

4. Growth of total output in the United States was accompanied by marked shifts in the composition of output. Agriculture and domestic service declined relatively, manufacturing rose and then leveled off, government service and some of the private service industries rose continuously. Within the manufacturing sector, output of capital goods grew faster than output of

consumer goods. Production of services now exceeds goods production in value, and will preponderate increasingly in the future.

5. In 1880 there were large regional differences in output and income per capita. But these differences diminished gradually up to 1940, and more rapidly since that time. The reasons are complex, but one major reason has been a more even diffusion of industrial activity throughout the country.

6. Our international economic position has changed from that of a debtor nation in 1900 to a large creditor nation today. We are continuing to build up our foreign assets by both private and government investment. We may in time reach a mature creditor position, in which the inflow of interest and dividend payments will exceed the outflow of new investment. But this stage is not yet in sight.

7. It is interesting that most of our exports and imports consist of manufactured goods; and that the bulk of our foreign trade is with the other industrialized countries. This suggests that the principal of comparative advantage continues to operate; and that the spread of manufacturing to all parts of the world is not incompatible with a growing volume of international trade.

27

The Soviet Experience: A Growth Race?

> The Dodo suddenly called out, "The race is over!" and they all crowded around it, panting, and asking "But who has won?"
>
> This question the Dodo could not answer without a great deal of thought, and it sat for a long time with one finger pressed upon its forehead (the position in which you usually see Shakespeare in the pictures of him), while the rest waited in silence. At last the Dodo said, "*Everybody* has won, and all must have prizes."
>
> *Alice's Adventures in Wonderland*

FROM the eighteenth century until World War I there was only one proven prescription for economic growth. Britain, the United States, Germany and other capitalist countries showed the way; and it was assumed that any other industrializing country would follow the same pattern.

But since 1917 a second prescription had been abroad in the world. Soviet economists maintain that this prescription is inherently superior. Under central planning, it is said, growth does not just happen. A planned economy can decide how fast it wants to grow. By setting the target high enough, it is possible to outdo anything that has been accomplished in the capitalist countries.

It is argued also that the Soviet prescription is preferable for the poor countries of Asia, Africa, and Latin America. Soviet bloc leaders say, "Of course it is possible for a poor country to lift itself by its bootstraps. We know how to do it. In fact we have done it in one country after another.

The requirements are government operation of all means of production, a national economic plan which emphasizes investment and restricts consumption, and rigid political discipline through a one-party system."

So it is important to ask what the Soviet system has actually accomplished over the past half-century. How rapid has been the growth in national output? How have the results been accomplished? Is the pattern of growth basically different from that in capitalist countries? Will growth continue at the same rate in the future, and will the U.S.S.R. eventually surpass the production levels of the U.S.A. and Western Europe?

The Measurement Problem

The student of Soviet growth is faced at the outset with a formidable problem of measurement. This is not due mainly to inadequacy of data on individual products. In the post-Stalin era, at least, Soviet economic statistics have been comprehensive and open to examination by Western scholars. While concepts and definitions differ somewhat from those used in the West, and while there may be some optimistic bias in the production totals, there is no reason to suspect extensive falsification.

The main problem is that the growth rate for individual products varies enormously. Output of power, metals, machinery, and other capital goods has risen very fast. Most consumer goods show much lower rates of growth. The increase in some types of agricultural output has been quite disappointing. So in calculating an overall growth rate for the economy, everything depends on how much *weight* one gives to each line of production. And since heterogeneous products can be added up only in value terms, this raises the question of the proper *price* to be attached to each product.

The characteristics of the Soviet pricing system were pointed out in Part One. Prices of capital goods are relatively low by U.S. standards, while prices of consumer goods are relatively high. The whole price structure has been revised on several occasions. So it makes considerable difference whether one makes comparisons in terms of 1937 prices, or 1950 prices, or 1962 prices. And if one valued Soviet production at U.S. prices the result would again be different.

Fortunately, while calculations on various bases differ considerably, the outlines of the story remain much the same. In what follows, I have tried to use the most plausible estimates by leading authorities, but anyone interested in the niceties of measurement should consult the original sources.[1]

---

[1] See in particular Abram Bergson, *The Real National Income of Soviet Russia Since 1928* (Cambridge, Mass.: Harvard University Press, 1961); and Abram Bergson and Simon Kuznets (eds.), *Economic Trends in the Soviet Union* (Cambridge, Mass.: Harvard University Press, 1963). These sources are referred to hereafter as *Real National Income* and *Economic Trends* respectively.

The Vagaries of History

Another important consideration is that Soviet history has been punctuated by war and invasion, and so economic progress has been jerky and discontinuous. From 1914 to 1928 the economy was ravaged by foreign war followed by civil war, and then recovered gradually under a regime which was still largely one of private ownership. From necessity rather than conviction, Soviet leaders left the peasants in control of the land while private trade and handicrafts flourished in the cities. Only factory industries were fully nationalized. Central economic planning was not yet born.

The year 1928 marks a decisive turning point. By this time Stalin had triumphed over Trotsky and other political rivals, and was in a position to shape the course of Soviet development. He announced a policy of rapid industrialization and complete socialization, applied both to industry and agriculture. The peasants were forced into collective farms amidst bloodshed and disorganization of production. Guide lines for the economy were laid down in a Five-year Plan for 1928–32, followed by a second plan for 1933–37, and so on. There was a rapid build-up of industrial capacity, particularly of industries producing capital goods and armaments. By the mid-thirties World War II was already visible on the horizon, and Soviet leaders were racing against time to achieve self-sufficiency in military production.

The storm broke in 1941. The most productive part of the country was invaded and occupied. Despite efforts to shift production to safe areas behind the Urals, Soviet output fell considerably and the population suffered severe hardships. But with the remaining production, and with massive aid from the West, Russia managed eventually to roll back the invading armies. When Talleyrand was asked what he had been doing during the French Revolution, he replied "I survived." Stalin might have given the same answer in 1945 in justification of his iron policies.

For several years after 1945 the U.S.S.R. was engaged in rebuilding the devastated areas, shifting population and production back to pre-war locations, and replacing wartime losses of machinery and equipment. In 1948 the average Soviet consumer was probably no better off than he had been in 1928, perhaps no better off than the average Russian of 1913. One could well ask, "What has the common man gained from the sacrifices and pressures imposed on him by the Soviet regime?"

Since the late 1940's, however, the picture has brightened considerably. Industrial and agricultural production have risen substantially, and consumers have begun to share in this larger output. Living standards are already well above 1950 levels, and the advance is continuing. It is this recent record which leads Soviet officials to proclaim optimistically that they will soon surpass the capitalist countries in per capita output.

Because of this roller-coaster pattern of economic growth, it is not very meaningful to discuss trends over the whole period since 1917. It is better to concentrate on periods of *peacetime development within the present institutional framework*. This means focusing on: (1) the years 1928–40, during which the institutional framework assumed its present shape, and the first great burst of industrial development was carried through; and (2) the period since 1950, which has been one of continued industrial development, accompanied for the first time by significant progress in agriculture.

THE PERIOD 1928–40: GREAT EFFORT, LOW EFFICIENCY

The story of these years is soon told. There was great effort to increase the productive resources of the economy—to enlarge the labor force, to bring more land under cultivation, to build factories and machinery. Total output rose at better than 4 percent a year. The striking

TABLE 27–1
Annual Percentage Rates of Change, 1928–40*

	TOTAL ECONOMY	INDUSTRY	AGRICULTURE
Output	4.2	9.8	0.3
Factor inputs	4.2	7.7	1.8
Labor input	3.7	6.6	1.1
Capital input	9.8	14.9	−0.4
Land input	. . .	. . .	2.3
Factor productivity	0.1	2.1	−1.4

* Data for this table and for the later table, 27–2, covering the years 1950–58 are drawn from essays by Raymond P. Powell (industry), D. Gale Johnson (agriculture), and Abram Bergson (total economy), in *Economic Trends*

thing, however, is that output rose at only about the same rate as resource inputs. There seems to have been virtually no gain in productivity over the period.

Another feature of this period was the divergence between the performance of industry and agriculture. Industrial output rose rapidly and productivity rose moderately, but agricultural production stagnated and productivity declined. This cleavage in the economy has persisted to the present day.

Looking first at industry, the industrial labor force doubled between 1928 and 1940. This vast transfer from country to city was accomplished partly by economic incentives. Skilled workers in industry, and production workers who were willing to work hard at piece rates, were relatively well paid. Meanwhile government paid the collective farmers such low prices for their produce that there was a strong economic incentive to leave agriculture. These incentives were reinforced by massive propaganda in favor of industrial employment. Women as well as men were urged to enlist in the labor force, and occupations from top to bottom of the economy were opened to women on an unprecedented scale.

The build-up of industrial capital also proceeded rapidly. From 1928 to 1940, capital in use rose about 15 percent per year, or fourfold over the period. This was accomplished through the industrial targets laid down in the five-year plans. The economy was deliberately oriented away from consumer goods production and toward coal, oil, electric power, steel, machinery, and other capital goods. Gross investment was raised from 12.5 percent of GNP in 1928 to 26 percent in 1937. Most of this investment went into heavy industry, power, and transport. Housing, agriculture, light industry, and other sectors were relatively neglected.

In view of this massive effort, it is not surprising that industrial production rose 10 percent a year. Yet productivity rose only 2 percent a year, and accounted for only one fifth of the increase in output. How can this be explained? During these years the U.S.S.R. was borrowing technical know-how from the West on a large scale. Western engineers helped build factories and power plants. Much foreign machinery was imported and later copied in Russian models. The growth of Soviet industry should also have produced economies of scale plus external economies which would show up as a rise in productivity.

Against this must be set the fact that industrial workers and factory managers were new and inexperienced. Many mistakes were made, and much effort went into training rather than production. Methods of central planning were new and primitive, leading to strategic errors and to the kinds of routine inefficiency described in Chapter 10. Another negative factor was the secret police activity and the bloody purges which marked the Stalin era. Fear of a Siberian labor camp or the firing squad did not prove a good stimulus to managerial efficiency.

While industry was advancing, agriculture lagged behind. During the collectivization drive, hundreds of thousands of the more prosperous and efficient peasants were shot or deported. Many peasants decided to eat their farm animals rather than turn them over to the collectives, and livestock numbers dropped sharply. Government policy toward the new collectives was discouraging to production. They were obliged to sell most of their produce to government agencies at artificially low prices. City workers enjoyed low food costs at the expense of the farmers. The amount of capital allocated to farm machinery, fertilizers, and other forms of agricultural investment was small compared to the heavy investment in industry.

The results stand out plainly in the production statistics. Between 1928 and 1940 crop production rose by one quarter, but livestock production fell by one sixth. Total farm output increased less than 5 percent, well below the 15 percent increase in population. Agricultural efficiency, measured by outputs per unit of input, fell by about 15 percent.[2]

Despite the lag of agriculture, *total* Soviet output rose from 1928 to 1940 at more than 4 percent per year. This is a respectable, if not a sensational, rate of economic growth. Where did the additional output go? Primarily, to capital formation and military production. Private consumption per capita in 1940 was probably at about the level of 1928.

It would not be fair to conclude that the Soviet consumer had gained nothing by 1940. Community consumption had risen substantially, amounting to 10.3 percent of GNP in 1940 compared with 4.6 percent in 1928. Educational facilities had been greatly expanded and were free of charge. Medical and hospital facilities were much enlarged and were also free. Greater attention was being paid to parks, cultural centers, recreational facilities, and vacation resorts. Low-rent housing developments benefitted the small percentage of families lucky enough to get into them.

Even so, the average citizen in 1940 might well have concluded that the industrialization drive had not paid off in direct benefits to him. The promised era of abundance was still a mirage.

THE YEARS SINCE 1950: RISING PRODUCTIVITY AND CONSUMPTION

The picture since 1950 has been considerably brighter. GNP has risen at about 7.5 percent a year. Almost half of this increase has come from greater productivity, indicating that the economy is gaining momentum on this front. The rise in productivity has extended to agriculture as well as industry. And consumers are getting enough of the increased output to permit a rapid rise of living standards.

The U.S.S.R. lost many millions of men during World War II and emerged with a seriously unbalanced population and labor force. In 1959 women constituted 48 percent of the working population. Women formed 39 percent of the workers in industry, 54 percent in agriculture, 61 percent in trade, service, and government administration, and 71 percent in education, science, and health. The low birth rates and heavy casualties of the war years have also meant a slow increase in the labor force since the war. During the 1950's the rate of increase was only 1.4 percent per year.

The capital stock has continued to increase at about its prewar rate. Emphasis on capital formation has not diminished. On the contrary, the investment rate has edged up as high as 28 percent of GNP in some years. The amount of land under cultivation also rose 3 percent a year during the 1950's through the settlement of large new areas in Kazakhstan and other eastern regions.

Since labor is still the main input, and since its rate of increase has

---

[2] For a more detailed analysis and a critique of the statistical sources, see D. Gale Johnson, "Soviet Agriculture," in *Economic Trends.*

been low, total factor inputs have increased less rapidly than before the war. Yet output has risen faster. This must have been due to substantial improvements in productivity. For the economy as a whole, productivity has been rising at about 3 percent a year. This is not an unprecedented rate of productivity increase, but it is on the high side. Japan is the only other industrial country which has approached this rate over a long period of time. Some of the Western industrial nations have approached it for 10 to 20 years during spurts of unusually rapid growth.

Since industry has consistently been given top priority, it is not surprising that output and productivity have risen faster in industry than in the economy as a whole. Factors contributing to higher productivity include: the large amounts of industrial equipment contributed by the Western allies during the war, or seized by the U.S.S.R. as reparations from occupied territories after the war; heavy Soviet investment in scien-

TABLE 27–2
Annual Percentage Rates of Change, 1950–58*

	Total Economy	Industry	Agriculture (Period 1950–59)
Output	7.2	10.5	4.9
Factor inputs	4.1	6.2	1.6
Labor input	1.4	3.8	−1.6
Capital input	11.2	11.5	7.9
Land input	...	...	2.9
Factor productivity	3.0	4.0	3.3

* Data from Bergson essay in *Economic Trends.*

tific research and education, with its payoff in technical progress; the fact that management and the industrial labor force is more experienced and educated than during the 1930's; continuing improvement in economic organization and planning; and easing of political repression after the death of Stalin in 1953.

There have also been substantial productivity increases in agriculture. Throughout the Stalin era agriculture stumbled along, undersupported and underrewarded, with output rising little and productivity stagnant. Livestock and dairy production fell far short of keeping up with population growth, so that the Soviet diet became increasingly dependent on cereals and potatoes. During the past decade these trends have been arrested and reversed. The Khrushchev regime has been strongly pro-agriculture. The collective farms have been given greater latitude in planning and managing production. The hateful supervision of the machine tractor stations has been removed. Farm prices and earnings have been much increased. Agriculture has begun for the first time to receive something like its share of the available investment funds. There has been intensive development of hybrid corn and of other improved crop and livestock strains.

These policies have had a marked effect on production. Farm output has been rising about 5 percent a year, and most of this is due to higher productivity. The number of workers engaged in agriculture leveled off in the mid-fifties and then began to drop. The proportion of the labor force engaged in agriculture, which had previously hovered around 50 percent, has now fallen below 40 percent. This is a major turning point, for it means that agriculture is now able to release more labor to industry, construction, and other sectors. Without this the Soviet economy would be hampered by a severe manpower bottleneck.

Soviet agriculture is still considerably below U.S. agriculture in yields per acre, and much below American agriculture in output per farm worker. It is doubtful, indeed, that the collective form of agricultural organization can ever be as efficient as the family farm. But the trend

TABLE 27–3

Relative Shares of Final Uses in Gross National Product, U.S.S.R., 1928–55
(Percent)

Outlay Category	1928	1937	1940	1950	1955
Household consumption outlays	79.5	52.5	49.4	45.7	48.0
Communal services	4.6	10.5	10.3	10.2	8.7
Gross investment	12.5	25.9	19.1	26.9	28.1
Government administration, including					
NKVD	2.1	3.2	3.9	4.3	2.1
Defense (as recorded in budget)	1.3	7.9	17.3	12.9	13.1
Gross National Product	100.0	100.0	100.0	100.0	100.0

Source: *Real National Income*, p. 237.
Calculations are in terms of 1937 ruble factor cost.

in the U.S.S.R. is upward, and the productivity gap will probably be narrowed gradually by mechanization, fertilizers, and other improvements.

Another notable development of the 1950's is that the Soviet system has finally begun to pay off in higher living standards. Tables 27–3 and 27–4 are interesting in this connection. Table 27–3 shows the distribution of Soviet GNP by final uses at various points of time. Note the sharp cutback in the share of household consumption between 1928 and 1937, and the sharp increase in communal services and in investment. The share of household consumption is still low, not very different from the 1937 level. But with GNP increasing so rapidly, an unchanged share means that consumption is also rising at about the same rate.

This impression is confirmed by Table 27–4, which shows the annual rate of increase in each component of GNP over vaious periods of time. Note that consumption per head fell slightly from 1928 to 1940, and fell sharply during World War II. From 1950 to 1955, however, household consumption rose almost 7 percent a year; and the rate of increase from 1955 to date is probably not much different. Both the statistics and the impressions of Western visitors confirm that living standards are well above those of a decade ago.

The pattern of consumption looks unbalanced to Western eyes. Food is adequate in calories, but not nearly as varied as in the West. Clothing is adequate, though rather standardized and unstylish. Health, education, and other public services are well provided for. Stores, restaurants, repair shops, and personal services are quite deficient. Housing is still scarce and crowded, and even with the present high rate of construction it will take many years to make up the deficit. Small consumer items such as radios, bicycles, and wrist watches are now available in volume. Washing machines, refrigerators, stoves, and other large consumer durables are still in short supply. Production of private automobiles is kept

TABLE 27–4

Average Annual Rates of Growth of per Capita GNP by Use, U.S.S.R., 1928–55
(Percent per annum)

Outlay Category	1928–37	1937–40	1940–44	1944–50	1950–55
Gross national product	4.5	1.0	−0.3	5.1	5.8
Household consumption outlays	−0.2	−1.0	−8.1	9.5	6.8
Communal services	14.6	0.4	−3.8	7.4	2.4
Gross investment	13.3	−8.8	−6.5	16.2	6.7
Government administration including NKVD	9.5	7.3	−3.2	9.2	−8.2
Defense (as recorded in budget)	27.9	31.1	29.8	−16.0	6.0

Source: *Real National Income*, p. 226.
Calculations are in terms of 1937 ruble factor cost. GNP figures for 1940–44 and 1944–50 refer to GNP exclusive of Lend-Lease.

low as a matter of policy, partly to avoid the heavy expenditure on roads and highways which the automobile has necessitated in other countries.

The Soviet consumer, almost completely insulated from the outside world, cannot compare his living conditions with those prevailing in other countries. To him, as to most of us, the important thing is whether his position is improving year by year. In these terms, he is making substantial progress and can expect more of the same. Remember also that the Russians have the highest standard of living in the vast section of the earth stretching from Berlin eastward to Peking. To a visitor from Chicago, the U.S.S.R. may seem a rather poor country. But to a visitor from Djakarta or Calcutta, it seems very prosperous.

SOME ELEMENTS IN SOVIET GROWTH

Two questions come forcibly to mind as one looks at the performance of the U.S.S.R. since World War II. How do they do it? And will they be able to keep on doing it, year after year, through the 1960's and 1970's?

To the first question Soviet economists have a pat answer: "Our production grows rapidly because we have a *socialist economy*. Socialist systems grow rapidly, while capitalist economies grow slowly or not at all." This answer does not explain very much. Why are some of the Soviet bloc countries growing faster than others? Why has the U.S.S.R. growth rate varied from time to time? Central economic planning obviously does not ensure any *one* rate of economic growth. Some of the capitalist countries are growing faster than others, and faster than some of the socialist countries. Why is this? A simple ideological answer does not tell us.

Nor is it sufficient to say that Soviet output grows rapidly because of *central economic planning*. We concluded in Chapter 10 that the degree of economic centralization prevailing in the U.S.S.R. is *per se* unfavorable to efficient use of resources. If the U.S.S.R. has grown rapidly, it has been *in spite of* the effort to run the whole economy as a giant corporation. There is nevertheless one element of truth in this explanation. Central planning makes it easier to organize a high rate of investment, which has been an important element in Soviet growth.

As one digs beneath these superficial explanations, one encounters more solid reasons for the rapid growth of Soviet output. It is important to sort these out, because some will continue to operate in the future while others may taper off or disappear. Thus our analysis of the past has a bearing on the outlook for the future.

1. It is important that Soviet leaders take the increase of material production as a major national objective. While Western countries attach importance to a high rate of economic growth, they do not pursue this goal with such single-minded attention. Moreover, the Soviet economic structure removes some of the restraints on maximum production which exist in capitalist countries. There is no problem of adequate total demand, since demand can readily be manipulated through the state budget and the state bank. The inflation problem is not eliminated, but it is more manageable because wage rates and prices are prescribed by government. An adverse balance of payments cannot lead to uncontrolled gold outflows, since foreign trade is handled by government organizations, and imports can be tailored to prospective exports.

2. In line with this objective of maximum production, there has been an effort to stretch the supply of productive resources to the utmost. The basic resource, and the ultimate check on expansion of production, is the supply of labor. There has been a particular effort to bring women into the labor force, partly by eliminating sex discrimination throughout the whole range of occupations, partly by setting up nurseries and canteens to reduce the burden of cooking and child care. The low level of Soviet wages provides a powerful incentive for the wife to contribute to the

support of the household. While employment of women in Russia may strike us as being beyond the optimum, it helps to stretch the production potential of the economy.

3. The determined effort to build up capital resources has already been noted. Gross investment, adjusted to Western definitions, typically ranges from 25 to 28 percent of GNP; and since the Soviet capital stock is new and depreciation relatively low, most of this also constitutes *net* investment. The only capitalist country with such a high investment rate is Japan.

The importance of high investment is obvious. If one continues to build power plants, oil wells, steel mills, electrical equipment, industrial machinery, and other capital goods at a high rate, this will add materially to future production.

4. In addition to the large volume of Soviet investment, the *productivity* of investment seems to have been unusually high. Kuznets estimates[3] that, in the U.S.S.R. from 1950–58, each new unit of capital added 0.33 units to national output. Only Japan and West Germany had equally high rates. By contrast, the yield of a unit of new capital during this period was 0.25 in France, 0.20 in the United States, 0.15 in the United Kingdom, 0.14 in Sweden, and 0.10 in Norway.

One reason for the unusually high yield of investment in the U.S.S.R. may be that Soviet industry is young and the capital stock is relatively small. The amount of capital per worker is well below that of the older industrial countries. The U.S.S.R., in short, is operating higher up on the marginal productivity curve of capital. The allocation of investment is also important. Two thirds of Soviet investment goes into industry and agriculture which have high yields per unit of capital—usually more than 1 in agriculture, and close to 1 for many branches of manufacturing. In the United States, on the other hand, only about 30 per cent of investment goes in these directions. We allocate considerably more to housing, stores, and office buildings which have a long life and a low annual yield.

5. The U.S.S.R. allocates substantial resources to higher education, scientific research, and technological development. While the productivity payoff from these expenditures is hard to estimate, it is probably substantial. Indeed, the transformation in the knowledge and skills of the Soviet population over the past 40 years may have been as important as the accumulation of physical capital.

Large resources have been put into higher education, and the orientation of the educational system is strongly vocational. Russian universities turn out few philosophers, literary critics, and other humanists. They do turn out large numbers of natural scientists, medical scientists, engineers, agriculturalists, teachers, accountants, and technicians of every sort. Moreover, graduates seem to be sorted out quite carefully for placement

---

[3] In his essay in *Economic Trends*.

on the basis of their academic records. An outstanding engineer may be recommended to a key factory in central Russia, while a poor student may find himself headed toward Irkutsk. This is about what would happen in a well-organized market economy.

Scientific research is organized through the Academy of Sciences of the U.S.S.R. in Moscow, and through similar academies in each of the republics. Within the Academy are specialized institutes for each branch of study. The research workers are full-time scholars, without teaching or other duties. They are well paid and are among the élite of Soviet society. They are relatively free from the political nagging and pressure to which most Soviet citizens are subject. It is not surprising that scientific careers are attractive and that they draw many of the best minds in the younger generation.

At a more applied level, each industry has one or more research institutes devoted to solving production problems of that industry. The number of people engaged in such activities probably compares well with the number of research and development people in American industry. Thus one can expect that the U.S.S.R., which for a long time was mainly a borrower of technical knowledge from the West, will in the future become increasingly a contributor.

6. The U.S.S.R. started from a relatively low level of managerial efficiency. In Chapter 10 we emphasized the inefficiencies in central planning and in the grass-roots management of Soviet enterprise. This line of argument cuts in two directions. The more badly you are doing at the moment, the more room you have for improvement in the future. There is doubtless a continuing advance in management efficiency and overall economic coordination, which may account for some of the observed rise in productivity.

In sum: There is no reason to be puzzled or overimpressed by the recent Soviet growth rate. There is nothing magical about it. It can be analyzed and understood on economic grounds. While we cannot weigh the exact importance of each contributing factor, taken together they provide an adequate explanation of what has occurred.

WHAT OF THE FUTURE?

Will the high Soviet growth rate of the 1950's continue during the decades ahead? The answer is of great political importance. In the past, shifts in the productive capacity of nations have been accompanied by gradual shifts in the world balance of power. In the eighteenth century, the fact that the Industrial Revolution occurred in Britain rather than France enabled the former to emerge triumphant from their long rivalry. The preponderance of German power in Europe after 1870 was associated with rapid industrialization. The emergence of the U.S.A. as the greatest power of the twentieth century was certainly connected with our production accomplishments. The world position of the U.S.S.R. in the year 2000 will depend very much on how its economy functions in the meantime.

There seems no logical reason why the Soviet growth rate *must* decline. True, the expansion rate of individual industries always slows down eventually. This may happen also for an entire sector, such as manufacturing. It does not follow that it must happen for output as a whole.

One can nevertheless think of reasons why Soviet growth *might* slow down within the next decade or two:

1. As capital accumulation continues the marginal productivity of capital will fall, unless this tendency is offset by rapid technical progress. The race between invention and accumulation is a basic fact for any economy, including a planned economy.

2. The rate of increase in other factors of production is likely to fall. The agricultural frontier will eventually be reached. The Soviet labor force can scarcely increase in the future as rapidly as in the past. The rate of population growth has now fallen to about the U.S. level. The possibilities of urging more women into the labor force must be nearly exhausted. The U.S.S.R. also seems about to emulate the United States by going in heavily for leisure. The work week in industry has been cut to around 40 hours, and there is talk of going to a 35-hour or even a 30-hour week. If this is done, it will slow down the rise of per capita output.

3. The rate of transfer of labor from agriculture to industry will also slow down eventually. Why is this important? Because output per worker in Soviet agriculture is only about one third as high as in industry. As a matter of arithmetic, then, moving a worker from agriculture to industry raises *average* productivity in the economy. As the agricultural sector shrinks, however, this source of productivity increase becomes less important.

4. Soviet leaders may eventually reduce their concentration on commodity production and become receptive to expansion of the service industries. As the income of Soviet citizens rises, their consumption preferences will certainly tend in this direction. So the question is really whether Soviet leaders will become more responsive to consumer preferences in the future. This would get them good marks in terms of consumer satisfaction, but it would cost something on the productivity side. The service industries are not very susceptible to mechanization, and their rate of productivity increase is low. Hence a dilemma: Giving consumers what they want may imply a lower rate of increase in the amount you can give them.

5. Productivity improvement in the past has depended a good deal on borrowing technical know-how from the Western countries. To the extent that Russia catches up and forges ahead in science and technology, the possibilities in this direction will diminish. The possibilities of im-

provement in economic organization and management methods will also diminish gradually. One can keep on improving forever, but it is hard to keep on improving *at the same rate*.

By giving heavy weight to these factors, one can make a case that Soviet output can't possibly keep on rising at the present rate. But the case is not conclusive. At least two things must be set on the other side. One is the continued heavy investment of resources in scientific research and technical development. The practical result of these activities is unpredictable. But it would be unwise to sell science short. It is conceivable that technical progress might be fast enough to offset all the unfavorable factors listed above.

Another important consideration is the flexibility of the Soviet investment rate. The economy is now rich enough that it can invest more heavily *and* continue to raise consumption levels. If the marginal productivity of capital should fall in the future, this might be offset by increasing investment to 30 or even 35 percent of GNP.

The division of GNP between consumption and investment is *the* political issue in communist countries. The government group typically contains some people favoring a "hard line" (a high investment ratio) and others favoring a "soft line" (less investment and more emphasis on immediate consumption). Depending on who wins out in the power struggle, decisions may veer in one direction or the other. The unpredictability of political developments in the U.S.S.R. makes economic prediction hazardous. Economics and politics, always inseparable, are particularly so in the communist setting.

RUSSIA AND THE UNDERDEVELOPED COUNTRIES

Russian growth is relevant to the less developed countries in two ways. First, the U.S.S.R. now has sufficient resources to extend large-scale economic aid to these countries. This will be examined in connection with our discussion of U.S. aid strategy in Chapter 30.

Second, Soviet leaders maintain that their system provides a model of effective economic development, and that the poor countries need only follow this model to succeed. This contention requires a word of comment.

We may note first that Russia in 1914 was already a richer and more developed country than are most of the underdeveloped countries today. The foundations of an industrial state had already been laid. There was extensive development of food processing, textiles, clothing, and other branches of light manufacturing. There was a rail network. Agriculture was sufficiently productive that Russia before 1914 was a large exporter of grain to the West. There was a long tradition of national patriotism and centralized government. So the task confronting Soviet leaders in the 1920's was considerably easier than that now confronting the new nations of Asia and Africa.

One can say further that Soviet planning methods, which involve prescribed targets for end products and centralized control of material flows, are not directly applicable to the less developed countries. They assume a framework of complete public ownership, while the underdeveloped countries are typically "mixed economies" with the private sector predominating. The kind of development planning required by these countries is quite different from Soviet planning, as will appear in Chapter 29. The skills needed for development planning, such as macroeconomic theory, interindustry economics, linear programming, and methods of project evaluation, have been developed mainly in the West. Soviet planners probably have little in the way of special expertise which is not known in other countries.

In most countries agriculture is by all odds the leading industry, and agricultural progress is a key requirement for economic development. But in this sector the U.S.S.R. has had only limited success, and some of the other communist countries have been spectacularly unsuccessful. It has yet to be demonstrated that collective farming can be combined with agricultural efficiency. On this front the poor countries can learn a good deal more from the West than from the East.

What, then, does Soviet experience show? It shows that, if a population can be persuaded to tighten its belts for 20 or 30 years and to work hard meanwhile, it can achieve a rapid build-up of industrial capacity. People must consume less, or at least refrain from consuming more, while effort is channeled heavily into capital goods production. There is nothing mysterious about this, and the moral is not confined to communist systems. But it is a discouraging lesson, and one which is not easy to apply in a poor country.

Soviet experience also underlines the fact that rapid development requires a strong government. But this need not be a communist government. True, a communist government by ruthless policing can enforce stricter belt-tightening than a more moderate regime. Communist economies grow just as Marx maintained that capitalist economies grow: by grinding the faces of the poor. The human costs are great, and only those who regard suffering lightly could view this as the easy way to economic progress.

RUSSIA AND THE WEST: A GROWTH RACE?

Russian output during the 1950's rose considerably faster than in most of the capitalist countries. Some calculations by Professor Kuznets on this point are reproduced in Table 27–5.[4] Note that most of the Western countries show annual increases of 3 to 5 percent in GNP, and 2 to 3.5 percent in GNP per capita. The figures for the U.S.S.R. are roughly double these levels.

---

[4] Simon Kuznets, "Quantitative Characteristics of the Economic Growth of the U.S.S.R. Compared with Those in Other Countries," in *Economic Trends*.

The performance of the British and American economies during the 1950's was particularly unexciting. If one wants to argue that capitalist countries can grow as fast as communist countries, one must point to Japan and West Germany rather than to the United States.

One cannot be sure that Soviet growth will continue at the same rate in the future, and one may hope that the American performance will improve. It still seems likely that the gap between Soviet and U.S. output will narrow considerably within the next generation. As nearly as one can capture things in figures, Soviet GNP was about half of U.S. GNP in 1960. Starting from this position, and assuming alternative growth rates, one can readily calculate "when the curves will cross." For example, if our

TABLE 27–5

Annual Percentage Increase in Total and per Capita Output
Selected Countries, 1950–58

COUNTRY	POPULATION	GNP	GNP PER CAPITA
1. West Germany	1.08	7.95	6.80
2. Japan	1.28	7.96	6.60
3. U.S.S.R.	1.74	7.50	5.70
4. Greece	0.97	6.71	5.68
5. Italy	0.56	5.58	4.99
6. France	0.83	4.30	3.44
7. Netherlands	1.27	4.46	3.15
8. Finland	1.10	3.97	2.84
9. South Africa	1.82	4.60	2.73
10. Sweden	0.70	3.03	2.31
11. Belgium	0.59	2.90	2.30
12. Norway	0.97	3.20	2.21
13. United Kingdom	0.31	2.24	1.92
14. Denmark	0.70	2.31	1.60
15. U.S.A.	1.74	2.86	1.10
16. Canada	2.76	3.78	0.99

GNP should grow at 4 percent and Soviet GNP at 7 percent, by 1975 their output would be three quarters of ours. By 1985, the output of the two economies would be roughly the same. Since the Soviet population is about one fifth larger, however, they would not equal our output per capita until sometime in the 1990's. Meanwhile, enough other things might happen to throw off these calculations entirely.

It may be better anyway to consider particular products or industries rather than total output. The emphasis of Soviet economic expansion is different from our own. In the products to which they attach highest priority—coal, steel, machinery, electric power—they may exceed our production level within the next 10 or 15 years. In fairness, one should add to this list health services, education, scientific work, and ballet performances. It will be much longer before they reach our per capita production of meat, fresh fruits and vegetables, housing space, furniture, and kitchen equipment. It is doubtful that they will ever reach our per capita output of automobiles, tires, gasoline, communication services, travel, retailing and repair services, and personal services. This is simply to say that the patterns of life will remain different in the two countries—so different that aggregative comparisons do not mean very much.

The U.S.S.R., being a late starter, is preoccupied with the growth race. Exhortations to "overtake and surpass the United States" appear on factories and buildings throughout the country. Predictions that this goal will be achieved by a specific date are used for propaganda effect at home and abroad.

It is doubtful that Americans need get very excited about all this. There is no military issue involved, since each country already has the capacity to annihilate the other. The United States is rich enough to match anything the U.S.S.R. might choose to do in scientific development, space exploration, economic aid to other countries, and so on. The U.S.S.R. might eventually gain a propaganda advantage by being able to say that its GNP was larger than ours, but even this is doubtful. Going around the poor countries of the world boasting about how rich you are isn't the best way to win friends and influence people. If and when the Russians do become as rich as we are, they may become equally unpopular.

GROWTH POLICY IN THE UNITED STATES

Quite apart from what may be happening in other countries, there is reason for concern about the recent performance of the American economy. Since the mid-fifties the economy has behaved rather sluggishly and the rate of increase in GNP has slowed down. Business cycle upswings have stopped well short of capacity operation. Full-time unemployment as a percentage of the labor force was 2.7 percent at the peak of activity in 1953. But it was 4.2 percent at the 1957 peak, 5.1 percent at the 1960 peak, and 5.8 percent at the end of 1962. The amount of slack in the economy has been growing.

The difficulties of the economy involve demand rather than supply. The question is whether aggregate demand will rise fast enough to hold the economy near capacity operation. The nature of this problem was explained in Chapter 25. As national income rises, saving seems to rise at about the same rate. So investment, which in our economy means largely private investment, must also rise at this rate if total demand is to be adequate. If investment fails to rise at the required rate, we shall see more of what we have seen over the past decade: weak upswings, below-capacity operation, chronic unemployment, and slow increase in GNP. It seems paradoxical that the remedy for *excess capacity* should be to build *addi-*

tional capacity at a faster rate than before. This would not work out for a single company or industry. But if everybody does it, it works out for the economy as a whole. It lifts the expenditure schedule to a level at which both the old and the new capacity can be profitably employed.

Since the behavior of private investment is a large part of the problem, we can begin by asking what can be done to encourage private investment.

1. Optimists place great faith in *scientific and technological research.* The expenditure figures are encouraging, at least on the surface. Total spending on research and development almost tripled between 1953 and 1960, rising from $5 billion to $15 billion. Most of this money ($10.5 billion) was *used* by business concerns, while most of it ($9.2 billion) was *supplied* by the federal government. But note that two thirds of the industrial research expenditure was concentrated in three industries: aircraft and space vehicles, electrical equipment and communication, and chemicals. Research was heavily oriented toward military objectives. And basic or "impractical" research, which produces most of the important discoveries, got only 9 percent of the amount spent.

Government might well provide more support for basic research, which is done mainly in universities and government laboratories rather than in industry. There is also need for effort to break the bottleneck in the supply of research workers. Research spending rose between 1953 and 1960 at the rate of 25 percent per year. Meanwhile, the number of available scientists and engineers was rising only 6 percent per year. This means that people were being pulled out of teaching and other important activities to staff new research teams. The result has been to undermine the educational process on which the future supply of teachers and researchers depends. We need to increase greatly the number of scientists, engineers, and technicians being trained year by year. This means money for fellowships, for adequate teaching salaries, for buildings and laboratory equipment.

2. The *federal tax structure* needs to be thoroughly re-examined. The present structure represents a mixture of opportunistic revenue hunting and equalitarian philosophy. The effect on investment has not been carefully analyzed. A rethinking of tax policy, taking high investment and rapid economic growth as central objectives, might suggest important changes. It should give one pause that the tax policies of West Germany, Sweden, Japan, and most other capitalist countries are more favorable to investment than is the case in the United States.

The trick is partly to find devices which encourage high investment by business concerns, but which do not permit unduly wide differences in personal income. We want to favor profits which are *reinvested*, rather than profits which go into luxury consumption. The tax changes initiated by the Kennedy administration in 1962 work in this direction. There was a general shortening of the depreciation periods allowed by the Bureau of

Internal Revenue, so that buildings and equipment can be written off more rapidly. This raises the tax-free amount which a company can set aside in depreciation allowances, and thus encourages replacement of obsolete equipment with the "latest model." This raises productivity as well as the level of investment.

A second change permits businesses to deduct 7 percent of any investment in eligible machinery and equipment from their income tax bill. This is a direct investment subsidy. It raises the prospective yield on new investment without permitting larger profits on old investment.

3. Making high investment a major objective also changes one's thinking about *control of cyclical fluctuations*. For example, it argues against heavy reliance on monetary policy to check an excessive upswing. Such an upswing typically involves a high level of planned investment which, when added to consumer and government spending plans, yields an excessive level of demand. Somebody's demand has to be reduced. Monetary policy operates to cut investment plans by raising interest rates and restricting credit. This may be quite undesirable in terms of long-run growth.

Suppose instead that government raised personal income tax rates to restrict consumer demand and produce a budget surplus. The money would be used to retire government securities, and would become available through the capital market to finance private investment. Business concerns would be able to carry out their investment plans, and the burden of restriction would fall mainly on consumption.

Thus the conclusion of Chapter 24 that monetary policy is the natural way to control a strong upswing needs to be modified when growth objectives are brought into the picture.

4. A device which is used increasingly in Europe is *business-government consultation on investment levels*. This is the essence of the "economic plans" of France, Sweden, and a number of other countries. Once a year each industry canvasses its members to determine their investment plans for the year ahead. Leaders of the major industries then sit down with economic officials of the government to see how this will work out for the economy as a whole. Suppose it appears that total demand will be excessive. Several things can be done: government can reduce its own investment plans; or government can move to restrict consumer demand; or government may check private investment by raising interest rates and restricting credit, at the same time making clear to the business community why such action is necessary. In the opposite situation, where demand threatens to be insufficient, government can prepare and discuss with industry a package of proposals designed to raise demand to the full employment level.

The essence of this procedure is *advance* consultation to ensure that business investment plans and government fiscal plans are consistent with each other and with the capacity limits of the economy. It has the advantage of reassuring business that the economy will operate near full capacity, and that they can safely make investment plans on this assumption. The nervousness which characterizes business investment decisions in the United States arises partly from the fact that business and government planners operate at arm's length, or even in an atmosphere of mutual distrust.

5. Efforts to stimulate private investment should be accompanied by a vigorous program of *public investment*. Without taking sides in the controversy over whether government has been "over-investing" or "under-investing" in the past, one can point to large areas of investment opportunity in highways, airports, navigation, and local transport; slum clearance, urban redevelopment, and low-income housing; construction of educational facilities at all levels from grade schools through medical schools; improvement of hospitals and other health facilities; funds for scholarships, fellowships, and basic scientific research; and natural resource conservation and development. We shall argue in Chapter 30 that there is also wide scope for mutually profitable loans to the less developed countries.

Government expenditures of an investment type can appropriately be financed through borrowing rather than from current revenue. The capital expenditures of our state and local governments are already financed in good measure through bond issues; and a steady rise in their debt, provided it is in line with their ability to meet interest charges, is accepted as normal. Only in the case of the federal government do we stigmatize bond financing by such terms as "unbalancing the budget" or "fiscal irresponsibility."

How much debt financing should be used is another matter. One cannot say that, if capital expenditures form 20 percent of government outlay, then 20 percent of government revenue should be raised by bond issues. The proper proportion of debt financing depends on what is needed to maintain capacity operation of the economy. The great strength of fiscal policy is its flexibility, the fact that the budget line (Chapter 20) can be shifted upward or downward to regulate total demand. At some times this may require a large amount of debt financing, at others none at all. Whether a full-capacity fiscal policy would involve a gradual creeping up of the federal debt is unpredictable, since it depends basically on the vigor of private investment and on how much government supplementing is needed.

A final word of caution: even if all these things were done, the results would not be spectacular. The rate of increase in GNP might be 1 percent a year greater than otherwise. This would be well worthwhile. But in a large and decentralized economy the growth rate cannot be changed suddenly or sharply by turning some magic key. And we would not really want the kind of economic organization in which such sharp changes are possible.

SUMMARY

1. Soviet growth is difficult to summarize, because it has been very uneven by sectors of the economy and also by time periods.

2. The year 1928 saw the initiation of central planning and a marked reallocation of resources toward capital goods production. From 1928 to 1940, GNP rose at about 4 percent a year. This seems to have been due almost entirely to larger labor and capital inputs. And progress was confined to the industrial sector, while agriculture stagnated and food consumption per capita fell.

3. Output fell considerably during World War II and recovered during the late 1940's. The period from 1950 to date has been one of substantial progress. GNP has risen at between 7 and 8 percent a year, and GNP per capita at almost 6 percent. Agricultural output has risen substantially, though not as fast as industrial output. And for the first time there has been a sustained rise in consumer goods output and in living standards.

4. Important factors in recent Soviet growth include a continued high rate of capital goods production, heavy allocation of capital goods toward directly productive uses in industry and agriculture, heavy investment in education and research, and improvements in economic planning and management making for greater efficiency.

5. There are a number of reasons for expecting that the Soviet growth rate will decline somewhat as the economy matures. But this is by no means certain, and the growth rate will remain high relative to most other countries.

6. During the 1950's Japan and West Germany had growth rates above the Soviet level. But most other capitalist countries, including the United States, were considerably below.

7. If present growth trends continue, Soviet GNP per capita will rise above the United States level before the end of this century. But this aggregate comparison is of doubtful significance. The uses of national output, the pattern of production, and the style of consumption will remain quite different in the two countries.

8. The United States growth rate could be increased, possibly by as much as 1 percent a year, by efforts to stimulate private investment, by adequate public investment programs, and by vigorous use of fiscal policy.

The Poor Countries

It is not the scarcity of money, but the scarcity of men and talents, which makes a state weak.

VOLTAIRE

In the infancy of societies it is the chiefs of the state who shape its institutions, and later it is the institutions that form the chiefs of the state.

MONTESQUIEU

THE North Atlantic countries, Japan, and the U.S.S.R. have one thing in common: economic growth can be taken for granted. It is built into the structure of the economy, and the only question is whether it will be slower or faster.

In large areas of the world, however, economic growth cannot be taken for granted. In some countries output per capita is stationary or even falling. In many others it is advancing only slowly and intermittently.

These countries are often called "underdeveloped"; but this term is invidious and has no clear meaning. A more descriptive term is "primary producing economies," since most people in these countries are engaged in agriculture. Our choice of "the poor countries" is intended to indicate sympathy rather than condescension, and they are indeed poor by any test. One might also call them "the countries of the South," since they lie generally to the south of the industrial nations.

Whatever the label, it is clear that we are talking about the countries of Central and South America, Africa (except for South Africa), and Asia (excepting Japan). Spain, Portugal, southern Italy, and Greece might be considered fringe members of this group.

The fact that we group these countries for discussion does not mean that they are highly similar. They are in fact so dissimilar that generalizations must be treated with caution. It will be useful at the outset to emphasize some of the major differences. These include differences in size, resource base, degree of population pressure, income level and growth rate.

SOME IMPORTANT DIFFERENCES

Size. India has a population of more than four hundred million, and a land area approaching that of the United States. Brazil, with a land area also about that of the United States, has some seventy million people. Pakistan and Indonesia have about a hundred million each. But most of the poor countries have populations below ten million, and some are quite tiny. British Guiana has about half a million people, Jamaica a million and a half, Sierra Leone two and a half million. Not only is population small, but *economic size* is very small. A country of ten million with a per capita output of $100 per year has a GNP of only $1 billion.

The economic significance of these differences is obvious. Countries such as India or Brazil can expect to become diversified and largely self-sufficient industrial economies. But this pattern of development is not feasible for Jamaica or Sierra Leone. Their domestic market is too small to support a full array of manufacturing industries. They must grow mainly by developing export specialties and by participating in international trade.

Resource base. The Congo basin has great mineral wealth. Thus far there is no indication of equivalent deposits in Morocco or Burma. Oil is found in some areas and not in others. The land area of some countries is 90 percent desert and mountains, while other countries are fertile and well-watered. Some climates are more favorable than others to health and productive activity. So there are permanent differences in the *economic potential* of countries. All of them can hope to become richer than they are now. But they will not necessarily reach the same income level even in the long run.

Population pressure. One sometimes thinks of all poor countries as overpopulated. This impression comes mainly from looking at India, Pakistan, and a few other Asian countries. In most parts of Africa population pressure is not yet severe, and this is true also of Latin America. Some Latin American countries still have an open frontier, with free land which requires only the effort of developing it.

It is hard to get an objective measure of population pressure, since this depends on the resource base and on the pattern of economic activity. Britain, Belgium, or Japan would be heavily overpopulated if they had to depend mainly on agriculture; but by development of manufacturing and other industries they can support a dense population at a rising standard of living.

For countries which are still primarily agricultural, the ratio of labor to farm land is significant. Table 28–1 suggests that serious population pressure is found mainly in Egypt, the Indian subcontinent, China, and southwest Asia. In southeast Asia, Africa, and Latin America the ratio of labor to land is not excessive. Low output per farm worker in these latter

TABLE 28–1

Males Engaged in Agriculture per Square Kilometer
of Standard Farm Land*

REGION	MALE FARM WORKERS PER SQUARE KILOMETER
Egypt	73.1
India and Pakistan	31.2
China	24.5
Southwest Asia (excluding India-Pakistan)	24.5
Philippines	7.5
Southeast Asia (excluding Philippines)	6.5
Africa: British areas	6.3
Indonesia	5.7
Central America and Caribbean	4.4
Africa: non-British areas	2.2
Argentina	1.8
Brazil	1.0
South America (excluding Argentina-Brazil)	0.8
U.S.S.R.	3.1
Canada	1.7
U.S.A.	1.2

* Colin Clark, *The Conditions of Economic Progress* (3d ed.; London: Macmillan, 1957), Table XXXIII, p. 308. A kilometer is roughly five eighths of a mile; thus a square kilometer is about 250 acres.

countries is due mainly to primitive agricultural methods and inadequate equipment.

Even when population pressure is not yet severe, the rate of population increase is often alarming. Most of the poor countries now have populations growing at 2 to 3 percent a year. Some are still below 2 percent, including Burma (1.0), Argentina (1.2), Chile (1.8), Tanganyika (1.8), and Nigeria (1.9). But a number of countries have climbed above the 3 percent level, including Malaya (3.0), Ecuador and Mexico (3.2), the Philippines (3.8), Venezuela (near 4.0), and Thailand (near

4.0). These high rates of population increase[1] mean that a country must run fast simply to prevent a fall in per capita income.

Income level. Some countries are much poorer than others. GNP per capita, converted to dollars at official exchange rates, ranges from about $60 at the bottom of the list to ten times that at the top (Table 28–2). Note that the level of incomes in Latin America is considerably higher than in Africa or Asia. Most Latin American countries are "middle class" rather than really poor. For purposes of comparison, the West European countries now have GNP's in the range of $1,000 to $1,500 per capita, while the U.S. figure is approaching $3,000.

TABLE 28–2

National Output per Capita, U.S. Dollars,
Selected Countries, 1957

Venezuela	648	Rhodesia-Nyasaland	135
Argentina	490	Indonesia	131
Chile	379	Ceylon	129
Malaya	356	Iran	108
Brazil	293	Thailand	96
Colombia	263	Kenya	87
Mexico	262	Nigeria	78
Philippines	220	India	73
Turkey	220	Pakistan	70
Ecuador	189	Uganda	64
Peru	179	Tanganyika	61
Ghana	172	Burma	57
Egypt	142		

Source: E. E. Hagen and M. Usui, *World Income 1957* (Cambridge, Mass.: M.I.T. Center for International Studies, 1959).

These comparisons should not be taken too seriously. National income estimates for the poor countries are crude, and they exaggerate the true size of income differences for reasons explained in Chapter 17.

Growth rate. Countries differ also in the rate at which they are progressing toward higher levels of income. The estimates shown in Table 28–3 are quite rough, and probably have an optimistic bias. Any government embarked on a development program likes to show that the program is succeeding, and a statistical demonstration of progress is helpful in securing continued foreign aid. So one suspects that some of the estimates are on the high side. And some of the high rates are explained by special circumstances such as oil in Venezuela and copper in Northern Rhodesia.

---

[1] Data are in most cases for 1950–60 and are based on the *U.N. Demographic Yearbook*, 1960, pp. 126–42 and the *U.N. Statistical Yearbook*, 1961, pp. 42–47. Even on something as definite as population, the estimates for some countries are still unreliable, and so the figures listed should not be taken as precise.

Disregarding these special cases, the remaining countries show a wide range of performance. A few, including Brazil and the Philippines, have been making appreciable gains in per capita output. A good many others—Ceylon, Pakistan, Argentina, Peru—have done little more than keep abreast of population growth.

TABLE 28–3

Average Annual Increase in Real Product, Selected Countries, 1951–59 (Percent)

COUNTRY	TOTAL OUTPUT	PER CAPITA OUTPUT
Venezuela	7.8	4.6
Rhodesia-Nyasaland	6.8	4.1
Turkey	5.9	2.9
Philippines	5.8	2.5
Brazil	5.7	3.2
Ecuador	4.8	1.6
Thailand	4.8	1.3
Burma	4.6	3.6
Colombia	4.6	2.3
Indonesia	4.2	2.2
Nigeria	4.1	2.2
Chile	3.5	1.1
India	3.3	1.3
Peru	3.2	0.9
Ceylon	3.0	0.4
Malaya	3.0	0.2
Pakistan	2.3	0.4
Argentina	1.7	0.1

Source: U.N. *Yearbook of National Account Statistics, 1961* (New York, 1962), pp. 303–4.

For most countries the data relate to gross domestic product, but in a few cases gross national product or national income was the only figure available. To minimize the effect of initial and terminal years, an average was first taken of the years 1950–52 and 1958–60, and centered at 1951 and 1959. The figures in the table are annual percentage rates of increase between these two averages. For a few countries data cover less than the full period.

So much for differences. What are the common characteristics which give the countries of the South a certain family resemblance to each other? They include:

1. Limited development of product and factor markets.
2. Importance of subsistence production.
3. Dominance of agriculture, combined with low productivity in agriculture.
4. Dependence on a few primary exports.
5. Inadequate tax systems and low levels of public expenditure.
6. Inadequate educational systems, leading to a shortage of professional and technical skills.
7. Marked inequality of income distribution.

8. Serious deficiencies of private business leadership.
9. A feudal social and political structure.
10. A low level of competence in public administration.

These features appear more acutely in some countries than in others, and they are interrelated in a complicated way. But they provide useful avenues for explaining the political economy of these countries.

LIMITATIONS OF THE MARKET MECHANISM

Recall the characteristics of a competitive market economy outlined in Part One. They include highly developed transportation and communication facilities, numerous competing producers in each industry, freedom of entrance for additional producers, freedom for workers to change jobs in response to economic advantage, and a financial system which mobilizes savings and channels them toward the most productive uses.

Such an economy has never existed anywhere in pure form. But in the Western industrial nations markets are *relatively* well developed, people are *relatively* free to respond to economic opportunities, and things happen *somewhat* as they would in a competitive market system.

In the poor countries, however, markets are typically rudimentary and imperfect. Transportation and communication facilities are sometimes so limited that one can scarcely speak of a national economy. Instead, one has a collection of village economies with little national linkage. Normal difficulties of distance may be compounded by topography. From Mexico to Chile mountain ranges split each country into valleys and highlands which can be linked only at heavy cost.

In the urban centers manufacturing, banking, and wholesaling are typically monopolized. Rarely does one find more than two or three concerns in the same line of business. Sometimes these are foreign concerns which established a dominant position during the colonial era. But in other cases, notably in the Latin American countries, influential local families have gotten control of particular industries. Free competition is viewed as undesirable, and the "ins" use their political and financial influence to bar outsiders. Management is a prerogative to be enjoyed, not a job to be worked at. Profit margins are high, and enterprisers are not very enterprising.

Financial institutions are little developed. Savings banks, insurance companies, securities markets, and other devices for mobilizing and transferring savings are scanty. Inadequate corporation laws, and reluctance to entrust money to anyone outside one's immediate family, make it difficult to amass capital for large ventures. The few commercial banks which exist are usually more interested in financing trade than in financing industrial or agricultural production. Availability of credit is heavily dependent on family and business connections. This is one of the many obstacles which make it hard for newcomers to break into established industries.

Turning to the labor market, most workers live in the country and are outside the money economy. They are physically isolated, largely illiterate, and often dominated by landlords in feudal fashion. Moving to the city is almost an act of revolt. Once in the city, access to jobs may be limited by racial or religious restrictions. In East Africa, for example, there is a long tradition that management jobs are done by Europeans, clerical jobs by Indians, and manual jobs by Africans. Upward movement to professional and administrative jobs is difficult. These are reserved for the educated, and educational opportunities are severely limited.

So in theorizing about, and developing economic policies for, one of these countries we cannot assume the flexible, self-adjusting market mechanism which we associate with industrial capitalist countries. But neither should we make the mistake of acting as though market linkages were entirely absent. The reality of market interdependence is shown by the fact that large budget deficits affect prices throughout the economy with surprising speed. Moreover, there is always the possibility that markets can be improved through deliberate effort; and this should be an important aim of government in any underdeveloped country.

SUBSISTENCE PRODUCTION: THE DUAL ECONOMY

A striking feature of the poor countries is the cleavage between the market economy and the subsistence economy. This is largely, though not entirely, an urban-rural cleavage. In the capital city of a South American country, one feels oneself in a sophisticated, Europeanized, and moderately prosperous environment. Twenty miles away one is in a world of rural poverty and primitive superstition, a world which seems to have no point of contact with the first.

Most people in these countries live on the land. They sell little to the outside world and buy little from it. The nearest city may be far away, and roads may be poor or nonexistent. This reduces the incentive to grow more than one can consume, or to work on improving productivity. The country people are largely illiterate, and politically inert and ineffectual.

This does not prove that they are unhappy. Anthropologists sometimes maintain that the subsistence villager, living in a stable and well-integrated culture, is better off than his brother who has gone to work for wages in the city. This question is not at issue. We are saying only that these people are outside the money economy, which accordingly is much smaller than the size and population of the country would suggest.

The money economy focuses on one or a few cities, typically on the seacoast where they have ready access to overseas trade. Here one finds traders and bankers, professional people, small manufacturers, rich landowners who prefer city life, and other members of the political elite.

The money economy may also include some primary production. In some countries one finds large oil or mining developments, typically in foreign hands. There may also be plantation agriculture—the tea estates of Ceylon and Kenya, the rubber estates of Sumatra and Malaya, the coffee plantations of Brazil—producing mainly for the export market.

This cleavage between subsistence and market production raises perplexing questions about the meaning of economic development. One logical sequence of development starts off from larger output and exports of minerals or plantation crops. These exports help pay for imports of machinery and materials to establish local industries. Industrialization yields higher incomes to employers and workers and larger tax revenues to government, which can be used to finance investment and public services.

But all this happens within the money economy. To what extent does it benefit the 75 percent of the population who live in the subsistence sector? Can one assume that progress in the money economy will spill over into the subsistence sector and raise income levels there?

In the United States, industrial progress, beginning in a few eastern centers, has spilled over into other regions and in the process largely eliminated subsistence agriculture. But remember that this happened with an adequate transportation network, an educated and mobile population, progressive business and farming institutions, and energetic support by government. One cannot assume that it will happen where these conditions are lacking. Instead one may get a lopsided development limited to a small minority of the population.

SOME CHARACTERISTICS OF LOW-INCOME AGRICULTURE

Denmark and New Zealand demonstrate that an agricultural country does not have to be poor. The countries of the South are poor, not just because they are agricultural, but because productivity in agriculture is so low.

What are the main reasons for agricultural inefficiency? In many countries most of the land is held by large landowners, who supply the equipment and working capital. The tenants provide labor power and receive part of the crop in return. The tenants' share is rarely more than one half and may be as low as one third. This pattern of landholding is particularly characteristic of Central and South America. In some of these countries 1 percent of the landowners control two thirds or more of the agricultural land. This pattern also prevails in most countries of the Near East and South Asia.

Under a landlord-tenant system, the tenant has little economic incentive. If he produces more, most of it will go to the landlord. Buildings, fences, drainage, and other improvements on the land belong to the landlord and not to him. So why should he put extra time into these things? He also has little choice of products or methods of production.

Any impetus toward greater efficiency must come from the landlord. But the landlord may not be interested. Landowners in these countries are not "maximizing men" on the pattern of the Western capitalist. They are often absentee owners who live in the city, where they engage in a business or profession. They cling to their land for security and prestige, but take little interest in its management. So long as it yields the customary income, they will not bother to squeeze out more production. They need enough for the town house in Caracas, the annual trip to Europe, the foreign education of their children. Why bother about more?

The situation is not necessarily better under a system of peasant agriculture. For here farms may be too small for maximum efficiency. In some Asian countries farms average only one to two acres. Even this small area may be divided into a number of separate pieces, as was true in Europe in feudal times. This wastes the time of the farm operator and consumes a good deal of land in boundaries and footpaths. If the legal system requires family property to be divided among the surviving heirs, landholdings may be split smaller and smaller with successive generations.

Land reform is often thought of as taking over large estates and dividing them into family-size farms. But creation of proper-sized farms may also require consolidation and enlargement of holdings where these have become too small over the years. Both lines of action may be necessary in the same country.

The rural population of these countries is dominated by a traditional culture little affected by events in the outside world. The South Indian villager knows nothing of the economic plans and pronouncements emanating from New Delhi. The Peruvian Indian in the high Andes scarcely believes in the existence of Lima. Rural children may go to school for a few years, but quickly slip back into the age-long illiteracy which surrounds them. Agricultural methods are handed down from father to son, and suggestions for change are resisted rather than welcomed.

The very poverty of the people acts as a barrier to change. Living close to the margin of subsistence, they are chronically in debt to the landlord or the local moneylender. Surplus income from a good crop year is immediately swallowed up in debt repayment. Their meagre resources do not permit even small capital outlays for tools, fertilizer, or livestock. They dare not risk new crops or methods because, if the experiment should fail, they would be left destitute. Thus poverty perpetuates itself in a way which has been familiar in these countries for centuries.

SPECIALIZATION AND EXPORT DEPENDENCE

In the primary producing countries exports typically form a high percentage of GNP (Table 28–4). Many countries export 10 to 20 percent of their output, and the proportion may run as high as one half.

Exports consist mainly of oil, minerals, foodstuffs, and industrial raw materials. Many countries get more than half their export revenue from a single product: rubber in Malaya and Liberia, rice in Burma, sugar in the Philippines, jute in Pakistan, oil in Venezuela and Iraq, copper in Chile and Northern Rhodesia, bananas in Central America, coffee in Colombia, cocoa in Ghana, cotton in Egypt and the Sudan.

This dependence on specialized exports raises both short-run and long-run problems. In the short-run, it leads to serious economic instability. The demand for primary products fluctuates with economic activity in the industrial countries, particularly the United States. A recession in the United States lowers demand for a wide range of raw materials. World output of agricultural products fluctuates considerably for climatic and other reasons. These shifts in demand and supply pro-

TABLE 28–4

Exports as a Percentage of GNP,
Selected Countries, 1958*

British Guiana	55	Peru	31
Belgian Congo	52	Burma	23
Rhodesia & Nyasaland	47	Egypt	19
Venezuela	41	Nigeria	18
Panama	38	Mexico	17
Ceylon	36	Philippines	14
Jamaica	34	Brazil	9
Ghana	32	India	7

Source: Charles .P. Kindleberger *Foreign Trade and the National Economy* (New Haven, Conn.: Yale University Press, 1962) p. 220.
* For a few countries earlier data were used when the 1958 figures were not available.

duce wide swings in the prices of primary products, much wider than in the case of manufactured goods.

Any of these countries, then, may suddenly experience a sharp drop in the value of its exports. If its foreign trade was previously in balance, it now has a balance of payments deficit. Unless this can be covered from reserves or borrowing, imports will have to be cut. This is unpleasant. Cuts in imports of consumer goods mean higher prices, speculation and profiteering, higher living costs and aggressive wage demands, and political unrest. Cuts in imports of capital goods may mean abandonment of important development projects.

Moreover, since these governments usually depend heavily on export and import taxes, a drop in exports means a drop in tax revenue. The government must then either cut its spending, including its development activities; or it must cover the budget deficit by borrowing from the central bank.

There is a characteristic difference between business cycles in industrial and nonindustrial countries. In the industrial countries, cycles occur mainly because of fluctuations in domestic investment. In the primary producing countries the impetus typically comes from the outside, from fluctuations in export revenues.

Over the long run, dependence on primary exports raises a different kind of problem. Suppose a country launches a development program designed to raise GNP 5 percent a year. Its import requirements will probably rise even faster, perhaps 7 or 8 percent a year. Most of the machinery, building materials, and other goods needed for industrialization will have to come from abroad. There will also be increased needs for fuel and materials to feed the new factories. As incomes in the country rise, there will be heavier demand for manufactured consumer goods; and import of many of these items cannot be resisted.

What are the chances that these import requirements can be covered by an equivalent increase in exports? World demand for primary products depends mainly on the rate of growth in the advanced countries. Suppose real GNP in these countries is rising 5 percent per year. Then their imports of primary products will probably rise by something less than 5 percent. Foodstuffs, which constitute a large share of primary exports, have a low income elasticity of demand. Demand for many nonfood products is also being reduced by new inventions—synthetic fibres instead of natural fibres, synthetic rubber instead of natural rubber, and so on.

It is also often argued that *price* trends are likely to be adverse to primary products over the long run. Prices of manufactured goods are often controlled by monopoly arrangements. Improvements in production methods are reflected in higher wages and profits rather than in lower product prices. Supply is adjusted to demand at a fixed price. It is much harder to control the world supply and price of rubber, coffee, or cotton. With uncontrolled supply and a slowly growing demand, there is chronic downward pressure on primary product prices. So the poor countries are likely to find the prices of their export products falling relative to the prices of the manufactured goods which they import.

A developing country, then, can find itself in a situation in which its import needs are rising 8 percent a year but it can increase exports only 3 percent a year. Something has to give. One possibility is to close the gap by loans or grants from abroad. This is a major reason why rapidly developing countries need foreign capital. Another avenue of adjustment is to reduce the need for imports by forced draft development of local manufacturing industries. This is termed *import substitution*. The strategy of successful import substitution will be examined in the next chapter.

TAX SOURCES AND GOVERNMENT EXPENDITURE

Many of the things necessary for development must be done by government. This takes money. So it is pertinent to ask where government revenues come from in these countries.

Most countries rely heavily on excise or sales taxes, and on export and import taxes (Table 28–5). These taxes are normally *regressive*. Moreover, indirect taxes are typically inflexible, that is, their yield rises less rapidly than national income. But if government is to meet its development responsibilities, it needs a tax system under which revenues will rise *more* rapidly than national income.

The industrial countries have such a revenue source in the personal

TABLE 28–5

Sources of Tax Revenue, Selected Countries, 1960–61*

COUNTRY	GOVERNMENT EXPENDITURE AS PERCENT OF GNP	PERCENT OF TAX REVENUE DERIVED FROM			
		Direct Taxes on Income and Wealth	Export and Import Taxes	Excises, Sales, and Other Taxes on Consumption	Other Sources
Asia:					
Burma	16.2	30.8	33.7	23.5	12.0
Ceylon	15.3	27.3	57.0	10.4	5.3
India	n.a.	30.2	13.0	23.4	33.4
Iran	n.a.	8.7	26.2	⟶	65.1
Malaya	12.6	22.0	66.2	3.2	8.6
Pakistan	n.a.	23.4	35.2	39.7	1.7
Philippines	8.7	16.5	40.8	17.2	25.5
Thailand	8.6	10.0	38.8	29.3	21.9
Latin America:					
Argentina	13.0	28.4	42.3	⟶	29.3
Brazil	11.3	20.1	7.4	⟶	72.5
Chile	9.3	34.8	20.2	⟶	45.0
Colombia	6.3	55.0	36.8	⟶	8.2
Ecuador	12.6	18.0	51.0	⟶	51.0
Mexico	6.1	39.9	24.9	12.4	22.8
Peru	11.9	53.6	12.5	⟶	33.9
Venezuela	21.1	55.1	31.2	⟶	13.7
Africa:					
Egypt	n.a.	29.6	⟶		70.4
Ghana	10.2	17.5	76.5	⟶	6.0
Kenya	n.a.	42.2	37.1	⟶	20.7
Rhodesia and Nyasaland	11.8	59.4	26.6	⟶	14.0
Tanganyika	10.2	36.0	43.6	20.3	0.1
Uganda	n.a.	20.3	56.4	⟶	23.3

* Sources: U.N. Economic Survey of Asia and the Far East, 1961.
 U.N. Economic Survey of Latin America, 1961.
 U.N. Statistical Yearbook.
 U.N. Yearbook of National Accounts Statistics.
 Data do not cover precisely the same time period for all countries. In most cases, however, they refer to fiscal 1959–60, calendar 1960, or fiscal 1960–61.
 n.a. = not available.
 ⟶ = combined total shown in right-hand column.

and corporate income taxes, whose yield rises more than proportionately
to increases in GNP. But the less developed countries draw little revenue
from these sources. The politically powerful landowners largely escape
taxation. High-income groups in the cities also pay little. There may be
a stiff income tax on the books, but the rates are not enforced. In some
countries it is said that only two groups pay the personal income tax:
foreign businessmen, who are fair game, and civil servants, whose incomes are a matter of public record. Much the same is true of taxes on
business income. Large foreign concerns pay the full tax. Large local
concerns may pay the tax, in whole or in part. Smaller local businesses
typically do not pay. The revenue yield is small, and falls mainly on the
most progressive businesses.

The difficulty of collecting taxes hampers the financing of development programs. In the industrial countries, government expenditures
usually form 20 to 30 percent of GNP. Yet in the poor countries, where
the economic tasks of government are even more critical, government
expenditures are typically in the neighborhood of 10 percent. Professor
Arthur Lewis has argued cogently that a country must raise its tax collections to around 20 percent of GNP if it is serious about economic
development.

With tax sources restricted, and with heavy pressure for expenditure,
many of these countries have large budget deficits. A little money can
be raised by selling government bonds to the public. But the main way
of closing the deficit is to borrow from the central bank. In some countries, the main function of the central bank is to finance deficits of the
national government. The higher level of spending, instead of raising
production, mainly pushes up the price level. Brazil, Chile, and several
other Latin American countries have suffered from inflation for decades.
This is true also of some of the Asian and African countries in the period
since independence.

Some economists believe that mild inflation can be helpful in the
early stages of economic development. But there would be little disagreement that inflation of 25 or 50 percent a year has a disorganizing effect on the economy. One effect is that the value of the country's
currency falls on world markets. If the country nevertheless maintains a
fixed exchange rate, this artificial rate has to be supported by government rationing of foreign exchange. This often involves favoritism, corruption, and an uneconomic allocation of the available foreign funds.

EDUCATION AND THE SHORTAGE OF SKILLS

Most of these countries have very inadequate educational systems.
On the economic side, this limits the skill and productivity of the
labor force. On the political side, an illiterate electorate provides a poor
foundation for stable democratic government.

In Iran, at the time of the most recent census, 85 percent of the population was illiterate. The corresponding percentages were 82 in India, 75 in Egypt, 65 in Turkey, 62 in Malaya, 51 in Brazil and Venezuela, and around 45 percent in Thailand, Burma, and Ceylon.[2]

In many countries only a minority of children ever attend school. In the late 1950's the percentage of children of primary school age who were enrolled in school was 65 in Ceylon, 63 in the Philippines, and 56 in Thailand. But it fell as low as 38 in Egypt, 33 in Brazil, 25 in Burma, and 18 in Iran. Moreover most pupils drop out so early that school leaves no lasting imprint. The proportion of children of high-school age enrolled in high schools is typically only 10 to 20 percent.[3]

Educational facilities are particularly inadequate in the rural areas. There are few teachers because of a shortage of teachers' colleges, and these teachers usually prefer to live in the city rather than in isolated rural areas. The outlook of the country people is usually indifferent or even hostile to book learning.

Only a small percentage of young people get the prerequisites for college training, and facilities for higher education are pathetically inadequate. The vast Republic of the Congo has one university, admitting a few hundred students a year. Indonesia, with 80 million people, has two universities. Universities are badly understaffed, and faculty salaries are usually so low that they must be supplemented from outside sources. In Latin America, college teaching is almost always a side-line occupation for people whose main job is in government, law practice, or business. Since most college students in Latin America also hold jobs and are studying on the side, their training is not very intensive.

The training provided in the universities often bears little relation to the needs of the economy. The ex-British colonies, notably India, have a surplus of liberal arts graduates who remain unemployed in the larger cities. At the same time there are crying shortages of engineers, scientists, doctors, and business executives.

Almost all these countries have severe shortages of the professional skills needed in a modern economy. There are far too few educated people fitted for business administration and government service. There are far too few engineers, architects, agronomists, teachers, economists, statisticians, medical technicians, scientific research workers. The gap can be only partially closed by sending students to Europe or the United States for training. At some stage there must be a massive effort to build up educational facilities within these countries.

THE DISTRIBUTION OF PERSONAL INCOME

In mature capitalist economies one sees a gradual leveling of personal incomes, for reasons examined in Chapter 15. But the poor coun-

---

[2] It should be added that some of these censuses are several years in the past, and that in most countries the situation is gradually improving.

[3] UNESCO, *Basic Facts and Figures, 1960*, Paris, 1961, pp. 22–24.

tries are still largely pre-capitalist. While information is scanty, it appears that income distribution is considerably more unequal than in the industrial nations.

Large landowners and businessmen receive high incomes which are not subject to effective income taxation. Doctors, lawyers, engineers, and other professional men are also well rewarded because of the serious shortage of these skills. White-collar workers and skilled artisans are typically better paid, relative to ordinary labor, than is true in industrial countries. At the bottom of the pyramid, the tenants and small peasants in the countryside and the unskilled workers in the cities are poorly paid. And there is often a large body of unemployed and underemployed who live only by charity.

The low income level of the bulk of the population has several unfortunate consequences. There is no mass market for anything but the simplest kinds of consumer goods, and this hampers the growth of local manufacturing. Most people cannot save, and this limits the financing of new investment. Low wage rates give the employer little incentive to use labor efficiently or to introduce modern management methods. When labor is so cheap, why bother to train or supervise it? The result is a dreary circle of low wage rates and living standards → low physical energy and effort → low productivity → low wage rates. There is no easy way of breaking out of this circle.

One might think that the high incomes of the wealthy at least have the advantage of permitting large savings, which can be tapped to finance investment. But in many countries one is denied even this consoling thought. Large land owners show a deplorable leaning toward jewelry and imported Cadillacs, chateaus on the Riviera, and safe deposit boxes in Swiss banks. Anything left over is apt to be put into city real estate in Karachi, Teheran, Caracas, or wherever. It is not easy to get the landowning class to invest in industrial activities.

Business profits are another matter. A good part of profits usually is reinvested, and thus one gets a gradual expansion of the industrial sector. But where this sector is small to begin with, internal growth is necessarily slow.

THE SUPPLY OF INDUSTRIAL MANAGERS

New industries require enterprise and management, but in the poor countries the supply of managerial talent is typically small. Nor can this shortage be corrected quickly by setting up business schools in all corners of the earth. It is deep rooted in history and in the social structure.

In Asia and Africa during the colonial period, most banks, plantations, and trading concerns were foreign-owned and were managed by men sent out from the mother country. Natives of the country were employed only as clerks, foremen, and laborers. Now that these countries are independent, foreign enterprise is suspect and generally discouraged; but local enterprise on any substantial scale does not yet exist.

The European colonial powers also exalted government service over business occupations, in accordance with the scale of values prevailing in the home countries. This is most noticeable in the former British colonies. If a young Indian finishes his university course with top marks, it is taken for granted that he will enter the Civil Service, which is considered the intellectual elite of the country. Business is not quite a fit occupation for a gentleman. The advantage of this tradition is that India has an honest and capable public service, which contributes to its chances of economic development. The disadvantage is that business enterprise does not get an adequate share of the top intellectual talent.

In some countries business has been dominated by groups which, while nationals of the country, are still regarded as "foreign." The Chinese have been the traders, bankers, and artisans throughout Southeast Asia. Indians have performed the same functions in Burma, East Africa, and Central Africa. This situation creates obvious tensions. The majority group in the country resent the strategic position and higher incomes of the "outsiders," and there is political pressure to get rid of them. The Indonesian effort to oust the local Chinese businessmen is a case in point. But since members of the majority group are inexperienced, the immediate result is a setback for business development.

This issue often underlies the debate over private enterprise versus government enterprise. Consider the case of Burma. Following the British tradition, intelligent and well-born Burmese typically go from the university into Civil Service. Thus anything operated by government is managed by Burmese. Private enterprise, on the other hand, is usually in the hands of Indians or Chinese. Thus when a Burmese politician argues for government operation of a certain industry, he is not necessarily arguing from socialist conviction. He is mainly arguing for Burmese control of the industry as against what he regards as foreign control.

A sizable indigenous business class is found only in countries which have long been independent, which means mainly the countries of Latin America plus Iran, Thailand, and a few others. But businessmen in these countries differ importantly from businessmen in the United States. They tend to be hereditary in origin, family-oriented, monopolistic, and traditional.

A business in these countries is usually a family affair. Facilities for selling stock to the public are poor, and it is also considered dangerous to share control with outsiders. You can't really trust anybody, but you can trust a brother or cousin more than a stranger. This limits the capital of an enterprise to what the family can raise. It also limits the recruitment of executives. You become a businessman by being born into the right family. There is no general market for executive talent such as exists in more industrialized and fluid societies.

Because of the small size of the domestic market, businesses are usually in a quasi-monopoly position. Competition is frowned on and profit margins are high. Monopoly positions are protected by working through political channels to get tariff protection, government contracts, or import quotas, and to deny these things to potential competitors. The leading business and political families are closely interrelated.

The outlook of management is paternalistic and traditional. Businessmen are not familiar even with the scientific management of 1910, let alone with recent developments in human relations and operations research. The head of the enterprise maintains tight one-man control. Workers are regarded as naive children, for whom the employer has a paternal responsibility, but whose function is strictly to carry out orders.

Development of a modern, efficient, enterprising business class remains a task for the future. In the Western industrial countries this was a slow process extending over generations. How far it can be accelerated in the newer countries by deliberate effort is something about which we know very little.

THE SOCIAL AND POLITICAL STRUCTURE

Most of the poor countries have a hereditary aristocracy. This is often associated with large landholdings. Below this comes a middle class of businessmen, professional people, and government officials. This class is numerous in most Latin American countries, indicating that they have already made progress in industrial development. It is considerably smaller in Asia, and very small in most parts of Africa.

At the bottom of the social pyramid are the bulk of the population, who are economically poor, socially unimportant, and politically passive. Movement from this group to higher levels occurs in a slow trickle. The social mobility and blurring of class lines which one finds in an industrialized society has not yet occurred. The social structure is closer to that of feudal Europe than of twentieth-century Europe or America.

This social matrix is not hospitable to political democracy. The rise of democracy in the West was *accompanied or preceded* by widespread public education, economic diversification, the growth of a middle class, and a sharp increase in occupational and social mobility. But in most of the poor countries these things have not yet occurred. So even when the forms of democracy have been established, the system remains ineffective in operation. Government is dominated by a small clique of the "right people"; and if power changes hands, it changes to another group not very different from the first. Most of the population remains illiterate, ignorant of public issues, skeptical of government activity, and with no feeling of participation in political life.

Some countries are of course closer than others to being functioning democracies. Mexico has well-established democratic institutions, with an active electorate which does influence the complexion and policies of the national government. (But remember that Mexico had a popular revolution in the 1910's, sweeping land reforms in the 1930's, and vigorous industrial development from 1940 to the present.) Two or three other Latin American countries may be approaching this degree of political sophistication and stability. At the opposite extreme, Saudi Arabia is a feudal kingdom with no popular participation. Most countries are still closer to Saudi Arabia than to Mexico in this respect.

A prominent feature of government in these countries is the political power of the armed forces. Military leaders frequently step in, oust the civilian government, and run the country for a longer or shorter period. It is too simple to view this as a substitution of dictatorship for democracy, for these countries are not very democratic to begin with. It is mainly a substitution of one ruling clique for another, and the new group may or may not be worse than the old.

If one wants to play devil's advocate, one can argue that the army is often the most democratic organization in these countries. It is drawn from all strata of the population, including the poorer classes. Indeed, it is almost the only channel through which a poor boy can get technical training and administrative experience. Military officers may be more honest than the civilian officials whom they replace. But one cannot condone the suppression of civil liberties and the physical violence which accompanies military rule. Even at best, military control is a stop-gap. The long-run problem is to create institutions for civilian government under effective popular control.

PUBLIC ADMINISTRATION

The weakness of political institutions in these countries implies a similar weakness of public administration. Again, the situation varies from country to country. The British encouraged higher education in their colonies, sent many students to Britain for training, and drew the best university graduates into a civil service patterned on British lines. Particularly in India and Pakistan and to a lesser extent in other ex-British areas, strong civil service staffs have been carried over from the colonial period.

The Belgians, Dutch, and Portuguese, on the other hand, followed a policy of not providing university education in their colonies. Natives of the Belgian Congo were not allowed to go abroad for training, and university training in the Congo was begun only in the last two or three years of Belgian rule. Indonesian students could work toward a degree in medicine, but not in other subjects. This barred local people from administrative positions, which were filled entirely by men from the mother country. When these men were withdrawn after independence, they left an administrative vacuum. The disorganization of economic administration in Indonesia stems directly from this source. Even more dramatic is the case of the Congo, which in 1960 was left completely stripped of trained leadership.

Even in areas which have long been independent, such as Latin America, one usually does not find a career civil service. Government jobs are frankly political, and it is taken for granted that they will change hands if the government changes. The main qualification for office is family and connections; and the upper administrative group is drawn from the educated, well-to-do elite of the country. Many of these people are able and conscientious. But their training and background bears little relation to the jobs they are supposed to be doing. Government appointments are in fact scarcely regarded as jobs. They are political perquisites, to which a man is entitled by belonging to a certain group. Under these conditions one cannot expect the continuity, efficiency, and professional spirit which marks the public services of the Western world.

This has serious implications for economic development. Carrying out a development program is a skilled and technical undertaking. It requires people with specialized education and administrative experience. In most countries of the South one finds only a handful of such people; and this shortage can only be partially remedied by borrowing foreign experts. Even the supply of foreign experts is getting spread very thin, as economists from Europe and the United States dash about the globe flinging advice over their shoulders and leaving do-it-yourself kits behind them.

One of the commonest and most discouraging experiences in these countries is to find impressive development plans and policy pronouncements emanating from the capital city, which have no practical effect because there is no administrative apparatus behind them. Building such an apparatus is a basic task which must at least be commenced before economic development can move forward.

THE PROSPECTS FOR ECONOMIC DEVELOPMENT

Because of these characteristics one should not assume that sustained growth will get underway quickly or easily in the poor countries. It cannot be assured simply by infusions of capital from the richer countries. The main impetus must come from within these countries themselves.

In most countries one finds considerable development ferment among political leaders, intellectuals, progressive businessmen, and other members of the urban middle class. But one also finds powerful groups which are uninterested in development or actively opposed to it. Why should the large landowners of Chile or Iran favor economic change? They are doing well as it is, and moves toward modernization of the economy will be to their disadvantage. Enlightened self-interest should perhaps lead them to cooperate in moderate reforms to ward off potential revolution, but this argument has rarely proven persuasive with ruling classes.

Traditional business concerns will also resist economic changes which might bring increased competition and an erosion of monopoly profits. Religious leaders, tribal chieftains, and other guardians of the traditional culture will usually oppose economic innovation. When these things are added together, we must expect that many countries will make no economic progress, or will make only slight and intermittent progress.

To do better than this requires profound social and political changes of whose nature we are as yet only dimly aware. One apparent necessity is a political leadership which is growth-oriented, and which is able to mobilize the progressive elements in the community for a long-run effort. Economic growth, since it requires a higher rate of saving and investment, involves restraining the urge toward consumption in the early stages. It may be several decades before there is a substantial payoff in consumer incomes and living standards. It takes unusual political skill to win public acceptance of such a program. It may even require a single charismatic leader—a Nasser, or Nehru, or Nkrumah—who is able to retain power for a prolonged period.

So when we turn in the next chapter to explore the strategy of economic development, we are talking about a process which is presently underway in only a minority of the poor countries. Concretely, we are talking about a number of the ex-British colonies, including India, Pakistan, Ceylon, and Malaya; about a few areas where there has been strong American influence, such as the Philippines, Taiwan, and Israel; and about Mexico, Brazil, and perhaps two or three other countries of Latin America. The discussion of development policy nevertheless has potential relevance to other countries, which may add themselves to the developing group over the course of time.

SUMMARY

1. The economies of Asia, Africa, and Latin America differ so greatly that it is artificial to group them together. Some have a long experience of political independence, while others are just emerging from the chrysalis of colonial rule. Some are considerably richer than others. Some are growing, while others are not. They differ widely in size, resource base, and degree of population pressure. There are nevertheless certain characteristics which appear in most of them in greater or lesser degree.

2. There is only a limited development of competitive markets for goods, labor, and capital. Hence it is questionable how far one can apply to these economies the "Western" economic principles expounded in Parts One and Three.

3. Most people are engaged in agriculture, and a large proportion of agricultural output is consumed on the farm. There is a distinct cleavage between the subsistence economy and the money economy, often termed *economic dualism.*

4. Productivity in agriculture is typically low. In some countries this is traceable partly to landlordism; but small, independent peasant agriculture can also be very inefficient.

5. Exports often constitute 10 to 20 percent of GNP, and are usually concentrated in one or two primary products. Fluctuations in export sales have the same unsettling effect on these economies that fluctuations in investment have in

the industrial countries. Over the long run, low income and price elasticity of demand for primary products poses a problem of how to increase exports fast enough to pay for the imports needed for economic development.

6. Tax revenue is typically only 10 percent or so of GNP, and comes mainly from commodity taxes rather than income taxes. Hence revenue may rise less than proportionately to increases in national income, seriously hampering development expenditures.

7. Educational facilities are increasingly inadequate as one proceeds from the primary to the university level. There are severe shortages of training capacity for the technical and professional skills needed in a modern industrial economy.

8. Income distribution is more unequal than in the industrial countries, and the high incomes of the rich tend to go into luxury consumption or hoarding rather than into industrial investment.

9. There is a serious deficiency of business leadership. In some countries most businessmen belong to foreign ethnic groups, which places them at a political disadvantage. Where there is a local business group, as in the Latin American countries, it is typically traditional and monopolistic rather than innovative.

10. The social structure of many of these countries is more nearly feudal than modern. Only a few of them yet have the prerequisites for democratic government. Rule by the wealthy or by the army is the general rule.

11. Government administrative staffs are poorly trained and selected, and are typically inept or corrupt or both. So even when a reasonable development program has been developed, little may come of it because of lack of an administrative apparatus.

12. Despite these difficulties, a minority of the poor countries are making substantial economic progress; and as their example spreads, others may join the developing group in the years ahead.

The Strategy of Economic Development

"Now *here*, you see, it takes all the running *you* can do to keep in the same place. If you want to get somewhere else, you must run twice as fast as that."

Through the Looking Glass

If to do were as easy as to know what to do, chapels had been churches, and poor men's cottages princes' palaces.

WILLIAM SHAKESPEARE, *The Merchant of Venice*

Whoever makes two blades of grass to grow where only one grew before renders a service to the State.

VOLTAIRE

PLACE YOURSELF in the position of the president of a poor country striving for economic development. You are beset by all the problems described in the last chapter. The country lacks virtually everything. Where do you begin? What do you set as high-priority objectives? How do you lay hands on the resources to work toward these objectives? Can you learn anything from the record of how growth occurred in other times and places?

SOME LESSONS OF EXPERIENCE

Lessons from the West

Rapid economic growth began in the West. Starting from England in the period 1750–1800, modern industry spread during the nineteenth century to the United States, Western Europe, and the British Commonwealth. It is natural to look first at the record of growth in these countries. What was their situation at the beginning of the modern era? How did growth get underway? What was the sequence of events during the crucial early stages? Is there any implication that newer industrial nations must follow the same sequence?

Conditions in the Western countries at the beginning of *their* period of rapid development were more favorable than those now prevailing in the poorer countries. Income per capita was considerably higher. It has been estimated that average income in Britain in 1800 was about at the level of Argentina or Chile today, which would place it well above most of Asia, Africa, and Latin America. So there was more margin for saving and capital accumulation, and also a wider market for manufactured consumer goods.

Population growth in Western Europe from 1750–1850 was typically less than 1 percent a year. At a later stage these countries experienced a "population explosion," because of rapid reduction of death rates. But they had entered a period of sustained economic growth *before* there was a rapid increase in population. The reverse is true in most of the poorer nations today. Modern medical science has arrived there in advance of any increase in economic productivity. The population of many countries is rising at between 2 and 3 percent a year. This requires considerable effort just to keep per capita income from falling.

The Western nations had other advantages in the early stages: political unification, which in some cases had existed for centuries; economic unification through a road network, to be followed in the nineteenth century by a rapid development of canals, railroads, and steamships; stable government, including guarantees for private property and business enterprise; and a sizable business class, which was to grow rapidly in social prestige and political power. Most poor countries today are less well off in these respects.

Starting from this advantageous position, the growth rates of the Western nations were not spectacular. Growth began gradually, and it was often a half century before one could be sure that a permanent acceleration had occurred. Even in more recent times, annual growth rates have not been high. Kuznets' calculations for the past century indicate that even in the fastest-growing industrial nations GNP has typically risen by 3 to 4 percent a year. In some countries (Britain, France, Holland, Australia) the average annual increase has been 2 percent or less.

The development plans of the poorer countries today often aim to increase GNP at 4 to 6 percent a year, i.e., more rapidly than the wealthier nations have done over the long run. This does not prove that the targets are unattainable. But to attain them will require a larger national effort than was made in the industrial countries at a corresponding stage.

As regards the *pattern* of growth in the Western countries, we may note first the existence of a progressive agricultural sector. In most countries there were important advances in agricultural productivity *before* there was much development of factory industry. The agricultural revolution typically led the industrial revolution. This was true not only in the West but in Russia, which had developed a large export surplus of grain before 1914. Without this initial cushion, the U.S.S.R. could scarcely have survived the shock of collectivization and the long neglect of agriculture during the 1930's and 1940's. In Japan, too, agriculture led the march of the economy into the modern era.

Second, growth was associated in many countries with increased opportunities for international trade. Ocean transportation became cheaper throughout the eighteenth and nineteenth centuries; improved roads, canals, and railroads lowered the cost of getting goods from the interior to port cities; tariffs and other trade restrictions among the advanced countries fell considerably; and colonization of many parts of the world by Europeans opened up trade opportunities in those areas. The countries which grew rapidly were typically countries which had something to sell abroad; textiles from England, timber from Sweden, foodstuffs from Denmark, grain from Russia and the United States, silk from Japan. Trade was an engine of growth.

Some economists argue that primary producing nations today do not have the favorable export opportunities which existed at an earlier time, and that it is particularly hard for them to break into the world market for manufactures. There is doubtless something to this. But the prominent role of trade in economic growth over the past two centuries suggests that one should not reject the possibilities of trade without careful examination.

Third, we may note the complex and pervasive nature of economic growth, the diffusion of pioneer activity throughout all branches of the economy. Economic historians tend to simplify the picture by focusing on major inventions or on new industries which were growing with particular speed—the "coal and iron age," the "railroad era," and so on. This overlooks the great amount of "follow-up investment" by innumerable small men in subsidiary lines of activity whose growth is necessary to support that of the major industries. It neglects also the gradual spillover of talent and capital from the leading sectors into other lines of industry.

Fourth, government played an important role in developing transport and communication facilities. Government took main responsibility for the network of roads and canals, the postal system, and other means of communication. It subsidized and protected merchant shipping in various ways. Railroads were a government monopoly from the beginning in most countries, and so was electric power at a later stage. Education and public health, so closely linked with the improvement of human resources, were mainly a government responsibility. It is thus inaccurate

to picture Western economic growth as arising solely from private initiative with government playing a passive role. The blend of private and
public activity naturally varied from country to country, depending on
national institutions and traditions. Government initiative was more important in Japan than in Europe, and more important on the Continent
than in Britain or the United States.

Finally, we may look at the financing of private capital formation.
The main source of finance in most countries was reinvestment of business profits, often termed the *classical process of capital accumulation.*
The way in which this process operated in the Western countries (and in
Japan after 1868) is well known. Inventions and improvements were raising productivity in both agriculture and industry. But real wages rose
only slightly. This lag of wages behind the increase of productivity
yielded large business profits. Rates of return on capital during the nineteenth century were substantially higher than they are today.

Most capitalists of this era were conscientious men, who lived well
but not wildly, and who put most of their profits into business expansion.
Hence, a cumulative process: profits were reinvested in plant and
equipment, to make still larger profits in the future, leading to more reinvestment, and so on and on. With profits forming an increasing share of
national income, and with most of these profits reinvested, it followed
that capital formation must also form a rising share of national income.
The rise in capital formation rates was one of the striking features of
nineteenth-century economic growth.

Why was the increase in national output not swallowed up immediately by wage increases, and thus channeled into consumption rather
than investment? There were several reasons. In some countries, agricultural progress was creating a surplus of landless workers who could be
drawn into urban industries at low wages. So long as this surplus continued, there was no need to raise city wages substantially. Another reason was the limited development of effective trade unions. Great Britain
did not have large-scale unionism until the 1890's, the United States not
until the 1930's, and Japan is only now reaching this stage. There seems
to have been a lag of about a century between the beginnings of large-
scale industry and the development of strong union organizations.

Nineteenth century wage earners took little part in politics and had
little influence on government policy. During the period of rapid industrial build-up there was no unemployment compensation, or old age pensions, or family allowances, or medical and hospital insurance, or other
appurtenances of the "welfare state." Nor was there a progressive income
tax to reduce inequalities of income.

For a considerable time, then, the laboring class enjoyed only limited participation in the benefits of economic growth. The welfare of the
average British worker seems to have risen only moderately between
1780 and 1840. But while the common man benefited little at the time,

the high rate of capital formation made possible larger output and higher living standards at a later stage. Without exploitation of labor in the nineteenth century, there would have been less product for the welfare state to redistribute in the twentieth. One difficulty in the poor countries today is that there is political pressure to legislate a wide range of welfare measures immediately, before productive capacity has risen to the point at which the economy can "afford" the promised increases in living standards.

These features of early industrialism in the West provide a useful background for our later discussion of development strategy. This is not to say that the future must repeat the past. But it would be surprising if the future were entirely *unlike* the past, and if the rules of economic growth had changed completely since 1945.

It is worth noting that the classical process of capital accumulation has operated in the U.S.S.R. somewhat as it operated in the Western countries at an earlier stage. Productivity is raised through investment and technology, while wages and living standards are held back. The result is a large profit gap, which in this case shows up mainly as tax receipts by the central government. A large share of these receipts is plowed back into industrial investment, leading to larger output and profits on the next round. This process operated so successfully from 1928 to 1950 that it has now become possible to relax the austerity of the Stalin era and to permit workers to share in the rise of productivity. The moral for the less developed countries is not so much that growth occurs through planning as that growth occurs through belt-tightening over a prolonged period.

Some Lessons from Japan

A nation embarking on economic development might well make a careful study of Japanese experience. A century ago Japan was a very poor country, with a feudal political structure and a substantial population confined in a small land area. Beginning with the Meiji Restoration in 1868, Japan proceeded to become a major industrial nation, which in recent years has had one of the highest growth rates in the world. How did they do it? Several points may be underlined:

1. While there is a widespread impression that Japan developed rapidly after 1868, early growth was in fact quite gradual. Industrialization did not really get underway until the 1890's, twenty-five years after the Restoration. Even then, industry meant mainly textiles. As late as 1930 Japan was not self-sufficient in steel, and far from it in machinery. Metals, machinery, and chemicals did not begin to rival textiles until the armament program of the 1930's, and did not outshine textiles until the 1950's. The sequence was from a primarily agricultural development (1868–90), to textiles and other light industries (1890–1930), and finally to heavy industry (1930 to date).

2. Early Japanese growth was marked by a sharp rise in agricultural output. Between 1878 and 1908, land under cultivation increased by 35 percent and output per acre by 80 percent, so that total output more than doubled. How was this accomplished? There was a basic land reform early in the period, under which government paid off the feudal land-owners with government bonds and resold the land to the cultivators, who had a more direct interest in raising productivity. There was also considerable public investment in irrigation, drainage, and land reclamation.

Within this framework productivity rose through a multitude of small improvements: increased use of fertilizers, better varieties of seeds, weed control, double-cropping of rice, better layout of plots, improved methods of cultivation. Government research and agricultural extension activities, which relative to Japanese national income have been even larger than in the United States, were important in promoting these improvements. Improved agricultural credit facilities, and efforts to raise the literacy of the rural population, were important. Farm incomes also benefited from sideline activities: a wide diffusion of handicraft production throughout the countryside, and the introduction of silkworms which gave Japan a major export product.

The government taxed away much of the increase in farmers' incomes to finance capital formation elsewhere in the economy. From 1878 to 1912 about two thirds of total tax collections came from agricultural sources. The tax burden on agriculture, as a percentage of agricultural income, was about three times as heavy as on other sectors of the economy. Thus the agricultural sector provided food for the growing population, a major source of exports, the main source of tax revenues, and a growing market for domestic manufactures. What more could one ask?

3. The influence of government on economic development was important but indirect. While the government started many model factories in the early stages of industrialization, most of these were sold in 1882 to private concerns. The government continued to operate only such things as railroads, the tobacco monopoly (for revenue purposes) and steel and munitions (for strategic reasons). The main thing government did was to create a unified internal market through improved transport and communications, an atmosphere of political stability, an enforceable tax system, corporation laws, and other prerequisites for the successful operation of private enterprise. The point has been well put by Patrick:

Flexibility in the utilization of factors was greatly enhanced by clearing away the legal and political obstacles to freedom of ownership of land, occupation, and movement for labor, and by institutional reforms in law, taxation, currency, banking and other areas. Consumption and saving relationships were altered, especially in the redistribution of income away from the *daimyo* lords and their retainers. A start was made at bringing in foreign knowledge and at disseminating it, both through a government drive at general basic literacy, and emphasis on a wide variety of technical skills through vocational schools, the hiring of foreign technicians, sending missions and students abroad, importing machinery, and so on.

By and large the state used the private market mechanism to allocate resources and to obtain its objectives generally, exerting its influence through the market (via tariffs, subsidies, differential tax rates, purchases, and the like), rather than replacing the market through government planning or production . . . except at the very beginning the government was not important as an industrial producer and its contribution to the growth of the economy did not lie in State-owned enterprise.[1]

4. The early Japanese entrepreneurs were mainly of rural origin— sons of country merchants, rich peasants, or landlords. "They were restless young men, with considerable education and early practical experience, who in a sense broke with the past, had great faith in Western methods, and who moved as young men to one of the large urban centers, in the quest of progress and personal advancement."[2]

Pursuit of private profit was fused with service to the Emperor and development of national power. It was taken for granted that "what is good for Mitsubishi is good for Japan," and vice versa. Development of large industrial enterprises was considered a national service. How pleasant to become rich and patriotic at the same time! The social structure of the country remained oligarchic, with close interlocking by marriage among the top business, political, and military families. This new ruling class rapidly assumed the position held by the feudal landlords before 1868.

5. Alongside the growth of factory industry, the small workshop has continued to play an important role in the Japanese economy. As recently as 1955, three quarters of manufacturing employment was in shops with fewer than 300 workers, and 40 percent was in shops with less than 30 workers. How have the small shops managed to survive instead of being squeezed out by mass-production enterprises? There appear to be several reasons. First, the surplus of labor and scarcity of capital in Japan favors labor-intensive methods, which usually means smaller production units. Second, small shops pay considerably lower wages than large ones. In 1954, manufacturing plants with 100 to 500 workers paid wages only 70 percent as high as plants with 1,000 workers or more. Plants with 10 to 30 workers paid only 55 percent as much as the largest establishments. Thus low wages serve as an offset to the lower productivity of the small shops.[3]

---

[1] Hugh T. Patrick, "Lessons for Underdeveloped Countries from the Japanese Experience of Economic Development," *Indian Economic Journal*, October, 1961, pp. 150–66. Excerpts from p. 151 and p. 157.

[2] *Ibid.*, p. 162.

[3] How are the small shops able to get by with these lower wage rates? Partly because of the chronic labor surplus in the economy, but also because the small plants are largely unaffected by union organization, which has been a strong factor in large-scale industry since World War II.

Third, small plants are not necessarily in competition with large plants. On the contrary, large factories often subcontract a good deal of their work to low-cost small producers. In assembly industries such as bicycles, sewing machines, radios, and electronics, the parts are often made in small shops and then brought to the central factory for final assembly. There may be lessons in this for some of the newly developing countries, which are apt to think of industrialization as synonymous with large-scale production.

6. Foreign trade was important in Japanese development. Before World War II Japan typically exported about 20 percent of her national product. But the character of this trade changed as Japanese manufacturing grew in diversity and competitive power. In 1880, Japan was exporting raw materials and importing both capital goods and manufactured consumer goods. By 1940 she was exporting primarily manufactures, while importing raw materials and even some foodstuffs.

Unlike the United States and many other countries, Japan did *not* depend heavily on foreign borrowing in the early stages of development. Capital formation came almost entirely from domestic sources: increased government tax revenues, reinvestment of business profits, and personal savings of the frugal Japanese people. It is interesting that the capital formation rate was not high in the crucial early decades. Gross investment seems to have been 10 to 11 percent, and net investment perhaps 6 or 7 percent, of national product from 1889 to 1914. The growth of national output seems to have been due mainly to technical progress and institutional changes, rather than to investment *per se*.

GOVERNMENT AND PRIVATE ENTERPRISE IN ECONOMIC DEVELOPMENT

Before examining what should be done to promote economic growth, a word about *who* is to do it. What functions can be performed most effectively by government? What things are best left to private initiative and management?

We have seen that government played an important role in the early growth of the older industrial countries. The burden falling on government in today's poor countries will be even heavier. This is partly because of the meagre development of modern politico-economic institutions in these countries, their lack of many things which existed in Europe and America before 1800. It is also because the intellectual climate of the poor countries today differs from that in the West during the formative stages of capitalism. In these countries *property* and *profit*, instead of being good words, are viewed with suspicion. The good words today are *national economic independence, planned development*, and *public welfare*. Private business activity will win acceptance only to the extent that it can be shown to contribute to these ends.

Granted that government must do a good deal in these countries, what concretely is it called on to do? The answer will differ from country to country. Some are more statist in outlook (Ghana, the United Arab Republic), while others are more inclined toward private enterprise (Malaya, Thailand, the Philippines). But certain basic functions would be widely accepted, and these deserve brief comment.

Providing Public Services

This is a noncontroversial activity in which all governments engage, but often at an inadequate level. Hardly any of the less developed countries are now doing as much as would be desirable in the areas of education, health and sanitation, and urban development. In some countries basic law and order is still precarious.

Social Overhead Capital

Development requires heavy investment in transportation, communications, power, irrigation, and the like. This investment is normally public, partly because more money is needed than can be raised from private sources, but also because these activities are considered to be of a public character.

Funds for Development

Government is always an important source of development funds, and often the largest source. Only government has the taxing power, and vigorous use of this power can raise the investment level substantially. Over the long run much can be expected from reinvestment of business profits; but this source will grow only gradually, and may never attain the dominant role which it played in the older capitalist countries. Government is also the main mechanism for securing loans and grants from the developed countries and the international lending institutions.

Initiating New Industries

Argument over public *versus* private operation of industry in these countries centers on a narrow range of activities. Few people would argue that government should *not* operate the railroads, the telephone system, the electric power network, and other public utilities. At the other pole, few would argue that government *should* operate farms, stores, service and repair establishments, handicraft shops, or light manufacturing industries. Controversy centers on steel, nonferrous metals, machinery, electrical equipment, and other branches of heavy manufacturing.

One must distinguish here between *initiation* of new enterprises and *subsequent operation* of these enterprises. Government will often be involved in launching a large new industry. The timing and location of the investment should be related to the national development plan. The enterprise may need government financing. Tariff protection and import quotas may be required. There may be no private business group prepared to participate in the venture in the first instance.

But government initiation of an enterprise is quite consistent with turning it over to private operation at a later stage. The Japanese government did this successfully in the late nineteenth century. More recently, this technique has been used in Pakistan through the Pakistan Industrial Development Corporation. A Canadian company, for example, is called in to construct a paper mill in West Pakistan. The P.I.D.C., a government-owned corporation, puts up the initial capital. It also negotiates a management contract under which the Canadian company agrees to operate the mill for the first few years, meanwhile training Pakistani managers to take over. With this breathing space, the P.I.D.C. scouts around Karachi to see whether some wealthy families may be willing to buy into the paper company. A sizable number of new industries have already been transferred to private operation in this way, freeing the P.I.D.C. funds to start additional industries.

The real issue, then, is whether government should sell off new industries as rapidly as feasible or whether it should continue to operate them as public enterprises. Socialists feel that basic manufacturing industries are power centers of the economy, which it is dangerous to leave in private hands. Public operation, it is argued, will make it easier to coordinate expansion of these industries with overall development plans. It is also argued that, since the ablest and best educated people are concentrated in government service, they can do a better job of industrial management than any other group. This is heard most frequently in the ex-British colonies, where the highest-ranking university graduates are normally channeled into the civil service.

But the past is not binding on the future. If it is true that talented people have been going heavily into government service, while business occupations are poorly staffed and poorly regarded, one might conclude that the system of education and recruitment needs to be changed. Perhaps steps should be taken to raise the prestige of business management and to draw more talent in that direction. The problem is in a sense opposite to that which exists in the United States. Here it is usually said that business management attracts most of the top talent, while government gets the leftovers; and that steps are needed to interest good men in politics and public administration.

It is often said that the less developed countries lack potential businessmen. It is no use appealing to private entrepreneurship, because it isn't there. It is hard to know what this argument means. A Burmese economist commented in conversation, "It amounts to saying that we are just stupid." If nationals of a country cannot manage production efficiently for a private company, how can they do so for a government department? One should remember also that inconspicuousness is a hallmark of the budding entrepreneur. You learn of his existence only after he has appeared and cashed in on some profitable opportunity. One school of thought maintains that there are many such people in the poor countries, presently engaged in trade or small manufacturing, but waiting only for opportunity to branch out and flourish on a larger scale.

The writer's judgment would be that it is wise to turn over manufacturing concerns as rapidly as possible to private operation. One reason is to economize the scarce administrative resources of government. No matter how able the civil service, it cannot do everything at once. Administrative talent is needed in a dozen directions: to do overall economic planning, to develop effective systems of taxation and government budgeting, to manage public utility enterprises, to cope with the intractable problems of agriculture, to strengthen education and other public services. If one adds to this the management of numerous manufacturing enterprises, government's personnel resources get spread very thin. Encouraging private industry enables the society to tap additional supplies of administrative talent, usually inconspicuous, often poorly educated, but shrewd and adept in responding to economic incentives. Other advantages of decentralized control of industry were emphasized in Part One and need not be re-stated here.

A Framework for Private Initiative

Government in these countries often leaves an industry in private hands, but with an air of reluctance and with restrictive controls which make efficient operation difficult. Here one gets the worst of both worlds. The decision to leave a certain activity in the private sector should be a *clean* decision. From that point on government should try to make private operation efficient and profitable. This involves doing certain things and refraining from doing other things.

On the positive side, government action is needed at dozens of points to set the stage for a fruitful development of private enterprise. The requirements include modernized property, corporation, and tax laws; widening of markets through improved transport and communication; development of market institutions—produce exchanges, labor exchanges, financial exchanges; mobilizing labor supplies through general education and technical training; mobilizing capital supplies through government lending institutions; encouraging competition and warding off the baneful effects of private monopoly.

On the negative side, government should avoid the petty and purposeless regulation of private decisions, the pettifogging bureaucracy, the maddening delays which can make business almost impossible. In most underdeveloped countries business is over-regulated at present, and regulated in a haphazard and arbitrary way which leads to private inefficiency and public corruption. This was, of course, the typical situation in eighteenth-century Europe. The sweeping away of needless restrictions by the laissez-faire revolution released a great wave of private initiative in

Europe and America. One would expect similar results to follow in other countries.

STRATEGIC ISSUES IN DEVELOPMENT POLICY

Let's return now to the problem of the President of Chile or Pakistan. What does he do for his own country, here and now? His government has limited resources of administrative talent as well as money. How should these resources be deployed for development purposes?

This may be viewed from one standpoint as a problem of *balance*. How can the growth of various sectors of the economy be made consistent and mutually supporting? From another standpoint it is a problem of *time sequence*. What activities, if started first, will be most conducive to later growth of other activities?

One is involved in a variety of issues: the balance between investment in direct production and in social overhead capital; the balance between agricultural and nonagricultural activities; the choice of industries for development; and the degree of emphasis which should be placed on foreign trade and development of export markets. On each of these matters there is considerable disagreement even among experts. This is one reason why economic development is an unusually lively area of economic study and practice. While we cannot resolve all disagreements in this area, we can at least try to clarify what the argument is about.

The Role of Social Overhead Capital

Industries may be divided into two broad groups:

1. Those which provide basic services required for the development of other industries. This includes electric power production; road, rail, air, and water transport; postal, telephone, telegraph, and radio communication; and technical education, scientific research, and extension services. The familiar term *public utilities* covers most of these industries. They are also sometimes called *economic infra-structure*, a military term which denotes the communications and supply network needed to support an army in the field. Another common term is *social overhead capital* (SOC), which one wit has defined as "anything for which the World Bank will lend money."

2. Agriculture, mining, manufacturing, and the like, and usually termed *directly productive activities* (DPA). This does not put the matter quite correctly, for public utilities are also productive. But the DPA industries are in a sense built on top of and serviced by the SOC facilities.

The development of social overhead capital is in most countries considered a function of government. Well-conceived projects can usually be financed by borrowing from the World Bank or other foreign sources, since they yield a cash revenue from which to pay interest and principal. But one cannot equate the economic return from a railroad or power project with the revenue from sale of its services. The benefit to the economy will usually be considerably larger than the cash revenue. This is because of the beneficial effects on other lines of production. If cheaper transport lowers costs and prices of manufactured goods, this means higher real incomes for the population, and a larger national output of manufactures.

To go back to the terminology of Chapter 10, an SOC project yields *external economies*. Its *social product* is typically a good deal larger than the *private product* which can be appropriated as profit by the operators of the project. So it is usually desirable from a national standpoint to invest *more* in such projects than one would do if the objective were to maximize private profit. This is one reason why decisions about the level of social overhead investment should be made by public authorities rather than private investors.

It seems sensible that SOC investment should proceed in step with development of manufacturing and other DPA industries. But precise balance cannot be attained at each moment of time. In addition to the usual difficulties of forecasting demand, many SOC investments are large and time consuming. A major hydro project can easily take 10 years from conception to completion. This raises a problem of strategy: is it better for social overhead investment to be somewhat *ahead* of investment in directly productive activities, or somewhat *behind* it? This question has been posed particularly by Hirschman,[4] who terms the former course *development via excess capacity* (of SOC), and the latter *development by shortages*.

The first strategy involves building railroads, highways, port facilities, and power plants ahead of immediate demand, in the hope that availability of these services will call forth investment in DPA industries. This is a safe strategy in the sense that *eventually* the country will grow sufficiently to use these overhead investments. The difficulty is that this excess capacity has only a *permissive* rather than a *compulsive* effect. One cannot be sure how quickly DPA investment will be forthcoming. If the lag is long, facilities may deteriorate for lack of use, and some of the premature investment will be wasted.

The opposite course is to push ahead as fast as possible with DPA investment, which will raise the demand for public utility services. Then, as shortages of these services become apparent, go ahead with SOC investment to overcome the shortages. The advantage of this *compulsive* sequence is that, if the first step is taken successfully, the second can be counted on to follow. As transport lines and power output become inadequate, there will be political pressure to do something about it and the necessary steps will be taken almost automatically. The disadvantage is

---

[4] Albert Hirschman, *The Strategy of Economic Development* (New Haven, Conn.: Yale University Press, 1958), chap. 5.

that, since SOC investment takes so long, an expansion undertaken only *after* shortages are visible means that these shortages will continue for several years. The existence of these bottlenecks will have a discouraging effect on further productive investment.

Despite these difficulties, Hirschman concludes that the second strategy is generally preferable:

> . . . if we endow an underdeveloped country with a first-class highway network, with extensive hydroelectric and perhaps irrigation facilities, can we be certain that industrial and agricultural activity will expand in the wake of these improvements? Would it not be less risky and more economical first to make sure of such activity . . . and then let the ensuing pressures determine the appropriate outlays for social overhead capital and its location? As examples of this type of sequence, one may cite the development of Japan, Turkey, and, to a considerable extent, of the U.S.S.R.[5]

Closely related to investment in physical overhead capital is expenditure on public health, education, technical training, and other things which improve the quality of the labor force. This is usually classified as current expenditure in government budgets, and is regarded as an addition to consumption; but it contains an important investment element. Giving people stronger physiques, more knowledge, and greater technical skill raises their productive capacity just as surely as giving them more elaborate tools and equipment.

The parallels between investment in social overhead capital and investment in human beings are in fact quite striking. Most countries regard both as normal functions of government. Both have widespread beneficial effects throughout the economy and encourage the growth of other industries. In both cases the social product of the investment is substantially greater than the private gain. There is consequently a danger of underinvestment, which can be averted only by farsighted government action.

Human investment raises two questions. First, *how much* should government spend in this direction? One can safely answer, "More than usually is spent." Even in the United States, with its elaborate educational system, the yield on investment in education is still high. One would expect it to be considerably higher in countries where educational facilities are severely limited. It seems likely that in most countries there is (relative) overinvestment in material capital and underinvestment in raising personal productive capacity.

Second, how should the health or education budget be distributed among *specific uses?* This raises intriguing issues which can only be suggested here. The answers depend partly on how highly one values the consumption aspect of these expenditures as against the productivity-raising aspect. In terms of personal happiness, national culture, and so on, one might wish to put as many people as possible through academic

---

[5] *Ibid.*, pp. 93–94.

high schools and liberal arts colleges. But in terms of maximum productivity gain, one might argue for more school training in manual and
clerical skills, and more technical and professional training in college.
These issues are important even in wealthy countries. In the poor countries they are very important, because the total resources available for
education are so limited. Similar questions arise in the area of medical
care. For example, how much should one allocate to caring for chronic
invalids in the upper age-groups as against improving the health of young
people with a long productive life ahead of them?

The Balance of Agriculture and Industry

Is it feasible for an economy to grow simply through industrial development, while agriculture continues in its traditional stagnation? Both
history and theory suggest a negative answer. In the older industrial
countries a transformation of agriculture typically accompanied, or even
preceded, the rise of factory industry. We can also suggest logical reasons
why rising agricultural output *must* accompany any sustained economic
growth.

Industrial development means among other things a transfer of manpower from country to city, the formation of an urban wage-earning
class. How are these people to be fed? It may be said that, since they
have simply moved in from the country, the food which they formerly
consumed on the farm is now "surplus." All one needs is some way of
capturing this surplus and shipping it to the city to be consumed there.
But this is not very realistic. As the number of mouths to be fed from
each farm plot declines, the people remaining on the land will probably
eat more than before. Conceivably, they may eat up all of the hypothetical surplus. Moreover, the people who move to the city are now
working harder and earning money wages, so their demand for food will
be higher than before. Thus the amount of food available must increase
if the economy is to remain in balance.

If domestic food production does not rise sufficiently, the increased
demand will spill over into foreign markets. Food imports will rise and
this, given a limited supply of foreign exchange, will reduce the country's ability to import capital goods for development. Alternatively, if
imports are restricted, food *prices* will rise, and this will act as a brake on
industrial development. Industrial wages will have to be raised to cover
the higher food costs, which will cut into profit margins and into the
funds available for reinvestment.

Rising domestic demand for food, then, is a basic reason why farm
output must rise as development proceeds. But there are other reasons as
well. First, agriculture produces not only food but also wool, cotton, flax,
hides, oilseeds, and other raw materials. Unless production of these things
is increased, the processing industries which depend on them either cannot develop or must use imported materials. Second, agriculture can

often be a source of the increased exports so desperately needed to finance imports of capital goods. Third, industrialization leads eventually to a shortage of labor. At this point improvements in agricultural productivity become necessary to release additional labor for urban employment.

This last point deserves further explanation. The poor countries are often said to suffer from *disguised unemployment* or *redundant labor* in the agricultural sector. One can distinguish these terms as follows: There is *redundant labor* if workers can be withdrawn from agriculture with no reduction in output, that is, if the marginal productivity of labor is zero. There is *disguised unemployment* if the marginal productivity of labor in agriculture is positive but below the worker's own consumption.

In a heavily populated country, both phenomena may be present.[6] But if agricultural workers can be drawn off into industrial employment faster than new workers are being added by population growth, the amount of redundant labor will gradually fall. Eventually one will reach a point at which redundant labor is exhausted. The speed with which this point is approached is a good indicator of the success of a development program.

Even after redundant labor is exhausted, it will still pay to continue transferring labor from agriculture to industry so long as there is any disguised unemployment. The people remaining in agriculture benefit, because the transferred workers were eating more than they were producing. National output benefits because the transferred workers are producing more in industry than they previously were in agriculture.

But since the disguisedly unemployed were adding *something* to agricultural output, their removal means that agricultural output will tend to fall. This must be offset by raising the productivity of those remaining on the land. Only thus can one reconcile the need for continued transfer of labor from country to city with the need for greater agricultural output.

It is much easier to demonstrate the need for agricultural progress than to devise ways of getting it. Basic organizational changes may be necessary—buying out absentee landlords, establishing efficient-sized farming units, and other things suggested in the last chapter. Given an effective institutional framework, the proper prescription for raising output depends mainly on the labor-land ratio. After the point of labor

---

[6] This point is controversial. The existence of redundant labor even in densely populated countries has sometimes been denied on one or both of the following grounds: (1) All the labor in agriculture is needed at harvest time and other seasonal peaks. In between these peaks one has *seasonal unemployment*, but not really redundant labor. (2) Strictly speaking the marginal productivity of labor is zero only if, as labor is withdrawn, output remains unchanged *with the same production methods*. It is often argued that labor can be withdrawn from traditional agriculture with no loss of output only if at the same time there are changes in methods and a redeployment of the remaining labor force.

shortage has been reached, it makes sense to replace farm labor by machinery. But up to that point, mechanization is inappropriate. What one wants in the early stages is not *labor-saving improvements* but *land-saving improvements*, i.e., measures which increase output per acre while requiring as much or more labor than before. This means fertilizers, irrigation, improved seeds and breeds of animal, improved cultivation methods, use of insecticides and pesticides, double-cropping where climate permits, systematic crop rotation, and the like.

A puzzling thing about agriculture in the less developed countries is that the techniques in use are so far behind those already known to agricultural scientists. In India, experts say that it would be possible to raise farm output 30 to 50 percent by using only known techniques and with no increase in the cultivated area. This would stave off the food problem for a generation and give the country an invaluable breathing space. Yet the potential gains in output are not being realized. Why not? What might be done to reduce the gap between the best-known techniques and the actual techniques?

One necessity is an effective agricultural extension service. The best agricultural methods are known mainly to scientists and other experts in the cities. If these methods are to become effective, they must be applied by millions of farmers in the rural areas. There is often an almost total lack of communication between the two groups. The job of the extension service is to break this impasse and to establish effective two-way communication.

This requires extension workers who are willing to dirty their hands working with the farmer. Too often the agricultural agent, having some education and being a government official, considers himself several steps above the peasant. He will pass out literature or issue instructions, but he will not get out in the field and use his hands. Thus effective communication is not established. The United States, with its long and successful record of extension activity, has a good deal to teach on this front.

Raising the level of agriculture also requires new rural institutions—land banks and credit cooperatives, purchasing and marketing associations, and so on. It is not enough to set the small farmer up on his land and urge him to produce. Particularly where he has been used to getting capital and instructions from the landlord, he is apt to flounder when left on his own. Efficient family farming requires that the farmer be surrounded by a network of servicing institutions organized on a larger scale, as is true in the United States and other advanced agricultural countries.

Investment is needed in several directions: new fertilizer factories; adequate roads from farm to market; warehousing, refrigeration, and processing facilities; agricultural colleges and experiment stations. The prime necessity, however, is organization and education. If this is done effectively, a small amount of capital put into agriculture may yield large returns.

Industrial Development

Establishment of manufacturing industries is considered a hallmark of economic development. But what industries are appropriate at a particular time and place? How does one decide whether to encourage textile mills or shipyards, radio plants or steel works?

Why can't we get the answer by following the usual business procedures for determining the worthwhileness of an investment? Estimate future sales revenues from the proposed enterprise, deduct production costs, and get the stream of expected future profits. Reduce this to a percentage rate of return on the initial investment. Then compare with the going rate of interest. If the prospective rate of return is above the rate of interest, go ahead with the project. If not, drop it.

This kind of calculation should certainly be made for any project, but the results are not conclusive. The businessman is concerned with maximizing the money return from a single act of investment. A government visualizing the future course of the economy faces the different problem of seeing that the country's resources are used most effectively from an overall and long-run standpoint. There are several reasons why these overall calculations may yield a different result from those of the individual businessman.

First, the businessman's calculations rest on market prices for the factors of production. But in underdeveloped countries the price system is often biased in such a way that factor prices do not accurately reflect resource scarcities. To estimate the true cost and benefit of a proposed project, one must adjust factor prices so that they do correspond more closely to the actual resource situation.

Consider the case of labor. In many countries the marginal productivity of labor in agriculture, and hence the opportunity cost of using it in industry, is close to zero. But the market price of labor cannot be zero, since workers must be paid at least a subsistence wage, and may be paid considerably more than this because of political and trade union pressure. Thus labor is "overpriced" from an economic standpoint. In calculating the yield on a proposed project one should value labor, not at the inflated market rate, but at considerably less than this.

Capital, on the other hand, is typically underpriced. Capital is scarce in the poor countries, and its marginal yield is high. But there are often political objections to allowing interest rates to rise to their natural level, and they are pegged at a lower level by regulation. Thus the market price of capital should be adjusted upward to reflect its true cost. When labor and capital have been revalued in this way, labor-intensive industries and production methods turn out to be more profitable from a national standpoint than they would appear to any one businessman.

Exchange rates may also be out of line. The domestic currency is often overvalued, which means that foreign currencies are undervalued. Dollars, pounds, and marks may be worth twice as much in actuality as they are at the official exchange rate. A recalculation based on actual values will make exports from the country appear more profitable, and imports more expensive, than they would be at the official rates. Thus correct calculation encourages economizing on imported goods plus a drive to raise the level of exports, which is sensible policy for most developing countries.

Second, the businessman's horizon is limited to his company and industry. Government must consider the interrelation of many industries, which are expanding together in a developing economy. New investment in one industry may be profitable if, and only if, certain related industries are also expanding at appropriate rates. Expansion of industry A may confer indirect benefits on industries B, C, and D. These are valuable to the national economy even though they do not add to industry A's profits.

From a national standpoint, then, one can scarcely calculate the profitability of each act of investment in isolation. It is more useful to calculate the joint profitability of alternative "bundles" of interdependent projects. At the extreme, one can regard all the industrial investment which is expected to be undertaken during the next several years as constituting a single "bundle," and compare the total yield with the total cost. One can then tinker with the bundle by adding and subtracting projects to see whether it is possible to get greater returns for the same cost.

Third, planning industrial development does not involve merely sorting out alternative investment projects *at a point of time*. It involves also determining the *sequence of events over time*. The decision is not just to accept or reject a particular project. An acceptable project can be started immediately, or it can be postponed. It is impossible to do everything at once, and this raises what Hirschman calls the problem of *efficient sequences* of investment.

An efficient sequence, in Hirschman's view, is one in which the early investments encourage and stimulate later investments. This may happen because of *backward or forward linkages* between industries. Building a plant to produce a raw material will encourage the development of industries using this material. This is forward linkage. Conversely, a factory producing finished goods and buying materials will stimulate the growth of plants to produce those materials. This is backward linkage, which is perhaps the more dependable of the two. A finishing industry *must* have materials to work with and, as it becomes large enough to use the output of an efficient-sized material producing plant within the country, this plant will be established quite naturally. Forward linkage, on the other hand, is permissive rather than compelling.

The commonest case of forward linkage in developing countries is the processing of agricultural raw materials by flour mills, sugar refineries, breweries, cotton gins, coffee roasting plants, and the like. Backward linkage often takes the form of a gradual substitution of home production for imports. A country has been importing, say, rayon and women's nylon clothing. As a first step, a clothing industry may be established which continues to use cloth imported from abroad. Next, cloth mills may be set up using imported yarn. Later, facilities for producing the synthetic yarn may be constructed, still using imported chemicals. Eventually the chemicals may be produced at home, and substitution is complete. This "nibbling away" at a sequence of related industries, starting with the finished goods end and working back toward basic materials, may prove quite efficient.

In sum, central oversight and calculation is necessary to determine what sequence of industrialization is most advantageous for a particular country. Central decision about which projects should be encouraged is of course quite compatible with having most of these projects carried out by private firms. Government can act as entrepreneur without becoming deeply involved in ownership or management of industry.

If a country makes accurate calculations along these lines, what pattern of industrialization will emerge as preferable? There is no general answer. It depends on circumstances, and particularly on the size of the economy and the supplies of the factors of production.

The size of the national market sets limits to what should be undertaken at a particular time. The optimum scale of plant varies widely from one industry to the next. It is quite small for vegetable canning or clothing, considerably larger for refrigerators or washing machines, still larger for machine tools and light machinery, and very large for basic metals, auto assembly, and heavy electrical equipment. Unless a country can foresee within the near future enough demand to support an efficient-sized plant, the plant should presumably not be built. Countries whose economic size is very small may be limited permanently to light consumer goods. Heavy industry is a practical proposition for only a limited number of the larger countries.

This picture may be altered, however, by export possibilities. Suppose the much-discussed Latin American common market developed to a stage at which one could consider the most efficient location of industries to serve a continent-wide market. Then some of the smaller countries might turn out to be good locations for very large plants, most of whose output would be exported. Southern Chile, which has an unusual combination of water power and forests close to ocean transport, might supply pulp and paper to the rest of the continent, although the Chilean market alone would not support such a development.

The supplies of the factors of production are also important. In a country with redundant labor, it would seem efficient to encourage *labor-intensive industries*, i.e., industries which use a high ratio of labor to capital. And within each industry, it would seem sensible to use simple, *labor-intensive production methods* rather than highly mechanized techniques.

This conclusion has sometimes been disputed. It is argued that capital-intensive plants have numerous indirect benefits. Investment in highly mechanized factories will mean substantial profits for the factory owners; and on the premise that capitalists save while workers do not, this will increase the funds available for reinvestment. Introduction of the most modern technology into a backward economy will also have important educational effects on managers, technicians, and workers. On these grounds some economists have argued that the limited amount of capital available for industrialization should be concentrated in plants of the most modern type, which will become demonstration centers for the remainder of the economy.

But need one go this far? Indirect as well as direct effects of a proposed investment should certainly be considered in estimating its yield. But after having done this, the choice among products or methods of production should be made on the usual productivity grounds. This will not necessarily lead to use of the most capital-intensive methods available.

At a factual level, it is argued that factor proportions are rigidly fixed by technology, and that there is little scope to substitute capital for labor or vice versa. There is some truth in this. But even where the central production operations are automatic, there is usually room to use more or less labor in subsidiary operations, such as getting raw materials and parts to the points where they are needed, removing finished products, overhauling and repairing equipment, packing, and warehousing. Russian steel plants use more labor in these subsidiary operations than do American plants, and Indian steel mills use still more. This is partly a rational response to relative factor supplies in the three countries.

There are also industries in which the main production operations can be done in a variety of ways. Cotton cloth can be woven on anything from the simplest hand looms to fully automatic power looms. A. K. Sen has made some interesting calculations[7] on the relative efficiency of these various methods in India, using actual output figures and experimenting with various "accounting prices" for labor and capital. It turns out that the most efficient technique is usually *neither* the simplest (which has very low output) or the most highly automatic (which has high capital costs), but something in between; and the choice is influenced by the prices assigned to labor and capital.

Another way of using additional labor is by subcontracting the manufacture of parts to small shops using simple hand methods. The parts are then brought together into a larger factory for final assembly. This "putting-out system" was important in the early stages of the Industrial

---

[7] A. K. Sen, *The Choice of Techniques* (Oxford, Blackwell, 1962), Appendix C.

Revolution in England, and it has also been used very successfully in Japan. Large plants using modern equipment are not necessarily an *alternative* to small handicraft shops. The two can often be combined so as to reinforce each other and to make effective use of available labor.

The Role of Foreign Trade

One of the most serious problems of the poor countries is the tendency for import requirements to expand faster than export earnings. Efforts to accelerate the growth of domestic production do not solve this problem. On the contrary, since growth depends heavily on imports of capital goods and industrial materials, more rapid growth will in the short run make the problem worse rather than better. So there is need for special effort to increase exports on the one hand, and on the other to reduce import needs by substituting domestic production wherever possible.

Planners in the developing countries sometimes take a dim view of the prospects for the primary exports on which they so largely depend. But indiscriminate pessimism is surely unwarranted. One can scarcely argue that the market outlook for *all* primary products is poor, while the outlook for *all* manufacturers is good. The demand prospects for coffee, bananas, and crude rubber may indeed be poor, while the prospects for tin, copper, and wood pulp may be much brighter. Instead of turning against primary products in general, a country should try to curtail output of products whose prospects are poor and to push those for which the demand situation is promising. A successful effort to raise export earnings contributes to development by enlarging the country's ability to import materials, machinery, and other things which cannot as yet be produced at home.

On the import side, one can expect gradually to replace imports of manufactured goods through the development of local industries, a process usually termed *import substitution*. But import substitution should not be pushed indiscriminately, as though any kind of industry had some magic quality. There is need for careful cost comparisons to select those industries in which the country has comparative advantage or can hope to attain such advantage within a reasonable period.

Even though a new industry has good prospects for the long run, it may require tariff protection in the early stages. The infant industry argument for protection, which now has little force in the older industrial countries, still applies in the countries of the South. These countries are emerging into a world in which there are many well-established manufacturers of most products, and in which ocean freight costs to remote areas, which once provided a substantial "natural" protection to local industries, are being steadily reduced. Thus a new national industry, if exposed immediately to the full force of world competition, may be undersold and swamped by imported goods. Yet if the industry can be given time to get on its feet, build up sales volume and master production and management techniques, it may be reasonably competitive with foreign producers.

Part of the output of these new industries may be exported, thus helping the country to move away from dependence on primary exports alone. Countries like Mexico, Brazil, India, and Pakistan, if their development proceeds successfully, will gradually show a rising proportion of manufactures in their export trade. True, it will be hard for them to export manufactures in volume to the United States, Germany, or Japan. But there will doubtless be a growing exchange of manufactures among the newer countries themselves, and this can be furthered by common market schemes which encourage trade within Latin America or Asia while retaining a tariff wall against the outside world.

MOBILIZING RESOURCES FOR DEVELOPMENT

We have begun with the activities which need to be initiated for economic development, and with problems of choice and selection among these activities. It would have been more conventional to begin on the resource side by examining the sources of finance for development. But this approach can be quite misleading. It implies that, if only enough finance is available, development will follow automatically. This is decidedly not the case. Nothing is easier than to waste money, and some countries have done so on a massive scale. Conversely, if funds are well applied, the amount required may be modest. Studies of Britain, Germany, Sweden, and Japan indicate that, during the crucial early decades of their development, net capital formation as a percentage of net national product, was typically in the range of 6 to 8 percent. Not until after 40 or 50 years, by which time they were well along in the growth process, did the percentage rise above 10 percent.[8]

But while one can be naïve in overemphasizing the role of finance, one can also go too far in debunking it. The fact remains that development requires capital formation, and that capital formation usually requires money financing. Where is the money to come from?

The sources of finance for capital formation can be classified into:

1. Direct, nonmonetary capital formation in agriculture and public works.
2. Private saving, business and personal.
3. Public saving from tax revenues and the profits of public enterprises.
4. Deficit finance.
5. Foreign capital, private and public.

While these sources are logically distinct, they cannot be separated neatly in practice. A tax on corporate incomes will reduce reinvestment of earnings. Taxes on consumers will affect the level of private spending

---

[8] See on this point Simon Kuznets, "Notes on the Take-off," presented at the 1960 meeting of the International Economic Association; to be published in the proceedings of this meeting.

and saving. Thus events in one sector interact with those in another. Bearing in mind this interdependence, let us examine each of the major sources.

Direct Capital Accumulation

Investment in agriculture often requires mainly the farmer's own labor. Fencing, ditching, drainage, tree planting, and additions to farm buildings are usually done in this way. One reason for giving farm operators security of tenure, and preferably outright ownership, is to provide maximum incentive for these types of improvement.

Road building and other public works can also be carried out on a nonmonetary basis. Until quite recently this was common practice in rural American communities. The town assessed taxes each year against the farmers. But each year also the country roads needed mending. So a farmer would turn out with his horses and equipment to grade the road, repair potholes, and spread gravel, receiving credit for each hour worked. Mysteriously, the farmer's credits were usually about equal to his tax bill. Little money changed hands, but the work got done. The farmer had been taxed in time rather than in money.

This is not very different from the system used in parts of Africa in colonial times. A small poll tax was placed on each man in a village. The man had no money to pay. So he was offered a chance to earn money by working on roads and other local improvements. When he had worked enough to earn his tax, he was free to quit.

The late Professor Nurkse argued that this principle could be widely extended in underdeveloped countries. His argument starts from the observation that many countries have redundant labor in agriculture. Suppose these people are withdrawn from agriculture and put to work somewhere else. The opportunity cost of doing this is zero, since output in agriculture will not fall. So if these previously useless people are put to work on roads, dams, irrigation ditches, schools, and other local improvements, whatever they produce is a net gain.

True, some money financing is required. The people transferred from agriculture were previously paid nothing. When they are employed on public works they must be paid a wage. Isn't this an added cost to society? A money cost, perhaps; but not a real cost. Remember that there are now fewer people left to be fed in agriculture, but just as much farm production as before. If the excess food—the food which used to be consumed on the farm by the people who have now been withdrawn— can be transferred and made available to these people in their new location, everything balances out.

One might do it this way: Put a tax on the people remaining in agriculture. They get the money to pay the tax by selling surplus food in town. The public works employees are paid from the proceeds of the tax, and then go to the store and buy the food which has been shipped in from the country. The flows of money and food just balance.

This is not quite as easy as it sounds. It will be hard to prevent the people who remain in the country from eating more, so it may be impossible to extract the full food "surplus" from them. The people who have moved are now doing hard physical work, so will need to eat more than they did when sitting around the farm. The country's total food requirements will probably rise. Moreover, the people employed on public works cannot work with their bare hands. There will have to be some investment in tools and building materials. So capital formation by the Nurkse route is not really *free*. But it is a very *low-cost* method, requiring mainly leadership and organization.

Private Saving

Business profits are high in the early stages of industrial development. The risks may also be high, but the successful enterprises pay off well. The first firms in a field have a semi-monopoly position. Labor is typically plentiful and wages low. This cheap labor, combined with modern factory techniques, yields large profit margins. Reinvestment of these profits yields still larger profits in the future, and so on through the classical process of capital formation.

The way in which this process might operate in the less developed countries has been suggested by Professor Lewis.[9] His reasoning can be explained with the aid of Figure 29–1. OS is the average income of workers in agriculture, while OW is the wage level for labor in the industrial sector. Factory wages must be above the agricultural level, partly to provide an incentive for people to transfer to industry, partly because of higher living costs in the city. But because there is a large surplus of underemployed labor in agriculture, and perhaps also in trade and service occupations, the supply of labor to industry is infinitely elastic along the line WW.

If the marginal productivity of labor in industry is shown by N_1N_1, the number of workers employed will be OE_1. Why only this number? Because if more were employed, the marginal productivity of labor would fall below the wage level OW. Employment of the extra workers would be unprofitable. The total output of the industrial sector will be $ON_1Q_1E_1$, of which the workers get OWQ_1E_1 (number of workers employed × the wage rate), while employers retain WN_1Q_1 as profit.

Now suppose the capitalists are frugal people and put most of this profit back into plant and equipment. Workers have more equipment to work with, so their marginal productivity rises to N_2N_2. (We may also, if we wish, admit technical progress as an additional factor raising the productivity curve over the course of time.) Now OE_2 workers are employed, and business profits are shown by the larger area WN_2Q_2. Re-

[9] W. A. Lewis, "Economic Development with Unlimited Supplies of Labor," *The Manchester School*, May, 1954, pp. 139–92; and "Unlimited Labor: Further Notes," *The Manchester School*, January, 1958, pp. 1–32.

investment of these profits raises labor productivity to N_3N_3, and so on in a cumulative process.

There are two main characteristics of this expansion. First, industrial employment expands *at a constant wage level*. So long as surplus labor is available from agriculture, there is no reason for wages to rise.

FIGURE 29–1
Economic Development with Unlimited Supplies of Labor

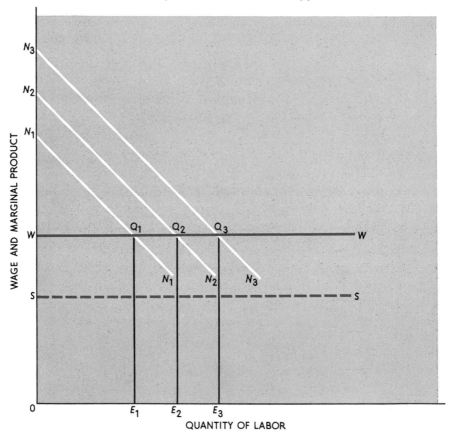

Industrial employers can hire as much labor as they wish at the wage OW. The marginal productivity of labor at the beginning is N_1N_1. So employment is OE_1, total wages are OE_1Q_1W, and profits are N_1Q_1W. These profits are reinvested in plant and equipment, which raises the marginal productivity of labor to N_2N_2. The result is employment of OE_2 and still larger profits, reinvestment of which raises marginal productivity to N_3N_3; and so on.

Second, business profits rise not only absolutely but as a proportion of national income; and this provides a reservoir for saving and capital accumulation.

Lewis contends that the savings level of a nation does not depend on its average per capita income or on the inequality of personal income distribution, but rather on the *functional class* to which income accrues.

Capitalists save. They have a passion for accumulation. Landlords, princes, salary earners, and wage earners do not save to any extent. The most effective way of raising saving, then, is to increase the profit share of national income.

Will Lewis's process of cumulative expansion go on forever? Certainly not at the same rate. Eventually the labor supply will run out. How soon this happens depends on the rate of industrial expansion, on the rate of population growth, and on developments within agriculture. At some point, however, agriculture will be sucked dry of both redundant labor and disguised unemployment. As urban employers are forced to compete with agriculture for scarce labor, the wage level OW will begin to rise. Moreover, labor scarcity will stimulate improvements in agricultural productivity. This raises OS, which also tends to force up OW. Profit margins will shrink, the profit share of national income will no longer be rising, and the momentum of expansion will slacken.

The expansion process may slacken also because of trade union or political pressures. Trade unions may force up industrial wages even before labor has become scarce. There may be political pressure for social security systems financed from employer contributions, which will also raise the cost of labor. This poses a strategy problem for a developing country. Increases in real wages and strengthening of social security systems are desirable objectives. The whole point of economic development is presumably to raise living standards for the mass of the population. But if these objectives are pushed too hard or too early, they can reduce the funds available for reinvestment and cut the rate of economic growth.

There is a similar dilemma as regards tax policy. Most developing countries urgently need larger tax revenues to finance investment as well as education, health, and other important services. Business profits provide an obvious and tempting source of revenue. But to the extent that this source is tapped, business concerns have less money for reinvestment, and this slows the expansion of the private sector. One should probably go lightly in taxing *reinvested* earnings, while being tough on profits which are withdrawn and used for luxury consumption. The latter problem might be handled either through the personal income tax or through heavy excise taxes on luxury goods.

While businessmen are the main source of private saving, there is some savings potential in other groups. Even in the wilder parts of Africa, people have been known to put money in a tin can and bury it in the ground. The impulse to save should certainly be encouraged and turned into constructive channels. This requires creation of appropriate institutions, such as savings banks, postal savings systems, and insurance companies, which can put savings to use and pay a return on them. Eventually one may reach the stage of organized securities markets and widespread public purchase of stocks and bonds, but at this stage a country can no longer be considered underdeveloped.

Government Revenue

In the early stages of development a good deal of capital formation must be financed by government. Government normally provides the basic transport and communications network, and other items of social overhead capital. It must maintain law and order, provide good general administration, and supply agricultural research and extension services. It must spend adequate amounts on health and education, which are important in raising the productivity of the population. It may be necessary for part of the capital needed in the private sector to be raised by government and then lent to private concerns.

All this takes money. We noted in the previous chapter that most of the poor countries have narrowly based tax systems which depend heavily on commodity taxes. This makes government revenue unstable in the short run and inflexible in the long run.

What can be done to diversify the tax structure and increase public revenue? First, the higher ranges of personal income should be taxed more effectively. It is hard to condone spectacular luxury consumption in the higher income brackets, while most people are very poor and the country is starved for development capital. Many countries have a graduated personal income tax on the books, but it is usually not enforced. If income tax enforcement is considered too difficult, one could try a general tax on *expenditures*. Luxury expenditures can also be reached to some extent by high commodity taxes—import duties in the case of imported items, excise taxes in the case of domestic products. In one way or another the upper income groups should be compelled to make a greater contribution than they typically make at present.

But "soaking the rich" is not enough. There aren't enough of them. A serious development effort requires "soaking the poor" as well. This may mean substantial sales or excise taxes on all but the most basic necessities. Something like the Russian policy in this respect may be essential for any country which wishes to force the pace of development. This policy is of course much harder politically with an "open" government, which must reveal what it is doing, than in the U.S.S.R. where turnover tax rates are virtually a state secret.

A serious problem in most countries is that farmers use their political leverage to avoid their share of the tax burden. If incomes in agriculture are low and static, it is of course hard to squeeze out much tax revenue. It becomes easier if agricultural incomes are being raised through technical progress, so that government is simply siphoning off part of the annual increase. The success of the Japanese government with this strategy during the nineteenth century has already been noted. Unless a country is able to step up agricultural output substantially, and then tax away a good part of the proceeds, the pace of development will be much reduced.

For farm products sold on the export market, it is possible to siphon off part of the income either through an export tax or through a government marketing agency which buys the produce at one price from the farmers and sells it at a higher price on world markets. But this by itself is not a satisfactory solution. If government does only this, the effect may be to discourage production of export crops and divert effort into other crops which are less advantageous to the nation. One needs a method of taxation which bears equally on farm income derived from any source.

Another possible revenue source is the profits of public enterprises. The government typically owns the railroad system, communication facilities, the electric power network, and sometimes mining, petroleum, and industrial enterprises. But there is often political pressure to operate these enterprises in an unprofitable way. If there is a surplus of unemployed labor, government industries will be pressured to employ unnecessary workers, and their power of layoff or discharge may be severely limited. Government will also be under pressure to serve as a "model employer" by paying above-average wages and fringe benefits. On the revenue side, price increases by a government enterprise are usually resisted, and may even lead to strikes and political demonstrations. These tendencies are particularly noticeable in Latin America. Railroads and other government enterprises, squeezed between inflated labor costs and rigid prices, often show large losses which must be covered from the general treasury.

There is no disagreement among experts that government should resist these pressures and should try to manage its enterprises on economic principles. This will not mean maximizing profits, as a private monopoly might do. It may even be desirable to sell below cost, as explained in Chapter 12. But the costs themselves should be held to a minimum, and any losses which are incurred should result from deliberate policy rather than haphazard pressure.

Deficit Finance

Even with maximum effort in these directions, government revenue will often fall short of desired expenditures. What then? Should government spend more than it is able to raise?

If a government deficit can be covered by selling bonds to the public, there is no problem. The buyers of the bonds give up as much money as the government receives, and there is no increase in money supply. Even in a poor country, there is usually some scope for sale of bonds to private savers.

If the deficit is larger than this, it will require sale of government bonds to the banking system, which typically leads to an increase in money supply. This will not necessarily cause a rise in the price level. In a growing economy, the volume of production is rising. If the money supply is increased no faster than production, prices can still remain stable.

One can be even a bit more venturesome. One feature of a developing economy is a gradual increase in the public's use of money. Goods which used to be produced and consumed at home now pass through the market. Barter transactions are replaced by money transactions. People in remote villages become used to the sight of money, and put some of it away under mattresses. So the demand for money rises, and an increase in money supply which simply matches this increase in demand creates no problem. Lewis estimates this possibility at perhaps 1 percent of national income per year during the early stages of development.

Suppose the deficit is still larger, and money supply rises at a rate which forces up the price level. Then we have the process of inflation which was explored briefly in Part Three. How far inflation is harmful to development, and whether it can even be helpful on occasion, is a subject of considerable debate among economists. As in the case of the developed countries, the answer depends partly on the *degree* of inflation. Most people would not be concerned over inflation of a few percent a year. But inflation of 50 to 100 percent a year, which occurs commonly in some of the Latin American countries, is another matter, and must surely have a disorganizing effect on the economy.

One of the more serious effects is that on trade relations with other nations. If a country inflates more rapidly than other countries are doing, the value of its currency will fall. Even if this were offset by frequent depreciations of the exchange rate, there would be currency speculation and additional risk in international dealings. But most countries dislike to depreciate their currencies frequently. So in countries with chronic inflation, the official value of the currency is typically above its true or free market value. This acts as a penalty on exports and a stimulus to imports, scarcely a healthy situation for a developing country.

Foreign Capital

The main function of foreign capital is to finance imports of machinery and other capital goods, plus industrial fuels and raw materials, which in the early stages of development must be obtained largely from abroad. An industrialization program requires machinery and building materials for the factories, generators and electric cable for the power projects, rails and rolling stock for the railroads. Operation of the new factories requires increased imports of fuels and materials. As industry becomes established, the country gradually becomes more self-sufficient and import needs taper off. But in the first few decades of industrialization they are likely to grow at a staggering rate.

The sources of foreign funds will be examined in Chapter 30, and can simply be enumerated here. They include:

1. Private investment by business concerns from the more developed countries.

2. Loans from international lending organizations, of which the most important is the International Bank for Reconstruction and Development.
3. Loans from the governments of the developed countries. The U.S.A., U.S.S.R., Britain, France, and West Germany are the largest lenders, but several other countries also make substantial contributions.
4. Outright grants of funds. These come mainly from the U.S.A., and are small relative to the volume of loan money.

Since foreign money usually comes in the form of repayable loans, a borrower country must estimate how far it can safely go into debt. It must estimate its future export earnings, and make sure that it has an adequate margin for payments of interest and principal. If debt servicing comes to absorb as much as 25 percent of normal export earnings, the country is in a precarious position. It is important also to ensure that foreign borrowings are used to increase productive capacity.

SUMMARY

1. The early stages of economic growth in the Western industrial nations and in Japan had several significant characteristics: the gradualness of the rise in per capita income; the importance of improvements in agriculture; the importance of foreign trade; the role of government in financing infrastructure investment; the growth of an influential class of business enterprisers; and the importance of profits as a source of finance for business investment.

2. Government action is needed in the less developed countries to strengthen basic public services, to mobilize funds for investment, to develop and operate public utilities, and to initiate modern manufacturing enterprises. There is disagreement over how far government need continue to own and operate industries outside the public utility sphere. There seems much to be said for turning over manufacturing industries to private operation as rapidly as feasible. Efficient conduct of private industry requires supporting action by government at various points, and elimination of needless restrictions and controls.

3. Efficient growth requires balance between investment in social overhead capital and in directly productive activities. Expenditures on health, education, and technical training contain an investment element and are analogous to social overhead.

4. Increases in agricultural output are needed to provide food for a rising population at higher income levels, to supply industrial raw materials, and possibly to provide additional exports. In the early stages of growth labor is often *redundant*, that is, its marginal productivity in agriculture is zero. So what one needs is *land-saving improvements* rather than *labor-saving improvements*. These involve organization and education plus some investment. When redundant labor is exhausted, however, labor-saving improvements become necessary to free additional workers for industrial employment. The speed with which redundant labor is being reduced is one index of the success of a development program.

5. Individual business decisions cannot be relied on to produce the most efficient pattern of industrial development, because of biases in market prices of the factors of production, the importance of interdependence of investments and external economies, and the need to consider the time sequence of investments over an extended period. Central oversight and calculation is desirable to determine what sequence will prove most advantageous. But this is quite com-

patible with having most industrial projects carried out and operated by private firms.

6. In countries with redundant labor, there is a strong case for emphasizing industries and production methods which use a high ratio of labor to capital. The practical possibilities in this direction are substantial, and the theoretical arguments against it are not very convincing.

7. There should be an effort to raise exports of primary products with good market prospects, and to substitute home production for imports of manufactured goods. Import substitution should be selective and guided by long-run comparative advantage.

8. Much capital formation in agriculture and public works can be carried out at low social cost by mobilizing unused reserves of labor.

9. Reinvestment of business profits can be looked to as an important source of capital formation, but it will probably not be as important as in the older industrial countries. There is often political pressure both to push up the wage level and to tax away business profits.

10. Government should tax heavily enough to provide adequate current services and leave a surplus for capital formation. Farmers and rich people are undertaxed in most countries. In addition to extracting more from these groups, however, the general public will have to contribute through taxes on mass consumption.

11. Moderate budget deficits can be financed in ways which may help the economy rather than hurt it. But very large deficits, financed by increasing the money supply, will push up prices at a rate which is disorganizing to the domestic economy and harmful to its trade relations.

APPENDIX: PLANNING FOR ECONOMIC DEVELOPMENT

Many countries now embody their development activities in a national development plan extending over five years or more. While the techniques of development planning may be considered too specialized or advanced for an elementary course, it seems desirable to add a word on them for those who are interested.

The Meaning of a Development Plan

Planning is a slippery term, with many possible meanings. When experts from the U.S.A. and the U.S.S.R. tour the underdeveloped countries, both groups asserting that planning is desirable, they do not mean the same thing. The methods of planning which are gradually being hammered out in the poor countries are quite different from the methods used in Soviet-type economies.

Soviet planning involves physical balance sheets for some seven hundred major product groups. It involves a detailed input and output plan for individual producing units, and central supervision of their operations. It involves centralized allocation of key raw materials and capital goods, and administrative control of their flow from suppliers to users. This is feasible because all producing enterprises are government owned. In the underdeveloped countries, however, the great bulk of economic activity is carried on by private farmers and businessmen. Rarely does government produce more than 10 percent of national income. In this setting detailed physical planning is not appropriate.

What kind of planning, then, is feasible in the poor countries, and what is actually being done? The more sophisticated development plans usually contain the following elements:

1. *A projection of the grand aggregates of the economy.* This usually runs for five years ahead, and covers total output, the distribution of output by

major sectors, private consumption, private saving, government receipts and expenditures, exports and imports, and so on. A serious limitation is that most countries are very short on reliable economic statistics. This makes it hard to determine what has happened in the past, and hence what it is reasonable to expect in future.

But the figures for the future are not just a mechanical projection of past trends. They contain also an element of hope, intention, and target-setting. The output and investment targets are typically set higher than the economy has been doing in the recent past, but not so high as to be clearly impossible of attainment. This often leads to complaints that the plan is overambitious and unrealistic, to which government leaders retort, "Of course we can do it if we just buckle down to the job."

In addition to being plausible, the projections must be internally consistent. Savings and investment must balance, expected imports must be offset by exports, grants, or loans, and so on. The problem of achieving an internally consistent plan will be considered in a moment.

2. *A plan for raising and using funds in the public sector.* This is the heart of the plan for practical purposes, since it covers the things which are under direct government control. The sources of funds include the estimated yield of existing taxes; additional amounts which might be raised by new or higher taxes; profits of public enterprises; loans and grants from other countries; domestic borrowings through bond issues; and (possibly) some deficit financing.

On the uses side of the budget one finds the cost of current government services; new investment in public enterprises; other public investment projects; and loans to private industry for investment purposes. This provides clues as to the government view of development strategy. The sectors which receive the main allocations of public funds are presumably those which it has been decided to push hard in the immediate future.

The line between current and investment expenditures is hard to draw and can be misleading. The costs of health services, education, scientific research, and agricultural extension are normally classified as current; yet insofar as they raise the productive capacity of the population they are akin to investment. Some governments recognize this by speaking, not of *investment* expenditures, but of *development* expenditures; and by including in the latter category current expenditures which clearly contribute to higher productivity.

3. *Targets for private investment and production.* Development plans normally profess to be comprehensive plans, covering events in the private as well as the public sector. In the official tabulations, the targets for private output and investment *look* just as firm as those for public expenditure. But in practice they are not equally firm. What happens in the private sector depends on a multitude of decisions by households and business concerns, and the course of events can differ widely from that envisaged in the plan.

In some cases, however, government consults private industry in the course of working up its estimates. The Indian Planning Commission surveys the investment intentions of each major industry and takes these into account in preparing the plan figures. Government also has levers which can be used to nudge the private economy in one direction or another. Certain industries can be encouraged by government loans, import quotas, building permits, and tariff protection. Other industries can be denied these advantages. So trends in private production can be semiplanned even if not fully planned.

Paper Plans and Operational Plans

It is not difficult to turn out a plan *document*. Put some bright young economists together in a room. Give them paper and pencils, a desk calculator, some rudimentary statistics about the economy, and a U.N. manual on development planning. In due course they will emerge with an elegant program, supported by many statistical tables and appendixes, showing what is supposed to happen in every corner of the economy over the next five years.

But this may or may not have anything to do with the real world. More often than not, the plan is filed away with due ceremony, while government continues with business as usual. There is a strong tendency toward what Latin Americans call *proyectismo*. This means taking the word for the deed, drafting up a program and convincing yourself that by drafting it you have also executed it.

Several things are needed to convert paper planning into operational planning. First, top government leaders must be committed to overall planning. They must be willing to participate in the planning work, to take responsibility for the product, and to take the administrative steps needed to carry the plan into effect. It is helpful in these matters if the planning organization is attached directly to the office of the president or prime minister. If it is tucked away in some department of the government, its recommendations are less likely to have practical effect.

Next, the totals in the plan should be based on calculations for individual investment projects. One must know when particular power developments will be started, how long they will take, and approximately how much they will cost. The plan total for power investment should be built up from the bottom in this way. Similarly for each other sector. Too often, however, the totals are constructed at the top and left hanging in air with no real foundation. A certain amount is allocated to steel or power or transportation, without engineering studies of specific projects, often without even knowing what projects are to be started. When micro-decisions are divorced from macro-decisions in this way, the latter cannot have much controlling force.

Third, one needs effective budgeting machinery within the government. Most countries do not have anything approaching the United States Bureau of the Budget, which reviews the expenditure programs of all agencies and puts them in shape for final decision by the President. In many of the poor countries, each government department simply spends whatever it can lay hands on. The Minister of Finance, who collects the money, is apt to have the dominant voice in its allocation. So the actual flow of funds may bear little relation to that set forth in the plan.

Finally one needs follow-up machinery to trace events during the plan period, to detect discrepancies and call them to the attention of the head of government, and to secure corrective action. Otherwise one comes to the end of the period and then discovers that things have not gone as intended. But one does not know why, and it is too late to do anything about it.

There is as yet no country which meets all these requirements. India has probably gone farthest, and a handful of other countries are making some progress. But in most countries one must look beneath the official plan to discover whether it has any actual effect, and one is usually disappointed by what one finds.

The Logic of Development Planning

Development planning involves projecting a limited number of economic aggregates in a way which is both plausible and internally consistent. The aggregates come from the national income accounts, with which we became familiar in Part Three. The chief difference is that the *foreign sector* needs more thorough analysis, since imports of capital goods are essential for development and a country's export capacity is not unlimited.

The main elements entering into most development plans are:

gross national product	imports (total)
consumption	imports of consumer goods
domestic saving	imports of capital goods
investment	foreign saving (= aid)
exports	

The planning problem is to get values of these variables which will be mutually consistent. How does one get consistent values? Logically, this involves setting up and solving a set of simultaneous equations. The number of equations must equal the number of variables to be determined, which in this case is nine. If the number of equations is less than this, the system is indeterminate. In practical terms, the plan is not *complete*. If there are too many equations, the system is overdetermined, and the results will be consistent only by chance. Concretely, the planning board is trying to *do too much*. There can be *overplanning* as well as *underplanning*, and one can determine by logical methods whether either of these mistakes is being made.

How does one get the equations needed to flesh out a planning system? They are derived from three sources:

1. *Accounting equations.* We became familiar with some of these in Part Three earlier. They are identities which must be true by definition. For example,

gross national product ≡ consumption plus investment
total imports ≡ consumer goods imports plus capital goods imports
investment ≡ domestic saving plus foreign saving

2. *Behavior equations.* These express structural relations in the economy, and are also familiar from our earlier discussion. One of the more famous is the *consumption function*. One can also set up an *output function*, relating investment in physical capital to increases in national output.

3. *Exogenous variables*, which are specified from outside the system. Thus one can say that GNP in future years *must* increase at some minimum rate, because this is the lowest rate which will be politically acceptable to the population. Or one can take the level of exports in future years as determined by world demand, and hence independent of anything the planners may do.

So it is easy to get enough equations to determine the major aggregates. In fact, it is too easy. It is possible to set up more equations than one needs to determine the system. This raises a problem of *planning choice*. It is the choice of a particular set of equations from among the many possible sets which gives a plan its specific coloration and strategy.

Concretely, some variables can be left free to be determined by the operation of the economy, or they can be set at a particular level by planning decisions. Consumption is a good example. One can say that consumption must attain a specified level for political reasons—for example, that per capita consumption must rise 2 percent a year. Alternatively, one can derive an estimate of probable consumption from the consumption function.

Or take the case of foreign loans and grants. One can estimate that just so much foreign aid will be *available*, and enter this as an exogenous variable. Alternatively, one can determine the level of imports required for the plan, subtract the estimated exports, and determine how much foreign aid is *needed* to close the gap. Whether one tailors the plan to a predetermined level of foreign aid, or whether one assumes that the richer countries will obligingly provide whatever amount of aid turns out to be needed, is obviously a critical decision.

Consider, for example, the Second Five-Year Plan of Pakistan, covering the period from mid-1960 to mid-1965.[1] Here the first step seems to have been an independently determined target for the rate of increase in GNP. Population was expected to grow at close to 2 percent a year, and a 2 percent annual increase in output per capita was judged the minimum necessary to generate public enthusiasm for the plan and to provide a noticeable improvement in living standards. So by multiplication one gets an increase in GNP of 4 percent a year, or about 20 percent over the plan period.

The Plan makes some provision for additional taxes and improved collection of existing taxes. So disposable personal income will rise less rapidly than GNP. The division of disposable income between saving and consumption seems to have been estimated from a consumption function. The calculations assume a marginal propensity to save of 0.25, which may well be optimistic. If the estimate is realized, domestic saving will rise from 6 percent of GNP in 1960 to 7.8 percent in 1965. Because of taxation and saving, per capita *consumption* is expected to rise by only 1.4 percent a year. While this involves some restriction of consumption, it is clearly not an austerity model of the Russian or Chinese variety.

The expected increase in output is distributed in the plan by major sectors of the economy, and by specific branches of manufacturing. The amount of new investment needed to produce these increases in output was calculated on the basis of engineering studies and past experience. Adding these amounts yields required investment for the economy as a whole. This is a weak step in the procedure, since investment-output relations are uncertain and often turn out considerably different from what was expected.

Having determined GNP, consumption, domestic saving, and investment, we turn to the strategic foreign sector. Since we now know consumption and investment, we can calculate the necessary volume of imports. Capital goods imports will equal total requirements of machinery and building materials less whatever amount of these things can be produced at home. Imports of finished consumer goods can be estimated from income elasticities of consumer demand. There will also be increased imports of raw materials, fuel, and other things needed for manufacturing within the country. Since the prospective increases in manufacturing output are known, one can derive the requirements for additional inputs.

Exports are typically taken as independently determined by world demand, and this procedure was used in the present case. Finally, one comes to the foreign exchange gap, which in this case is quite startling. Exports over the plan period are estimated at 10,050 million rupees, while prospective imports total 18,050 million rupees. This leaves 8,000 million rupees, or close to $2 billion, to be secured through loans and grants from other countries.

Foreign aid, in short, emerges as a residual. It is the amount of capital which the rest of the world must put up if the output targets are to be met. Foreign aid is expected to adjust to the size of the plan rather than vice

---

[1] The interpretation given here follows Gustav Ranis and John Fei, *Planning Methodology with Special Reference to Pakistan's Five-Year Plan* (Karachi: Institute of Development Economics, Monograph 1, 1960). It should be emphasized that this is a private interpretation, which has no official status.

versa. The calculations in the Second and Third Indian Five-Year Plans were essentially similar.

Pakistan government leaders realize, of course, that there is some limit to what the traffic will bear. So the aid figure which appears in the Plan should perhaps be construed as the maximum which the government can hope to secure from other countries by skillful negotiation. (The Plan document itself is of course an important instrument in such negotiation.) Once this essentially political calculation has been made, the remainder of the Plan can be tailored to fit under the aid ceiling.

The Largest Plan: India 1961–66

India is the world's second most populous country, with more than 400 million people. It is an extremely poor country, where life in the villages has changed little for generations or even centuries. Rough estimates indicate that during the first half of this century output per capita did not increase at all. Despite recent emphasis on industrialization, the country is still basically agricultural. Agriculture employs about 70 percent of the labor force and produces about half of the national product. There is heavy underemployment of labor in agriculture and a large amount of open unemployment in the cities. Population growth is accelerating because of a fall in death rates, and the rate of increase during the 1960's is expected to exceed 2 percent per year. This puts heavy pressure on the country's productive resources.

On the positive side, India has a stable and broadly based political system, dominated by the Congress Party. It has a well-trained civil service, and better economic and statistical staffs than any Asian country except Japan. Its political leaders have been working energetically to set the sluggish economy in motion and to initiate a process of sustained growth.

The First Five Year Plan of 1951–56 was mainly an estimate of the future rather than a true plan. Production nevertheless advanced considerably, aided by several good harvest years. The Second Plan of 1956–61 contained a larger degree of control, including an ambitious program of public investment. The actual development of the economy over these years, however, differed substantially from the plan figures. The government was unable to mobilize domestic savings on the intended scale, and even with the help of expanded foreign aid, public investment fell short of the targets. Private investment, on the other hand, rose considerably above the planned level. About three quarters of household saving seems to have been reinvested directly in small businesses and farms, and there was also substantial reinvestment of corporate earnings. Both agricultural and industrial output rose less than had been planned. Output of the service industries, on the other hand, rose more than was expected, perhaps reflecting a drift of unemployed labor into these industries.

Despite this limited success of planning, the economy did grow during the 1950's. GNP rose at an average rate of 3½ percent a year, which with a population increase of 2 percent meant an annual increase of 1½ percent in per capita output. Particularly encouraging is the fact that agricultural production kept ahead of population growth, enabling people to eat better and reducing the need for food imports. About half of the increased output, however, came from increased acreage under cultivation. The problem of raising yields per acre has not really been solved.

On the employment front, the economy lost ground during the 1950's because of rapid population growth. It is estimated that at the end of the Second Plan there were 9 million workers completely unemployed and 15 to 18 million underemployed in agriculture and elsewhere. The situation is expected to deteriorate further during the Third Plan. Even if Plan targets are fully met, the number of new jobs created will fall short of the increase in the labor force. The goal of full employment seems to be receding over the horizon.

The Third Five Year Plan, like the Second, is basically a program of public investment plus some projections for the private sector. The investment target is about $21 billion over the years 1961–66, which would be more than one third higher than the level of the Second Plan. About two thirds of this investment would be in the public sector, one third in the private sector. The latter figure relates to the so-called *organized* private sector of medium and large-scale industries. Investment in farms, retail shops, and small handicraft operations, which still provide about half of India's manufacturing output, is difficult either to estimate or control.

This level of investment, it is hoped, will raise GNP by 5½ percent a year, which would mean an annual increase of 3 percent in per capita output. What this means in physical terms is suggested by the following figures:

ITEM	PLANNED PER-CENTAGE INCREASE, 1960–61 TO 1965–66
Total agricultural production	30
Food grain production	32
Total industrial production	70
Steel ingots	163
Aluminum	332
Machine tools (value)	445
Petroleum products	70
Cloth	24
Coal	76
Exports	32
Power: Installed capacity	123
Railways: Freight carried	59
Road transport: Commercial vehicles on road	74
Students in schools	47
Hospital beds	29
Consumption levels per capita:	
Calories per day	10
Yards of cloth per year	11

In interpreting the figures for industry, one must remember that industrial production is increasing from a very small base. The large percentage increases are rather small in absolute terms. If the targets are achieved, however, they will mean a rise in the relative importance of the industrial sector and some change in its complexion. Factory industry at present produces only about 10 percent of national output. Three quarters of this consists of light consumer goods. Ninety percent comes from privately owned factories, less than 10 percent from government enterprises. The objective is a gradual shift toward heavy industry and, since there is more government participation in heavy industry, this will mean some rise in the government share of manufacturing output.

The proposed distribution of investment funds, compared with the actual distribution from 1956–61, is as follows:

SECTOR	PERCENT OF TOTAL INVESTMENT	
	Actual 1956–61	Planned 1961–66
Agriculture, community development, irrigation	18.6	20.3
Large industry and mining	22.9	24.7
Small industries	3.9	4.1
Power	7.2	10.2
Transportation and communication	20.8	16.7
Social services	19.1	16.2
Inventories	7.5	7.8
Total	100.0	100.0

This seems a reasonably balanced distribution, particularly when one remembers that agriculture and small industry will receive a good deal of unplanned private investment. The main changes from earlier years are a moderate shift toward agriculture, factory industry, and electric power, and a tapering off in railroad construction and equipment.

Where is the money to come from? In particular, how will government raise the $15 billion or so which it plans to invest? About one quarter of the total is expected to come from government saving. Tax revenues will rise both because of rising national income and imposition of additional taxes. There is a promised effort to hold down current government expenditures so as to leave a margin for investment. It is hoped also that rising profits of government enterprises will permit substantial reinvestment from this source. During the Second Plan, however, rising tax revenues and profits barely kept pace with rising current expenditure, and government saving was negligible. The Third Plan may do better, but it is doubtful whether it will do as well as projected.

About 40 percent of the total is expected to come from internal borrowing. The rate of domestic savings is expected to rise from 8.3 percent of national income at the end of the Second Plan to 11.5 percent at the end of the Third Plan. This assumes that households will save more than 20 percent of the *increase* in their incomes over the plan period; and it is hoped that the great bulk of these savings can be transferred to government through bond sales, the postal savings system, and so on. Again, the assumptions seem optimistic. During the Second Plan households showed a strong disposition to reinvest their savings directly in small private businesses, and government was able to mobilize only about two thirds as much as it had planned to get from this source.

This leaves about 35 percent of public investment, or about a quarter of total planned investment, to be financed through loans and grants from abroad. Even with optimistic assumptions about exports and minimal estimates of imports, the foreign exchange gap over the five years is estimated at $6,750 millions. But the response of other countries to this need has been encouraging. About $5,000 million had already been pledged from various sources by the end of 1961, including $2,345 million from the U.S.A., about $1,000 from other Western countries, $500 million from the U.S.S.R., and $400 million from the I.B.R.D. and I.D.A. Aid from non-Soviet sources is coordinated through a consortium, commonly dubbed the "aid to India Club," which meets to discuss the overall aid level and how much each country should contribute.

The Third Plan bears a strong family resemblance to the Second Plan, and it would not be surprising if by 1966 one found the same kinds of deviation between plan and performance. The rise in agricultural and industrial output may be less than expected. Private investment may once more be higher than the targets, public investment lower. The foreign exchange gap may be larger and the need for foreign aid greater than the Plan suggests.

This would not mean that the Plan had been unsuccessful. The Plan is mainly a systematic effort to increase the funds available to government and to ensure an economic allocation of these funds among investment projects. This is clearly worthwhile. The growth rate of the economy will almost certainly be higher with planning than without it, even if the ambitious targets are not fully achieved.

If the Plan has been criticized as too large in some respects, it has been criticized as too small in others. The size of the Plan has been geared partly to the estimated availability of foreign aid and foreign capital equipment. But agricultural improvements, community development, local public works, irrigation schemes, and road building can be carried through without much machinery. They require mainly an organizational effort to mobilize the vast amount of unused labor time in the Indian countryside. Some critics feel that more could be done in this direction than is presently being done.

Looming always in the background of economic discussion is the population question. During the Third Five Year Plan alone the Indian population will grow by an amount equal to the whole population of Britain or France. To absorb this massive increase and to prevent living standards from falling is in itself a major task. Unless the birth rate drops significantly, improvement of Indian living standards will be very slow and there can be no hope of full employment for decades to come.

The above was written before the Indian-Chinese border conflict became acute in late 1962. This has brought a considerable diversion of resources to military production, and reduced the chances that the other output targets set for 1966 will be achieved.

Economic Development and
the American Interest

Now it is not good for the Christian's health to hustle the Aryan brown,
For the Christian riles, and the Aryan smiles, and it weareth the Christian down;
And the end of the fight is a tombstone white, with the name of the late deceased,
And the epitaph drear, "A fool lies here, who tried to hustle the East."
RUDYARD KIPLING

MOST of the resources for economic development come from inside the developing countries, but a critical proportion must come from outside. A country with little industry must import tools and machinery in the first instance. Industrial development also means increased imports of fuel and raw materials. As development proceeds and personal incomes rise, part of this will spill over into demand for imported consumer goods.

These imports must be paid for. The poor countries must somehow acquire dollars, pounds, marks, and so on to finance the inflow of goods. What are the main sources of foreign currency at present? Are these sources adequate to the need?

SOURCES OF FOREIGN FUNDS

The main sources of foreign currency are shown in Table 30–1. They include:

1. *Export Earnings.* This is the largest single source and will presumably remain so. Hence the problem of expanding and stabilizing export earnings is very important.

2. *Private Investment.* This was the main way in which Britain and Europe contributed during the nineteenth century to economic development in the U.S.A., Canada, and Australasia. While private investment still contributes substantial amounts, its relative importance has diminished. In some of the poor countries political instability is a serious deterrent to private investment. Others do not welcome private capital because it carries overtones of colonialism and foreign domination.

TABLE 30–1

Inflow of Foreign Funds to Underdeveloped Countries, 1960

Source	Amount (Millions of dollars)
Export receipts	27,300
Private net long-term investment	2,022
Government loans and grants:	
From U.S.	3,436
From other Western countries	1,900
From Soviet bloc	1,063
International Organizations	832
Total	36,553

Sources: U.N. *Statistical Yearbook*, 1961. U.N. *International Flow of Private Capital*, 1959–60, June, 1961. Data on private investment relate to 1959 rather than 1960.

3. *Government Loans and Grants: The U.S.A.* During the years 1948–53 the United States made massive loans and grants to Western Europe for postwar reconstruction under the Marshall Plan. Since that time our activities have shifted mainly to Asia, Latin America, and Africa. We operate at three levels:

a) Hard loans. These are loans on a straight business basis, at rates of 4 to 6 percent, repayable in dollars, and usually for projects which yield a cash return. The Export-Import Bank and the Inter-American Development Bank are the main vehicles for this type of lending. In addition, we supply about one third of the capital for the International Bank for Reconstruction and Development, which is also a hard loan agency.

b) Soft loans. These are loans for longer periods and at lower interest rates; and they are sometimes repayable in the currency of the borrowing country, which is much easier than repayment in dollars. While they are sometimes tied to specific projects, they may also provide general support for a development program. They are made principally by the Agency for International Development (AID).

c) Grants. These are used mainly in countries where there is no realistic prospect of repayment in the near future. They are used also for sending U.S. experts abroad and for other forms of technical assistance. Over the years, grants have diminished and soft loans have risen as a percentage of our aid activity. Grants are handled largely by AID.

The total of these activities is less than popularly supposed. The figure that runs in one's mind from Congressional debates is $4 to $5 billion a year. A large part of this, however, has consisted of military supplies to allied nations plus semi-military assistance which goes largely to South Korea, South Vietnam, and Taiwan. Loans and grants for development purposes have typically been between $2 and $3 billion a year.

4. *Government Loans and Grants: Britain, West Europe, Japan.* Most of these countries are gradually increasing their lending to the less developed countries. They are under pressure to do so from their business communities, which want export markets in these countries but can find them only if someone will provide the necessary financing. This commercial motivation has not been absent in the United States. The Export-Import bank was established specifically to promote American exports, and the dollars loaned or granted by AID are usually tied to purchase of American products. Loans by the other Western countries and Japan are typically hard loans.

5. *Government Loans and Grants: The Soviet Bloc.* Since the mid-1950's, the Soviet bloc countries have stepped up their lending activities. The total now exceeds a billion dollars a year and is still rising. More than three quarters of this comes from the U.S.S.R., but several of the East European countries make sizable contributions.

The Soviet bloc lending program has several distinctive characteristics. First, it is a concentrated program. More than three quarters of the money has gone to India, United Arab Republic, Indonesia, Afghanistan, Iraq, and Cuba, though there have been smaller loans to about 15 other Asian and African countries. The program aims at maximum leverage in a few countries which are considered especially susceptible to Soviet political influence.

Second, the program consists almost entirely of soft loans. Grants are avoided, except for an occasional showpiece project. The loan terms are liberal. Loans usually run from 10 to 30 years. The interest rate is typically 2½ percent, but has sometimes been as low as 1 percent. And the loans are normally repayable in local currency or local products. These are essentially barter transactions in which the donor supplies industrial materials and equipment, technical assistance, and sometimes military assistance, receiving mainly agricultural products in return.

The inefficiency of agriculture in the U.S.S.R. gives it a certain advantage over the U.S.A. Since the U.S.S.R. is short of foods and fibres, it needs just those things which the borrower countries can most readily supply—wheat, rice, cotton, sugar, and the like. One can imagine the outcry in Congress if the United States began to import these things in repayment of our foreign loans.

Finally, Soviet bloc loans are typically made for particular projects, such as the Aswan dam in Egypt, or a steel mill in India. And Soviet officials appear to accept the priorities of the borrower countries without question. If a country says, "This is what we need most," the U.S.S.R. agrees. United States aid officials, on the other hand, usually try to form an independent judgment of the country's needs.

6. *International Organizations.* The largest international lending organization is the International Bank for Reconstruction and Development, usually called the World Bank. Its capital has been raised by stages to $10 billion, of which the United States has provided about one third and West Europe most of the remainder. The Soviet bloc countries do not participate. The Bank has authority to raise additional money by selling its own bonds in the leading money markets, and has done this on a substantial scale. Its loans to mid-1961 were about $6 billion, and were widely distributed around the world.

The World Bank is a hard loan agency, and normally lends for completion of a particular project. It has a strong preference for revenue-yielding projects such as power developments, railroads, telephone systems, and manufacturing plants. Two thirds of its funds have gone into transportation and electric power. The loan is normally limited to the amount of foreign exchange required to import machinery and other components for the project. The borrowing country is expected to finance local currency costs from its own resources. Loans usually run from 15 to 25 years, carry interest of $4\frac{1}{2}$ to 5 percent, and are repayable in the currency borrowed.

Some countries are not able to take on additional debt commitments, and some projects do not meet banking standards of low risk and assured yield. So there has been pressure to set up a soft loan organization operating parallel to the IBRD. In 1960, the International Development Association (IDA) was established. It can make loans for as long as 50 years, with a grace period of up to 10 years before repayment begins, and can charge interest or not as it sees fit. While its activities are still small relative to those of the IBRD, they will doubtless increase in the future.

The United Nations is important mainly in the area of technical assistance, where it operates through a variety of agencies including the regular technical assistance program, the Special Fund for Economic Development, the World Health Organization, the Food and Agriculture Organization, and the regional economic commissions. Through these agencies the United Nations maintains training and research centers in the less developed countries, sends nationals of these countries abroad for technical training, and supplies thousands of experts and advisers from the more developed countries. The cost of these activities is not large relative to the other items in Table 30–1, but they are often of key importance.

What does this list of sources boil down to, from the standpoint of the recipient countries? A country which is able and willing to assume the obligations of a hard loan has many possibilities open to it. It can go to the World Bank, or the United States Export-Import Bank, or the governments of France, Britain, West Germany, Japan, or a dozen other countries. If it wants a soft loan, the possibilities are more limited. Only the U.S.A. and the U.S.S.R. are in this business on a substantial scale. And only the U.S.A. provides much money in outright grants.

There is no international agency for overall review and coordination of aid programs, but there is some degree of coordination among the Western powers. The Organization for Economic Cooperation and Development, which includes the United States and Canada along with Britain and the West European countries, maintains a standing Development Advisory Committee (DAC) at its Paris headquarters. DAC is now a focal point for discussing the capital requirements of the less developed countries. The other focal point is the IBRD. Where there is a well developed economic program requiring large foreign resources (The Indian Third Five-Year Plan, the Pakistan Second Five-Year Plan, the Indus River Valley Project), the World Bank often takes the lead in organizing a *consortium* of lending countries. In the three cases mentioned, the U.S.A., Britain, West Germany, several other countries, and the Bank agreed to share the total loan required.

There has been much discussion of whether the volume of government loans and grants now flowing toward the less developed countries is adequate to their needs. The core of the problem is the present capacity of these countries to use foreign capital productively, sometimes referred to as *absorptive capacity*. On this there is wide disagreement. A study by Professors Millikan and Rostow in 1957 set the figure at $6.5 billion a year.[1] A more recent analysis by Professor Rosenstein-Rodan came up with a total of $5.7 billion.[2] Several U.N. studies, on the other hand, have arrived at estimates in the range of $15 to $20 billion a year. But these studies tend to assume that all the poor countries are ready to embark on economic growth, that capital is the sole bottleneck, and that additional investment will yield proportionate returns in output. These assumptions are questionable, and the estimates flowing from them seem considerably exaggerated.

---

[1] M. F. Millikan and W. W. Rostow, *A Proposal: Key to an Effective Foreign Policy* (New York: Harper & Bros., 1957).

[2] P. N. Rosenstein-Rodan, "International Aid for Underdeveloped Countries," *Review of Economics and Statistics*, May, 1961, pp. 107–38.

The question cannot really be answered without some specification of the *terms* on which funds are to be made available. If one thinks of hard loans, at high interest and repayable in hard currencies, the poor countries are probably already getting as much as they can prudently borrow. The lending capacity of the IBRD and other hard loan agencies is far from exhausted. On a soft loan or grant basis, the borrower countries doubtless could use more funds to advantage. So how "soft" does one want to get? And what order of risk are the lending countries willing to accept? In many countries it is an open question whether the country will or will not move ahead economically. How far are we willing to gamble? The answer could make a difference of several billion dollars in the estimate of absorptive capacity.

THE POSSIBILITIES OF PRIVATE INVESTMENT

Loans and grants are only one way for the poor countries to get hold of foreign funds. Another important way is to increase exports. But there is not too much that the developed countries can do about this directly. They can try to keep their own economies growing rapidly, thus providing a growing market for primary products. They can reduce tariffs and other barriers to imports. They can take a sympathetic interest in efforts to iron out the wide price fluctuations for primary products, which wreak such havoc at present. But the main effort must come from the poor countries themselves, through development of their productive capacity in export industries.

In the area of private investment, the developed countries can perhaps take more initiative. We shall speak here particularly about American investment, which provides about one third of the private capital flowing to the less developed countries and may be of two sorts:

1. *Portfolio investment* is where an American buys securities issued by a foreign government or corporation. This was the main way in which European investors contributed to financing development in the United States, Canada, and other countries during the nineteenth century. Today, American investors buy Canadian and European securities in considerable volume. But securities from Asia or Latin America are usually too risky for private buyers, and few such securities are issued in the American market.

2. *Direct investment* occurs when an American corporation sets up a subsidiary or affiliate in another country and contributes to its initial capital. This is now the main form of private investment and, in the less developed countries, almost the exclusive form. The present distribution of U.S. direct investment is shown in Table 30–2. Most of our funds have gone to the economically advanced and politically stable areas of Canada, Britain, and Western Europe. Sizable amounts have gone to Latin America, relatively little as yet to Asia or Africa. In the less developed areas, our investments have been strongly oriented toward primary production. Oil is much the largest item, with mining second.

There are economic reasons for this distribution of investment. Capital will move abroad only if the prospective return, adjusted for risk, is at least equal to what can be earned at home. This argues for Canada and Western Europe, where domestic markets are growing rapidly, property is secure, and there are adequate supplies of trained labor and management. Investment in the less developed countries is inherently more risky. Where an American concern goes in to exploit oil or mineral resources, the risk is limited by the fact that the size of the resources is known and the product can be sold on the world market. To set up a manufacturing concern in Colombia or Thailand producing for the *domestic* market is quite another matter. The rate at which the domestic market will grow in the future, and possible difficulties with labor supply, local management, and government regulation, are hard to estimate in advance. Thus the

TABLE 30–2

U.S. Direct Investment Abroad, 1959
(Millions of dollars)

Geographic Area	Total, All Industries	Petroleum	Mining and Smelting	Manufacturing	Public Utilities	Other
Total, All Areas	29,737	10,423	2,859	9,691	2,413	4,351
Canada	10,171	2,465	1,090	4,558	636	1,422
Latin America	8,218	2,963	1,258	1,405	1,101	1,491
Europe	5,300	1,453	50	2,927	44	826
Africa	843	338	255	120	5	125
Asia	2,235	1,662	20	248	95	210
Other	2,970	1,542	186	433	532	277

Source: Samuel Pizer and Frederick Cutler, *U.S. Business Investments in Foreign Countries*, U.S. Department of Commerce, 1960, p. 89.

venture will be undertaken only if there is a possibility of extraordinarily high returns, say 20 to 30 percent a year on invested capital instead of the 6 or 8 percent which might be considered adequate at home.

Another factor conditioning private investment is the attitude of governments in the recipient countries. Many of these countries have recently won political independence and are strongly nationalist in outlook. They are suspicious of U.S. private investment in their countries, not so much because it is *private* as because it is *foreign*. They view it as a kind of "economic colonialism" which may retard development of locally owned industries and even threaten their political independence. Antipathy to foreign control is stronger in some areas of investment than in others. It is strongest in transportation, communications, power, and other public utilities. There is also growing opposition to foreign exploitation of oil fields, mineral deposits, and other national resources. These views may be shortsighted and unwise, but they are deeply held. And so foreign control of public utilities and natural resource industries can probably not continue over the long run, except in places like the "oil sheikdoms" which make no pretense of economic independence.

Even if these areas are gradually closed off, U.S. private investment can make an important contribution in less sensitive sectors, and particularly in manufacturing. The contribution of private investment in this area is not so much that it provides capital, but rather that it provides technology and management. If the United States government lends money to the government of Ceylon to start a cement industry, Ceylon still has the problem of getting the plants built, staffed, and into operation. But if an American company comes in, *it* takes responsibility for getting the plants built and for providing experienced management until local executives can be trained to take over. The training of managers as well as workers, and the establishment of modern production and personnel methods, are probably the main contributions of American private enterprise abroad.

There are several things which the United States government can do to help realize the potentialities of American private investment. The most obvious is providing information about investment opportunities. This is one function of the economic staffs of our embassies and AID country missions. The government can also use AID funds to pay for technical surveys of the feasibility and cost of proposed investment projects.

Our government can negotiate with foreign governments over the treatment of American investors in their countries. If a country decides to admit foreign capital to certain areas of the economy, it should provide fair and nondiscriminatory treatment. United States companies should not be subjected to special taxes, penalties, or regulations beyond those imposed on locally owned enterprises. There should be security against arbitrary seizure of property. And there should be provision for converting a reasonable share of local profits into hard currencies for transfer to the parent company.

There are other ways of reducing the risks of foreign investment. AID now operates an insurance system under which an American company operating abroad can, by paying a modest premium, insure itself against losses from expropriation, property damage arising from war or insurrection, and inconvertibility of its foreign earnings into dollars. This comes close to eliminating all but the normal commercial risks of overseas operation, and should make it worthwhile for American capital to go abroad at lower expected profit rates.

AID is contributing increasingly to the financing of development banks and other intermediate credit institutions in the less developed countries. The main function of these banks is to finance locally owned business concerns. But they can also lend to American-owned subsidiaries in the country, or to joint ventures combining American and local capital. The United States also owns large amounts of local currency in some countries, arising mainly from sale of our surplus agricultural products. Our foreign aid legislation provides that up to 25 percent of any currency acquired in this way may be used by AID for loans to American business concerns operating in the country. This is a useful source of supplementary finance.

There is general agreement that we should do what can be done along these lines, and that American private investment will continue to make an important contribution to economic development. But it is equally clear that it cannot do the whole job. There are certain kinds of industry to which American private capital will not be admitted. Nor can private capital be used to finance government programs of education, public health, agricultural development, and the like. Needs of these types require government-to-government loans or grants.

UNITED STATES GOVERNMENT PROGRAMS: RANGE OF ACTIVITIES

Our main foreign aid agency has had a long and alphabetical history. Originating in Marshall Plan days as the Economic Cooperation Administration (ECA), it became successively the Mutual Security Administration (MSA), Foreign Operations Administration (FOA), International Cooperation Administration (ICA), and most recently (1961) the Agency for International Development (AID). After some experiments with independent status, it has settled down as an arm of the State Department, under an AID Administrator who ranks as an Under-Secretary of State. The AID mission chief in each country operates under the American Ambassador, though he also reports directly to AID headquarters in Washington.

Several other agencies also operate in this area. The Export-Import Bank operates independently, though in close cooperation with AID. The Department of Agriculture manages the supply side of our surplus disposal operations, though decisions about amounts of agricultural produce to be sent to recipient countries are handled by AID. The Department of Defense handles transfers of military equipment but coordinates with AID on the economic implications of these transfers. The Peace Corps operates a separate program of technical assistance.

At the height of the Marshall Plan in 1950, foreign economic aid was about $5 billion a year. It declined after that, and in recent years has rarely exceeded $3 billion. There have also been important changes in geographic emphasis. As European activities tapered off, emphasis shifted to the Near East and South Asia, which now receive about half the funds. India and Pakistan alone absorb close to $1 billion a year, and significant amounts go to Greece, Turkey, the U.A.R., and Iran. Latin America was relatively neglected before 1960. Since then activity has increased considerably and Latin America now receives close to $1 billion a year through AID, the Export-Import Bank, the Inter-American Development

Bank, and other sources. Little aid money has gone to Africa, though a beginning is now being made in Nigeria, Tunisia, and the Sudan. Opportunities for effective use of capital in Africa will undoubtedly grow as the new governments of that continent become more firmly established.

Aid expenditures in fiscal year 1962, by type of activity, were as follows:

U.S. Loans and Grants for Economic Development
Fiscal Year 1962
(Millions of dollars)

Loans: AID	1,301
Grants: AID	306
Agricultural surplus disposal	1,400
Supporting assistance	538
Contributions to international organizations	154
Contingency fund	275
Total*	3,974

* Exclusive of Export-Import Bank loans.

Let us see what is involved in each of these activities.

Hard Loans: The Ex-Im Bank

Partly because of Congressional objection to "give-away programs," partly on grounds of economic policy, aid activities have shifted increasingly from grants to loans. Much the greater part of our aid is now repayable in one form or another.

The Export-Import Bank makes business-style loans to American or foreign private companies, or to foreign governments and their agencies. In recent years it has made net new loans of around half a billion a year, and its total accumulated loans are above $10 billion. It lends mainly for industrial and public utility projects requiring machinery and equipment from the United States. The loan usually finances only the foreign exchange cost of the project, though AID sometimes cooperates in financing local costs. Loan periods are typically 8 to 12 years for industrial projects, but as much as 16 to 20 years for hydroelectric projects. Interest charges cannot be more than 2 percent above the cost of money to the U.S. Treasury, with a ceiling of 5¾ percent. Most loans in recent years have been at the ceiling figure. Loans are repayable in dollars.

Semi-Soft Loans: AID

These differ from Ex-Im or World Bank loans in two ways. First, loan terms are more liberal. For countries with low repayment capacity, AID can lend for as long as 40 years, with a 10-year grace period before repayment begins, and with interest as low as ¾ of 1 percent. For countries in a stronger position, AID usually sets terms of 15 to 25 years, with perhaps a 5-year grace period, and interest of 3½ to 5 percent. These loans are repayable in dollars, and so can be considered semi-soft rather than really soft.

Second, the purposes for which loans can be used are broader. AID loans are sometimes made for specific projects. But they may also provide support for an overall development program, as has typically been the case in India and Pakistan. AID loans are not limited to meeting the direct foreign exchange cost of the investment program, but may exceed this amount. This flexibility is necessary because an active development program raises local purchasing power, which in turn generates pressure for larger imports. While this pressure can be partially contained by import quotas and exchange controls, it may not be wise to cut it off entirely. So the borrower country may need dollars for general import purposes in addition to those needed to buy equipment for specific projects.

AID loans can be made to tide over balance of payments crises, provided the country is meanwhile taking steps to bring its accounts into balance. Loans can be made for social as well as directly economic purposes —for schools, hospitals, housing, adult education, or community development. Many of these purposes could not be financed from the Ex-Im Bank or the IBRD.

Where a country needs a loan for a specific industrial or utility project, it is expected to canvass the Ex-Im Bank and the IBRD first to see whether they will support it. Only if the proposal fails to interest the banks can it get consideration from AID. Anyone who criticizes AID loans as being of dubious profitability should remember that this is their purpose. AID provides a second line of defense for countries whose immediate repayment capacity does not warrant taking on heavy interest obligations, and for projects whose benefits are so diffused throughout the economy that they are not bankable by ordinary standards.

Really Soft Loans: The Agricultural Surplus Program

An act of 1954, usually referred to as Public Law 480, authorized several methods for disposing of surplus agricultural products abroad. Food may be donated free for famine relief or for distribution by private American relief agencies. Produce may be sold for dollars under long-term supply contracts. Most important, however, is the provision for sale of agricultural products in exchange for local currency. This involves no dollar financing, and hence no foreign exchange problem for the recipient country.

The United States turns over several million tons of wheat, say, to the Indian government, which sells the wheat for rupees in the Indian market. What happens to the rupees after that? Some may be used to meet expenses of United States government agencies operating in India, and some may be set aside for lending to subsidiaries or affiliates of American business concerns. As much as 50 percent of the proceeds of each sale can be set aside for these purposes. The actual percentage is usually considerably lower, since United States need for rupees is limited. Rupees not used for these purposes may be re-lent to the Indian government for development activities on a long-term, low-interest basis, repayable eventually in rupees rather than dollars. Outright grants may also be made where this seems preferable.

It is an interesting question how far the United States will ever be able to use the local currency which other countries owe us under this program. What can we do with large amounts of Indian or Iranian or Brazilian currency? A good deal of this may eventually be written off, and some loans will turn out to have been grants. But meanwhile we have gotten rid of some of our farm surplus and also helped the economies of the recipient countries.

Activities under P. L. 480 have in recent years amounted to between $1 billion and $1½ billion a year. The great bulk of this represents wheat shipments, though there have also been sizable transfers of cotton and feed grains.

How do these food shipments aid economic development in the recipient countries? We saw in the last chapter that a vigorous development program raises the demand for food. If there is no outside aid, and if local agriculture cannot produce enough extra food to match the increase in demand, food prices will rise. This will cause social unrest, force up the money wage level, and hinder the development program. Food imports under P. L. 480 can prevent these undesirable tendencies by closing the gaps between local food production and the rising demand for food. They permit a country to go ahead with industrial development *without* the prior progress in agriculture which is a normal prerequisite.

The limitations of the program are also apparent from this description. Since the United States imports are sold through normal commercial channels, they affect the price level of agricultural products. Unless sales are carefully managed, they may depress prices to a degree which discourages local production. Moreover, if a country can meet its food deficit in this way year after year, it may continue to neglect the problem of raising agricultural output within the country. At some point the agricultural problem must be faced if development is to continue, and it should be faced sooner rather than later. Another common criticism is that P. L. 480 reduces the export market for wheat exports from Canada, Australia, Argentina, and other producers. True, P. L. 480 provides that we will ship food only in addition to what the recipient country would normally buy on a commercial basis. But this line is hard to draw, and our program doubtless does reduce commercial exports. This is a continuing source of friction between us and other agricultural exporters.

Development Grants

Development grants are mainly a way of financing technical assistance to countries which are at such an early stage of development that it would not be realistic to expect repayment. Technical assistance means providing support in such areas as general and technical education, health and sanitation, agricultural research and development, public administration, development planning, and industrial technology. It includes the cost of sending American experts to work in the country; building schools, hospitals, research facilities, and other physical structures; training local personnel within the country; and sending people to the United States for specialized education. The interchange of personnel under this program is substantial. Thousands of foreign nationals are in the United States each year for advanced training, and thousands of American experts are out working in the poor countries.

This is a program of human and institutional development. It is intended to establish the pre-conditions for economic growth, and to move more countries to the point at which they can absorb increasing amounts of physical capital.

In addition to AID, the Peace Corps is an important channel of technical assistance. Young Americans are now being sent at the rate of more than a thousand a year to work abroad as teachers, agriculturalists, engineers, technicians, and craftsmen. The United States also contributes about 40 percent of the amount spent on technical assistance by the United Nations. The U.N. program is mainly a two-way exchange of personnel: teachers and technicians, mainly from the developed countries, going out to work in the less developed, while students and trainees from the less developed countries go abroad for advanced training.

Supporting Assistance

Under this label about half a billion dollars a year has been going to South Korea, South Vietnam, and Taiwan. These countries have become military and economic dependencies of the United States. We give them large quantities of military hardware and supplies. They maintain standing armies considerably larger than they could support from their own resources. So we bolster their economies with dollar grants which allow them to supplement their domestic production by importing fuel, food, and consumer goods from the United States. There may be an incidental contribution to economic development, but the primary purpose is to maintain the present governments in power and prevent a communist takeover. With careful planning, our aid could probably contribute more to economic growth than it presently does; and policy toward these countries is under frequent review with this object in mind.

Contingency Fund

This is a fund which can be drawn on to meet special emergencies. Our ambassador to Ruritania cables Washington that the country is in dire straits. The prices of its export products are falling. It has a balance of payments deficit. Food stocks are low. Social unrest is growing. Local communist groups are active. "Do something!" he urges. The something often turns out to be a dollar grant, large enough to tide over the immediate crisis, but unrelated to any broader development program. Some countries have managed to draw on the United States in this way fairly heavily, without showing much progress toward better economic management or sustained growth. Whatever the justification of these grants in terms of international politics, they can scarcely be classified as development assistance.

Even this brief review indicates the diverse content and rationale of our foreign economic activities. They range all the way from orthodox bank loans to emergency political handouts. And the emphasis is different in each country with which we deal. It is too simple to ask: Are we spending too much or too little on foreign aid? It is more meaningful to ask whether we are putting too much into certain types of program and perhaps too little into others, and whether the allocation of aid by countries is correct.

UNITED STATES GOVERNMENT PROGRAMS: SOME POLICY DILEMMAS

Several issues arise repeatedly in discussions of aid policy. Perhaps they recur because there is no final answer to them. Why are we in the foreign aid business anyway? What standards can be applied in allocating aid among countries? To what extent should loans be based on specific projects, to what extent on the needs of an overall development program? What kind of economic and political strings should be attached to American aid? Given our balance of payments position, can we afford the present level of aid expenditures?

The Objective of Aid Policy

Why are we in the aid business? The program may gain us something in international goodwill, but it can also backfire. It is proverbial that the feeding hand shall be bitten.

The program can be justified to some extent in terms of economic self-interest. Raising the national income of other countries makes them better customers and better suppliers, and we can increase trade with them to our mutual advantage. But it is impossible to translate this into a percentage return on our capital or to deduce from it the proper size of aid program.

The main justification of the program is doubtless political. It rests on a belief that nations which are advancing economically stand the best chance of maintaining political stability and independence. This will contribute to a stable and peaceable community of nations, the kind of community in which Americans would prefer to live.

The objective can also be put in balance of power terms. We would prefer to have as few countries as possible undergo communist revolutions. Experience indicates that static, feudal, agricultural nations are most vulnerable to communist penetration. As a country industrializes and as economic growth becomes a routine affair, it strengthens its chances of maintaining a mixed economy and a liberal political system.

This assumes that most poor countries have the *capacity* to make economic progress and finally to reach a stage of self-sustained growth. There may be some which are too barren of resources, or too hopelessly misgoverned. But the belief is that most countries, given temporary help in education, technology, and capital equipment, can mobilize effectively and begin to lift per capita output. For most of the world this is still an act of faith, and the aid program is basically a gamble. But even if the gamble pays off only partially, we may eventually be proud to have made it.

The Problem of Aid Criteria

Suppose Congress next year appropriates $3 billion for loans and grants to other countries. How should this be divided among the dozens of underdeveloped nations of the world? What standards can be used as a guide to proper allocation?

The poverty of a country and the need of its population cannot be taken as a guide. Foreign aid is not a community chest. Even the great resources of the United States cannot have much immediate impact on global poverty. The function of aid is to accelerate capital formation and economic growth in countries where the pre-conditions of growth already exist. It aims to provide that critical margin of resources which may lift a country over the hump and enable it to move forward under its own power.

It follows that aid should go mainly to countries which are making a successful effort to help themselves, as measured by the capital formation rate, marginal rate of saving, rate of increase in GNP, and other indicators. These will probably not be the poorest countries, but they are the countries which can make best use of additional capital. Aid allocations should be based on a *productivity* criterion rather than a *need* criterion.

In stagnant economies where the prospect of growth is slight, it may still be desirable to make token grants to maintain what State Department people call "an American presence" in the country. The most useful thing in these circumstances may be grants for education and other types of technical assistance, which may gradually establish a favorable climate for economic growth.

Where economic growth is already underway, one could in principle apply a productivity test to determine the proper size of aid allocation. The more outside capital is put into a country, the lower will be its marginal yield. So one must set up a standard of expected marginal yield, and one can argue that this standard should be uniform for all countries. If we are willing to provide Brazil with capital up to the point at which the marginal social yield falls to 5 percent, we should be willing to do the same for India or Nigeria. This is the principle which applies to capital allocation among industries within the United States, and it serves the same purpose of maximizing the expected return on capital.

Although the principle can be simply stated, it is hard to apply. The yield of additional American capital supplied to Nigeria is harder to estimate than the yield of additional investment in automobile manufacturing within the United States. It depends on the amount of aid which other countries are supplying to Nigeria, the amount of local resources which Nigeria is able to raise, the effectiveness of the development planning organization in the country, and other things. It is particularly hard to estimate the return on investment in human beings and in social overhead facilities. But the fact that a judgment is difficult does not remove the necessity of judgment. Any decision that so many million dollars of aid should go to Nigeria implies a judgment about yield. The judgment should be made self-consciously, with as much documentation as possible, rather than casually and intuitively.

How high should one set the standard of expected return? This depends partly on the size of the aid appropriation. If the appropriation were large enough, we could saturate other countries with capital to the point where its marginal yield fell to zero. This seems to be what some economists have in mind when they speak of the *absorptive capacity* of the underdeveloped countries. (It is meaningless to speak of absorptive capacity without at the same time defining a standard of expected yield. A zero marginal yield will give the maximum estimate of absorptive capacity. The higher the expected yield is set, the smaller the amount of capital the country can absorb.)

While we could doubtless saturate the underdeveloped world with capital, this might not make good economic sense. In any event, Congress will certainly not be this generous. Appropriations will be small enough relative to world needs that AID officials will have to apply a positive rate of expected return. The smaller the appropriation, the higher the standard which must be imposed. The point of having a standard is to provide a basis for rationing capital among countries, *not* to assess interest charges against the borrowers. What interest rate should be charged in each case is a separate problem, with no bearing on the allocation decision.

Project Support versus Program Support

The productivity test can be applied in various ways. One can ask the borrowing country for a list of proposed investment projects, each of which can be reviewed on its merits. Or one can ask the country to come in with an overall development program, specifying the resources which it expects to have available from domestic and foreign sources, and the way in which these will be allocated among sectors of the economy. AID can then review the total program, analyze its foreign exchange implications, and decide how much dollar support should be made available.

In the past there has been heavy reliance on the project approach, partly because few governments have had the capacity to draft and administer an overall program. AID officials have often preferred the project approach because it gives them something concrete to work with. It is easier to appraise the cost and yield of a new textile mill than to say whether the Second Five-Year Plan of Pakistan makes sense. It is also argued that the project approach gives the United States greater leverage over the use of its funds. AID can urge that some projects be stricken from the list and others added, and so influence the shape of the development program.

But there are serious limitations to this approach. Granted that most countries are not yet able to draft overall development programs, it is not certain that they are further advanced in the art of defining feasible projects. Estimates of project costs and time schedules have often proven wide of the mark, and in some countries United States officials have virtually had to compile the project list because the country itself was unable to do so. Moreover, the yield of a particular project cannot be judged in isolation. It depends partly on what is going on elsewhere in the economy. A list of isolated projects may not add up to a consistent and optimal development program. It is doubtful also whether the project approach really gives us much control over a country's development activities. Rarely does our support amount to more than 5 or 10 percent of the country's investment program. If we insist that our funds be used only for certain projects, the government will withdraw other resources from those projects and shift them to the uses which *it* prefers. So we may be deceiving ourselves about the extent of our influence.

In recent years we have urged the countries with which we deal to draft comprehensive development programs, in the belief that systematic planning makes for better use of resources. It gives AID officials a picture of where the country thinks it is going, and a better basis for estimating the dollar resources required for success of the plan. For reasons already explained, the foreign exchange requirements of a plan are typically *greater* than the direct cost of the machinery and other capital goods which must be imported for specific investment projects.

While the program approach seems generally preferable, it also has limitations which make it unwise to rely on it exclusively. There is always a danger of leading countries to expect a certain level of United States aid, year in and year out, which then becomes difficult to reduce. The danger is less if aid is tied to projects with a definite completion date. Support for specific projects is easier to dramatize to the American public and to Congress. It is also easier for the United States to get credit abroad for having financed identifiable projects, instead of simply contributing dollars which get lost in a general resource pool. The U.S.S.R. finances almost exclusively projects which can be dramatized effectively in the recipient countries.

For these reasons we shall probably continue a mixed policy of furnishing some aid linked to major projects, plus some funds intended to close the foreign exchange gap in an overall development program.

What Kind of Strings?

What can we reasonably require of countries which depend heavily on us for economic aid? It is scarcely feasible to insist that these countries take our view of international politics, or that they enter into military alliances with us. It is doubtful whether we can expect a country to have a government of which we completely approve, a government which observes Western standards of personal liberty and responsible government. Most underdeveloped countries do not have this kind of government, and may not have it for a long time to come. The practical choice is often between nice autocrats and nasty autocrats.

One can make a good case that we should aid a benevolent autocracy which is following intelligent economic policies designed to benefit the mass of the population. Here one can hope that economic improvement will gradually broaden the base of political participation. By the same token, we should withhold aid from a government whose economic policies are backward-looking and ineffective. There are countries in which the governing group is so incompetent that it is likely to be overthrown within the foreseeable future. Here it may be more to our interest to have friends among the groups which will be in power a generation from now.

How far should we expect to influence the shape of the development programs financed in part with our aid? Here one can distinguish between deciding the *goals* of economic policy and criticizing the *means* for attaining these goals. In the former category are such issues as the extent to which investment should be raised by enforcing austerity in consumption; the emphasis to be placed on industrial development as against agricultural development; the boundary line between the public and private sectors; and foreign trade and exchange policies. These are choices which a sovereign government will insist on making for itself, and on which our advice will be resisted and evaded.

We are on firmer ground in criticizing ways and means. It is legitimate to say, "We accept your economic objectives. But the program you have laid out will not attain these objectives." One can point out that the development program is incomplete or contains internal inconsistencies; that the estimate of internal resources is overoptimistic; that the capital-output ratios assumed in the plan are out of line with experience elsewhere; or that underallocation of investment to certain industries will produce bottlenecks as the plan goes into operation. Friendly criticism at a technical level is a necessary part of responsible aid administration. If the gaps in a country's program are glaring, and if the government is unresponsive to advice, curtailment of aid may be the most sensible course.

Can We Afford Foreign Aid?

It is sometimes said that, while foreign aid is a fine and desirable thing, it imposes an undue strain on our resources. We just cannot afford to continue the program at its present level. In terms of actual resource use, this argument is untenable. Economic aid in recent years has amounted to about half of 1 percent of GNP. This is considerably less than we are now spending to land on the moon. It is much less than we devote each year to frivolous consumer expenditures. It is much less than the amount of output lost in most years through underutilization of our productive capacity. For the richest country in the world to say that it cannot supply a small fraction of its output to the poorer countries is factually wrong and morally indefensible. We could, in fact, increase foreign aid to several times its present level without serious pressure on our resources.

But there is one sense in which the argument that "we can't afford aid" contains a grain of truth. We usually provide other countries with dollars rather than directly with goods. If the recipient countries are free to spend these dollars anywhere, and if they actually spend them outside the United States, this can worsen our balance of payments position.

What happens when we lend or grant a million dollars under the foreign aid program? This appears as a negative item in our balance of payments statement, since it gives other nations a dollar claim against us. Now suppose the million dollars is spent immediately on American wheat, steel, or machinery. Then our exports rise by a million dollars, this appears as a plus item on the payments statement, and everything remains in balance. We have in effect provided the aid in commodities.

But suppose the recipient country is free to spend the dollars anywhere, and decides to buy machinery from Britain or Sweden. In this case our exports will not necessarily rise, and our balance of payments position may be worsened.[3]

The problem is not as large as one might think, for most of our aid is tied directly to shipments of American commodities. This is true of the agricultural surplus disposal program. It is true of the military aid program, which involves a direct turnover of military hardware to friendly nations. Loans by the Export-Import Bank are normally tied to exports of American merchandise. Even in the case of AID loans and grants, experience indicates that two thirds or more of the dollars come back as increased orders for American products. Thus although military and economic aid together come close to $5 billion a year, the potential balance of payments deficit arising from the program could scarcely exceed $1 billion.

---

[3] Britain or Sweden may, of course, use the dollars to increase their purchases from the United States; but they may also withdraw gold or accumulate dollar balances.

Considering the thin ice on which we have been skating in recent years, even a billion dollars could be troublesome. What to do? We could reduce the size of the aid program. But since there is no difficulty as regards our real resources, it seems a pity to cut the program below what is judged desirable on other grounds. We could make only tied loans and grants, which require the recipient countries to spend the money on American products. But this runs counter to our general policy of greater freedom of international trade and it is only partially effective.[4] Since 1960 we have taken steps to tie a larger proportion of AID loans and grants, but this is a device of expediency which hardly anyone considers desirable.

The most desirable solution would be for the other Western industrial nations to engage in aid programs which, relative to their GNP, are as large as the U.S. program; and to give this aid on an untied basis. We could then feel safe in untying our own aid dollars. The flow of dollars going to the underdeveloped countries and re-spent on foreign goods would be offset by the flow of pounds, marks, francs, and so on going to the underdeveloped countries and re-spent on American products. Things would balance out, provided our capital goods industries remain competitive with those of other countries.

The financing problem, in short, does not seem serious enough to be given prime place in determining the scale of our aid program.

A Word of Caution

The foreign aid program is important and would seem to merit continuation. But it should not be sold under false pretenses. Proponents of foreign aid sometimes speak as though it will yield rapid results and will be all over in a decade or two. We need only prime the pump for a short time, after which the poor countries will be able to go ahead under their own power. Since many Americans seem to believe this, it is only natural that the borrowing countries should sing the same tune. One development plan after another asserts that the country will be independent of further aid in 10 or 15 years.

This is quite unrealistic. As a country's growth begins to accelerate, its ability to absorb capital rises sharply. Its capacity for saving also increases, but less rapidly. So the gap remaining to be filled from foreign sources increases instead of diminishing. Remember that the United States, where development occurred under unusually favorable circumstances, remained a large net borrower for about 70 years. It would be unreasonable to expect today's poor countries, starting from a lower level and with many handicaps, to work their way to economic independence in a decade or two.

---

[4] Most countries have some *free dollars* earned through exports to us. So if we prevent them from spending AID dollars in Germany or Sweden, they may simply shift more of their free dollars to purchases from those countries.

There is every prospect that we shall be in the foreign aid business for many decades to come. This is not surprising, since the task is nothing less than equipping two thirds of the people on earth with the knowledge, skills, and equipment of modern industry. The prospect should be challenging rather than alarming. But the long-run nature of the effort should be recognized, lest the program collapse in disillusionment because we have not set the world right by next year.

SUMMARY

1. The poor countries have access to foreign exchange from several sources: export earnings, private investment, loans and grants from national governments, and loans and grants from international organizations.

2. The present level of receipts seems undesirably low relative to the rising import needs of the developing countries, but the size of the gap is unclear. The answer depends partly on whether one is thinking in terms of hard loans at normal interest rates, or soft loans at lower rates; and partly on one's optimism about the ability of specific countries to use capital effectively.

3. Private investment can make a valuable contribution to economic development, especially in manufacturing. Nationalist feeling is likely to exclude foreign investors increasingly from public utilities and natural resource industries. The United States government can encourage American private investment in the less developed countries by providing information on investment opportunities, negotiating with foreign countries for nondiscriminatory treatment of our investors, granting concessions as regards United States taxation of foreign earnings, lending local currency through AID to American companies operating abroad, and insuring them against expropriation and other special risks.

4. The United States foreign aid program embraces a wide spectrum of activities: normal business loans through the Export-Import Bank; dollar loans on more liberal terms through AID; shipments of surplus agricultural products, which are paid for largely in local currency; outright grants, mainly for technical assistance; special assistance to countries such as South Korea, South Vietnam, and Taiwan, for politico-military purposes; and emergency handouts to tide over economic or political crises. Each activity has somewhat different objectives and rationale. It is not clear what part of the total should be considered foreign *economic assistance*, or what the size of the aid program really is.

5. Administration of foreign aid raises numerous policy issues, on which there is far from complete agreement. What are the main objectives of the program, and in what ways can the United States expect to benefit from it? What criteria should be used in allocating the aid budget among individual countries? Should aid be extended on the basis of specific investment projects or as general support for a comprehensive development program? What kind of political or economic strings can be, or should we, attach to our economic assistance? How large an aid program is justifiable in terms of world need and United States resources? Should balance of payments difficulties be a major consideration in determining the size of the program, and how can these difficulties be minimized?

6. We should beware of expecting large and quick returns from the aid program. Some countries will prove incapable of using aid effectively. Even where aid is well used, it may be 20 or 30 years before one sees a substantial payoff in terms of economic growth. If the program is worthwhile, it will need to be continued for as far ahead as one can see.

INDEX

Index

*This book has been set on the Linotype in
10 point Janson, leaded 2 points, and 9 point
Janson, leaded 1 point. Part numbers and titles
and chapter titles are in 24 point Alternate
Gothic; chapter numbers are in 48 point Alternate Gothic. The size of the type page is
27 by 47 picas.*